SOCIAL AND
PSYCHOLOGICAL ASPECTS
OF AGING

AGING AROUND THE WORLD

*Proceedings of the Fifth Congress of the
International Association of Gerontology*

SOCIAL AND PSYCHOLOGICAL ASPECTS OF AGING

SOCIAL WELFARE OF THE AGING

BIOLOGICAL ASPECTS OF AGING

MEDICAL AND CLINICAL ASPECTS OF AGING

Social and Psychological Aspects of Aging

EDITED BY CLARK TIBBITTS AND WILMA DONAHUE

 1962

Columbia University Press

New York and London

The Congress, including the preparation and publication of this volume, was supported in part by a grant (H-5058) from the National Heart Institute and a grant (R. G. Mult. 6239) from the Division of General Medical Sciences, Public Health Service. Contributions to the support of the Congress were made also by The Ford Foundation, The Kaiser Foundation, and The San Francisco Foundation.

The International Association of Gerontology

THE International Association of Gerontology came into existence in Liége, Belgium, in July, 1950. The rapid rise of longevity, shared by many countries of the world during the preceding quarter century, led to a surge of new research interest in the nature of the aging process and in the clinical manifestations of disease in the aging organism. By the late 1940s, gerontological societies had appeared in at least seventeen countries and Dr. V. Korenchevsky had initiated a movement to create an International Association of Gerontological Societies. The growing recognition of the need for an international facility for exchange and cross-fertilization of ideas resulted in the Liége meeting which was to become known as the First International Congress of Gerontology. The ninety-five research workers in attendance formally organized the Association and elected Professor L. Brull to its presidency.

The aims of the Association, reaffirmed at the 1960 Congress, are:

(1) . . . promote gerontological research in the biological, medical and social fields, carried out by gerontological associations, societies, or groups, by all possible means, and in particular to promote cooperation among the members of these societies, associations, or groups;

(2) . . . promote the training of highly qualified professional personnel in the fields of aging. . . .

The Second International Congress was held in St. Louis, Missouri, in 1951, under the presidency of Dr. E. V. Cowdry. Growing research interest in the psychological and social science aspects of aging prompted Dr. Cowdry to make provision for a social science division parallel to the sections on biology and clinical medicine. The new section responded by presenting a full complement of papers from western Europe and the United States.

The Third Congress took place in London in 1954 with Dr. J. H. Sheldon as its president. All divisions had scientific programs which kept the participants busy for four full days. Just prior to this Congress, international research seminars were held by small groups of biologists and social scientists, the latter sponsored by the Nuffield Foundation. The social science seminar led to the establishment of a permanent Social Science Research Committee which, like the Biological and Clinical Medicine committees, assumed responsibility for arranging the scientific programs of future congresses.

The Fourth International meeting took place in Merano and Venice, Italy, in 1957 with Dr. E. Greppi as president. The program was extended to six days in order to accommodate the growing volume of papers. The 1957 Congress afforded evidence of large-scale development of research in what had come to be known as the field of social gerontology and of the need to give greater recognition to its applied aspects. Accordingly, the Governing Body of the Association created a Division of Social Welfare.

The Fifth International Congress of Gerontology met in San Francisco during August of 1960. Each of the four divisions— Biology, Clinical Medicine, Social Science, and Social Welfare—had a program extending over the entire period. Research workers from thirty-two countries presented a total of 394 papers. Representatives of fifty nations contributed to an attendance of more than 1100 individuals. Recognizing the increasing depth and breadth of gerontological interest, the Board of Governors of the Association adopted a new set of by-laws designed to accommodate the growing number of societies throughout the world and to encourage greater activity on the part of the research committees.

The proceedings of the Fifth Congress appear in four volumes under the general title *Aging Around the World*. They have been prepared for publication under the direction of an editorial committee consisting of Clark Tibbitts and J. H. Sheldon, co-chairmen, and Gordon J. Aldridge, Jerome Kaplan, Herman T. Blumenthal, Nathan W. Shock, and Wilma Donahue. On behalf of the entire Association, I wish to express profound gratitude to them and to the scores of individuals who contributed to the success of the program and these publications. Special thanks are also due to the National Institutes of Health of the Public Health Service, U.S. Department of Health, Education, and Welfare, The Ford Foundation, The Kaiser Foundation, and The San Francisco Foundation for their generous contributions to the support of the Congress.

Sacramento, California   LOUIS KUPLAN
February 20, 1961   *President*

Foreword

THE social and psychological research program of the Fifth International Congress of Gerontology was organized under the auspices of the Social Science Research Committee of the International Association of Gerontology. Organized in 1956, the Committee has set forth its objectives and functions as follows:

1. To stimulate, plan, and facilitate research, including parallel and cross-cultural studies in the anthropological, economic, political, psychological, psychiatric, public health, and sociological aspects of aging;

2. To facilitate exchanges of approaches, concepts, conclusions, and methodologies through seminars, international exchange of personnel, and other appropriate ways;

3. To develop and conduct the social gerontology (psychology, social sciences, and related disciplines) section of the program, in connection with the triennial meetings of the International Gerontological Congress.

In order to facilitate its work, the Committee has a European Branch and an American Branch. The two branches work closely together, initiative moving from one to the other dependent upon where a particular activity is to take place. The European Branch has held two all-Europe conferences and planned the social research program for the Fourth International Congress of Gerontology held in Italy in 1957. The two branches jointly planned and conducted research seminars in 1957 and in 1960.

Since the 1960 Congress was being held in the United States, organization leadership became the responsibility of the American Branch. Responsibility for developing the program of each of the six sections was vested in a member of the American Branch assisted by a European counterpart. Their work was coordinated by Clark Tibbitts, the Committee's Secretary. The sections and their respective leaders were: Population and Social Organization, Leonard Z. Breen and Pierre Naville; Economics of Aging, Seymour L. Wolfbein and Henning Friis; Housing, Family, and Social Relationships, Wilma Donahue and Peter Townsend; Personality Theory, Attitudes, Roles, and Adjustments, Bernice L. Neugarten and Jean-René Tréanton;

Mental Health and Rehabilitation, Richard L. Williams and Martin Roth; Psychology of Aging: Experimental Studies, James E. Birren and Alan T. Welford.

The 1960 program achieved a new level of diversification and excellence, reflecting the expanding interest in social gerontology and the gradual accumulation of scientific work in the field. It is particularly gratifying that the program included several papers by research workers in Asia, the Pacific area, and the Near East. Grants from the National Institutes of Health made it possible to extend invitations to twenty of the foreign scientists who participated in the social science program.

The Congress was preceded by a Seminar on Psychological and Social Aspects of Aging in Relation to Mental Health. The Seminar, conducted jointly by the Committee and the National Institute of Mental Health, brought together eighty scholars who spent four days discussing conclusions, methodological problems, and research needs. The availability of the Seminar participants helped to enrich the program of the Congress. The report of the Seminar will appear in a separate volume entitled *Psychological and Social Processes of Aging*.

It is agreeable to note, as the present volume goes to press, that the first application for support of an internationally developed research project has been submitted.

Chicago, Illinois   ERNEST W. BURGESS
March 1, 1961   *Chairman, American Branch*

Preface

THIS compilation of papers presented in the Social Research Division of the Fifth International Congress of Gerontology provides, in essence, a report of the sweep of current worldwide scientific investigation of the social and psychological facets of aging. The subject matter ranges from that of psychological studies of the aging individual to broad matters of group behavior and societal action. It is thus well representative of the emerging field of social gerontology as well as of the evolving intradisciplinary research interest in aging.

Basically the book is organized, as was the program, with reference to six subject-matter areas: population and social organization, economics and employment, family relationships and environmental aspects of living, personal and social attitudes and adjustment, personality changes and mental health, and changes in psychological capacities and performance. Within each of these areas, critical questions are examined from a variety of approaches. One of the major contributions of the volume is that it brings together reports of research currently in process in many parts of the world. Gerontologists and the scientific community generally are indebted to the program organizers in the United States and abroad who planned the content of their sections and sought out, from the world over, the researchers active in the field.

The program of the Social Research Division included, also, a Symposium on Meaningful Uses of Free Time. The papers in the Symposium constitute a preview of a (United States) Gerontological Society project aimed at conceptualizing the research field of the uses and meaning of free time to older people and suggesting fruitful lines of scientific inquiry. The papers are a useful addition to the volume.

The present compilation includes the full texts of virtually all of the papers presented in the Social Research program of the Congress. The following papers were presented at the Congress but are not included in this volume: Brian Abel-Smith, "Recent Developments in Income Security Programs in the United Kingdom"; Seymour L. Wolfbein, "Work Patterns among Older Persons"; Rudolf Tartler, "The Older Persons in Relation to Family, Community, and Societal Factors."

A few of the papers were first presented at the pre-Congress research seminar. They are represented by abstracts or shortened versions in the present volume and will appear in full in the seminar report, *Psychological and Social Processes of Aging*. All of the papers appear in English although several of them were given in the usual language of the investigator.

The Editors wish to express their appreciation to the section organizers who developed their programs, assembled the participants and their papers, and accomplished the preliminary editing and translations. Great credit—for final editing, reference checking, proofing, and indexing—goes to the experienced Staff of the Division of Gerontology at The University of Michigan, Ann Arbor. The Editors and the Social Science Research Committee are pleased to have this opportunity to acknowledge their gratitude to the Division for its expert and painstaking work.

Washington, D.C.   CLARK TIBBITTS
October 1, 1961   WILMA DONAHUE
                                     Co-editors

Contents

Contents xvii

POPULATION AND
SOCIAL ORGANIZATION

Organized by
LEONARD Z. BREEN
Purdue University, Lafayette, Indiana
PIERRE NAVILLE
Centre National Recherche Scientifique
Paris, France

Some Features of Aging in the French Active Population

PAUL PAILLAT

TO anyone interested in economic and social consequences of aging, France offers an outstanding example for study because (a) the proportion of aged people is one of the highest in the world (12 percent of people aged 65 and more) and (b) this country is an important industrial power.

If it is true that aging is a phenomenon of the population, linked with industrialization and the development of a consumers' society, the case of France might prove thought-inspiring for those who observe the beginning of the same process in their own country. A better knowledge of the population age structure can then lead foreigners—as well as Frenchmen—to useful learning.

It is not the author's intention to cover the whole problem in this paper. Less ambitiously, he wishes to stress some key features, some peculiarities of the economically active population which are not only the result of demographic evolution but which also reflect historical accidents or economic pressures. The major source of information is the 1954 Census, though its tables on the age structure of the active population are in press.[1] The whole picture regarding the location of people has rather changed since 1954, but age distribution and patterns are still of interest. In any case it will be the only source available for some years, aside from the limited information provided by other institutions (social security, pension funds, etc.).

AGRICULTURE
Age Distribution of the Active Population

In France, as in the other Western countries, the farming sector's importance relative to other economic activities is constantly decreas-

---

[1] Data have been kindly provided by M. Febvay, Head of the Population Department, Institut National de la Statistique et des Etudes Economiques (I.N.S.E.E.).

ing. In 1954 it employed, however, 27 percent of the active population. Progress in productivity, especially by mechanization, implies less manpower, and the "freed" laborers have to look for employment in towns or industrial areas. The rural out-migration has a less known cause: the aging of the farm population and particularly that of farmers. The higher proportion of aged people in rural districts is due not to better health conditions but to the *migration of the younger generations.* When the 20–35 group clears out too quickly, the population ages and this development cannot be inverted. Those who do not leave the farms before the age of 35 stay in this sector and, as usual, work longer than in other economic activities. The best way to be sure of this fact is to compare age distribution of males in the active agricultural population and in the active nonagricultural population, as is shown in Table 1.

Table 1. Percentage distribution of active male population by age, 1954

Population	Age					
	Under 25	*25–34*	*35–44*	*45–54*	*55–64*	*65 and over*
Agricultural	18.6	20.8	14.3	21.7	14.5	10.1
Nonagricultural	15.2	26.4	19.7	22.7	11.8	4.2

It is even more significant to compare activity rates after 55 in the active agricultural population and in the whole active population (see Table 2).

Table 2. Activity rates of males at upper ages, 1954

Population	Age			
	55–59	*60–64*	*65–69*	*70–74*
Agricultural	95.2	87.6	72.8	63.0
Total	82.2	68.0	49.5	33.5

In this farm population, it is necessary to distinguish between two usual categories: on the one hand, farmers (and their families), and, on the other hand, farm workers. Men only will be taken into consideration because the statistical treatment of active women not earning wages is always a tricky problem; it is difficult to know what belongs to their housework and what belongs to their farm work, and census instructions vary, making time comparisons almost impossible (Table 3).

Farm workers are less and less numerous in the new generations: the percentage under 25 is significant. Specialized studies (Febvay, 1956) have shown that only 39 percent of farm workers' sons keep on

Table 3. Active agricultural population: percentage distribution according to status, males only, 1954

	Age				
Status	*Under 35*	*35–44*	*45–54*	*55–64*	*65 and over*
Farmers	34.6	13.5	23.0	16.2	12.7
Farm workers	50.8	16.3	18.6	10.3	4.0

farming and that very few are promoted to the status of farmer. It means that, while members of the farmer's family are needed more and more, at the same time trends are the opposite. Because of the lengthening of life of adults, farmers stay in the ruling position for a longer period, and the eldest son, usual but not privileged heir, must wait longer until he becomes the boss. He does not always wait. His younger brothers, often under the influence of their wives, leave the family farm after their compulsory service in the armed forces and always before the age of 35. For that reason it is clear that rural out-migration will go on. Who could wonder at that, even if it is well known that in censuses some old men, because of self-pride, state they are "farmers" when in fact they depend on sons who are the actual bosses of the farms? In many cases, the son is not as free as if he were alone, particularly when he has to buy costly equipment or to change farming techniques. No doubt aging is a factor in rigidity, a factor partly explaining why agriculture makes slower progress than the over-all economy, an overlooked cause of dissatisfaction among farmers.

It is easy to understand the troubles raised in a small township or in a village by the almost complete absence of young adults. The distribution of public expenses is difficult; it cannot be the same. A village's fate is written in tomorrow's tables: the fewer the young couples, the lower the birth rate, and the increased likelihood of an insufficient reproduction rate, while towns and industrial areas expand abnormally. This phenomenon can be observed in Brittany, a part of France famous for its fertility: the birth rate there is decreasing while in the industrial districts of eastern France it is increasing. This is in contradiction to the widespread idea that children are a lighter charge for peasants or for well-to-do persons than for low middle-income people who strive for a better standing in society. This factor still has some influence upon employees and is perhaps beginning to affect farmers and farm workers, though they are less familiar with contraceptive methods than town dwellers. Nowadays children constitute less easily (and less early) a supplementary and cheap source of manpower, and for that reason parents, more and more, do not let nature play unrestricted.

The farming population rises and falls, with gaps in some young age groups.

Regional disparities

Such aging of the agricultural sector also explains disparities which accentuate regional differences and make the job of authorities in charge of town and country planning more difficult. Indeed, the "old-young" ratio varies noticeably from one "département" (France is divided into 90 départements) to another. In order to show clearly this time and space evolution, we have selected the 16 départements where 50 percent of active men work in agriculture (agricultural départements) and the 17 départements where 40 percent of the whole active population works in industry (industrial départements); and we have compared the "old-young" and "old people-total population" ratios in 1936 and in 1954 (see Table 4).

As a first comment, in 1936 the proportion of old people varied from 1 to 2 in agricultural départements (e.g., from Côtes-du-Nord, No. 22, to Gers, No. 32), as in industrial départments (e.g., from Moselle, No. 57, to Aube, No. 10); in 1954 maximum differences were only 79 percent in the first case and 56 percent in the second case. The "old-young" (O/Y) ratios covered a range in 1936 from 236 to 589 in agricultural départements (difference: 150 percent), and from 183 to 391 in the others (differences: 114 percent); in 1954 such differences were much reduced: from 332 to 586 for the first ones (difference: 76 percent) and from 249 to 434 for the others (difference: 74 percent). In other words, the new upward trend of the birth rate has slowed down aging more in industrial areas than in farming areas. Compare, for instance, Moselle's ratio of 249 with Creuse's (No. 23) ratio of 783: in the first case there are only 82 old people for 1000 inhabitants, whereas there are 190 in the second case. Curiously enough, in both départements the O/Y ratio has increased at the same rate. If we exclude the special case of Paris and neighboring suburbs (No. 75 in Table 4), we find again Aube (No. 10), where the O/Y ratio has made practically no change in 18 years: with the same rate of variation, this ratio is still 20 percent lower than the ratio of Tarn-et-Garonne (No. 82).

It is somewhat peculiar to note that, although aging is generally linked to industrialization (lesser fertility, better sanitary equipment), the most aged départements in France belong to the agricultural sector and are aging more rapidly than industrial départements. One might hastily conclude that the industrial society exerts its influence by

Table 4. Aged people in agricultural and industrial départements, 1936 and 1954

	AGRICULTURAL "DÉPARTEMENTS"						INDUSTRIAL "DÉPARTEMENTS"				
	1936		1954		O/Y: 1936 = 100		1936		1954		O/Y: 1936 = 100
Number[a]	O/T[b]	O/Y[b]	O/T	O/Y		Number[a]	O/T	O/Y	O/T	O/Y	
11	127	469	153	566	121	08	105	329	115	348	106
12	120	380	149	518	136	10	117	391	127	408	104
19	119	399	158	571	143	25	83	246	105	314	128
22	86	236	113	348	147	38	102	325	115	370	114
23	153	573	190	783	137	42	100	341	120	399	117
24	121	402	146	505	126	54	74	222	96	294	132
32	162	589	159	586	100	57	62	183	82	249	136
40	127	454	153	578	127	59	87	278	110	345	124
43	126	413	151	505	122	60	106	327	128	383	117
47	132	463	151	515	111	62	71	192	91	260	136
48	118	348	155	510	147	67	75	230	108	355	154
53	92	265	106	308	116	68	82	265	114	396	149
61	103	305	112	332	109	69	84	304	111	399	131
79	114	361	139	435	120	75	69	296	102	434	147
82	136	481	150	501	104	78	81	268	109	363	135
85	107	408	127	370	91	88	98	303	107	301	100
						90	81	273	99	314	115

Average increase 122   *Average increase* 125

[a] Numbers are those of the alphabetic order of the départements adopted for statistical purposes, e.g., 11 is Aube; 59 is Nord; 75 is Paris, etc.

[b] O = population 65 and over; T = total population; Y = population under 25; ratios are per 1000 of the base population.

radiation rather than on the very spots of its activity. This is only an apparent contradiction: migrations from rural districts to towns play the main role; they make the conditions worse in the rural areas and lighten the burden of older people on young shoulders in the towns. Paris is an interesting case: though the proportion of aged people is lower than the national average (10.2 against 12), the O/Y ratio is by far the highest of all industrial départements. In such a case, comparison should bear on the "old" and "adult" groups. The picture is quite different when one considers the Lille area (No. 59), where fertility is high.

The agricultural départements (11 out of 17) where there is more than one old man or woman for two young people are in a very serious situation, especially Creuse, Gers, Landes, and Aube. Creuse holds the record in aging, with a rate of 19 percent. According to Mr. Pressat (1957 *a* and *b*), in the list of départements where the active farm population should decrease the most (with the influence of the demographic pattern) between 1954 and 1964 are Corrèze (No. 19), Creuse (No. 23), Gers (No. 32), and other départements, in which the O/Y ratio is higher than 500, whereas Mayenne (No. 53) and Côtes-du-Nord (No. 22), which should have an increasing population of that type, is low. Migrations play a significant part in Côtes-du-Nord, where the O/Y ratio, though average, has increased at the quickest rate in spite of a fertility which is slightly higher than the average.

Behind these demographic statistics may be hidden the future of French agriculture. When the observation concerns not départements but smaller districts, some natural and traditional areas appear where farmers are striving hopelessly because they know that no one will follow after them. In that respect, the building of new factories in rural areas is not always planned according to population forecasts and could accentuate the existing ill-balanced trend.

INDUSTRY

If industrial départements appear to be aging less rapidly than agricultural ones, it would be wrong to assume that industry as such is immunized against aging pressure or to believe that such a phenomenon develops at an even pace. As for individuals, some activities are "aging" more than others, and this is particularly true in a long period of quick technical progress.

Age distribution by collective activities

In Table 5 are given the percentages of employed wage earners of some age groups according to branch of collective activity, classified according to the I.N.S.E.E. code.[2] Later, greater differences will be underlined in a paragraph dealing with various types of personnel.

Table 5. Employed male wage earners: Percentage distribution by age and by collective industrial activity, 1954[a]

Activity[c]	Number	Age[b]			
		Under 25	45–54	55–64	65 and over
1. Coal mining (G.S.)[d]	256,380	15.4	23.8	2.8	
2. Metal manufacture (ore and metal processes)	418,820	17.7	20.9	12.3	2.7
3a. Machinery construction	146,520	17.4	20.0	12.1	3.6
b. General engineering	124,760	29.6	16.1	9.0	2.7
c. Motor vehicles	272,440	26.2	17.2	8.6	2.2
d. Electrical engineering	137,160	19.8	18.5	10.9	2.7
4a. Building	786,140	28.3	17.9	8.2	2.2
b. Civil engineering (private sector)	176,880	17.2	20.0	8.7	1.7
c. Civil engineering (G.S.)[d]	100,880	6.5	30.6	17.6	2.2
5. Chemicals	143,420	10.5	24.4	13.3	3.9
6. Textile industry	203,240	19.1	20.9	14.2	4.7

[a] Source: 1954 Census (I.N.S.E.E.) Table DA f₁.
[b] 25–44 omitted.
[c] Grouped according to I.N.S.E.E. code: 1 = 11; 2 = 16, 18, 19, 20; 3a = 21; 3b = 22; 3c = 26; 3d = 28; 4a = 33; 4bc = 34; 5 = 35–36; 6 = 47.
[d] G.S.: government sector.

The main differences, observed in Table 5, may be explained by several factors:

a. Special pension scheme. Such a scheme may provide for a younger than usual retiring age. In coal mines, for instance, nobody works after 55, with the exception of a few people in the managerial group.

b. Recently expanding activity. The "young" group is important; the aged group is limited. This is the case for motor vehicle manufacturing. It is significant to compare this industry with machinery construction, at both ends of the age scale. Electrical engineering occupies an intermediate situation since there the 25–34 group is more important than in other modern types of production. The building

[2] Data have been kindly supplied by M. Febvay, Head of the Population Department, Institut National de la Statistique et des Etudes Economiques (I.N.S.E.E.).

trade is exceptionally young. This is owing to the development of
dwelling projects (against the housing shortage), to the easy hiring
of unskilled young fellows, and to working conditions not proper for
older workers (sheltered jobs are rare).

c. Declining trade. The textile industry still attracts many young
people (is it because it is their first job?) but employs mainly aged
workers. The female staff constitutes the majority (53.3 percent)
and among employed women the percentages by age group after 45
are, respectively, 18.6, 13.0, and 3.1. The two last figures are extremely high when compared with other industrial activities.

d. Various causes. In spite of its recent expansion, the chemical
products industry is rather "old" if one notes that the ratio between
"55 plus" and "under 25" is much higher than 1 (exactly 1.6),
whereas it is 0.4 in the motorcar industry and only 1 even in the aging
textile industry. The high level of skill of common manpower perhaps
operates against the young. This is true for skilled workers, and is
also true for the engineers[3] (*ingénieurs*) as compared, for instance,
with their colleagues in electrical engineering, but both categories are
only a small part of the personnel. Maybe automation is a factor:
reliable, steady workers are required for control jobs—in other words,
people with somewhat long experience.

Age distribution in social-status categories

The significance of such large and heterogeneous groupings is, of
course, limited because important phenomena may be overlooked.
For instance, it is impossible to detect an abnormal and unfortunate
aging of the managerial staff (executives) if the *common* manpower
has a good-looking age distribution. It is then useful to consider the
age distribution, on the one hand, according to the status *and* the
branch, and, on the other hand, according to the individual occupation.

As far as the status-branch classification is concerned, noteworthy
differences appear among private undertakings, government-owned
enterprises, and public administrations. In both latter cases, differences come partly from staff regulations and special pension schemes
which provide for a retirement-age scale according to occupation and
rank. The recruitment policy is also a factor. For the sake of financial

---

[3] In France, the use of the *"ingénieur"* title is ruled by law. It covers individuals with advanced scientific studies and/or graduates of some high-
standing schools. The word "engineer" is thus often misleading (for instance,
in international comparisons). Here it means only *ingénieur,* as above specified.
"Technicians" occupy an intermediate situation between supervisors and engineers.

economies, recruitment may be stopped for a while and the retiring age may be lowered for some categories of staff; the middle group is then abnormally inflated without consideration of the fact that this policy will have, in the long term, extremely serious effects on the pension scheme (see abstract of author's paper on "Old Age Pensions and Allowances in France" in this volume). Insufficient resources have to be made up by budgetary subsidies; in other words, the whole national economy contributes to balance the scheme. This matter will be considered later in this paper under the section on "Services."

Since the war more attention and effort have been given to vocational training, for instance, in metallurgy. The percentage of young skilled workers is notably higher than the percentage of young specialized operatives (semi-skilled workers) or laborers, but it is consistent with the national level; on the contrary, above 55, in the same industry, they are only 2.1 against 12.2 in the whole private sector (Table 6).

Table 6. Employed male working population: percentage distribution by age and social status category and activity[a]

		Age[b]				
Social status category	Number	Under 25	45–54	55–64	65–69	70 and over
Status 2: Industrial employers	70,740	0.5	34.1	32.6	6.4	**5.6**
Status 5: Wage earners, private sector						
Engineers	77,700	2.5	24.6	12.8	2.2	1.3
Managerial staff	104,360	0.8	29.5	21.2	4.3	2.4
Skilled workers in metal manufacture and metal working	605,940	23.6	17.4	9.0	1.5	0.6
Semi-skilled workers in metallurgy	260,640	16.5	21.0	10.7	1.7	0.5
Unskilled in metallurgy	136,080	17.2	20.3	14.2	2.8	1.3
Skilled workers in building and civil engineering	431,140	26.4	17.9	7.8	1.4	0.6
Status 7: Wage earners government sector						
Coal miners	236,360	11.8	16.6	1.7		

[a] Source: 1954 Census (I.N.S.E.E.), Table DS f₃.
[b] 25–44 omitted

Laborers (i.e., unskilled workers) should be the matter of a special survey. It is worrisome to note the high percentage of metallurgy laborers aged 55 or more (18.3), because their pensions will be extremely small (it is computed on the mean wages earned during the last 10 years, i.e., usually between 55 and 64). At this age, possibilities of a better training are quite limited, and it would be interesting to know how many of them were formerly skilled workers unable to keep the pace. In the private sector male unskilled workers are about 870,000, of which 15.8 percent are aged 55 or more; the percentage in metallurgy is then much higher than the average of people belonging to this category (or classified as such). The percentage of older female laborers in this branch is also high (20.9 percent), but they are not so numerous. In the whole group of women in this case (245,000), 25 percent are aged 55 or more, which frankly is a painful figure, even if it is understandable.

Incidentally, in older ages the age distribution of employers in industry is the same for the whole French population, which means that age-specific activity rates are very high.

An analysis of percentages of every year after 65 shows that all categories lose more than half of their population between 65 and 70. The pace is sometimes quicker: for instance, skilled metal workers from 1660 at 65 are no more than 420 at 69. At this stage the downward trend cannot be explained by upgrading or by a change of status; it is due to retirement or to death.

Examples of individual occupations

Some individual occupations are worth consideration. With the exception of machine-loom weavers, who in the proportion of 17.8 percent are 55 years old and more (men as well as women), there are few manual occupations with a much higher percentage than the average of all workers (11.9). We can mention skilled workers in chemicals, blacksmiths, forgemen (14.8), moulders (14.6), and semi-skilled workers in textiles (14.4). Among low percentages are (coal miners excluded) the welders (4.8) and electrical equipment installers and maintenance men (5.2).

Engineers (in the French meaning) are numerous at middle (25–34) or mature ages (45–54) and very scarce later. Of course, they switch from production to management and are then classified as "top managerial staff" or even as "employers." In the first case, 28 percent are aged 55 and more. It is interesting to note that, against a little more than 17 percent of chemical or civil engineers aged 55 or more, less than 13 percent of electrical engineers are in the same age category; most of them belong to the 25–34 group (40 percent), which is an almost unique figure. In the private sector, technicians are, as expected, more than 50 percent in groups under 35 and only 12.7 percent over 55. It is the proof of a temporary occupation and partly results from a very active recruitment during the last decade. This is a promising outlet for the younger generations, since they are the most wanted in France.

Comparative aging index (CAI)

To make comparisons easier, we have devised an index which, for synthesizing age distribution, is based on the ratio between "under 35" and "55 plus" types of working people. Both limits are, of course, arbitrary (and might be changed later if needed) but with the former it is possible to include young engineers, for instance, and to cover all individuals able to switch from one employment or activity to another; the latter include all categories of personnel whose age makes any transfer difficult, a new employment uneasy (e.g., administrators and engineers), and possibilities of promotion for rank-and-file workers almost nonexistent. The ratio between the two categories in the active nonagricultural population (i.e., 39 for men; 45 for women in France, 1954) is made equal to 100. Nobody then will be surprised to note that engineers' CAI is 110, while technicians' is 62; or that metal unskilled workers' is 64 instead of 78 for their textile colleagues.

Table 7 gives a selection of significant indexes corresponding to various groupings or occupations considered in preceding paragraphs.

SERVICES

Because of their population or economic role, railways (government-owned network), house servants, and agriculture and food (distributive) trades constitute the most interesting cases.

It is impossible not to notice the very low percentage of older workers in the French railways (S.N.C.F.) and the corresponding figure for young workers. Pension schemes and recruitment policy have acted in the same direction. The ratio between contributing staff and pension-holders is already less than 1. In 1964 all members of the 45–54 group will belong to the retired 55–64 group; the picture will be worse inasmuch as the active 25–34 group will at that time be rather small. Special advantages granted to the railways' personnel (including clerical workers) have been and will have to be paid more and more by the whole French economy since the S.N.C.F. cannot cover the extra burden. In that respect the praiseworthy efforts which the S.N.C.F. still makes toward improving its productivity are counter-balanced or even offset by the demographic pattern of its personnel.

Table 7. Selected comparative indexes of aging

Category	Men	Women	Category	Men	Women
Social status			*Wage earners by*		
Employers	315	289	*industrial field*		
Top managerial staff	351		Metallurgy	69	60
Engineers	110		Motor vehicles	49	56
Executive staff	110	67	Electrical engineering	67	45
Clerical employees	92	63	Civil engineering		
Technicians	62	71	Government sector	190	
Workers (total)	62	89	Private sector	54	
Foremen and			Textiles	110	69
skilled workers			Printing	92	56
(G.S.)[a]	54	140			
Foremen and			*Individual*		
skilled workers			*occupations*		
(P.S.)[b]	64	87	Underground coal		
Semi-skilled			miners	13	
workers (G.S.)[a]	121	111	Semi-skilled metal		
Semi-skilled			workers	64	
workers (P.S.)[b]	67	80	Fitters	41	
			Tool makers	56	
			Electrical engineers	74	
			Electrical equipment		
			installers	23	
			Skilled chemical		
			workers	110	
			Semi-skilled textile		
			workers	74	78
			Civil engineers	126	

[a] G.S. = government sector.
[b] P.S. = private sector.

If, with the exception of engine drivers and firemen, the common pension scheme had been in force (with the normal retirement age of 65), the 55–64 group would have amounted at least to 45,000 instead of 21,000; about 20,000 retired people would have kept their jobs (in 1957 average retiring age: 55 years, 9 months). How many of them, still in good physical condition, find other occupations and draw, at the same time, pensions and wages?

House servants are mostly female (95.1 percent). Besides a very high percentage of young ones (32.2 percent), there are many in the 55–64 group, and house servants hold the record of aged active people (farming excluded); 7.9 percent are aged more than 65 (see Table 8). Among the young, it can be mentioned that many girls start in this occupation and leave it afterward. Among the oldest, they are either old family servants (a constantly decreasing type) or widows who become charwomen in order to get necessary means of living. It is thus easy to understand why the 25–44 groups are small.

Food servicing and distributive activities (and distributive trade in

Table 8. *Percentage distribution of employed wage earners in service activities, by age*[a]

		Age[b]			
Service activity	Total number	Under 25	45–54	55–64	65 and over
Railways (G.S.),[c] males	408,640	4.5	30.6	5.1	0.1
House servants, females	532,820	32.2	18.2	20.2	7.9
Food servicing and distributive trade					
Males	245,560	26.6	16.8	8.3	3.0
Females	109,360	32.0	19.2	10.0	2.2

[a] Source: 1954 Census (I.N.S.E.E.), Table DA f₁.
[b] 25–44 omitted.   [c] G.S. = government sector.

general) have a pattern similar to that of servants; they draw young people, mostly girls (anyone may observe the large numbers of female shop assistants or clerks in all Western countries); but possibly owing to the question of appearance, the percentage of aged female employees is low. More elaborated series would help to account for the difference, at this age, between common employees and the managing staff. Standing jobs, very common in shops, are of course improper for women after a certain age. The CAI in trade is 67 for men and 51 for women.

CONCLUSION

The analysis of aging in the active population (at least in France) is made more difficult by several factors.

Statistical reasons

Although the latest census was undertaken in 1954, no age-specific series are yet available on an area basis. It is not possible to check the existence of discrepancies in age structure of the whole population and also in that of the total working population (or that of the active population in such and such branch) or to determine whether they are more accentuated in some areas. Obviously the hiring of young people coming from rural districts hides the aging of some collective activities. It would be necessary to complete census data (as far as census instructions do not change) by periodical surveys on employment or by special surveys of branches or occupations. The "Enquête sociale sur la situation des ingénieurs diplômés" (1958, Fédération des associations et sociétés françaises d'ingénieurs diplômés) opens the way in that direction.

Extra pension schemes could provide valuable information, in spite of differences of classification.

Economic growth

Since the war, many activities have expanded so much that the gap between the total population and the active population has been widened to such an extent that, in some instances, the usual holes in the age pyramid do not exist. The appeal of up-to-date production plays a role in hiring [CAI in motor vehicles is 49 (m), in electrical engineering 67 (m)], but the absence of training or information also explains the abnormal inflation of young personnel in shops. If tomorrow the "secondary" sector does not offer a sufficient number of jobs, young manpower, as a wave, will flood the "tertiary," already too heavy in the French economy.

Role of the government sector

The rules in force in the government-controlled sector have an influence on the evolution of individual careers; they appeal to people looking for stable employment; they serve as a basis for claims (see Table 7). The number of wage earners in this sector bears on the whole economy. Examples given by public undertakings such as that at Renault might be dangerous for firms of a lower standing. By the way, a very small staff turnover at Renault is a cause of aging which can counterbalance the gains in productivity, and this is a source of worry for the management.

Size of undertakings

It would be very useful to study the demographic pattern of big concerns over several years in order to check whether they offer more or fewer possibilities of employment to older workers (say, after 55) than small or middle-sized undertakings. Many steps advocated in favor of this type of personnel cannot be implemented under a minimum size unless difficult clearing mechanisms are provided.

The study of demographic aging in economic activities is only in its initial phase. The field is wide open for research.

REFERENCES

Febvay, M. 1956. La population agricole Française-structure actuelle et évolution. Etudes et conjuncture, 11: No. 8 (Août), 707–39.

Pressat, R. 1957a. La population agricole en France: structure actuelle et prévisions jusqu'en 1966. Population, 12: No. 1 (Janvier-Mars), 17–35.

——— 1957b. La population agricole des départements structure actuelle. Evolution jusqu'en 1964. Population, 12: No. 2 (Avril-Juin), 209–36.

The Aging of Human Populations:
Mechanisms of Change

CLYDE V. KISER

THE aging of individuals and the aging of populations are two distinct but interrelated problems. By definition, a living individual's chronological age increases with the passage of time. The problems in the aging of the individual are those of biological and psychological changes inherent in passage from infancy to old age. The aging of a population, in contrast, refers to the *increase of the proportion* of old people and *decrease of the proportion* of young people in the total population of an area or society. Thus the passage of time per se does not necessarily bring an aging of the population. The age distribution of a population may remain virtually unchanged for a long period. In fact, the population might even become younger, for a period at least, with the passage of time.

The age structure of a population has much to do with its form and functioning. A society with a high proportion of young people may be expected to differ in its outlook and way of life from one that has a high proportion of older members. Changes in the age composition of a society may be expected to produce adaptive changes in many areas of behavior.

In this paper we shall consider, with special reference to the United States: (1) the trends in aging of the population, (2) the mechanisms of change, (3) differentials in aging, and (4) some demographic characteristics of aged people.

TRENDS IN AGING

The number and proportion of aged persons—i.e., those 65 years of age and over—have increased continuously in this country for well over a century (Thompson and Whelpton, 1933; von Mering and Weniger, 1959). As late as 1900, however, there were only about 3.1

million people 65 years of age and over in the United States and they constituted only 4.1 percent of the total population. In 1958, according to estimates of the Bureau of the Census, there were some 15.0 million people 65 years of age and over and they comprised about 8.7 percent of the population (U.S. Bureau of the Census, 1959). The 1960 Census is expected to show that persons 65 years and over number about 15.8 million and constitute about 8.8 percent of the total population. There is a sounder basis for estimating the number of aged persons 15 to 25 years in the future than the percentage that they will form of the total population because of uncertainties as to the course of fertility. Estimates of about 21.9 million aged persons constituting 9.0 to 10.1 percent of the population have been made for the year 1975 (U.S. Department of Health, Education, and Welfare, 1960).

Trends in the age distribution of the whites and Negroes of the United States during 1880–1958 are shown in Fig. 1.[1] This chart shows the changing proportions of the population in four broad age groups: under 20; 20–44; 45–64; and 65 and over. These groups are sometimes labeled, respectively, children and youth, the younger working force, the older working force, and the aged. The proportion of persons under 20 years old declined continuously until 1950. It subsequently increased because of the increases in fertility that have been under way since 1940. In contrast, there have been continuous increases in the proportion of persons 45 years of age and over. For both whites and Negroes the proportion of persons in the younger working force, 20–44, remained fairly constant until about 1950 when the small crop of babies born during the thirties began advancing into the 20–44 bracket and being replaced in the under-20 category by the larger cohorts of the baby boom.

The nature of the recent changes induced by changing fertility may be illustrated more clearly by comparing the age pyramids for the United States for the years 1900, 1940, and 1958, shown in Figs. 2, 3, and 4. Age pyramids are simply devices for showing the age-sex distribution of a population at a given time. They may indicate absolute numbers in given age-sex categories, or, as in the present instance, they may indicate the percentage that a given age-sex group forms of the total population.

As indicated in Fig. 2, the population profile for the whites in this country in 1900 was that of a virtually perfect pyramid. With advancing 5-year age groups, there were successively smaller proportions of

[1] The data for the years 1880, 1890, and 1958 are for nonwhites instead of Negroes.

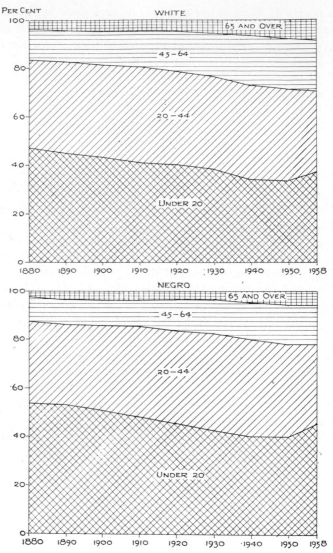

Fig. 1. The aging of human populations: mechanisms of change
Composition by broad age groups of the white and Negro population of the
United States, 1880–1958. The data in the lower section for 1880, 1890, and
1958 relate to nonwhites.

people. The base of the pyramid is broad, reflecting high birth rates,
and the top of the pyramid tapers off sharply and consistently. The
age pyramid for the Negroes in 1900 was much like that of an underdeveloped country. The relatively broad base reflects the high birth

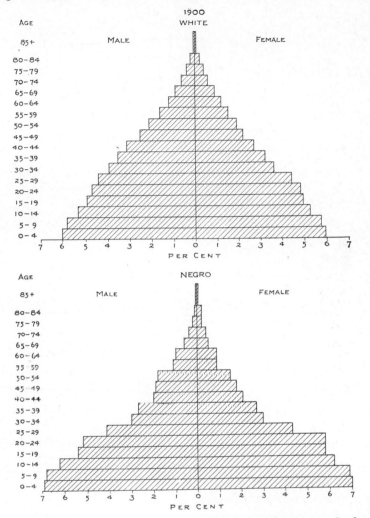

Fig. 2. The aging of human populations: mechanisms of change
Age pyramids for the white and Negro populations of the United States, 1900.

rates of Negroes, who in 1900 were largely concentrated in the rural areas of the South.

The 1940 pyramid, depicted in Fig. 3, shows marked erosion of the base, due to the sharp declines in fertility that had been under way during the twenties and thirties. In 1940, because of 2 decades of sharp declines in birth rates, there were fewer white people 10–14 than 15–19, fewer 5–9 than 10–14, and fewer under 5 than 5–9. To some extent this situation also prevailed for Negroes in 1940. The

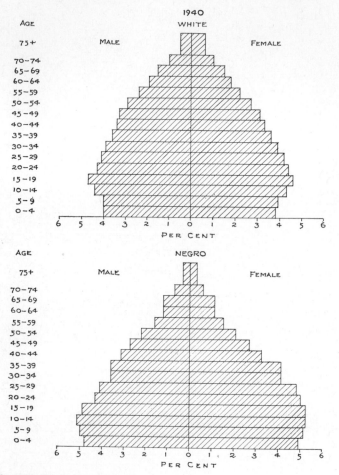

Fig. 3. The aging of human populations: mechanisms of change
Age pyramids for the white and Negro populations of the United States, 1940.

decrease in the proportion of children and youth rather automatically increased the proportion of persons in the other age categories because the percentages add to 100.

The 1958 age profile in Fig. 4 reflects the restorative effect of the baby boom on the base of the pyramid. If we conceal the data for the whites under 20 years old, we see again the shape of the 1940 pyramid. The gash that is in the pyramid because of the low birth rates of the previous times will travel upward in the pyramid with the passage of time.

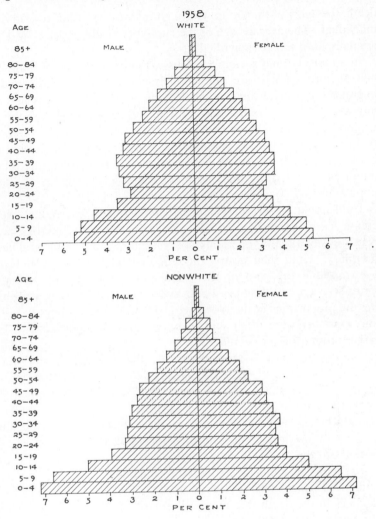

Fig. 4
Age pyramids for the white and nonwhite populations of the United States, 1958. Estimates of population from U.S. Bureau of the Census, *Current Population Reports,* Series P-25, No. 193 (February 11, 1959).

MECHANISMS OF AGING OF POPULATIONS

Attention may now be turned to the components of population change and their effects on the age structure. If a group of young men of precisely the same age are imprisoned or put on an island for life, with no further admissions and with no departures except through death, the aging of the group will be the same as that for any surviving individual. The average age of the survivors would increase by 1 year annually until the last one died.

In a more normal society, of course, there are people of both sexes and all ages. There are annual increments through births and in-migration and there are annual decrements through deaths and out-migration. Births, deaths, in-migration, and out-migration are the four components of population change, and they have bearing on composition as well as size of the population. Consideration of migration may be deferred for the moment and attention will be given to the relative importance of fertility and mortality trends on the aging of human population.

Until about 10 years ago most demographers interpreted the increase in the proportion of old people in Western countries as the result of the jointly operating declines in fertility and declines in mortality. Until then it was thought that while declines in fertility were eroding the base of the population pyramid, the declines in mortality were enabling people to live longer and hence were enhancing the proportions in the older ages. In this sense declines in fertility and mortality were often said to be working hand in hand to bring larger proportions of people into the older age groups.

During the past decade, however, the researches of Valaoras (1950), Lorimer (1951), Sauvy (1954), Coale (1956*a* and *b*), Stolnitz (1956), the United Nations (1954, 1956), and others have demonstrated that *past* increases in proportion of older persons in the United States and other Western countries have been a result almost entirely of declines in the fertility rate and virtually not at all of declines in the mortality rate.

It should be emphasized that this statement refers to *past* trends and more specifically to trends up to about 1940. In the future, declines in the death rate may well emerge as the dominant factor in the further aging of the population in this country.

The *past* reductions in mortality rates have been concentrated heavily at the young ages. They have been especially marked among infants and children. As a consequence, the *past* declines in mortality in this country have had much the same effect that increases in the birth rate would have. Hence, they have tended to increase the proportion of youngsters and to retard rather than to accelerate the aging of the population. Thus the declines in mortality in the past have not contributed to any appreciable increase in the proportion of older people because there has thus far been relatively little decline in the mortality rates at the older ages. If the *future* declines in mortality are concentrated largely in the older age groups, as indeed they might well be, the declines in mortality will produce an older population.

Empirical evidence of the irrelevance of *past* mortality trends to the aging of the population has been supplied by Coale who demonstrated that with the existing declines in fertility in Sweden since 1860 the age distribution in 1950 would have been virtually what it actually was in 1950, even if mortality had remained at the 1860 levels. He has also shown that with the existing declines in fertility since 1860, the age distribution in 1950 would have been approximately the same as the actual for 1950, even if mortality had been at the 1950 level throughout the entire period of the preceding 90 years. To generalize, the life table of Sweden for 1860 with a life expectancy of about 45 years, and that for 1946–1950, with a life expectancy of about 72 years produce about the same age distributions when combined with the same fertility schedule (Coale, 1957).

In a recent report, the Population Branch of the United Nations has provided similar findings. Figure 5 shows the composition by broad age groups of model stable populations corresponding to given levels of fertility and mortality, as computed by the Population Branch (United Nations, 1956). Under similar gross reproduction rates above 1.0 the proportions of the stable population 60 years of age and over are much the same with increasing expectation of life at birth. In fact, the proportion of people 0–14 tends to increase with rise of expectation and constancy of reproduction.

In contrast, with lowering of reproduction and constancy of mortality there are marked reductions in proportions 0–14 years old and increases in the proportion of persons 60 years old and over. This is evident by comparison of the four panels in Fig. 5.

The United Nations report carefully points out that age structure is not simply a function of existing levels of expectation of life and reproduction rates. It is rather a function of the past levels of these variables. Nevertheless the data demonstrate the sharper relevance of declines in fertility than of declines in mortality to the past aging of populations.

It is also emphasized that since 1940 the increases in fertility in the United States have served to increase the proportions of people in the young age groups and to lower the median age of the population; although the proportion of people 65 years of age and over continued to increase.[2]

---

[2] In terms of age differentials in rates of growth, since 1940 the United States population has increased most at the two extremes, i.e., the young and

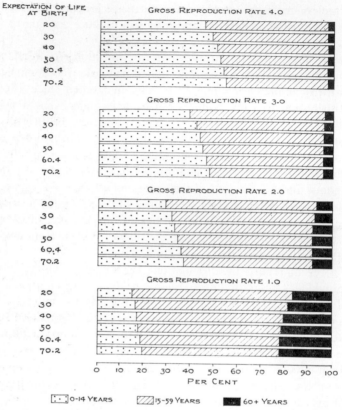

EXPECTATION OF LIFE AT BIRTH

GROSS REPRODUCTION RATE 4.0

20
30
40
50
60.4
70.2

GROSS REPRODUCTION RATE 3.0

20
30
40
50
60.4
70.2

GROSS REPRODUCTION RATE 2.0

20
30
40
50
60.4
70.2

GROSS REPRODUCTION RATE 1.0

20
30
40
50
60.4
70.2

O   10   20   30   40   50   60   70   80   90   100
PER CENT

0-14 YEARS   15-59 YEARS   60+ YEARS

Fig. 5

Composition by broad age groups of model stable populations corresponding to different levels of fertility and mortality. Based on "The Aging of Populations and its Economic and Social Implications," *Population Studies*, No. 26, United Nations, New York, 1956, p. 26.

The writer realizes that people in medical and health circles may be surprised to learn that declines in mortality have had very little to do with past aging of the population of modern Western countries. Some of them have tended to attribute most of the responsibility for aging to declining mortality. In this connection, much depends upon what one means by *aging* of the population. If we mean increase in expectation of life at birth, the declines in mortality rates are obviously the virtually sole factor. Declines in fertility may be indirectly involved in that the spacing of births may facilitate declines in mortality.

the old. Thus, during 1950–1958 the estimated increase was 15 percent for the total population. It was 29 percent for those under 20, 1 percent for those 20–44, 15 percent for those 45–64, and 23 percent for those 65 and over.

Nevertheless, mortality rates alone form the basis from which average length of life is computed by actuarial methods.

Also, if by aging of the population we mean the increase in sheer numbers of old people, declines in mortality again constitute the responsible agency. In this connection we may also acknowledge that the growing numbers of the aged in this country and the outlook for still larger increases make the problem a massive one. When one considers costs of programs of medical care for the aged, for instance, the future trends in the number of aged are factors of major concern. It is the sheer magnitude of the expected numbers of aged persons that baffles those concerned with future problems of chronic disease and mental illness.

However, when the demographer speaks of the aging of populations he generally means the increase in the proportion of people in the older age groups. He does not mean increases in the expectation of life or increases in sheer numbers of old people.

Migration

Most of the recent studies of the relative roles of declining fertility and declining mortality on the age structure of the population have utilized closed population models or countries with relatively little immigration or emigration in order to rule out the factor of migration. This has not been based on any assumption of the unimportance of migration. It has been prompted instead by recognition of the complexity of the factor of migration and the desire to avoid this complexity in the assessment of the relative roles of fertility and mortality.

Since both international movements and internal migrations of human populations are frequently selective with respect to age, these factors often affect the age distribution of both sending and receiving areas.

With respect to international movements, the sudden stoppage of immigration to this country in the twenties means that the existing foreign-born population has aged considerably and is now concentrated largely in the older ages. In considering the effects of migration from abroad, however, we should remember that, without getting credit for it, the native children of foreign-born parents have to some extent mitigated the effects of the foreign-born on the age distribution of the United States in recent years.

Internal migration frequently has bearing on the regional and urban-rural differences in age distribution to be discussed later.

Another aspect of this question is the mobility of the aged people themselves. The aged persons in 1950 were somewhat less mobile during the preceding year than were the younger people. It will be recalled that in the 1950 Census, people were asked where they were living 12 months previous. The replies were tabulated in terms of same or different house, same or different county, and same or differ- ent state. About 90 percent of the aged males and females were classified as nonmovers as compared with 78 percent for males 20–64, and 81 percent for females of this age. Only about 5 percent of the aged as compared with 7–9 percent of the persons 20–64 reported that they had lived in a different county 1 year previous.

DIFFERENTIALS IN AGING
Aging in relation to modernization

In general the proportion of population aged 65 and over tends to be directly related to degree of modernization. Data for nations as units probably would show that the proportion of aged persons in the population is directly related to the percentage of the population that is urban. It tends to be directly related to the educational attainment of the population. The percent of population 65 and over is inversely cor- related with magnitude of the birth and death rates. There is good reason to believe that the inverse relation with the death rate simply reflects the relation with modernization; the causal relation stems from the declines in the birth rates. At least this has been the case in Western countries in the past, up to about 1940.

To some extent the positive relation of aging with modernization helps to explain some of the detailed correlates with aging, such as color, region, and urban-rural status. However, the detailed correlates may also reflect other factors, especially selective factors.

Color

The process of aging has advanced further among the whites than nonwhites in the United States. Thus in 1950 about 8.4 percent of the whites and 5.7 percent of the nonwhites were 65 years old and over. However, the gap between the two groups has narrowed con- siderably. The differential has been due to the greater lag in the decline of the birth rate among the nonwhites than among the whites.

In terms of distribution of the aged by color, in 1950 about 93 percent were white and 7 percent were nonwhite.

Nativity

Differences in age composition of the native and foreign-born reflect periods and ages of migration, historical trends in immigration policy, and differences inherent in the definitions of the terms. In the nature of the case the foreign-born population includes relatively few infants; children born in the new country are natives of it. Since the large migrations from Europe to this country were virtually stopped by the quota laws of the twenties, a heavy proportion of the foreign-born residents of this country are in the older age groups. In 1950, about 27 percent of the foreign-born whites as compared with 7 percent of the native whites were 65 years old and over. The median age was 56 for the foreign-born whites and 29 for the native whites. It is because of their relatively high proportion of older people that the foreign-born whites contributed 18 percent of the deaths in the United States in 1950 although they constituted only 7 percent of the total population. As already noted, if the offspring of the foreign-born people in this country could be allocated to their parents, a considerable part of the difference between the natives and foreign-born with respect to age structure would be eliminated.

Urban-rural residence

The age distribution by urban-rural residence reflects differences in fertility rates in the past. It also reflects age selections in the past migrations from rural to urban areas. Thus the base of the age pyramid tends to be broader in rural than in urban areas, reflecting the higher birth rates in the rural areas. The high proportion of youngsters is especially prominent in the rural-farm areas.

The relatively high proportion of young adults in urban areas reflects the migration of youngsters to the cities. The rural-farm population is especially short on this segment of population.

In terms of distribution, the aged are somewhat less urbanized than the general population. Among 11 million whites 65 years old and over in 1950, about 64 percent were in urban areas, 22 percent in rural-nonfarm areas, and 14 percent in rural-farm areas. The nonwhite aged are more rural. Among the 900,000 nonwhites 65 years old and over in 1950, 57 percent were in urban areas, 22 percent were in rural-nonfarm areas, and 22 percent were in rural-farm areas.

Regional differences in age structure

Regional differences in age structure reflect regional differences in fertility and in composition of the population by color, nativity, urban-rural residence, and migration status. Thus the South ranks above average in proportions rural and nonwhite. It is an area marked by a long period of high fertility and high natural increase but also of out-migration of both whites and Negroes to other regions.

The attractiveness of certain areas with mild winters to the older people sometimes serves noticeably to inflate the proportion of older people within given states and regions. However, the influence of this factor on the proportion of older people is not as strong as one might think. In 1950 persons 65 years of age and over comprised 8.5 percent of the population in California, 8.6 percent in Florida, and 8.1 percent in the United States as a whole. California is attractive to older people but it is also attractive to the middle-aged and younger people. Some cities in Florida cater to the older people but in the state as a whole there are also many inducements for younger people.

DEMOGRAPHIC CHARACTERISTICS OF AGED PEOPLE
Sex in relation to aging

Because of their greater longevity, females are conspicuously more numerous than males among the aged. In 1958, among 15 million persons 65 years old and over in the United States slightly fewer than 7 million (46 percent) were males and over 8 million (54 percent) were females. The sex ratio, i.e., the number of males per 100 females, was 84 for all persons 65 years of age and over. By specific age group, the sex ratio was about 90 at ages 65–69, 85 at ages 70–74, and 76 at ages 75 and over. Further details are given in Table 1.

By residence, the number of males per 100 females 65 years old and over in 1950 was lowest in urban areas (79), intermediate in rural-nonfarm areas (95), and highest in rural-farm areas (126). Stated differently, among the males 65 years of age and over in 1950, 60 percent were in urban areas, 23 percent were in rural-nonfarm areas, and 17 percent were in rural-farm areas. Among the females the corresponding percentages were 67, 21, and 12.

Marital status

The high proportion of broken marriages complicates the problem of the aged. In 1950, among the persons 65 years of age and over,

Table 1. Sex ratios (males per 100 females) by age, residence, and color, United States, 1950[a]

Age	TOTAL			URBAN			RURAL–NONFARM			RURAL–FARM		
	Total	White	Nonwhite	Total	White	Nonwhite	Total	White	Nonwhite	Total	White	Nonwhite
All ages	99	99	96	95	95	92	104	104	103	110	111	103
Under 5	104	104	101	104	104	100	104	105	101	104	105	101
5–9	104	104	100	103	103	98	104	105	100	105	106	101
10–14	104	104	101	102	102	98	105	105	103	108	109	105
15–19	100	101	95	92	93	86	108	109	102	118	121	107
20–24	95	97	86	90	91	78	104	103	109	117	122	95
25–29	95	96	90	93	94	86	99	98	108	101	103	91
30–34	96	96	88	93	94	85	101	101	103	99	100	90
35–39	96	97	90	93	94	87	104	105	102	103	105	93
40–44	99	99	96	95	95	94	107	107	104	108	109	101
45–49	100	100	98	96	96	96	107	107	103	109	110	103
50–54	100	99	102	96	96	102	105	105	102	111	112	104
55–59	101	100	107	97	96	104	103	103	107	118	118	119
60–64	101	100	105	95	95	100	102	102	101	127	127	127
65–69	94	94	93	86	86	86	98	99	89	131	132	124
70–74	91	91	101	81	81	89	100	100	101	135	134	137
75–84	85	84	99	74	73	84	100	99	109	126	125	131
85+	70	70	72	60	60	62	85	84	86	95	97	80

[a] Source: U.S. Bureau of the Census, *1950 Census of Population*, Vol. II, *Characteristics of the Population*, Part 1, "United States Summary," Washington, D.C., U.S. Government Printing Office, 1953, Table, 38, p. 1-91.

about two-thirds of the males and only one-third of the females reported themselves as married in the 1950 Census. About one-fourth of the males and over half of the females were widowed. Only about 8 percent of the males and females 65 years of age and over reported themselves as single and about 2 percent as divorced.

Several factors account for the higher proportion of widowhood among aged females than aged males. Wives tend to outlive husbands because they have the dual advantage of younger age at marriage and longer expectation of life. Furthermore, remarriages are more frequent among aged males than among aged females because the males tend to choose brides under age 65.

Widowhood among the aged is more pronounced among the non-whites than among the whites. Thus among males 65 and over in 1950 the percent widowed was 24 for whites and 29 for nonwhites. Among females it was 53 for whites and 66 for nonwhites. For whites and nonwhites widowhood among the aged is more pronounced in urban than in rural areas. Thus, among males 65 years of age and over, the percent widowed in 1950 was 25 in urban areas, 24 in rural-nonfarm areas, and 21 in rural-farm areas. Among the females it was 57 percent in urban areas, 52 percent in rural-nonfarm areas, and 45 percent in rural-farm areas.

Relationship to the head of the house

Largely because of the greater prevalence of widowhood among aged females than males, the old women live in the homes of their children and other relatives to a greater extent than do their male counterparts. In 1950, about 9 percent of the aged males and 21 percent of the aged females were living with their children, i.e., they were in households in which they were reported as parents or parents-in-law of the heads of the household (Table 2). An additional 4 percent of the males and 7 percent of the females were in homes of other relatives. The remaining 11 percent of the males and 9 percent of the females were enumerated in households of nonrelatives or in institutions of various types.

As expected, within the age groups 65 and over, the proportion of males and females reported as living in their own households (head or wife of head) declines sharply with age. Among the aged people in urban areas in particular, the proportion reported as living in their own households was somewhat higher for whites than for nonwhites. This may be partly a function of the lower proportion widowed.

Table 2. *Percentage distribution of persons 65 years old and over by relationship to head of household, by sex, residence, and color, United States, 1950*[a,b]

Relation to head	WHITE		NONWHITE	
	Male	*Female*	*Male*	*Female*
	All residences			
Head or spouse	76	63	75	59
Parent or parent-in-law	10	21	7	22
Other relative	4	7	5	9
Other	11	9	13	10
	Urban			
Head or spouse	74	62	69	56
Parent or parent-in-law	10	21	8	23
Other relative	4	7	5	9
Other	12	11	18	12
	Rural-nonfarm			
Head or spouse	78	68	80	70
Parent or parent-in-law	8	16	6	15
Other relative	4	6	4	7
Other	11	10	10	7
	Rural-farm			
Head or spouse	80	63	83	59
Parent or parent-in-law	11	27	8	27
Other relative	5	8	5	11
Other	4	2	4	3

[a] Source: U.S. Bureau of the Census, derived from *1950 Census of Population*, Vol. II. *Characteristics of the Population*, Part 1, "United States Summary," Washington, D.C., U.S. Government Printing Office, 1953, Tables 107 and 108, pp. 1-192, 1-205.

[b] Percentages have been rounded off.

However, the differences are not great when age and type of community are held constant.

By type of community, the proportion of aged persons living in their own households (head or wife of head of the household) was 67 percent in urban areas, and 73 percent in both rural-nonfarm and rural-farm areas. In rural-farm areas it is probably physically easier to "take in" the aged parent or relative. In urban areas and particularly in apartment houses there is less likely to be an extra room or an extra bed that the aged parent could use. Perhaps partly for this reason the proportion of oldsters living in institutions is higher in urban than in rural areas. It is recognized, of course, that nursing homes and institutions are more likely to be in urban areas. It is also recognized that it may be easier to continue housekeeping activities in small towns than in cities.

The foregoing data on marital status of the aged and their relationship to household heads probably add up to a situation of loneliness for many of the aged. Elderly men frequently undergo a change of role from economically productive citizens to inactive ones, from that of head of a family to an onlooker, from an active to an inactive role in the church and community. Women do not so frequently face the sharp transition from full-time employment to economic inactivity, but for them the problem of loneliness may loom larger because of the greater degree of widowhood. For men and women loneliness may be increased with the onset of disabilities and defects such as deafness. A substantial proportion of old people are victims of degenerative diseases like heart diseases and cancer, or succumb to mental illness. Many are in hospitals for chronic diseases and in mental institutions.

Through strengthening the provisions of social security we may mitigate some of the economic hardships faced by the aged. Through advances in the treatment of chronic illness, we may add more years to the lives of the aged. We may even find it possible to improve the mental health of the aged. Through community efforts we may help the aged in various ways. But in all these efforts we would perhaps do well to remember that the aged are human beings who want to lead useful lives and who want to be respected, recognized, and loved, perhaps especially by their own children.

Acknowledgment. The author wishes to acknowledge the invaluable assistance of Miss Vivian Small in collecting the data for this paper.

REFERENCES

Coale, A. J. 1956*a*. The effects of changes in mortality and fertility on age composition. Milbank Mem. Fund. Quart., 34: 79–114.
——— 1956*b*. The effect of declines in mortality on age distribution. *In* Trends and differentials in mortality, pp. 125–32. New York: Milbank Memorial Fund.
——— 1957. How the age distribution of a human population is determined. Cold Spring Harbor Symposia on Quantitatve Biology, 22: 83–89.
Lorimer, F. 1951. Dynamics of age structure in a population with initially high fertility and mortality. (Population Bulletin, No. 1.), December, 31–41. New York: United Nations.
Mering, O., von, and Weniger, F. L. 1959. Social-cultural background of the aging individual. *In* J. E. Birren (ed.), Handbook of aging and the individual, pp. 279–335. Chicago: University of Chicago Press.
Sauvy, A. 1954. Le vieillessement des populations et l'allongement de la vie. Population, 9: 675–82.

Stolnitz, G. J. 1956. Mortality declines and age distributon. Milbank Mem. Fund Quart., 34: 178–215.

Thompson, W. S., and Whelpton, P. K. 1933. Population trends in the United States. New York: McGraw Hill Book Co.

United Nations. 1954. Population Division. The cause of the aging of populations: declining mortality or declining fertility? (Population Bulletin, No. 4), December. New York: United Nations.

———— 1956. Department of Economic and Social Affairs. The aging of populations and its economic and social implications. (Population Studies, No. 26.) New York: United Nations.

U.S. Bureau of the Census. 1959. Current population reports. (Series P-25, No. 193.) Washington, D.C.: The Bureau.

U.S. Department of Health, Education, and Welfare. Social Security Administration. 1960. Health, education, and welfare trends. Washington, D.C.: Government Printing Office.

Valaoras, V. G. 1950. Patterns of aging of human populations. *In* Social and biological challenge of our aging population, pp. 67–85. New York: Columbia University Press.

Longevity and the Never-Married

BELLE BOONE BEARD

THIS paper proposes for further study what appears to be a new population phenomenon—the increasing number of never-married in the second half of the life-span. Although various sociological studies have shown that the mortality rate of married women is less than that of single women in the years from 15 to 40, recent investigations into the life-span of alleged centenarians indicate that the trend is reversed in the later years. Previously it had been assumed that the advantage of marriage continued throughout life and that having been married increased one's life chances. In other words, singleness was thought to be negatively correlated with longevity. This paper seeks to show that the reverse is true.

Many studies of marriage have been made. This is the first study of singleness in relation to longevity.

Since the validity of a thesis depends upon the accuracy of classification, one may well ask: Can marital status be ascertained with certainty? Authentic classification of marital status is sometimes difficult to obtain since social and economic and perhaps political factors affect the accuracy of reporting. "Single" is used as synonymous with "never-married." In the official recording of marital status in all countries cited, persons who have ever been married are expected to use the appropriate classification: "married," "separated," "divorced," or "widowed." Annulment is the only exception; annulment invalidates the marriage and returns the person to his previous marital status. When the term "married" is used it applies to a person living with spouse; otherwise the term "never-married" is used or previous marriage is indicated. The most we can say of some of the data presented here is that the classification used is the one by which the individual is officially known or which he prescribes as applying to himself.

The custom of designating females who have ever been married as

This investigation has been facilitated by assistance from the Mary K. Houck Foundation, Mrs. Leslie McCurdy, The National Institutes of Health, and The Southern Fellowships Fund.

"Mrs." and ones who have never been married as "Miss" gives a clue to the marital status of females which is not available for males. Males are indiscriminately designated as "Mr." whether single, married, divorced, etc. In some societies only the title "Mrs." is used, it being assumed that females without a title are unmarried. There are chances of error in such reporting. There may be deliberate falsification. Married persons for professional or other reasons may report themselves as single. Single women—as, for example, unwed mothers—may use the title "Mrs." Some divorced persons may have reported themselves as single. We have accepted marital status as reported. Among the 450 centenarians on whom the author has made detailed investigation, no case of misrepresentation regarding marital status was found.

Essentially the question treated in this paper is not "What effect does marriage have on the life-span?" but "What effect does singleness have?" No attempt has been made to analyze the relative weights of first, second, third, or subsequent marriages, or of widowhood, separation, or divorce with or without remarriage. It is well known that the mortality rate of persons married and living with spouse is lower than the mortality rate of single, widowed, and divorced. However, when the married lose this status through death or otherwise they lose their mortality advantage. Widowhood for the female is the giant killer. It is not the purpose of this paper, however, to evaluate marital status other than to differentiate between the life-span of the never married and the married.

Normally the percentage of single in the population is expected to decline progressively, since people do get married even after 100 years of age. And if singleness were dysgenic, as previously supposed, we would expect that the percentage of single would decline more rapidly as age advances. Actually the percentage of single in the later years is increasing in many countries. The percentage of single decreases through marriage and death; the percentage of single increases only by relatively more deaths among those who have married.

In order to isolate the issue, the hypothesis to be examined is: Single persons in their later years outlive those who have married. It is concerned with one factor, the effect of singleness on the life-span.

Three types of evidence are presented to test the hypothesis that the single have greater longevity than the married:

1. Official census data from twelve countries[1];

[1] Official Census Reports furnished by:
S. R. Carver, Commonwealth Statistician, Census of the Commonwealth of Australia, June 30, 1954. (a) "Males Classified According to Age in Conjunction with Conjugal Condition," (b) "Females Classified According to Age in

2. Enumeration of centenarians in various limited populations;
3. Personal investigations of specified older populations.

Table 1 presents the percentage of single in Australia, Canada, England and Wales, France, Germany, Hungary, The Netherlands, New Zealand, Norway, Sweden, Switzerland, and the United States, according to the latest available census reports. There is no claim that the countries mentioned here are typical. The presence or absence of a country has no special significance. In late 1959 letters were sent to all United Nations countries requesting data on marital status by age and sex. Twenty-one countries replied that they had no official

Conjunction with Conjugal Condition," (c) No. 120a "Deaths: Males, Age and Conjugal Condition at Death, Australia, 1958," (d) No. 120b "Deaths, Females, Age and Conjugal Condition at Death, Australia, 1958."

M. Paul Paillat, Institut National d'Etudes Démographiques, Ministère de la Santé Publique et de la Population, République de Française, Paris, France, "France: Total Population by sex, age and marital status, Jan. 1, 1955."

Dr. Schwarz, Statistisches Bundesamt, Federal Republic of Germany, Wiesbaden, Germany. "Statistik der Deutschland, Band 35." nock 2.: Die Bevölkerung im Bundesgebiet (ohne Saarland und Berlin) nach Altersjahren und Familienstand am 13, 9, 1950."

U.S. Dept. of Commerce, Bureau of the Census, Washington, D.C. "The Population of Hungary," International Population Statistics Reports, Series P-90, No. 9, p. 160, Table 26. "Marital Status of the Population 15 years old and over, by age and sex: 1949."

Dr. J. Ch. W. Verstege, Deputy Director-General of Statistics, Central Bureau voor de Statistiek, The Hague, The Netherlands. "Bevolking naar Leeffÿd Geslacht en Burgerlÿke ataat, 31 December, 1958."

A. E. Edridge, Acting Government Statistician, Department of Statistics, Wellington, New Zealand. Table 1, "Marital Status of New Zealand Population (Including Maoris) 50 years and over—1956 Census."

Signy Arctander, Statistisk Sentralbyra, Oslo, Norway, 1953. Norges Offisielle Statistikk XI. 146. "Folketelligen 1, Desember 1950. p. 12 Tabell j. Gifte og for gifte pr. 1 000 i de enkelte aldersklasser, 1900–1950."

Statistisk Tidskrift NR 5, Maj. 1957 Statistiska Centralbyran, Stockholm, 22 Sweden. "Folkräkningen, den 31 December 1950. V Totala Räkningen, Folkmängden efter Ålder, Kön Och Civilstand. p. 33 Tab. U. "Relativa civilstand fördelningen inom olika aldersgrupper, aren 1945 och 1950."

E. Zollinger, Bureau Federal de Statistique, Bern, Helvetia. "Wohnbevolkerung der Schweiz nach Geburtsjahr, Geschlecht, Heimat, Zivilstand 1950." P. 48 "Mannliche Bevölkerung der Schweiz nach Fünjahresklassen und Zivilstand." P. 49 "Weibliche Bevölkerung der Schweiz nach Fünjahresklassen und Zivilstand."

Census of Canada, 1956, Population: "Marital Status by Age Groups." Dominion Bureau of Statistics, Ottawa, Canada, 1957.

Statistical Review of England and Wales, Table A3, "Estimated Total Population of England and Wales by Sex, Age and Marital Condition, as at 30th June 1958," General Register Office, London, W.C. 2, England.

U.S. Dept. of Commerce, Bureau of the Census. Washington, D.C. 1950 United States Census of Population, Table 102, "Marital Status, by Age and Sex, 1890 to 1950, and by Color, 1950 and 1940, for the United States," pp. 1–179 and 1–180.

data on this subject. The data presented, unless otherwise indicated, were supplied by the official population statistics bureaus of the designated countries. To date, replies have been received from less than half of the nations of the world. As this preliminary draft is written we have no data on the Orient, Africa, South America, or on the U.S.S.R. The countries cited here as showing the greatest increase in singleness in the later years are, for the most part, of Western, Indo-European culture; and, for the most part, they are countries which are urbanized and industrialized.

We are concerned primarily with the proportion of single in the second half of life but have included the total age span when available in order that the reversal of the curve of singleness may be seen. It will be noted that there is wide variation among countries in the percentage of the population who marry. For example, the percentage of single in Hungary declines with age, leaving only 2.9 percent of males single at 65 and over, whereas the percentage of single males in Sweden in the 65–69 age bracket is 13.8 percent and in Switzerland is 12.2 percent.

A similar disparity is found in the percentage of single females in the later years. Only 4.6 percent of females are reported single when 65 and over in Hungary as compared with 21.5 percent of females in Norway 65 and over and 21.0 percent of those 65–69 in Sweden. While these age groupings are not identical, they give a general picture of the situation.

In Switzerland the picture is confused; a low of 11.8 percent is found among males in the 55–59 age group followed by 12.0 percent at 60–64 and 12.2 percent at 65–69. After this spurt upward, the percentage of single declines to a low of 2.7 percent in the 95–99 bracket. In Sweden the single males decline to a low of 9.7 percent in the 85–89, with an increase to 10.1 percent among the 90 and over. This picture is somewhat similar to that in Australia, where the single males are 10.8 percent at 65–69, increase to 12.0 percent at 80–84, drop again to 10.7 percent at 90–94, and increase to 19.6 percent when 95–100, and to the extraordinary figure of 28.0 percent for persons 100 and over.

The picture of the single female is quite different. Only in Hungary does the ratio continue to decline. Again we wonder whether a breakdown of older ages might not show an increase of single.

There is considerably more uniformity in the pattern of singleness among females than among males, especially in the peak of singleness. In Australia, Canada, England and Wales, The Netherlands, Norway, and Sweden the peak of singleness is in the age group 35–39. From

*Table 1. Percentage of single in designated countries classified
by sex and age*

Age group	Australia (1954)	Canada (1957)	England & Wales (1951)	France (1954)	Germany (1950)
Male					
15–19	99.1	98.9	99.4	99.3	
20–24	74.0	72.1	76.2	80.7	
25–29	36.3	33.9	34.8	37.4	
30–34	19.5	18.7	18.9	18.9	
35–39	13.9	13.7	13.2	14.3	
40–44	12.3	12.2	10.8	12.2	
45–49	11.5	11.9	9.1	11.0	
50–54	11.7	12.4	8.6	9.6	5.3
55–59	11.3	12.1	7.7	7.8	4.6
60–64	11.0	11.6	7.9	6.7	4.7
65–69	10.8	11.5	8.7	6.6	4.9
70–74	11.5	11.8	8.4	6.4	4.6
75–79	11.6	11.1	8.2	6.2	5.5
80–84	12.0	10.3	7.4	6.0	5.6
85–89	11.0	9.8	6.6	5.1[a]	6.0
90–94	10.7	9.2	6.2	5.6[a]	5.8
95–99	19.6	9.1	6.6	11.3[a]	10.0
100 and over	28.0		28.1	28.6[a]	7.1
Female					
15–19	93.0	91.6	95.5	96.2	
20–24	40.9	44.2	51.7	57.0	
25–29	14.9	18.2	21.7	22.7	
30–34	9.6	11.6	14.5	13.5	
35–39	8.6	10.2	13.2	10.8	
40–44	9.1	10.5	14.2	9.7	
45–49	10.3	10.8	15.2	10.0	
50–54	11.2	10.9	14.9	10.6	12.6
55–59	11.7	10.1	15.5	11.3	12.6
60–64	12.5	9.9	15.5	11.4	11.6
65–69	13.0	9.5	15.3	10.8	10.7
70–74	13.6	9.9	17.2	9.9	10.3
75–79	14.4	10.1	16.4	10.0	12.3
80–84	14.7	10.9	16.3	9.8	10.4
85–89	13.5	11.2	17.0	8.7[a]	10.3
90–94	12.6	11.4	17.3	8.3[a]	10.7
95–99	11.0	10.9	17.2	8.3[a]	21.2
100 and over	15.2		19.8	24.5[a]	10.7

[a] Figures for 1954 are used to "80 and over." In order to have comparative statistics the 1946 figures are used from 85 to "100 and over."

age 40 on to 100 and over the ratio of single increases more or less regularly. Apparently the single woman surviving to age 40 takes a new lease on life and from then on outlives the "ever-married." A comparable low point is not reached in the United States until 50–59 when single females constitute 7.7 percent of the female population. A decline in the percentage of single is a result only of marriage or

Hungary (1949)	Nether-lands (1958)	New Zealand (1956)	Norway (1950)	Sweden (1950)	Switzer-land (1950)	United States (1950)
98.9	99.7		99.7	99.6		96.7
75.7	86.5		88.0	84.4		59.1
40.8	40.3		54.7	48.6		23.8
19.4	15.9		30.2	26.9		13.2
12.1	9.9		20.2	19.8		10.1
8.9	7.9			17.0		9.0
6.7	7.8		16.2	16.1		8.7
5.1	7.6	9.4		15.1	12.5	8.3
4.6	7.2	9.7	14.1	14.2	11.8	8.3
3.9	7.0	9.5		13.9	12.0	8.6
2.9	7.1	10.1	13.2	13.8	12.2	8.7
	7.9	9.9	10.7	13.1	11.1	8.3
	8.3	10.6		12.2	10.8	8.1
	8.8	10.9		11.1	10.4	7.4
	10.7	11.0		9.7	9.1	7.7
		7.6		10.1	8.7	
		10.6			2.7	
		28.5				
88.5	97.4		96.9	96.3		82.9
46.6	63.7		65.6	59.6		32.3
21.9	22.4		33.3	26.4		13.3
13.9	12.6		20.1	15.8		0.3
10.7	10.8		17.3	14.3		8.4
9.4	10.8			15.8		8.3
8.4	11.6		19.4	18.4		7.9
8.0	12.1	11.0		19.8	19.1	7.7
7.1	12.2	11.4	21.2	20.4	18.9	7.7
6.1	12.1	12.1		21.3	18.4	8.2
4.6	12.7	12.3	21.5	21.0	17.8	8.4
	13.2	12.8	21.1	21.0	16.6	9.0
	13.5	13.5		20.9	16.8	9.4
	13.9	13.9		20.7	17.6	9.4
	14.2	12.8		20.0	18.2	9.7
		12.4		18.4	17.6	
		8.5			20.0	
					11.1	

death. We do not know without considerably further investigation whether the American female between 40 and 60 years of age marries later than her European counterpart or whether she is more prone to die.

If the increased survival of the single is a general trend as it appears to be, then The Netherlands stands out as the prime example. Only in this country is there a continuous trend for increased longevity of the single, both male and female, after middle age. But even here the single female shows this advantage earlier than the male. Single women in The Netherlands increase regularly from a low of 10.8 percent at age 35–39 to a high of 14.2 percent at 85 and over. The single males increase from a low of 7.0 percent at 60–64 to a high of 10.7 percent at 85 and over. The difference of 25 years in the peak of singleness is more pronounced here than in most countries. In Germany, for example, the peak of singleness for both men and women is in the 70–74 age category and in both cases rises irregularly to a high at 95–99.

In the United States both male and female singleness reaches a low at 50–59. The males increase irregularly while the females increase in each decade from a low of 7.7 percent to 9.7 percent at 85 and over.

MARITAL STATUS OF ALLEGED CENTENARIANS

Since the official statistics do not always report marital status in extreme old age we present the next data on alleged centenarians. If it is true that the single outlive the ever-married there should be a larger proportion of single among the survivors of mankind, those over 100 years of age.

Table 2 shows the number of males and females in each universe enumerated together with an indication of the relative number of single and "ever-married" females. The information for these reports is taken largely from newspapers and other mass media.

These lists of centenarians are not mutually exclusive. There is probably some overlapping between the Bird collection and the New York Times Index and possibly some overlapping of the first three with the Beard list, though the latter covers a much wider geographic distribution including all the states.

In Pennsylvania it is the custom of each county medical society to honor, by the presentation of a plaque, the persons within that county who reach the age of 100 years. From January 1, 1948 to July 1, 1959, 437 persons were so honored in Pennsylvania. Of these 96 were male and 341 female. Seventy-two women or 21.1 percent were recorded as single and 269 or 78.9 percent ever-married.

Farmer and La Staiti made a tabulation of centenarians indexed in the section on longevity of the New York Times Index for 1950 through 1957. This listing included 730 persons, 319 of whom were males. Of the 411 females, 82 or 20.0 percent were designated as "Miss," 329 or 80.0 percent designated as "Mrs."

Table 2. Marital status of female centenarians[a]

Source	Total	MEN Total	WOMEN Never-married Number	Never-married Percent	Ever-married Number	Ever-married Percent	Unknown Number	Unknown Percent	Total Number	Total Percent
Pennsylvania Medical Society Centenarians, Jan. 1, 1948 to July 1, 1959[b]	437	96	72	21.1	269	78.9	0	0	341	100
New York Times Longevity Index, 1950 through 1957[c]	730	319	82	20.0	329	80.0	0	0	411	100
Grace E. Bird, clipping file, 1930 to 1955	773	338	50	11.5	365	83.9	20	4.6	435	100
Belle Boone Beard, Centenarian File, United States	3445	1635	221	10.5	1859	87.4	42	2.0	2080	100
Foreign										
Canada	38	11	6	22.2	21	77.8	0	0	27	100
England	70	16	10	18.5	41	75.9	3	5.6	54	100
Other	119	52	8	11.9	41	61.2	18	26.9	67	100

[a] As reported by mass media, 1930–1960.

[b] Mr. Roy Jansen, Director of Public Relations, Pennsylvania Medical Society, Harrisburg, Pa., "Centenarians Honored by the Pennsylvania Medical Society, Jan. 1, 1948 to July 1, 1959."

[c] Alice Cary Farmer and Sanra La Staiti, "The Validity of the New York Times Index as an Inventory of Centenarians," unpublished senior seminar paper, Sweet Briar College.

One of the first persons to "collect" centenarians was Dr. Grace E. Bird of Providence, Rhode Island. The author inherited her collection, which consists of obituary notices and other brief articles appearing, for the most part, in newspapers in New England and the Middle Atlantic states from 1930 to 1955. This collection contained 773 names half of whom, 338, were males. It will be seen that this listing as well as the New York Times Index is skewed in favor of males since the proportion of males to females in the general population is nearly 1 to 2. Of the females 11.5 percent were referred to as "Miss," 83.9 percent as "Mrs.," and 4.6 percent had no marital designation.

The author's file of centenarians in the United States contains 3445 names, 1365 or 38.7 percent of which are males. Of the 2080 females, 221 or 10.6 percent are listed as single, 1859 or 87.4 percent ever-married, and 42 or 2 percent unknown.

In a miscellaneous file of notations regarding centenarians in other countries 227 were distributed as follows: 38 from Canada, 70 from England, and 119 from other countries largely from Russia and the Balkans. Of the Canadians 22.2 percent were listed as "Miss" while 18.5 percent of those from England and 11.9 percent of the other foreign were so listed.

In comparison, the percentage of single females 55–59 years of age in 1890 in the United States population was 6.8 percent, and in 1900, 7.6 percent. In other words, all of these enumerations of centenarians reported in the press contain much larger percentages of single than their age cohorts contained at an earlier period. A question arises as to whether the single centenarian is favored by the press. It is unlikely that the single would have been given preferential listing since it is usually the children of centenarians who instigate public recognition of 100th and subsequent birthday celebrations. The unmarried lack this publicity medium.

GERIATRIC SURVEYS

As further indication of the trend toward increasing longevity of the never-married we cite four recent research investigations all of which were conducted by personal interview (Table 3).

The Duke University Geriatric Research Program has been engaged for several years in an intensive study of men and women in the older age brackets. A recent report supplied by Miss Frances Jeffers[2] lists

[2] Miss Frances Jeffers, Duke University Geriatric Research Program, Durham, N.C., Participants of Community Health Study by Age, Sex and Marital Status."

Table 3. Marital status by age and sex in designated research investigations

Research study	Total	MEN						WOMEN					
		Never-married		Ever-married		Total		Never-married		Ever-married		Total	
		Number	Per-cent	Number	Per-cent	Number	Per-cent	Number	Per-cent	Number	Per-cent	Number	Per-cent
Duke University													
65–74	139	1	1.4	68	98.6	69	100.0	9	12.8	61	87.2	70	100.0
75–84	58	0	0.0	30	100.0	30	100.0	4	14.3	24	85.7	28	100.0
85 and over	13	0	0.0	7	100.0	7	100.0	1	16.7	5	83.3	6	100.0
Total	210					106						104	
Gallup-Hill													
95 and over	392	9	6.1	138	93.9	147	100.0	30	12.2	215	87.8	245	100.0
Kips Bay-Yorkville													
60–90	500	21	11.2	167	88.8	188	100.0	59	18.9	253	81.1	312	100.0
Pinellas County													
65–74	344	6	3.6	160	96.4	166	100.0	5	2.8	173	97.2	178	100.0
75–84	126	2	3.2	61	96.8	63	100.0	7	11.1	56	88.9	63	100.0
85 and over	16	0	0.0	7	100.0	7	100.0	2	22.2	7	77.8	9	100.0
Total	486					236						250	

210 persons ranging in age from 65 to 94. A relatively disproportionate number of these, 106, are males but they contain only one man listed as single (less than 1 percent). On the other hand, 13.4 percent of the females are single. When broken up into 10-year groups, 12.8 percent of those 65–74 are single while the comparable figures are 14.3 percent for 75–84 and 16.6 percent for 85 and over.

A recent highly publicized survey of older persons was conducted by Dr. George Gallup by means of his Public Opinion Surveys, Inc., published by Dr. Gallup and Evan Hill (Gallup and Hill, 1959) in the *Saturday Evening Post* under the title "The Secrets of Long Life." A memorandum from Dr. Gallup gives a detailed breakdown of the marital status of 392 of the 402 persons interviewed.[3] Although this sample was chosen to be representative of the 29,000 persons in the United States 95 years of age and over, his 6.1 percent unmarried males is below the national average while the 12.2 percent single among the females is somewhat larger than "expected."

A survey made by Kutner and others (1956) of the Kips Bay-Yorkville Health District of New York City covered 500 persons over 60 years of age. Of the 188 males 11.2 percent were single while of the 253 females 18.9 percent were single.

Dr. Irving L. Webber[4] has supplied tentative data on the Pinellas County (Florida) Health Survey. The percentage of single among the white males is small and decreases in successive age brackets. The percentage of single white females is 2.8 percent at 65–74, 11.1 percent at 75–84, and climbs to 22.2 percent at 85 and over.

It is easy to see why the theory that marriage fosters longevity has been so widely accepted. Earlier studies of longevity state unequivocally that the married live longer than the single. Invariably their authors, calling attention to the fact that the persons who had married outnumbered the single, concluded that marriage was conducive to longevity. They failed to compare the percentage of single among centenarians with the percentage of single in their age cohorts at earlier periods. The following studies in Table 4 are illustrative of this fallacy.

Eugene Thomson (1875) published an article on longevity in *Scribners Monthly* listing 36 males and 18 females. Of the 18 females marital status was given for 10—2 single and 8 married or widowed.

Frederick H. Nash (1884) published a pamphlet on "Ye Old

[3] Dr. George Gallup, Public Opinion Surveys, Inc., Princeton, N.J., Memorandum *re:* "Marital Status of Males and Females 95 Years and Over," 1959.
[4] I. L. Webber, Research Social Scientist, Pinellas County Health Department. "Table 19. Marital Status by Race, Sex and Age," Pinellas County Health Study Subsample, 1959 (Florida).

Table 4. *Marital status of female centenarians as reported in studies of longevity*

| Author | Total | Men | Women | WOMEN (KNOWN MARITAL STATUS) | | | |
| | | | | Single | | Ever-married | |
				Number	Percent	Number	Percent
Thomson	54	36	18	2	20.0	8	80.0
Nash	20	8	12	1	8.3	11	91.7
Smith	12	6	6	2	33.3	4	66.7
Bowerman	8	1	7	1	14.3	6	85.7

Folks of Connecticut with Ye Sketches of Twenty Living Centenarians." He mentioned 8 males and 12 females; of the women 1 was single and 11 had been married.

Colonel Nicholas Smith (1905) published his *Masters of Old Age* in which he names 6 men and 6 women who died between 1888 and 1905 in the United States at ages past 100. He gives the marital status of only 1 man, but mentions that 2 of the women had never married.

Walter G. Bowerman (1939), Actuary of the New York Life Insurance Company, published a study of "Centenarians" in which he reported on eight persons 108 or older whose ages he had verified. He believed these to be the only authenticated cases at that time of those who had reached 108. Of the eight, 7 were women—6 married and 1 single.

Although the numbers are small and therefore the percentages have little reliability, it is clear that in each case the percentage of single is actually *large* in relation to the "expected" percentage: 20 percent in the Scribner list; 28.3 percent, Nash; 33.3 percent, Smith; 14.3 percent, Bowerman.

It is unfortunate that earlier studies of longevity which listed larger numbers of people did not record marital status with any consistency. Easton (1799), for example, listed "1712 persons who attained a century and upwards from A.D. 66 to 1799." Atkinson's (1894) study in the United States and Young's (1899) in England also inventoried hundreds of alleged centenarians but did not classify them.

CHANGES OVER RECENT YEARS

That the increasing longevity of the single female is a twentieth-century phenomenon is shown by Table 5. In these shortened age

Table 5. *Percentage of female population in designated countries by age, 1860–1950*

Country	1860	1880	1890	1900	1910	1920	1930	1940	1946	1950
England and Wales										
55–64	10.9	10.9		11.7	13.2	15.3	15.6			15.5
65–74	10.5	10.4		11.1	12.1	13.9	15.8			15.6
75–84	10.2	9.7		11.1	12.0	13.2	14.7			16.4
85 and over	9.1	9.1		11.9	12.6	13.0	14.2			17.2
Norway										
35–39				25.1	25.9	26.5	26.8		21.6	17.3
40–49				20.0	21.6	22.2	23.5		22.0	19.4
50–59				16.7	18.2	19.8	20.8		21.8	21.2
60–69				15.3	16.3	17.5	19.7		21.2	21.5
70 and over				13.1	14.6	15.0	17.9		19.7	20.1
Switzerland										
65–74	16.1	16.9		17.5		16.7	17.4	16.9		17.2
75–84	15.5	16.0		17.7		16.0	17.0	17.6		17.1
85 and over	14.6	13.0		11.1		17.9	17.4	15.7		18.2
United States										
55–59							9.0	8.7		7.7
60–64			5.8	6.6	7.1	8.4	8.9	9.3		8.2
65–69							8.4	9.4		8.4
70–74			5.6	6.0	6.3	7.1	8.4	9.5		9.0
75–79							7.3	9.2		9.4
80–84								9.2		9.4
85 and over								8.0		9.7

sequences the increase in single males in the later years is not shown. But since the longevity bonus of the female appears at an earlier age than for the male, census data from England and Wales, Norway, Switzerland, and the United States show this change.

In England and Wales as early as 1900 the oldest bracket, 85 and over, showed an increase over the younger groups. After declining in 1920 and 1930 this oldest group again shows a larger percentage of single in 1950. In Switzerland the single female shows relative increase after age 70 in 1920 and 1930, while in Norway an increase is shown beginning with 1930. Of the countries cited the United States is the latest to exhibit this phenomenon, as it is only in 1950 that the females increase in percentage in the oldest age category.

CONCLUSIONS

Although the trend is by no means uniform, the hypothesis is verified.

We have shown that since the turn of the century a change has gradually taken place in the relative number of single and married surviving to old age. In all countries the trend is more pronounced for females than for males. The reversal of the singleness curve also comes later in life for males. The tendency for the single to increase proportionately to the ever-married is shown by all types of evidence examined: census data, lists of centenarians compiled by various persons, research investigations of persons under 100, as well as studies of centenarians, past and present.

The explanation of differential mortality is beyond the scope of this paper. Undoubtedly many factors—physiological, psychological, and sociological—affect the situation. Likewise a desire to evaluate the possible consequences of prolonged life of the bachelor and spinster has been curbed. Increased longevity of the never-married raises many social and economic problems.

The function of this paper is merely to indicate that a change is taking place in the composition of older populations. It is conceivable that this knowledge might be of concern:

1. To the 10 percent or more of the population who never marry;
2. To the relatives of older unmarried people who have a responsibility or concern for their welfare;
3. To actuaries who may need to revise their life-expectation tables for the single;
4. To insurance companies who offer life insurance and annuities for sale;
5. To the makers of tax laws (at present the single are penalized);
6. To a social security agency;
7. To other social agencies planning recreational programs, counselling services, case work, etc. for the aged;
8. To Blue Cross and Blue Shield and other health and hospitalization agencies.

REFERENCES

Atkinson, A. 1894. Longevity with a list of persons known to have lived one hundred years or more. Virginia Med. Month. (February).

Bowerman, W. G. 1939. Centenarians. Trans. Actuarial Soc. American, 40, II.

Easton, J. 1799. Human Longevity. Salisbury, England: J. Easton.

Gallup, G., and Hill, E. 1959. The secrets of long life. Saturday Evening Post, 232: August 15, 17–19; August 22, 22–23; August 29, 30.

Kutner, B., Fanshel, D., Togo, Alice M., and Langner, T. S. 1956. Five hundred over sixty: a community survey of aging. New York: Russell Sage Foundation.

Nash, F. H. 1884. Ye names and ages of all ye old folks in every hamlet, city, and town in ye state of Connecticut now living with ye sketches of twenty living centenarians. New Haven, Connecticut: Price Lee and Co.

Smith, N. 1905. Masters of old age. Milwaukee: The Young Churchman Co.

Thomson, E. 1875. The curiosities of longevity. Scribner's Monthly (November), 32–42.

Young, T. E. 1899. On centenarians and the duration of the human race. London: C. & E. Layton.

A Critique of Papers Presented by P. Paillat, C. V. Kiser, and B. B. Beard

POUL MILHØJ

DR. KISER points out right from the beginning that the past trends toward an increase in the proportion of older persons have been due almost entirely to declines in the fertility rate and virtually not at all to declines in the mortality rate. What the future will bring, we still do not know. Dr. Kiser says: "If the future declines in mortality are concentrated largely in the older age groups, as indeed they might well be, the declines in mortality will produce an older population." But one might question the possibilities for future decline in mortality among older people. There is, in the figures we have collected for the latest years, a tendency toward rising mortality, at least among older men. This may be due to a more severe stress for the modern man. It may also be due to the fact that the past reduction in mortality rates has been concentrated heavily in the young ages. This might, in the long run, produce weaker cohorts of older people, because they have—compared with former cohorts of older persons—been, so to speak, kept artificially alive. If this, at least to some extent, holds true, there is a risk that old people in the future will have rather high mortality rates.

Dr. Paillat's paper shows how economic growth and shifts in economic structure affect age composition of the labor force in different occupations and in different branches of industry. And in doing so, he points up the fact that the differences in age structure from one occupation to another represent a warning against using present age structure to indicate in what way the present labor force in an occupation will die out. This means that if you find, within a group in the labor market today, a steep decline in the number of people 60 years old or older as compared with the number of 50-year-old people, you are not allowed to predict that in 10 years nearly all the people 50 years old today will have disappeared from the group. In other words, care has to be taken in making life tables for particular occupations.

From Dr. Beard's paper it must be concluded, first, that the percentage of never-married is increasing in the second half of life; and, second, that the percentage of never-married among people in the second half of life has been increasing for many years and in many countries. But it is insufficiently proved that never-married persons nowadays to a large extent outlive their married contemporaries. When it is found that single persons evidence rising percentages in the second half of life, it may simply be explained by the fact that smaller percentages of the now old cohorts married when they were young. It does not necessarily follow that it *must* be explained that way.

Table 5 in Dr. Beard's paper shows that the percentage of single women out of all women in the older age groups has been rising throughout this century. This development cannot, it must be admitted, be explained by a general tendency toward increasing marriage frequency. If fewer persons got married in the cohorts who were young, say 100 years ago, than among the cohorts who were young, say 30 years ago, the proportion of never-married should be *decreasing* from one census to another in the twentieth century.

But of course, if the results recorded by Dr. Beard in Table 1 are explained by an increasing marriage rate in the younger cohorts in the past, say 30 years, that does not exclude the possibility that the marriage rate was decreasing in the second half of the last century and in the beginning of this century. If that is the case both Tables 1 and 5 may be explained by variations in marriage rates in the past. And then, there is perhaps no reason for life insurance companies or for relatives of never-married persons to expect that the unmarried person they hold insured or intend to take care of is going to live longer.

This interesting paper, therefore, calls for studies partly of marriage rates in the past and partly of varying death rates within each age group and within each group varying by marital status. Before such further study is done, it is, in fact, impossible to see to what extent the tendencies pointed out in the paper will hold for the future.

Normative Aspects of Retirement

HAROLD L. ORBACH

RETIREMENT represents the creation in modern society of an economically nonproductive role for large numbers of persons whose labor is not considered essential or necessary for the functioning of the economic order. While departure from a life long career may serve as the basic operational indicator of retirement, sociologically retirement raises problems of the dynamics of social and institutional roles and relationships of a more basic nature than those associated with mere occupational role change. As a social process, retirement is the prescribed transition from the position of an economically active person to the position of an economically nonactive person in accordance with the norms through which society defines and determines the nature of this change.

From this standpoint, the basic problems of retirement must be approached in terms of the issues involved in the transition from one social role to another with the consequential implications of changes in status which accompany this role change. On the individual level this means the problems of varying conceptions and definitions of appropriate role behavior for the individual which are derived from the person's self-concepts growing out of his total social life experience. In this process, the norms for behavior of significant others and of significant reference groups play a crucial part in determining what the nature of one's social role is and ought to be. It is here that the specifics and details of one's retirement role are conceived, refined, and in practice organized into a coherent pattern.

On the societal level this raises the issue of the basic social definition

This study is a condensed version of a longer paper presented to the International Research Seminar on Psychological and Social Aspects of Aging in Relation to Mental Health, Berkeley, California, August 1–7, 1960. The full paper appears in *Psychological and Social Processes of Aging: An International Research Seminar,* edited by Wilma Donahue, C. Tibbitts, and R. H. Williams (to be published).

[1] For a fuller treatment of these issues, see the discussion in Donahue, Orbach, and Pollak (1960), in which more detailed presentation of a number of the arguments presented in this paper may be found.

of retirement and calls into focus the value orientations underlying the retirement policies and attitudes of society at large and of major organizations directly concerned with retirement systems such as business and labor organizations. It is here that the fundamental framework and nature of retirement as a societal phenomenon is structured.

THE INSTITUTIONALIZATION OF RETIREMENT

Retirement is a phenomenon of modern industrial society. This emerging pattern of social life has no precedence in the past, and represents the development of a new and distinct social role available universally for ever increasing numbers of persons. While prior socioeconomic systems have had varying numbers of older people, none has ever had the number or proportion of aged that obtains in the industrialized societies of the present, and, more important, the older persons of previous societies were not retired persons. There was no such thing as a retirement role in the past (Simmons, 1945).

The development of retirement is a result of the complex series of interrelated changes in the technological, social, political, and demographic character of modern society. We can attempt to summarize these changes as follows:

1. The creation of a state of technology based on the scientific approach to knowledge which has shattered and continues to shatter prior conceptions of the potentialities for the production of the food and goods necessary for the sustenance and improvement of the conditions of life.

2. The development and extension of political and social order through powerful national states. This is a corollary of the growth of rational methods of economic life inherent in industrialism, which have been able through modern technology and communication to exercise an ever-increasing degree of purposeful control over man's natural and social environment over a vast area of the earth.

3. A demographic revolution unique in man's history which has witnessed the growth of human population in the last 100 years in a measure unheard of in all previous time. This, as industrial societies have matured, has ushered in the phenomenon of the aging of populations.

4. The reorganization of man's economic and social life as a consequence of the new systems of production and consumption into a distinctly new set of social roles based on an altered relation between man and the tools he works with and, in consequence, the manner and form in which he reaps the rewards of his labor. The industrial system of production with its rational division of labor, separation of the laborer from control of the instruments of production, and wage system of economic exchange has altered the older systems of social relationships which were built upon the existing state of the economy and profoundly changed the structure of the institutional arrangements in man's life.

Each of these has contributed in part the necessary economic, social, and political conditions for the institution of retirement. Modern society can support a nonworking segment by virtue of its productive capacity; the political organization of the national state provides a structural means for the operation of universal retirement systems; the demographic revolution has created a segment of society, a large number of whom will live far beyond their years of maximally potential economic life; and the changing social relationships which have arisen to meet the structure of the industrial system have rendered untenable the types of social and economic accommodations which previous societies made for their older people.

As is usually the case in human affairs, the values and norms of behavior have not kept pace with the changes in our material conditions of life, and our patterns of social life have in consequence been in a state of change and flux. We are in the process of adapting to the new conditions which have been thrust upon us. The result is the lack of any clear-cut role for the retired person; there is an ambiguity and lack of clarity in the behavioral expectations for the members of this new social position.

Unlike other social role changes throughout the life-span which are marked by a series of role transitions and gradations from one more or less clearly defined social role to another and which encompass various forms of anticipatory socialization for the role-to-be through informal antecedent preparation, the retirement role is beset with a lack of socially defined appropriate behavior inasmuch as it also lacks a clearly defined social position in the structure of society. In one sense, retirement is a negation of the traditional values surrounding the place of work in Western society, and men are loath to surrender the identifying position in society which a job bestows. The notion of organized preparation for retirement which has received so much attention in recent years is an attempt to fill the gap in the normative structure of the present by defining and preparing the individual for this new social role.

Insofar as one of the most crucial sources of role expectations and behavior comes from the members of the reference group of position holders of any social role, one of the problems of the retirement role has been the lack, in the past, of a viable group of persons in this category itself. This feature is, of course, rapidly changing today due to the maturation of the institutional basis of retirement in the United States. As a consequence of the inauguration of Old-Age and Survivors Insurance and the industrial pensions since the end of World

War II, we have witnessed the growth of an economic institutional foundation for retired persons within a span of 20 years.

While preoccupation with retirement began as a concern for the protection of the wage earner and his family when health and age no longer made it possible for him to continue working for a living, there has arisen the phenomenon of retirement today which involves matters of general social policy and institutional needs and demands as well. Old-Age and Survivors Insurance was adopted in the United States, in part, to relieve the pressures of unemployment during the great depression of the 1930s, and it was structured and has been viewed in these forms throughout its short history. Similarly, industrial pensions and executive retirement represent calculated decisions of policy for the renewal and replacement of labor, skills, and vitality in the market place. Finally, the growth of unionization and its cardinal principle of seniority have begun to generate pressures along similiar lines for the opening up of opportunities through the retirement of senior workers holding advantageous and prized positions.[2]

The development of institutionalized retirement has created a situation with more far-reaching consequences than was intended by the mechanisms through which it was brought about. The continuing changes in society being accentuated by our new demographic characteristics and the technology of automation have served to create a series of further demands for more extensive retirement even as they have raised questions of changes in the general conditions of work. And yet, we have seemed unwilling or unable to adjust our work related values to acceptance of retirement as a desirable conclusion of the working life. We are faced with demands both for the seemingly contradictory freedom of prolongation of working life and for the extension of retirement at the same time.

SOCIETAL VALUE ORIENTATIONS
TOWARD RETIREMENT

Part of this problem can be traced to the basic value orientation which underlies the conception of retirement as a form of social life. The worker of today still, by and large, sees retirement in terms of negative features (Tuckman and Lorge, 1953; Donahue, Orbach, and Pollak, 1960). These include economic deprivation, loss of status and function, and lack of anything to do with one's free time.

[2] See the paper by Breen (to be published) for an analysis and discussion of these functional aspects of retirement.

These are issues related to the social and individual definition of the retirement role, based on a quite realistic appraisal of the status and position of the retired person in today's society.

However, basic societal values which underlie the institutionalized retirement system also are operative. The role of government in acting as an agent to ensure the welfare and well-being of its citizens is a major issue, as is the social nature of retirement itself, and, thus, the character of pensions or retirement benefits.

On the one hand, conceptions of social responsibility have from the earliest pension schemes been clear in expressing the character of retirement pensions as a form of social welfare or assistance which society undertakes to grant as a measure of charitable and self-interest. On the other hand, more recent trends have suggested that retirement pensions are a form of social reward or deferred pay—a form of social justice—which accrues as a matter of right.

Shenfield (1957) has put this issue clearly:

Are pensions to be regarded as a way of discharging community responsibility to those unable to maintain themselves in the same way that support is organized for other disabled persons, or are they a reward for a lifetime of effort, a kind of deferred pay to which everyone should be entitled after a named period of work attendance and contributions? If the latter, then pension schemes should create a right to retirement for all workers on a pension which is adequate to meet their basic needs, while they enjoy their well-earned rest. Those who choose voluntarily to continue to work should gain, either by receiving pension and wages, or by a deferred pension ultimately drawn, in recognition of the surrender of leisure which might otherwise have been enjoyed. The notion of creating a "right" to a pension at a certain age is emphasized by the device of insurance as a method of financing old age. [pp. 103–4]

It would appear that we in the United States have in effect, institutionalized a system of rights without correspondingly accepting the values and normative system that is implied. While we maintain a dual system of insurance plus welfare assistance, the insurance system has an underlying orientation of "basic subsistence" rather than providing a reasonable measure of income for a decent standard of living. But, retirement systems organized on an insurance basis or involving a notion of social reward should tend to provide such a standard as a matter of consistent policy, and in point of fact the German and Swedish systems have moved in this direction. The point of view has been well put by the pronouncement of the German Federal Republic (Achinger, 1959): "A pension is no longer a grant-in-aid toward a person's subsistence, but will in future ensure maintenance of the living acquired" (p. 26). The growth of industrial pensions has arisen to fill this gap in the United States, but while unions look upon pensions as a right in the form of deferred pay, there is no similar inclination presently expressed on the part of employers. In point of fact, of course, it is only since the 1949 decision of the U.S. Supreme Court in the Inland Steel case, that the right to bargain collectively for pensions has been recognized. This gave rise to the tremendous growth of retirement systems in the 1950s just as the development of unions themselves followed similar legal decisions in the late 1930s.

It must be recognized that retirement must obtain a positive value and be endowed with sufficiently rewarding economic, social, and cultural values if it is to serve as an acceptable institutional form of social life for the older person. This implies a further movement toward "equality of rights" in respect of retirement since, although the basic support for private retirement systems comes from tax-exemptions to employers for contributions and thus the general public indirectly (Witte, 1951), only one-third of the labor force is currently covered by private or public pensions supplementing social security benefits (Holland, 1959).

EFFECT OF DIFFERENCES IN ORGANIZATIONAL ATTITUDES ON RETIREMENT SYSTEMS

An indication of the differences in attitudes and consequent policy between labor and management at present concerning freedom of choice of retirement can be obtained by observing the figures in Table 1. The two studies of retirement policies which are compared are of interest because in the first (Brower, 1955) nonunion companies comprised 29 percent of the total while the pension plans of the others were not necessarily developed under union-management negotiation. In the second, carried out by the U.S. Bureau of Labor Statistics (Levin, 1959), only union-negotiated plans were sampled. The striking differences in the percentage of workers covered by involuntary or compulsory retirement practices represents differing conceptions of the locus of norms for decisions of retirement. At the same time, the union-negotiated plans containing involuntary provisions also have greater flexibility in that only 19 percent of the employees have conditions of automatic retirement at a given age without the possibility of continued employment for an additional number of years, while 67 percent of those in the other plans are so governed.

Table 1. *Types of retirement provisions and practices in private pension systems, 1954 and 1958 by plans and employees covered, percentage distribution*[a]

Type of provision or practice	BROWER, 1954		BUREAU OF LABOR STATISTICS, 1958	
	Companies N = 327	Employees N = 4.1 million	Plans N = 300	Employees N = 4.9 million
No involuntary fixed-age retirement	25[b]	10[b]	40	45
Involuntary (compulsory)	67[b]	83[b]	60	55
Automatic retirement	48	67	23	19
Nonautomatic retirement	19	16	37	36

a Source: Adapted from Brower, F. Beatrice, *Retirement of Employees—Policies—Procedures—Practices.* (Studies in Personnel Policy, No. 148), National Industrial Conference Board, New York, 1955, Table 5; and Levin, H. L., "Involuntary Retirement Procedures," Mon. Labor Rev. 82 (1959), Table 2.

b Eight percent of the companies have a combination of both involuntary and noninvoluntary policies for different categories of workers; these cover 7 percent of the employees.

These differences suggest that the influence of unions in obtaining pensions as rights is matched to some degree by a demand for greater freedom of choice in exercising these rights.

The effects of unions and unionization can be measured in other ways. For example, a New York State Department of Labor (1957) study found that, while 89 percent of establishments with 2500 or more employees had pension plans, the figure was only 14 percent of establishments with less than 20 employees. The relation to unionization which is more prevalent in large firms is quite apparent. Pension coverage also varies considerably with type of industry, another feature obviously related to the extent of unionization—compare the steel or auto workers with service or domestic workers.

Generally unions have opposed compulsory retirement as a negation of the worker's seniority rights, thus presenting another area in which the worker's economic security must be protected. This does not imply opposition to compulsory retirement as such but to employer imposition of the conditions of retirement under circumstances which result in involuntary economic deprivation of the worker. Therefore, it is not surprising that "as retirement incomes have risen, so has union acceptance of automatic retirement schemes" (Bers, 1957, p. 83). The expression of union attitudes has clearly reinforced the willingness of labor to accept compulsory retirement systems under conditions approved and sanctioned by union members (Bers, 1957). This means, however, restriction of management's right to unilateral decision on the criteria of continued employment for older workers which many managements have been reluctant to accept.

An interesting case example of the effect of the institutionalization of a retirement system and the provision of more adequate retirement benefits can be obtained by examining the changes in retirement practices of auto workers covered under the "Big Three" auto companies' pension plans with the United Auto Workers. The UAW has, since its original pension plans were negotiated, obtained improvements in benefits and coverage at each of its bargaining talks with the automobile manufacturers. In addition, the UAW has operated a very active retired-worker's program, including preparation for retirement courses, drop-in centers for retired workers, and numerous other programs and activities designed to assist their members' adjustment to conditions of retirement.

In the light of these facts, it is of interest to observe the changes in the auto workers' retirement patterns since 1953 (Table 2). It is evident from the data that there has been a definite decline in the proportion of workers in all three companies who wait for the compulsory retirement age of 68, and an increase in the proportion of those electing early retirement benefits. In all three companies, too, the number electing early retirement with reduced benefits has shown a steady if slow progression. The special early retirement which is under conditions of mutually satisfactory agreement or company option and covers mainly employees in failing health who are not eligible for disability benefits, serves to control early retirement for health reasons. When these cases are removed in General Motors, we still are left with a continuously increasing proportion of early retirees over a period of 8 years in all three firms, and a complementary decline over the same period in those waiting until the compulsory age. If we view the combined totals for the "Big Three" as an indicator of the auto industry as a unit, a clear trend is in evidence since 1953, the year in which automatic retirement at age 68 was accepted by the UAW as a concession for better pension arrangements and more adequate benefits.

This study suggests that, as has been discovered in other cases (Baker, 1952; Donahue, Orbach, and Pollak, 1960), increasing the financial rewards of retirement tends to make it more acceptable. Further and more detailed study of the auto workers' pension experience and similar studies of other industries would go far in helping to establish a more coherent picture of the relative effects of

Table 2. Nondisability retirements in the "Big Three" auto companies under United Auto Workers negotiated pension agreements, 1953 and 1956–1959, percentage distribution[a]

	Early retirement age 60–64[b]			Normal retirement age 65–67[c]	Automatic retirement age 68	Total	Number of retirements
	Regular	Special	Total				
Chrysler Corporation							
1953	2		2	50	48	100	508
1956	5		5	64	31	100	1172
1957	8		8	67	26	101[d]	1204
1958	10		10	70	20	100	1462
1959	14	10	24	67	9	100	1774
Ford Motor Company							
1953	c		c	57	43	100	1996
1956	4		4	67	29	100	2075
1957	5		5	75	20	100	1926
1958	7		7	81	12	100	2376
1959	6	9	15	75	10	100	2160
General Motors							
1953	3	4	7	39	54	100	2088
1956	5	7	12	57	31	100	2824
1957	6	8	14	58	28	100	2820
1958	6	9	15	62	23	100	2959
1959	7	12	19	61	20	100	3085
"Big Three" combined							
1953	2	2	4	48	48	100	4592
1956	5	3	8	62	30	100	6071
1957	6	4	10	65	25	100	5950
1958	7	4	11	70	18	100	6797
1959	8	11	19	67	14	100	6989

[a] Source: Communications from the United Auto Workers, Chrysler Corporation, Ford Motor Company, and General Motors Corporation to the author.

[b] All three of the auto companies have had since 1950 a system of regular early retirement at age 60–64 with actuarially decreased benefits. In addition, General Motors has had a special early retirement system with retirement at the option of the company or by mutually satisfactory agreement which provides double the normal age 65 retirement pension until the retiree reaches age 65 and attains social security, at which time the pension is reduced to the normal rate. This system was incorporated in the Ford and Chrysler systems beginning in 1959.

[c] Less than 0.5 percent. [d] Differs from 100 due to rounding error.

financial incentive, retirement planning, and the general atmosphere of stable institutionalized retirement systems on individual and societal attitudes and values.

SUMMARY

The development of retirement as a new social role is an outgrowth of the vast changes which have occurred in human society since the industrial revolution. More recently, in the last two decades of this century, we have witnessed the development of an institutional basis for retirement life and with its maturation the emergence of retired persons as an important social category.

These phenomena have created problems of social role changes which have as yet not been assimilated into the normative structure of society and thus made part of the general socialization process. The result is that the role transition to retirement is one involving a large degree of uncertainty and ambiguity of the retired person's position and status in the social structure.

One aspect of this problem which is of great importance is the generalized value orientation of society as to the nature and character of retirement as an institutionalized form of social life. While we have developed a concept of retirement pensions as a social right, partly in consequence of the structures we have evolved to deal with the problems of retirement income, this concept has lacked positive development, and older orientations and values viewing retirement pensions as a form of welfare or assistance are current and influential in shaping our attitudes toward retirement. It is suggested that the further institutionalization of retirement must result in the development of clear and positive values attached to the retirement role if it is to serve as a suitable form of social life for older persons. One central feature of this development is the increase of retirement income to a point affording a reasonable standard of living rather than present subsistence levels and the equalization of retirement rights throughout the entire population. The experience of the auto industry in this respect shows a development in this direction.

REFERENCES

Achinger, H. 1959. The economic resources of old age. *In* Proceedings of the Fourth Congress, International Association of Gerontology, Merano, Italy, Vol. 3, 17–29. Fidenza: Tipografia Tito Mattioli.

Baker, Helen. 1952. Retirement procedures under compulsory and flexible retirement policies. Princeton, N.J.: Princeton University, Department of Economics and Social Institutions.

Bers, M. K. 1957. Union policy and the older worker. Berkeley: University of California Institute of Industrial Relations.

Breen, L. Z. Retirement: norms, behavior and functional aspects. *In* Wilma Donahue, C. Tibbitts, and R. H. Williams (eds.), Psychological and social processes of aging: an international research seminar. To be published.

Brower, F. Beatrice. 1955. Retirement of employees, policies-procedures-practices. (Studies in Personnel Policy, No. 148.) New York: National Industrial Conference Board.

Donahue, Wilma, Orbach, H. L., and Pollak, O. 1960. Retirement: the emerging social pattern. *In* C. Tibbitts (ed.), Handbook of social gerontology, pp. 330–406. Chicago: University of Chicago Press.

Holland, D. M. 1959. What can we expect from pensions? Harvard Business Rev., 37: 125–40.

Levin, H. 1959. Involuntary retirement provisions. Month. Labor Rev., 82: 855–60.

New York State Department of Labor. 1957. Division of Research and Statistics. Pensions: larger plans in New York State. (Special Bull. 232.) Albany: The Department.

Shenfield, Barbara. 1957. Social policies for old age. London: Routledge and Kegan Paul Ltd.

Simmons, L. W. 1954. The role of the aged in primitive society. New Haven: Yale University Press.

Tuckman, J., and Lorge, I. 1953. Retirement and the industrial worker: prospect and reality. New York: Columbia University, Bureau of Publications, Teachers College.

Witte, E. E. 1951. Comments. *In* Proceedings of a conference on problems of older workers. Madison: University of Wisconsin, Industrial Relations Center (processed).

The Role of Institutions in Fixing the Upper Limit of Productive Ages

PIERRE NAVILLE

THE conditions for fixing an age or several determined ages of retirement for "old" people has been the object of many studies. These have shown above all that at the moment we do not have at our disposal universally accepted methods for measuring all the forms of "withdrawal from the active population," and less still methods for establishing scientific criteria justifying the age limits of this withdrawal.

In industrially developed countries the work rates by age produce a declining curve beginning at about 50–55 years. The decline of this curve varies sharply according to type of work, occupational categories, social groups, sex, geographic region, etc. If we have such curves for sufficiently varied and precise criteria at our disposal, we can deduce from them the dynamics of withdrawals from the active population with the help of age coefficients of retirement.

However, the factors which influence the progressive decline of work rates are numerous and varied. One can distinguish the following types of factors: biological—death, sickness, disablement, whatever the causes may be; work—wear and tear, fatigue, change of capacities; institutional—rules of retirement, legislation regarding private or public pensions; economic—wage labor or private exploitation of the means of work, saving, etc.

We may well note other interfering factors of a structural character —like the existence of families of varying sizes—or of a conjunctural character, e.g., wars or underemployment.

Moreover, in the majority of cases this withdrawal is progressive. Except for serious or total invalids, most persons do not stop all occupational activity on the day after retirement. Ordinarily, they leave their "principal activity" in order to free themselves for secondary activities which they abandon gradually.

Thus, it is necessary, in order to be rigorous, to distinguish a work rate for the total population (T_1) and a work rate for each person (or by groups, T_2) at different ages. The T_1 can be measured by the relation between active and inactive people, that is to say, between two quantities of persons. The T_2 cannot be measured in the same way; it can be measured by the number of hours devoted to remunerative work, or by means of a rule of derivation in accordance with the "principal activity."

The complexity of the factors involved in retirement has led demographers, statisticians, and economists to simplify the problem by evaluating the age of retirement as a function of a total criterion relative to the economic situation—*activity* or *productivity*. However, these two aspects of the criterion do not, strictly speaking, overlap each other.

In any case, the problem again becomes knowing how to measure the upper limit of activity, thereby first of all defining the object of the measure.

The active population is ordinarily defined by an economic criterion —remuneration. Active persons are those who are paid in one form or another for work, whatever its nature may be. But this economic criterion is transformed into a demographic criterion by the change to the number of remunerated persons *of a given age*. The economic conditions of activity then become the limits (lower and upper) of the productive or active ages. The criterion is finally chronological.

As a result of this transformation we attempt to act on the volume of the productive ages rather than on income and the cost of living at all ages. Institutions strive to modify the social cost of "inactivity" by modifying the relative volume of productive ages, i.e., by raising the work rate in the upper ages, especially after ages 55–60.

However, this demographically based policy has given no positive results up to now, and the public and private collectivities now appear to envisage the policy of retirement as taking economic and institutional requirements into consideration, at least as much as demographic and chronological conditions. The upper limit of the productive ages is regarded more and more as a function of institutional policy which does not rest on purely chronological facts.

If we consider the case of France, we observe that since 1921 work rates for both men and women over 65 have been falling regularly. For the age group of 55–64 years, this decline is noticeable only since 1936 for men, while for women the work rate hardly varies (Table 1).

A decrease in the work rate is also observable for all persons 55 years and over through the same period in which the proportion of persons 55 years and over in the total population has increased. This

Table 1. Work rate (per thousand) for age groups, by sex and year of census, France[a]

Age group	1896		1906		1921		1926		1936		1946		1954	
	Men	Women	Men	Women	Men	Women	Men	Women	Men	Women	Men	Women	Men	Women
Total population	637	329	682	390	711	423	702	375	654	342	676	376	622	299
Below 15	295	226	385	259	92	62	76	53	49	35	30	23	502	334
15–24	}	}	}	}	893	601	889	555	844	532	844	593	}	}
25–34	915	446	964	536	965	549	969	484	970	488	965	487	966	404
35–44	920	426	966	535	970	545	967	489	963	480	972	504	967	423
45–54	930	427	915	499	959	546	951	486	929	470	949	509	953	466
55–64	864	381	}	}	890	495	861	425	790	396	814	433	788	390
65 and over	667	250	662	282	674	313	622	251	537	208	548	226	362	133

[a] Source: L. Cahen, "France," in Institut National d'Études Démographiques, *Migrations professionnelles*, The Institute, Paris, 1957, pp. 145–47. The category "age not ascertained" has been omitted.

double tendency is even more marked for persons 65 and over. These represented 8.3 percent of the total population in 1896, 9.9 percent in 1936, and 12.1 percent in 1954. But their work rate was 667 per 1000 in 1896 and 362 in 1954, a reduction of almost one half. The reduction in the work rate for persons 65 and over is more pronounced for men than for women. This means that in France the aged segment of the population, while proportionately larger, is working less.

On the other hand, the work rate of those between 20 and 64 has varied little for 60 years, despite changes in the age-group composition of the total population, which confirms the law of Sundbörg once more.

The decline in work rate varies sharply according to the type of occupational activity. It is more rapid in the tertiary sector (transportation and communication) and much slower in agriculture. Furthermore, there are differences according to professional and technical categories. Miners and teachers, for example, retire at about the same age (starting at 55) due to special legislation covering their pensions, whereas these two groups belong to completely different branches of work. Farmers work longer than urban wage earners because their activity is dependent, in the great majority of cases, on an enterprise which is their own private property. Moreover, farm work is so varied that the farmer can maintain himself for a long time by gradually giving himself over to those tasks which are compatible with his declining capacities.

The differential development of the work rate shows how difficult it is to set a uniform upper limit for the productive ages. It is, moreover, just as difficult to fix a lower limit given the progressive and varying character of the amount of time spent in professional training after the final threshold of compulsory education.

There is another reason why it is difficult to measure the productive ages by the number of persons of a given age. It is because the number of working hours per week (or per month or per year) varies a great deal, not only according to the branch of work, but also by age in each branch. Table 2, for example, gives some information relative to occupational groups where working hours normally undergo important fluctuations.

It is evident that weekly work hours are rather unequally distributed according to age. In other words, productive work is unequally distributed according to age even within the same given productive ages. Still, the concern here is with the people who work. But layoffs or

Table 2. Percentage distribution of the number of weekly working hours, by selected occupational groups, France, December, 1951[a]

Occupational groups	0	1-14	15-16	17-31	32-39	40	41-44	45-47	48	49-55	55	56	Not ascertained	Total
Agriculture, forestry, fishing (workers)	4.7	3.0		14.2		4.1		11.0	13.1	19.3	30.6			100.0
Agriculture (women, employers)	0.3	13.6		35.4		6.9		8.8	8.5	8.8	15.6		2.1	100.0
Domestic services, sanitation		1.7	10.4	15.5	12.5	11.9	5.9	3.5	5.2	9.9		23.3		99.8
Housemaids		21.1	35.0	12.7	7.5	4.2	2.9	3.6	4.2	3.6		5.2		100.0

[a] Source: Ministry of Labor, Quarterly Survey of Employment, December, 1951.

permanent underemployment tend to add their contingent of non-active persons, at least temporarily, within active age groups.

A third reason which makes the assimilation of productive forces with quantities of persons at a given age rather arbitrary is the modification undergone by the qualitative structure of the activities. This modification is obvious in branches of industry, occupational groups, and even individual concerns, but it will suffice to refer to three large classical categories of economic activity. It will be seen that the growth of the tertiary sector tends to modify the equilibrium of direct productive functions and economically unproductive or indirectly productive functions on the national scale.

In France the relationship of the three sectors has been modified in the following fashion over the last century (Table 3).

Table 3. Percentage distribution of the total active population in terms of the three major sectors of activity, France, 1856–1954 (unemployed omitted)[a]

	1856	1906	1954
Primary	51.4	43.2	31.4
Secondary	31.1	29.0	33.6
Tertiary[b]	17.5	26.1	33.8
Difficult to classify		1.7	1.2

[a] Source: L. Cahen, "France," in Institut National d'Etudes Démographiques, *Migrations professionnelles*, The Institute, Paris, 1957, p. 150.
[b] Includes transportation and communication.

As in many other countries, the proportion of the "tertiary" sector has almost doubled. Now, it is in this sector that we find the largest proportion of occupations which are considered to be unproductive (whatever the precise definition we take, either from the point of view of the economy or the character of unproductiveness). The nonproductives form a part of the active population located particularly in office work, retail trade and commerce, and certain learned and intellectual professions.

It is thus certain that within the "productive ages" and the active population of the census are numerous persons whose active output is occasionally quite meager and often nothing. This is another reason for doubting that chronological age can be considered as a uniform upper limit of activity.

Various authors have proposed abandoning the relationships between *active/inactive* and *adult/aged* (and *youth*), which are based on the numbers of individuals at a constant age. Mackenroth (1954), Luzzato-Fegiz (1954), Winkler (1954), and Mortara (1958) in particular, have supported this point of view, which we consider entirely justified according to French data.[1] Moreover, it has been confirmed through the calculation of work-life expectations, in particular by the work of Wolfbein and Depoid.[2] The assimilation of the active and inactive populations into determinate age groups (the inactive ages being distributed among the youth and the aged) may present some interest for facilitating theoretical research using simplified models. However, in this case it is preferable to resort to the actual volume of employment and unemployment at all ages rather than to cross section of ages—presumed to be representative of activity and inactivity.

[1] Mackenroth (1954) estimates that the relation of life expectancy to expected active life has remained largely the same for almost a century (but he obtains this result, which is probably not exact, by considering the group 15–65 years as potentially active and constant during this period of time). In any case, he admits that it depends on the manner in which these systems of old age and invalidity insurance are conceived whether the economy benefits or not from a possible lengthening of the active period of life.

Luzzato-Fegiz (1954) has pointed out that instead of arbitrarily choosing clear-cut limits between productive and unproductive ages, one must determine according to the statistics of wages and other incomes, the net value of production as a function of age. In order to do this, one must calculate the annual cost of children and men and different ages; one would thus obtain an equation giving net yields as a function of age.

Winkler (1954) emphasizes also that it is arbitrary to assimilate the volume of the active population defined by two age limits and the volume of the truly productive population. According to him there are two methods, that of age-characterized groups and that of data on remunerative employment, which complement one another. The age-characterized groups serve as a demographic frame and represent the potential labor force, while the data on effective employment indicate the use of this potential determined by economic and social conditions.

Mortara (1958) has presented an index of productive capacity and consumer needs characteristic of each age, taking as standard the highest productive capacity and the maximum consumer need at the adult age. Thus he obtains for France in 1954, in large age groups, the following percentage distribution of units of income and expenditure:

Age group	*Unit*	
	Expenditures	*Income*
0–14	13.08	2.19
15–64	75.30	89.86
Over 65	11.62	7.95

There remains the problem of establishing indices by much more differentiated age groups and branches of activity. In this connection see Naville (1959).

[2] The work-life expectancy being calculated to take into account all forms of withdrawal from activity, including death, for each year of age, implies, as does the series of work rates, abandoning the principle of a uniform age limit of activity. This is perhaps the reason why work-life expectancy has not been taken into consideration up to now by authors who have tried to justify fixing an upper age limit for activity through demographic considerations, although work-life expectancy is derived nevertheless from survivors tables of the demographic and chronological type.

But on the grounds of statistical material utilizable by planning institutions and by the perspectives of plans for economic development, it would seem to be preferable to renounce definitely all calculations based on the existence of a relationship between actives and inactives taken to be identical with a relationship between persons of two given age groups. This is, moreover, what occurs in practice. The planning institutions for retirement and old age security take into account the curve of effective work rates and life expectancy (and work life), and not total theoretical relationships between activity and inactivity by age groups.

The upper age limit of activity then appears variable according to multiple criteria (age, occupation, income, etc.) which signalized the effect of factors which can be combined, neutralized, or contradicted.

Thus, on the one hand, the conditions of increasing work incapacity with advancing age and the willingness to withdraw from activity as a function of savings contribute to fixing the actual and gradual times of retirements. On the other hand, when retirement rules are fixed institutionally (on the level of companies or public collectivities and the government) they often cause or oblige individuals to retire from active life sooner than if they were constrained only by the regular conditions of physical incapacity.

In summary, the time of withdrawal appears more and more to have the character of a *mobile point of equilibrium* between the curve of retirement exigencies (of all causes) and the curve of retirement possibilities (offered by means of personal or collective subsistence). Age is the reference axis of the curves, but it is not the factor determining their form. It is properly as a consequence of age that most cases of withdrawal from active life occur. But this does not mean that age in itself is the essential cause in all cases.

More precisely, one must say that age, or rather old age, is a condition on which institutional factors act. But this condition is not absolutely determined because it varies considerably according to groups, individuals, and economic and occupational circumstances. On the other hand, the action of institutions can be determinant since they can dictate precise rules of employment or nonemployment (or partial employment) at advanced ages. The real problem, then, consists in knowing what institutional form of withdrawal is the most compatible with both economic circumstances and the needs of the individual person.

Let us examine the situations which allow a person to withdraw finally from the active population. We will put aside the case of persons who retire gradually, those who are semiactive for a certain time.

We can classify in the following fashion the situations compatible with withdrawal from the active population:

a. Death in the course of active life;
b. Personal possession of an income (whatever may be its nature and source, provided that it is private);
c. Allocation of an income by a family or public collectivity, unrelated to work furnished during active life.

Two of these three classes of circumstance, b and c, can be combined, but these are the only types of existing possibilities. So long as a person is living, when he voluntarily or involuntarily leaves the active population three, and only three, are open to him: death, voluntary or not (a); subsistence on a personal income (b); subsistence on an income allocated by a collectivity (c). In case c withdrawal occurs as a result of a social requirement or a right (the principal of mutualism or *l'étatisme*).

From a theoretical point of view all other circumstances of withdrawal, complex or combined, can be reduced to the three cases, a, b, and c. In effect, a cancels all the other circumstances which could have been produced; b permits a person to cancel the effect of all other circumstances, as does c. Case b is compatible, within certain limits, with c and conversely, c with b (leaving aside the fact that b, in the case where a is produced, can be transferred from one person to another person).

These indicated relations between types of subsistence of persons who withdraw from the active population are, at least in theory, independent of age. In fact, there exists a dependency between age and appurtenance to the active population for the major part of the population. But the development of actual work rates (taking into account layoffs and permanent and temporary disability) shows that a uniform upper limit does not exist as a result of purely biological and physiological factors. The development of work rates according to social, occupational, and economic situations shows that factors of income and property are just as important, and even that they assume an increasing importance. This fact is rather evident if one considers the case of farm owners, industrial workers, or civil servants.

It is the operation of this double series of factors (biological and economical-institutional) which in the end determines the character of work rates at different ages. It is then a question of knowing which series of factors must take precedence in the process of drawing up rules.

Almost everyone today is in agreement in recognizing that the growth of longevity, due essentially to the lowering of the mortality rate, must not necessarily imply a proportional lengthening of the active life. In fact, in France as in the United States, active life has lengthened less quickly than biological life. The main reason for the relative increase in retirement life must be sought in the growth of resources which modern productivity puts at the disposal of society as a whole. The possibilities of accumulating a capital fund which allows the individual to live on personal incomes have greatly declined in the past 30 years, at least in Europe. On the other hand, resources concentrated in insurance and mutual societies of various types, and in public collectivities (such as social security in France) or even the state budget (such as for pensions of civil servants or for all wage earners in the Soviet Union), all have been considerably augmented. It is this augmentation, itself dependent on increasing productivity and national income, which is the essential reason for the lengthening of the average retirement life.

This fact deserves examination since numerous authors still reckon that the lengthening of the duration of active life is a natural and biological phenomenon, just like the lengthening of the total life span—the human organism, having physical strength available over a longer period of time, would also for a longer period of time have the strength to sustain work. However, the lengthening of the average life-span itself is not a simple biological phenomenon. The decline in mortality also has social sources (the progress of curative medicine, changes in working and living conditions, social hygiene) and directly economic sources (the growth of investments devoted to hygiene and to private and public care). The lengthening of active life obviously also has causes which are linked to the social causes which have brought about a lengthening of the total life-span. In fact, social hygiene, preventive medicine, etc., do not contribute only to greater longevity; they bring about, at the same time, better average health for persons in the active ages despite the worsening of certain working conditions in some occupations (notably those which involve nervous strain on the part of the workers). At the same time, modern hygiene facilitates the utilization of modern mechanical equipment for greater productivity and thus plays a part in increasing the national income. And it is clearly the growth of national income which allows collectivities to serve the needs of persons insofar as they are unproductive (whether they are at an active age or not).

The state of resources of the collectivity thus opens a *possibility,* if not a right, to unproductiveness for a part of the population whatever their age may be. It is natural that this possibility be open above all to the young, because they must be preparing themselves for work, and to the aged who have the right to a final period of inactivity exactly as they have the right to intermediate periods of inactivity and rest each week, each month, and each year. However, national resources also permit inactivity of certain persons during the active ages, as is the case with paid holidays, vacations, and leaves for sickness or accidents.

Clearly, the demographic data do not furnish a general framework of solid data on which economic and social institutions are able to estimate the differential *possibilities* of withdrawal from active life as a function of productivity, net national product, and net national income (and even international, as can be shown in the case of the European Community). It thus would be logical for the progressive development of withdrawals, no longer following a narrow demographic imperative, to become elastic and flexible as a function of the quantity of collective resources. The mobility of differential ages of retirement would be more the effect of a spontaneous equilibrium between age and personal and collective resources. Withdrawals would no longer be fixed once and for all by a legal or contractual means as a function of specific ages. Mobile thresholds could be anticipated by economic and social development plans and programs, just as programs for productive and indirectly productive employment (even unproductive) are beginning to be elaborated in a more and more systematic fashion as a function of general economic growth.

REFERENCES

Cahen, L. 1957. France. *In* Institut National d'Etudes Démographiques, Migrations professionnelles. Paris: The Institute.

Luzzato-Fegiz, P. 1954. La place des personnes âgées dans une société civilisée. *In* Institut National d'Etudes Démographiques, etudes européennes de population. Paris: The Institute.

Mackenroth, C. 1954. L'importance de la limite de l'âge dans le rapport population active/population inactive. *In* Institut National d'Etudes Démographiques. Paris: The Institute.

Mortara, G. 1958. Aspetti economici della composizione per eta della populazione. Giornale degli Economisti (Nov.-Dec.).

Naville, P. 1959. Measurement of working life and employment of older workers in France. *In* C. Tibbitts (ed.), Aging and social health in the

United States and Europe, pp. 74–95. Ann Arbor, Michigan: Division of Gerontology, The University of Michigan.

Winkler, M. 1954. L'évolution de rapport population active/population inactive en Autriche de 1910 à 1960. *In* Institut National d'Etudes Démographiques, Etudes européennes de population. Paris: The Institute.

Joint-Holding of a Retirement Pension and Gainful Employment

LÉON-ELI TROCLET

THE development of the gerontological sciences on the one hand and of social security on the other poses the increasingly acute problem of the simultaneous holding of gainful employment and of a retirement pension. Accordingly, two-thirds of the countries with legislation on old age or retirement pensions regulate this type of joint-holding through some sort of retirement test. On this point, it is impossible to establish a distinction between the Western democracies and the Communist countries. This fact is without doubt the best proof of the existence of this problem.

ACTUALITY, COMPLEXITY, AND RELATIVITY

Citing the experience of the country the author knows best, it should be pointed out that in Belgium two legislative proposals initiated by the Parliament were tabled solely because of this question of joint-holding. This is why in 1959 a scientific conference at the Solvay Institute of Sociology was organized, devoted to this subject (Institut de Sociologie Solvay, 1959).

Similarly, the French National Center of Scientific Research has carried out an investigation under the direction of Dr. J. R. Tréanton (1958) to learn the causes of retirement of elderly Parisian workers.

Since the French social security system permits joint-holding and the Belgian system permits it only for a part-time job (one-fourth of time), the Solvay Institute of Sociology likewise carried out a survey in Belgium to determine the opinions of workers and some union leaders on the subject of joint-holding. Analysis of this research is not entirely completed, and the results will appear in a second volume.

The result of these studies, which are still very incomplete, is that the question of the envisaged joint-holding must be approached under numerous very diverse aspects and that a simple solution seems to be excluded.

Retirement or old age pensions have become a besetting social problem, and when the question of joint-holding with gainful employment is posed, everyone is tempted to answer yes or no without hesitation. This spontaneous reaction is rarely the fruit of reflection, however short, if it is given by a lay person. It will be almost a professional reflex if it is furnished by one or another of the specialists in any of the numerous branches of the social sciences. When the answer comes from a layman it will reflect either his personal situation or his own individual feelings because of some circumstance that he has known or that has stuck in his mind. Men of science will be similarly divided.

However, one can attempt to advance some provisional conclusions that may help in developing the study of this question, drawing one's inspiration from the great contemporary current of altruism and humanism, which is also a current of social personalism tending to the recognition of a guaranteed right, which is thoroughly embodied in the concept of social security.

DISCREPANCIES

A certain number of discrepancies are set up in the examination of this problem, and sometimes errors of perspective give a misleading picture of the question under consideration. There are errors of perspective when we speak of the larger categories and forget the numerous particular cases which are not included, or when we speak of a large group as if it encompassed everyone. There are discrepancies when in arguing we give different content and meaning to the same formula.

Pensioners and elderly persons

The most frequently encountered discrepancy occurs when we think of "older persons" in talking about a problem limited to "pensioners." There is no need to complain of this as such, but one must be aware in his reasoning that he is passing from one category to the other. It is, in fact, evident that most pensioners are older persons and that the problems of the latter are problems of the former, with the exception, for example, of the case of pensioned noncommissioned officers, invalid mine workers, or widows. It is, therefore, fatal to see one category as infringing upon the other. It cannot be forgotten that for the specific problem under study there are aged persons who are not pensioners and there are pensioners who are not aged; i.e., military men, policemen, and widows.[1] One of the results of this discrepancy is that little is said of these categories, which pose, however, even more complex and delicate problems than the others.

With the benefit of these observations provisional conclusions may be classified according to whether they concern the medico-physiological aspect, the legislative, juridical, and technical aspects, or the economic and social aspects.

Occupational therapy

On the medical and physiological plane "occupational therapy" has been rightly placed in evidence for its actual merits which are also psychological and react in this respect upon the somatic state. We should not be especially deluded by the term therapy, because its techniques and its effects are not limited to sick persons, but are equally efficacious for healthy persons. Furthermore, in most cases this technique aims as much at *occupation* as at work properly speaking and thus does not necessarily constitute an answer to the problem of joint-holding of a retirement or old age pension and of gainful employment.

Thus, for example, certain older persons devote the leisure of their retirement to various types of pursuits and activities, and certain intellectuals to research and studies which they had to postpone during their careers. In this connection someone said to us recently that he had never had so much work as since his retirement. But here naturally it is a question of *nonobligatory* work, of truly free occupations that one begins and ends whenever one wishes, that are developed at the rhythm one likes, and that one chooses according to one's own taste. It is without doubt the most suitable occupational therapy and also the most efficacious.

However, this deals with activities and possibilities adapted to a minority of intellectuals or to a very restricted number of persons capable of accepting the requisites of doing creative work.

[1] Under Belgian law the widow has a right to survival pension at 45 years and even before that age if she is responsible for a child or if she is stricken with a disability of at least 65 percent.

Leisure-time activities

It may be answered also that besides this kind of activity, there are still others to encourage, such as gardening and small-stock breeding. Also, depending on the case, one may devote himself to certain occupations of an intellectual nature, such as reading. If we add to these possibilities certain activities of relaxation (movies, theater, etc.), it does not seem impossible to "occupy" a great part of one's disposable time. It has been said that *ennui* is the number one enemy of the pensioner.

Finally this problem of occupational therapy must be posed in terms of individual circumstances, and the diversion should be total, slight, or partial according to the case.

It seems then that an occupation may often be useful, in truth necessary, but it would doubtless be excessive to conclude that the medico-physiological aspect of the problem requires authorization of the joint-holding of a remunerative activity for persons pensioned at the normal age.

Subjection and gainful employment

Does this mean that remuneration would never play any role in this occupational therapy? "Never" would surely be an extreme term. We are willing to admit that in certain cases profit would serve as a continuing stimulus, especially when age has slackened energy. But the effect of such a stimulus is singularly attenuated, even destroyed, when it has as an opposing factor the prolonging of a patronal subjection or, in a more general way, an absence of that freedom to which so many workers aspire when they dream of their approaching retirement. We believe we are correct in finding in the psychology of the retired person (at least if he has a pension at a normal rate), the deep satisfaction, even if unexpressed, of feeling himself freed from obedience and constraint. It seems that technical progress should not in any way lessen this aspiration of the worker toward liberation.

This need of freedom is doubtless curious, even paradoxical, at first sight among people who feel that they are slowed down by age and physical weakness. But research in psychoanalysis and depth psychology could probably demonstrate the mechanism of the accumulated reactions and reveal the deep-seated justification of this attitude. Except where individual needs very obviously exceed income, it does not seem that the stimulus of remuneration can counterbalance the hope for freedom of retirement. It would necessarily, therefore, be a question of an activity that is remunerated but essentially free. We will agree that these two conditions are rarely combined and that they could satisfy only an extremely small number of pensioners, creating an injustice for the others.

Also the problem would certainly be different for self-employed workers, although a number of them, especially among the poor, also have a feeling of subjection, but with respect to the clientele. Here there will often be years of repressed impatience which are to be liberated by retirement.

Therefore, occupational therapy merits being examined thoroughly not only as to its potentialities, its limits, and its modalities, but also as to its interferences as much on the plane of individual psychology as on that of social psychology. The latter comprises interpersonal psychology as well as the psychology of the working mass. The study of occupational therapy must be pursued, but in all its aspects.

TWO OPPOSING CLAIMS: TOTAL JOINT-HOLDING AND LOWERING OF PENSION AGE

An observation of quite another kind should also arouse reflection. Two contradictory claims are formulated with noticeably equal frequency. Some claim the right to joint-holding (they understand by that *total joint-holding* of gainful employment and pension),[2] while others claim the lowering of the retirement age. One supposes that the same people are not drawing up these two claims simultaneously— with the exception of some demagogues who fish for favors in all directions, even if they are irreducible.

In fact it is mainly, but not exclusively, among pensioners (perhaps also some workers near pension age) that we find those who want joint-holding, while it is among those who will still be working for a few years that the partisans of lowering the pension age are recruited. It is doubtless unnecessary to emphasize that most of the latter either are suffering from some health deficiency or else feel no "joy in work," either for personal reasons or because of the unhealthiness of the job, or as a function of bad "human relations" at the job site. But whatever the categories into which the one group or the other falls and whatever may be the explanations of the attitudes taken, these are not less contradictory or more exactly opposed.

[2] Among those who formulate such a claim there are those who have found it absolutely impossible to accumulate any savings (because of adversities under minimum wages). Such situations should disappear progressively with the setting up of pension laws and with the development of social security.

Joint-holding and wages

One can hardly conceive in any case that the lowering of the retirement age will be accompanied by total freedom of joint-holding. We shall not consider here the problem of retirement age, which would require at this point insertion of a series of considerations foreign to the present purpose. It is proper however to emphasize that the more the retirement age is lowered the larger becomes the pyramid of ages which must be taken into consideration. This entails very numerous consequences from the point of view which concerns us: the number of job seekers increases rapidly, their physical strength is diminished accordingly, and unless a policy of broad economic expansion is concurrently achieved, we would surely move toward a reduction of wages by way of the double economic mechanism of a mounting unemployment and a system of odd wages.

It truly seems that the right to total joint-holding and the lowering of retirement age are irreconcilable, and that if one of the two claims were to win out it could only be, socially, to the detriment of the other. Therefore, it would be necessary eventually to make a choice.

Income of young people and income of elderly persons

In other respects, to permit joint-holding at an earlier age would correspond to raising the incomes of the aged person who would practice joint-holding, to the detriment of the younger ones who still have family burdens. That would appear quite difficult to defend in the framework of a social equilibrium.

The opinion of "on-the-job" workers

If it is a question of making a choice, it is difficult to imagine it entirely free, devoid of all "relations of power." With the latter in play, we may easily imagine that the point of view of the active workers will predominate not only by reason of the reception of their spokesmen but also because in fact they are more efficient, and, moreover, at the same time they are the ones who make the financial contributions. The system of assessment, which, under a compulsory program, is taxed more and more by the state of business affairs, can only accentuate their influence upon the solution of the problem.

The least that we can say is that, in view of the arguments that can be invoked on either side, a compromise solution is doubtless indicated in the direction of a cautiously determined partial joint-holding.[3]

Prolongation of normal activity

When we come to the problem of joint-holding, a confusion often establishes itself in discussion, at least in Belgium. We talk of retirement age as if it were imposed by law. Now it is nothing of the sort, no more moreover, if we are well informed, than in most other nations. Thus, if a worker invokes a state of flourishing health at the age when he *can* retire, nothing prevents him legally from continuing his work, this under the benefit of some adjustments[3] which follow. But before these adjustments, it must be emphasized that in principle nothing deters him from pursuit of full-time gainful employment beyond the legal and normal pension age, 65 years for men and 60 for women. Under Belgian law this age is only a minimum condition of the "commencing of the right." Henceforth if his physical condition permits and, if, psychologically, he does not very keenly desire the liberation of retirement, a worker may continue to earn his full salary. These cases are not so rare; a little less than one-third of men prolong their work life beyond age 65 and more than one-third of women beyond age 60. The difficulty of the problem of joint-holding is then eliminated, and the question of occupational therapy is generally solved for this "older person."

ALLOWANCE FOR DEFERRED PENSION

This observation leads us to the first of the adjustments. Under Belgian law early retirement results in a reduction of 5 percent per year in the normal pension in consideration of the double phenomenon of the enlarging of the age pyramid and the earlier cessation of payment of contributions. Thus one could quite validly defend an inverted system by which the voluntary retardation of the age for receiving a pension would give rise to a larger pension. This would be justified also by the double inverted phenomenon: prolonging of the period of contributions (which Belgian law requires but without a corresponding rise of the pension) and shrinking of the age pyramid.

[3] Since calculation by the day presents some difficulty (Belgian law permits accumulation of 6 days per month), a spokesman of the Belgian employers to the National Council of Labor proposed substituting a right to joint-holding of 4 hours per day at pay rates fixed by the parity commissions.

But it is just to say in passing that shrinking of the pyramid seems to create less pension right than enlarging removes.

Against this system, there appears to be only one objection, of a psychological nature, mainly raised by those whose state of health compels them to take the early pension but also by other pensioners: A certain feeling of frustration based upon an injustice of fate obliges the weakest to be content with a lower pension for the rest of his days. It is not rare either for this social discomfort to be felt by the physically deficient with respect to those who are healthy and who practice joint-holding effectively within the present limits of the law. Many anonymous denunciations have just this origin, and it is not rare for signed denunciations to express this reaction against the inequality resulting from joint-holding in which some may engage and others not.

FORCED RETIREMENT BY THE EMPLOYER

There is another adjustment to make, but of a very different nature. In a certain number of businesses it is the employer who makes retirement compulsory at the age permitted by law. Even before the law provided for early retirement certain businesses set retirement prior to the legal age—often with compensation—which posed further problems. Without any studies having been made, we have the feeling that this practice of compulsory retirement is spreading. In this case, it is not the law but the employer who reduces the worker to inactivity. It is difficult to justify this practice if the worker has maintained his full or almost full work capacity, and in the Keynesian perspective this practice seems assuredly less defensible than prohibition of joint-holding. Action by the employers' associations would be needed to counteract this tendency,[4] concurrent with an effort toward economic expansion.

RECLASSIFICATION OF OLDER PERSONS

Dismissal of those workers who have reached the prophetic age brings us to a third adjustment, that of unemployment and the occupational characteristics of elderly persons. The growth in unemployment

[4] It is answered by the employers that such pressure upon businesses is unnecessary because the company head himself will see to it that a particularly useful worker is not dismissed even if he has passed the age of 65. However, we know of many big businesses where dismissal is automatic and where even the company manager is retired the same as are all the specialized workers.

of older persons has been so often emphasized that it is unnecessary to recount here all the data gathered on this subject. In connection with our problem, and especially the dismissal of workers at the normal age taken currently for the regular pension even though some may have maintained their total work capacity, it must be noted that reclassification will generally be very difficult for those who would like to take up other work. Doubtless the only exception will be in the case of some highly qualified workers, or, in even rarer situations, cases involving the influence of parents or friends or when certain factors make it a social case taken into consideration by some sentimental employer.

THE WORK OF OLDER PERSONS

The hypothesis of the great qualification of older workers evokes an argument that has often been placed in evidence: older persons like the handicapped are generally, at least within the limits of their individual capacity, more assiduous and more conscientious workers, an easily explainable phenomenon which requires no further commentary. However, it seems necessary to reconsider the problem of the quality and quantity of older workers' production. It is useful to establish a distinction between the aged who produce more and those who produce less.

The first will generally be those who, having maintained full physical capacity, are skilled workers. Over the years they have had a very rich and varied experience in specialized and diversified work situations. Their years of work have given them knowledge of difficult problems and the solutions discovered, and they have developed the celebrated "quick trigger ability" which has naturally changed in the course of the decades but remains a symbol, valid and utilizable, of the abilities developed through long practical experience.

Others will see their productivity decline with age. This will apply especially to those who are limited to jobs in which physical strength plays an important if not preponderant role, or work which creates nervous tension. Many of these jobs are low paying and have hardly permitted the workers to save anything for their old age, since their income scarcely exceeds their basic needs.

JOINT-HOLDING AND ITS INFLUENCE
ON LOWERING OF SALARIES

The economic and social problems raised with respect to joint-holding are numerous and diverse. One objection frequently heard against the practice in the development of the trade-union position in its most recent phase relates to the negative influence that the work of pensioners may have upon wage scales. Mayors, local trade-union leaders, people deeply immersed in daily social life cite numerous specific cases. This opinion has been vigorously attacked and when taking a stand on the basis of economic theory, it tends largely to be destroyed. Nevertheless there remains, it seems to us, two reservations that cannot very well be eliminated. The one deals with economic theory, the other with social practice.

Reasoning on the level of economic theory takes place in the framework of a necessary policy of economic expansion such as is wished for but scarcely practiced. Under this latter hypothesis the justifications for joint-holding no longer have the same foundation, and, alas, it is this absence of economic expansion policy which is the reality in very many countries.

On the plane of social practice we must admit that the marginal occupations and the mechanism of the "odd wages" are overlooked by general economic reasoning. We have a tendency to believe that the whole game of wages is ruled by collective agreements, because they always concern large masses or important groups. In neglecting the fact that for workers in full health the "individual wage" generally differs from the "conventional wage," which is less often the case for the workers of meager capacity like most pensioned workers, it is necessary to take into account two factors which while very different are acting in the same direction.

SMALL BUSINESSES AND MARGINAL WORK

There are more marginal occupations or positions than one would imagine at first sight. It is doubtless difficult to determine the number. It is not sufficient to add up the number of workers registered in the few principal occupations and subtract that sum from the aggregate number of wage earners, because each of these subtotals includes marginal workers who as a matter of fact are placed outside the scope of the collective agreements. To these unascertainable categories, we must then add the difference between the wage earners and the sum of the subtotals that we have just mentioned. The error that one would be tempted to make is of the same nature as the current error that leads us to believe that the great majority of workers are employed by big businesses because some of these are impressive due to their size and the large number of their employees. On the contrary, the great majority of workers are dispersed in very numerous small and average-sized businesses, which much more easily escape the embrace of the collective agreements. By means of this relative individual freedom and by the phenomenon of sliding from category to category, well known in social practice, we cannot completely exclude the pressure of the remunerations of these marginal jobs upon the general level of wages. If this downward pressure seems certain to us, we have no intention of exaggerating it. It has only a relative importance, but it exists above all in the realm of unskilled occupational activity.

INFLUENCE OF ODD WAGES

Another downward pressure—also relative of course—results from the existence of odd wages. Studies on the determination of pay for women's work have often brought out the fact that women's wages have frequently been set much lower than those of men for the same work, because for a good number of women (notably young girls and married women) the pay serves only as spare money to the family income and especially to that of the head of the family. These women workers tend to accept a lower pay in order to be certain of getting it, taking into account the normal income of the father.[5] These *"salaires an rabais"* (cut wages), as Gemahling called them, have an influence upon the wages of workers engaged in the same business or a very closely related one, but who, in order to live, have full need of regular pay for their work. Of course we must refrain from generalizing. But we can no longer deny this phenomenon nor the fact that, with regard to the number of available jobs, even a small percentage of "cut wages" acts quickly upon the general level of the occupational category and even upon allied categories.

Now the pay for pensioners' work is established in the same climate as that of odd wages: the same compliance, the same desire not to let the money escape because of exigencies judged excessive by the partner, the same supplementary character with regard to income, the

[5] There are naturally other social situations which likewise give rise to odd wages.

same psychological state in the pensioned worker and in the employer too easily tempted to profit from the situation. This state of affairs is felt by those who are bent under the daily reality of social life even when they have not thought out the problem. This is why the trade unions have not ceased to protest against the employment of retired military career men and policemen; this is why in the last stage (or next to the last according to case) of the development of their position, the unions have wanted joint-holding to be limited; this is why, in order to combat the disadvantages of "black work," [6] employers demand as a major principle that, for equal work, wages and social costs be equal; this is why many countries have been led to prohibit or to regulate and limit joint-holding. It would doubtless be difficult to think that all these fears are absolutely without foundation. In truth the daily reality of social life nourishes such apprehensions. At most it might be admitted that they are a little exaggerated, but they have not arisen without any foundation.

FEELING OF INEQUALITY DUE TO THE RIGHT OF JOINT-HOLDING IN GOVERNMENT SERVICES

Those who are in daily contact with workers and who strive to isolate the most active psychological factors will generally recognize that ideas of justice and equality surpass the others. Ideas of a definite justice and a definite equality moreover, because it cannot be concluded that this need goes so far as requirement of absolute justice and equality; popular psychology accepts certain differences. But beyond these differences, a deep aspiration toward justice and equality is keenly felt, and the realm of pensions is not excluded. Thus, in Belgium, even among those who do not wish to work during retirement, this tendency is frequently expressed through a comparison which offends them—between the prohibition of joint-holding prescribed for retirees of private industry and the unlimited authorization of joint-holding for pensioned government employees, since this is the situation under Belgian law. The social unrest corresponding to this difference of regulations falls into the psychological framework of what we would propose to call the psychological need for individual equity.

[6] "Travaux noir," i.e., work performed in violation of labor codes and regulations covering the given type of activity, especially the payment of minimum wages and the social insurance costs of the employer.

NATURE OF THE RIGHT TO PENSION
AND ITS CONSEQUENCES

The only, but important, legal problem posed relates to the nature of the right to a pension. At the outset of legislation—as is still the case for the self-employed—when pensioners made no payments because they had reached retirement age before the law went into effect, the pension was actually only public assistance carried out by the government. Since then, the compulsory mechanism with its system of individual capitalization has contributed to the growth among some people of the belief in a property right when what is at stake is a "claim right" (*droit de créance*). This practice has supported in certain circles, especially in one category of employees and among many self-employed workers, an individualistic feeling which reacts upon the question of joint-holding.

If the constituted capital is the property of the contributor, the payment of income cannot be subjected to any condition, and therefore those who support this interpretation admit neither prohibition nor limitation of joint-holding. This is a judicial view of the situation, but an inaccurate one.

When the pension system, at least in the area of wage earners, has continuously called for more assessments of taxes, the judicial error on the nature of the right no longer seems possible since it is the contributions of the active workers that allow the payment of the pensions for the inactive. But here a new fact is added to the problem of joint-holding: can pensioners compete at all with the regular active workers who finance their pensions, without precautions being taken?

BLACK WORK

Another problem is that of "black work." In a system of economic freedom, some people regret this expression born spontaneously out of economic and social experience. The systematic growth of parity commissions and collective agreements as well as the introduction of social security have brought about this notion of fraudulent work. It is understood that employers of the work areas concerned are conscious of this, and experience leads us to recognize good grounds for the worries of small and average-sized businesses that are hurt by the appearance and spread of these fringe activities.

The majority of workers in the work areas concerned worry less about the problem because they do not feel, generally and individually, the immediate effects. However, if black work spreads, its consequences would react unfavorably upon the financing of social security by progressively deteriorating it, and exercising a downward pressure with respect to wages, with further interference on contributions apportioned according to pay.

Even if the pressure was not very strong and only slightly affected the big businesses, it would be felt very quickly in the small and average-sized businesses, which on the whole employ the greatest number of workers, especially in construction. Employers and workers are in agreement in fearing this danger.

INCREASE OF THE BURDEN UPON THE ACTIVE STRATA

Examination of the difficulties relative to joint-holding allows us to recall an already well-known observation. The constantly improved pensions of the elderly increase the burdens that rest upon the young. Raising the age of compulsory education will contribute to increasing the burden of the active strata of the population, just like the constant lowering of the mortality age. From these points of view, it is still less fitting that pensioners should profit from the fact that when they add to the advantage of their pension through gainful employment, they generally content themselves with an odd wage, thus reducing the receipts of the pension coffers.

BURDENS AND AGING OF THE POPULATION

As for the demographic diminution in the number of young producers in comparison with the aged strata, a situation currently called the "aging of the population," it seems that to a great degree the increase of productivity can furnish an important compensation. But it is evident that this increase cannot, socially, be devoted entirely to pensions. Some good souls, animated by the desire for social progress, insist upon "the importance of studying and achieving a rational allocation of jobs between the various age groups."

UNEMPLOYMENT OF YOUNG PEOPLE

"Unemployment of the young" is always brought up when joint-holding is discussed. The psychological reactions of workers, especially during an economic crisis, are generally hostile to joint-holding, starting with that now banal consideration that it is not sound for pensioners to be working when young people are reduced to unemployment. This is a question not only of the physical power that is unused, but also of the burdens of young people who have a home to establish.

PROMOTION OF YOUNG PEOPLE

Along the same line, attention is drawn to the necessity of not retarding the promotion of younger people. But it is fair to note that this objection is just as valid when it applies to unpensioned workers who prolong their working life beyond the usual age. Therefore, the objection does not specifically apply to joint-holding. But it is contrary to the physiological and psychological considerations which tend to permit a prolongation of the work life. This conflict between contradictory arguments is not easy to resolve, but we must nevertheless put it in proper perspective.

These specific questions of unemployment of young people, of prolongation of work life of those who have reached pension age, and of joint-holding of gainful employment with a retirement pension are entangled with the often-studied problem of the discharging of older persons. Confronting these problems together would doubtless permit us to throw a little light upon the ensemble of these apparently contradictory elements.

On the economic level we may certainly say, in a Keynesian perspective, that work brings work.[7] But should or can this axion be understood as favoring joint-holding or prolongation of the work life? Is work carried on under joint-holding with an undercutting pay, as much in direct wages as indirect, in the long run more profitable than injurious for wage levels and social security receipts, at least in periods when the economy is not expanding? Would it be possible to strike a balance between economic benefits and disadvantages?

[7] If the Keynesian formula tends to reabsorb unemployment, it is inscribed in economic liberalism and does not convey the certainty of full employment.

WORK OF PENSIONED WIDOWS

Joint-holding by pensioned widows is located on the social level. It is very difficult to untangle the skein of varying individual cases, and doubtless one would solve it only at the cost of a very expensive survey accumulating data about numerous infinitely varied situations and proceeding methodologically by successive classifications. In the present state of social knowledge, all conclusions would be risky.

But we can say that the problem is important since in the Belgian workers' social security system the burden of survival pensions represents 28 percent of the total number and 40 percent of the costs of retirement, percentages which may not be startling at first sight, but which are bound to be interpreted as a function of the survival pension rate, which stands at about 33 percent of the family pension.

JOINT-HOLDING AND PENSIONS AT THREE-FOURTHS OF WAGES

Under Belgian law, the progressive raising of pensions for the various classes of wage earners, with the purpose of winding up with a rate corresponding to 75 percent of the average pay over the work life, makes the solution of the problem of joint-holding more difficult. The normal work life taken into consideration being 45 years, the holder of a full pension receives about 60 percent of his pay at retirement. The worker called on to take his pension the following year will find it set at a slightly higher rate, and so on from year to year. If we consider that a pension of 60 percent is insufficient and that it is justified to add to this through paid employment, this justification fades away over the years pursuant to the annual accession of new generations to their pension. At what point between the rates of 60 and 75 percent can joint-holding seem less justified, if we consider that 25 percent represents the inherent burdens of daily work (transportation, clothing, etc.)? And when one is already at 75 percent— which is practically the case for former common laborers with low wages—do not the authorized 6 days per month represent the 25 percent difference from the previous working income? Finally, what about the coexistence of many annual generations of pensioners who, having taken their pensions in different years, have differentiated pensions? If it is necessary to permit joint-holding in order to allow an augmenting of income because a man is getting in under the law at its inception, when will this justification have disappeared? If it is never to disappear, we will again be faced with the same general problems discussed above.

PROGRESSIVE INCAPACITY AND PROGRESSIVE PENSION

The setting up of a progressive pension as a function of progressive incapacity has been suggested. Assuredly it is a rational solution. Is it not a little too much so in the face of a social reality so varied and so shifting, that does not allow itself to be encompassed by pure reason? Experiments have been attempted on a system of part-time work. These would merit being followed up in order to gain experience in ascertaining how a rational formula may be adapted to the concrete conditions.

PROVISIONAL CONCLUSIONS

There are many other aspects of the problem of joint-holding than those discussed above. These are, however, the ones most frequently met, and they suffice to demonstrate its complexity and delicate character.

If we wish to retain the necessary objectivity and reject every preconceived idea, we must recognize that we do not yet have in sight a solution that gives full satisfaction. Certainly, this objectivity can be more easily achieved if the study bears upon one single aspect among those recognized, because each science, each discipline, possesses its own set of norms and useful criteria. Nonetheless, such objectivity risks being fallacious because it is pointed toward only one limited aspect of the problem. Since the solution demands recourse to numerous disciplines, or more precisely cannot ignore their precepts, the true difficulty appears when we must objectively assess the influence of each of these in order to arrive at a socially acceptable over-all solution. This assessment requires preliminary examination of these diverse precepts so that we may evaluate and weigh them. Contradictory interests are present, and the solutions, for example, which an ideal economic organization would indicate do not correspond to a nonideal situation. Individuals are far from having an identical degree of physiological or psychological resistance, are far from having the same level of intellectual development, or the same personality.

Over and above these differences every solution must meet two golden rules: to subscribe to a perspective of social progress encompassing all workers, and to draw inspiration from the necessity of respect for mankind, because there is no social law other than for man. Human progress is identical with social progress. It behooves both politicians and practitioners reaching into their experience and their humanitarian feeling to seek the most measured and balanced technical formulas, those most adaptable to the considerations placed in evidence and most compatible with pension levels and with individual and social requirements, in order that they may arrive at the most socially just and practical solution for a society that is seeking order and equilibrium.

REFERENCES

Institut de Sociologie Solvay. 1959. Cumul d'une pension de retraite et d'une activité lucrative (Editions de l'Institut de Sociologie Solvay, Recueil des Travaux). Brussels: The Institute, Université Libre de Bruxelles.

Tréanton, J. R. 1958. Les réactions à la retraite: une enquête psychosociologique. Revue français du travail, 12: 149–65.

A Critique of the Paper Presented
by L.-E. Troclet

MARGARET S. GORDON

THE issue with which Professor Troclet's paper is concerned is usually referred to in the United States as the question of the retirement test. In other countries it is sometimes characterized as the question of an earnings test or a limitation on earnings of pensioners. Somewhat related is the question of an income test, such as the one imposed for old age pensions in Denmark. Although there are important conceptual differences between an income test and an earnings test, the differences in practice may not be very great, since relatively few older persons have investment income in appreciable amounts.

Professor Troclet has presented an exceedingly interesting and thoughtful discussion of the considerations that enter into debates over this issue. He seems, on net balance, to lean toward an earnings test. He has particularly stressed, in the context of Belgian conditions, the fact that elimination of the restriction on earnings would greatly increase the cost of the pension system. This would be especially true, he points out, if the retirement age were also lowered, as some groups in his country seem to be urging. He has also indicated that, under conditions of less than full employment, permitting old age pensioners to work without any restrictions might have a depressing effect on wages and an adverse effect on employment opportunities for young persons.

The considerations stressed by Professor Troclet have likewise been emphasized by those who are opposed to elimination of a retirement or earnings test in the United States and elsewhere.

Although decisions in every country must be made on the basis of conditions prevailing in that country, a broad analysis of the issue will take account of the fact that the actual effects of an earnings test are likely to vary substantially from country to country. Differences will tend to be related, not merely to the level of employment, but also to retirement practices in industry and to the various provisions of the national old age pension program. The impact of the earnings test may be affected by the level of pension benefits in relation to average earnings of employed workers, the amount of permissible earnings associated with the test, the minimum pensionable age, and the extent to which benefits may be increased by postponing receipt of pensions beyond the minimum pensionable age. In other words, the earnings test is just one of a number of features of a country's retirement policy, any one of which must be considered in relation to each of the others.

This general principle is most easily illustrated with reference to the minimum pensionable age. The later the pensionable age, the less difference the existence and restrictiveness of a retirement test is likely to make. Professor Troclet's remarks have taken this into account in relation to proposals to lower the retirement age, but the principle is clearly true in a more general sense. If, for example, the pensionable age is 70, as it is in a few countries, average life expectancy is approximately that prevailing in western Europe and the United States, *and* if pension benefits provide a reasonably adequate retirement income, relatively few persons are likely to continue working beyond the pensionable age. In this situation, the presence or absence of an earnings test is unlikely to make a great deal of difference. However, in most countries of western Europe and the United States, the minimum pensionable age is 65, and the question as to whether or not an earnings test should be imposed is more critical. Where the minimum pensionable age for men is below age 65, average life expectancy tends also to be somewhat lower, and this factor will affect the impact of an earnings test. And yet, there is the further complication that, as average life expectancy increases, the proportion of persons who are able to continue to work beyond the minimum pensionable age may rise, and provisions with respect to the pensionable age, an earnings test, and other features of a pension program may require reexamination.

The relationship of an earnings test to the average level of pension benefits presents greater complexities. One finding that seems to be emerging from recent research is that prospective retirement income does have an important influence on decisions to retire, although the influence of the income factor must be analyzed in relation to other factors. A recent paper (Gordon, to be published) has shown that, among industrialized countries, the higher the level of pension benefits in relation to average earnings in the country, the smaller the proportion of elderly men in the labor force is likely to be. The ratio of pension benefits to average earnings, for example, is relatively high in Belgium, the proportion of men aged 65 and over in the labor force is comparatively low, and the limitation on earnings of pensioners is relatively restricted. In this type of situation it seems rather unlikely that a large proportion of elderly men who are out of the labor force would seek work if the restriction on earnings of pensioners were removed, and yet the cost of providing pensions for those who are still working full time or nearly full time would be appreciable. Meanwhile, the existence of a limitation on earnings of pensioners represents a less severe hardship than in countries in which the ratio of average pension benefits to average earnings is much lower.

The case of France is very different. There average pension benefits are relatively low in relation to average earnings of employed workers, a substantial proportion of pensioners continue to work while receiving their pensions, and the imposition of an earnings limitation on pensioners would represent a severe hardship.

The United States would appear to represent a case somewhere between Belgium and France. The U.S. Department of Health, Education, and Welfare has presented data indicating that the number of elderly persons who are apparently limiting their earnings because of the restrictions imposed by the retirement test is relatively small (U.S. Congress, 1960). And yet to provide full retirement benefits to those potentially eligible elderly persons who are continuing at work and have not yet applied for benefits would substantially increase the cost of the OASDI program. The Department takes the position that, in view of the inadequacy of social security benefits for those elderly persons who must rely almost entirely on this source of income, it would be better, at least for the present, to incur increased costs for the purpose of raising the general level of benefits rather than for the purpose of removing or substantially liberalizing the retirement test.

Studies of the impact of changes in earnings tests on the labor-force participation of elderly persons are clearly needed, although it is nearly always difficult to separate the influence of these changes from other changes occurring at the same time. Abel-Smith (to be published) has recently completed an interesting analysis for Great Britain indicating that the age distribution of persons awarded national insurance pensions has remained remarkably stable in the postwar period despite a series of increases in the amount of pension benefits, the amount of permissible earnings of pensioners, and the increments for postponement of retirement. However, he points out that the fact that these changes in pension provisions did not seem to affect retirement behavior does not prove that much larger increases in pensions would have no effect.

These examples illustrate the difficulties and complexities involved in any attempt to arrive at generalizations about the impact of an earnings or retirement test. As we proceed with studies of the factors that influence older persons in their decisions to retire or continue working, we are gradually developing more sophisticated methods of analysis and are becoming increasingly aware of the interaction between health status, income status and other important determinants of these decisions. The earnings test is one element that requires careful analysis, but it is becoming increasingly clear that it must be analyzed in relation to all the other factors that affect retirement behavior.

REFERENCES

Abel-Smith, B. State Pensions and the age of retirement. *In* Wilma Donahue, C. Tibbitts, and R. H. Williams (eds.), Psychological and social processes of aging: an international research seminar. To be published.

Gordon, Margaret S. Income security programs and the propensity to retire. *In* Wilma Donahue, C. Tibbitts, and R. H. Williams (eds.), Psychological and social processes of aging: an international research seminar. To be published.

U.S. Congress. 1960. Senate. Subcommittee on Problems of the Aged and Aging of the Committee on Labor and Public Welfare. The aged and aging in the United States: a national problem. (Report 1121, Appendix III, 86th Cong., 2d sess.) Washington, D.C.: Government Printing Office.

One Aspect of the Problem of Older Persons: Housing Conditions

G. R. CHEVRY

A REAL economic and social problem of the aged arises in most of the Occidental countries. These are the countries which have known, at the same time, a progressive decrease in the birth rate during the nineteenth century and the first third of the twentieth, and a lengthening of the average duration of human life coinciding with a fall in mortality. These countries record a regular increase in the number of persons aged 65 and over, as well as a growth of the proportion of these persons in the whole population.

In France, for example, the number of these persons has increased from 2,316,000 in 1851 (6.8 percent of the total) to 5,179,000 in 1954 (11.5 percent) and will probably reach 6,592,000 in 1981 (12.8 percent).

It is understandable that these older persons, growing in number and proportion, most of whom are economically inactive and live on retirement pensions or social security allocations which are often insufficient, are the cause of a number of problems. This is due to the fact that their conditions of life are mediocre, causing them to be under-consumers, and, on the other hand, that their life must be assured by an active population whose relative importance does not stop decreasing.

In England, where these problems arise as in France, a National Consultative Commission on the employment of older persons was formed in 1953 to find solutions. In France the government constituted by a decree of April 8, 1960 a study committee on the problems of the aged; its duty is to study "the problems arising from the employment and the conditions of living of the aged, and to propose to the government the solutions to be given to these problems in the frame of a general policy." Although the considerable increase, in absolute as well as in relative value, of the number of the aged [1] sets

---

[1] In all that follows, the term "aged persons" concerns, except on contrary indication, persons of 65 years of age and over.

by itself economic and social problems, one may wonder whether these problems are not aggravated in France by the housing conditions of many of these persons, conditions which have been changing for the last century.

The proportion of the population of all ages living in rural communities (less than 2000 inhabitants agglomerated in a *cheflieu*) has not stopped decreasing, moving from 72.7 percent in 1856 to 59.1 percent in 1901, 50.9 percent in 1926, and only 44 percent in 1954. At the same time, the part of the population living by agriculture in the total population has fallen from 52.9 percent in 1856 to 23.2 percent in 1954. Concerning especially the persons aged 65 and over, the proportion of those who live in cities of over 10,000 inhabitants has doubled between 1901 and 1954 as is shown in Table 1.

Table 1. Progress of urbanization: proportion of persons aged 65 and over living in cities of over 10,000 inhabitants, France

Age group	1901	1954
65–74	21.1	41.7
75 and over	19.3	37.2
Total, 65 and over	20.6	40.1

It appears, thus, that the number of aged persons living in the country has notably decreased, while the number of those living in cities increased in a large proportion.

It seems incontestable that the living conditions of old people are much more difficult in the city. In small communities, old persons generally live in their own homes, have produce from a family garden, and are near their children, if they have any. On the other hand, thinking has changed on this matter, and there are very few young couples who decide to live with their parents when the housing crisis does not oblige them to do so.

These circumstances seem to create difficulties particular to the aged who live in cities.

In order to better specify the housing conditions of the aged, we shall refer to certain results of the 1954 Census. A sample of 1/20 and a subsample of 1/100 of the collected documents have been subjected to specific measurements which have permitted an intensive study of the composition of "households" and of the "nuclear family" which may constitute them. Conventionally, the following terms have been defined thus:

"Household": the group of persons who live in the same house (dwelling) including the subtenants, but not including the servants and salaried people living in.

"Principal core of the household": the group of persons with the head of the household and including all the household, except the persons who constitute secondary cores.

"Secondary core": a group of persons forming part of the household, formed either by a couple other than that of the head of the household and having or not having children belonging to the household, or by a person other than the head of the household, nonmarried (bachelor, widow, or divorced) having at least a child forming part of the household.

Thus, a secondary core always includes at least two related persons, while the principal core may comprise only one.

All the results presented below concern persons aged 65 and above on May 10, 1954.

DISTRIBUTION ACCORDING TO TYPE OF HOUSEHOLD

The 1954 Census distinguished ordinary households and collective households, the latter being constituted by groups of persons lodging in certain institutions (hospitals, asylums, boarding schools, religious communities, and big hotels) who often take their meals together. The following collective households have been identified: (1) boarders in hospitals or asylums who had no other residence elsewhere; (2) the staff in these institutions who lived in; (3) the members of religious communities; (4) the faculty and staff of boarding schools; (5) the staff of big hotels.

We must mention, moreover, that in all the following tables the term "nonmarried" includes bachelors, widows, and divorcees.

Table 2 shows first that the population of old persons amounts to

Table 2. Distribution of persons aged 65 and over by sex, type of household, and marital status (simplified), France, 1954 (in thousands)

	ORDINARY HOUSEHOLDS			COLLECTIVE HOUSEHOLDS		
Age group	*Married*	*Non-married*	*Total*	*Married*	*Non-married*	*Total*
Men						
65–74	982	296	1278	6	30	36
75 and over	379	282	661	5	31	36
Total	1361	578	1939	11	61	72
Women						
65–74	738	1173	1911	6	57	63
75 and over	181	921	1102	4	88	92
Total	919	2094	3013	10	145	155

more than three million women for only two million men, that is, three women for two men, and that this disproportion continues to increase with those aged 75 years and over (1,195,000 women against 697,000 men), a fact which may be explained by masculine over-mortality.

Also, a total of 1,372,000 married men is found against only 929, 000 married women. This difference may be astonishing, but it must be remembered that married men are often older than their wives; a large number of married men over 65 years may have a wife less than 65 years old.

Table 3. Marital status and type of household of persons aged 65 and over, by sex, France, 1954, percentage distribution

	MARITAL STATUS		HOUSEHOLD TYPE	
Age group	*Married*	*Nonmarried*	*Ordinary*	*Collective*
Men				
65–74	75.3	24.7	97.3	2.7
75 and over	55.0	45.0	94.8	5.2
Total over 65	68.3	31.7	96.4	3.6
Women				
65–74	37.7	62.3	96.8	3.2
75 and over	15.5	84.5	92.2	7.8
Total over 65	29.3	70.7	95.1	4.9

According to Table 3 old men are married in the proportion of 63.6 percent, while only 29.3 percent of old women are married; and this difference is accentuated for persons over 75 years of age (55 percent of married men against 15.5 percent only of married women).

It has also been ascertained that life in collective households affects only a small proportion of aged persons (less than 5 percent); it is more frequent with women than with men, and the frequency of this way of life doubles for each sex when passing from the age group 65–74 to 75 years and over.

Table 4 presents the distribution in percentage of aged persons living in collective households according to four categories of these households.

One may see that, in this particular group of aged persons, religious communities shelter between 3.9 and 5.6 times more women than men; but on the other hand, more than half the men (living in collective households), and almost two-thirds of those beyond the age of 75, land in the almshouse; the proportion is much less for women (35 percent for those between 65 to 74 and a little more than half for those over 75 years old).

Table 4. *Percentage distribution of persons aged 65 and over living in collective households, by sex and type of collective household, France, 1954*

TYPE OF COLLECTIVE HOUSEHOLD

Age group	Religious communities	Homes for the aged	Hospitals, clinics	Other
Men				
65–74	3.2	52.3	36.0	8.5
75 and over	3.6	63.6	24.3	8.5
Total over 65	3.4	58.0	30.0	8.5
Women				
65–74	17.9	35.0	40.2	6.9
75 and over	14.0	51.7	26.5	7.8
Total over 65	15.6	45.0	32.0	7.4

HOUSING AND LIVING CONDITIONS OF PERSONS LIVING IN ORDINARY HOUSEHOLDS ACCORDING TO THE CATEGORY OF COMMUNITIES OF RESIDENCE

The aged persons of each sex are classified in Table 5 according to their matrimonial state (simplified) and according to their residence either in the country or in the city. However, it has seemed useful to make a distinction: for the rural population, between farmers and nonfarmers; for the urban population, between the Parisian region and the other cities; hence four categories of population.

This table shows that, although exactly half of all aged women live in rural communities, a slightly larger proportion of aged men is found (56.4 percent). Besides, residence in the country becomes more frequent with age, the proportion among the rural reaching 62.5 percent for men 75 years old and over and 52.8 percent for women the same age. One notices also that the Parisian region and the other cities shelter, whatever the age may be, a larger proportion of aged women than of aged men.

On the other hand, one may derive the distribution of aged persons according to their place of residence, compared to the distribution of persons of all ages. This is shown in Table 6.

Thus it is shown that cities in general have a proportion of aged persons less than their share in the total population, especially as the persons are more aged. This is due in a small part to the return to the country of a number of urban retired persons, and mostly to the fact that the emigration toward the cities, and especially toward the Parisian region, has increased during the last 100 years. The oldest

Table 5. *Distribution of persons 65 years of age and over living in ordinary households, by sex and age group according to marital status (simplified) and type of community, France, 1954 (in thousands)*

Age group and marital status	RURAL COMMUNITIES		URBAN COMMUNITIES		
	Farmers	Nonfarmers	Paris	Other cities	Total
Men					
65–74					
Married	280	232	129	341	982
Nonmarried	95	74	38	89	296
Total	375	306	167	430	1278
Percent	29.3	24.0	13.0	33.7	100.0
75 and over					
Married	136	96	34	113	379
Nonmarried	107	75	23	77	282
Total	243	171	57	190	661
Percent	36.6	25.9	8.7	28.8	100.0
Total, 65 and over					
Married	416	328	163	454	1361
Nonmarried	202	149	61	166	578
Total	618	477	224	620	1939
Percent	31.8	24.6	11.6	32.0	100.0
Women					
65–74					
Married	116	262	91	269	738
Nonmarried	195	355	178	445	1173
Total	311	617	269	714	1911
Percent	16.3	32.3	14.0	37.4	100.0
75 and over					
Married	31	70	18	62	181
Nonmarried	171	310	111	329	921
Total	202	380	129	391	1102
Percent	18.3	34.5	11.7	35.5	100.0
Total, 65 and over					
Married	147	332	109	331	919
Nonmarried	366	665	289	774	2094
Total	513	997	398	1105	3013
Percent	17.0	33.1	13.2	36.7	100.0

Table 6. *Urban-rural percentage distribution of persons aged 65 and over compared to persons of all ages, France, 1954*[a]

Place of residence	65–74 years	75 years and over	All ages
Rural			
Farmers	21.5	25.1	22.6
Nonfarmers	28.9	31.3	23.7
Urban			
Non-Parisian	35.9	33.0	38.5
Paris	13.6	10.6	15.2

[a] Source: derived from Table 5.

generations are less well represented in the cities than the younger generations.

Finally, we must note an anomaly shown in Table 5: the number of married men agriculturists is larger than that of married women classified as agriculturists, while the difference is in the opposite direction for the married nonfarmers. This is mostly due to the fact that a great number of farmers' wives have registered as inactive and have consequently been classified as "rural nonfarmers." We must recall, besides, that an aged man aged 65 and over may have a wife less than 65 years old who does not figure in the table.

Heads of households and of secondary cores

Table 7 classifies only the aged persons who are heads of households or of secondary cores, according to the category of place of residence.

Table 7. Rural-urban distribution of persons aged 65 and over living in ordinary households as head of household or of secondary core, France, 1954 (in thousands)

	RURAL COMMUNITIES		URBAN COMMUNITIES	
Household status	*Farmers*	*Nonfarmers*	*Paris*	*Other cities*
Men				
Heads of household				
Having no secondary core	421	382	189	508	1500
With secondary core	78	26	15	47	166
Total	499	408	204	555	1666
Heads of secondary core	39	15	6	16	76
Total	538	423	210	571	1742
Total number of persons 65 and over living in ordinary household	618	477	224	620	1939
Women				
Heads of household				
Having no secondary core	193	417	208	499	1317
With secondary core	25	25	13	37	100
Total	218	442	221	536	1417
Heads of secondary core	5	5	2	4	16
Total	223	447	223	540	1433
Total number of persons 65 and over living in ordinary household	513	997	398	1105	3013

The differences between the general totals furnished by this Table 7 (1,742,000 men and 1,433,000 women) and the corresponding totals of Tables 2 and 4 represent for the masculine sex, isolated aged men, sheltered by a principal family core and who, owing to their isolation, do not constitute a secondary core. They are 193,000 in number. For the feminine sex there are, on the one hand, isolated aged women, sheltered by a principal core (712,000), and, on the other hand, the aged wives of a head of a household, or of a head of core (919,000, according to Tables 2 and 4).

There the balance is not made exactly with the general total of aged women, due to the fact that a small number of married women declared themselves heads of households or heads of a secondary core, and consequently appear at the same time among the 1,433,000 women heads of a household or of a core, and among the 919,000 married women.

One may notice that 90 percent of the aged men living in ordinary households are heads of a household or of a core and 86 percent are heads of a household. For women, the proportions are much less: 47 percent of heads of household or of core, and 45.5 percent of heads of household.

Different types of households in which aged persons live

The particular situations being extremely diverse, it has been necessary to classify them as the following types:

Restricted households constituted either by: a man alone, a woman alone, or a couple alone.

Simple households constituted by other persons not forming a secondary core (children, grandchildren, parents, or other) and the following: an unmarried man head of household, an unmarried woman head of household, or a married couple.

Complex households constituted by one or several secondary cores and, eventually, other persons not forming a secondary core (children, grandchildren, parents, or other) and the following: an unmarried man head of household, an unmarried woman head of household, or a married couple.

Let us recall that a secondary core is always composed of at least two persons (for example, a married couple, with or without children, a widowed daughter and her children, etc.).

Table 8 shows the distribution separately for aged nonmarried men, aged nonmarried women, and aged married men, according to their place in the household and by category of place of residence. As for the analogous distribution of aged married women, in principle it must be the same as that of aged married men, but a large number of married men over 65 years of age have a wife who has not reached

Table 8. *Rural-urban distribution of persons aged 65 and over*
living in ordinary households, by marital status and
household status, France, 1954 (in thousands)

| | | RURAL | | URBAN | |
Household status	Total	Farmers	Non-farmers	Paris	Other cities
Nonmarried men					
Living alone	222	62	63	29	68
Head of simple household	116	37	28	16	35
Head of complex household	47	19	12	2	14
Sheltered by a principal core	193	83	46	14	50
Total	578	201	149	61	167
Nonmarried women					
Living alone	948	139	315	143	351
Head of simple household	332	54	90	52	136
Head of complex household	102	26	26	13	37
Sheltered by a principal core	712	146	234	81	251
Total	2094	365	665	289	775
Married men					
Living alone[a]	17	5	5	3	4
Head of restrained household (couple)	802	193	219	103	287
Head of simple household	332	116	71	38	107
Head of complex household	125	62	17	12	34
Head of a couple forming a sheltered core	85	40	17	7	21
Total	1361	416	329	163	453

[a] This case constitutes an anomaly, but in fact a certain number of men have
declared themselves both "married" and "living alone."

this age. We have seen above that there were in 1954 only 919,000
aged married women against 1,361,000 aged married men.

The commentaries drawn from Table 8 are the following.

Nonmarried men. Of a total of 578,000 men, 350,000 (60.6
percent) live in the country and 228,000 (39.4 percent) in cities; on
the other hand, 222,000 (38.4 percent) live absolutely alone and
193,000 (33.4 percent) have been given shelter in a home. Besides,
one may note that if 57 percent of the 385,000 nonsheltered live in
rural communities and 43 percent in cities, of which 13 percent are
in the Parisian region, the proportions are entirely different for those
who have been given shelter: 67 percent in the country and only 33
percent in cities, of which only 7 percent are in the Parisian region.
This confirms what has already been said, that the acceptance of an
aged person by a younger couple is rarer in a city, and notably in
the Parisian region, than in rural communities.

Nonmarried women. The distribution of nonmarried women according to the category of their place of residence and according to their place in the household is quite different from what we have just noticed with nonmarried men; 49 percent of these women live in the country and 51 percent in cities; besides 948,000 (45 percent) live absolutely alone and 712,000 (34 percent) have been given shelter by a younger couple.

This last result is quite remarkable if compared with the analogous result obtained with sheltered men (33.4 percent). One might think *a priori* that nonmarried old women would be more willingly accepted by young couples than old men because of the greater services a woman may offer (household duties, baby-sitting, increased freedom from work for the wife). We see that this is not so; apparently proving that the families who accept an aged parent in their homes are less selfish than is usually believed.

We must point out, however, that an old woman lives absolutely alone more easily than an old man. This consideration, doubtless, is not without influence in the frequency of acceptance of an aged man in the home of one of his children.

Besides, we observe that of the 1,382,000 nonsheltered women, 732,000 (53 percent) live in cities, of which 15 percent are in the Parisian region; and the 712,000 sheltered women live in cities in a proportion of 46.5 percent and in the Parisian region, in a proportion of only 11.4 percent.

By computation, besides, we find that of a total of 100 nonmarried aged women, 15.7 are sheltered in an urban community and 3.9 are sheltered in the Parisian region, while of 100 nonmarried old men, only 11.1 percent find shelter in a city, and of these, 2.4 percent are sheltered in the Parisian region.

Married men. Out of the 1,361,000 married old men, 745,000 (that is, almost 55 percent) live in rural communities, and 163,000 (12 percent) live in the Parisian region. Only 85,000 (6.25 percent) are the heads of a sheltered couple; 33 percent live in cities, of these only 8 percent are in the Parisian region.

These results are not surprising. In a town, especially in Paris, it is more difficult to welcome an aged couple than a lone person.

Proportion of aged persons owning their homes

Table 9 presents for the three simplest types of households the proportion of heads of households who own their homes with the usual distribution by category of place of residence.

For the whole of France, the proportion of owners varies between

Table 9. Rural-urban percentage distribution of heads of households aged 65 and over owning their homes, by age group and type of household

Household type	Total	RURAL		URBAN	
		Farmers	Nonfarmers	Parisian region	Other cities
65–74 years					
Man living alone	47.9	67.2	56.9	38.5	20.0
Woman living alone	42.2	65.9	59.3	32.5	15.1
Couple living alone	56.0	75.2	67.1	33.4	45.7
75 years and over					
Man living alone	55.8	71.3	59.9	44.2	28.0
Woman living alone	46.1	64.1	60.6	34.1	17.7
Couple living alone	59.6	73.6	67.3	32.3	48.9

42 and 60 percent. It is larger for persons aged 75 years and over than for persons 65 to 74 years old. In each age group, women who are alone are less frequently owners, and couples are most frequently so.

We observe, besides, that the highest proportions concern farmers (64 to 75 percent), which should not be surprising; next come the rural nonfarmers. The Parisian region shows proportions between 32 and 44 percent, while other cities show the lowest proportions (down to only 15 percent for single women from 65 to 74 years of age) except for couples which include 45 to 49 percent owners.

To complete the information presented above which has been drawn from the 1954 Census, it has seemed useful to add some data from various sources which are also concerned with the housing conditions of the aged.

Percentage of aged persons having no child living and of couples having one single living child

The sheltering of an aged person in the home of a younger couple, which is most often that of a married child, was quite frequent long ago. We showed, above, that in 1954 it was not rare since it occurred with one nonmarried person out of three, but that it had become difficult in urban agglomerations. Yet, for this shelter to be possible, it is necessary for the aged person to have at least one living child, although a younger brother or sister, a nephew or a grandson, etc., may shelter the old person; these cases are, however, rare.

Tables 10 and 11 give the proportion, by age group and by sex,

Table 10. *Proportion of aged persons having no child surviving in 1946, France*

Age group	Men	Women	Total
60–64	25.7	28.3	27.1
65–69	25.4	28.4	27.2
70–74	24.6	28.6	27.0
75–79	24.3	29.7	27.5
80 and over	23.8	29.2	27.4

Table 11. *Proportion of couples having only one child surviving in 1946, France*

Husband's age group	Percent
60–64	27.5
65–69	26.6
70–74	26.0
75–79	25.2
80 and over	25.0

of old persons having no living child and that of couples having only one living child.

These proportions are drawn from the results of the 1946 Census, the question relative to the number of children still living was not asked in the 1954 Census. But the date of the information seems without importance, the proportions changing only very slowly with time, especially with older generations.

We may see that this proportion of persons having no living child is, at each age, a little higher for women than for men, which seems due to the fact that women get married generally at an earlier age than men; the average age of children of a woman 70 years old, for example, is higher than that of children of a man the same age; consequently, there is a stronger probability for the woman's children to be deceased earlier. The proportion varies very little with age.

It may be said roughly that one old person out of four has no living child and that the others have only one living child, a fact which greatly limits the possibilities of shelter in the home of a child.

Aged persons occupying new homes

An investigation in 1959 based upon interviews with the occupants of homes built since the 1954 Census in cities of over 50,000 inhabitants showed that, out of every 100 occupants, 3.7 were over 65 years old, this proportion being 1.6 percent in the Parisian region. The percentage of aged persons in the total population was 11.6 percent in 1960.

At the beginning of this study we asserted that the life of old persons of modest means meets special difficulties in large cities, unless they are lucky enough to have large enough homes which they may sublet in part. It would be interesting to know the proportion of these persons who leave the city to retire in the country. Unfortunately, because of lack of declarations of changes of residence, no complete data exist on internal migration. Only a few very imperfect and fragmentary indications exist, furnished by the changes made in the home address at time of registration at the polls.

In 1958, when these changes were numerous because of the importance of the elections, the net balance of arrivals and departures of persons over 65 years old, registered in rural communities, by the urban communities (except Paris) and even by the suburban region of Paris, were all insignificant and positive. On the other hand, the agglomeration of Paris saw 14,973 departures as against 8433 arrivals, that is, a net emigration of 6518 persons. This number, however, represents only 1.3 percent of the population of those over 65 years old living in the Parisian agglomeration. Out of these 6518 persons, 3739 (over half) retired in rural communities and 1101 in the suburban zone of Paris.

Thus, the return of older persons to the country is quite rare. However, we may say that many of these persons were born outside of Paris. A comparison of the distribution by age of the persons examined in the census for the Parisian region in 1921 and 1926 shows that the net immigration, between these two dates, of persons 20 to 25 years old [2] was 45 percent for men and 30 percent for women of populations of the same age group as in the 1921 Census.

[2] In 1960, these persons will be 60 to 65 years old.

Income and Living Conditions of Older Persons Receiving Public Assistance in Milan

UGO M. COLOMBO

THIS is a study of the income and living conditions of 300 persons, 65 years of age or older, selected by a scientific sample from persons regularly receiving assistance from the Milan Municipal Department of Assistance. All these persons live in their own homes and receive monthly economic assistance. This assistance is primarily in the form of money, but also includes, especially in the winter, benefits in kind, e.g., food, clothing, and sometimes meals.

The study was carried out through questionnaire interviews held in the person's home during the first few months of 1960. Milan, while the second largest city in population (1,500,000 inhabitants), is the most important industrial and commercial center in Italy.

CHARACTERISTICS OF THE SAMPLE

The general characteristics of the sample are shown in Table 1. The total of the sample represents slightly more than 4 percent of the 6875 (male: 2335; female: 4540) persons 65 years of age or older receiving assistance. Older persons comprise 55.5 percent of all persons receiving assistance through the Department.

Table 1. General characteristics of the sample, percentage distribution

Age		Length of residence in Milan (in years)	
65–70	26.0	From birth	24.5
71–75	30.0	Over 50	37.0
76–80	25.0	20–49	34.5
81–85	16.0	10–19	3.0
86–90	2.0	5–9	1.0
Over 90	1.0		
Sex		Marital status	
Male	33.0	Unmarried	23.5
Female	67.0	Married (living with spouse)	20.5
		Separated	4.5
		Widowed	51.5

While there is a large annual immigration to Milan, especially from southern Italy, with a net rate of 14.55 per thousand, the overwhelming majority of these are young persons and adults (72 percent being between 15 and 44 years of age), and persons over 65 constitute only 175 per thousand of the net rate. This helps to explain the sample population's very long residence in the city.

The health conditions of the interviewed persons are, in the majority, satisfactory, given the age of the subjects. While many of them have irregularities of sight or hearing, in general, 60 percent can be classified as in normal health.

LIVING CONDITIONS

Over two-thirds of the sample (67.5 percent) live alone in single dwelling units. Of these, women outnumber men 6 to 1. About one-quarter (25.5 percent), most of whom are now living with their spouses, live in two-person households. Only 5 percent live in three-person households, and 2 percent live in households of four or more persons. Generally these are persons living with children or relatives.

The predominance of individuals living alone or as couples is typical of large urban areas and illustrates the strong inclination of older Italian people toward an independent family system.[1] Not only do older people preserve autonomy in their family life, but they also refuse, as long as possible, residential accommodations in institutions or rest houses. The percentage of older persons living in institutions is very low throughout Italy, being less than 4 percent of persons 65 years of age and over. Increases in the number of admissions to public or private institutions have been mainly among persons with chronic diseases.

One factor supporting this phenomenon has been the system of rent control which has allowed only a moderate and gradual rise in rent which in the case of poor persons and old pensioners has been quite minimal. This has also encouraged continued residence in the same dwelling. If rents had been allowed to rise in the same degree as other costs of living for goods and services, the individual and social implications would have been quite striking.

[1] The general population receiving assistance through the Department of Assistance confirms this phenomenon. Family units receiving monthly allowances are distributed as follows:

Household	Percent	Household	Percent
Single-person	56.2	Four-person	4.7
Two-person	25.0	Five-or-more-person	5.2
Three-person	8.9		

Finally, another factor involved in this continuity of dwelling place, even under unsatisfactory conditions, is the extreme difficulty faced by single persons and couples in gaining admittance to the new low-rent public housing projects. Social priority has been up to now given to larger family units, those with three or more persons.

Table 2 shows the length of residence in their present dwelling unit of the sample.

Table 2. Length of residence in present dwelling units,
Milan, Italy, percentage distribution

Length of residence (*in years*)	Percent
50 or over	9.5
30–49	26.0
20–29	29.0
10–19	16.5
5–9	8.0
2–4	7.5
Under 2	2.5
No answer	1.0

The low grade and unsatisfactory character of the dwelling buildings is indicated in Table 3.

Table 3. Selected characteristics of present dwelling units

Characteristic	Percent	Characteristic	Percent
Type of building or place		Floor of dwelling unit	
"Deluxe"	5.5	Ground floor	14.0
"Middle"	18.0	First floor	27.0
Old public housing	56.0	Second floor (with elevator)	0.5
New public housing	7.5	" " (no elevator)	15.5
Smaller public housing	1.5	Third floor (with elevator)	1.0
Attic	7.0	" " (no elevator)	20.5
Underground floors	1.0	Fourth floor (with elevator)	1.0
Dormitories	0.5	" " (no elevator)	11.0
Other	3.0	Fifth floor or higher (with elevator)	3.0
Number of rooms		Fifth floor or higher (no elevator)	6.5
One	59.5		
Two	31.3	Running water	
Three	6.2	Indoor	64.0
Four	1.5	Outdoor	36.0
Five or more	1.5		
Heating		Toilet facilities	
Central	13.0	Indoor	36.5
Stove	82.0	Outdoor	63.5
Chimney	1.0		
Other	1.5	Bathing facilities	
No heating	2.5	Bath	13.0
		Shower	1.5
Lighting		No indoor bathing	85.5
Electricity	98.0		
Other	2.0		

PRERETIREMENT OCCUPATIONAL STATUS

The preretirement occupational percentage distribution of the sample members shown below illustrates the lower class status of most of the subjects:

I. Agriculture	4.0	III. Tradesmen	3.0
Unskilled workers	41.5	Clerks	3.0
II. Skilled workers	31.5	Teachers	1.0
Foremen	0.5	Other professions	9.0
Artisans	3.0	No occupation given	3.5

With respect to the reasons for retirement, these are detailed in Table 4. In considering work status it must be realized that under

Table 4. Reasons for retiring, percentage distribution

Closing of factory	5.0
Reduction in number of jobs	0.5
Resignation for personal reasons	2.0
Resignation for health reasons	32.0
Attainment of pension age	26.5
Dismissal because of age	7.5
Other causes	12.5
Undetermined	14.0

Italian law, the minimum retirement age for workers in private industry is very low (60 years for men, and 55 for women), although workers can postpone retirement for 5 years more than the given minimum age. Consequently, the number of persons economically active after age 65 is necessarily limited, all the more so as the single largest group of aged persons is composed of unskilled workers who find it extremely difficult to compete with the better trained younger generations of today. It should also be noted that our subjects are persons on public assistance and that, for many, poverty is generally a result of employment difficulties. Among a similar sample of persons not on the public assistance rolls, the proportion of those still employed in some fashion would be higher.

Nevertheless, the number still economically active (including part-time work) is remarkable (Table 5).

Among the part-time or occasional workers, 27 (6 men and 21 women) declared that their activity was equivalent to their preretirement occupational status; 16 (3 men and 13 women) were engaged in activity that was different and required a lesser degree of skill, and 17 (7 men and 10 women) were engaged in work which was quite inferior to their previous occupational status.

Among those who were inactive, 72 percent were not interested in

Table 5. *Current work status of 289 older persons*

		Economically active			
Age group	Full time	Part time or occasional	Housewives	Inactive	Total
65–70	4	29	6	40	79
71–75	3	21	4	60	88
76–80	1	6	4	59	70
81–85	1	4	2	39	46
86–90			1	4	5
91 and over				1	1
Total	9	60	17	203	289
	(M = 4; F = 5)	(M = 16; F = 44)		(M = 68; F = 135)	

regular work, either full or part-time. Only 4 percent were interested in full-time employment, and another 4 percent in part-time employment. The others did not give any answer to this question. The length of time that these people had been inactive since retirement or interruption of work is shown in Table 6.

Table 6. *Time passed since retirement or last work, presently inactive persons*

Time since retirement or last work (in years)	Male	Female	Total
Less than 1		4	4
1–2	4	13	17
3–5	6	14	20
6–10	25	24	49
Over 10	33	80	113
Total	68	135	203

BUDGET AND DIETARY STATUS

Our research into the budgets of the older people followed the general criteria presented in the author's previous study of "Budgeting Surveys" given at The Copenhagen Seminar in 1956 (Colombo, 1958).

The data of Tables 7, 8, and 9 give a general picture of the standard of living of these older people.

The amount of monthly cash grants from public assistance to the subjects is shown in Table 10. In addition, cash grants are made to 50 percent of the sample for heating, to 17 percent for rent, and to 8 percent for lighting. Supplementing this, grants in kind of food are made to 49 percent, while luncheons in public restaurants are received by 7 percent of the subjects.

Table 7. Total family monthly income

Monthly family income (in liras[a])	Percent
Under 5000	9.5
5001–10,000	14.5
10,001–15,000	38.5
15,001–20,000	17.5
20,001–25,000	9.5
25,001–30,000	4.5
30,001–40,000	2.5
40,001–50,000	1.5
Over 50,000	1.0
No answer	1.0

[a] One U.S. dollar equals 833 Italian liras.

Table 8. Aged persons' share of total family income

Share of monthly family income (in percent)	Percent
Total family income	84
Over 50	4
40–50	3
30–40	2
20–30	2
10–20	1
Under 10	3
No answer	1

Table 9. Percentage distribution of older persons having income from monthly pensions and wages

Amount (in liras)	Monthly pension	Monthly wage
Under 5000	4.0	8.5
5001–10,000	38.5	9.5
10,001–15,000	18.5	6.0
15,001–20,000	5.0	1.0
20,001–30,000	1.5	0.5
Over 30,000		
No income	31.0	73.5
No answer	1.5	1.0

Table 10. Amount of monthly cash grants to old age public assistance recipients

Amount of monthly grant (in liras)	Percent receiving
1000–2000	61
2001–3000	26
3001–5000	9
Over 5000	4

Food and rent represent the basic expenditures of these persons. Tables 11 and 12 present the distribution of monthly expenditures for these items and the percentage which these items represent of total monthly expenditures.

Table 11. Percentage distributions of amount of monthly expenditure for food, and percentage of food expenditures to total expenditures

Amount of monthly food expenditure (in liras)	Percent	Food expenditures as percent of total expenditures	Percent
Under 5000	14.0	Under 50	25.5
5001–10,000	43.5	51–60	25.0
10,001–15,000	19.5	61–70	25.5
15,001–20,000	10.5	71–80	12.0
20,001–25,000	1.0	81–85	2.5
25,001–30,000	2.5	86–90	0.5
Over 30,000	1.0	Over 90	1.0
No answer	8.0	No answer	8.0

Table 12. Percentage distributions of amount of monthly expenditure for rent, and percentage of rent expenditures to total expenditures

Amount of monthly rent expenditure (in liras)	Percent	Rent expenditures as percent of total expenditures	Percent
Rent free	6.0	Rent free	6.0
Under 1000	12.0	Under 5	9.5
1001–2000	32.0	6–10	22.0
2001–5000	34.0	11–20	30.0
5001–10,000	8.5	21–30	15.5
10,001–20,000	1.5	Over 30	12.0
20,001–30,000	0.5	No answer	5.0
Over 30,000	0.5		
No answer	5.0		

If we take account of the number of calories necessary each day for an individual 65 years of age or over living a sedentary life (2500 for men and 2100 for women), then the diets of a large group of our subjects are unsatisfactory (Table 13). In fact, only 31 percent of the men and 53 percent of the women have or exceed the above stated

Table 13. Percentage distribution of daily calorie intake of older persons

Under 1500	25
1500–2000	22
2001–2500	20
2501–3000	15
Over 3000	15
No answer	3

daily minimum calorie intake. Similar data were found with respect to other food needs. Daily protein, fat, and carbohydrate intake is shown in Table 14. Only 22 percent of the men and 30 percent of the women have sufficient protein in their diet. Daily fat intake showed that 57 percent of the men and 43 percent of the women did not have the minimum daily amounts necessary. Carbohydrate insufficiency was found in 54 percent of the men and 47 percent of the women.

Table 14. Daily protein, fat, and carbohydrate contents of diets of older persons

Daily intake (in grams)	Percent
Proteins	
Less than 50	38
51–70	29
71–100	17
101–120	8
Over 120	4
No answer	4
Fats	
Less than 50	46
51–75	28
Over 75	21
No answer	5
Carbohydrates	
Less than 100	4
101–200	16
201–300	30
301–400	21
401–500	15
501–600	6
Over 600	3
No answer	5

In Tables 15–17 we have a picture of the place in these persons' budgets of expenditures for clothing, personal needs, and recreation as well as the extent of their possession of means of recreation in the home, radio, television, and record players.

Finally, in Table 18 we see that despite the meager character of their livelihood, more than half these persons have a deficit in their income. They face the terrible problem of how to meet the basic necessities of life. In spite of this, only a small minority of 4 percent are forced to pawn possessions while another 18 percent have contracted debts, generally of very small amounts. The majority of budget deficits are balanced through invisible channels (private charity, help from relatives and neighbors, dissavings, and sale of possessions, etc.).

Table 15. Percentage distribution of amount of monthly expenditures for clothing as percentage of total monthly expenditures

No expenditure	38.5
Under 5	40.5
5–10	7.5
11–20	4.5
21–30	2.5
Over 30	0.5
No answer	6.0

Table 16. Percentage distribution of monthly expenditures for personal needs and recreation

Monthly expenditures (in liras)	Percent
Personal needs	
No expenditure	40.0
Under 500	26.0
501–1000	12.0
1001–2000	8.0
2001–3000	2.5
Over 3000	3.5
No answer	8.0
Recreation	
No expenditure	59.0
Under 500	22.5
501–1000	4.5
1001–2000	2.5
Over 2000	3.5
No answer	8.0

Table 17. Possession of radio, television, and record player

Item	Percent
Radio	31.8
Television	0.1
Record player	0.1
None	68.0

CONCLUSION

This study concerned itself with very poor old people, on the rolls of the Department of Public Assistance. Consequently, their standard of living could only be quite modest. Their living conditions are extremely distressed as is confirmed by the revealed deficiencies in housing, diet, personal, and recreational expenditures, and in the general standard of living.

The subjects were indeed very simple and honest persons. When

Table 18. Comparison of income and expenditures

Relation of income and expenditures	Percent
Equal	7.0
Income exceeds expenditures	35.0
Expenditures exceed income	55.0
No answer	3.0

asked if they would accept shelter in a poor home, almost all replied negatively and some wept at the mere allusion. When asked about the sufficiency of their present standard of living, only 9 percent felt that it was sufficient. The distribution of incomes desired by the others is shown in Table 19.

Table 19. Monthly income desired by aged recipients of public assistance

Monthly income (in liras)	Percent desiring
Under 10,000	10
10,001–20,000	42
20,001–30,000	32
30,001–40,000	8
Over 40,000	5
No answer	3

These are very modest requests indeed. The more so, since 67 percent of the subjects indicated they would be satisfied if the standard of assistance were slightly inferior to the above figures.[2]

Economic assistance in Italy is rather neglected even if the general system of social security covers appreciable sections of the population and several improvements have been made in the last few years. Along with other experts in the social sciences, I have continuously striven for better standards and benefits for old age recipients. In my opinion, the results of sound social research would help facilitate the attainment of needed radical improvements.

Acknowledgments. The interviews for this study were carried out by the social workers of the Municipal Department of Assistance (Ente Communale di Assistenza). The author wishes to acknowledge his appreciation to them and to the students of the Schools of Social Service in Milan who cooperated in the early stages of the study.

---

[2] A confirmation, although hardly necessary, of the inadequacy of domiciliary economic assistance is given by comparing it with the cost for older persons admitted to rest homes or institutions. The daily rate now, in Milan, is 800 liras per person. The global expenditure at home could not be less than that amount, but the Department of Public Assistance is not able to provide a corresponding amount.

The Municipal Bureau of Statistics provided assistance in the analysis of the data.

REFERENCE

Colombo, U. M. 1958. Budgetary surveys. *In* The need for cross-national surveys of old age, pp. 22–26. Ann Arbor: University of Michigan, Division of Gerontology.

ECC

OF

Orgai

SEYM

U.S.

HENN

Danisl

Copen

Some Policy Issues in Social Security Programs for the Aged

WILBUR J. COHEN

WHEN President Franklin D. Roosevelt signed the Social Security Act in 1935, he prophetically called it the "cornerstone in a structure which is being built but is by no means complete. . . ." In the 25 years which have passed since the Social Security Act first became law, many significant changes have taken place in the legislation, in socio-economic conditions in the United States and throughout the world, and in the role of gerontologists in tackling problems with which the Social Security Act attempted to deal.

Today the social security program is taken for granted by the community as a basic part of the warp and woof of the "American way of life." But it was not always so. As in the case of any great social reform, there were many powerful influences prior to 1935 opposing the basic principle of public responsibility embodied in social security. Even at the present time there are influential groups in the community power structure who, unable or unwilling to be specific about programs or provisions they dislike, attack "the welfare state" in general and the cost of welfare programs but, in times of recession, highly praise "built-in stabilizers" for their contribution to the resurgence of the free-enterprise economy.

Perhaps no other single piece of social legislation concerned with domestic policy adopted in the past quarter-century has been more far-reaching than the Social Security Act in helping to promote the well-being and happiness of the American people and to preserve our economic and political system. Under this one Act, there exist programs of old age, survivors, and disability insurance; unemployment insurance; federal grants to the states for the needy aged, the blind, dependent children, and the permanently and totally disabled; and maternal and child health, crippled children, and child welfare services. It can be said unequivocally that the social security system of nationwide social insurance and federal grants-in-aid programs for public welfare has become a permanent part of the basic fabric of the nation's social institutions. Moreover, it is now clear that these programs have the support of both major political parties and the overwhelming majority of the American people.

Twenty-five momentous years of social security have been completed. Much has been accomplished in this time, more than many people expected when the limited program was initially established in 1935. The vision of the framers of the social security system has provided a basic structure which has remained unchanged. Yet there are important gaps and striking inadequacies which still require solution. As the program enters its second quarter-century, what does the social security balance sheet show in terms of assets and liabilities? What changes in program emphasis are required to meet the challenges, the problems, and prospects, in the decades ahead? How can we meet the needs of our growing aged population while, at the same time, meeting the needs of children and families?

BROADENING OF SOCIAL SECURITY OBJECTIVES

The Social Security Act of 1935 was passed by Congress and became law on August 14, 1935, with the objective of meeting certain specific immediate needs and helping to prevent some types of future want and dependency. Through the federal-state partnership implemented by federal grants-in-aid, assistance became available early in 1936 under the federal-state program for needy persons in three groups of the population that, in good times as well as bad, have little or no capacity to earn their own living—the aged, the blind, and children deprived of parental support or care through the death, absence from the home, or physical or mental incapacity of a parent. Longer-range provisions of the Act were designed to provide insurance benefits for employees in commerce and industry that would furnish some income in old age retirement and during limited periods of unemployment.

The term "social security" widely used throughout the United States has often given exclusive emphasis to the income-maintenance provisions in the legislation for the aged. This is not a correct estimate of the social security program. It is highly significant that the original law recognized the need for a balanced program and also included grants-in-aid to the states for maternal and child health and welfare services, public health services for the whole community, vocational rehabilitation services, and financial support for the expansion and maintenance of a nationwide employment service. The aid to dependent children (ADC) and child health and welfare provisions of 1935, the survivors insurance provisions of 1939, the amendments of 1956 incorporating social service objectives in the public assistance program, and the broadening of child welfare services in 1958 illustrate the important role that the welfare of the entire family has had in the original and subsequent development of the law.

During the past 25 years, many important and far-reaching changes in the social security law and administrative organization have been made. Most of these have been beneficial—but not all of them. There are some legislative changes since 1950 which should be repealed or modified. But, on the whole, the changes made reflect not only amendments to keep the programs in line with rising levels in earnings and living costs and with administrative experience, but also reflect a broadening and changing character, scope, and concept of "social security." These trends are most likely to continue.

A MORE FAMILY-CENTERED PROGRAM

Over the years the social security program, step by step, has given increasing recognition to the significance of the family as a unit and to the importance of family welfare. This trend is becoming more apparent in some programs than others. But there are also serious blocks to further progress in this area which require removal.

The public assistance provisions in the original law affirmed the importance of family life by limiting the use of federal funds for needy aged or blind persons to those who were not inmates of public institutions. Moreover, the Act affirmed the dignity and responsibility of recipients by specifying that aid was to be given in the form of money which the receiver was free to spend as he deemed best for his welfare, rather than as aid in kind, such as orders for groceries or fuel, which too often reflected condescension and unwarranted suspicion of the recipient in past relief administration.

The emphasis in old age insurance was shifted from the individual to the family by the legislative changes made in 1939. Benefits were added for the aged wife and minor children of a retired insured worker and for family dependents of insured workers who die either before or after retirement. Insurance benefits to dependents and survivors were broadened and increased by the amendments of 1950, 1954, 1956, and 1958; and disability insurance benefits to insured disabled persons age 50 and over were added in 1956 and broadened to include dependents in 1958. Amendments are pending in Congress to eliminate the age 50 restriction so that disability insurance benefits will be available irrespective of the arbitrary age provision.

Survivors insurance benefits, aid to dependent children, and child welfare services are all parts of the social security program designed to aid in preserving and strengthening family life.

Despite the limitations of existing programs, in countless homes insurance or assistance payments mean that an aged couple can live out their remaining years together in a familiar setting, near their relatives and friends and with their cherished possessions; that many families in which earned income has been cut down or cut off by disability or old age have an assured income that they can use just as others in the community use their money, continuing to plan and manage their own family affairs.

The $55 billion paid out under the OASDI program since it was established can be added, and so can the number of persons to whom these payments have gone. Equally important is the self-respect and peace of mind which these programs make possible in homes into which pay envelopes no longer come, the strain and worry and humiliation averted from parents and from children whose lives might otherwise have been scarred by the anxieties of their elders or by separation from home and parents. It is well to remember the great number of homes where high standards of conduct have been upheld in the face of adverse circumstances, frequently with the aid of the modest social security payments and limited social services provided during the past 25 years.

While the social security program has done much to help in strengthening family life, there are vast problems still unsolved. There are still many low-income families. There is still a substantial amount of uncompensated wage-loss caused by sickness and disability. There are many areas without trained public assistance workers. Health, welfare, recreation, and other social services are not available to all aged persons in every community. Social insurance benefits are inadequate in many cases. Social objectives are subordinated to fiscal considerations in some instances. Medical care of high quality is not actually available to all who need it. These are some of the unfilled needs and controversial areas with which we must deal in the decade ahead.

TOWARD UNIVERSAL COVERAGE

Just prior to the 1950 amendments, old age insurance was a relatively small program. Benefits at that time averaged only about $26 a month for a single retired individual compared to $82 a month for those first drawing benefits in May, 1960. Total disbursements under the program in early 1950 were running at about three-quarters of a billion dollars annually, less than 10 percent of the nearly $12 billion is currently being paid out. And the number of persons receiving old age assistance on a needs-test basis exceeded the number of aged persons drawing old age insurance up until 1951.

Congress made a vital decision in 1950 "to reaffirm the basic principle that a contributory system of social insurance . . . is the most satisfactory way of preventing dependency." It decided that old age and survivors insurance really would be the first line of defense in meeting the income-maintenance needs of retired aged persons. By 1951 the number of aged person receiving old age insurance had exceeded the number receiving old age assistance. The reiteration and extension of the 1950 policy in 1954 by a new administration, after careful study and review of the controversies of the previous 18 years, enabled the system to accelerate the performance of the far-reaching role set out for it by Congress in 1950. In May, 1960, there were over 14 million persons drawing OASDI benefits at an annual rate of nearly $12 billion.

Today, Old Age, Survivors, and Disability Insurance (OASDI) is the largest and most important social insurance program in the United States, dwarfing any other social insurance program and even the veterans' programs.

In protection afforded to employees and their wives, it exceeds the coverage and protection of all private pension plans in the United States.

In protection afforded to widows and orphans, it is equivalent to the face value of all the private life insurance protection in the nation.

In protection afforded to the permanently totally disabled, it exceeds the coverage and protection of private insurance.

It does all this in a way which has not adversely affected initiative or thrift and has preserved emphasis on self-responsibility and wage differentials. It has operated at the phenomenally low administrative cost of only about 2 percent of disbursements, while paying benefits totaling over $50 billion on an efficient basis without any taint of political manipulation or scandal. Moreover, the expansion of OASDI has not adversely affected private insurance for old age, survivorship (life insurance), or disability. Private provisions for old age retirement have grown spectacularly in the past 10 years. The post-war expansion of private-group pension plans brought the number of aged beneficiaries of such plans in December, 1957 to 1,250,000, the majority of whom also received OASDI.

A group of business executives appointed in 1957 by the Secretary of Health, Education, and Welfare surveyed the operations of the Bureau of Old-Age and Survivors Insurance. They found that the Bureau is "carrying out its mission in a sound and vigorous manner" and commented favorably on their "impression of both efficiency and friendliness created by the typical OASI district office."

It is this enviable record that makes it possible to discuss the issues involved in still further broadening, expanding, and improving the insurance program to cover new risks.

The studies by the Committee on Economic Security in 1934, preceding the establishment of the social security program, recognized that the risk of loss of livelihood in old age was so nearly universal that the coverage of the old age insurance program should be as broad as possible. Administrative considerations, however, dictated the decision to initially cover only employees in commerce and industry. These were groups for which wage reporting and collection of contributions could be organized with less difficulty than in such excluded areas as agricultural employment, domestic service, and self-employment, even though workers in these and other excluded fields also needed protection because of their generally low earnings and irregular employment.

Administrative considerations were of particular importance at the start of the program because the insurance system relates benefits to individual earnings and hence keeps an individual record of covered earnings for each of millions of workers throughout their working lives. Some pessimists predicted that such a system could not be maintained at all or, if so, only at exorbitant cost. Despite those dire predictions, payment of benefits, including the added benefit for dependents and survivors, was started at an earlier date than had been initially scheduled, and the system has continued to operate efficiently and economically as coverage and benefits broaden, demonstrating the feasibility of operating a vast public program efficiently and economically and, at the same time, with courtesy and individualization. With this background and experience, it is now possible to add health insurance benefits to social security beneficiaries and to administer such benefits at less cost than they can be provided through private auspices.

With the major extensions of coverage in 1950, 1954, and 1956, coverage of substantially all gainful work in the United States under the OASDI system is within sight—a goal that seemed politically and administratively unattainable 25 years ago. There are still some hurdles to overcome in reaching the goal of universal coverage. But further progress in extending coverage appears possible in the future.

BLANKETING-IN

During the past 10 years, attention has been given to proposals that all aged persons not eligible for old age, survivors, and disability insurance benefits or for benefits under a public retirement program, be "blanketed-in" under the insurance program and receive a minimum monthly benefit. There are considerable numbers of aged persons who were never eligible for old age, survivors, and disability insurance; the largest group among them consists of widows whose husbands died before coverage was extended to the husband's particular occupation. Minimum benefits for this group could be considered as analogous to the past service credits under some private pension plans.

Although the issue has been explored by Congressional committees, and various public groups, no official body has recommended blanketing-in. The Advisory Council on Public Assistance considered the matter last year in relation to reducing the number on old age assistance. It concluded at that time:

> But we have not recommended blanketing-in. Many among the ineligible group have been able to make independent provision for their old age and are reasonably well-to-do; others can rely on sons or daughters or other relatives. Using public funds to provide them with a small pension does not seem to us to rate high priority among social objectives. Moreover, any blanketing-in plan likely to be feasible would still leave a substantial need for public assistance; most of the persons now on old-age assistance are getting payments considerably higher than those proposed as the minimum pension, and would continue to need supplementary income for maintenance as well as for medical care and social services.
>
> Probably the most serious objection advanced to blanketing-in was that a minimum pension from old-age, survivors and disability insurance funds, for those who have made no direct contribution to old-age, survivors and disability insurance, would be a very real threat to the wage-related, contributory character of the insurance program. The consensus was that the possible advantages of blanketing-in, at the present time, are far outweighed by the importance of preserving and strengthening the

basic social insurance program. [U.S. Advisory Council on Public Assistance, 1960, p. 32]

However, in the light of any amendments enacted by Congress this year, it may be wise to reexamine the question in the light of the provisions in any social security and health bill, the status of the OASDI and public assistance programs, including their adequacy in promoting health and well-being, the formula for Federal financial participation in public assistance costs, and their relationship to social insurance programs.

DISABILITY INSURANCE PROTECTION

From the outset, the social security program has recognized the individual and social importance of meeting risks of disability and prolonged illnesses, not only in the provisions for services for maternal and child health and for crippled children, but also in those for assistance to the needy blind and to children whose need arose from the parent's physical or mental incapacity. In 1950, resources to counter need arising from disability were augmented by the establishment of federal grants for public assistance for needy adults who are totally and permanently disabled. As of May, 1960, about 360,000 disabled persons were receiving disability assistance in addition to about 110,000 blind persons.

In 1952, Congress first enacted a "disability freeze" provision in the insurance program, but it did not become operative. Then, in 1954, Congress made the provision effective. Periods in which a worker has been totally disabled, as defined by the law, are omitted in computing his insured status and the average earnings on which his eventual benefit and benefits to his dependents or survivors are based.

A program of cash benefits for periods of extended total disability passed the House of Representatives in 1949 but failed to be enacted. Legislation to provide cash benefits, as part of the Old-Age and Survivors Insurance system, to insured persons totally disabled for an extended period of time beginning at age 50, was enacted into law in 1956. This was an important step in the development of social insurance. The disability insurance provisions were adopted in the Senate by a close vote of 47 to 45 after a vigorous debate and controversy. What originally began as a limited old age insurance system in 1935 became a broad social insurance program by 1956, covering three

with public assistance
ress made has been
substantial increases
the states and localiti
to meeting the needs
estimates are sufficie
met is staggering. S
public support of the
large part of the need
must be overcome t
areas.

Since future public
medical care needs :
operation with nong
role in stimulating
quality, including pre

Steps should be ta
toward assuring tha
recipients are compr
ments in medical car
payments to recipien

The federal gover
lating and encourag
improve the quality
made on behalf of
end, federal leaders
states for evaluatin
of medical care; (?
amounts of medical
lishing periodically
and other informati
about needed medic

The federal agen
care advisory comn
public assistance.

INCREASING
SERVICES

Services to indiv
portant in all aspec

"vendors" (that is, providers) of medical care, such as physicians, dentists, nurses, hospitals, or druggists.

In amending the law in 1950, Congress narrowly limited the federal financial share for direct payments for medical care. In 1956, the law was amended to provide a specially earmarked arrangement for medical care ($6–$3 matching plan). Outside of, and in addition to, whatever federal funds were available for money payments to needy individuals, the federal government offered to share in state payments to the vendors of medical care. The federal government, however, limited its financial responsibility in both cases by setting up certain maximums beyond which a state could not claim reimbursement. These provisions were very substantially changed and improved by legislation in 1958 in two respects:

1. The maximums in the federal law on the payment to the recipient, and on the vendor expenditures made in his behalf in the form of medical care in which the federal government will participate, are combined into one *average* maximum for all recipients in a state, which maximum is applicable to the entire assistance expenditure, including both money payments and medical care. For old age, blind, and disability assistance, this maximum was placed at $65 a month.

2. The federal share is determined in part by the relative fiscal ability of the state as measured by state per capita income.

The federal share of assistance expenditures for the aged, blind, and disabled was continued at four-fifths of the first $30 of the average monthly assistance expenditure. Federal participation in the assistance expenditures made above these maximums (but within the over-all limits determined by multiplying by $65 the number of persons receiving old age, blind, and disability assistance each month) is increased above the previous 50–50 matching for the lower income states. Federal participation in such payments is 50 percent for states whose per capita income is equal to or above the per capita income for the United States, ranging upward to 65 percent for states whose per capita income is below the national average.

These changes in 1958 were the result of protracted efforts to improve public assistance. Still further changes are needed and will undoubtedly be given consideration by the Congress during the next few years. Federal sharing in general assistance and the removal of residence and settlement laws so that assistance can be given solely on the basis of need are of special concern. The absence of comprehensive health insurance coverage protecting the lowest income groups in the population requires additional funds and program planning in public assistance. At the beginning of 1960, an Advisory

Counci
change
conside
sive pu
suranc

Des
needy
help.
progra
becaus
able to
are en
suppor
not or
ineligit
receive

Five
All ha
same
the ne
monly
old ag
aid to
federal
special
consid
nature
of cer
eligibil

As
assista
helpin
availal
assista
young
can cc
family
menta
state c
the sta

The
payme

of preventing or mitigating economic and social insecurity. Close coordination of services and benefits has always existed in the employment security program. Workers who claim unemployment benefits must report and register for work at public employment offices, thus initiating efforts that may get them what is better than a benefit —a new job. The employment service aids in counseling and placing workers, giving particular attention to older workers and other workers requiring special service. Increasing attention is being given by the employment service and other community agencies to services for older persons.

The 1954 and 1956 amendments relating to disability insurance recognized the importance of rehabilitation services by providing for the referral of disabled persons to state vocational rehabilitation agencies. These agencies will be in an increasingly better position to recognize and aid, frequently in an early phase, persons for whom appropriate medical and vocational counseling may prevent more serious disability or restore working capacity. There is similar collaboration between the state public assistance and vocational rehabilitation agencies in locating and assisting incapacitated assistance recipients.

The statements of purpose in all four public assistance programs were amended in 1956 to specify that, in addition to enabling states to give financial assistance to needy people, the purpose is also to enable states to furnish appropriate public welfare services to help assistance recipients toward independent living. In the program for the aged, blind, and disabled, the amendment makes it clear that services should be directed to assisting individuals toward self-support or self-care.

Many states are now beginning to give wider recognition to services focused on rehabilitation and prevention in their public assistance programs. Under the 1956 amendments, states are required to outline the services, if any, that are provided under each of the assistance programs and the steps taken to assure maximum use of other agencies providing similar or related services. The amendments also make explicit that the federal government shares in the states' costs in providing appropriate services, as well as assistance, to needy people.

It appears, however, that if the total caseloads on public assistance are drastically reduced, particularly for old age assistance, public welfare agencies could then begin to provide, finance, and staff social services on a broad, high-quality, comprehensive basis.

GOALS FOR SOCIAL SECURITY IN THE COMING DECADE

During the next 10 years the productivity of our nation should continue to grow, because of automation, research, inventions, new processes, products, and services. It should be possible, therefore, for our country to afford improvements in our social security system from these increased resources so that every aged and disabled person will have sufficient income to enable him to live in health and decency. By the end of the decade a series of periodic legislative changes by the Congress should result in the following:

1. An increase in social security benefits averaging about 40 to 50 percent above present levels so that the average insurance benefits will be about $175 a month for a couple;

2. An increase for widows somewhat larger than the average because their incomes are now the lowest among any of the aged;

3. The payment of a regular monthly insurance income to all those who are totally disabled for any extended period of time irrespective of age or the type of disability;

4. The financing of the insured disabled individual's retraining and rehabilitation through the OASDI program, thus helping him wherever possible to regain independence, become self-supporting, and return to independent living;

5. The social security system taking on a major share of the responsibility of financing hospital and nursing services for the aged and the disabled. By financing these heavy costs through pooling employee and employer contributions, some of the heaviest financial burdens of medical care should be spread over an individual's entire working lifetime and over the entire nation.

The decade of the sixties should be a period of continued economic growth. At the same time, we must make sure that we have an equitable method of distributing this increasing production to our aged and disabled, to our widows and dependent children, and to the unemployed and their families. Social security programs—public and private—assure us all that there will be a fairer distribution of goods and services in the economy. It is not a handout; it is a cooperative social insurance program that relates benefits to costs on a sound long-run financial basis.

Even those who have vigorously opposed basic provisions of the social security program in the past will now admit that it is here to stay in some form or other and that it will be expanded and strengthened in the light of experience. Social security is recognized as necessary to the effective functioning of our economy. It is both a businesslike and humanitarian approach to problems affecting millions of people.

The economic problems of the aged, the disabled, widows, and orphans are part of the problem of persistent poverty in the midst of plenty. We must more vigorously attack the problems of dependency. The United States can, if it wishes, accomplish the abolition of poverty and financial dependency—including our aged and disabled persons—before any other country does it. This objective, like flying to the moon, has been a dream in the past. There is no reason why the United States should not make as its goal the accomplishment of both objectives during this coming decade.

REFERENCE

U.S. Advisory Council on Public Assistance. 1960. The report of the Advisory Council on Public Assistance containing findings and recommendations. (S. Doc. No. 93 [86th Cong., 2d sess.].) Washington, D.C.: U.S. Government Printing Office.

Income Needs and Adequacy of Pension Systems

HENNING FRIIS

IN most Western countries the financial impact of pension programs for the elderly is increasing, not only because the number of elderly persons is growing, but because there is a continual urge to increase the pension rates. The question, therefore, arises in every country: What is the right level of pensions?

The answer depends on so many sociological and economic variables that it cannot be given in a general form. It is possible, however, to give the policy-makers and the general public some information which can be applied when decisions are taken regarding the level of pensions.

Calculations of "minimum standards" have been one of the main points of departure when efforts have been made to find a basis for fixing pensions. Calculated minimum standards were used by William Beveridge for the benefit proposals in his famous Report on Social Insurance and Allied Services in 1942 and they are used in the United States in fixing benefit rates for old age assistance ("budgeting"). Even at this minimum level a number of subjective judgments are involved on which it is difficult to reach agreement (Townsend, 1954). Furthermore, the use of calculated minimum subsistence levels may often be of limited practical value.

In connection with the planning of a social security scheme for Egypt, studies were undertaken with a view to estimating the minimum means on which sedentary persons in Egypt can subsist (Friis, 1951). Results of the findings showed that the estimated minimum monthly cost of living was much higher than the minimum wage for industrial workers fixed by the government. The suggestion to the Ministry of Social Affairs, therefore, was that when fixing the maximum for the benefits the main emphasis be placed on the legal minimum wage as the level of pensions should not in any case be higher than the minimum wage.

This is only an example, drawn from a country with a rather low general level of living. At the other scale of the balance, cases could be drawn from more developed countries showing that the pensions are already higher than what would usually be considered a minimum level of living. Here again, calculations of minimum budgets in the traditional sense are of very little use when making decisions on the level of pensions.

However, there are other possibilities of throwing light on pension levels than a calculated minimum standard. The criteria to be discussed here are based on comparisons between the level of living of persons involved in national retirement pension schemes and the level of living of other groups in the population.

COMPARISONS BETWEEN NATIONAL RETIREMENT PENSION AND OTHER SOCIAL SECURITY BENEFITS

A national retirement pension scheme may be considered either in isolation from social security schemes (as deferred wages) or as an integral part of a comprehensive social security system. Where the latter is the case, as in Denmark, it is natural to compare the level of national retirement pensions with the level of benefits under other social security schemes.

In fundamental considerations concerning the fixing of the level of the benefits, two divergent points of view have predominated. One is that social benefits should be higher where the case of need is of brief duration (illness and unemployment) than in cases of permanent need (disablement and old age). The reasoning is that in the short run it is a greater hardship and more undesirable that a family's subsistence level should be considerably pressed down than in cases of permanent loss of earnings, such as the coming on of old age, for which the persons in question have had time to prepare and adjust themselves. The other point of view, which was advocated by Beveridge, among others, is that benefits should be uniform, irrespective of whether the case of indigence is of short or long duration. "There is no difference between the subsistence level of those affected by different forms of interruption of earnings which is large enough and clear enough to justify a differentiation of benefits." (Beveridge, 1942, pp. 54–55.)

It is doubtful whether the fixing of the level of social benefits in Denmark was originally based on any fundamental considerations such as these, but as a matter of fact the social security legislation of 1933 did fix benefits in short-term cases of need at a higher level than the benefits in more permanent cases of need, as will be seen from Table

1 which shows the levels of social benefits in 1934 and 1958. In 1934 the old age pension was the lowest of all social benefits.

Table 1. Levels of social benefits in Denmark, 1934 and 1958

	COPENHAGEN				PROVINCIAL TOWN			
	Kroner		*Index*		*Kroner*		*Index*	
Type of social benefit	*1934*	*1958*	*1934*	*1958*	*1934*	*1958*	*1934*	*1958*
National retirement pension (married couple)	1053	5316	100	100	885	5040	100	100
Disablement pension (both spouses qualify)	1230	6324	117	119	1050	6048	119	120
Municipal relief (married couple)	1230	4519	117	85	1050	4284	119	85
Tuberculosis patients	1230	6044	117	114	1050	5740	119	114
Daily cash benefit under the industrial injuries scheme[a]	1734	6617	165	124	1734	6617	196	131
Maximum daily cash benefit under the health insurance scheme[a]	2184	2184	207	41	2184	2184	247	43
Daily cash benefit under the health insurance scheme plus daily benefits from the Sick Leave Fund[a]		6216		117	2184	6216	247	123
Unemployment benefit (breadwinner)	1440	5503	137	104	1440	5503	163	109

[a] The benefits are calculated as paid for 12 months, irrespective of waiting period and limiting period.

However, it will be seen from Table 1 that today the differentiation is not quite so clear. The retirement pension is still lower than most other benefits. The relative levels of the benefits are now rather fortuitous, and there is a very great need for a reconsideration of the criteria for fixing the relation among the benefits, based on concrete studies of the relative needs of the different groups.

COMPARISON WITH THE LEVEL OF LIVING FOR THE LOWER INCOME BRACKETS IN THE ACTIVE POPULATION

As long as nothing more is required of the old age pension than meeting a certain minimum standard which is below the subsistence level in active population groups, there is not direct need, in fixing the level, for comparisons with these groups. In fact, careful comparisons of this kind have not normally been made. For the purpose of international comparisons, more superficial calculations have been carried out, primarily in connection with I.L.O. Convention No. 102 concerning minimum standards of social security. As a control figure for the level of old age pensions in the countries that ratified the convention, it was here decided to have the old age benefits for a married couple measured against some typical workers' wages; for systems constructed like the Danish system the benefits were measured against the wages received by a fully employed unskilled worker in 1 year.

Such a comparison shows in the case of Denmark that the national retirement pension for a married couple in 1958 amounted to approximately 43 percent of the wages received by a fully employed unskilled worker. By way of comparison it may be mentioned that in 1934 the old age pension for a married couple amounted to approximately 33 percent of the wages of an unskilled worker.

Such schematic comparisons, however, do not give any very valuable illustration of the level of living of pensioners relative to the level of living of employed persons, since they do not take into account the fact that a given income covers many different subsistence levels. This is primarily due to differences in the burden of family responsibilities, but there are also many other reasons, including differences in rent levels. As far as retirement pensioners are concerned, such comparisons rarely allow for the fact that old people on various points have lower expenses, apart from the fact that as a rule they have no children to support if they have retired from active work; for instance, their transportation cost is lower and they are spending less money on food away from their homes. In budgeting, the elderly are not burdened with acquisitions of durable or semi-durable goods to the same extent as younger people, and a great many of them have supplementary incomes, as from boarders and lodgers, from property, and from the more or less regular contributions of their children. However, payments from old people to their children also occur (Townsend, 1957).

In order to illustrate the differences in the levels of living of the old age pensioner and the unskilled worker (with average unemployment) I have made some calculations of disposable income after deduction of various fixed expenses.

The comparison is based on four basic types: families with and without children and families living in newly built or old flats. Table 2 is related to childless families in Copenhagen in 1958.

In old flats, the actively employed breadwinner has 2800 kroner more surplus than the age pensioner. In new flats, for instance, if the age pensioner is living in a flat designed for pensioners where the rent is comparatively low, the worker has some 1300 kroner more.

Table 2. *Childless families in Copenhagen, 1958*

Income and fixed expenses	Married unskilled worker		Married old age pensioner	
	Old flat	New flat	Old flat	New flat[a]
Earnings + unemployment benefit	11,680	11,680		
Pension, etc.			5520	5520
Fixed expenses				
Rent and heating	1200	2400	1200	910
Social insurance contributions	940	940	200	200
Workingclothes, transport, food	900	900		
Taxes	1770	1770	50	50
Total fixed expenses	4810	6010	1450	1160
Disposable income	6870	5670	4070	4360

a In special apartment houses for pensioners.

For workers with children, the disposable amount is reduced by expenses on the children's consumption of food and clothes and by the extra expenses of a larger flat, including a larger heat consumption. On the other hand, these families are granted family allowances, tax reduction, and may have smaller expenses owing to free school meals, free summer camps, and free dental treatment for the children. In addition, families with three children occupying flats of a reasonable standard are entitled to a special rent allowance.

The budget of the worker with three children as compared with that of the childless family is given in Table 3.

It will be seen that the worker with three children in an old flat has more left over than the old pensioner in an old flat, though the difference has been reduced to only about 400 kroner, whereas the worker occupying a new flat has some 400 to 500 kroner less at his free disposal than has the old pensioner.

However, a family like the one mentioned will have children's expenses for only 20–25 years; of this there will be expenses for three children at the same time for only approximately 10–15 years; and therefore it must be expected that the disposable income will rise about their fortieth year.

If we consider the same worker's family as before, but without children, the disposable amount for this family in a new flat will rise from about 3800 kroner to about 5600 kroner. The increase is not greater because the rent allowance ceases and taxes go up as the children grow up. From the time when the support of the children is supposed to cease, the worker will thus have a disposable amount that is 1100–1200 kroner higher than that of the old pensioner.

However, the difference between the disposable amounts before and

Table 3. Comparison of disposable income of married unskilled
worker with three children, according to residence
in old or new flats, in Copenhagen, 1958

Fixed expenses and additional income (earnings of 11,680 kroner)	Residence	
	Old flat	New flat
Fixed expenses for childless workers	4810	6010
Extra expenses (because of children)ᵃ		
Rent and heating	240	300
Other expenses	3800	3800
Total	8850	11,110
Extra income or savings		
Rent allowance		740
Free meals at school ⎫		
Free summer camp ⎬	500	500
Free dental treatment ⎭		
Deductions and allowances in respect of children under Taxation Acts	1010	1010
Children's allowance during periods of unemployment	90	90
Total	1600	2340
Fixed expenses + extra income or savings	7250	7770
Disposable income	4430	3910

ᵃ On the basis of Swedish and Danish calculations, these expenses for each child
account for about 14 percent of the income.

after the children have grown up is, if anything, smaller than stated,
because some adjustments of the income in later years must be made.

It must be taken into consideration that a married couple who has
had three children in the home must expect some expenses for new
acquisitions when the children leave home, because furniture, carpets,
etc., will have become more or less worn out. Moreover, it must also
be considered that many people buy durable goods, or in some other
way lay something by for their old age, for quite a number of years
before they are to retire on pension. This means, then, that the slightly
higher disposable income during these years is to go back to the time
when there were children in the house and also ahead to their old
age. As the difference between the disposable amount of old age and
that of the preceding period was only slightly more than 1000 kroner,
there seems to be a tendency toward parity between subsistence levels
in the different age groups.

COMPARISONS WITH EARLIER LEVELS OF LIVING OF PENSIONERS

Many national pension systems, including the recent British and Swedish systems, aim at compensating for an appreciable part of the income that ceases when the working capacity fails owing to old age. In the decision regarding the level of pensions in such systems two factors are involved: (1) a criterion for earlier income, and (2) a compensation percentage.

In the new Swedish law, for example, the first criterion has been fixed as the average income of 15 years with the highest earnings.

From the desire to avoid a sharp fall in income owing to retirement on account of old age, it would seem more natural to use as the criterion the subsistence level in the years immediately preceding the pensionable age. This would be most advantageous to groups whose incomes rise as they grow older, such as public servants and many salaried employees of private firms. On the other hand, it would be disadvantageous to many wage earners and some salaried employees whose earnings decrease as they grow older, among other things owing to increasing unemployment.

In fixing the compensation percentage it will, in principle, be reasonable to make comparisons of the type described earlier, so that allowance can be made for differences in expenditure requirement before and after the pensionable age, including possible savings through retirement from work, special tax reductions for the aged, etc.

COMPARISONS WITH PENSIONS OF OTHER OLD PEOPLE

Comparisons of the pension level of a group of old people with what others receive in pensions actually take place. One of the chief motives for carrying through the recent Danish National Retirement Pension Scheme was that the old age pensioners compared their circumstances with the pensions to which public servants are entitled. This comparison led to the result that all old people were to have retirement pensions. The result achieved so far has been a token amount of 1300 kroner to those who are entitled to receive only the minimum. It must therefore be expected, and in fact the original proposal of the Social-Democratic Party aimed at this, that constant increases in the minimum amount will be demanded, so that in the end everybody will get the same amount of national retirement pension. Even this, however, will not place national retirement pensioners on an equal footing with public pensioners as the pensions of the latter are fixed in proportion to earlier income. This form of comparison therefore leads into schemes corresponding to those recently introduced in Sweden and Britain. Such a development based on comparisons between the pension levels of different groups of old people will in future be intensified by the increasing number of superannuation schemes for salaried employees of private firms.

How far such a comparison leads is difficult to say. The retirement pension of a Danish public servant may, under the recently enacted change in the Civil Servants Act, amount to 75 percent of the special base salary. Since the pensionable share of the salary falls as the salary rises, this means that the pension from a salary of 10,000 kroner amounts to about 71 percent, but that from a salary of 20,000 kroner amounts to about 64 percent, and from a salary of 30,000 kroner it will be 60 percent. These percentages are increased because the public servant is entitled to national retirement pension (as a rule only the minimum amount) but, on the other hand, they are actually lower in proportion to the total earnings of the public servant, since extra income is not pensionable. This means, particularly for the higher income groups who have the highest extra incomes, that the pension may be considerably less than 60 percent of total earnings.

An examination of a large number of Danish private superannuation schemes shows that the pension percentage varies considerably, namely from 45 percent to 80 percent; but most of the schemes tend to be based on 66⅔ or 70 percent. In some cases this means that the pension is actually about 70 percent of the terminal salary, but in the majority of cases it is considerably lower, because the pension basis has rarely been brought up to date with the increases in prices and wages that have occurred since the establishment of the scheme.

To enable a correct comparison to be made between the national retirement pension scheme and public and private superannuation schemes, it would be desirable if a study were to be made of the actual compensation percentages in the different schemes.

Several other criteria for comparisons could be set up, but those discussed above reflect the tendencies that have appeared in the care of the aged during the last 10–15 years.

The first step has been pensions which guarantee a certain recognized minimum standard somewhat below the subsistence level of the lower income groups in the active population.

The next step brings this minimum standard up to the typical subsistence level of the lower income groups.

The third step aims at ensuring a subsistence level for the aged which is close to the subsistence level previously achieved by each pensioner. The comparisons with the earlier levels of living discussed previously correspond to this step; whereas while the comparison with the income from pensions of other old people is irrelevant in connection with the goal indicated, it is of very great importance from a sociopsychological point of view.

REFERENCES

Beveridge, W. 1942. Social insurance and allied services. New York: Macmillan Co.

Friis, H. 1951. Report to the United Nations on technical assistance in public assistance and related social services to Egypt, 1950. United Nations. (T.A.A. 335/1/01. Egypt Reports. Restricted.)

Townsend, P. 1954. Measuring poverty. Brit. J. Sociology, 5: 130–37.

——— 1957. The family life of old people. London: Routledge & Kegan Paul Ltd.

Pensions for Dependent Wives

BRIAN ABEL-SMITH

IN several European countries there have been movements in recent years to provide pensions which represent a high proportion of retirement earnings. Such movements can be seen for example in Germany, Sweden, and the United Kingdom. In addition there has been a tendency for countries which have traditionally had flat-rate pensions to introduce an element of wage-related pension. This step has already been taken in both Sweden and the United Kingdom and the comparative merits of wage-related and flat-rate systems of state pensions are now being carefully considered in Canada.

These trends can be attributed to many different forces—the growth of occupational pensions, the effects of inflation, the political power of an increasing proportion of elderly persons in the population, and a variety of other social, economic, and political changes. One important basic issue seems to be raised by these developments. It has certainly raised complex and conflicting problems of equity among those engaged in pension planning in Great Britain. This is the problem of fitting married women into a pension scheme which provides a high level of benefits.

Essentially the problem is whether society should give separate recognition to the needs of a pensioner's dependent wife. If her needs are to be recognized, there arises the further problem of devising a means of doing so which does not (1) do an injustice to the wife who has chosen to go out to work and (2) give an "excessive" pension to married couples. In both Great Britain and the United States the proportion of married women at work has been increasing to such an extent that the problem can no longer be ignored.

The problem not only arises in social security benefits, but is to be found also in income tax law. For many years the needs of the dependent wife in Great Britain have been given some recognition in the form of a higher allowance of tax-free income for a married man than for a single man. The married man's allowance has, however, always been lower than the allowances for two single people. At present the married man receives an allowance of £240 as compared to the single allowance of £140. Thus, by implication, the marginal needs of a wife are about 70 percent of those of a single person.

The recognition of the wife in the British social security system occurs only for men who are dead, sick, unemployed, or over pensionable age. While a family allowance is payable for the second child and subsequent children to the wife of a man who is under 65 and at work, there is no such allowance for the wife herself. The standard rates of social security benefits in Britain are 50*s.* per week for a single person and 80*s.* for a married couple. Thus, by implication, the marginal needs of a wife are about 60 percent of those of a single person.

CROSS-NATIONAL COMPARISONS

From the publication of the Social Security Administration (1958) of the U.S. Department of Health, Education, and Welfare "Social Security Programs throughout the World," it is possible to see to what extent the dependent wife is recognized in different programs for income maintenance of the aged. This does not take account of amendments to different schemes since the report was published.

Information was published for 58 countries out of which there was specific mention of provision for a dependent wife in the pension programs of 26 countries. A very few of the 32 countries for which there was no clear indication of provision for a dependent wife met the needs of the aged solely by assistance services; they, therefore, may have been giving more to a married couple than to a single person under these services. But the vast majority of the countries, without additions to benefit for a wife, had wage-related programs.

Out of the 26 countries with a wife's benefit, 10 gave the wife less than 45 percent of the single person's benefit, 14 gave the wife between 45 percent and 65 percent of the single person's benefit, and 2 gave the wife the same as her husband. It is significant that all the countries with a wife's benefit of less than 45 percent had wage-related schemes. The most popular rate for a wife among this group was 10 percent as in East Germany, Iran, Nicaragua, and the U.S.S.R. Peru and the Dominican Republic gave less, while Belgium gave 25 percent. The 2 schemes which gave the wife the same as her husband took no account of contribution records of any kind—that is, the old age pensions' scheme of Canada and the gradually growing superannuation benefit of New Zealand.

The 14 countries with benefits for the wife of between 45 percent and 65 percent of the husband's benefit fell into these groups. One group consisting of Australia, Denmark, Iceland, and the United Arab Republic had an income test. The largest group of 6 countries (Finland, Israel, The Netherlands, Norway, Sweden, and the United Kingdom) had flat-rate schemes without an income test. The third group consisted of 4 countries with wage-related schemes—France, Greece, Switzerland, and the United States.

There seems to be a certain logic in these provisions. The 2 countries who give the wife the same as her husband think of pensions as a right of citizenship and attach no contributory conditions to it. While it is obviously true that 2 old people sharing a home can live more cheaply than if they live apart, this is true of all old people living together, not just of married couples. Thus it may be argued that paying a lower pension to a dependent wife than to a single person is not a very exact way of adjusting pensions to need.

It is noticeable that of the 14 countries paying the dependent wife between 45 percent and 65 percent of what her husband receives, 10 are flat-rate systems with or without an income test. It appears, moreover, that all flat-rate systems of pensions pay the dependent wife more than 45 percent of what her husband receives. The philosophy of flat-rate pensions is that minimum needs are broadly the same for all pensioners. Once pensions become thought of in terms of minimum needs in this sense it is logical to accept that a married couple's needs are more than those of a single person and less than those of 2 single persons.

The question comes to mind whether the differences in the proportions of the husband's benefit paid to a wife among these countries represent different costs of minimum needs. Thus one questions whether shared costs (rent, heating, etc.) play a larger role in Australia where the wife gets 50 percent than in Iceland where the wife gets 60 percent. And why is there almost as large a difference between the figures for adjacent Norway and Sweden? If subsistence needs underlie the figures, how much research has there been to establish the appropriate relationship for the dependent wife's benefit?

The majority of the countries with wage-related pension schemes give no benefit for the dependent wife—most of the minority that do give such a benefit keep it small. These countries have no doubt been influenced in their decisions about pensions by the practices of private insurance companies. But to rationalize the philosophy that underlies these schemes, perhaps need is seen as varying to some extent between individuals. Thus need is thought of wholly or partly in terms of the standard of living which has been enjoyed before pension became due. As the existence of a dependent wife did not, by definition, augment income before pensionable age, there is no justification for extra income after pensionable age on this account.

Four countries with wage-related schemes, however, do pay substantial benefits to a dependent wife—France, Greece, Switzerland, and the United States. There are no obvious similarities among these countries or among their pension schemes. Thus the Swiss scheme is partly supported by a government contribution but the other three schemes are not. The French scheme is strictly wage-related while the other three schemes appear to give advantageous terms to lower paid employees.

THE PROBLEM POSED BY GENEROUS PENSIONS

Where pensions represent quite a low level of earnings, the pension for a dependent wife does not create special problems. Some may choose to think of need entirely in terms of accustomed standards of living and therefore provide no benefit for a dependent wife. Others may think of need in terms of survival and therefore recognize that two need more to survive than one. It is also possible to combine these ideas and thus argue that need is partly a function of survival and partly a function of accustomed standards. This leads to a wage-related pension with a supplement for a dependent wife. But once it is intended to provide a pension which represents a high proportion of earnings, a generous pension for a dependent wife seems anomalous.

Many considerations are involved in determining the "ideal" relationship between pensions and earnings while at work. Much will depend on whether family allowances are provided and at what level, on the availability of services in kind for old people, and on the extent of help available from the wider family circle. Perhaps we can assume, and it is an assumption, that pensions should not normally provide a higher level of living than has been enjoyed while at work or is currently being enjoyed by those at work. Perhaps the aged need somewhat less as they do not incur the same expenditure on insurance contributions, on travel to work, and on other items (such as meals away from home and special clothing). But whatever is the appropriate level for a maximum pension, it follows that if this level is paid to a man with a dependent wife, the effect of a separate wife's allowance is to make the pension for the single person lower than it otherwise could have been.

The question of dependent wives' pensions raises many emotional reactions. The dependent wife, particularly the wife who has the care of dependent children, undoubtedly contributes to national wealth even though her contribution is not normally recorded in national income statistics. But it is an odd society which chooses to recognize this contribution, not at the time when it is being made, but in old age. If cash allowances were provided for the dependent wives of men of working age, these allowances would logically be brought into account when considering the ideal pension for married couples in old age. When there are no such allowances and where pensions represent a high proportion of earnings, a pension for dependent wives is hardly justified.

THE PROBLEM OF THE TRANSITION

If these broad principles are accepted, if it is agreed that a dependent wife's benefit is not consistent with a high level of pension, the conclusion may be of no practical value unless a solution can be found to the problem of the transition. The literature of social security is not lacking in theoretical argument. In practice, however, it is extremely difficult to withdraw a benefit which has been enacted. This is largely a consequence of the heavy stress which is laid on the insurance analogy. Social security schemes in many countries are haunted by the mistakes of the past, by provisions which remain even though they are clearly unsuited to current social circumstances.

The United Kingdom has already undergone, almost unnoticed, the transition from equal pensions for men and women to a wife's benefit of about 60 percent of her husband's benefit. It has also undergone a transition from sickness and unemployment benefits without benefits for wives to a system which provides such benefits. The history may therefore be worth relating. Moreover, it may prompt others to tell of the experience of their own country in this respect.

In the first legislation for noncontributory old age pensions in 1908, the standard pension was 5s. per week and was provided subject to a test of means and subject to other conditions. This pension did not intend to provide more than part maintenance. The bill which was introduced in Parliament provided that where there were two or more pensioners living in the same household their pensions should be reduced to 3s. 9d. per week. This had been for many years the principle of the poor law under which the needs of the indigent aged had been met before 1908. It was pointed out during the debate that such a provision created anomalies, evasions, and administrative difficulties (Great Britain, House of Commons, 1908). Accordingly the bill was amended to provide a pension of 5*s.* per week to men and women whether or not they were married. It was a pension by right of citizenship with an income and other tests.

When contributory pensions were introduced by the Act of 1925, it was hardly possible to refuse equal pensions to dependent wives. The precedent had been established and there was no proposal to increase at this stage the level of pensions. Fundamentally the wife's pension was as high as her husband's because the 1908 Bill had been unwisely drafted.

The legislation of 1911 which introduced contributory insurance for sickness and unemployment provided benefits only for the insured person. No addition to benefit was made for a dependent wife. This remained the position in sickness insurance until 1948. Allowances were, however, introduced for wives and children in unemployment insurance in 1919. There was a curious reason for this breach in the principles of private insurance. A special benefit or "dole" was given to demobilized soldiers after World War I and to "certain workers thrown out of work through the change from war production to peace production." The benefit for a demobilized soldier was based on the army terms of service and therefore included a benefit for the soldier's family. It soon became anomalous to have some of the unemployed with benefits for wives and children and others with benefits only for themselves. The principle of dependents' benefits had to be extended to all the unemployed.

The Beveridge plan of 1942 aimed to provide the minimum income needed for subsistence. Thus, his proposals logically involved allowances for dependent wives in all benefits. He was able to alter the relationship between the pension for a dependent wife and that of her husband, as his ultimate proposals involved quite a large increase in the level of pensions. Thus, he gave a figure at 1938 prices of 17*s.*10*d.* for the subsistence requirements of a retired man, to which he added 11*s.*10*d.* or 66 percent for a dependent wife. The whole weight of his reasoning was on the subsistence argument. The fact that he was proposing such a small increase in pension for the dependent wife was barely mentioned.

When legislation was introduced in 1946 based largely on Beveridge's proposals, the pension for a dependent wife was put at 61 percent of her husband's—16*s.* compared with 26*s.* This proportion has been roughly maintained in the subsequent changes in pension rates. The broad principle underlying the pensions bill of 1908 was successfully introduced in 1946.

While the logic of subsistence benefits required Beveridge to recommend a benefit for the dependent wife, in the process he created an anomaly in the case of married women who go out to work. As a wife was entitled to some pension whether she worked or not, the advantage of paying a contribution of her own was much less than in the case of a single woman. Thus at present a dependent wife is entitled to a pension of 30s. whether or not she works. If she chooses to pay the same contribution as a single woman she can add only 20s. to her pension while a single woman gets the full 50s. for her contributions. It is true that a married woman who contributes can receive her pension at age 60 irrespective of her husband's age, instead of waiting until her husband is 65. But this is a material consideration in only a minority of cases.

This anomaly has grown in importance as the proportion of married women going out to work has steadily increased. In 1911 and 1921 less than 10 percent of married women worked outside their homes. By 1955 nearly 30 percent did so. Plans for pensions can no longer ignore the problem of the married woman who goes out to work. It is no longer realistic to regard the great bulk of married women as dependents. One possible solution to this problem would be to require the married woman to pay a contribution adjusted to the additional pension she would gain by going out to work.

CONCLUSION

British experience shows that it is not difficult to make the transition from equal pensions to a lower proportionate level of pension for a dependent wife. This could presumably be done in Canada or New Zealand, if the increase in the basic benefit were considerable and provided the whole emphasis were placed upon this aspect of the change.

It would seem more difficult to dispose altogether of the wife's allowance, particularly if it were separately paid out to her. If there were a sufficiently large increase in the basic benefit, it might be acceptable to enact that in future the wife's allowance would be deducted from her husband's benefit. Another possibility would be to place a limit on the joint benefit which could be received. Such a "stop" could be fixed in terms of the previous earnings of the beneficiaries. Either solution might create political difficulties.

If no solution can be found to the problem of the transition, this paper must end with a paradoxical conclusion. The more generous the provision made for dependent wives in programs for the income maintenance of the aged, the lower must be the general level of benefits which can be attained by the program.

REFERENCES

Great Britain. House of Commons, 1908. House of Commons debates, Cols. 1786–1787, June 24.

U.S. Social Security Administration. 1958. Division of Program Research. Social security programs throughout the world. Washington, D.C.: Government Printing Office.

Standard Budgets for Elderly Persons: Problems of Concept, Method, and Interpretation

HELEN H. LAMALE AND EWAN CLAGUE

ALTHOUGH the first of the so-called "standard" budgets was developed about 60 years ago, they have dealt almost exclusively with the problems of families in the lower- or middle-age ranges, or with dependent families, and only in recent years have the problems of living costs for self-supporting elderly persons received much attention in standard budget research.

In 1943, the Social Security Board published budgets for an elderly man living alone and for an elderly couple, which were intended to be comparable to the Works Progress Administration (WPA) Maintenance Budget for a four-person city family. This budget was described as "less liberal" than the "health and decency" level of budgets for workers' families developed in the 1920s.

In 1946–1948, the Bureau of Labor Statistics (BLS) developed a new budget for the four-person city worker's family, and the Social Security Administration concurrently developed the Elderly Couple's Budget. These budgets have been used to measure income needs for a wide variety of purposes, ranging from evaluation of national needs for legislative purposes to appraising individual family needs in administering welfare programs.

The improved financial position of elderly persons in the postwar years, and the resulting changes in their standards of living have shifted the emphasis from minimum subsistence needs for dependent elderly families to adequate standards for self-supporting families. Not only has very little analytical work been done with respect to the income requirements of elderly persons to maintain an adequate standard of living, but it is only in recent years that basic statistical data have been summarized in sufficient detail to give valid data on

An expanded version of this paper was presented at the Fifth Congress of The International Association of Gerontology.

Table 1. *Annual costs of the retired couple's budget, by major components, five large cities and suburbs, Autumn, 1959*[a]

Item	Washington, D.C.	Houston	New York	San Francisco	Chicago
Food and beverages[b]	$ 864	$ 758	$ 945	$ 920	$ 889
Food at home[c]	816	711	892	866	838
Low-cost plan	685	595	776	755	743
Moderate-cost plan	948	827	1009	976	933
Food away from home	29	28	32	32	33
Housing	1163	928	1124	1172	1331
Rent, heat, utilities[d]	921	694	849	919	1067
House furnishings	95	99	99	107	100
Household operation and communications	147	135	176	146	164
Clothing	216	197	215	224	232
Husband	80	76	83	82	84
Wife	106	92	101	106	114
Clothing materials and services	30	29	31	36	34
Medical care	271	260	262	346	317
Transportation[e]	176	161	134	174	195
Automobile owners	583	530	652	627	653
Nonowners of automobiles	61	57	50	46	66
Other goods and services	357	337	364	387	402
Reading and recreation	102	95	111	114	124
Personal care	78	75	69	86	83
Tobacco	32	41	39	34	35
Gifts, contributions, etc.	145	126	145	153	160
Total cost of goods and services	3047	2641	3044	3223	3366
Estimated annual cost comparable in content with original budget[f]	2770	2390	2812	2949	3112

[a] The family consists of a retired husband and wife, aged 65 or over. For items and quantities included in the various categories and annual costs for Cleveland, Detroit, Kansas City, Los Angeles, Minneapolis, Philadelphia, Pittsburgh, Portland, Oregon, St. Louis, Scranton, Seattle, Atlanta, Baltimore, Boston, and Cincinnati, see Stolz, Margaret S., The BLS Interim Budget for a Retired Couple, Monthly Labor Review (November, 1960), 1141–57, Tables 2, 4–6.

[b] Includes small allowances for guest meals and for alcoholic beverages.

[c] The cost of food at home used in the calculation of the total cost of the budget is an average of the low- and moderate-cost food plans, including the suggested additional allowance of 10 percent for small families.

[d] Average contract rent for tenant-occupied dwellings that conform to the housing standards specified for the budget plus the cost of required amounts of heating fuel, gas, electricity, water, and specified equipment.

[e] The mode of transportation within metropolitan districts is related to location, size, and characteristics of the community. The average costs of automobile owners and nonowners were weighted by the following proportion of families: for New York 14 percent for automobile owners, 86 percent for nonowners; for the remaining cities, 22 percent and 78 percent, respectively.

[f] Costs based on the low-cost food plan, and excluding allowances for automobile ownership and alcoholic beverages.

the financial position of elderly persons and families and a reasonably sound basis for evaluating their consumption needs.[1]

DEVELOPING AND USING CURRENT BUDGETS
Problems of concept and definition

No standard budget can serve equally well the many purposes for which it is needed and will perforce be used. It is necessary, therefore, first to determine and explicitly describe the level of living which the budget goods and services will provide, and to define the size, age, composition, and employment status of the family members and the general nature of the household in which they live.

Since World War II, standard budgets have generally been defined as providing a "modest but adequate" level of living for the family, i.e., the goods and services necessary to provide an adequate level of living as determined by prevailing standards of what is needed for health, efficiency, social participation, and the maintenance of self-respect and respect of others. This standard was adopted for the Elderly Couple's Budget developed in the Social Security Administration in 1946–1948. Descriptions of this standard quite clearly state that it is not "minimum" in the narrow sense of that term. In addition to the requirements for physical subsistence, the concept of this budget recognizes psychological and social needs and includes goods and services which will provide a reasonable participation of the elderly couple in community life. It assumes that the couple will be a self-supporting couple, aged 65 or over, with the husband retired or with very occasional employment, in reasonably good health for persons at this age, and able to take care of themselves and manage the home.

The budget provides an estimate of the total cost of a representative list of goods and services considered necessary by retired elderly couples to maintain a level of adequate living according to standards prevailing in large cities of the United States. Such a list of goods and services is not an absolute and unchanging thing since "the prevailing judgment of the necessary will vary with the changing values of the community, with the advance of scientific knowledge of human needs, with the productive power of the community, and therefore with what people commonly enjoy and see others enjoy."

[1] The report on the revised budget appeared in the November, 1960 issue of the Monthly Labor Review. Budget estimates for five cities are shown in Table 1. These cities were selected to represent high-, low-, medium-cost cities among the twenty cities and to give an estimate for one city in each of the four major regions of the country.

Two courses are open to the budget-maker in determining the amounts and kinds of items to include in the budget. For goods and services for which objective scientific standards are available, such as food and housing, the budget quantities can be derived with reference to such standards, but for other categories of the budget— accounting for about two-fifths of the total—no generally recognized scientific standards exist, and the budget quantities must be determined in other ways.

Even for the categories for which scientific standards have been developed, it is necessary to relate the specific items used in estimating budget costs to the actual practices of families being considered.

Problems of translating concepts into budget quantities

Adequate food. Continuous research by the Department of Agriculture (USDA) has provided widely accepted food plans which comply with the Recommended Dietary Allowances and reflect the food-preference patterns of nonfarm families. The most recent food plans were developed from the 1955 Household Food Consumption Study. The suggested quantities of food for 18 sex-age groups which will provide a nutritionally adequate diet at low-cost, moderate-cost, and liberal-cost levels were published in July, 1959. The food-consumption patterns representatives of the choices of nonfarm families in the lower, middle, and upper thirds of the income distribution in 1955 provided the guide in specifying the quantities of specific foods for the three plans. Regional preference patterns in the selection of specific foods to meet the nutritional standards are also provided by the Department of Agriculture study.

Thus, the budget-maker has available authoritative and generally accepted source data for establishing the food standard. There is still, however, the problem of the selection of the particular food plan which will be consistent with the overall concept of the budget level. The revised food component is based on an average of the cost of the low- and moderate-cost plans, adjusted to provide for meals away from home and snacks.

Adequate housing. Scientific standards which specify the essential characteristics of adequate dwellings have been developed by the American Public Health Association and the U.S. Public Housing Administration. City families almost universally live in individual homes either in apartments or houses, and family privacy is believed to be so important that other living arrangements are considered only as a last resort. Many studies in recent years have provided evidence of the fact that when income permits, families at all age levels generally prefer to live apart from other family groups.

For the elderly retired couple the standard for shelter specified in the original Elderly Couple's Budget and retained for the current revision of this budget is a two- or three-room unfurnished rental dwelling with kitchen facilities, a complete private bath, and central heating in areas of the country where temperature requires this, and which is located in a structure and neighborhood which meet specified health and safety standards. The problem in the use of the scientific standard for the Elderly Couple's Budget does not lie in the basic characteristics of the dwelling as defined by this standard, except indirectly, but rather in the fact that elderly couples, when income permits, are predominantly homeowners. In the BLS Survey of Consumer Expenditures, in 1950, about 70 percent of the elderly retired couples whose expenditure patterns were analyzed in the derivation of the revised budget quantities were homeowners. Owned dwellings in most areas average five or more rooms and may be of better quality than the average rental unit specified for the budget standard. Also, they frequently represent a major part of the assets of the retired couple and an important psychological consideration in the family's social and economic status.

Although a detailed discussion of the relative cost to the occupant of owned and rented shelter, including heat and utilities, is beyond the scope of this paper, some guides to developing procedures for adjusting the rental budget cost to approximate the costs for homeowners may be found in data from the Bureau's Survey of Consumer Expenditures in 1950. In the large and small cities (places over and under 50,000 population) in all regions, at this age level and in income classes from $2000 to $5000, owner expenditures for current housing costs, heat, and utilities were less than those of renters. The owners' average annual expenditure for shelter, heat, and utilities by families with head aged 65 to 75 years and 1950 income of $2000 to $3000 ranged from about 65 to 85 percent of renting families' expenditures for these items.

Adequate medical care. While much progress has been made in medical-care research, completely objective standards, comparable to those for food and housing, have not been developed. The incidence of medical-care expenditure is unpredictable, and expenditures for medical care vary widely for those families who have this expense in a particular year. In recent years, development of budget standards for medical care for young families has been somewhat simplified by the possibility of including a medical-care or hospitalization insurance plan in the budget. This procedure raises considerable question, however, in the development of an adequate medical-care budget for an elderly couple because substantially fewer families among the elderly couples have medical-care insurance, and frequently such families are not eligible for insurance. Furthermore, it does not cover the cost of many items such as dental care, drugs and medicines, physical examinations, physicians' visits, etc. For the interim revision of the Elderly Couple's Budget, it was decided to estimate medical care costs for the family in two alternative ways. One method assumes insurance coverage for hospitalization; the other, that all medical-care items are budgeted and priced on a pay-as-you-go basis.

Adequacy for other goods and services. For other categories of the budget, including clothing, house furnishings, household operation, transportation, communications, personal care, reading, recreation, tobacco, gifts, contributions, and miscellaneous expenses, there are no scientific standards to serve as guides. In these areas, psychological and social requirements are more important than physical needs, and even among families at the same economic level there is considerable variation in what is considered necessary for clothing, transportation, recreation, etc. For goods and services other than food, shelter, and medical care, the revised quantities were derived, primarily by examining the quantity-income elasticities of the expenditures of retired couples, with head aged 65 or over, as reported in the BLS Survey of Consumer Expenditures in 1950. This technique is objective in that it uses the consumers' collective judgment as to what is adequate for such items as clothing, house furnishings, etc.— a standard determined by the families themselves.

In this analysis, the quantities of various items purchased at successive income levels are examined to determine the income level at which the rate of increase in quantities purchased begins to decline in relation to the rate of change in income, i.e., the point of maximum elasticity. The average quantities and kinds of items purchased at these income levels are the quantities and qualities specified for the budget.

Pricing the budget

The problems of sampling and estimating prices are varied and complex and present a formidable task even when carried out within the framework of an established program for the collection of price data. In the revision of the Elderly Couple's Budget, the Bureau made extensive use of its established pricing program for the Consumer Price Index in twenty large cities, as the foundation on which to develop the budget pricing program. The price data were collected from the Bureau's regular sample of retail stores and service establishments with only such expansion as was required to obtain sufficient price quotations to provide reliable averages.

DIRECTION OF FUTURE RESEARCH

As previously mentioned, there is need for a comprehensive review and reappraisal of the concepts and methods of budgets for elderly persons in light of their current and future financial status and manner of living. Data from the continuing surveys of OASI beneficiaries and from the BLS expenditure surveys programmed for 1961–1962 will contribute greatly to this. Research to develop short-cut techniques for estimating total budget costs or for adjusting the costs for differences in family composition or from place to place is also needed.

Extensive research has been directed toward a proper definition of "income" for use in evaluating the well-being of elderly persons. There is less recognition of the fact that determining the adequacy of that "income" is dependent upon appropriate measures of income need. Standard budgets are general-purpose statistics and are not valid for specific uses without careful consideration of their appropriateness for the specific purpose. Appropriate measures can be developed only if program goals are clearly defined and the level of living consistent with those goals is specified.

Old Age Pensions and Allowances in France

PAUL PAILLAT

ONE of the most "aged" countries in the world, France has an extensive, but quite uneven, network of pensions and allowances for old people. This deliberately factual paper gives a picture of a nonlogical situation resulting from conflicts between social ambition and sectorial (professional) interests. In a condensed form, principles governing the main schemes covering wage earners as well as nonwage earners are explained. Statistical information is given concerning statutory and average retirement ages in various schemes. The amount of pensions and allowances is compared with wages: the sharp decline in the standard of living appears clearly, inasmuch as no scheme is yet fully operating and retired people draw more allowances than what could properly be called pensions.

Today every worker, whatever his status, contributes to a compulsory pension fund, but the protection against "old age" risk is not the same—hence the development of extra pension schemes, more or less on a voluntary basis (Collective Labor Agreement can make them compulsory for a branch).

The data only make it clear that pensions and allowances do not meet the needs of old people in France since, for instance, the maximum workers' pension cannot reach the minimum wage rate and since no one is yet entitled to draw such "maximum" pension.

Allowances are only a temporary device and a rough one. Some feel they "segregate" old people who have to accept controls after a long, hard life at work. Allowances, even when generously granted, cannot be compared with proper pensions which are partly based on personal contribution.

There is also the unfair character of this uneven pension network.

The full text of this paper is contained in Wilma Donahue, C. Tibbitts, and R. H. Williams (eds.), *Psychological and Social Processes of Aging: An International Research Seminar* (to be published).

With a similar contribution the difference at the same retiring age may be abnormally wide if one individual is enrolled with the "general scheme" and the other with a "special scheme" (many extra advantages of the latter being, in some way, paid by taxpayers).

Basic Issues Regarding Levels of Living in Old Age

SVEN HYDÉN

THE International Social Security Association initiated its work regarding pension by examining the pension systems in accordance with stipulations in the International Labor Office (ILO) conventions, starting with the well-known Convention No. 102, "Objectives and Minimum Standards of Social Security."

The minimum standard of pension asked for in this convention is 40 percent of a certain standard wage. The International Labor Office has not sought to establish any minimum level based on a demand and has for that reason recommended not a flat-rate pension but a pension related to wage level.

Studies by the ILO and other international bodies have not been grounded on investigations into the actual income requirements of older persons. Problems of care and the need for occupation and social contacts are not considered.

A difficulty in solving the problems is that they have been tackled on a political basis.

A scientific way of solving the problem of levels of living in old age would be to determine the requirements of different groups of old persons and to draw up budgets.

A comparison between methods and standards prevailing in various countries is given in Table 1.

The full text of this paper is contained in Wilma Donahue, C. Tibbitts, and R. H. Williams (eds.), *Psychological and Social Processes of Aging: An International Research Seminar* (to be published).

Table 1. Pension provisions in various countries

Country and quantitative criteria[a]	Basic pension level[b]	Maximum and minimum income qualifying for pension[c]	Adjustment to economic conditions
Europe			
Austria (yc + e)	40.5 percent (miners 45) of the wage during last 5 years (drip)	Max.: 79.5 percent (miners 87.5) (iqpm) Min.: 40.5 and 45 percent	Special decision
Belgium (yc + e)	60 percent for single persons, 75 percent for married persons of the average annual income after 45 and 40 yc for men and women respectively (drip)	Monetary maximum and minimum	Automatic
Czechoslovakia (yem + e)	5–20 yem → pension in proportion to time; after 20 years an increase based on occupational category	Min.: after 5 yc: 15, 13.75, and 12.5 percent in various categories	Special decision
Federal Republic of Germany (yc + e)	For workers and salaried employees 1.5 percent (for miners 2.5) of average earnings during time of employment; after 40 years and age 65 → 60 percent respectively, 100 percent of average earnings (drip)	Workers and salaried employees monetary maximum	Automatic (price level) Special decision (adjustment to wages)
France (yc + e + ra)	At age 60, 20 percent of average wage during the last 10 years (drip, decrease for a qualifying period less than 30 years)	40 percent of average wage during last 10 years (iqpm) Monetary minimum	Special decision
Israel (yc + ra)	Certain monetary amount; every insurance year over 10 raises the pension by 2 percent up to a given maximum (drip)	Monetary maximum	Automatic
Italy (yc + ra + e)	(drip)	Max.: 80 percent of the average wage of the last 5 years Monetary minimum	Automatic

Table 1. (Continued)

Luxembourg (yc + e)	Combination of basic monetary amount — supplement in percentage of wages (special rules for agricultural workers)	Max.: 83.33 percent of average wage during last 5 years as ceiling Monetary minimum	Automatic
Netherlands (yc + e)	Nominal basic pension + supplement percentage based on wages and ye	No maximum or minimum	Automatic
Poland (yem + e)	Two categories of persons; pension in relation to earnings over last 12 months with 60 and 40 percent of wages up to a certain income level and 20 and 15 percent for top incomes	Monetary maximum	Special decision
Portugal (yc + e)	From 20 up to 80 percent of average wage for the whole career (drip)	Max.: 80 percent of average wage for whole career up to a certain maximum No minimum, but minimum 10 years → 20 percent of average wage for whole career	Special decision
Sweden (yc + e)	60 percent of average income from work during the best 15 years + basic pension (drip)	Monetary maximum and minimum	Automatic
Switzerland (yc + e)	No basic pension level; premium 4 percent of income; pension based to some extent on actuarial data	Monetary maximum and minimum	Special decision
Turkey (yc + ra + e)	With a minimum of 25 yc a rate of 35 percent for single persons and 50 percent for breadwinners at pension age of 60 (drip); earlier pension reduces payment		
U.S.S.R. (yem + e)	Pension in relation to last 12 months' income; amount from 100 percent of a low income to 50 percent of a relatively high income	Monetary maximum and minimum	Special decision

Table 1. (Continued)

Country and quantitative criteria[a]	Basic pension level[b]	Maximum and minimum income qualifying for pension[c]	Adjustment to economic conditions
Yugoslavia (yem + e)	The average wage for the last 3 years allots the persons concerned to one of 21 classes of pension	Monetary maximum and minimum	Special decision
America and Asia			
Brazil (yc + e)	66 percent of average wage during last 3 years before minimum pension age (60 years for commercial workers, 65 for both male and female industrial workers)	Monetary maximum (66 percent of three times the legally prescribed minimum wage) Min.: 70 percent of the legally prescribed minimum wage	Automatic
Chile (yc + e)	Basic amount = 50 percent of average earnings during the last 5 years prior to pension age (65) + increment of 1 percent of average earnings for every qualifying year over 10	Max.: 70 percent of average earnings Min.: 56 percent for men, 50 for women, of average earnings	Special decision
Costa Rica (yc + e)	Basic amount = 40 percent of average earnings during last 10 years prior to pension age (65 years) + increment of 1.5 percent of average earnings for every qualifying year over 3 (drip)	Max.: 90 percent of average earnings; monetary maximum Min.: 58 percent of average earnings	
Dominican Republic (yc + e)	Basic amount = 50 percent of average earnings during the last 4 years + increment of 1 percent for every qualifying year over 16	Max.: 70 percent of average earnings No minimum	
Japan (yc + e)	A flat amount = about 12.5 percent of the wage of industrial workers + $\frac{1}{2}$ percent of average earnings for every qualifying year (60 years for men, 55 for women)	No maximum or minimum	

Table 1. (Continued)

Nicaragua (yc + e)	Basic amount = 30 percent of average earnings + increment of 1.5 percent of average earnings for every qualifying year over 3	Max.: 80 percent of average earnings; monetary maximum
Panama (yc + e)	Basic amount = 50 percent of average earnings + increment of 2 percent of average earnings for every qualifying year over 20	Monetary maximum
Paraguay (yc + e)	Basic amount = 30 percent of average earnings during last 3 years + increment of 1 percent for every qualifying year over 15	

[a] Here e = earnings or amounts of contribution; ra = retirement age, yc = years of contribution, and yem = years of employment.
[b] Here drip = deferred retirement increases payment.
[c] Here iqpm = income qualifying for pension maximum.

Occupational Mobility and Old Age

SVEN FORSSMAN

OCCUPATIONAL mobility may consider (1) change from one type of industry to another, (2) change from one factory or other place of employment to another within the same type of industry, or (3) change from one occupation to another within the same place of employment. Studies on labor turnover normally deal with alternatives (1) and (2).

In studying the potentiality of occupational mobility of old people, one must consider the nature of handicaps related to aging (disability) as well as the ability and working capacity of old people. Aging changes the working ability in many ways such as gradually reducing the maximum physical working capacity and, on the mental side, reducing the capacity to work constantly at high speed, combining and memorizing new information, etc. Many of these changes of the working capacity with increasing age may, however, to a certain extent be compensated for through the experience of the older worker, making it possible for him to plan his work in a way that suits his reduced capacity.

However, the handicaps of the aging population may be caused more by the increasing incidence of disease in higher age groups than from aging as such. There is, for instance, above 40 to 50 years of age a higher incidence of disease of the heart, blood vessels, lungs, organs of movement, and central nervous system. It has been shown, however, in studies of workingmen that those with diseases of the heart and blood vessels may be able to do even heavy physical work, and to a much higher degree than would be expected from the results of the medical examinations (Åstrand, 1958). This will call for individual evaluation of working capacity of old workers and great care must be taken not to generalize the findings of the average working capacities of different age groups, because the range of these average values is considerable.

Utilizing scientific laboratory studies on the influence of aging on physical and mental working capacity (Welford, 1958) as well as practical experience of old workers in places of employment (mostly industries), one can summarize the positive and the negative aspects of old people from the point of view of their ability to work. Negative aspects are such items as reduced maximum physical working capacity, dark adaptation and near vision, increased need for illumination, reduced capacity to work at constant high speed, ability to memorize and combine new information, adjustment to changes of environment, increased need of time to learn new working methods, etc. Positive aspects of old workers are experience which may compensate for some of the above-mentioned handicaps, capacity to carry out work demanding a high degree of accuracy, responsibility to work, low labor turnover, low number of absences (especially short-term absences) and usually a low number of lost days due to sickness and accidents. Old workers are on the whole absent less often than young workers but the duration of each sick absence increases with age, especially in higher age groups.

It is possible in many cases to place old people in jobs according to their abilities and experience, in spite of the disability related to aging; this is confirmed by practical experience in industry and other places of employment. People of higher age groups thus have a great potentiality for occupational mobility, even if practical experience recommends first trying to keep the old employees on the same work as before but with a reduced work load.

In studying the potentiality of occupational mobility of old age, certain principles could be worked out for job placement of old people, considering influence of age upon health and working capacity. It is thus advisable that when old people change occupation it should be from heavy to light work, from high-speed work to work with less speed, with a possibility of having pauses and intervals, and from piece rate to time rate. Old workers should not be placed in groups of young workers, if the latter decide the speed of work. For psychological reasons, however, it may not always be advisable to put all old workers together, but rather to mix them with younger workers. Reports from special workshops for old people have been favorable in some countries but not in others. Reassignment should be prepared well in advance and the old worker should be informed in due time, in order to make it possible for him to adjust to the new conditions. Old people are sensitive about doing useful work and playing important roles in the working group and they should not be placed in jobs with a lower prestige value, according to their own attitude and the attitudes of others. The experience as well as the responsibility of old workers should be utilized as far as possible in the reassignment of jobs. If replacing old workers must be combined with retraining, this should be planned early and not delayed until the time of change. Considering the difficulty which old people experience in adjusting to changes of work and environment, it seems desirable that old workers should be informed well in advance of their replacement.

Considering what has been mentioned above concerned potentiality of occupational mobility of old age, it is interesting to study the reality of occupational mobility and the situation of old people at work in industry and other places of employment. It is generally known that old people normally do not change work or occupation. Labor turnover generally decreases with increasing age. For instance, it was shown in a study of Swedish industries (Forssman, 1957a, 1957b) of all male employees above 60 years and all female employees above 55 years, that old employees form a stable population with low labor turnover. The average time of employment for old male office employees was 35 years and for old male industrial workers, 26 years; similar but somewhat lower figures were found for female employees. When time of employment was related to age, it was found that male employees 60 years old got their employment in the same factory, on the average, at the age of 33 years. The corresponding figure for female employees of 55 was 43.

A recent study in all Swedish industries (Hydén et al., 1960) shows that labor turnover decreases rapidly with increasing age, especially over 45 years old (Table 1).

It is interesting to note in this study that all those who left their employment during the observation period had a rather short average time of employment; however, this was more pronounced in younger than in older age groups.

There is a trend showing lower labor turnover among workers over 45 years of age in larger factories (more than 500 workers) as is shown in Table 2.

A study of older workers in industry (Forssman, 1957a, 1957b) showed that there is, for health reasons, a certain occupational mobility among old workers within the same factory. According to this study 6 percent of male office employees and 31 percent of male workers above 60 years of age had been placed in their present jobs in consideration of age, health, and working capacity. This change had been mostly from work with stress or from heavy physical work to light work. It must be mentioned that this study was carried out in factories with well-developed industrial health services.

The professional distribution of the higher age groups of a population shows in all countries that the frequency of older workers is high

Table 1. *Percentage distribution of male workers who have left their employment during the one-week observation period in May, 1959, in Swedish industries, by industry and age groups*[a]

Industry	Number of workers (in thousands)	24 and under	25–34	35–44	45–54	55–64	65 and over	Total[b]
				Age groups				
Metal (and machine industry)	944	47.5	27.6	12.0	5.2	3.7	4.1	100.1
Paper (and pulp industry)	116	43.9	18.1	13.8	12.1	4.3	7.8	100.0
Food industry	164	43.9	32.9	15.2	3.0	1.2	3.7	99.9
Textile industry	132	35.6	22.8	12.1	15.9	10.6	3.0	100.0
All industries[c]	2091	44.4	23.6	14.9	9.4	3.6	4.3	100.2

[a] Source: S. Hydén et al., *Medelålders och äldre arbetskraft*, Stockholm, 1960.
[b] Totals differ from 100 due to rounding errors.
[c] Includes all industries, including those listed above.

in some professions such as agricultural workers, watchmakers, violin makers, watchmen, etc., and low in others such as miners, foundrymen, dockers, building workers, merchant navy, etc. (Le Gros Clark and Dunne, 1956). Workers usually retire earlier in some professions than in others. This difference may be due to the fact that the demands of the work are too high for most old people, but many social and economical factors are also of importance.

In spite of the good results that many industries have obtained in

Table 2. *Percentage distribution of male workers who have left their employment during the one-week observation period in May, 1959, in Swedish industries, by year of employment and age groups*[a]

Year of employment	24 and under (N = 925)	25–34 (N = 493)	35–44 (N = 312)	45–54 (N = 194)	55–64 (N = 73)	65 and over (N = 89)
			Age groups			
1957 or later	77.4	72.4	63.8	59.8	45.2	14.6
1954–1956	18.5	17.2	14.1	11.9	9.6	12.4
1951–1953	4.1	3.4	10.3	8.2	6.8	4.5
1946–1950		4.7	7.1	3.6	9.6	13.5
1945 or earlier		2.2	4.8	16.5	28.8	55.1
Total[b]	100.0	99.9	100.1	100.0	100.0	100.1

[a] Source: S. Hydén et al., *Medelålders och äldre arbetskraft*, Stockholm, 1960.
[b] Totals differ from 100 due to rounding errors.

the proper placement of older workers, and in spite of the fact that it may be of value to the health of old workers to keep them at work as long as they are able, there are many practical difficulties and prejudices to be overcome, especially when old people are looking for new jobs.

It is often mentioned that old workers will have difficulty in adjusting themselves to new conditions or new working processes, and that it would be difficult and costly to train them. This seems to be one of the most common objections to employing old people. It has been recently shown in a Swedish study (Hydén *et al.*, 1960) that unemployment in different occupations is much more common among people over 40 and that people of higher age groups stay unemployed for a longer time than younger ones.

Practical experience in industry in many countries shows that old people, in spite of skill and experience, often have difficulty in competing with young workers and therefore may be found in jobs involving heavy physical work or low pay.

CONCLUSIONS AND SUMMARY

In studying occupational mobility and old age it was found that there are theoretically many possibilities for old people to change jobs or to find new occupations if their abilities and disabilities related to aging are considered.

However, practical experience shows that occupational mobility decreases with increasing age for psychological, financial, and social reasons and that the decrease is also due to prejudices against employing old people and to practical difficulties in finding suitable jobs for older employees. Old people will often have difficulty in competing with young people in the labor market, with low labor turnover in higher age groups as a consequence.

REFERENCES

Åstrand, I. 1958. Clinical and physiological studies of manual workers 50–64 years old at rest and during work. Acta Med. Scand., 162: 155–64.

Forssman, S. 1957a. Health problems of the older worker: a study in Swedish industry. Trans. Assoc. Industrial Med. Off., 7: 9–21.

—— 1957*b*. Old people in industry. (In Swedish.) Stockholm: Publikationer från Svenska Arbetsgivareföreningen.
Hydén, S., Bengtsson, S. F., Edgren, G., and Lundgren, I. 1960. Middle-aged and old labour force. (In Swedish.) Stockholm: Bröderna Lagerstrom Boktryckare.
Le Gros Clark, F. and Dunne, A. C. 1956. Ageing in industry. New York: Philosophical Library.
Welford, A. T. 1958. Ageing and human skill. London: Oxford University Press.

Occupational Mobility in Aging

POUL MILHØJ

EVIDENTLY rather few attempts have been made to analyze whether the labor market is accommodated to old persons finding work, even if they are well qualified. A medical certificate of working ability is not sufficient to enable old people to find employment if, simultaneously, the labor market bars their way. As far as can be seen a good deal of research is needed concerning the structure of the labor market in relation to the employment of the aged.

The following is based on the assumption that the majority of old people—say beyond 65—are able to work. This implies that physical and psychological hindrances to participation in industrial life may be overcome by a majority of the old.

The question to be discussed, but far from answered, is whether there are employment possibilities for old persons in a modern society. This depends partly on the general level of employment and partly on the structure and institutional establishment of the labor market.

The significance of the level of employment is evident and will be touched upon only briefly.

If a high and stable employment exists for a long period, or if there is actually a certain excess demand for labor, the labor market always makes use of its reserves. There may, however, be countless obstacles to this benefiting the employment of the old—fixed age of pensions, educational monopolies, and so on. But a sufficiently long-lasting, unsatisfied demand for labor will always accelerate employment of the marginal labor force. And it is in this category that the old presumably belong. This does *not* mean that all unemployed old people get work. But it does mean that more old people get started than when the level of employment is generally low.

However, if the significance of the level of employment for the occupational possibilities of the old were to be seriously explained, many things would have to be taken into consideration.

A series of variations of the state of full employment would have to be examined. It would also be necessary to investigate the influence of a general boom on pensions and incomes from interest. Incidentally, it must be emphasized that the road to high employment is often paved with a rise in prices, and this reduces the buying power of non-price-regulated pensions and fortunes which often are the most important basis of support for the old. Consequently, during a boom it will often be seen that the chances of employment of the old are improved while, simultaneously, the buying power of their pensions is lowered. Therefore, when employment rises, there should be two factors that draw the old into the labor force or postpone their retirement.

At this point the paper turns to an analysis of the possibilities for employment that a modern society of the Western type offers older people. The level of employment is then taken for granted.

When old people are really able to work and wish to do so, they will probably continue in the positions they have previously held.

This is, however, not always possible. There are only a very few wage earners who may continue their work in old age. Nearly all civil servants and other salary earners are forced to retire at a fixed pension age; workers are less often submitted to a compulsory pension age. But experience shows that older workers often have to retire because it becomes more and more difficult for them to return to their original work when, after reaching old age, they are hit by unemployment or illness. For independents there is usually no outside obstacle to prevent them from continuing work, even far into old age. The statistics on occupation show that the groups of independents, on the whole, contain most old people.

The compulsory pension age and the difficulty in returning to the original work after a long absence thus create the first obstacles to the employment of the old. For one may well assume that by and large it would be easiest for most people if they wish to work during old age to continue to do so in the work to which they are accustomed and which they can manage. The working capacity of an old person may also be discussed. However, the facility of an old person for readjusting himself to an entirely new kind of work, appears to be even more disputable. And, presuming that the new work is easy to learn and to adjust to, it will probably very often involve a lower social status. It may also be difficult for the old to adjust to this.

Many arguments can be advanced against forcing the old out of their previous work. On the other hand, it is not possible to disregard the fact that if the aged are to remain in the labor force there are also certain advantages attached to forcing them to find a use for their decreasing strength in new and successively easier positions.

Whether there is some advantage to forcing aged wage earners out of their previous jobs must remain doubtful. This practice is considered by some as a drawback; however, it is obvious that this does happen to wage earners.

Consequently, the problem of occupational possibilities for the old will, to a large extent, be identical with the problem of the possibility of their taking up new jobs, i.e., the problem of occupational mobility in aging.

In order to throw at least some light on this problem, an attempt will be made to classify some of the positions at hand in some main categories and to judge the possibilities of the old getting work in these categories if they have not had it before.

There is no chance whatsoever of being transferred to *skilled* trades. This, in any case, applies to the conditions in the Danish labor market, not only for old people but for everybody, as soon as they are over 20 years of age. Only the old person who transfers to other work within his own trade is able to get a new job as a skilled worker. In advance one would believe that industry could often utilize the experience of the old workers as superintendents or the like. In this connection it seems especially reasonable to emphasize the importance of *advancing technical development*. Naturally all firms do not simultaneously pass over to a new technique; there will always be some within a branch who are behind in transferring to new techniques. Such firms should be natural meeting places for the older skilled workers who are familiar with previous techniques.

Although mobility of this type should be possible, the trade unions are often opposed to the gathering of older people in certain areas inside the profession. One reason is that it is difficult to overlook the consequences of this for wage policy.

As for *unskilled* work there is no institutional barrier, if only one is able to manage the job. Here, competition for vacant jobs is open to everyone, regardless of age. Much of the unskilled work, however, requires a long adjustment period, and often puts great demands on physical strength. This implies that independents, salary earners, and skilled workers do not have the physical strength to take up unskilled work when old.

Nevertheless, there will probably be a good deal of unskilled work which the aged may do regardless of their previous occupations, that does not demand too much physical strength or too much speed. But such work will very often mean a loss in social status which will be difficult to accept for any but previous unskilled workers.

Salaried work often requires so much training that it is difficult for the old with no previous experience to enter. Furthermore, many salaried positions are obtained by promotion from lower ranks and therefore cannot be taken over by people entering late in life. Finally, it is exactly within the salaried groups that you most frequently meet the compulsory retirement age—which is, of course, also applicable to newcomers.

However, it is also true for the salaried workers that continual change to new methods of production should increase the possibilities of employment of the aged in those establishments that lag behind in industrial change. There is not much reason for training young technicians nowadays in working with steam engines and steam locomotives. Nevertheless, steam power is still used in a lot of plants and, in the author's opinion, creates a demand for old technicians who have grown up with this technique. This also applies to office machines and so on.

While it is difficult for the old to find new work as wage earners once they have left their usual occupation, it probably happens quite often that the old start firms or shops of their own after retirement. Among wage earners, skilled workers and some specialized salary earners are especially able to establish themselves in small individual firms where they can make use of their professional knowledge.

Factory and shop owners and other independents are seldom forced to retire at a certain age. If they are stricken by illness, or if sales are falling, it is often possible to adjust to the new situation by taking over a smaller business within the same branch. Frequently this is easier for independents than for wage earners, because they more often possess capital from their previous business.

CONCLUSIONS

Thus, in summary, the author is rather pessimistic about the possibilities of occupational mobility in aging.

Both educational claims and professional monopolies prevent the old from entering *skilled* and *salaried* work; only unskilled work or establishing firms of their own remain. However, the physical claims of unskilled work and the prospect of a lower social status are hindrances.

In facing the question of whether this pessimistic picture will also hold for the future, one is, as far as can be seen, confronted with two adverse tendencies.

On one side, it is probably easiest for old wage earners to transfer to unskilled work—especially if they have previously held unskilled positions. Modern big industry seems to some extent to eliminate narrow professional training. This ought to increase the possibilities of mobility of the aged. On the other hand, there seems to be an increasing percentage of wage earners who are salaried workers. This development may create new groups of specialists whose occupational mobility in aging is small. Furthermore, the number of smaller firms seems to be decreasing. This seriously diminishes the possibilities of mobility because independents take over smaller firms and aged wage earners establish themselves as small dealers or the like.

The present fluctuations in industrial structure do not point toward an improvement of occupational mobility in aging. Wishes for gainful employment of the aged must be accommodated by eliminating as many as possible of the obstacles that prevent able old persons from remaining in their jobs. Toward the same end, one may accept a selection of types of work especially suited for the aged and reserve these jobs for them. This may be done in different branches of the labor market and in any given establishment.

The possibilities here are numerous. The realization of a long-lasting high level of employment will also cause them to be utilized.

Age and Disability

I. M. RICHARDSON AND R. D. WEIR

ECONOMIC prosperity, changes in population age structure, and the development of health services have deepened interest in the problems of disabled people in general and the older disabled worker in particular. National and local efforts have been made with considerable success to improve the occupational lot of those who, by reason of injury or disease, encounter difficulty in obtaining or keeping employment. In the now voluminous literature dealing with this subject reference has often been made to the special difficulties of older disabled people. It is only within the last 10 years that studies (Welford, 1958) have begun to show more precisely how aging itself, quite apart from disease, may modify working capacity.

In discussing the problems of older disabled people, we are therefore dealing with two fairly distinct effects, namely, those of normal aging and those produced by pathological processes. For example, it is now well known that older people often encounter difficulty in jobs where speed of operation is stressed but that greater accuracy may, at least for a time, compensate for this difficulty. If to this normal effect of aging is added some physical handicap, such as cataract, deafness, or arthritis, which interferes with reception of information or with the execution of finer movements, compensation may be impossible. An occupational problem is the result.

Although this paper is not directly concerned with the changes produced by normal aging, these changes, and the measures which may be applied in industry to mitigate their effects, are highly relevant to the occupational problems of older disabled people. Difficulties posed by high-speed operations, bonus plans, and heavy muscular work, for example, are probably aggravated by certain physical handicaps. It is, therefore, very important in studying the problems of disability to bear in mind research in industrial gerontology (Murrell, 1959; Clay, 1960) and to try to apply the findings in programs of rehabilitation.

THE NATURE OF THE PROBLEM

It is difficult to be sure how many older people have occupational problems attributable wholly or in part to disability. The presence of disease or pathological defect is, by itself (except in the case of gross impairment), not a reliable guide to the existence of an employment problem; the attitudes of employee and employer, experience and training, availability of alternative employment, and quality as well as availability of medical care interact with the physical situation. It is the product of these factors which determines the degree of disability which is present.

For the purposes of social policy and practice, some sort of arbitrary working definition is necessary; in Great Britain the Disabled Persons' Employment Act of 1944 describes a disabled person as one who:

on account of injury, disease or congenital deformity, is substantially handicapped in obtaining or keeping employment, or in undertaking work on his own account, of a kind which apart from that injury, disease or deformity would be suited to his age, experience and qualifications.

At present in Great Britain just over 700,000 such people are voluntarily registered as disabled persons and, of these, nearly 60,000 are unemployed. Age distribution of the total registrations is not normally available, but it was estimated (Le Gros Clark, 1956) that about 22 percent of all registered disabled men (both employed and unemployed), or around 164,000, were aged 60 and over. A Ministry of Labour analysis of unemployed registered disabled showed that about half are over the age of 50. Since registration is voluntary it is very likely that these official data underestimate the prevalence of disability at all ages; it was to throw some light on the true situation that we undertook a regional survey some years ago in Aberdeen (Richardson, 1956). Two groups were interviewed at random, the first made up of 200 men aged 30 and over who had been out of work for at least a month, and the other consisting of 254 men age 30 and over drawn from industrial firms in the city. Interviews covered health, occupational history, attitude toward work, and some personal and domestic particulars.

Fitness for work was graded in three categories and the results are shown in Table 1.

Due to sampling difficulties the total age distributions of the subjects are not quite representative of the populations concerned, but care was taken to ensure as far as possible that there was no selection

Table 1. *Proportion of disabled employed men and disabled unemployed men by age, Aberdeen Sample Survey, 1955, percentage distribution*[a]

Age	No disability		Moderate disability		Severe disability		Number of men	
	Employed	Unemployed	Employed	Unemployed	Employed	Unemployed	Employed	Unemployed
Totals	78	55	21	41	1	4	254	200
30–39	90	62	10	36		2	38	50
40–49	87	58	13	38		4	54	71
50–59	78	45	22	53	1	2	80	51
60–64	53	50	42	39	5	11	45	28

[a] Source: I. M. Richardson, "A socio-medical study of 200 unemployed men," Med. Officer, *96*, 165–70 (1956). Data are reproduced with permission of the Medical Officer.

within age groups. If the proportions of disabled men within each age group are applied to the employed male population of Great Britain, we arrive at a rough estimate of nearly one million men over age 50 who have some physical disability. What proportion of this total have encountered, or are experiencing, occupational difficulties is unknown, but clearly the potential problem is no mean size.

Next we looked at the medical nature of these disabilities. Among both employed and unemployed men, heart disease (especially coronary disease), respiratory disease (especially bronchitis), chronic peptic ulcer and its complications, and locomotor disorders such as arthritis accounted for the majority; the findings are in line with those published by the Ministry of Labour (Great Britain, Ministry of Labour, 1955) and with the results of a small intensive study by Weir (1957). Although the general pattern of disability was similar in the employed and unemployed groups, this does not mean that the severity of disablement was equal. It is very difficult indeed to measure this quality, but our impression certainly was that the unemployed man with coronary heart disease or bronchitis was a good deal more restricted in his capacity for effort than his counterpart in employment. Be that as it may, other factors bearing on disability such as skill and attitude toward work, must be examined.

Using the Registrar General's Social Classification, the unemployed men were divided into two grades, those whose former occupation was skilled, in the sense that a period of 3 or more years' training had been required, and those who had either no training or a very short period of training. Attitude toward employment was graded as good, fair, or poor on the basis of replies to questions about the efforts made to find work, why the individual thought he had been unsuccessful, and what help the Employment Exchange had given him. When these retrospective data were related to length of the current spell of unemployment, a fairly clear trend emerged which can best be presented in the form of a contrast:

Fourteen percent (3 out of 22) of men age 30–49 who were fit, skilled, and had a good attitude toward work had been unemployed for 1 year or more.

Seventy-two percent (47 out of 65) of men age 50 and over who were disabled, unskilled, and whose attitude toward work was fair or poor had been unemployed for 1 year or more.

Because official records of unemployed men are confidential, we could not check the accuracy of statements about duration of unemployment; furthermore, it seemed desirable to test the validity of our assessments of attitude toward work. A follow-up study was therefore planned in which our social worker visited the homes of the men 1 month after the initial interview (which took place in the hospital out-patient department). During this period 31 men had obtained work and when this group was compared with those still unemployed after 1 month, we again found that it was the older, unskilled, disabled man with a poor attitude toward work who was least likely to be reemployed.

It is also worth mentioning that comparison between the unemployed group and either the sample of employed men or the city population as a whole showed an excess of single men, of divorced or separated men, of large families, and of domestic overcrowding, among those who were out of work. It is perhaps hardly necessary to point out that these associations with unemployment are usually not directly caused—they are but some of the factors in a complex human problem called unemployment, which often seems to have its roots far back in the individual's life history. While interviewing these men we were often struck by the possibility that unemployment in older disabled men is really the end result of a set of forces whose origins were lost in the mists of time. Why, for example, did this man break off training in youth for a skilled trade and take up heavy laboring, or that man change from being a steady worker with a stable home to a chronically unemployed casual worker, living in a common lodging house, who did not know where his family was? Such speculations are not entirely idle. Improved vocational guidance in youth, the growth of marriage guidance services, and the spread of rehabilitation programs for disability in its early stages, make it likely that (economic considerations apart) some of the situations which have contributed to unemployment in the past may arise less frequently in the future and thus reduce in some measure the number of older disabled unemployed men. We estimated, for example, that thorough rehabilitation and retraining could have salvaged about one-third of these unemployed men if facilities had been available when occupational difficulties first appeared, although for many of them this would probably have involved moving from northeast Scotland where unemployment is twice the national average to areas with a more favorable economic situation.

Resettlement clinic

While these field studies were going on, we had been exploring the possibility of helping disabled hospital patients who had employment problems. An experimental resettlement clinic was started in 1954. The team consisted of a social worker, a Ministry of Labour representative, and the honorary consultant in Social Medicine. Patients were referred from various departments in the general hospital and, after thorough documentation and discussion of the problem, we made recommendations and then followed up the patients for 6 months. Analysis of the first 84 cases (Richardson and Weir, 1956) showed that the older unskilled man with a doubtful or poor attitude toward resettlement fared worst of all as measured by the proportion still unemployed after 6 months. Nevertheless, 6 years of experience in the work of such a resettlement clinic suggests that a concerted diagnosis of the exact nature of the older disabled man's problems, followed by an intensive search for suitable employment, can make a significant contribution to the solution of his difficulties. It was, however, realized that the ex-hospital patients referred to such a clinic were an unrepresentative group; they were mostly men (only one or two women were included) who had already experienced difficulties which they could not overcome unaided. We were aware that an unknown proportion of all men discharged from hospital either succeeded in resettling themselves or were too disabled to be eligible for work. The next step in our program of study was, therefore, to obtain an over-all picture of the resettlement problem of the hospital patient.

The hospital follow-up

In 1954 a report on the progress of some 700 patients discharged from a Scottish hospital (Ferguson and McPhail, 1954) aroused considerable interest. The findings from a 2-year follow-up led the authors to conclude: "In many cases early recurrence of breakdown came of bad social and environmental conditions rather than of any inevitability on medical grounds."

It was, however, realized that the results in one city are not necessarily a guide to the situation elsewhere, and the Nuffield Trust therefore decided to sponsor further studies of this kind. In Aberdeen, 500 male patients from surgical and medical wards were interviewed in hospitals and have been seen in their own homes at intervals of 1, 3, and 12 months after discharge. Although strict random sampling was impossible, every effort was made to exclude bias, and comparison between the sample and the whole hospital population shows that representativeness has been attained. All ages from 15 upward were included, but we report here only a preliminary analysis of patients age 55 and over.

The broad aims of the study were to observe what happened to these patients after they left the hospital and to seek explanations for the events observed. At the first interview in the hospital a detailed medical, occupational, and personal history was recorded; at the subsequent home interviews medical, occupational, and other personal developments were systematically explored, using a standardized recording procedure. Cooperation was excellent, but formidable difficulties have sometimes to be overcome in such studies since the contrast between a patient in bed in a fine modern hospital and the same person in his own home may be extreme.

Results

Men age 55–59. Seventy men were between ages 55 and 59 on admission to the hospital; of these, 9 were unemployed and 61 were working. The situation 12 months later is shown in Table 2. Further analysis showed that, whereas 36 of the 61 employed men had suffered from some chronic disability for at least 2 years prior to the hospital admission, no less than 7 of the 9 unemployed men had been disabled for at least 2 years. Furthermore, the proportion of skilled men in the employed group was 45 percent as against 27 percent in the unemployed group. These findings suggest again that the combination of disability and lack of recognized occupational skill may, quite apart from age, produce employment problems.

Men age 60–64. Of the 44 men in this age group, 14 were not at work before admission to hospital and 30 were. The observations a year later are shown in Table 2. In this age group, as in the previous one, the proportion of men suffering from a chronic illness was higher (12 out of 14) in the unemployed group than in those who were working prior to admission (17 out of 30). Only 4 out of the 14

Table 2. *Situation on admission to the hospital and one year later*

ONE YEAR AFTER LEAVING HOSPITAL

ON ADMISSION	Dead Number	Per- cent	Unfit for work Number	Per- cent	Working Number	Per- cent	Not employed Number	Per- cent	Retired
Men, age 55–59									
Employed									
(N = 61)	8	13	8	13	42	69	3	5	
Not employed									
(N = 9)	3	33	3	33	2	22	1	11	
Men, age 60–64									
Employed									
(N = 30)	6	20	8	27	13	43	1		2
Not employed									
(N = 14)	3*	21	4	29	1	7	3		3

men were skilled workers as compared with 16 out of 30 employed men.

Thus both age groups are alike in suggesting that the major occupational difficulty among ex-hospital patients is found in unskilled men with a chronic disability who have been out of work before admission. But, as measured by the proportion who are at work 1 year later, the men age 60–64 fared worse than those who were on the average 5 years younger; it would be easy to attribute this to age and leave the matter there, but age by itself can hardly be the explanation and some further analysis is necessary to show which of the many changes with age might be responsible.

Severity of illness is one likely factor. Mortality and morbidity rates increase rapidly after middle age so that a difference in the *degree* of disablement might account for the above results. Severity of illness is notoriously difficult to measure but there are at least two indices which may be tried. First, the median duration of stay in hospital: for the 55–59 age group this was 15 days, for the 60–64 age group the figure was 21 days. Second, capacity for movement was rated at each of the follow-up interviews: both at 3 and 12 months after discharge the younger age group recorded a higher proportion (67 percent) of men with unlimited mobility than did the men age 60–64 (54 percent). There is, therefore, some evidence to support the view that more severe illness is a factor accounting for the observed age difference in return to employment. An additional factor likely to be important is nearness to retirement age; three men approaching 65 casually mentioned this and there is an impression in our data that others who did not go back to work tended to be nearer 65 than 60. Such a suggestion needs confirmation, but it seems reasonable that a man who had planned to retire at minimum pension age anyway might feel inclined to regard a few months' work after hospitalization as hardly worthwhile.

Men age 65–69. As would be expected, the occupational pattern changed after age 65. Of the 31 men in this age group only 8 were in full-time work prior to admission to hospital; 1 year later 4 of the 31 were dead, 5 were in full-time work, and the remainder were partly or wholly retired. Perhaps the most surprising finding was that in only 3 cases had the illness changed the pre-hospital occupational pattern; these 3 men had all been working prior to admission and had hoped to return to work, but 2 decided to retire after the permanent effects of the illness became apparent, and the third was quite unfit for work.

Men age 70–74. Of the 27 men aged between 70 and 74, 21 were retired before the illness which led to their admission to hospital. One year later, 5 were dead, 2 were still working full time, and the remainder were mainly or completely retired. Two men previously working were found to have retired 1 year later, but in neither case was the retirement attributable to the hospital illness—one man had gone back to work but gave up following a minor accident, the other did so because he disliked the job.

Self-employed men

Quite early in our studies we noticed that some self-employed men, such as farmers and shopkeepers, seemed to show a different pattern of resettlement. The pattern over 65 was complicated by part-time jobs but, if these are included, the proportion of self-employed men doing some work was approximately double that of employees. Moreover, the difference between the self-employed and the employees, in respect of the proportion working 1 year after leaving hospital, became greater as the age group increased, a finding consistent with data extracted from the 1951 British Census (Richardson, to be published). Why this should be so is a matter for speculation; the economic incentive to go on working may be greater in those who own their business, but it is also likely that the disabled self-employed man can sometimes delegate work in a way that the similarly disabled employee cannot. Certainly we came across a number of instances where a son took over the main responsibility, including any heavy work, leaving his father to look after the administrative side of the farm, shop, or business; we also observed graduated retirement along the same lines, especially among farmers. We think these differences between self-employed men and employees merit further study.

Remedial action

This preliminary analysis of the pre- and post-hospital experience of older men suggests one main conclusion, the need for vigorous rehabilitation in the *earliest* stages of those diseases that are liable to recur. Just as there is growing awareness of the potential value of forestalling the effects of aging by modifying job situations before age changes produce difficulties, so we must try to predict which patients may encounter occupational problems and prevent or mitigate these by appropriate action when the disability first appears. For example, the shipyard worker who develops bronchitis in his forties may well feel able to return to his dusty strenuous job and his physician may see no reason to advise him otherwise. The chances are high, however, that 5 to 10 years later he will be in hospital with chronic bronchitis (emphysema) and then his resettlement is a problem because, in addition to his disability, he has to contend with age prejudice and a severely reduced capacity for effort. Had he been advised and helped to move to a dust-free and less continuously heavy job 10 years previously, the probability of later trouble could have been much reduced. The same kind of argument applies to many of the other disabilities which are associated with employment problems of older men. To some extent this policy does operate in industry already; we ourselves as honorary medical advisers to two companies in Aberdeen are not infrequently asked to see middle-aged men returning to work after illness and to advise whether some job modification or change is appropriate. But until medical services in industry are more widespread, hospital specialists and domiciliary physicians will have to assume greater responsibility for the *early* detection and prevention of the kind of difficulties described in this paper, and it is to them that industry should be able to turn for help. At present the liaison between medicine and industry is too often distant and indirect. Such experiments as the rehabilitation center at Vauxhall Motors in England have clearly shown what can be achieved when cooperation is close; rigorous and planned therapy accompanied by careful assessment of working capacity—present and future—and vocational selection are the keys to successful resettlement of the disabled at all ages but particularly in middle age and beyond. If rehabilitation facilities are to become generally available, however, much more precise evaluation of their claims is needed; in Britain, "clinical impression" rather than statistical demonstration is too often the basis for advocacy of extended provision of rehabilitation centers. What little evidence there is certainly confirms the opinions of those of us who have observed the results of good rehabilitation units, but only further well-designed operational research studies will supply the facts on which socio-medical policy can be based.

REFERENCES

Clay, H. M. 1960. The older worker and his job. London: H. M. Stationery Office.

Ferguson, T., and McPhail, A. N. 1954. Hospital and community. London: Oxford University Press. (Nuffield Trust.)

Great Britain. Ministry of Labour. 1955. Statistics of the Disabled Persons' Register. Ministry of Labour Gazette, 63: 274–75.

Le Gros Clark, F. 1956. Employment problems of elderly men. London: Nuffield Foundation. (Mimeographed.)

Murrell, K. F. H. 1959. Major problems of industrial gerontology. J. Gerontol., 14: 216–21.

Richardson, I. M. 1956. A socio-medical study of 200 unemployed men. Med. Officer, 96: 165–70.

———— Occupation and Health. In Wilma Donahue, C. Tibbitts, and R. H. Williams (eds.), Psychological and social processes of aging: an international research seminar. To be published.

Richardson, I. M., and Weir, R. D. 1956. An experiment in resettling the disabled. Rehabilitation, 17: 2–8.

Weir, R. D. 1957. A study of 108 registrations under the Disabled Persons (Employment) Act. Rehabilitation, 23: 16–27.

Welford, A. T. 1958. Ageing and human skill. London: Oxford University Press.

Semi-Skilled and over Forty

ALASTAIR HERON AND SHEILA M. CHOWN

THE purpose of this paper is to promote realism when considering future research on the life pattern after 40 of male manual workers. It has been stimulated by some findings of a recent survey carried out by the authors and their colleagues in over 20 manufacturing firms located in Merseyside, the heavily industrialized area surrounding Liverpool.

A start can be made by posing the problem in the context of the present concern, which is with the health aspects of income, employment, and retirement. What steps should be taken by industry to promote the well-being of manual workers as they move through the second half of life?

The dependent questions have been well stated by Murrell (1959), in a thoughtful paper to which too little attention has been paid, and these questions can later be employed as a useful focus of existing knowledge of our recent findings and of the difficulties facing future investigators. In order to use this integrating device, however, it will first be necessary to provide the reader with minimal information about the sources and methods which were employed in the Merseyside survey of aging in manufacturing industry.

SOURCES AND METHODS
IN THE MERSEYSIDE SURVEY
The firms

Twenty-one firms were approached and 20 of these agreed to participate. Each firm was drawn from a different sub-class within 9 of the 13 "manufacturing" orders of the Industrial Tables, 1951 British Census. Of these 20 firms, 7 were in industries over-represented in Merseyside compared with England and Wales, the remaining 13 industries being typical. This was a deliberate compromise between the conflicting needs for local involvement and for wider generalization of the findings. Between them the 20 firms employed approximately 25,000 hourly paid people of whom about two-thirds were men. Fifteen employed between 400 and 1000, three between 1000 and 2000, and two over 2000. In this connection it should be noted that although only 6 percent of manufacturing establishments in England and Wales employ more than 400 persons, nevertheless, half the working population of manufacturing industry is to be found in this minority of larger establishments. Industries represented included chemicals, rubber, food, light sheet metal, electrical equipment, paper and printing, and clothing. The percentage of male shop-floor workers over 40 years of age proved to be 47.7, slightly below the national average of 50. In 7 firms, more than half the men were over 40, one firm having 70 percent above this age; at the other extreme there was a firm with only 32 percent over 40. When the figures were further broken down into age groups, it was found that some firms had a great many men over 55, while others had a preponderance in the 40–54 age group. No firm had less than 11 percent of men over 55.

Scope and methods of inquiry

Information was sought on company policy: on age differences in employee behavior, on working conditions and job demands, and on the attitudes of departmental managers and foremen toward age changes in their men.

Use was made of three distinct methods of inquiry, these were (a) examination of records, (b) interviewing, and (c) inspection of actual operations. No one of these methods on its own is ever wholly satisfactory. Records kept by industrial firms for their own use vary widely in their completeness and accuracy; information obtained during interviews is liable to distortion from several causes; and evaluation of working conditions and job demands should ideally be based on wholly objective physical and physiological measurements which are too time-consuming for extensive use. But methods of field study must be practicable, and strict precautions were taken in the planning and execution of this investigation to maximize the reliability of those used. Information obtained is compared wherever possible. A fourth method, involving the measurement of individual productivity, was considered but found quite impracticable in the face of the almost universal group incentive payment systems current in British manufacturing industry.

For the purposes of this paper, the data obtained on company policy through interviews with top management and on that obtained on working conditions and job demands through inspection of actual operations will be drawn upon. The latter requires some definition and explanation before the findings can be utilized for the present purpose. In the job study all the 526 semi-skilled jobs under those foremen who had been interviewed in 19 of the survey firms were examined. The term "semi-skilled" was defined by exclusion, in that no jobs were studied that could be "picked up in a day," and, at the other extreme, none for which the usual apprenticeship was required. This definition provided a relatively comprehensive coverage of the heterogeneous activities on which the majority of men in manufacturing industry are engaged. The 526 jobs studied involved 2774 men in the age range 16 to 74 years.

To ensure comparability of job studies across the firms, no assessments were sought from employees of the firms themselves. Instead, two members of the research team examined and assessed each job simultaneously but strictly independently. They subsequently discussed each job until agreement was reached on all differing assessments. In the first 11 firms a third rater attended this discussion to serve as a referee. All jobs were assessed in respect of four working-condition variables, which were: (1) dust and fumes, (2) heat, (3) noise, and (4) draughts; and five job-demand variables, defined as follows:

1. Fineness: the degree of precision or accuracy involved in any type of discrimination which could be based on the fineness of material dealt with;

2. Pacing: speed of work when the control of this emanates to varying degrees from "outside" the worker. This includes machine or process pacing, pacing by the expectations of others, piece work, etc.;

3. Need for responsible behavior, especially when the safety and welfare of other people is involved;

4. Sustained care and concentrated attention: the extent to which close application to the job is necessary, i.e., the duration and degree to which one must continuously pay attention to the job;

5. Physical effort.

Full details of the rating system and its evaluation appear elsewhere (Featherstone and Cunningham, 1959); it will suffice to say here that the average reliability of the assessments before discussion was 0.61 (range 0.54 to 0.72). It should be noted that only 15 percent of the 526 jobs studied involved 10 men or more, 54 percent being represented by fewer than 4 men. These facts, which run counter to popular misconceptions of the modern factory as a place where hundreds of people do identical work, must be borne in mind when assessing the results presented.

Age and the manual worker

There is no need to rehearse here in detail the firm knowledge already in our possession. It is readily available in a book by Welford (1958), a paper by Murrell (1959), and in a chapter by McFarland and O'Doherty (1959), to mention but three recent sources.

It is proposed instead to quote verbatim and then to discuss the eight topics listed by Murrell (1959) as follows:

1. "What are the factors in the work situation which cause difficulties to older men? How can they be remedied?" Clay (1960) summarizes the position as follows:

a. "The older worker may find it difficult to keep up with the demands for speed, whether these are made by the machine he operates, or by the team he works with, or by a payment system."

b. "Provided he is not debarred from heavy physical work on medical grounds, the older worker finds its demands less exacting than those made by lighter work involving pressure for speed."

c. "Changes in mental ability that are found as one grows older reduce a worker's efficiency at jobs where he has to remember information for a short time before he makes use of it, or where he has to translate or alter the information in some way mentally before he can take the appropriate action."

A tendency was found for significantly fewer men under 25 and more men over 40 to be employed on semi-skilled jobs carried out under bad working conditions. Similarly, significantly more men over 40 were on jobs demanding much responsible behavior, such jobs occurring more often under bad working conditions. Fewer older men were on jobs making severe demands for attention to fine detail or involving sustained care and concentration, or on those severely paced.

When one remembers that these findings are based on over 500 jobs involving over 2700 men, in firms representing 20 different manufacturing industries, it is clear that a real but still submerged problem on a large scale awaits attention. How can the adverse conditions and demands be remedied? They can be remedied by general improvement of working conditions, by taking care to see that older men are not left behind to "silt up" in old shops when new ones are built, and by modifying specific jobs so as to reduce the strain caused by pacing, sustained concentration, or fine detail. While general improvement of working conditions is going on all the time, industry may not be conscious of—and if conscious, not anxious about—older men being under the worst working conditions. With regard to modifying jobs in favor of older men, it must be reported that not one manager in the 116 who were interviewed had ever done so.

2. "What avoidable long-term health hazards (other than toxic hazards) are present in a work situation?" Research evidence from long-term studies of individuals and their jobs is lacking. Meanwhile there is no answer beyond the common-sense inference that some ill health and debility in the later years may be attributable to the cumulative effect of bad working conditions and severe job demands which become less tolerable from middle life onwards. If this inference is accepted, then "avoiding long-term health hazards" may mean planned job change in the late forties or early fifties. Change to what? This question will be deferred for consideration until Murrell's third question has been examined.

3. "What is the effect of bonus schemes on older men?" Again, this is not known; but, as Murrell rightly suggests, the effect will be related to the "tightness" of the rates. In the majority of firms studied in the Merseyside survey, group bonus schemes were in operation and individual piecework was a rarity; but rates did not in general appear to be tight enough to affect the older members of the group. One instance was encountered of an assembly department where the bonus target was set by the informal leaders of the teams; one or two of these would not "carry" a slowing member, and the firm reported having to move several men each year, usually in their low to middle forties, almost always to a lower-paid job. A return to the question, "Change to what?" is now in order.

It is not so easy to transfer a semi-skilled worker to less demanding work without loss of earnings, as might be imagined. Even where this is achieved, it is nearly impossible to detect for the simple reason that most internal transfers on the shop floor of manufacturing industry are informal, unrecorded, and certainly not attributed to age effects.

4. "What are the determining factors in promotion, and how do they discriminate against the older man? What is the role of 'status' in job satisfaction?" In a pilot survey which preceded the main inquiry, departmental managers were asked what factors they took into account when selecting men for promotion from the shop floor. The factors most often mentioned were suitable personality, leadership qualities, and ability at their present job. Seniority (or length of service) was only rarely taken into account.

Senior management in the main survey, interviewed on company policy, sometimes mentioned a desire to obtain a minimum number of years of service from a man in a new appointment. Departmental managers mentioning an age bar for promotion to foreman volunteered such reasons as "a general preference for younger men"; "difficulties encountered with entry to a staff pension scheme"; "lack of ability"; and that "a man is not worth promotion" if he has not gained it by the age specified.

An age bar was mentioned by senior management in 12 of the 20 firms in the survey, 6 giving 55, and 3, 50 as their limit. When the inquiry was repeated in the same firms at the departmental manager level, asking "Is there in practice (as distinct from policy) an upper-age limit for promotion?", it was found that half the managers said there was no age limit and a quarter gave one above 50.

By ascertaining the actual promotion ages of all the 547 present foremen in 18 firms, it was possible to show that fewer than 1 in 5 had reached foreman status after the age of 45, 1 in 10, after 50. Average age at promotion was 40.4 years. Thus, whereas three-quarters had gained promotion between 30 and 50, three-quarters of the departmental managers said there was no upper age limit or gave an age over 50.

Murrell raises an important question by asking about the role of status, both formal and informal. It is probable that as people get older they acquire some perspective about status, both through achievement and by acceptance of their limitations; but that perspective is not likely to include ready acceptance of any lowering in the esteem of their peers. He is surely right in suggesting that one of the aims in attempted transfer to less demanding work should be the provision of equal or greater status, even if no pay increase be involved.

5. "To what extent can older men be re-trained? What age-group is, economically, most worth training?" The dearth of evidence concerning the training or retraining of older people is well known but nonetheless painful. We can contribute to an understanding of this dearth by summarizing the evidence on company policy and supervisory attitude obtained during the Merseyside survey. Of the 20 manufacturing firms, only 2 ran special courses for semi-skilled workers, and 2 others had courses for training foremen how to give on-the-job instruction. In most of the other firms it was thought that "training schemes are unnecessary" because the semi-skilled work is "easy to pick up." Not a single firm had considered making any special provision for training or retraining men over 40, although well over a

third of their supervisors had noticed that above the age of 40, men were slower in learning unfamiliar jobs.

As Murrell points out, the answer to his subsidiary question is, at present, the traditional one: "Catch them young," because you will get more return for the cost of training, provided your labor turnover is low and you are not likely to initiate major process changes in the near future. The managers and foremen interviewed mostly preferred that new recruits for semi-skilled jobs be in the 26–35 age group, old enough to have "settled down a bit," young enough to be "adaptable." But in 1957, the full year preceding this survey, 29 percent of the 25–39 age group left the 17 firms for which reliable data were available, compared with only 11 percent of the 40–54 age group. It should be made clear that the populations at risk were closely comparable in size: 25–39 years, 5363; 40–54 years, 4731.

6. "What is the basis of discrimination against older workers in employment policy? What are the attributes of older men which make them worth employing?" Only 2 of our 20 firms had no age limit for new starters; the others varied from 35–60, the ages of 45 and 50 being mentioned by 5 firms each. The direct question "Is the maximum starting age linked to pension age in any way?" elicited affirmative replies from 11 firms. In 3 further firms, where the age limit was not linked to pensions, it was imposed as "a means of redressing the age balance in the work-force." Reference has already been made to the belief that adaptability is less after 40 years of age; to this one should add the generally held view that "slowing-down" is the principal feature of getting older on the shop floor.

In our other paper in this volume we deal fully with the favorable attitudes of managers and supervisors toward older men. It will suffice to say here that these are broadly based and widely held; if we attempt to sum them up in a single sentence, it would be to say that: "Older men work with a supervisor with the common aim of getting the job done, while younger men work more for themselves." To this, one should add objective evidence of better timekeeping, reduced frequency of absence, and the lower labor turnover already mentioned.

7. "What is happening to men who give up their accustomed jobs because they can no longer cope with them?" More than half the managers and foremen said that in their departments it was not usual to have to transfer men from jobs because the jobs had become too much for them. There would seem to be alternative explanations for this: either most older semi-skilled workers can continue to do all the jobs, in some cases more slowly, in others without showing clear

signs of distress, or transfer was taking place unrecognized in the general course of rearrangement of work.

When asked about jobs to which men were transferred, a fifth of the supervisors (about half those responding on this topic for the reason just given) mentioned "lighter" or "less strenuous" work. Similarly, when asked about work in their department considered "specially suitable for older men," half of those responding again mentioned "lighter work." A list of all jobs actually mentioned by name contains a very high proportion of manual and low-grade jobs. It is probable that an absolute shortage of such "alternative work" is one of the factors tending to prevent earlier transfer and to encourage firms in the direction of a compulsory retirement policy, usually at 65 years of age. Only 6 of these 20 firms had a genuine policy of flexible retirement; in 7 firms there was a rigid age bar, at 65, while the remaining 6 had an age limit to which some exceptions were made. During the last 10 years 4 firms had made it harder for men to stay on after 65.

The data on alternative work provide support for the statistical analysis of Le Gros Clark (1955) who came to the conclusion that "Somewhere around 15 or 20 percent of all men in their early and mid sixties probably need to be given either the chance of a new job or working conditions better suited to their age," and that "We are near exhausting all the traditional avenues of transfer to light work." (Le Gros Clark, 1956, pp. 20–21.)

Consideration of Murrell's subsidiary questions under this heading, and of his last main question, is deferred to the next section of this paper, since for these we have no new direct evidence to offer from the survey.

DISCUSSION

We have used some recent findings from a survey of aging among semi-skilled workers in manufacturing industry to extend our understanding of future research needs. This represents a small but perhaps significant contribution to what Murrell describes as "an enormous program of research" implied by his list of questions. But the main purpose of this paper is to bring us squarely up against the problems facing those who attempt industrial research on aging. Some of these were brought forcibly to our attention in planning and executing this survey, in analyzing our data, and in comparing our findings with existing knowledge and recognized needs. What are these obstacles to research and to its application?

First, we think it vital to face the fact that industry in general simply does not acknowledge a problem of aging. This is not just pigheadedness or lack of imagination; the consensus of research data so far available would appear to sustain a view that the effects of aging are very gradual, are diffused by enormous individual differences, are minimized by informal processes of group adjustment, and are concealed by attribution, rightly or wrongly, to other causes.

Second, account must be taken of the general attitude of industrial management toward the effective utilization of manpower resources in the unskilled and semi-skilled categories which form the bulk of the labor force. It is not an implied criticism of management to recognize their preoccupation with "high production at minimum cost": after all, that is what the consumer expects of the producer. The cumulative efforts of industrial psychologists, work-study engineers, personnel managers, industrial medical officers, and human-relations consultants have partly convinced some industrial managements, mainly of large corporations, that this preoccupation can defeat its own end. But there remains a massive scepticism which largely determines the climate for research proposals on any aspect of the "human factor."

Let us consider a single but highly relevant example, quite unspecific however to aging or the older worker. A survey of industrial in-plant training programs in seven European countries was published by the European Productivity Agency (Organization for European Economic Cooperation, 1957). The concluding section of that report opens with three paragraphs which justify quotation here in full.

This survey has made it abundantly clear that as yet, industry in general in the countries concerned has done very little to provide training for semi-skilled and unskilled workers on a systematic basis. It can be said that the situation differs from industry to industry in that in most countries experience showed that it was easier to find examples of systematic training in the textile and wearing apparel industries, in the electrical and transport equipment industries and in the chemical industry than in others.

The fact that systematic training is so little developed must reflect the attitude of managers to the question of training for the kind of work with which the inquiry has dealt. This attitude seems to stem from a number of ideas, of which four were the most commonly referred to in the reports of the national institutes.

The first was that semi-skilled and unskilled work were so simple that they could easily be learned without any training, and that this in fact was one advantage of modern production methods, which provide for a very fine sub-division of labour. Secondly, there was the fear expressed of the disadvantages of being first in the field with systematic training, namely that workers who were trained would be enticed away to other firms, perhaps at higher wages. An associated idea was that because the rate of labour turnover was very high, it was not worthwhile attempting to improve the training of new workers. Lastly was the notion that systematic training is necessarily elaborate and expensive. This stems from the lack of information on training methods and their applicability to different kinds of situation with their relative advantages and disadvantages. [Organization for European Economic Cooperation, 1957, p. 75]

If this is the general picture, can we be surprised to find no thought of training or retraining middle-aged workers, as in our recent study or the attitude reported by Shenfield: "Most firms were suspicious of the idea of re-training well before retirement age, considering it impracticable and unnecessary." (1957, p. 202.)

Third, we have to reckon with the widespread reaction of industrial managements to the social consequences of the shorter day, shorter week, shorter working-life trend. If this reaction takes the form of regarding the problems created for older people by enforced earlier retirement as a fair charge on the community at large, rather than on industry in particular, who can wonder? Since almost all the "problems of the older worker" which management has actually encountered on a large scale seem to arise at about 60 years of age, will there not be a natural temptation to use the trend as a "solution" preferable to the preventative measures advocated by such as ourselves?

This brings us to Murrell's remaining questions. Of these, the first is "What can be done to help men over their first and subsequent retirements?" He is here referring not only to the usual final retirement, but also to the earlier "retirement" when a man changes his job because of age difficulties, whether or not these are appreciated as the cause. It looks as though the help needed for this latter problem is the kind we have just recognized as being not likely to come from industry itself, at least not at all widely. Murrell and others therefore suggest that government training centers now concentrating on the disabled should offer their facilities to meet this new and growing need. This suggestion would in our view be most acceptable if the scheme enabled firms to send men on short courses, or on a "day-release" basis; it should not be thought of solely or mainly as a rehabilitation service for men who had become unemployed.

What about final retirement from full-time work? Here a start has been made, through industry itself, with schemes of preparation for retirement; but as Wermel (1960) has shown, there is wide variation among firms in the perception of this idea. It is likely that only a few large firms have actually launched and kept going successfully any detailed scheme, involving group discussion and individual counseling, which starts long enough before retirement to be fully capable of utilization. The first, and so far the only, scheme in Great Britain is, however, of this type.

Murrell goes on to inquire "What is the extent of the skill lost to the community due to these retirements, (and) what are the economic consequences?" We are sure that no one can answer these two questions at present, and we venture to doubt whether an objective answer to either can be envisaged. If the economy of a country is in such a position as to put a premium, however small, on the increment of production added by the work of each additional member of the labor force, i.e., if there is full employment and an expanding market, then obviously that country loses economically if the skills and experience of its mature adult workers are not utilized. But the interests of a particular firm, industry, or locality, are often not perceived as identical, at any given point in time, with those of the country as a whole.

The final questions will serve to close the circle: "What are the bases of the present attitudes of industry towards the older worker? What is needed to alter these attitudes and to produce personnel policies more sympathetic to older workers?"

On the basis of the evidence at present available to us from close and frequent contact with the management of some representative manufacturing industries in Great Britain, it seems that present attitudes are based on an almost total acceptance of inevitable and natural, though gradual, deterioration with age. The power of ancient clichés is tremendous: "old dogs can't learn new tricks"; "too old at forty"; "older people are set in their ways"; "training is for the young"; "light work for the elderly." Personnel policies are in general "sympathetic" toward older workers; the problem is to make them realistic toward the "not-so-old." What kinds of research then are most likely to be both practicable and effective in the industrial situation? We suggest the following.

Long-term follow-up studies, based on cohorts of individuals in the same firm (replicated in additional firms), designed to establish what job changes, whether attributed to age or not, actually occur, and at what ages these begin and become most frequent. Where possible, study of the working conditions and job demands should be carried out along the lines reported in this paper.

Laboratory investigations of learning, involving miniature work situations as well as verbal learning, are needed to generate hypotheses which could be tested under industrial conditions in those few firms which take systematic training of the semi-skilled seriously.

Opportunistic follow-up studies of the effect on workers of different ages involved in major process changes within the firm could serve as pointers to the need for retraining procedures in advance of such changes.

Schemes of preparation for retirement, provided they are started early enough in the working life—say at 50—could serve as "action research" projects, offering opportunities for study of immediate problems of job change as well as for long-term work up to and beyond retirement.

SUMMARY

This paper has utilized recent findings from a survey of manufacturing industry in reconsidering the research strategy necessary and practicable for improving the prospects of the older worker.

Previously available data are confirmed and extended; in particular, attention has been drawn to the danger of older men being exposed to unfavorable working conditions, and to their being discriminated against when recruitment, promotion, and training are being considered.

Evidence is produced to suggest the increasing difficulty of finding suitable alternative work for men in their fifties and sixties, and for the exacerbation of this problem by the inability of managers and foremen to perceive the nature and extent of the underlying problems, or of the need for preventive action.

Types of research considered necessary and largely practicable are recommended.

REFERENCES

Clay, H. M. 1960. The older worker and his job. London: H. M. Stationery Office.

Featherstone, M. S., and Cunningham, Catherine M. 1959. Age of manual workers in relation to conditions and demands of work. Bull. Brit. Psychol. Soc., 38: 3a. (Abstract.)

Le Gros Clark, F. 1955. New jobs for old workers. London: Nuffield Foundation. (Mimeographed.)

——— 1956. The employment problems of elderly men. London: Nuffield Foundation. (Mimeographed.)

McFarland, R. A., and O'Doherty, B. M. 1959. Work and occupational skills. *In* J. E. Birren (ed.), Handbook of aging and the individual: psychological and biological aspects. Chicago: University of Chicago Press.

Murrell, K. F. H. 1959. Major problems of industrial gerontology. J. Gerontol., 14: 216–21.

Organization for European Economic Cooperation. 1957. The training of workers within the factory. Paris: O. E. E. C.

Shenfield, Barbara E. 1957. Social policies for old age: a review of social provisions for old age in Great Britain. London: Routledge & Kegan Paul Ltd.

Welford, A. T. 1958. Ageing and human skill. London: Oxford University Press.

Wermel, M. T. 1960. Personal communication.

The Matrix of Health, Manpower, and Age

WALT R. SIMMONS

ACTION initiated by an individual in support of his well-being as an older person, as well as policy and programs undertaken by societies for the same purpose, should be selected first for their human values and second for economic and sociological considerations. Within this context, wise decisions can be made only when they are based on facts.

Facts, truth, concepts, and measurement

A considerable part of the effort expended throughout history in religious, philosophical, and scientific endeavor has been the search for truth and for facts. These primary values are not easily determined. Lest there be any misunderstanding, it should be stated immediately that the present paper does not presume to engage in analysis of so fundamental a matter as the nature of truth or the determination of facts. However, it will be useful to consider briefly a few topics which are peripheral to these questions and basic to the point of view I wish to take concerning information about the matrix of health, manpower, and age. We proceed with a good bit of caution but still optimistically recalling Aristotle's observation: "The search for truth is in one way hard and in another easy. For it is evident that no one can master it fully nor miss it wholly."

Concepts and relevant facts. In the study of populations, an idea or concept of the working population or the labor force has emerged. To many millions of people this notion of a labor force, under one label or another, has meaning. But the concept differs between classes of consumers, and within a class among the members of the class, and even within a single person from one time to another and from one purpose to another. The kinds of data which may be assembled on the matter and the types of measurement of presumptive facts are

An expanded version of this paper was presented at the Fifth Congress of The International Association of Gerontology.

similarly varied, and of differing relevance for the different circumstances.

HEALTH IN RELATION TO WORK STATUS
OF THE AGING
The matrix of health, manpower, and age

The title of this paper, "The Matrix of Health, Manpower, and Age," might suggest to some persons a mathematically precise functional relationship among three social variables. That is not the intention behind the title. The relationship among these factors is multidimensional and highly complex. It is not expressible in any single equation or statistic, or even in a single mode of evaluation. The economist will emphasize one set of features of the interrelationships of health, age, and work force; the sociologist quite a different set; and still other aspects will gain the special attention of the physician or the psychologist.

Truth with respect to this complex topic is a many-sided matter, and it should be stressed that contrasting and alternative points of view are not only acceptable but even necessary if understanding is to be gained of relationships among health, manpower, and age.

As a further illustration of this thesis note how information about many health phenomena can be expressed in distinctly separate forms and thus emphasize different facets. Consider the matter of days spent in bed as a consequence of illness. The presence of disease and associated bed-days is literally a vital matter to the person with the health problem. A prime form of information is that of the specific individual case: the medical diagnosis, the treatment, the social, psychological, and financial impact on the person who is ill, and on the people close to him. This type of information is unique to each person and condition; it is of paramount or supreme importance to the individual; it cannot be reflected in statistical terms because it is unique. As one seeks to draw conclusions from statistics in the field of health, he should never lose sight of this first form of information which is critical to the individual human being.

Another useful form of information is the statistic, which marshals myriads of individual instances into a structure more comprehensible to men's minds. The statistic itself can appear in many dresses. Thus it may be said, in global manner, that in the United States in 1958 persons 65 and over experienced 237 million man-days of bed-disability.

Since such aggregates, lacking scale, may be difficult to evaluate, statistical relatives are also useful. In health statistics the relative number often is expressed in terms of the incidence, prevalence or experience *per person,* and given greater perspective by comparison of such a rate for a defined group with corresponding rates for other groups. Thus for the group over age 65 the 1958 bed-day annual rate per person has been estimated at 16.3. This compares with a rate of 7.8 days for all persons in the United States, and with a rate of 5.2 days for males under age 5 living in the United States (U.S. National Health Survey, 1959).

Definition of health

The phenomenon of health itself or of the absence of health is very difficult to define. The formulation of a procedure for measuring defined health is equally difficult.

Suppose a person is given an extensive medical and physical examination. Such an examination would reveal the presence or absence of certain classes of morbid conditions. Positive findings might lead to a particular diagnosis and to the declaration that the examinee or patient was ill. The types of conditions revealed would depend not only upon their "existence" in some undefined real sense, but also upon the nature of the examination and perhaps upon the skill of the physicians, nurses, and technicians administering the examination. The variety of possible outcomes of this medical examination could be elaborated at some length. Medical sciences and arts have advanced since the eras of witch doctors. Indeed, generally speaking, the judgments of physicians and clinicians are accepted as determinations. But the physician's diagnosis or prognosis usually is subject to some measure of uncertainty. It should be made clear that the uncertainty of diagnosis is not merely a function of the state of the arts and of the practice and ability of the physician, but also of the fact that for extremely obscure reasons a given pattern of physical conditions will affect the health of different individuals in different ways.

In quite a different manner the health of a person can be judged not by the pronouncement of his physician, but by the actions the person takes. A given individual may at any point in time go about his usual activities; or he may not; he may stay in bed; he may consult a physician; he may be absent from his regular job; he may take medication; he may not be able to sleep; he may not eat; he may use a wheel chair, or a crutch, or eyeglasses; he may be unable to lift weights; he may be very active with apparently unlimited energy; he may die. Many of these actions can reasonably be considered observable facts, and can form the basis of relatively objective measures of physical well-being.

Many other possibilities for evaluating the health of a person can be cited, but perhaps my point has been made.

History of statistics on manpower, health, and age

A review of the history of statistics on labor force and health in the United States reveals interest and activity since the start of the nation. In human affairs statistical knowledge is never sufficient. But with respect to labor force and employment, the scope, quality, and detail of information are better than in most areas of social inquiry. A contrasting picture prevails for statistics on the health of the United States population. Despite many praiseworthy efforts, over-all knowledge of health conditions has been regrettably thin until quite recently. Even today, development in the area of health statistics, if beyond its infancy, is better thought of as being in a stage of childhood rather than maturity.

THE U.S. NATIONAL HEALTH SURVEY

Following 6 years of intensive developmental study, the U.S. National Health Survey was inaugurated in the summer of 1957, having been established through Congressional legislation.

Several provisions of the law deserve special mention for their impact on informational relationships among age, manpower, and health. The most important of these is that the Surgeon General of the Public Health Service is directed to maintain a *continuing* survey to provide statistical information on the amount, distribution, and effects of illness and disability in the United States, and the services received for or because of such conditions. The law also recognizes the difficulty of this task and the need for more powerful measuring techniques, and therefore explicitly directs that methodological research be a part of the operating program.

Leading tenets of NHS policy

Statistics reflect in some degree the principles which motivate the collecting agent. For this reason, several leading tenets of the U.S. National Health Survey are identified.

Health is a diverse phenomenon. It was emphasized earlier that there is no unique determination of health; that health has many aspects and forms. This principle is fully accepted by the NHS. Thus we like to emphasize that the NHS is itself not a single survey, but rather a family of undertakings which collectively are expected to present a useful statistical summary of illnesses, injuries, impairments, and related health matters for the civilian population of the United States.

Evolutionary pattern. Continuity and comparability of estimates for different time periods are desired objectives, but they do not have overriding priority. A substantial portion of the resources and energy of the NHS, at least during its early years, is being devoted to studies and evaluation of quality of data input, to efficiency of collection and processing, and to usefulness of output. It is expected that with these activities, guided by the active and constructive criticism of users, and its own research, the NHS operates a program which is changing in response to need in scope, content, method, and specific product.

Impartial intelligence vehicle. The very choice of which phenomena are to be measured and the selection of general techniques for attempting the measurement necessarily represent judgments rather than chance. However, a fundamental of the NHS is that the Survey is not an advocate of any particular health doctrine or policy. The Survey is an impartial fact-finding agent. With substantial aid from both governmental and public advisory committees representing many points of view, the Survey attempts in collection and in analysis to present evidence in as unbiased a manner as ability allows. In particular, social and medical interpretations are left to consumers.

Data for the entire population. While not a characteristic of every project of the NHS, most Survey activities measure a defined health experience for the entire civilian population rather than restricting coverage to persons who are ill. It is believed that better balance in analysis results when it is known, for example, that although 100 million bed-days per year result from impairments, nearly 90 percent of the population reports no impairment in NHS surveys.

The household interview survey

One of the major projects of the NHS is a continuing household interview survey of the civilian noninstitutional population.

There are limitations to the accuracy of diagnostic and other information collected in household interviews. For diagnostic information the household respondent can, at best, pass on to the interviewer only the information the physician has given to the family. For conditions not medically attended, diagnostic information is often no more than a description of symptoms. However, other types of facts such as those concerning the circumstances and consequences of illness or injury and the resulting action taken or sought by the individual, can be obtained more accurately from household members than from any other source since only the persons concerned are in a position to report all of this type of information. Furthermore this type of survey facilitates greatly comparison of the ill population and the well population, and assessment of relative impacts of a variety of illnesses and impairments.

The continuity attribute. The interview survey is not only a continuing project, but has from the statistician's viewpoint the rather striking characteristic of being *continuous.* The survey is not a one-time tally of the population, not even an intermittent activity, but rather is taking place yesterday and today and tomorrow on a flow basis. This process is accomplished in the following manner. Each week a sample of about 700 households or 2300 persons is drawn in such a manner that though small it is representative of the national population, and is additive with other similarly selected weekly samples. For example, a single week's sample may be used alone, or combined with 13 or 52 other weekly samples. In a year, the process includes some 38,000 households and 120,000 persons. Thus the design permits both continuous measurement of characteristics of high prevalence or incidence in the population, and through the larger consolidated samples more detailed analysis of less common characteristics and small categories.

Interviewing. Interviews are sought for all persons in the sample households. Each person 18 years or older, available at the time of interview, is interviewed for himself. Proxy respondents are accepted for children and for adults not available at the time of interview, provided the respondent is closely related to the person about whom information is being obtained.

The questionnaire. The questionnaire carries some 40 items for identification of households and persons and socio-demographic description of respondents. There follows a group of about a dozen illness-recall inquiries. Another 50 questions for the most part elicit information related to the health conditions identified in the recall part of the interview. The questions seek to discover such facts as whether the condition was medically attended; what the diagnosis is; whether the condition caused restriction of activity, confinement in bed, or work-loss; whether it led to other limitations in daily behavior; and what use has been made of dentists, physicians, and hospitals.

The health examination survey

A second major phase of NHS activity is a Health Examination Survey. In this continuing project, a probability sample of persons from the noninstitutional civilian population is offered a limited physical examination. Contrasting with the Household Interview Survey in which a third of a million persons have been interviewed, the Health Examination Survey is just beginning.

The Examination Survey as compared with the Interview Survey is intensive rather than extensive, and is directed at types of information for which a household interview is not an appropriate technique. The examination secures a variety of physical and physiological measurements, including such items as weight, height, blood pressure, visual acuity, a test for hearing, several blood analyses, skinfolds, and a variety of frame measurements. It encompasses x rays of hands, feet, and chest, a 12-lead electrocardiogram, a dental examination, a glucose-tolerance test, a medical history, and a limited general physical examination. The primary immediate objectives in the first cycle are to obtain distributions of the population—well and unwell—by the measured physical and physiological characteristics, and to arrive at estimates of prevalence of certain classes of impairments and chronic conditions, with special emphasis on cardiovascular and arthritic and rheumatic conditions.

Additional NHS undertakings

The Household Interview Survey and the Health Examination Survey are the first two major activities of the NHS. My full paper identifies a number of other NHS undertakings in various stages of planning and operation.

DATA ON AGE, HEALTH, AND WORK STATUS

Statistics in any detail on health by age and work-force status cannot be presented at this time. Some data are offered in my full paper, and a good many more in an official publication of the U.S. National Health Survey, now in press. The NHS publication will treat chronic and acute disease as well as injuries and impairments. Measures of prevalence, incidence, disability days, limitation of activity, and use of medical, dental, and hospital facilities are offered. An overlook at a very few highlight numbers may serve here to fix the scale of magnitude in a few of the possible dimensions of interest.

There will here be no debate of who should be included in the group "older persons." For convenience, the ensuing statistics apply to the age group 65 years old or older. It is suggested that many topics will be best understood when separate data are presented for the entire population in 5-year intervals.

The U.S. has a civilian noninstitutional population of roughly 176 million persons of which something like 9 percent, or more than 15 million, are over age 65. About one-third of these are over 75. Note that these and later data quoted exclude the institutional population.

For the 15 million persons in the group 65 years or older, typically today:

Three million usually were working over the past year, 6 million usually were keeping house, 5 million were retired, and 1 million were in miscellaneous groups.

Some 2 million characterize themselves as unable to work at all and another 3 million say they are limited in amount or kind of work they can perform.

Three out of 4 report the presence of one or more chronic conditions.

The incidence of acute conditions is no higher among older persons than among younger adults.

Older persons show higher rates of utilization of physicians and hospitalization, but variations are substantial by rural-urban residence, by income, and by other factors.

The group of persons age 65 or over experiences annually: 600 million days of restricted activity, 200 million bed-days of disability, and 50 million work-loss days.

SUMMARY

Both individuals and societies seek improved health of the population. Effectiveness of the search should be judged first in terms of human values; second in terms of economic and sociological considerations. Efficiency of the effort is likely to be determined by the degree to which plans and actions rest upon factual evidence.

Correspondence between evidence and truth in a real world is an elusive and ambiguous relationship, classically and pervasively difficult to establish in both philosophical and scientific domains. In particular, one should not expect to discover a simple unique formula which explains interaction among age, health, and manpower of a people. Rather it is that understanding will be promoted through multiple measurements and descriptions of health and work-force status.

Among prominent modes of measurement, but certainly not exhausting avenues of insight, are those processes to which special attention has been called in this review. The United States is fortunate in its variety and extent of data on labor force, including decennial population censuses, quinquennial industrial censuses, annual and quarterly tax returns under social security systems, monthly reporting of selected items by employers, monthly sampling of the population through household interviewing, and many more specialized studies by local and national groups, among which private and public employment offices, universities, and nonprofit organizations are particularly notable.

Health of a person or population is outstandingly a many-valued phenomenon. The range of measures includes individual clinical, physical, and physiological tests; medical diagnosis; observed or recorded actions such as admission to a hospital, use of a prosthetic device, or absence from work; expressed opinions of persons; and an extensive variety of types of statistical absolutes, averages, relatives, and rates.

Statistical knowledge of relations among age, health, and work-force status is now being augmented by continuing projects of the U.S. National Health Survey. These activities emphasize the advantages in perspective obtained by studying representative samples of all persons, both well and ill, in a population, thus permitting association of morbidity measures with demographic, sociological, and economic characteristics. The Health Survey utilizes techniques of physical examinations, interview, and record sampling.

This paper has attempted little substantive analysis of data on health, work-force, and age. But to analysts of many disciplines, the challenge of data now available is strikingly exhibited by such contrasting pieces of evidence as these: (a) the civilian noninstitutional population of the United States, age 65 and over, loses annually over 200 million person-days through bed-disability, and three out of every four persons in this population block have one or more chronic illnesses or physical impairments; (b) yet the usual activity of nearly 40 percent of males age 65–74 is working in a job or business, and for this group work-loss per person due to health conditions is but

2 weeks per year, and only a third more than for males in the next younger 10-year cohort.

Surely this evidence points both to the existence of very serious problems, and to reasonable hope for resolution of those problems.

REFERENCE

U.S. National Health Survey. 1959. Health statistics from U.S. National Health Survey: Disability days, United States, July, 1957–June, 1958. (Series B-10.) (Public Health Service Pub. 584–B10.) Washington, D.C.: Government Printing Office.

The Aging of the Italian Population: Its Causes and Consequences with Particular Emphasis on Pension Eligibility

ROBERTO CUZZANITI

OBVIOUSLY the phenomenon of "aging" can be analyzed from various points of view, some of which are the biological, collective, and demographic. This paper will take up exclusively points connected with the demographic process according to which the numerical consistence of the different age brackets of a population, and especially of the Italian population, changes progressively and predominantly, in the older brackets.

When is a person old? Biologists and doctors, very cautiously, do not impose exact limits. However, laws made by men establish a precise limit: they say that at a certain age a worker is no longer of use in the productive effort of the collectivity and therefore has need of certain security, according to modern ideas of social security.

All the same, even in this field, opinions are not in agreement. Even if our inquiries are to be confined to western Europe (Table 1) it is found that the pension age is 65 years in the greater number of the countries which have been taken under consideration; it is a bit higher

Table 1. Old age pension eligibility according to social legislation, western European countries

Nation	Age of pension eligibility		Nation	Age of pension eligibility	
	Men	Women		Men	Women
Austria	65	60	Ireland	70	70
Belgium	65	60	Italy	60	55
Denmark	65	60	Luxembourg	65	62
Finland	65	65	Portugal	70	70
France	65	60	Spain	65	65
German Federal Republic	65	65	Sweden	67	67
Greece	65	60	Switzerland	65	63
Holland	65	65	United Kingdom	65	60
Iceland	67	67	Yugoslavia	55	50

in the countries of northern Europe; while an age limit of 60 years is found only in Italy and Yugoslavia.

In about half the countries which have been considered, the activity of women and men workers stops at the same age; in the others, eligibility for old age pensions dates from a few years before, with a difference which varies between 10 and 2 years when women are compared to men.

In almost all the countries, workers of both sexes can, with the authorization of the employer, postpone taking their retiring pension: for 5 years in Denmark, Finland, Italy, and the United Kingdom; for 8 years in Iceland; and for an unlimited period in the German Federal Republic, Austria, Belgium (confined to white collar workers), France, and Portugal.

In the greater part of the countries, this delay in benefiting from old age pension programs results in an income which at the actual time of work cessation is greater than that which the worker would have been entitled to if he had retired at the age provided for by the social security laws. Naturally, it appears logical that whether or not the worker avails himself of this possibility depends on a variety of factors, of which some personal ones (condition of health, physical efficiency, good will, etc.) have certainly had much less weight than environmental ones. Some of these factors can be indubitably favorable (interest of the employer in keeping elderly workers) while others play a completely contrary role in the greater part of western European countries (labor market, national economic situation, predominant features of the economy of the country, industrialization, etc.).

In regard to Italy, old age pension eligibility begins at 60 for men and 55 for women provided that certain conditions as to contributions have been fulfilled. It is interesting to recall that in 1898 an optional old age pension scheme was started for workers, with a minimum eligibility age of 60 years.

With the adoption of compulsory social insurance, which dates back to 1919, it was established that eligibility for old age pensions started at 65 years for men and 60 for women. The age limit for pension eligibility, at present in force, was ratified with the amendment of the social security law introduced in 1939.

It must also be noted that the age limits of 60 and 55 years, respectively, for men and for women, apply to workers, clerks, and laborers employed in private enterprise, who without doubt represent the bulk of the nation's labor force.

At the same time, the recent law which extends the rights of old age pensions to farm owners, farm hands, sharecroppers, and artisans established an age limit of 65 years, but gave women the opportunity of retiring 5 years earlier if desired.

Equally, the civil servants, i.e., civilian employees of government administrations, are generally eligible for pensions when they have reached 65 years. However, there are some exceptions in relation to rank and duties of certain special brackets for which the age limit is brought up to 70 years.

In the same way, the law has provided special measures for military personnel in permanent active service; however, this obviously covers a very small minority.

The degree of aging of the Italian population, taken as a demographic process, will be compared with what has occurred in other countries.

It is a fairly well-known fact, and one which has for some time been attentively studied by scholars of social problems, that the world population has grown enormously since the beginning of the history of our times. According to a very recent survey made by the FAO, the population increase in future years is going to take on a dizzy trend; in fact, if today the inhabitants of the world are nearly 3 billion, in the year 2000 they will be 5 billion; in 2050, 10 billion; and in 2100, 20 billion.

The estimates recently given by Baldi are in part the same (Table 2).

Table 2. World population estimates, 1650–2000

Year	World population (in millions)	Year	World population (in millions)
1650	545	1950	2500
1800	906	1980	4280
1850	1094	2000	10,000

Closely linked to this general demographic factor is another, also well known, which is the aging of the population. This is understood to mean the change in the composition of the age brackets of the population, with an increase in the percentage of the aged, or, in other words, of those who have lived more than a certain number of years. These changes are much more evident among the populations of Western civilization, particularly in those of "old" Europe.

This is clearly shown in Table 3, taken from a recent study by Tizzano (1958*b*). From this table it is obvious that the proportion of old people is the highest in France; this was true in 1900–1901 and remained so until 1930–1931. Recently Belgium has caught up with the country in question, for there the percentage of aged has nearly doubled in about a half century.

Table 3. Proportion of persons over 60 years of age of the total population, 1900 to the present, selected countries[a]

Country	1900–1901	1930–1931	Recent figures
Austria			16.0
Belgium	9.4	11.8	16.2
Canada		8.3	11.3
Czechoslovakia		10.2	
Denmark	9.8	10.8	13.7
Finland			11.3
France	12.4	14.0	16.2
Germany	7.8	11.0	14.4
Great Britain	7.8	11.6	15.6
Greece			9.7
Hungary	7.5	9.7	
India			5.7
Italy	9.6	10.8	12.0
Japan	8.3	7.4	7.9
The Netherlands	9.2	9.4	11.6
New Zealand	6.7	10.5	
Norway	10.9	11.6	14.0
Portugal	9.7	9.6	10.5
Spain			10.3
Sweden	11.9	12.8	15.0
Switzerland	9.2	10.7	15.1
United States	6.5	8.5	12.4
U.S.S.R.	7.0	6.6	6.6

[a] Source: A. Tizzano, "La durata naturale della vita umana," Difesa Sociale, *37*, 22 (1958).

Listing the different European countries according to the respective percentages of old people, it can be noted that this index does not show substantial changes from 1900–1901 to 1930–1931.

An examination of the data extracted from the most recent statistics, particularly when compared with those of 1900–1901, reveals that in some countries there has been a notable increase among the aged (Great Britain, Germany, Belgium, and Switzerland); on the contrary the percentage of old people in Greece, Spain, Portugal, and the Netherlands is very low.

For the whole of western Europe, the number of people aged 60 and over is found to be equivalent to about 140 per thousand inhabitants; from which stems the observation that Italy with its 120 old people per thousand inhabitants occupies an intermediary position among the countries of western Europe.

Again on the basis of Tizzano's data, it can be noted that, notwithstanding the fact that only somewhat fragmentary and incomplete factors are available, a progressive increase is seen in the percentage of the aged even in other parts of the world; this is particularly evident in the United States, followed by Canada and New Zealand.

In Japan and the U.S.S.R., on the other hand, an appreciable decline can be noted in these percentages and probably, apart from other considerations, the destruction of human life which occurred during the Second World War may have had an influence on it.

As is known, there are two demographic factors which have the greatest influence on the natural movement of populations—these are birth and mortality rates. Their influence before and after the eighteenth century has been very different, so much so that it has been said that during that period there was a genuine demographic revolution.

The very marked progress of medicine, hygiene, and techniques which has taken place beginning with the nineteenth century has brought about a notable decline in mortality; this is shown by the fact that the population of western Europe, which at the beginning of the nineteenth century numbered 125 million inhabitants, now after 150 years, is about 310 million. On the contrary, a high mortality rate directly connected with the embryonic condition of medical knowledge at that time, and with the frequent famines and epidemics, not to mention wars, characterized the historical period which drew to a close at the end of the eighteenth century. Births, too, which were extremely high up to the end of the 1700s, have shown a progressive decrease since the beginning of the nineteenth century.

Going on to a more thorough analysis of the Italian demographic situation, it can be seen that starting from the middle of the 1800s, exact data have been available on the size of the population, on its composition by sex and age, as well as on its birth and death rates.

Table 4 gives data which, though summarized, are sufficiently repre-

Table 4. Evolution of the age composition of the Italian population, 1861–1951, number (in thousands) and percentage distribution[a]

AGE GROUP

	0–14		15–39		40–59		60+	
Census date	Number	Per-cent	Number	Per-cent	Number	Per-cent	Number	Per-cent
31/12/1861	7446	34.2	8861	40.8	4043	18.6	1428	6.5
31/12/1871	8703	32.5	10,422	38.9	5336	19.9	2339	8.7
31/12/1881	9156	32.2	11,042	38.8	5707	20.1	2554	8.9
10/2/1901	11,070	34.4	11,856	36.5	6362	19.5	3157	9.6
10/6/1911	11,734	33.8	12,704	36.6	6594	19.0	3519	10.2
1/12/1921	12,018	31.1	15,048	38.9	7114	19.1	4024	10.4
21/4/1931	12,443	29.7	16,463	40.0	8016	19.5	4454	10.8
21/4/1936	13,165	30.9	16,650	38.1	8466	19.8	4711	11.2
4/11/1951	12,422	26.1	18,416	38.8	10,904	22.9	5774	12.2

[a] Source: A. Tizzano, "La composizione della popolazione italiana par età e sesso," Notiziario dell' Amministrazione Sanitaria, *11*, 93 (1958).

sentative of the variations which have occurred in the different age brackets of the Italian population from 1861 to 1951, the date of the last census.

During this period of time the number of inhabitants has gone from 21,777,300 units in 1861 to 47,525,500 in 1951 with an increase of more than 100 percent.

The following facts should be emphasized:

1. Children and adolescents (from 0 to 14 years) have dropped from 34.27 percent in 1861 to 26.1 percent in 1951.

2. Individuals comprising the 15-to-40-year bracket formed 40.8 percent in 1861 against 38.8 percent in 1951; that is, during the 90 years under examination this group remained fairly constant as regards the total number of its components.

3. The 40-to-60-year bracket went from 18.6 percent to 22.9 percent, the percentages found, respectively, in 1861 and 1951. It is interesting to note that, if a comparison is made between the numbers of the individuals belonging to the different 5-year periods starting from 15 years of age, a progressive percentage increase can be noted in the groups after the forty-fifth year, as was shown by Perez and Alisi (in press) (see Table 5).

Table 5. Changes in the distribution of the working population, by age groups, Italy, 1861–1951, number (in thousands) and percentage distribution[a]

| Age group | 1861 | | 1951 | |
	Number	Percent	Number	Percent
20–24	1848.5	17	4031.5	16
25–29	1856.4	17	3898.1	15
30–34	1425.7	13	2816.6	11
35–39	1692.2	16	3390.5	14
40–44	1111.6	10	3344.3	13
45–49	1212.6	11	2865.4	12
50–54	841.1	8	2499.4	10
55–59	878.0	8	2124.1	9

[a] Source: M. Perez, and A. Alisi, "Invecchiamento demografico della popolazione italiana: rilievi statistici," in press.

4. The percentage increase, already appreciable in individuals between 40 and 60, is particularly marked in those of the 60-and-over bracket, which with the passage of 90 years has gone from 6.5 percent to 12.2 percent of the whole population.

In other terms, Italy too has undergone a progressive demographic aging similar, although with a certain delay, to what has occurred in the whole of the western world.

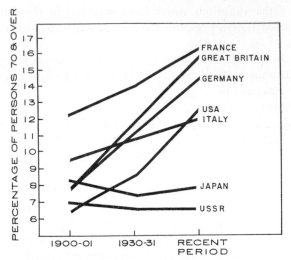

Fig. 1. Changes in the proportion of persons 70 years of age and over, selected countries, 1900–1901 to 1961

Source: A. Tizzano, "La durata naturale dell a vita umana," Difesa Sociale *37,* 22 (1958).

This trend is clearly seen in Fig. 1, plotted on the basis of Tizzano's (1958*b*) data.

The demographic aging of the Italian population, taken in itself,

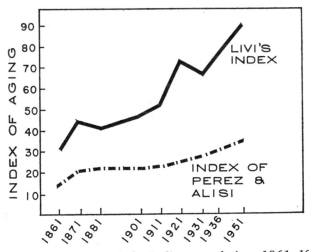

Fig. 2. Indices of aging of the Italian population, 1861–1951

Source: M. Perez, and A. Alisi, Invecchiamento demografico della popolazione italiana: rilievi statistici, to be published. Livi's index: (population 65 and over)/(population 0–5) × 100; Perez and Alisi: (population 60 and over)/ (population 0–20) × 100.

is, among other things, shown very clearly in Fig. 2 in the curves plotted by Perez and Alisi on the basis of the two indices of aging computed from the data of the different censuses of the Italian population from 1861 to 1951.

What are the causes of this trend? Undoubtedly the mortality rate has declined; in fact from the 828,992 deaths in 1887, equivalent to a mortality rate of 2799.2 per hundred thousand inhabitants, it has dropped to 446,689 deaths in 1955 equivalent to a rate of 912 per hundred thousand inhabitants.

All the same an examination of the mortality rates in the single age brackets (Table 6) clearly shows that the progress of medical science and technique has enormously reduced deaths in the very young groups, i.e., before the age of procreation. On the contrary, the percentage figures of deaths record an increase, in the period nearest to the present, of mortality in the oldest brackets, evidently because of a decline in that natural selection which mowed down the weakest subjects who formerly died at a very early age.

Table 6. Changes in mortality rates by age and sex,
Italy, 1881–1882 to 1950–1953

	MEN				WOMEN			
	1881–	1950–	Change		1881–	1950–	Change	
Age	1882	1953	Absolute	Percent	1882	1953	Absolute	Percent
0	212.4	67.5	−144.9	−68.8	191.3	58.8	−132.5	−69.4
1	109.2	10.2	−99.0	−90.9	108.2	10.4	−97.8	−90.6
2	53.3	3.5	−49.8	−93.4	53.6	3.3	−50.3	−93.8
3	33.1	2.1	−31.0	−93.7	33.6	1.9	−31.7	−94.3
4	23.9	1.6	−22.3	−93.3	24.6	1.4	−22.6	−94.2
5	17.9	1.3	−16.6	−92.7	18.7	1.1	−17.6	−94.1
10	5.9	0.8	−5.1	−86.5	6.5	0.6	−5.9	−90.8
15	5.0	1.0	−4.0	−80.0	6.1	0.7	−5.4	−88.5
20	8.2	1.5	−6.7	−81.7	7.0	1.1	−6.8	−86.1
25	8.7	1.7	−7.0	−80.5	9.1	1.3	−7.8	−85.7
30	7.9	2.0	−5.9	−74.7	9.8	1.6	−8.2	−83.7
35	8.7	2.5	−6.3	−71.3	10.5	2.0	−8.5	−81.0
40	10.6	3.3	−7.3	−68.9	10.9	2.6	−8.3	−76.1
45	13.3	5.5	−7.8	−58.6	12.0	3.8	−8.2	−68.3
50	17.4	8.7	−8.7	−50.0	14.6	5.3	−9.3	−63.7
55	23.3	12.8	−10.5	−45.1	20.8	8.0	−12.8	−61.5
60	31.7	19.3	−12.4	−39.1	30.1	12.7	−17.4	−57.8
65	48.5	29.0	−19.5	−40.2	49.5	22.2	−27.3	−55.2
70	70.0	46.1	−27.9	−37.7	79.7	38.8	−40.0	−51.3
75	105.7	79.1	−26.6	−25.1	113.9	69.5	−44.4	−39.0
80	145.2	128.2	−17.0	−11.7	151.3	115.4	−35.0	−23.8
85	193.6	198.8	+5.2	+26.8	196.9	176.4	−20.5	−10.4
90	248.6	282.4	+33.8	+13.6	246.5	247.7	+1.2	+0.5
95	307.1	370.7	+63.6	+20.7	297.3	321.6	+24.3	+8.2
100	365.6	453.7	+88.1	+24.1	347.4	391.2	+44.1	+12.7

The direct consequence of the variations which have occurred in the mortality rate is that in these last decades a much greater number of individuals have reached a more advanced age; however, it is theoretically possible that before becoming old, these individuals, in addition to increasing the ranks of the younger groups, may appreciably increase the very young groups through an increase of births.

It appears obvious from the above discussion that the decrease in the death rate could not have caused the aging of the population which has been observed, if two other factors had not been present, namely, the decline of births and emigration.

Table 7. *Variations in the crude birth rate, Italy, 1871–1955*

Years	Birth rate	Years	Birth rate
1871–1880	36.9	1941	20.9
1881–1890	37.8	1942	20.5
1891–1900	35.0	1943	19.9
1901–1910	32.7	1944	18.3
1911–1920	27.3	1945	18.3
1921–1930	28.6	1946	23.0
1931	24.9	1947	22.7
1932	23.8	1948	22.0
1933	23.8	1949	20.4
1934	23.5	1950	19.6
1935	23.4	1951	18.4
1936	22.4	1952	17.8
1937	22.9	1953	17.5
1938	23.8	1954	18.0
1939	23.6	1955	17.7
1940	23.5		

Table 7 shows clearly the downward trend of birth rates; this is particularly evident from 1930–1935 on as a result of the limitation of births, a practice which unfortunately has also been spreading in Italy in these last decades (Occhiuto, 1956).

In a recent survey made by the FAO, it is stated that the problem of hunger is not inherent in the growth of the population but rather in the deficiency of agricultural production and, I might add, in technical progress which is still insufficient in spite of the marvels which have been accomplished in these last years.

Also appreciable, although in a much less degree, has been the influence of emigration; Table 8 shows the migratory trend over a

Table 8. *Variations in the number of Italian emigrants, 1871–1955*

Decade	Average annual emigration	Decade	Average annual emigration
1871–1880	117,596	1911–1920	382,807
1881–1890	187,920	1921–1930	257,844
1891–1900	283,473	1931–1940	70,265
1901–1910	602,669	1946–1955	248,405

period of time which has contributed to raising the age level of the population by subtracting from it a certain number of working-age individuals, i.e., between 20 and 60, which form the numerically largest group of emigrants.

As we have set forth the degree to which the Italian population has been affected by the process of demographic aging which has been seen in the whole Western world, let us now look at the consequence of this. It can be summed up in the realization that what 90 years ago was an individual problem confined to a limited number of elderly or old people is today, on account of the absolute and percentage increase of old people, a problem which involves the whole collectivity.

If up to 90 years ago it was enough that the problems of the aged should be dealt with through the efforts of individual charitable institutions, today it is absolutely necessary in Italy, as elsewhere, that this question be handled through an organized plan guaranteeing, on account of the demographic aging of the population, that these shall be classified with priority among the most urgent problems which scourge society.

At present in Italy the security law covering old age pensions protects those old people leaving the labor force who, having complied with the conditions of contribution, are eligible for the pension; for other old people who have not earned their eligibility to the pension the legislation on public assistance applies, according to which the old people are included in the much wider category of those unable to work.

Confining our investigations to the first group, notably more consistent than the second, we can see that the worker, having reached 60 years of age, is declared no longer suitable for work and is pensioned.

According to a recent survey made by the I.S.S.A. in Italy, the holders of old age pensions derived from compulsory insurance in 1956 numbered 2,198,000, equivalent to 20.7 percent of all insured workers. In financial terms, in 1956 in relation to a national income of 12,640,000 million of which 47.4 percent was represented by earned income (I.S.S.A.), the outlay for old age pensions was 179,717 million, equivalent to 1.42 percent of the national income.

The situation has been further aggravated during these last years; at the end of 1958 the number of holders of old age pensions deriving from compulsory insurance was around 4,000,000; the increase recorded at that date is due, in addition to the natural increase in pensioners, to the extension of the security protection to farm owners, farm hands, and sharecroppers. To the above figure must be added about a million and a half pensioners who are former civil servants and employees of local "Enti" or government recognized organizations, etc.

Apart from these figures, including in our field of observation the old people who for some reason are not eligible for the benefits provided for by the law, we must point out that on the basis of just the data from the last census (1951) individuals over 60 years old represented 12.2 percent of the population, while those between 20 and 60 years represented 53 percent, and those between 0 and 20 formed 34.8 percent.

In other terms, very little more than one-half of the population must provide for the needs of the other half and without doubt the relation will change appreciably when it is considered that not all individuals in the age bracket between 20 and 60 are productive (unemployed, disabled, etc.)

Such a situation is undoubtedly onerous, particularly in a country like Italy which has a somewhat low national earned income per inhabitant.

In confirmation of this it is enough to glance at the amounts of the old age pensions derived from compulsory insurance; according to the data of July, 1958, 70.52 percent of these pensions were less than 10,000 liras a month, 20.73 percent were between 10,000 and 19,999 liras monthly, 6.65 percent were between 20,000 and 29,999 liras monthly, while only 2.1 percent reached or exceeded 30,000 liras monthly.

The direct consequence of such a situation is that a number of the old age pensioners are obliged in order to satisfy the most elementary requirements of life, to seek work, even if only modestly. According to a recent survey by Petrilli (1959), it appears in fact that 90 percent of the individuals between 60 and 65 who enjoy the old age benefits still continue to work. And it may be added that the greater part of these pensioners work in conditions of underemployment which are damaging to themselves and to the entire economy of our country where there is always a certain number of unemployed and where the rising generation of workers finds jobs only with difficulty (altogether the number of unemployed and those in search of their first jobs amounted in 1958 to 1,300,000 units).

This situation, if it is serious today, will become ever more so in the future if, as is probable, the statistical estimates of the actuaries prove correct, according to which the proportion of the 60-and-over age bracket will go up from the 12.2 percent of the 1951 Census to 15.7 percent in 1971 (Somogyi, 1957). According to Baldi (1960), the over-60 group will rocket up from 6,400,000 in 1961 to 10,-650,000 in 2001.

Therefore it is clear that if society is not already providing adequately for the needs of the aged worker, the situation will deteriorate in future years with serious repercussions for the national economy.

But, in addition to this, we cannot remain indifferent when faced with the drama of those who after a life spent in work suddenly, on account of the inexorable arrival of the age limit, are the responsibility of a society which, among other things, is not in a position to reimburse them for the salary they have lost.

Now if we consider that the Italian economy has almost reached the limit of supporting the security burdens, we might make our own interpretation of this extract from the English White Book on pensions, where it is stated: "No rich country can level out the alarming deficits created . . . by a decrease in the workers and an increase in the number of pensioners and the duration of their lives. . . ." which has been quoted by Baldi. It is therefore useless to count on an effective improvement in the pension income; there is nothing to do but examine the possibility of a better redistribution of this income, bringing the pension age (with a few exceptions for given categories of workers) to at least 65 years.

This, far from proposing measures damaging to single individuals, would enable avoidance of the damage of what might be defined as the crisis of pensioning which arises when the worker, still physically efficient, is deprived of his work and placed in a condition of financial need.

If we do not want our old people in future years to curse the advances in medical science and techniques which have enabled them to reach a very advanced age, we must seriously think, first of all, of giving them freedom from want, in their own interest and in that of the whole community, by keeping them in the productive cycle of the nation for a longer period.

Medicine tells us that the 60 and 65 year olds can still work and therefore, let us not forget, produce wealth. This is because they can overcome the weakening of physical forces, which is inevitably and undeniably linked to aging, with experience. All of this has been thoroughly confirmed by the already numerous investigations carried out during recent years in the United States, Sweden, and Belgium (not to mention other countries) and also by the social legislation of the majority of Western countries which has brought the age for pension eligibility to 65.

To this must be added, according to a recent study, that in 1951 the over-65 age bracket represented 15.4 percent of the self-employed and 1.7 percent of employees; it is clear that the difference between the two groups is a direct consequence of the absurd limit of the existing law, and it is equally clear that in 1951 a high proportion of the over-65 group nɔt only was working, but also was capable of organizing, managing, and usefully performing its own work.

Nor can it be said that keeping older people at work represents a danger for young workers. Work produces wealth and, thus, the retiring of individuals who are still potentially active is translated on one side into a burden and on the other into a particularly serious loss. This will become more pronounced in the future, since progress in techniques requires a long period of training for young people who remain for a longer time dependent on society than in the past.

A similar argument can be advanced concerning the unemployed. It is certainly not sound economics to give work to the unemployed who, in addition to everything else, often lack specialized training. This is at the cost of dismissing the older worker, who is still efficient, from his job and providing him with insufficient economic independence if he is pensioned. The dismissed worker will do everything possible to return and take his place in the productive cycle. In many cases he will succeed, but only at the high price of accepting a situation of underemployment which constitutes an effective and real damage both to the old workman and to society.

Lastly, attention should be drawn to the fact that the elderly workman, even when he is no longer capable of keeping his job, can still continue to bring the useful, indispensable contribution of his experience to society for a long time. This is particularly needed at a time like the present when, because of technical progress, the lack of specialized elements to train the rising generation of workers is keenly felt.

This is especially true in Italy which has not only the highest percentage of illiterates (13 percent against 2 percent maximum for the other countries in western Europe) but also the lowest percentage of trained and specialized young workers. According to the data given by Baldi, 46 percent of Italians attended only the first three elementary grades in schools, 30 percent have nothing more than an elementary school certificate, and less than 2 percent have attended a professional training school.

The National Institute for Pensioners of Italy has used every effort to meet the most imperative needs of old workers and to promote investigations and discussions of the subject. The achievements made in the last 5 years are a clear demonstration that in Italy work, and serious work, is being done. It is with the peace of mind which comes from the conviction of having done one's duty that everyone in Italy dedicates himself with enthusiasm and faith to the accomplishment of the work undertaken.

REFERENCES

Baldi, G. M. 1960. Una svolta storica: la realtà biologica, demografica ed economica modificano i termini e le dimensioni dei problemi previdenziali. Milano.

Occhiuto, A. 1956. Invecchiamento della popolazione italiana e cause che lo determinano. Previdenza sociale, 12: 619.

Perez, M., and Alisi, A. Invecchiamento demografico della popolazione italiana: rilievi statistici. (In press.)

Petrilli, G. 1959. Intervento nella sezione sociale del II° Convegno O.N.P.I. Atti del II° Convegno medico-sociale O.N.P.I. Ed. Il Pensiero Scientifico. Roma.

Somogyi, S. 1957. Fertilità umana e trasformazione economica con prospettive demografiche per l'Italia. Ed. Ist. Medicina Sociale. Roma.

Tizzano, A. 1958a. La composizione della popolazione italiana per età e sesso. Notiziario dell' Amministrazione sanitaria, 11: 93.

——— 1958b. La durata naturale della vita umana. Difesa Sociale, 37: 22.

Some Problems in Measuring the Economic
Status of the Aged in the United States

LENORE A. EPSTEIN

Insofar as a society fails to identify, by fact and not by inference, its contemporary social problems it must expect its social conscience and its democratic values to languish. [Titmuss, 1960, p. 8]

WITH these words, Richard M. Titmuss of the London School of Economics recently challenged the social scientist to provide the hard facts of poverty and dependency. There can be no doubt that the precision with which the incidence of poverty and the levels of living of the dependent can be measured influences the character and development of programs designed to resolve or alleviate the problem.

The purpose of this paper is to lay out for inspection various measures relating to the economic status of persons aged 65 years and over in the United States, in particular, to indicate the problems created by varying definitions of the income-receiving unit and the significance of diverse concepts of income and method of its allocation among family members. The national debate during the past year on the medical-care cost problems of the aged provides telling illustrations of the diverse inferences that can be drawn from the same data.

Economists and statisticians specializing in the field of national income research have been wrestling for decades with problems connected with the measurement and interpretation of the distribution of income.[1] They have generally taken a very broad view, however, focusing on the projective value of the distributions, the consumption-saving function, and the implications of the apparent degree of inequality for national welfare.

Relatively little attention has been directed to the problems peculiar

---

[1] See, for example, *Studies in Income and Wealth,* published by the National Bureau of Economic Research, New York, for the Conference on Research in Income and Wealth (formed in 1936), particularly Volumes 5, 13, and 15, and *Income and Wealth,* published by Bowes and Bowes, London, for the International Association for Research in Income and Wealth (established in 1947), particularly Series 6.

to handling data bearing on the well-being of the aged. It is these which shall be considered. First to be taken up will be different definitions of the recipient unit and the related question of the method of allocating income (however defined) among family members. Second, various possible definitions of income will be discussed and an attempt will be made to assess the effect of broadening the concept not only to include current cash receipts but also to reflect asset holdings and/or income in kind, as from home ownership or home-food production. This seems a prerequisite to definition of terms in ways that are precise and yet adapted to the practical needs of social policy making.

Certain inherent limitations of surveys shall be ignored because they are not peculiar to measuring the economic status of the aged. One is the fact that samples do not represent very accurately the small number of cases with very large incomes, which makes them poor bases for estimating national aggregates. Another is the tendency of field surveys to exaggerate somewhat the proportion of units having little or no income, because income received in small amounts may be forgotten.

The sources from which an aged person derives his income have an important impact on his welfare in the sense that some can be depended on for life and some are clearly temporary. This is not the subject of this paper; however, it has received considerable attention (Steiner and Dorfman, 1957; Epstein, 1959). Suffice it to note here that much of the analysis of data for those 65 years and older would be more meaningful if these people were subclassified by degree of attachment to the labor force. This, however, would open up questions as to the suitability of present labor-force concepts in studying the aged that might well be the subject of a separate paper.

THE RECIPIENT UNIT
The conceptual question

The recipient unit suitable for analysis of income data obviously depends on the focus of the analysis. For study of the age-employment-income cycle, the individual is of course the most suitable unit. If, on the other hand, interest centers on the level of living, then the consuming unit is the most suitable (Miller, 1955; Sheldon, 1958).

But what is the appropriate consuming unit? The three-generation family has become less and less common in the United States. Nevertheless, of all persons aged 65 and over in 1959, 24 percent with no spouse shared a home with children or other relatives, and about the same proportion of the aged couples had children or other relatives in the home (U.S. Bureau of the Census, 1959). In some cases this represents a "normal" relationship, i.e., a son or daughter has not yet left the parental home. More often, however, the joint living arrangements reflect the need of an elderly person for financial support or physical care, desire for companionship, or a combination of reasons. More than one-fifth of all aged couples last year shared a home with a child or other relative who was over 24 years of age (or married if younger), and therefore likely to be in the labor force.

The crucial question then is whether it is useful for social policy determination to take account of the resources of all related persons who live together or whether the analyst should try to segregate the resources of the aged from those of adult children and other relatives. In my judgment, in a society which expects the retired worker and his widow to have a modicum of financial independence, the second approach is by far the more useful. As Dorothy Brady demonstrated with cogency:

If incomes imposed no limitation on the living arrangements, the number of consumer units would tend towards a maximum defined by the distribution of the members of the family by type, sex, and marital status. . . . With sufficient income a man can contribute to the maintenance of his parents and of a grown son or daughter in separate living quarters but low incomes may impel the three generations to dwell in one household. . . . Separate households are the rule when both the children and their parents can afford them and seem to prevail when one or the other has sufficient income to help finance more than one consumer unit. [Brady, 1958, pp. 269, 271, and 274]

Attesting to Dr. Brady's thesis is a decline from 33 percent to 24 percent in the proportion of nonmarried aged persons who shared a home with relatives, during the 9-year period 1950 to 1959, when incomes of the aged were rising (Sheldon, 1958).

Definitional problems of available survey data

Census income surveys. The Census Bureau series on income include distributions for men and women aged 65 and over not in institutions, also for families with head aged 65 and over, and separately for aged individuals who are living alone or lodging. The family income data are widely quoted, but they are difficult to interpret both because the family members may not constitute a meaningful economic unit and because the designation of the head may be somewhat arbitrary, particularly when a household contains one elderly parent and adult children.

The 1958 family income data, for example, represent 6 million families with head aged 65 and over. They were distributed by type as follows (in millions):

Total families	6.0
Husband-wife families	4.6
With no other adults	3.5
With one or more other adults	1.1
Other families	1.4
Male head	0.4
Female head	1.0

The husband-wife families that include other members 18 and over (1.1 million) and those with nonmarried aged persons as head (1.4 million) of course varied widely in size and composition. In all, the 6 million families with head 65 and over included 6.5 million members under 65 and 9.1 million older members. In addition to these 9.1 million aged persons, there were 2.3 million aged persons living in families with younger heads. One may well ask whether or not there is a really significant difference in the economic status of the 1.4 million aged persons reported as nonmarried family heads and the 2.3 million reported as relatives (other than wives) of the family head, since the designation of the head varies with the person who replies to the enumerator's questions, depending as much on ethnic background and mores as on economic relationships. It is clear, however, that the 2.3 million are in effect lost in the family income analysis, and such persons are likely to have smaller incomes than those who are married or the nonmarried who live alone.

Information collected by the Census Bureau for the Steiner-Dorfman study of the resources of the aged in 1951 demonstrates clearly that income data for Census-type families with an aged head should not be taken to represent the situation of all aged persons. In Table 1 the income of couples living alone is compared with that of couples who share a home with relatives. As might be expected, those who share tend to have smaller incomes. On the other hand, the total family income is very much larger for those who share than for couples alone.

Special tabulations of the 1956 Census income data (purchased by the Social Security Administration) bear out these findings (see Table 2 and Fig. 1). They not only show the differences in the reported income of husband-wife families with and without grown children or other relatives in the home, but they also indicate clearly why

Table 1. Income and living arrangements: percentage distribution by money income in 1951 of couples with head aged 65 and over and other aged men and women by presence of relatives, and percentage distribution by total money income in 1951 of families that include aged persons (continental United States, noninstitutional population)[a]

| | MARRIED COUPLES | | | NONMARRIED MEN | | | NONMARRIED WOMEN | | |
| | | Sharing a home with relatives | | | Sharing a home with relatives | | | Sharing a home with relatives | |
Money income (in dollars)	No relatives in home	Own income	Income of family	Living alone or lodging	Own income	Income of family	Living alone or lodging	Own income	Income of family
Less than 500	15.2	26.4	5.7	33.2	47.6	4.2	46.0	72.6	7.7
500–999	20.1	18.1	4.6	35.5	24.0	11.8	34.9	18.3	9.3
1000–1499	16.2	13.7	9.1	9.7	11.8	8.5	8.2	3.0	6.6
1500–1999	10.4	10.9	7.6	5.8	4.3	8.9	4.8	2.4	7.7
2000–2499	8.4	9.3	6.1	4.2	3.1	8.5	2.6	0.6	5.4
2500–2999	5.3	5.3	8.4	3.1	2.0	7.0	0.9	0.8	5.8
3000–4999	15.9	12.4	27.1	6.2	3.2	23.2	1.3	2.1	31.5
5000 or more	8.5	3.9	31.3	2.4	4.0	27.8	1.4	0.3	26.1

[a] Source: P. O. Steiner, and R. Dorfman, The Economic Status of the Aged, University of California Press, Berkeley, California, 1957, Table 202 for own income of couples and nonmarried persons; family income data unpublished.

Table 2. *Income and family type: percentage distribution by money income in 1956 of all families with head aged 65 and over, of husband-wife families by presence of relatives, and of other families with aged head (continental United States, noninstitutional population)*[a]

| Money income (in dollars) | All families | Husband-wife families | | | Other families |
		Total	No relatives in home	Relatives in home	
Under 1000	15.1	14.4	16.1	9.7	17.2
1000–1999	24.6	27.2	32.2	13.6	16.9
2000–2999	16.6	17.4	19.3	12.4	14.2
3000–3999	11.6	11.0	10.4	12.4	13.4
4000–4999	8.3	7.9	7.0	10.3	9.5
5000–5999	7.3	6.8	5.6	10.1	8.8
6000–6999	3.6	3.0	2.1	5.6	5.4
7000–9999	8.0	7.1	4.0	15.7	10.6
10,000 or more	4.9	5.2	3.3	10.1	4.0
Median income (in dollars)	2550	2420	2080	4200	3120
Number in population (in thousands)	5741	4292	3071	1221	1449

[a] Source: U.S. Bureau of the Census, *Current Population Reports: Population Characteristics*, Series P-20, No. 83, and *Consumer Income*, Series P-60, No. 27; and unpublished tabulations prepared for the Social Security Administration.

family-income data raise problems of interpretation that plague their users, i.e., why data for all families with an aged head cannot be interpreted with precision as relating specifically to the aged population or to any particular type of family. The fact that for the aged the family income distribution is more favorable for broken ("other") than for husband-wife families—contrary to the situation in the general population—suggests that much of the income of the former is contributed by members other than the head. The fact that three-fourths of the "other" families had an aged woman as head and barely one-fifth reported the head as employed supports this inference. Unfortunately, comparative income data have not been tabulated for families with head under 65 and at least one member 65 and over.

The 1951 study, however, permits comparison of the income of aged nonmarried persons who live alone and those who live with relatives—and with the income of the entire family, regardless of who might have been reported as family head (Table 1). The data suggest that low income is probably more of a factor in the decision to join up with relatives for nonmarried than for married persons. Data from this study indicate also that aged persons reported to the Census enumerator as family heads are likely to have somewhat more

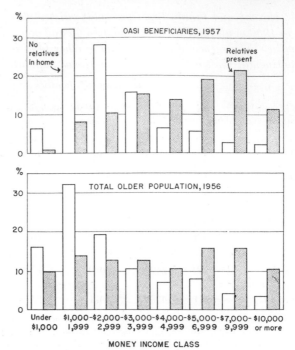

Fig. 1. Income of husband-wife families with aged head, by presence of relatives, percentage distribution.

income than those reported as parent or other relative of the head, as shown by the following median income figures, in dollars (Steiner and Dorfman, 1957):

	Men	Women
Family head	769	302
Parent of head	352	0
Other relative of head	500	136

Survey of consumer finances. Income data collected for the Federal Reserve Board in the Surveys of Consumer Finances, for a relatively small sample, are usually presented for spending units (including one-person units), which by definition have fewer income recipients than families as defined by the Census. The spending unit classification goes a step further toward identifying the precise group that pools income to form an effective consuming unit, and therefore might be considered more meaningful for analysis of economic well-being. But this classification scheme, or at least the manner of its use, also raises problems in interpretation, especially when dealing with data on the resources of the aged. Thus, it is estimated that the 1958 survey data for spending units with aged head covered only about three-fourths of the aged population of 15 million. Excluded from the survey by definition were persons living in large rooming houses or other transient quarters, as well as those in institutions—some 650,000 aged persons according to Census Bureau estimates. Of the 14.3 million aged in private households, about one-fourth, it is estimated, were members of spending units headed by a person under 65; they did not have more than $15 income per week or they pooled any income they had with that of the primary spending unit.

Table 3 provides a comparison of the distribution of 1958 income for Census families and for spending units. Spending units appear to be more concentrated in the $1000 to $4000 income range, with fewer reporting less than $1000 and more than $6000, when the distributions for 1-person and 2-or-more-person units are compared with Census individual and family income distributions, respectively. When family data from the Survey of Consumer Finances (not previously available by age of head) are compared with Census data for families, the differences are accentuated, because the family includes more income recipients.

Among the factors believed to account for the smaller number with very low incomes shown by the Survey of Consumer Finances are the greater detail on income sources in that survey, which places its main emphasis on financial information, the exclusion of the lodging-house population, and, on the other hand, the larger total number of unattached individuals accounted for in the Census survey.[2]

Consumer expenditure surveys. For its 1950 survey of consumer income and expenditure, as for several earlier ones, the Bureau of Labor Statistics used a classification based on a consumer-unit concept. Data were collected for consumer units as they existed throughout the survey year, not necessarily at the time of interview, that is, for "reconstructed" units (Lamale, 1959). They are presented for families of 2 or more related persons who pooled income for their major items of expenditure, and for persons living alone or with nonrelatives, termed 1-person families. Persons who were related and living in one household were considered as forming one family

[2] For comparisons of Census and Survey of Consumer Finances data and a discussion of conceptual and statistical differences, see the following papers: Goldsmith, 1951, 1958*b*; M. G. Sirken, E. S. Maynes, and J. A. Frechtling, 1958; and R. Wasson, A. Hurwitz, and I. Schweiger, 1951.

Table 3. Income of families and spending units compared: percentage distribution by money income in 1958 of families and unrelated persons with head aged 65 and over and of spending units with head aged 65 and over (continental United States, noninstitutional population)[a,b]

Money income (in dollars)	BUREAU OF THE CENSUS Families and unrelated individuals			SURVEY OF CONSUMER FINANCES[b] Spending units			Families		
	Total	Families of 2 or more	Unrelated individuals	Total	Units of 2 or more persons	1-person units	Total	Families of 2 or more	1-person families
Less than 1000	28	13	54	20	8	38	18	7	39
1000–1999	26	25	29	34	29	40	30	27	38
2000–2999	14	18	7	17	22	9	16	20	8
3000–3999	9	12	5	12	15	7	12	14	8
4000–4999	7	9	2	6	8	2	6	8	3
5000–5999	4	6	1	4	5	2	4	6	1
6000 or more	11	17	2	8	13	2	13	20	2
Number (in millions)	9.5	6.0	3.5	8.6	5.1	3.5	8.0	5.3	2.7

[a] Source: U.S. Bureau of the Census, *Current Population Reports: Consumer Income*, Series P-60, No. 33, for data for families and unrelated persons; combined distribution derived by weighting by population estimates in the same report; U.S. Board of Governors of the Federal Reserve System, "1959 Survey of Consumer Finances," *Federal Reserve Bulletin*, July, 1959, Supplementary Table 2 for all spending units, unpublished data made available by the Federal Reserve Board.

[b] Data relate only to persons in private households.

unless it was clear that some of the group, such as married children, kept their finances separately. Never-married children were always included as members of the parents' family.

The significance of this classification is indicated by a special analysis of these data by Eleanor M. Snyder, for the Franklin D. Roosevelt Foundation, which shows that in 1950 in the United States "6.4 million urban families and unrelated individuals had permanent low-income status. . . . If a nuclear family concept is adopted (this definition counts separately each family in a doubled-up unit) the total of substandard units is raised to 8.5 million." (Givens, 1958.)

Survey of Old-Age and Survivors Insurance beneficiaries. Periodic surveys of the characteristics and resources of aged beneficiaries under the Old-Age, Survivors, and Disability Insurance program—the last two undertaken late in 1951 and 1957—have taken as the unit for analysis the beneficiary group, that is, the person entitled to benefits as a retired worker (and his or her spouse, if any) or as a widow, including those in institutions. Income data are available separately for beneficiary couples and nonmarried beneficiaries classified by presence of adult children or other relatives in the home.[3] The findings further illustrate some of the pitfalls that result from using family income data regardless of family status and living arrangements. As in the case of the 1951 Steiner-Dorfman study, the 1957 beneficiary survey not only permits comparison of the incomes of couples and other aged persons who live alone and those who share a home with relatives, but it allows comparison of the family's income and the personal income of the aged couple or individual who shares a home (see Table 4). The general findings parallel closely those of the 1951 study. The difference between the distribution for aged couples living alone and those sharing a home with relatives is much greater, however, for OASI beneficiaries than for other aged couples (see Fig. 1).

Allocation of income among members

It has been customary when considering programs designed to meet the needs of the indigent aged to estimate the number who are needy from Census Bureau reports on the income of individuals, because annual income data have not been available for couples and separately for other aged persons, regardless of their living arrangements. This practice has been roundly attacked as misleading on the ground that married women without income fall in the low-income group regardless of the husband's income.

[3] Couples with minor children were excluded from the surveys.

Table 4. Income and living arrangements: percentage distribution by money income in 1957 of retired couples and nonmarried OASI beneficiaries by presence of relatives, and percentage distribution by total money income in 1957 of families that include aged beneficiaries (OASI beneficiaries aged 65 and over)[a]

| | RETIRED COUPLES | | | NONMARRIED BENEFICIARIES | | |
| | | *Sharing a home with relatives* | | | *Sharing a home with relatives* | |
Money income[b] *(in dollars)*	*No relatives in home*	*Own income*	*Income of family*	*Living alone or lodging*	*Own income*	*Income of family*
Less than 1000	6.6	9.0	0.7	38.6	57.5	1.5
1000–1499	16.1	20.2	2.8	27.6	19.4	5.0
1500–1999	16.3	21.1	4.7	15.4	10.0	5.9
2000–2499	16.5	16.2	4.5	7.9	5.7	5.2
2500–2999	11.8	9.6	5.2	3.5	2.3	4.8
3000–3999	15.6	11.0	14.5	3.0	1.6	10.9
4000–4999	6.3	6.8	12.9	1.3	1.6	11.5
5000–6999	5.7	3.8	18.1	1.3	0.9	24.0
7000–9999	2.7	0.9	20.4	1.0	0.5	16.7
10,000 or more	2.3	1.4	10.8	0.4	0.4	8.8
Unknown			5.4			5.7

[a] Source: Social Security Administration, U.S. Bureau of Old-Age and Survivors Insurance, *National Survey of Old-Age and Survivors Insurance Beneficiaries*, 1957, unpublished data.

[b] Income during a 12-month period from Fall, 1956, to Fall, 1957.

It has been necessary to rely on Census income data for individuals (such as are shown in Table 5) because the regular Census tabulation program has not allowed for matching the reports of husbands and wives to obtain a composite income figure for aged couples.

Analysis of the special tabulations of 1956 Census data for aged couples do suggest, however, that income data for individuals yield a remarkably good approximation to the actual situation with regard to the size of the low-income aged population. Based on the tabulations for individuals, in which wives supported entirely by their husbands are treated as having no income, the proportion of all aged persons with less than $1000 income for 1956 comes to 61 percent. The family data for the same year show 48 percent of the couples living alone had total money incomes of less than $2000 for the year, i.e., less than $1000 per person, and 57 percent of the individuals alone or lodging with nonrelatives had less than $1000. The incomes of aged couples and other aged persons sharing a home with relatives were not tabulated separately, but as noted above, both the Steiner-Dorfman and the beneficiary surveys indicate that such aged persons are more heavily concentrated at the low income levels. Even if we

Table 5. *Income of persons: percentage distribution by money income in 1958 of persons aged 65 and over, by sex (continental United States, noninstitutional population)*[a]

Money income (in dollars)	Total	Men	Women
Less than 1000	57.0	32.4	77.5
Zero	16.4	3.8	26.9
1–499[b]	14.4	8.7	19.2
500–999	26.2	19.9	31.4
1000–1999	22.8	32.1	15.0
1000–1499	14.6	20.0	10.2
1500–1999	8.1	12.1	4.8
2000–2999	7.9	13.4	3.3
2000–2499	4.9	8.3	2.1
2500–2999	3.0	5.1	1.2
3000–4999	8.1	14.3	2.8
5000 or more	4.2	7.7	1.4
Median income (dollars) for			
All persons	870	1440	560
Income recipients	1040	1488	776
Year-round full-time workers	n.a.[c]	3561	2291
Number in population (in thousands)	14907	6770	8137

[a] Source: U.S. Bureau of the Census, *Current Population Reports: Consumer Income*, Series P-60, No. 33, "Income of Families and Persons in the United States: 1958," January 15, 1960, Table 24.

[b] Includes a few persons reporting a net loss.

[c] n.a. = not available.

assume, for purposes of estimation, a somewhat more favorable income situation than probably existed for those sharing a home,[4] it nevertheless appears that some 58 percent of all aged persons had less than $1000, compared to the 61 percent calculated from the income data for persons.

In special studies of the aged, income reports are sometimes obtained for a couple rather than for the members separately. This was the case in the study of the health needs of the aged, undertaken by the National Opinion Research Center for the Health Information Foundation in 1957. Their first report on the financial resources of the sample population, however, did not provide the data on the income of couples and of other aged persons but instead an income size distribution for aged persons with income, in which the couple's

[4] The following three assumptions were made: (1) that the proportion of couples with less than $2000 was the same for those who shared a home as for those living apart from relatives, (2) that aged nonmarried persons classified as family heads were distributed by income as aged persons living alone, and (3) that the proportion having personal incomes of less than $1000 was only half again as large as in the case of other aged persons living with relatives as in the case of individuals who lived independently.

income was treated as the husband's and married women were excluded. As the author said, this procedure of course had "the result of increasing the median income of both men and women with income. In the case of men, this is because higher total incomes than are actually correct for individuals have been reported; in the case of women, the small amounts of OASDI and OAA benefits received by married women would lower the median, were they to be included in the tabulation (Shanas, 1959, p. 4, Table 30).

Unpublished tabulations of data from this survey, recently made available, provide the sort of information needed for program planning, i.e., the income of couples, subclassified by whether the wife is under or over 65, and the income of nonmarried men and women, further cross-classified by the main source of income (see Table 6).

Table 6. Income of couples by age of wife and income source: percentage distribution by money income in 1956 of couples with head aged 65 and over, by age of wife, and by main source of income (continental United States, noninstitutional population)[a]

MARRIED COUPLES WITH HEAD AGED 65 AND OVER

		Age of wife		Main source of income[b]		
Money income (in dollars)	Total	65 and over	Under 65	Employment	Social insurance and related programs	Public assistance
1–499	4.1	4.8	3.4	3.9	2.2	8.5
500–999	12.7	14.3	10.9	6.8	14.6	31.9
1000–1999	26.3	25.4	27.3	10.7	41.0	53.2
2000–2999	19.8	25.8	13.4	12.2	29.8	6.4
3000–3999	12.0	13.1	10.9	18.5	7.9	
4000–4999	8.4	5.6	11.3	15.1	3.4	
5000–5999	5.5	4.4	6.7	10.2		
6000–6999	2.7	2.4	2.9	5.4	1.1	
7000–9999	5.1	2.8	7.6	9.8		
10,000 or more	3.5	1.6	5.5	7.3		

[a] Source: National Opinion Research Center, *1957 Survey of the Health Needs of the Aged,* unpublished tabulations made available by the Survey Director.
[b] Couples whose main source of income was from private pensions, investments, or relatives not shown separately because of small number.

A rough calculation from these tabulations yields about the same proportion of persons aged 65 and over having incomes under $1000 as was obtained by adding to the group reporting money income of $1 to $999 those reporting zero income (including wives whose total income was allocated to the husband).

Income per equivalent adult

Another approach, instead of trying to isolate statistically the income of the elderly couple or individual, is to convert incomes to an adult-equivalent basis. A scale of equivalence which takes account of variation in needs with the number and age of family members can be a useful tool for analysis. Certainly, it permits maximum exploitation of data when the sample is small—apart from any question of tabulation time and cost. Such a device has been used effectively in several recent studies.

The University of Michigan Study of Hospital and Medical Economics with a sample of only 1031 families (253 with head aged 65 and over) containing 3516 individuals (424 aged 65 and over), produced some useful analytical tables on ability to pay for medical care and the amount of medical care consumed or needed for families and individuals classified by age of head and income per equivalent adult (McNerney, 1960, pp. 311–28).[5] Admittedly, the adjustment for the effect of family size on the adequacy of income to provide for the needs of the family was rough, with children under 12 and the second adult in each family counted as half an adult and all other family members counted as a full adult. The differences between the relative distributions by total family income and by adjusted family income for three broad age groups are noteworthy nevertheless (see Table 7). Being smaller, the older families are less heavily concentrated at the bottom of the income scale when income is adjusted than when it is not. But the shift is less than is often implied in debates on the interpretation of available family income statistics. Indeed 2 in 5 of the aged families, compared with less than 1 in 6 of the younger families, had adjusted incomes of less than $1050, "a point below which almost any family can be presumed to have a hard time making ends meet." (McNerney, 1960, p. 312.)

While analysis on an adjusted-income basis has obvious virtues for analytical use, there are two practical limitations: first, the data available for measuring equivalence in level of living are limited. A measure of variation in family needs with family size that has been widely used is a scale prepared in 1957 by Dorothy S. Brady on the basis of consumption survey data for the mid thirties and early forties (U.S. Bureau of Labor Statistics, 1947). This scale does not, however, take explicit account of age differences. Subsequent changes in

[5] It should be noted that aged persons and those hospitalized were over-sampled.

Table 7. *Income, age of head, and family size: percentage*
distribution of families classified by age of head, money income
in 1957–1958 as reported and as adjusted to an adult-equivalent basis
(state of Michigan, noninstitutional population)[a]

Money income as reported and as adjusted to an adult-equivalent basis (in dollars)[b]	*Age of family head*		
	Under 35	*35 to 64*	*65 and over*
Total family income			
Under 2000	7.9	6.3	46.8
2000–3999	24.8	18.6	33.6
4000–5999	33.6	32.3	9.0
6000–9999	28.1	32.5	7.8
10,000 or more	5.5	10.1	2.7
Adjusted family income[b]			
Under 1050	14.2	16.1	39.8
1050–2449	47.8	40.1	35.3
2450 or more	38.0	43.8	24.8
Average family size	3.9	3.6	1.8

[a] Source: University of Michigan, *Study of Hospital and Medical Economics,*
Michigan Population Survey, Tables 1, 2, and 12, statement of Walter J.
McNerney in Hearings before the Senate Subcommittee on Problems of the Aged
and Aging, April, 1960.
[b] Family income was adjusted to an equivalent adult basis by counting as
one-half an adult the second adult and each child under 12 years.

family composition and age at retirement may well mean that the
ratios are no longer appropriate. But even given a scale based on
more up-to-date data and refined to represent different family types,
adult-equivalent income measurement would not be very useful for
identifying the needy aged for program purposes.

THE INCOME CONCEPT

Just as the definition of the recipient unit affects the inferences
drawn as to the well-being of the aged, so the income concept influences the conclusions.

The concept of resources that is most common is the narrowest.
It relates to current cash receipts during the survey period—usually
a year—taking no account of capital gains and losses, large gifts and
inheritances, financial asset holdings, funds obtained through borrow-
ing, or income in kind. Finally, it is only rarely that any serious effort
is made to identify the "permanent-income component" or long-term
income prospects of the recipient.

Money income and other cash funds

Money income defined. Money income is defined in most field surveys to include wages, salaries, entrepreneurial earnings, interest, dividends, net rents and royalties, all types of social insurance benefits, pensions and compensation for veterans, private pensions, annuities, periodic payments under insurance settlements, public assistance, private charitable contributions, allotments, alimony, and contributions by relatives or friends not living in the same household.[6] This definition is common to all the surveys referred to in discussing the recipient unit, except that the beneficiary surveys also include the value of bills (other than medical) paid by relatives.

Capital gains, inheritances, and lump-sum insurance settlements have usually been excluded from income as defined in field surveys because traditionally they have been concerned either directly with the relationship between income and consumption expenditures, or else the level of living implied by the income figures. On the other hand, the growing tendency to favor deferred income and fringe benefits and to convert ordinary income into capital gains for the tax-saving effect has suggested to many students of income-size distribution that for certain analytical purposes the money income definition needs broadening.[7] Since many persons save for retirement it might be appropriate to include capital gains also when assessing the welfare of the aged. The effect on the size distribution for the aged would of course depend in part on the extent of asset holdings, discussed below.

Asset holdings. In our national debate on the medical-care-cost problems of the aged, some have contended vigorously that money income statistics for the aged are misleading and that asset holdings are a more appropriate measure of their financial resources (Kemp

[6] The Office of Business Economics of the Department of Commerce releases each year estimates of the size distribution of family personal income, defined as the current income received by families and unattached individuals from all sources, including in addition to money income certain nonmoney items such as wages in kind, the value of food and fuel produced and consumed on farms, the net imputed rental value of owner-occupied homes, and imputed interest. The money-income component differs from that of most field surveys in that it is net of social security taxes and does not include contributions for support from relatives and friends (Goldsmith, 1958a). The method of estimation is such that it does not permit cross-classification even by such characteristics as age of head, so that it is not relevant to the issues under consideration in this paper.

[7] See Joseph A. Peckman's "Comment on Mrs. Goldsmith's Paper," in *Studies in Income and Wealth,* Vol. 23, 1958.

et al., 1959; Campbell and Campbell, 1960), emphasizing the fact that older persons tend to have larger asset holdings than younger persons.

It is generally recognized that many older persons have acquired savings and property which could in some measure offset the reduction in current cash income that follows retirement. The question is how to quantify this, i.e., how to "add" assets to current income. Whatever the answer it must reflect the fact that older people have behind them their days of accumulating assets.

Assets and income. Although comparability of statistics from different studies is hampered by differences in definitions as to what constitutes the consumer unit and which assets are counted, one broad generalization emerges: those aged persons, families, or spending units whose incomes are lowest, and who would benefit most from assets readily convertible to cash, are the least likely to have them. By the same token, those with relatively high incomes are most likely to have financial assets, as suggested by data from the Survey of Consumer Finances for spending units in two broad income classes. The 1959 Survey of Consumer Finances shows, for example, that 21 percent of the aged spending units with 1958 incomes of $3000 to $5000, compared to 46 percent of those with smaller incomes, had less than $200 in liquid assets, and 28 percent compared to 14 percent had $5000 or more in such assets—defined as bank accounts, savings and loan shares, and U.S. savings bonds (Table 8). A special tabulation from the 1947 Survey for finer income classes shows the following proportions of aged spending units within two income groups having specified liquid assets (Fisher, 1952):

Money income in 1946 (in dollars)	Less than $500	$500– 1999	$2000 or more
Less than 1000	70	20	10
3000 or more	20	22	58

The pattern is about the same when financial assets, including stocks and bonds of corporations and marketable government bonds, are considered in addition to liquid assets. In 1957, the latest date for which statistics on holdings of total financial assets are available, there were practically no aged spending units with marketable securities that did not have some liquid assets (U.S. Board of Governors of the Federal Reserve System, 1957). In all, only 11 percent of the aged spending units owned stock, and few if any of those with liquid asset holdings of less than $2000 owned enough marketable securities to move them into a higher bracket when classified by total financial assets.

Table 8. *Liquid assets and income: percentage distribution
of spending units with head aged 65 and over, by amount
of asset holdings in early 1959, by money income of 1958
(continental United States, population in private households)*[a]

	Spending units with head aged 65 and over		
Amount of liquid assets (in dollars)[b]	Total[c]	Less than $3000	$3000–4999
No liquid assets	29	37	16
Some liquid assets	71	63	84
1–199	8	9	5
200–499	8	9	9
500–999	9	10	4
1000–1999	12	11	16
2000–4999	14	10	23
5000–9999	8	7	16
10,000 or more	11	7	12
Median holdings,[c] all units (in dollars)	780	330	2000
Units with assets (dollars)	1800	1320	3040

[a] Source: U.S. Board of Governors of the Federal Reserve System, *1959 Survey of Consumer Finances*, unpublished data made available by the Board.

[b] United States savings bonds, checking accounts, savings accounts in banks, and shares in savings and loan associations and credit unions; currency is excluded.

[c] Interpolated from distribution.

Data from the survey for Michigan likewise show sharp differentials with respect to asset holdings when elderly families with large and small incomes per equivalent adult are compared (see Table 9).

Data from the 1957 survey of Old-Age and Survivors Insurance beneficiaries (which covered more than 1800 retired couples and 2200 other aged persons) suggest a very close correlation between current income and ownership of income-producing assets. The proportion having $25 or more in income during the year in the form of interest, dividends, or net rents is shown in Table 10 by total money income class. For couples, for example, this proportion increased about 4½ times from 18 percent for those with less than $1200 total money income to 82 percent for those with $5000 or more.

The finding of a strong relationship between assets and income is, of course, not unexpected. Income and assets both, after retirement, are related to earnings in earlier years and to the opportunity they afforded for accumulating savings. Furthermore, to the extent that the assets held are themselves income-producing, the very fact of having them will raise total income.

Assets prorated. If we wish a distribution of aged persons by potentially available funds, it would be best to analyze each individual

Table 9. Liquid assets and income: percentage distribution of families
with head aged 65 and over, by amount of liquid asset holdings
in fall 1958, by money incomes per equivalent adult, 1957–1958
(State of Michigan, noninstitutional population)[a]

	Money income of family per equivalent adult[c]		
Amount of liquid assets (in dollars)[b]	Under $1050	$1050– 2449	$2450 and over
No liquid assets	44.7	27.8	14.8
Some liquid assets	55.3	72.2	85.2
1–199	1.1	6.8	6.3
200–499	13.8	9.0	6.3
500–999	15.1	7.9	6.3
1000–2999	11.1	18.3	20.1
3000–4999	6.2	11.0	19.0
5000 or more	4.0	12.1	24.0
Amount not ascertained	4.0	6.6	3.1

[a] Source: University of Michigan, *Study of Hospital and Medical Economics,
Michigan Population Survey*, Table 8, statement of Walter J. McNerney in
Hearings before the Senate Subcommittee on Problems of the Aged and Aging,
April, 1960.

[b] Liquid assets were defined for the survey as bank deposits, United States
savings bonds, and deposits in building and loan associations.

[c] Family income was adjusted to an equivalent adult basis by counting as
one-half an adult the second adult and each child under 12 years.

Table 10. Asset and total money income: percent of retired couples
and nonmarried OASI beneficiaries having asset income, by total
money income in 1957 (OASI beneficiaries aged 65 and over)[a]

RETIRED COUPLES		NONMARRIED BENEFICIARIES		
			Men	Women
Money income (in dollars)[b]	Having asset income[c]	Money income (in dollars)[b]	Having asset income[c]	Having asset income[c]
Total	50	Total	29	41
Less than 1200	18	Less than 600	9	17
1200–1799	36	600–899	10	28
1800–2399	46	900–1199	26	43
2400–2999	57	1200–1499	28	46
3000–4999	67	1500–2399	41	60
5000 or more	82	2400 or more	70	83

[a] Source: Social Security Administration, U.S. Bureau of Old-Age and Survivors
Insurance, *National Survey of Old-Age and Survivors Insurance Beneficiaries, 1957*,
unpublished data.

[b] Income during a 12-month period from Fall, 1956, to Fall, 1957.

[c] Income of $25 or more during the survey year from assets of any one kind,
either interest on savings accounts, dividends, or rental income. An additional
9 percent of the couples and the nonmarried men and 11 percent of the nonmarried women derived some income from assets, but not as much as $25 from
any one type.

report, and add to current money income a prorata share of financial assets, with the share computed on the basis of the life expectancy of the individual, but taking into account the fact that once income-producing assets are liquidated, future income is reduced. Since it has not been feasible to do this, presented here instead is a crude approximation for the 8.6 million spending units with head aged 65 and overrepresented in the 1959 Survey of Consumer Finances. The money income distribution (shown in Table 3) was transformed by reference to the cross-tabulation of income and liquid assets shown in Table 8. The median age of all persons 65 and over (in 1958) was 72 years, implying an average remaining lifetime at present survival rates of about 10 years. When one-tenth of liquid-asset holdings was added to income, the distribution compared as in Table 11 with the published data by money income.

Table 11. Money income of aged spending units, 1959: percentage distribution of money income with approximation of distribution allowing for liquid asset holdings[a]

Amount of income (in dollars)	Money income	Money income plus one-tenth of assets
Less than 1000	20	17
1000–1999	34	31
2000–2999	17	17
3000–3999	12	13
4000–4999	6	6
5000 or more	12	17

[a] Source: U.S. Board of Governors of the Federal Reserve System, *1959 Survey of Consumer Finances,* unpublished data made available by the Board.

This rough calculation (which makes no reduction in current income because of use of assets) suggests that only a small proportion of spending units would be moved out of an income class that might be termed marginal or uncomfortably low to a more favorable financial situation.

A somewhat analogous analysis based on data collected in the 1951 study of Old-Age and Survivors Insurance beneficiaries showed relatively little shift up the retirement-income scale when it was assumed that liquid assets would be used up at a constant rate over a 10-year period (Wentworth, 1954).

Instead of trying to prorate assets over the remaining lifetime, Steiner and Dorfman used in their study of the aged a classification by total receipts, to supplement their analysis by money income. They defined receipts as the sum of (1) money income as defined by the Census, (2) occasional cash gifts, (3) lump-sum receipts (such as insurance payments or inheritances), and (4) savings or assets used to meet current living expenses (Steiner and Dorfman, 1957). While it is tautological to define available funds as equivalent to expenditures (except that outlays financed by unsecured debts were not included), the authors found the measure useful for comparison with budget costs. For our purposes, however, it is useful to compare the distribution by amount of receipts with the distribution by amount of current income. As shown in Table 12, while the addition to money

Table 12. Money receipts compared with money income:
median receipts and median incomes (in dollars)
in 1951 of couples with head aged 65 and over and
of other aged men and women, by presence of relatives
(continental United States, noninstitutional population)[a,b]

Living arrangements	Married couples		Nonmarried men		Nonmarried women	
	Receipts	Income	Receipts	Income	Receipts	Income
Total	1490	1390	730	660	400	270
Living alone or lodging	1600	1460	800	740	660	560
Sharing home with relatives	1290	1200	630	550	230	80

[a] Source: P. O. Steiner, and R. Dorfman, *The Economic Status of the Aged,* University of California Press, Berkeley, California, 1957, Tables 202 and 302.
[b] Receipts are defined as the sum of total income (as defined by the Census Bureau), occasional cash gifts, lump-sum receipts such as insurance payments or inheritance, and dissaving, i.e., the use of savings or assets to meet living expenses.

income of dissavings and windfall receipts slides the distribution of the aged upwards, the difference is not enough to alter any generalization regarding the concentration of the aged in the low income groups.

Income in kind

Difficult as it is to translate asset holdings into measures of currently available resources, it is more difficult to determine the effective cash equivalent of home ownership, home-grown food, etc. This results both from problems of data collection and complexities of valuation (Reid, 1951; Kyrk, 1950).

Income in kind is of three main types, the use value of owned homes and other durable goods, the value of home-grown food and, theoretically, of various services performed by the housewife or householder, and the value of meals, lodging, etc., that are furnished in lieu of cash wages to some employees.

For the aged, wages in kind are of negligible importance because so few are still in the labor force, and they may be ignored. So too may be services performed in and about the home, and the use value of durable goods other than the home. Our concern, then, is with home ownership and home-produced food.

Money equivalent of home ownership. An owned home is undoubtedly the most common asset of the aged and in many ways the most important. It provides a measure of financial security, particularly when, as is so often the case among the aged, it is owned free and clear. To the extent that home ownership reduces out-of-pocket housing costs, it releases funds for other items and makes a given income go further. To the extent that equity in an owned home makes it possible to borrow money for an emergency, it also represents a potential net addition—though a temporary one—to current income. Outright sale of the home would of course produce the largest immediate increase in available funds. The relatively low value of the homes owned by the aged, however, and the high cost of the rental units which would probably replace them suggests that sale of the home would not work to the long-run economic advantage of many aged persons.

Early in 1959, according to the Federal Reserve Board's Survey of Consumer Finances, two out of three nonfarm families with an aged head owned their home, with 83 percent of the homes owned mortgage-free. The average equity of the debt-free homes was about $10,600, and the owner's equity in the mortgaged homes averaged about $200 less. Of the nonfarm homes owned by old persons who were Old-Age and Survivors Insurance beneficiaries interviewed in 1957, 87 percent were mortgage-free; the medium equity for all owners was $8100 for couples, and less than this for nonmarried beneficiaries.

As in the case of financial assets, those with limited cash resources, who might benefit the most from an owned home, are least likely to have one. As shown by the data in Table 13, nearly eight of every ten retired beneficiary couples with money incomes of $5000 or more in 1957 owned their homes, whereas this was true of fewer than two in three of those with less than $1200 cash income. (For beneficiaries not living with a spouse, the differences were even more striking.) The situation is analogous when resources are measured in terms of liquid assets. Unpublished data from the 1959 Survey of Consumer Finances for nonfarm spending units with head aged 65 and over, show that half of those with no liquid assets or less than $200 rented their quarters or shared a relative's home, while two-thirds of those with $200 or more in liquid assets owned their homes (Table 14).

The differential rate of home ownership with cash income would be greater were it not that in rural areas and small towns incomes are

Table 13. *Income in kind and money income: percentage*
of retired couples and nonmarried OASI beneficiaries
having housing and food in kind, by money income
in 1957 (OASI beneficiaries aged 65 and over)[a,b]

| | | | Food | |
Money income (in dollars)	Owned home	Free housing[c]	Total[d]	Some home-grown
Retired couples				
Total	70	4	29	26
Less than 1200	64	11	53	46
1200–1799	68	5	38	34
1800–2399	71	3	26	25
2400–2999	71	3	26	24
3000–4999	72	2	17	15
5000 or more	78	1	9	9
Nonmarried men				
Total	32	6	19	12
Less than 600	27	14	33	21
600–899	26	7	18	9
900–1199	25	5	20	13
1200–1499	34	8	21	12
1500–2399	39	5	15	10
2400 or more	46	3	11	9
Nonmarried women				
Total	38	6	15	6
Less than 600	29	7	18	11
600–899	37	8	14	4
900–1199	38	5	16	4
1200–1499	42	3	13	7
1500–2399	41	8	13	4
2400 or more	53	6	14	5

[a] Source: Social Security Administration, U.S. Bureau of Old-Age and Survivors Insurance, *National Survey of Old-Age and Survivors Insurance Beneficiaries, 1957,* unpublished data.

[b] Income during a 12-month period from Fall, 1956, to Fall, 1957.

[c] Housing provided without charge by agency, employer, or other person outside household.

[d] Food raised for home use or provided as gift or pay.

lower, on the average, than in large cities, whereas home ownership is more common.

The community-size differential in ownership is illustrated by comparing in Table 15 the percentage distributions for OASI beneficiary couples in two income groups.

The proportion of beneficiaries living in rural nonfarm areas, where ownership is so widespread, was only half as large in the $3000-and-over income group as in the under-$1800 group (13 versus 27 percent) whereas the proportion living in big cities was two-thirds larger

Table 14. Homeownership and liquid assets: percentage distribution by tenure of nonfarm spending units with liquid assets of more and less than $200; asset holdings in 1959 and income in 1958, by tenure (continental United States, population in private households)[a]

Tenure	Liquid asset holdings in early 1959		Median amount (in dollars)	Median money income (in dollars)
	Under $200	$200 or more		
Total	100.0	100.0	710	1880
Home owners	49.6	68.3	1070	2160
Renters	34.7	18.7	120	1760
Others[b]	15.7	12.9	c	c

[a] Source: U.S. Board of Governors of the Federal Reserve System, *1959 Survey of Consumer Finances*, unpublished data made available by the Board.

[b] Spending units that live with relatives, receive housing as part of compensation, live temporarily in houses they have sold, etc.

[c] Insufficient cases for computation of median.

in the upper-income group than in the lower (51 versus 30 percent).

Investment income. One method of imputing income from home ownership is to consider equity as an investment and to compute the expected return on an equivalent sum invested in another form of relatively low-risk saving. For example, the mean owner equity of about $10,000 reported in the Survey of Consumer Finances for the homes of families with head 65 years or older could yield about $500 a year in interest.[8] This is just about the same as the $46 median monthly rent reported by aged nonfarm families (in the same study) who were renting their housing.

Table 15. Home ownership of OASI beneficiary couples, by size of community and money income, percentage distribution[a]

Money income and tenure (in dollars)	Cities of 100,000 or more	Cities of less than 100,000	Rural nonfarm places
Under 1800	100	100	100
Home rented	50	37	21
Home owned, mortgaged	8	5	4
Home owned, mortgage-free	42	48	74
3000 and over	100	100	100
Home rented	35	18	15
Home owned, mortgaged	16	12	11
Home owned, mortgage-free	48	69	74

[a] Source: Social Security Administration, U.S. Bureau of Old-Age and Survivors Insurance, *National Survey of Old-Age and Survivors Insurance Beneficiaries, 1957*, unpublished data.

[8] Assuming an interest rate close to 5 percent, the current going rate for relatively low-risk investment. David estimated imputed rent as 5 percent of the reported value of the owner-occupied dwelling (David, 1959).

The net effect on the income distribution of the aged of allowing for the estimated return to home owners on their investment can be approximated using data from the survey of Old-Age and Survivors Insurance beneficiaries, which showed the medium equity at $8100 for home owning couples, $7250 for the nonmarried women and $6100 for the men. By assuming all equity at the median—an overstatement at the low incomes, and an understatement at the upper incomes—and a 5 percent rate of return, every home owner's income would be increased by about $400 in the case of a couple, and $350 and $300 for a nonmarried woman or man, respectively. The figures in Table 16

Table 16. Money income of retired OASI couples, home owners and non-home-owners with and without imputed income from home ownership, percentage distribution[a]

Amount of income (in dollars)	Money income	Money income plus imputed income from owned home
Less than 1200	13	6
1200–1799	22	20
1800–2399	20	20
2400–2999	14	17
3000–4999	21	26
5000 or more	10	11

[a] Source: Social Security Administration, U.S. Bureau of Old-Age and Survivors Insurance, *National Survey of Old-Age and Survivors Insurance Beneficiaries, 1957*, unpublished data.

illustrate how the addition of these amounts to the income of home owning couples would change the income distribution for all retired couples (home owners and non-home-owners combined.)

At the lower incomes home ownership is considerably less common among nonmarried than married persons, and consequently the imputation of income from home ownership results in less shift out of the bottom income group. This is illustrated by the data for nonmarried women on the beneficiary rolls in 1957 as shown in Table 17.

Net rental income. The data from the 1957 beneficiary survey make possible another estimate of the money equivalent of home ownership, namely, the difference between housing expenditures incurred by owners and what they would have to pay if they were renting the same house. The outlay for housing was obtained directly from the owners, including expenditures for repairs, taxes, and interest, but excluding mortgage principal payments. The owner was also asked to estimate how much the premises would bring in monthly if rented. Over the long run, the rent that an owner would charge is greater than the out-of-pocket expenses incurred by the owner-

Table 17. *Money income of nonmarried women OASI beneficiaries,
with and without imputed income from home ownership, 1957,
percentage distribution*[a]

Amount of income (in dollars)	Money income	Money income plus imputed income from owned home
Less than 600	17	14
600–899	28	20
900–1199	17	20
1200–1499	12	14
1500–2399	18	19
2400 or more	9	13

[a] Source: Social Security Administration, U.S. Bureau of Old-Age and Survivors Insurance, *National Survey of Old-Age and Survivors Insurance Beneficiaries, 1957,* unpublished data.

occupant. In any single year, however, there are owners whose expenses exceed "receipts" as measured by estimated rental value. Actually, for the survey year 1956–1957, about one in five of the beneficiary home owners reported such a net loss. (There was no appreciable difference with income in the proportion reporting a loss.) The average amount of "profit" per home owner was not tabulated.

Net reduction in out-of-pocket costs. An alternative way of estimating "real" income from home ownership is to compare expenses incurred by the owner with what he would be likely to pay if he did not own a home. This is indicated not by the estimated rental value of the owned home, but by the expenditures of families of the same composition and the same money income, in the same type of community, who rent their quarters. As an approximation, it has several advantages. First, it avoids reliance upon what is often little more than an uninformed guess: many owners have no basis for knowing what they could charge as rent. Second, long-time owners may well be living in places quite different from those they would currently select. This is particularly likely for aged home owners now living alone, but still occupying a home they bought when they were raising their children. Comparing the costs of ownership for such families with the rent paid by families in similar circumstances yields the most reasonable assumption of the "extra" spendable funds which a home owner enjoys. Other aspects of ownership—the psychological satisfaction of familiar surroundings or, alternatively, the inconvenience of a house too large for comfort—cannot be appraised in dollars.

The Old-Age and Survivors Insurance beneficiary survey data on housing costs make it possible to compare outlays by renters and owners during the survey year. To make the comparison as meaningful as possible, only beneficiaries living alone and maintaining the same living arrangements throughout the survey year are considered. Homes owned outright are classified separately from those with mortgage-debt, and rental housing limited to houses, apartments, or house-keeping rooms rented unfurnished. (Furnished rooms and boarding house accommodations are not included.) Costs for the renters represent space rent and charges for heat, light, and cooking fuel. Costs for owned homes were defined as taxes, maintenance, heat, light, and cooking fuel and in case of mortgage, interest—but not principal—payments on the debt.

As might be expected, owners still paying off a mortgage had the highest out-of-pocket costs for housing, and owners of mortgage-free homes, the least. Among the couples, for example, median housing expenses were about $34 a month for homes owned outright, $57 for those rented, and $75 for mortgaged homes—somewhat more in large cities, and somewhat less in small cities and towns. Both owner and renter outlays tended to rise with rising income, but in terms of the ratio of owners' costs to those of renters, there was no consistent pattern with income. On the average, an elderly beneficiary couple renting a place to live was spending about two-thirds again as much as one owning a paid-up house, but about one-fourth less than a couple still paying off the mortgage.

For the nonmarried beneficiaries, data from the survey were more fragmentary than for couples because fewer live alone in owned homes, and a number of the renters, particularly among the men, occupy furnished rooms rather than housekeeping facilities. On the whole, however, the ratio of owner-renter costs was just about the same as for the couples, with renters spending about two-thirds again as much as those owning a home free and clear, but about one-third less than the few owning their homes and still paying on a mortgage.

No attempt has been made to adjust the income distribution for the demonstrated saving in out-of-pocket housing costs made possible by home ownership. It is obvious that assuming for all home owners a saving of about 40 percent of average rent would affect the income distribution less than the hypothetical return on investment.

Food in kind.   Noncash income in the form of food is unique in that it is more common at low than at high money-income levels. This reflects the fact that persons receiving food as pay or gift are likely to be marginal workers and those able to garden or raise chickens, for example, are more likely to live in rural than in urban areas and hence to have relatively small cash incomes.

According to the 1957 survey of Old-Age and Survivors Insurance beneficiaries, some food was received without direct expense by 29 percent of the retired couples, 19 percent of the nonmarried men, and 15 percent of the women beneficiaries, most often food they raised themselves. The beneficiaries were not asked to try to evaluate the food, and no office estimate was made. United States Department of Agriculture studies suggest, however, that the net effect of home-grown food on the family grocery bill is apt to be less than a dollar-for-dollar saving (Orshansky, 1956). In other words, when the value of home-produced food is added to money income, it tends to overstate the effective income of families that raise food in quantity. They may have better diets but they do not necessarily have the equivalent in cash to purchase other goods and services. This is particularly true if the value of food raised for their own use by farm families is valued at retail rather than at farm prices.

SUMMARY

Before summarizing the conclusions reached, attention should be called to two facets of assessing economic status of which no mention has been made. One is the relative tax advantage of persons aged 65 and over, which is an important consideration when comparing their gross income with that of younger persons. The other is the determination of need, which, like measuring the size of resources, involves a complex of problems—accentuated because need is interrelated with place of residence, living arrangements, family status, health, and for the retired, the level of living maintained before retirement. Standard budgets can be very useful in assessing the sufficiency of an aged person's resources.

In this paper an attempt has been made to indicate that data presented on a family basis (as defined by the Census Bureau) and on a spending-unit basis (as defined for the Surveys of Consumer Finances) both tend to overstate the resource level of the aged population as a whole. This is in part because those with the least resources—elderly persons living in the homes of younger relatives—are lost in such an analysis. Furthermore, although the aged who share a home with relatives generally have smaller incomes than those who are living alone or lodging, the total family income tends to be larger on a per capita basis for families with an aged couple or nonmarried aged person reported as head than for the aged living alone or with non-relatives. The "extra" income is not necessarily at the disposal of the aged family members.

For social planning, the most generally useful units for analysis are the nonmarried aged person (whether in an institution or a household) and the couple, whether or not there are relatives in the home, provided proper account is taken of the family comprising elderly parents with dependent children. In the absence of data for units so classified, income distributions for aged persons serve remarkably well as indicators of the size of the low-income aged population.

Although the aged have somewhat larger liquid-asset holdings than younger persons, on the average, it is usually those with relatively high incomes who have accumulated the savings. Similarly, older persons are likely to own their homes mortgage-free, and a paid-up home can mean relatively small out-of-pocket expenditures for housing. Yet those with the most limited financial resources are least likely to have this advantage, whether resources are measured in terms of income or of financial assets.

Home-produced food in the 1960s is an important consideration for only a small fraction of the population. In any case, however, it appears that the funds that home-grown food would release to purchase other goods and services are apt to be somewhat less than the retail value of the food.

The importance of the source of an aged person's income insofar as it relates to its probable continuity should be reiterated. Thus, to appraise the resources of a retired individual it is desirable to look separately at his more-or-less permanent income, i.e., his retirement benefits, annuities, and returns on his investment—as has been the practice in surveys of Old-Age and Survivors Insurance beneficiaries. For an over-all view of the economic situation of the aged population, however, it is desirable to encompass resources of all types because there are always some retired persons who have earnings and some who receive assistance of one sort or another. It has been suggested that for most purposes separate analyses should be made for the retired and for those in the labor force. For welfare program planning it is useful to further subclassify those no longer in the labor force by whether or not they receive assistance.

REFERENCES

Brady, D. 1958. Individual incomes and the structure of consumer units. Am. Economic Rev., 48: 269–78.

Campbell, W. G., and Campbell, Rita R. 1960. Voluntary health insurance in the United States. Washington, D.C.: American Enterprise Association.

David, M. 1959. Welfare income and budget needs. Rev. of Economic Statistics, 41: (November) 393.

Epstein, Lenore A. 1955. Economic resources of persons aged 65 and over. Social Security Bull., 18: (June) 3–19.

————— 1959. Money income of aged persons: a 10-year review, 1948–1958. Social Security Bull., 22: (June) 3–11.

Fisher, Janet A. 1952. Income, spending and savings patterns of consumer units in different age groups. *In* Studies in income and wealth, 15: 75–102. New York: National Bureau of Economic Research.

Givens, M. 1958. Discussion of papers on income and consumption. Am. Economic Rev., 48: 304.

Goldsmith, Selma F. 1951. Appraisal of basic data available for constructing income size distributions. *In* Studies in income and wealth, 13: 266–373. New York: National Bureau of Economic Research.

————— 1958a. Size and distribution of personal income. Survey of Current Business, 38: 14.

————— 1958b. The relation of census income distribution statistics to other income data. *In* Studies in income and wealth, 23: 65–107. New York: National Bureau of Economic Research.

Kemp, A., Martin, L. W., and Harkness, C. 1959. Some observations on financial assets of the aged and Forand-type legislation. J.A.M.A., 171: 1228–31.

Kyrk, Hazel. 1950. Income distribution as a measure of economic welfare. Am. Economic Rev., 40: 342–55.

Lamale, Helen H. 1959. Methodology of the survey of consumer expenditures in 1950. Philadelphia: University of Pennsylvania, Wharton School of Finance and Commerce.

McNerney, W. J. 1960. Health needs of the aged and aging. Hearing before the Subcommittee on Problems of the Aged and Aging of the Committee on Labor and Public Welfare, U.S. Senate, 86th Congress, 2d Session, April, 1960.

Miller, H. P. 1955. Income of the American people. New York: John Wiley & Sons, Inc.

Orshansky, Mollie. 1956. Trends in farm family food practices. *In* 34th Annual Agricultural Outlook Conference, Washington, D.C. Washington, D.C.: U.S. Department of Agriculture. (Mimeographed.)

Reid, Margaret G. 1951. Distribution of nonmoney income. *In* Studies in income and wealth, 13: 125–85. New York: National Bureau of Economic Research.

Shanas, Ethel. 1959. Financial resources of the aging: reported resources available to those aged 65 and over in meeting medical costs up to $500.00. Research Series 10. New York: Health Information Foundation.

Sheldon, H. D. 1958. The older population of the United States. New York: John Wiley & Sons, Inc.

Sirken, M. G., Maynes, S. E., and Frechtling, J. A. 1958. The survey of consumer finances and the census quality check. *In* Studies in income and wealth, 23: 127–68. New York: National Bureau of Economic Research.

Steiner, P. O., and Dorfman, R. 1957. The economic status of the aged. Berkeley: University of California Press.

Titmuss, R. M. 1960. The irresponsible society. Fabian Tract 323: (April) 8.

U.S. Board of Governors of the Federal Reserve System. 1957. 1957 Survey of consumer finances: the financial position of consumers. Federal Reserve Bull., 43: 878–901.

U.S. Bureau of the Census. 1959. Current population reports: population characteristics. (Series P-20, No. 96.) Washington, D.C.: The Bureau.

U.S. Bureau of Labor Statistics. 1947. Workers' budgets in the United States: city families and single persons 1946 and 1947. (BLS Bull. 927.) Washington, D.C.: Government Printing Office.

Wasson, R., Hurwitz, A., and Schweiger, I. 1951. Field surveys of income: an appraisal. *In* Studies in income and wealth, 13: 482–554. New York: National Bureau of Economic Research.

Wentworth, Edna C. 1954. Economic situation of aged insurance beneficiaries: an evaluation. Social Security Bull., 17: (April) 13–30.

Scope, Goals, and Methodology for a Study of Retirement Policies and Practices in the American Economy

FRED SLAVICK, PATRICIA CAIN SMITH, EDWIN B. SHULTZ, AND JOHN W. MCCONNELL

NATURE, SCOPE, AND OBJECTIVES OF THE STUDY

THE rate of exit from the labor force on the part of individuals 65 years of age and over in the United States has been increasing steadily since the turn of the century. For example, of all males 65 and older, approximately two-thirds were in the labor force in 1900. At present the figure is approximately one-third. This long-run increase in the rate of retirement is probably due to a complex of factors, including urbanization of the population, unemployment due to technological displacement combined with discrimination against older workers in hiring, and the growth of public and private retirement systems.

With the liberalization of Old-Age and Survivors Insurance and growth of private pension plans since World War II, retirement at age 65 appears to be becoming formalized, and compulsory retirement of individuals at that age regardless of their health or competence has become common in American industry. Many employers, however, have some degree of flexibility as to the age at which retirement of employees occurs. This flexibility ranges from retirement on a completely voluntary basis, as long as the employees concerned are physically and mentally capable of performing their work, to selective types of flexibility by which some proportion of the older employees are continued beyond an established normal retirement age, as long as they are needed or until they reach a later compulsory retirement age.

The nature of the retirement policies of employing organizations has important implications for the welfare of the individual older employee, as well as for the employing organizations themselves. Continued employment or retirement is the major determinant of the income and material well-being of most persons in their later years. Moreover, retirement policies of employing organizations may be an important factor influencing the adjustment of individuals to the social and psychological problems of aging.

Retirement age policies may also have a wider significance. To the extent that they affect the withdrawal or retention of older workers, these policies have a direct impact on the nature of our labor force and the productivity of our national economy.

For the employing organization the nature of its retirement policy may have an important bearing on the effectiveness of its work force and its resulting ability to achieve its basic objective, whether this be profit or public service, or a combination of these.

As private pension plans have grown and as retirement age policies have been formalized, interest among employing organizations in programs which seek to assist employees to prepare for retirement has increased slowly but steadily. The potential of these programs for facilitating the adjustment to retired status may be significant, but we need to know much more concerning their nature, content, and actual effectiveness.

The purposes of our study are (1) to bring together in a systematic fashion the basic and relevant information about retirement age policies and practices currently being followed throughout the country by all types of employing organizations, including business, government, and private nonprofit agencies; (2) to analyze and assess in a limited sample the experience and satisfaction of organizations and individuals operating under various approaches to retirement, including the impact, if any, of retirement age policies on the satisfaction of individuals in retirement; and (3) to explore and analyze the content, nature, and effectiveness of programs aimed at helping employees prepare for retirement. We hope, moreover, to formulate and, as far as possible, to check hypotheses concerning the underlying factors which determine the effectiveness and impact of policy in different situations.

Policies with respect to retirement age

The principal reasons given by employers for utilizing compulsory retirement at a fixed chronological age have been the desire to avoid the difficult administrative decisions involved in selective retirement and the belief that compulsory retirement is necessary to keep open the lines of promotion for younger employees, thereby maintaining their morale and incentive for improved performance. It has also been suggested that employees are less insecure and anxious when they know in advance the date and situation of their retirement, and that the resentment of retired persons is reduced when, because of an absolutely uniform policy, there is no implication that the person who is retired is less competent than others who are retained after normal retirement age.

The actual reactions of retirees, present employees, employers, union officials, and other individuals under compulsory policies need to be ascertained; insofar as possible, these subjective reactions should be evaluated in the light of objective experience in terms of cost of turnover, training, and pension contributions.

Selective or flexible retirement has also been held, on the other hand, to improve employee morale, the satisfaction of retired persons and the efficiency of an enterprise. Some employers believe that selective retirement reduces the dollar cost of pensions and retains in productive employment a large number of employees who are eligible to retire but prefer not to do so. Again, the relation of policy to the satisfaction of employees, union officials, retired persons, and policy-makers should be investigated.

Administration of selective retirement policies involves a more complicated procedure than administration of compulsory retirement. We hope to ascertain the factors used in making the decision to retire or to retain individuals and the procedures developed by which these selections are made. We are aware that, in spite of continuing research, objective criteria other than chronological age have not, as yet, been established. Nevertheless, selections are being made, and it is our objective to determine the factors and methods which seem generally used in the selection process and to gather together the accumulated experience of employers and unions (where relevant) with the emergence and solution of problems encountered in administering policies of various degrees of flexibility in retirement.

Preretirement planning

Whatever the policy as to flexibility regarding the age at which employees are retired, it is possible that adjustment of retired persons may be improved by a program which prepares them to face retirement. An increasing number of employers, top personnel specialists, and unions are manifesting interest in such programs.

The methods and contents of these programs thus far have been experimental, and no obstacles should be placed in the way of continued experiment. However, it is important to ascertain what can be learned from the experience of existing programs. We hope to assess the advantages and disadvantages which have been revealed by the use of different approaches to retirement preparation, such as personal counseling, lectures, discussion groups, and distribution of literature. Can these programs be competently directed by personnel in the organization whose primary responsibilities lie in other functions, or do they require special training and skill which must be secured or employed from outside? Can the leadership be dispersed and thereby be closer to the operating lines or should it be a centralized function? What training is believed to be useful for leadership in such a program? What subjects should be covered? Have the subjects dealt with been based upon a survey of the interests and circumstances of those being prepared to retire or have they been selected from other sources? Were there significant subjects of general enough interest to permit group discussion? What types of employees participated in these programs?

The final test of a program, of course, is in the years after retirement. Have those who participated in programs of preparation for retirement made any better adjustment to retirement than those who did not participate? What evidence can be found in specific patterns of behavior? Have they managed their financial affairs more astutely? Have they found more satisfying ways of using their leisure? Do they report more frequently that they feel useful and needed? Are they fitting more smoothly into their family situation or creating a problem there?

Because of the diversity of planning programs and their relative newness, it is likely to be difficult to obtain sufficient data for valid statistical comparisons of effectiveness. To some extent, therefore, criteria for evaluation of such programs will have to be set up in a manner somewhat similar to those used for evaluation of other educational procedures. In other words, criteria will have to be based upon the extent to which the programs are designed to meet standards which have been generally agreed to be desirable. For example, there should be provisions in the program designed to remove some of the uncertainties that cause older employees to worry during their later years of employment; they should have provisions to encourage employees toward a realistic understanding of their financial resources for retirement; they should attempt to lead employees to recognize the value of postretirement participation in activities that are to them positively enjoyable (not passively accepted in the absence of something else) and socially useful; they should help employees to recognize the role of retirement in the entire process of aging.

To move in this direction realistically, prospective retirees must come to grips with such probable realities as a somewhat lower expendable income, the loss of older friends and loved ones, and decreasing vigor and stamina, if not actual serious illness. A sense of hope and interest in the future with realistic planning will not avoid such difficulties, but may provide an antidote which will enable them to take such difficulties in stride.

We intend to explore the acceptability of these goals to the persons who are going to make decisions about retirement-planning policies and shall seek to determine whether it is practical to establish reasonably reliable criteria for determining whether a given program has been set up to meet these goals.

We assume that a good preretirement planning program will modify the expectations of the individual in the direction of reality; he will be able to predict more accurately his own postretirement feelings and situation, and those of others like him. Using this approach to reality as a criterion, and parts of our retirement satisfaction questionnaires as measures, we should be able to obtain a more objective index of effectiveness of the programs.

Evaluation of impact of policy

The nature of evaluation. A retirement policy may be judged to be good, bad, or indifferent according to the extent to which it leads to improved satisfaction of the people concerned with it. These people include, primarily, present employees, retired persons, and policy-makers. The first step in evaluation of a policy, therefore, is to obtain a reasonably well-controlled estimate of these satisfactions. This means that evaluation must be made primarily in terms of the subjective report of the satisfaction of the people involved. It would be preferable, scientifically, to be able to rely on objective measures rather than upon opinion. Preference is, however, a subjective phenomenon, and it is this subjective feeling on the part of the worker, the retired person, and the employer which is related to his overt actions. Wherever possible, it will be desirable to relate subjective opinion to such objective indices of action as turnover, absence, transfer, and the like. Final reliance will have to be made, however, in the long run, on the influence of policy on people's subjective feelings.

The emphasis on the subjective reports of the people involved in a program should not lead to confusion with evaluations based upon the opinion of observers of such programs. It is very difficult to ascertain whether a program in serving the needs of the people involved simply

on the basis of even the most sophisticated and well-meaning observations of the nature of the program itself. A careful distinction
must be made between approval of the nature of the program on the
basis of the sincerity and thoroughness of the attempt on the one hand,
and its actual effectiveness in changing the attitudes and satisfaction of
the people involved on the other. The same distinction may be made
between the accreditation of schools on the basis of the quality of the
faculty and the courses offered, and the evaluation of their effectiveness
in terms of the actual increase in information, skills, and knowledge
which graduates of the program demonstrate.

In general, a very large number of variables need to be controlled
in any such study. The results should be general and should not be
specific to any one kind of firm, individual, or situation. Such possibly distorting influences as the attitude of the community and
especially of the reference groups of the retirees, the over-all personal
optimism or pessimism of the individual reporting, the availability of
other sources of income, alternative activities and pursuits, the education, hobbies and interests, and personality characteristics of the retiree should be equated or controlled insofar as possible. The methods
by which such control can be exerted will be outlined as we discuss the
measurement of satisfaction of the various individuals involved.

Evaluation of satisfaction of employees. The satisfaction of presently employed workers must be defined according to the report of
these employees concerning their satisfaction. There are two clearly
separable areas which must be evaluated. The first is concerned with
satisfaction with retirement policy as such. The second involves satisfaction with the job, including pay, supervision, task, and conditions
of work. Separate schedules will be constructed for both these measures, and their relationships to such variables as general rating tendencies, individual characteristics, and actual differences in policy will
be evaluated.

A certain amount of validation of these measures of satisfaction can
be obtained by correlation of degree of reported dissatisfaction with
amount of absenteeism, turnover, complaints, grievances, or other
objective measures. Such empirical objective validation of the subjective indices will be attempted in every case possible.

Evaluation of satisfaction of retirees. The satisfaction of this
crucial group must be defined in terms of their report of their satisfaction with existing policy. Again, two aspects of satisfaction must be
distinguished, that concerned with satisfaction with retirement policy
as such and that concerned with satisfaction with life in retirement.
In these two areas it is particularly important that some sort of

correction be made for over-all tendency of the person to rate all aspects of his life either favorably or unfavorably, although account must also be taken of the realities of the situation which are beyond the realm of inclusion in retirement policy. We plan to try to predict the retirement satisfaction of an individual on the basis of all the known variables in his background and his situation, and to utilize the *difference* between this predicted satisfaction and his actual reported satisfaction as a basis for comparison of different policies. This is a complicated approach to the problem but also, we feel, a realistic one in view of the fact that almost certainly retirement policy can have only a relatively minor impact on the total adjustment of a given individual. The minor nature of this impact does not, of course, imply that the policy-maker should ignore its influence, since it is at least under his control.

It is difficult to evaluate the validity of these subjective measures for retired persons. Possibly, an extremely effective policy might reduce the frequency with which retired persons seek secondary jobs or might increase their participation in community affairs. A comparison of these measures will be made.

Evaluation of satisfaction of policy-makers. It is, in any case, dissatisfaction of those who influence policy-making (whether company manager or union official) which will determine changes in eventual retirement policy. It is crucial, therefore, that such satisfaction be evaluated. It is not reasonable to expect the average management or union policy-maker to conduct a careful research study concerning the effectiveness of his retirement policy. He will, however, have an opinion about it. A consolidation of such opinions concerning the effectiveness of various kinds of policies in previous situations in which they have been introduced should be useful. Again, controls must be introduced for any such grading of satisfaction in terms of the tendency of the rater to give an over-all high or low rating and to be conservative or liberal in his judgment of difference.

The accuracy of the opinion of the policy-maker can, in many situations, be checked against the actual cost, actual reported satisfaction on the job, etc. Replacement of workers is expensive, as are pension costs. On the other hand, lack of flexibility in the labor force may also be expensive. The objective facts will be ascertained wherever possible.

Relevance of results to particular groups or situations. The generality of our findings concerning satisfactions will, unfortunately, be limited to particular kinds of groups or situations. To generalize, we must be able to classify different subcategories of companies, communities, individuals, and situations within which effects of policy will be similar. For example, different companies will not only have different policies concerning retirement but also various over-all personnel philosophies and different policies concerning other matters such as upgrading, transfer, insurance, profit-sharing, and discharge. Not only will philosophies differ but also such demographic characteristics as size, nature of industry, location, and the like. The effectiveness of a retirement policy can be predicted only in the context of the constellation of these other variables.

METHODOLOGY

Collection and analysis of data will proceed along two lines: (1) a nationwide questionnaire survey of employing organizations, and (2) an intensive study of 25 to 40 employing organizations involving personal interviews with management and labor representatives, present employees, and retirees. In addition, we are considering the possibility of surveys in a number of communities where the intensive studies are being carried out in order to ascertain the attitudes toward retirement held by nonretired elements of the community population and the services and facilities available to older people. Although a decision has not yet been reached concerning this phase of the study, it would be the objective of such surveys to examine the relationship of community attitudes, services, and facilities to the degree of satisfaction with given types of retirement policies and to retirement adjustment.

National questionnaire survey

We expect to gather facts by a national mail questionnaire survey of employing units as to retirement age policies in effect, trends in retirement policies based on recent or contemplated changes, existence and size of retirement benefits, and the content and methods of programs of preparation for retirement where these exist.

Sample design

Questionnaires will be mailed to local employing units of business organizations, government agencies, and nonprofit institutions. The local employing unit (i.e., plant or business establishment) has been selected as the focal point for study since it is at this level that the actual application, administration, and implementation of retirement policy takes place, and where the impact of retirement is experienced by the organization, its employees, and its retirees.

A plan of sequential sampling of employing units is to be carried out. A basic sample of approximately 20,000 establishments stratified by four size categories (i.e., number of employees) will be drawn. From this sample a subsample of approximately 2000 firms will be selected at random for the first questionnaire mailing.

The analysis of returns from this first subsample will have two objectives: (1) to present a picture of current retirement policies and practices for the United States as a whole, and (2) to identify those variables which appear to be significant in the determination of retirement policy and experience. This initial subsample of 2000 establishments is unlikely to be of sufficient size to enable us to establish causal relationships, but should yield sufficient information to identify the more significant variables by which subsequent subsamples might be selected or stratified. Thus, the first subsample will serve as a means of developing hypotheses. Subsequent subsamples of 2000 establishments each will then be drawn from the remaining 18,000 units in order to test these hypotheses and develop further factual information concerning retirement practices and experience. The number of subsamples (and, therefore, the total sample size) is not known as yet. The total size of the sample and its composition will be determined by the number and nature of the variables which appear to warrant investigation and their variance, and the decision concerning this must await the returns from at least the first subsample.

Our decision to employ sequential sampling is the result of the dearth of information concerning the variables which are actually of significance in determining whether or not organizations have pension plans, the nature of retirement age policies utilized, and experience thereunder. Thus, it is extremely difficult to determine an initial relevant basis for stratification. It would appear, for example, that factors such as size, skill requirements, profitability and rate of expansion in the industry, rate and nature of technological change, and extent of unionization would, to varying degrees, be key factors affecting the existence of pension plans and influencing retirement policy. But how is one to determine the *particular* industries which should be lumped for stratification purposes? To adopt arbitrarily the Budget Bureau's Standard Industrial Classification for purposes of stratification opens up the possibility of serious sampling diseconomies. Thus, for example, while the Standard Industrial Classification combines coal mining and crude petroleum production in its "Division B—

Mining," a combining of these industries for purposes of studying retirement policies is likely to be highly inappropriate.

It is our hope and expectation that the procedure of stratifying initially by size only and drawing the first 2000 establishment subsample randomly from these will provide an effective means of determining the relevant variables upon which to select or stratify subsequent subsamples. We can also intercorrelate various organizational characteristics in an attempt to formulate a clearer basis for classification of organizations.

Development and testing of research instruments

Survey questionnaire. A major portion of our efforts thus far has been devoted to the development and testing of questionnaires which will serve as the principal research instruments for the national survey. Since it is our objective to obtain detailed information concerning the retirement policies, practices, and experience of employing organizations, these questionnaires are somewhat detailed and complex.

In order to minimize the length and complexity of the questionnaires, it was decided to utilize a preliminary one-page instrument which would elicit information on the basis of which organizations could be classified as to basic types of retirement policies. Each organization is then to receive a longer questionnaire designed specifically for its category. The one-page preliminary questionnaire will request the following information:

1. Whether employees are covered by a formal pension plan other than Old-Age and Survivors Insurance;
2. Which of the following types of retirement policies is being followed:
a. All employees required to retire upon reaching a specified age
b. Employees permitted to work as long as they are willing and able to perform satisfactorily
c. Certain classes of employees required to retire upon reaching a specified age, while other classes of employees permitted to work beyond that age
d. No definite retirement age policy formulated;
3. The normal retirement age and, where applicable, the age at which all employees must retire[1];
4. Whether the organization has a preparation for retirement program (other than merely explaining the benefits for which the employees are eligible) and, if not, whether the organization is seriously considering the establishment of such a program;

[1] "Normal retirement age" is defined as the age at which employees are eligible for the full retirement benefit with no reduction because of age.

5. Whether the respondent would be willing to provide further information if requested.

This preliminary short-form questionnaire was sent to 132 firms in Elmira, New York; 27 firms in Binghamton, New York; 25 firms in St. Louis, Missouri; and 36 firms in Tennessee (primarily Knoxville). St. Louis and Knoxville were selected in order to test our questionnaires in cities sufficiently distant from Ithaca so that firms located there would not be influenced (either positively or negatively) by their proximity to and familiarity with Cornell University. No attempt was made at this time to obtain a representative sample of firms, but merely to pretest the questionnaire for quality and quantity of response.

The responses after one follow-up ranged from 61 percent in Elmira to 83 percent for Tennessee firms. The quality of response was generally good, although a number of minor changes in the questionnaire are indicated. The responses from Elmira (which were received before questionnaires were mailed to the remaining cities) indicated that small independent firms in that city generally did not have pension plans or formalized retirement age policies. Such firms, therefore, did not provide a good test for a questionnaire dealing with details of pension and retirement policies. In order to obtain a more adequate test of the questionnaires, these were sent only to firms of 200 or more employees in the other three test cities. Should our national survey indicate that small independent firms generally do not have pension plans or formalized retirement age policies, separate questionnaires will have to be developed to obtain detailed information as to their methods and experience in dealing with superannuated employees.

Based on the responses to our short form, we have developed four alternate long-form follow-up questionnaires, each of which is being sent to firms in the appropriate category. The four categories of organization are as follows:

1. Organizations which require all employees to retire at normal retirement age irrespective of their health or competence;
2. Organizations which permit employees to continue in employment beyond normal retirement age as long as they are willing and able to perform satisfactorily;
3. Organizations which permit employees to work beyond normal retirement age, but require all employees to retire upon reaching a later age;
4. Organizations which require certain classes of employees to retire at the normal retirement age, but permit other classes to work beyond normal retirement age.

The responses to these questionnaires will represent the principal test of the detailed follow-up questionnaires to be used in our national survey. A separate questionnaire dealing with preparation for re-tirement programs is being developed and will be sent only to those organizations which indicated on the preliminary short form that they have such programs.

Where the basic unit of study is the local plant or establishment, the use of a mail questionnaire to obtain information poses some major difficulties over and above those ordinarily involved in the use of this method of obtaining data. The special problems stem from the fact that some 19,000 of the approximately 60,000 business establishments in the United States with more than 50 employees are divisions of multiunit organizations.

Where multiplant organizations are involved, it is probable that only a portion of the information elicited in the questionnaire will be available at the local institution, with the remainder having to come from the headquarters office of the parent organization. Thus, for example, data as to the number or average age of individuals retired during a given time period or the number of exceptions to a com-pulsory retirement policy may be on file at company headquarters, while information concerning the relation of a particular retirement age policy to a local plant's labor supply problem is more likely to be answered best by local plant management. Moreover, even if all the desired information can be supplied by the local plant management, company policy may require that information provided by local man-agement be cleared through the firm's headquarters office.

The information sought in the preliminary short-form question-naire was sufficiently brief to enable one individual, whether at the local plant or national headquarters, to complete it in its entirety. This may not be possible for the longer follow-up questionnaire, however, and the necessity of its being routed to appropriate in-dividuals at the various levels and geographic locations of the or-ganization may prove to be a problem of major proportions.

In testing the follow-up questionnaire, our approach will be to mail the appropriate form to the particular individual who completed the preliminary questionnaire, accompanied by a request that he fill it out as far as possible and, if necessary, route it to whoever can best complete the remaining questions. We are hopeful that, having indicated on the preliminary questionnaire a willingness to provide further information, the respondent will make the effort necessary to ensure that the long form is completed and returned to us. Within a month the quantity and quality of the response should indicate whether alternative methods of securing responses from multiunit organizations will have to be investigated.

The questionnaires discussed above are designed for private commercial and manufacturing organizations. Mail questionnaires will also be utilized in our survey of retirement policies and practices in national nonprofit organizations and governmental units. These questionnaires will parallel those for profit-making institutions, and where appropriate, will permit the aggregating of information for all types of organizations. The questionnaires for nonprofit organizations and governmental units will differ from those for private organizations only insofar as is necessary to take account of the major differences between these types of institutions.

Test development. The goal of this phase of the project was to develop an evaluation criterion of perceived satisfaction resulting from various types of policies in various settings. The first step in this phase of the project was an extensive literature survey and compilation of a bibliography on multidimensional scaling and other approaches to measurement of job satisfaction. From this survey we set forth the scaling problems likely to be encountered and the proposed methods of handling them.

Following are desirable characteristics of satisfaction scaling instruments:

a. Scales personally relevant to respondents
b. Low verbal content
c. Avoidance of long questions involving several modifiers and qualifying phrases
d. Self-administering format
e. Scaling technique applicable to wide range of satisfaction, as with various aspects of jobs, life in general, and retirement
f. Applicability of some scales to wide range of socio-economic and job levels
g. Avoidance of rating errors
h. Independence of subscales to allow pattern analysis
i. Conformity with discrimination and validation criteria
j. Ordered metric scale.

As a starting point in the attainment of these goals, we decided to develop a scale for job satisfaction, then to generalize the method to other areas. Our subscales in the area of job satisfaction were task, supervision, work groups, and economic aspects. The choice of these subareas was based on fairly consistent results of factor analytic studies done in the area of job satisfaction. The decision was made to use adjective check lists with forced responses in order to reduce the verbal level of the material. The respondents chose their own anchor points for each scale in terms of the job they would like best and the job they would like least, in order to obtain measures which were personally relevant. The proposed scoring system is objective and involves similarity of present job to least desirable job and most desirable job as chosen by the respondents.

A series of pretests are being conducted. First, lists of adjectives were drawn up for each of the four areas. These lists were pretested on two groups of janitors to: (1) assess difficulty level of adjectives and instructions; (2) assess feasibility of testing technique, administration, etc.; (3) clarify and improve areas of questioning; and (4) clarify and improve the over-all format of the test.

Based on the results of the first pretest, some changes in adjectives were made, a self-administering format was drawn up and the instrument was administered to 30 secretaries at the School of Industrial and Labor Relations of Cornell University. Attempted validation of the scoring system was carried out against rankings by judges and selves regarding satisfaction and importance of subareas.

From these results the item content was improved in each of the subareas and the scales were balanced as to length. This new form was then administered to 317 college students and workers, with prospects of testing policemen, firemen, and some elementary school teachers in the near future. From these data we will determine item clusters and validate over-all test score and subscores against modified self-rating scale of importance and satisfaction with subareas.

Pilot intensive studies

From the firms responding to the long-form test questionnaire, six will be selected for detailed analysis through the media of personal interviews with company and union representatives, present employees and retirees, and collection of data at the source. These will serve as pilot studies in preparation for the intensive investigations of firms selected from respondents in the national questionnaire survey. The pilot studies will seek: (1) to help determine the nature and limitations of the data which can be collected in the intensive studies, (2) to facilitate the development of interview instruments, and (3) to provide information which will aid in revisions of the mail questionnaire should this prove necessary.

Intensive study of selected samples

By intensive study and questioning, members of the retirement study staff following a uniform plan will seek to understand and report on a relatively small number of organizations (22 to 40) representing as large a number of the significant independent and control variables as possible. Information will be sought from employers, employees, and employee representatives with respect to their opinions of the specific retirement age policies in effect in their organizations. We hope, thereby, to give an account of the advantages and disadvantages of these policies as seen by the parties affected.

The general satisfaction of employees and retired persons will be evaluated and related to the policies, and every attempt will be made to control for the effects of other personnel policies of the company. In each of the locations of these intensive studies, an appraisal may be made of community attitudes toward older people and retirement, the facilities for their participation in community enterprises, and provisions for recreation, housing, and maintenance of health.

In those organizations studied intensively which have a program of preparation for retirement, a study will be made of these programs. A study may also be made of other such programs in the community if this appears to offer an opportunity for the enrichment of the very limited knowledge available concerning their effectiveness in assisting persons in making satisfactory adjustments to retirement. This will require a follow-up of those retirees who have retired since participation in a program of preparation. Also, to round out our knowledge of such plans, we may undertake a subsequent longitudinal study of those about to participate in the programs, of their attitudes during final years of employment, and of adjustments made in moving from active employment to retirement.

We will also try to learn about problems of adjustment encountered by retirees for which their preparation program gave no, or inadequate, help. If this type of longitudinal study is undertaken, we would also wish to include comparable employees who had no opportunity to participate in preparation programs in order to get some basis for judging what contribution was made by the program to the participants.

Because of the large number of variables being compared, no statistical significance can be attached to any differences found on these first samples of intensively studied firms. We will, therefore, wish to repeat the comparisons which appear to be significant on a second, independent sample to furnish replication or cross-validation of the findings and to permit a safe generalization from our results.

PROPOSED CONCLUSIONS

On the basis of our studies we hope to measure the impact of various aspects of retirement planning or policy upon the adjustment of older persons who have retired under any given kind of policy in contrasting types of organizations and community situations. We want to be able to make similar conclusions about the effects upon the satisfaction of present employees and of policy-makers. Restricted as these conclusions may be, we hope that they will serve as a guide to employers who are attempting to make policies.

Our studies are also concerned with trends and with frequencies of policies. They should furnish tabulations and cross-tabulations of the frequencies with which various policies occur in different kinds of companies and situations. We want to know the extent to which these frequencies reflect the effectiveness of various policies in different operating situations.

We hope that we shall be able to formulate and possibly test hypotheses concerning the reasons for the relative reported effectiveness of different policies in contrasting organizations and their interaction with other important variables. This may make it possible for policy-makers and theoreticians to generalize beyond these particular situations which we will have investigated. In addition, we shall seek to formulate hypotheses as to the reasons which organizations have had for the adoption of policies of various kinds.

Methodologically, we hope to develop and utilize a procedure for the classification of organizations, the classification of policies, and the classification of situations. We hope that we will, by this analysis, devise a new method of control of personal and situational factors in determining satisfaction. Moreover, we hope that we shall have devised a new method for measuring satisfaction in worker retirement which will reflect the individual's own personal values in terms of the weights which we will assign to different factors in his over-all satisfaction.

Unemployment, Retirement, and Pensions

A. J. JAFFE AND J. R. MILAVSKY

EARLIER the authors had carried out two studies of unemployed workers who were receiving unemployment insurance benefits in New York State, during 1957 and 1958 (Columbia University, 1958, 1960). These studies revealed clearly that the economic effects of extended unemployment were quite different for various types of beneficiaries and families. The age and sex of the beneficiary, whether or not he was the only worker in the family, and the number of dependents are nonjob attributes of the unemployed person which are related to his adjustment toward unemployment as such and toward the time when unemployment benefits expire. Most workers, of course, ordinarily return to work before their benefits expire; this paper is not concerned with such persons.

A number of the unemployed, however, become chronically unemployed, i.e., they are still unemployed after exhausting all benefits. In New York State benefits in most instances are paid for 26 weeks (excluding special programs such as the Federal Temporary Unemployment Compensation Act of 1958). Accordingly, attention was addressed to persons who were likely to be chronically unemployed but who were still under the retirement age of 65. For the purposes of the study we defined such persons as men in the age group of 55 to 64 years.

The purpose of this study then consists of:

1. A brief examination of the available data which might indicate the extent to which the unemployed 55 to 64 year old men become reemployed;
2. With regard to those who become chronically unemployed, examination of the resources they may have to fall back upon with respect to:
a. Sources of family income other than unemployment insurance benefits;
b. Savings, if any, which may be available;
c. Family composition to ascertain the extent to which other family members might contribute to the support of the family;
3. Drawing such implications as seem to emerge, particularly with

regard to the Old-Age and Survivors Insurance (retirement pension) system.

Sources of data and methodology

The New York State Department of Labor, Division of Employment, has carried out a number of studies based primarily on the information ordinarily collected during the operations of the unemployment insurance program; these studies are referred to in the various footnotes. Further information is available from the special sample population census conducted in New York State in 1957. Also, the information which was collected in the study of Utica, New York, in 1958 was utilized; this information was obtained by means of interviews with almost 800 persons who had been drawing unemployment benefits for 5 weeks or longer prior to the interview, and who were still drawing such benefits as of the time of the interview (Columbia University, 1959).

The methodology consists of the calculation of various rates for three age groups of men: 45 to 54 years, 55 to 64 years, and 65 and over. In all tables where findings from the Utica study are presented, we have standardized the data within each age group for type of family,[1] so that this factor is held constant. Data obtained from other sources could not be standardized for this factor.

EMPLOYMENT AND UNEMPLOYMENT EXPERIENCES
Employment experiences prior to the last layoff

Older workers, in comparison with younger ones, tend to remain with the same employer, unless laid off. There is much less voluntary mobility, i.e., shifting from one job to another, among older workers (Palmer, 1954)[2]. Part of this, of course, it related to the fact that it is

---

[1] Types of families are defined as follows: (a) one-person families; (b) families of two or more adults in which no one was employed during the month prior to the interview; (c) families of two or more adults in which one or more persons other than the beneficiary were employed during the month prior to the interview. See also Appendix—A Note on the Utica, New York, Study.

[2] The Palmer study shows the mean number of jobs held per male worker (durng the decade 1940–1949) by age as follows:

Age	Jobs
25–34	3.4
35–44	3.0
45–54	2.3
55–64	2.0
65+	1.7

more difficult for an older man to find an employer who is willing to hire him. Part of this lesser mobility also stems from the fact that many of the older workers have accumulated seniority rights in particular establishments, together perhaps with pension and other fringe benefits; taken together, these various benefits tend to tie the employee to a particular job.

The unemployed men in the Utica survey apparently had about the same employment histories as others in the United States and as reported in Palmer's and other studies. This emerged in answer to the question: "During the last three years (prior to the onset of the present period of unemployment), for how many different employers have you worked?" (Table 1). Clearly, older men tended to remain with the same employer.

Table 1. Number of employers worked for in the last three years unemployed men, by age, Utica, 1958, percentage distribution

Age of respondent	Number of employers		
	1	2	3 or more
45–54	46	32	22
55–64	66	19	15
65+	77	12	11

The men were also asked for the number of periods during the last 3 years in which they had collected unemployment insurance benefits (Table 2). The fact that older men had fewer periods of unemployment reflects in part their tendency not to change jobs, if possible.[3]

In short, there is reason to believe—and the Utica study provides no contradictory evidence—that, at least up to the age of 65, the older

Table 2. Number of periods during which unemployment insurance was collected, unemployed men, by age, Utica, 1958, percentage distribution

Age of respondent	Number of periods		
	1	2	3 or more
45–54	59	35	6
55–64	66	21	13
65+	69	16	15

[3] Fewer periods of unemployment in the past may also reflect the fact that this group of beneficiaries was selective, by the very nature of the New York State unemployment insurance system. Any worker who had been laid off in the past (i.e., at least one year prior to the study) and had not been reemployed, could not be in the sample. Hence, as of any one date, age cohorts who have trouble in obtaining employment will have lesser proportions of persons who have collected unemployment benefits several times in the past.

worker will remain at his job, unless mass layoffs occur, or unless he becomes physically incapacitated. Beyond age 65, when he is eligible to collect his retirement pension, he may be asked to retire, as many of our older respondents reported, or lose his job via a mass layoff, as happened to others of our respondents.

Unemployment experiences

Unfortunately, there are always many firms which fail and go out of business; other firms move from one city to another; recession periods come when many are laid off; and other calamities do occur which result in unemployment for all, or most, of the workers of a given establishment. When such occurs the older man, with or without seniority rights, as well as the younger man, loses his job. In addition, sickness may result in job loss; this is more likely to affect older than younger workers.

Now some of these men who have lost their jobs find new jobs within such a short period of time that they do not collect unemployment benefits and are not recorded as unemployed (on the basis of the unemployment insurance system) (New York State Department of Labor, 1959a). Those who remain out of work for a week or longer and file then become recorded as unemployed.

For total New York State, older men have higher unemployment rates in terms of the unemployment insurance system. Those 65 and over have the highest rate, followed by those 55 to 64 years; at all ages below 55 the unemployment rates are still lower (Table 3).

Furthermore, and what is most significant, is the fact that a much larger proportion of the older men (than of the younger) who have become unemployed, exhaust their benefits. This means that these older men have been unemployed for a longer time, generally at least 26 weeks. This would seem to indicate that older men have more trouble than do younger men in finding new jobs.

There is further evidence that older unemployed men have more difficulty in finding jobs than do younger men (Sheppard *et al.,* 1960; Cohen *et al.,* 1960; New York State Department of Labor, 1959b). Among older men a much higher proportion of those who have exhausted their benefits retire from the labor force within a year after exhausting unemployment benefits (Table 3).

Among men age 65 and over, retirement from the labor force may be genuine in the sense that it indicates a preference to retire and live on their pensions, a decision perhaps reached after months of in-

Table 3. *Estimated unemployment, exhaustion, and retirement rates among male covered workers, by age, New York State, 1954 and 1956*[a]

Category	1954					1956				
	25–34	35–44	44–54	56–64	65 or over	25–34	35–44	45–54	55–64	65 or over
Percent of covered workers who became beneficiaries anytime during the year[a]	11	9	10	14	22	9	7	8	10	20
Percent of beneficiaries who exhausted their benefit rights[b]	12	10	13	17	39	8	9	12	16	41
Percent of exhaustees who withdrew from labor force within 12 months following exhaustion of benefits[c]	8	8	9	23	62	NA	NA	NA	NA	NA

[a] Sources: Number of workers who received benefits estimated from data presented in an unpublished study of the New York State Department of Labor, Division of Employment, "Labor Market Experience of Beneficiaries Who Exhausted Benefits in New York State, January 1954 through June 1955"; and from a published mimeo report of the same agency, "Persons Who Received 20 or More Weeks of Unemployment Benefits in New York State, Benefit Years Ending in 1954, 1955, 1956, and 1957," Bureau of Research and Statistics, December, 1958. In addition, number of covered workers by age and sex estimated from data in previously cited unpublished document and from data in published mimeo report. "Statistical Tables (Actual Sample Data) from the Sample Survey of the Labor Force in New York State by the U.S. Bureau of the Census, February–March 1957," Bureau of Research and Statistics, October 31, 1958; these various data adjusted in accordance with employment data present in various issues of the Labor Market Review, published by the New York State Department of Labor, Division of Employment.

[b] Sources: estimated from data presented in "Labor Market Experience of Beneficiaries Who Exhausted Benefits . . ." and "Persons Who Received 20 or More Weeks of Unemployment Benefits . . . ," see footnote a.

[c] Source: estimated from data presented in "Labor Market Experience of Beneficiaries Who Exhausted Benefits . . . ," see footnote a.

effective job seeking. Among men in the age group 55 to 64, however, very few have pension rights, and for this group, withdrawal from the labor force generally means inability to find new employment. There is but a thin line separating the chronically unemployed from those out of the labor force; the chronically unemployed who become despondent and quit looking for work are then regarded as having retired from the labor force.

Other evidence of the fact that older unemployed men have trouble obtaining reemployment is afforded by data from the seven-city study. The percentage distributions of hires by age as compared with that of all unemployed men (in total United States) are as shown in Table 4. Clearly, older unemployed men, particularly those 55 and over, are less likely to be hired than are younger men[4]; men 55 and over constituted 19 percent of the unemployed, but only 9 percent of the hires.

[4] "Thirty-six percent of the women and 28 percent of the men were still unemployed three months after separation; 41 percent of all those 45 years and over were among the unemployed, as against 26 percent of those 25 to 44 years, and 32 percent of the 17 to 24 age group!" ("Unemployed experience of separated federal workers," 1954, p. 660).

Table 4. Percentage distribution of hiring by age groups compared to percentage of all unemployed men, seven cities, United States, 1956[a]

Age group	Hires	Unemployed
Under 25	21	27
25–34	31	20
35–44	24	16
45–54	15	18
55–64	7	13
65 and over	2	6

[a] Source: "Studies of the Aged and Aging," Employment, Selected Documents, compiled by the staff of the Committee on Labor and Public Welfare of the U.S. Senate, November, 1956, Government Printing Office, Washington, D.C., 1957, Vol. IV, p. 57, Table 20. The distribution of all unemployed men is taken from the Current Population Reports, Labor Force, "The Monthly Report on the Labor Force," January and February, 1956, U.S. Bureau of the Census Series P-57, Government Printing Office, Washington, D.C.

FINANCIAL RESOURCES
Amount and sources during employed period

During the employed period the families of the men in all three age groups—45–54 years, 55–64 years, and 65 and over—had approximately the same median monthly income, a little over $400. These are the families of the unemployment insurance beneficiaries interviewed in Utica.

The sources of this income, however, varied considerably for families of men under age 65 as compared with men aged 65 and over. Among families having beneficiaries under age 65, between 4 and 5 families in 10 had been dependent entirely on the wages or salary earnings of the man who subsequently became unemployed and received unemployment insurance benefits (Table 5). The remaining half of the families received their income either from the combined wages of two or more workers, or from wages and other sources of income, such as profits from private business, rental income, veterans' and other pensions, etc. (By definition, of course, no family had exclusively nonwage income; such a family could not have appeared in the Utica study.)

Among families having beneficiaries aged 65 or over, in contrast, only one-quarter had been dependent entirely on the wages of the man who subsequently became an unemployment insurance beneficiary. Furthermore, about 6 families in 10 had income from sources other than wages and salaries. Among these families, old age pensions were a very important source of additional income; either the unemploy-

Table 5. *Sources of family income (for identical families)*
during employed and unemployed months, for male unemployment
insurance beneficiaries, by age, Utica, 1958, percentage distribution[a]

Employed month

| Age of beneficiary | Income from wages only | | Income from wages plus other sources |
	Beneficiary only	Beneficiary plus other members	
45–54	46	23	31
55–64	42	15	43
65 and over	24	15	61

Unemployed month

| Age of beneficiary | Income from unemployment benefits and wages | | Income from benefits, wages, and other sources |
	Benefits only	Benefits plus wages	
45–54	35	28	37
55–64	33	19	48
65 and over	2	1	97

[a] Source: Unpublished information from Utica survey (*Unemployment Benefits and Family Finances: A Study of Incomes and Expenditures of Beneficiaries and Their Families in Utica, New York*, Bureau of Applied Social Research, New York, 1960).

ment insurance beneficiary or some other member of his family had qualified for such pensions.

Furthermore, during an average month of employment, from 4 to 6 families in every 10 at each age group added to their savings. Only about 2 families in 10 used part of their savings, and perhaps one family in 10 had no savings at all. In short, the majority of families accumulated savings during periods of employment.[5]

Amount and sources during unemployed period

With the onset of unemployment, families tried to make financial adjustments in several ways, including: (a) cutting down on expenditures, (b) drawing on accumulated savings, (c) sending additional family members out to work, (d) utilizing hitherto unused pension rights, and (e) other ways.

The combination of the effects of the last two mentioned factors— sending other family members out to work and utilizing hitherto un-

[5] No effort was made to try to learn how much savings these people had. It was found in the pretest for the Utica survey that such questioning generated too much hostility.

used pension rights—becomes readily apparent in examining the sources of income during unemployment. Among families containing beneficiaries under age 65 only about one-third were dependent for their family income entirely on the unemployment insurance benefits. Compare this with the employed period when almost half the families were exclusively dependent on the earnings of the man who subsequently became a beneficiary (Table 5).

Among families with beneficiary aged 65 or over, full advantage was taken of OASI pension rights. During the unemployed period virtually no families were dependent entirely on unemployment insurance benefits or wages earned by other family members.[6]

Most families drew on past savings (in addition to any other adjustments they may have made) during the unemployed period. Among families containing beneficiaries aged 45 to 54 years, about half the families had used from half to all of their savings (from the onset of unemployment to the time of the interview); among families having beneficiaries aged 55 to 64 years about one-third had used half or more of their savings; and among families with beneficiaries aged 65 and over, about one-quarter (Table 6).

Apparently there was little difference in use of savings by age of beneficiary among families in which the beneficiary was under 65 years old. Perhaps a few more of the families in which the beneficiary was aged 55 to 64 had larger savings, in comparison with the families having younger aged beneficiaries. The more striking differences appear among families having beneficiaries aged 65 and over. Since these people took up their pension rights (with the onset of unemployment) they had less reason or need to use their past savings. Indeed, there is reason to believe that they were hoarding their savings against the time when unemployment benefits might be exhausted, leaving them chronically unemployed and with meager income resources.[7]

[6] Among all unemployment insurance claimants in New York state in August, 1959, the following proportions of men in each age group were receiving pensions:

Age group	Percent
Under 55	0.1
55–64	5.7
65 and over	72.1

Furthermore, of men receiving pensions, over 9 in 10 were receiving OASI (with or without other pensions) (New York State Department of Labor, 1960, Tables 1 and 2, p. 32).

[7] Home ownership, in theory at least, is one form of savings. To what extent it may be useful as a source of fluid emergency funds, however, depends on the size of the equity and the ease with which it can be converted into cash. Home ownership in Utica was much more prevalent among men over 55 years

Table 6. *Use of savings during unemployed period, for male*
unemployment insurance beneficiaries, by age, Utica, New York,
1958, percentage distribution[a]

	Age of beneficiary		
Use of savings	*45–54*	*55–64*	*65 or over*
Had no savings at onset of unemployment	15	7	8
Had savings at onset of unemployment	85	93	92
Did not use any	15	21	32
Used savings	70	72	60
Used all savings	21	12	4
Used more than half	25	15	8
Used just half	10	10	14
Used less than half	14	35	34

[a] Source: unpublished information from Utica Survey, Bureau of Applied Social
Research, *Unemployment Benefits and Family Finances: A Study of Incomes and
Expenditures of Beneficiaries and Their Families in Utica, New York, 1958*, The
Bureau, New York, 1960.

Families dependent exclusively on unemployment benefits

From the limited viewpoint of need only, we can assume that those
families dependent entirely on unemployment benefits may be in the
most precarious financial position. Families in which other members
are employed or which have nonwage sources of income will still have
some funds if and when the beneficiary exhausts his benefits and still
remains out of work. Where benefits are the only source of income,
however, we can assume that the family will be in serious financial
straits when and if the benefits are used up and the man becomes
chronically unemployed. Accordingly, let us turn to an examination
of the savings situation of those families dependent exclusively on unemployment insurance benefits.

We saw (Table 5) that among families with beneficiary under age
65 about one-third were dependent entirely on such benefits. Among
these families it would appear that about 1 in 10 had no savings at
the onset of unemployment. Of those families with savings (at the
beginning of the period of unemployment) two-thirds reported that

---

of age, among whom 7 in 10 reported owning their own homes; among men
45 to 54 years, only 5 in 10 reported home ownership. It is our belief that
such "savings" were of little use in helping to pay for the daily living expenditures (with the exception of housing expenditures). On the negative side, home
ownership may make it somewhat more difficult for some older men to find
new jobs. Sometimes a man may find employment by moving to another city;
a home owner, however, may find it so difficult to dispose of his house and
move, that he may simply remain where he is and continue to be unemployed.

they had used up half or more of such savings between the onset of unemployment and the time of the interview (an average of about 4 months). In short, it would appear clear that if unemployment were to continue much longer most of these families (dependent entirely on unemployment benefits) would become destitute. In this regard families having beneficiaries aged 55 to 64 were no different from families in which the beneficiary was younger. Only families in which the beneficiary was old enough to qualify for a pension were in a "sounder" financial condition.

EMPLOYMENT OF OTHER FAMILY MEMBERS

One way in which families might try to adjust to the unemployment of the head is to send additional members into the labor force. In order to investigate this point among the Utica respondents, we selected out the husband-wife families in which the husband was the unemployment insurance beneficiary and examined the employment status of other family members aged 14 and over, during both the period of the husband's employment and that of his unemployment.

Employment of wives

During the period when the husband was employed it was found that among husbands aged: 45–54 years, 4 in 10 of the wives were also working; 55–64 years, 2 in 10 of the wives were also working; and 65 and over, 1 in 10 of the wives was also working. Clearly, among older women fewer were employed; this is a finding to be expected on the basis of all other information we have on the employment of women (Bancroft, 1958).

With the onset of the husband's unemployment some wives previously not employed entered the labor force and found jobs. The proportions by age of husband were as follows: 45–54 years 3 in 10 of the wives not previously employed, found jobs; 55–65 years, 1 in 10 of the wives not previously employed found jobs; and 65 and over, *almost none* found jobs. Since older women, like older men, have difficulty in finding employment, it would seem that families of older beneficiaries—say, 55 and over—cannot expect as much financial aid via the employment of the wives as can be counted on by families with younger beneficiaries.

Employment of other family members

During the period when the husband was employed we find that among husbands aged: 45–54 years, 4 in 10 of other relatives in family were also working; 55–64 years, 7 in 10 of other relatives in family were also working; and 65 and over, 6 in 10 of other relatives in family were also working. Quite evidently, among the families with older heads, most other family members who were aged 14 and over and were able to work (except the wives) were employed. These other family members were grown children still living at home, siblings of the head or his wife, and sometimes a parent of the head or his wife. With the exception of any aged person (say, 65 and over) we should expect that most of these other family members would be in the labor force, and probably employed.

Among the younger families, i.e., those in which the head was aged 45 to 54 years, the other family members (except the wives) were more likely to consist of teenage children who were probably not working as long as the head had employment.

With the onset of the husband's unemployment, it would appear that among those families in which the husband was aged 55 and over, there were but few other relatives who could have found employment in an effort to make up for the husband's loss of wages. These other relatives were either employed already, or probably physically unable to find employment, probably because of advanced age or sickness.

Among families in which the head was under 55 years, however, there were a number of younger persons who could and did find jobs; consequently, during the period of the husband's unemployment we find the following proportions of other relatives employed (compare with the proportions during the employed period): 45–54 years, 7 in 10; 55–64 years, 8 in 10; and 65 and over, 6 in 10.

In short, it would appear that only families in which the beneficiary was under age 55 might expect to try to adjust to the unemployment of the head by having additional members find jobs. Among older families there were virtually no such unused labor resources.

CONCLUSIONS AND IMPLICATIONS

There appears to be a "no man's land" among beneficiaries just under the pension age of 65, where the problems of chronic unemployment and retirement form a morass in which victims are caught.

In this study, the age group 55 to 64 years was arbitrarily used; whether this "no man's land" should be limited to the age group 60 to 64, or extended to younger ages, it is hard to say.

The important facts which seem to emerge are:

1. With increasing age it becomes much more difficult for men to obtain employment, so that many of the older men who lose their jobs become chronically unemployed.

2. If the unemployed person is aged 65 or over, in the event that he cannot obtain reemployment, he can fall back on his retirement pension; it is impossible to say whether such pensions are adequate for his needs, but they are certainly better than no pensions.

3. Men under age 45, or perhaps 50 or even 55, are much less likely (than are older men) to become chronically unemployed, assuming no devastating depression as that of the 1930s. For most of these men the unemployment insurance programs, at least that of New York State, will help tide them over until they become reemployed. Furthermore, the wives of such beneficiaries are generally young enough so that many can obtain employment and help add to the finances of the family during the husband's unemployment.

4. Men in the age group just under 65, however, are probably just as likely to become chronically unemployed as are the men over 65, but have no pensions to fall back upon. Some of these unemployed men (just under age 65) are in families in which others are employed, and a few may have sufficient savings to tide them over a long period of time; these families, then, do not become destitute immediately upon the exhaustion of the unemployment insurance benefits. There are a minority of families however (in which the beneficiary is just under age 65), which have no savings, have no other family members who can find employment, and have no members who are old enough to qualify for a retirement pension. Chronic unemployment in such families means complete destitution.

The implications, therefore, seem clear. The chronically unemployed just under age 65 should be allowed to retire and collect pension benefits. Adequate safeguards to prevent abuse would have to be built into such a program, but this would appear to be a relatively simple thing to do; such safeguards might parallel those built around the disbursement of unemployment insurance benefits. Furthermore, the amount of pension benefits could be reduced in accordance with the age of the person, as is customary now in calculating pensions.

Acknowledgment.   The authors wish to thank especially Miss Irma Rittenhouse, Director of the Bureau of Research and Statistics, New York State Department of Labor, Division of Employment, for her kind cooperation and for making available to us various data, both published and unpublished, about beneficiaries in New York State.

APPENDIX: A NOTE ON THE UTICA, NEW YORK STUDY

Almost 800 persons who had been unemployed for 5 weeks or longer and who were receiving unemployment insurance benefits were interviewed in Utica in the fall of 1958. Included in this group were persons who had been unemployed for over 26 weeks (ordinarily the maximum number of weeks to which a person is entitled) but who qualified under the Federal Temporary Unemployment Compensation Act of 1958 for a maximum of 39 weeks of benefits.

Detailed inquiry was made regarding their total family income and the sources of such, during: (a) the month preceding the interview, which is always a month of unemployment, and (b) the last month prior to the onset of unemployment in which they worked full time.

Additional questions were asked regarding: (a) the employment experiences of each family member aged 14 and over during these 2 months; (b) the extent to which these families had used savings between the onset of unemployment and the date of the interview; (c) the personal characteristics of the beneficiary; (d) composition of the beneficiary's family; (e) a number of other areas bearing on unemployment but not referred to in this present paper.

The number of cases of male beneficiaries in the three age groups presented here are: 45–54 years, 73 cases; 55–64 years, 69 cases; and 65 and over, 130 cases.

REFERENCES

Bancroft, Gertrude. 1958. The American labor force: its growth and changing composition. New York: John Wiley & Sons, Inc.

Cohen, W. J., Haber, W., and Mueller, Eva. 1960. A report of nationwide surveys of unemployment, unemployment insurance, and attitudes of the unemployed. Printed for the Special Committee on Unemployment Problems of the U.S. Senate, June, 1960. Washington, D.C.: Government Printing Office.

Columbia University. 1958. Bureau of Applied Social Research. Benefits, incomes and expenditures of unemployed workers: experience of a group of unemployment insurance beneficiaries in Albany-Schenectady-Troy, Spring of 1957. New York: The Bureau.

——— 1959. Bureau of Applied Social Research. Unemployment insurance beneficiaries in Utica, New York. Procedural report of a survey of the New York State Department of Labor. (Mimeographed.) New York: The Bureau.

———— 1960. Bureau of Applied Social Research. Unemployment benefits and family finances: a study of incomes and expenditures of beneficiaries and their families in Utica, New York, 1958. New York: The Bureau.

New York State Department of Labor, Division of Employment. 1959*a*. Claimant's booklet of information: unemployment insurance benefits for workers in New York State.

———— 1959*b*. Claimants for extended benefits in New York State under the Federal Temporary Unemployment Compensation Act of 1958. (Mimeographed.)

———— 1960. Pensioners and unemployment insurance.

Palmer, Gladys L. 1954. Labor mobility in six cities. New York: Social Science Research Council.

Sheppard, H. L., Ferman, L. A., and Faber, S. 1960. Too old to work—too young to retire. Printed for the Special Committee on Unemployment Problems of the U.S. Senate, December 21, 1959. Washington, D.C.: Government Printing Office.

Unemployment experience of separated federal workers. 1954. Monthly Labor Review, 77: No. 6, June.

The Age Factor in the Sheffield Cutlery Industry

CHRISTOPHER E. FLEMING

THIS is a brief report from a pilot study of six medium to large cutlery companies in the city of Sheffield. The preliminary findings show that Sheffield cutlery manufacturing is one of the oldest industries in Great Britain in many senses. This area has been famous for its knives for over 600 years. In 1386 Dan Chaucer, describing the Miller's dress and accouterments, said "A Sheffield thwytil (general purpose knife) baar he in his hose." Also, the Sheffield cutlery male work force is outstandingly "old" in the proportions of such operatives in various later-age groupings.

Although there exists no satisfactory statistical report on the age structure of the cutlery industry, it was possible to collect some data incidentally in connection with another study (Fleming, 1955) which reveals the high proportion of male cutlery workers in various later age groupings in 1952. The relatively high age level of the male cutlery work force in Sheffield in comparison to the age of the male labor force in general is shown in Table 1. Some individual cutlery firms

Table 1. Proportion of older age groups of male workers, Sheffield "cutlery workers" compared with national industrial workers, Great Britain, 1952

Age group	Sheffield	Great Britain
45 and over	56	38
55 and over	34	17
65 and over	16	4

had appreciably higher later-age proportions; for example, in one firm employing 246 men the proportion 45 years of age or over was 61 percent, 55 years and over was 37 percent, while that of 65 years and over was 21 percent.

An expanded version of this paper was presented at the Fifth Congress of The International Association of Gerontology.

PILOT STUDY

Recently a field study was made including 82 male workers aged 55 years and over (about 10 percent of the total male cutlery work force in the Sheffield area) in 6 companies (about 27 percent of the sample's male work force). A 20-item questionnaire designed for "more adult workers" was administered to 61 men aged 55 to 80 years. It must be mentioned that in some cases the conditions for interviewing the workers were excellent but in other instances the questioner had to shout against a terrific noise, sometimes in hot workshops, and with the operative more or less going on with his regular job during the 5- to 10-minute interview. No attempt will be made here to report on the answers to all questions, or to show correlations between summed answers to particular questions, or between the various individual replies to particular questions.

In designing the "more adult worker" questionnaire, there were two main orientations of inquiry. One of these revolved around the question of health, particularly psychological health. How do the nature, circumstances, and conditions of the job affect the emotional-mental well-being of the older worker? The other was directed to gauging the older worker's equipment for, and attitude toward, the particular "life crisis" of retirement from the job—of departure from his accustomed socio-industrial behavioral pattern.

Occupational "setup" and health

One of the specific questions was a self-health-assessment (i.e., "excellent," "good," "poor"); this was linked with an inquiry into "Any particular health trouble?" Ideally, this self-health-assessment should have been checked, in each case, by the assessment of a properly qualified medical practitioner—or the worker's own physician. But the limitations of resources and circumstances precluded such an adventure in interdisciplinary socio-medical inquiry. However, the departmental managers gave their own assessments of the older workers' health status, without seeing the "private and confidential" papers of the men concerned.

There was a remarkable similarity between the older workers' self-health-assessments and the departmental managers' assessments of the workers' health.

The great majority, 80 percent, of the 61 workers rated their own health as either "excellent" or "good" (for their age, of course)—19 put "excellent," and 30 put "good." The departmental managers put 76 percent of these older men in either the "excellent" or "good" health category.

It was felt that in the great majority of cases the investigator unquestionably had the confidence of the questionee concerned, and that he was given an honest answer to the inquiry, "Have you any particular health troubles?" Only a few seemed to have any serious health disability. One man had a double rupture, 2 had ulcers, and 2 had a touch of tuberculosis. A few mentioned the effect of war wounds and 5 complained of bronchitis in the winter. One man of 59, both deaf and dumb from birth, indicated, cheerfully, that he was "as fit as a fiddle!"

This self-health-assessment question tied up with another, "Do you feel your job to be a strain?" and "If so, what manner of strain?" Only 10 percent of the 61 admitted to job strain and this was chiefly put down to "nervous strain" due to the tediousness of repetition. Only one man actually admitted to not liking his job—though "liking the job" ranged from "very much" to "fair enough" or "passable." Comments and observations elicited observations which linked up with the more direct questions on the relation between the conditions of work and health: five men complained of unduly noisy machinery which made it difficult for craftsmen to concentrate on fine work, such as filing. Quite a number of the men, also, commented on the poor light and dirty windows of many *other* cutlery firms.

Equipment for an attitude toward retirement

The "attitude toward retirement" question showed that three-quarters of the men were *not* looking forward to retirement. It must be mentioned that 27 of these 61 men were aged 65 to 80—that is, more than 4 in 10. Incidentally, a minor sampling of some men in the 40 to 56 year age grouping indicated that a greater number looked forward to retirement in the earlier later-age period.

Those *not* looking forward to retirement were asked, "How long would you like to go on working?" The two predominant answers were, "As long as I am reasonably healthy" (25), and "Indefinitely" (20). In some cases *both* answers were given. The majority of those looking forward to retirement indicated that "lack of money" could induce them to postpone retirement.

Most of the men questioned emphasized the inadequacy of the National Retirement Pension obtainable at 65 which is £2.10 a week for a single man and £4 a week for man and wife (one pound is roughly

$3). Quite a number stressed the desirability of some company super-annuation scheme and one man suggested such a scheme financed by the Trade Union from extra contributions.

The "Have you a plan for retirement?" question linked up with the one on "What are your hobbies?"—that is, active hobbies. Only 3 of the 61 men had anything approaching a plan for retirement. Two anticipated taking up gardening full time, and one man wanted to set up for himself doing odd jobs, such as sharpening lawnmowers, raking leaves, etc.

Most of the men had active hobbies of some kind, i.e., 54 of the 61. "Gardening" was mentioned as the hobby or one of the hobbies by 36 men. The next favorite hobby was "fishing" (22 men). Most of the fishing is done some little distance from Sheffield itself and although fishing appears an excellent hobby for "later maturants," it would seem that the meager National Retirement Pension will restrict this hobby when they leave paid work. "Music" and "painting water-colors" were mentioned as hobbies by some, but only one man mentioned "reading."

"What will you miss most when you finally retire?" More than half the men (32) said that what they would miss most would be the company of their workmates—the companionship of the workroom floor. But a sizable section (12) stressed that what they would miss most on retirement would be the work itself—the definite routine of the job.

The job and the cutlery trade

Comments and observation on the job and on the cutlery trade as such were very revealing. But only a few major strands of opinion can be indicated here. While it was appreciated that conditions and hours of work had improved greatly in the cutlery trade over the past 50 years, it was felt strongly that there was still room for much improvement—especially in some of the "industrial slum" cutlery workshops. Almost all the men questioned stressed the comparatively low wages for skilled men in the industry. This appears due to the undercutting of prices by the many "little meister" cutlery firms (and "out worker" teams) which have no idea of costing, and in which the hours of work are abnormally long. One man commented on the low piece-work rates by saying that he always kept going during the ten-minute "tea breaks" in the mornings and afternoons so as not to lose the money. Quite a number criticized the trend toward mass production and the consequent depreciation of the quality of Sheffield cutlery. But others looked for more machinery to "take the hard work out of the job," and some stressed the need to combine, or reconcile, the skills of the craftsmen and those of the engineer.

Policy and practice regarding the industry's
utilization of older manpower

Ten executives in the industry answered a fairly searching questionnaire. They included the senior executives (i.e., the proprietors, managing directors, or general managers) for each of the six companies studied. The information so obtained was supplemented by the author's discussions with several dozen other executives, a number of working foremen, and various officials knowledgeable in the industry. Mention should be made of N. C. Baker's recent survey of managerial opinions in the cutlery industry for the insight it afforded into the attitudinal characteristics of the industry (Baker, 1957).

In broad terms, what is the attitude of management in the industry toward the older workers? It seems to be similar in character to that indicated in two research studies dealing with an industrial gerontologic survey of certain Merseyside firms.

In one of these papers, A. Heron and S. M. Chown (to be published) made the statement that "Industry in general simply does not acknowledge a problem of ageing"; this would be a difficult task in the Sheffield cutlery industry but the human mind has an amazing capacity for evading reality! In the other paper the authors report "We have found supervision to be benevolent but unimaginative on this question of the older worker" (to be published) with supervisors apparently taking their cues in this regard from the views and actions of top management.

In considering the attitude of management in the cutlery industry toward the older worker it has to be borne in mind that there is a general labor shortage in Sheffield, and especially a pressing shortage of skilled cutlery workers. This has meant that very few of the Sheffield cutlery companies appear to have a fixed retirement age, and few, if any, have an upper age for engagement. Four of the six companies instanced the engagement, during recent years, of operatives past the national pensionable age. The normal working week is 44 hours (soon to be 42 hours). Five of the six firms allowed (as offered) part-time work for middle-aged women and men of pensionable age; as one manager put it, "Half a loaf is better than no bread."

Labor turnover, earnings, etc.

Most of the executives commented warmly and spontaneously on the stability and reliability of the older male operatives. This was in marked contrast to the high labor turnover rates for juveniles, especially girls, and also for married women earning "pin money" by part-time work. This low labor turnover rate for middle-aged-to-older men was confirmed by the figures given by most of the men for their years of service in the firms concerned.

All the firms studied combined a piecework wage system with a day-rate wage system and one had a system of day rate plus bonus. At the prevailing day rates even a skilled Grade I cutler (the key worker of the industry as it has operated for hundreds of years) cannot earn more than about £8 for a 44-hour week (Great Britain Wages Councils, 1959), that is, about $23. Unskilled laborers in Sheffield can earn £8.10 for the same working period.

There are some fifty different types of jobs in the Sheffield cutlery industry, but inquiries were made about the average and maximum weekly piecework earnings of what appeared to be five main job categories. The average of such weekly wages for such skilled male cutlery workers appears to be a little over £12 ($34); an unskilled labor on piecework, with 6 hours overtime, can earn £11. The maximum piecework earnings in the cutlery industry seems to be about £15. ($42) per week. Apart from their other reasons for wishing to postpone retirement, it is not to be wondered at that most men in the cutlery trade feel that they will never be able to save enough to retire in reasonable comfort.

Work study and job analysis

Some form of work study or job analysis seems to be carried out in all firms in the industry, at least in those of any size at all. A few of the larger firms are highly mechanized in all aspects of the manufacture of cutlery, and apparently there are very few firms which have not introduced some feature of job "breakdown" and mechanization.

For the sample studied, this mechanization was primarily with regard to the preparation of parts, secondly for finishing processes, and thirdly for the intermediate stage of the assembly of parts. The executives and others with whom the author discussed the possibilities of further mechanization in the industry considered that there was still considerable scope for this but that the character of the industry imposed limitations on this trend. There was need to retain flexibility and to safeguard quality.

*Special work features and special welfare facilities
for older operatives*

Apart from part-time work there appear to be no special work features for older operatives in the industry. There is certainly no element of retraining middle-aged to older workers. Indeed, until quite recently there has been no other system of training in the industry (even for cutlers *per se*) than "training by exposure." But in recent decades the industry has started to rehabilitate itself; there is now a Cutlery Research Council and Laboratory, for handling technical problems, operated by the Sheffield Cutlery Manufacturers Association. In 1955 the first indentured apprentice for a hundred years made his appearance in the Sheffield cutlery industry. There are now about 30 such indentured apprentices working under a planned system of training and day-release technical education, and about the same number of unindentured apprentices.

The statement that there are no special welfare facilities for the older workers in the industry has to be qualified in that most managements are accommodating to the shortcomings of the aging individual. But welfare features in general seem to be very uneven in the industry. Some few firms have excellent canteens, very good natural and artificial lighting, and other amenities, while others are "industrial slums" (Great Britain, Ministry of Labour and National Service, 1946). The latter characterization of some Sheffield cutlery firms is not necessarily confined to the minute, back-alley "little meister" firms. One of the fairly large companies visited had apparently not had its windows cleaned for years, while its general "housekeeping" left much to be desired.

Managerial attitudes toward aging of workers, etc.

One of the questions asked the executives was: "Have you had occasion to consider the question of work-force aging in your own operative work force?" Apart from the odd abnormally "young" firm, this phenomenon has been generally observed and is the occasion of some concern. But little appears to have been done about it other than some drive for youth recruitment. The problem of how to use a somewhat elderly work force in the best interests of productivity and efficiency, and with due regard to the best interests of the later-age workers themselves, has not been faced.

In 1952 the government set up a National Advisory Committee on the Employment of Older Men and Women; the Committee published two reports. Also, some few months ago, the Department of Scientific and Industrial Research published a booklet, "The Older Worker and His Job." One of the questions asked of the executives was whether they had read these publications. Only one in ten had done so, and this appears to overemphasize the extent to which socio-industrial gerontologic data has found itself on the desks of management in the industry. Yet from conversations with executives in the industry it seemed evident that many of them would welcome pertinent scientific data on aging in relation to occupation, presented in a readily intelligible language.

REFERENCES

Baker, N. C. 1957. Human factors: a survey of managerial opinion. Birmingham, England: Cutlery Research Council.

Fleming, C. E. 1955. Age composition of the British iron and steel industry. *In* Old age in the modern world, pp. 300–02. Edinburgh: E. & S. Livingstone.

Great Britain. Ministry of Labour and National Service. 1946. Industrial conditions of the cutlery trade. London: H. M. Stationery Office.

Great Britain. Wages Councils. 1959. The wages regulations (cutlery) order 1959. Statutory instruments. No. 2. London: H. M. Stationery Office.

Heron, A. and Chown, Sheila M. The expectations of supervisors concerning older workers. *In* Wilma Donahue, C. Tibbitts, and R. H. Williams (eds.), Psychological and social processes of aging: an international research seminar. To be published.

——— Semi-skilled and over forty. *In* Wilma Donahue, C. Tibbitts, and R. N. Williams (eds.), Psychological and social processes of aging: an international research seminar. To be published.

HOUSING,

FAMILY, AND

SOCIAL RELATIONSHIPS

Organized by
WILMA DONAHUE
The University of Michigan, Ann Arbor, Michigan
PETER TOWNSEND
London School of Economics, London, England

substantial commitment of effort and resources which inevitably will be directed toward the meeting of the complex housing needs of the elderly in the decades ahead.

DEPENDENCE ON PAST EXPERIENCE

In any nation, and indeed in any community, as it becomes apparent that significant numbers of older people are in dire need of suitable shelter, steps are taken in one fashion or another to try to meet them. All too often the initial efforts tend to fall back upon past experience and past solutions. Hence, it is not surprising that the first wave of activity rather commonly concerns itself with the provision of additional institutional-type facilities. Later, attention begins to be directed toward exploring other avenues for the meeting of the shelter needs of older people. Here again, unfortunately, there is a tendency to look to what has been successful in the past, rather than to attempt to pioneer new approaches.

In the field of housing, perhaps more so than in almost any other area of service to the elderly, the adherence to past solutions rather than the seeking of new answers can have long-term stultifying implications for the effective meeting of the shelter needs of the elderly. A physical structure built to house older people has a useful life of upwards of 50 years. Once the structure is built, it is only with costly alterations that its basic character and the character of its services can be changed. Hence, each time another institution or project for the shelter of older people is built, just so much more is the pattern of living for additional numbers of elderly people substantially frozen for the next half century or so. Whenever interest in the provision of housing for older people is active and expanding, as it certainly is in the United States and in many European countries, there is a need for a better understanding of how best to deal with the problem. This understanding can be brought about only through adequate and timely research.

Here in the United States, and we believe elsewhere as well, there is generally an unfortunate tendency to fail to look at the full depth of the shelter needs of the elderly. Understandably, a major emphasis is placed upon meeting the urgent needs of the currently ill-housed aged, especially those who are just reaching age 65 and those who are at a particular economic disadvantage. The preoccupation with meeting the needs of these most extreme cases has meant that insufficient attention has been or is being given to the question of how best to provide suitable living environments for all people at all stages in the aging process. As a matter of fact, so much attention is directed toward initially meeting this critical need that many observers of the situation are drawn into the common trap of feeling that the housing needs of the elderly are static and hence amenable to a single permanent solution. Put the 65-year-old into a living environment suited to his immediate needs and think no more of him! Unfortunately this is anything but the truth, as those who have had experience in this field well know. Actually the housing requirements of any family or individual are extremely dynamic, changing slowly, sometimes almost imperceptibly, over time. Housing arrangements that are ideal for the recently retired couple at age 65 can, and most likely will, be completely unsuited to the frail survivor of that marriage at age 80.

FOUR PHASES OF AGING AS THEY RELATE TO SHELTER NEEDS OF FAMILIES

Rather than beginning, and too often ending, at age 65, the attack on meeting the housing needs of the elderly should start as people reach middle age and should extend through the balance of the life cycle.

So that we may all have a common understanding of the span of life within which, in our judgment, the shelter needs of the aging should be considered, let us review briefly what appear to be the four phases of aging as they relate to the housing of family groups.

Middle age

The first phase comes when the family head reaches what, for lack of a better label, we have called "middle age." It is here that attention should first be directed to the housing requirement of people as they grow older. This is the period in which children are growing up, getting married, and establishing homes of their own. As a result the house which was perhaps scarcely large enough for the parents and their children now begins to provide more space than is actually needed for the remaining family group.

However, few families at this stage in their lives even entertain the idea of moving into smaller quarters. Their roots are generally well-established in the community. There are many sentimental attachments which hold them to their present quarters. There is a certain sense of satisfaction at having ample room in which to live in greater comfort than was perhaps possible at any other time in their married lives. Since as a general rule their health is still good, most of the principal wage earners are still employed and their incomes are still at or near their peak; thus there is little immediate pressure to make a change. This is ironic, since at this point in the family cycle the couple is probably in the best economic position to make a housing shift or to adapt its present quarters to meet later requirements.

Later maturity

All too commonly, however, families drift on from middle age to what is coming to be identified as "later maturity" without having made any changes in their living arrangements. By this time all the children have left home. Many of the principal wage earners either have retired or face an early retirement. As a result income is definitely lower for most families than it was in middle age. Physical changes have taken place as well. The individuals have begun to "slow up." A growing number have definite physical ailments which limit activity. Those with two-story homes are beginning to find the stairs a bit hard to climb. Progressively more and more find the house too big or too expensive to keep up, the yard too large to maintain, the furnace too difficult to tend. A study by Hunter and Maurice (1953) in Grand Rapids, Michigan, shows that during later maturity better than two-fifths of the families begin to report some problems with their living quarters.

By this time more families are beginning to think about changing their living arrangements. Yet most of them never get beyond the discussion stage. Corson and McConnell (1956) in their study of *Economic Needs of Older People* found that even after retirement seven out of every ten couples were still living in the residences they had occupied when the husbands were still employed. While there is still a significant group of these couples in late maturity who have the economic strength to make a satisfactory readjustment, the proportion is less than it was in middle age; as couples advance through later maturity, they find that despite social security benefits and industrial pension programs, their ability to negotiate a satisfactory readjustment in their independent living arrangements slowly lessens.

It is at this point that there begins to be an active interest, on the part of those in the upper end of the economic strata, in finding houses in a warmer climate or making arrangements for getting into some type of retirement housing facility. However, among those at the lower end of the economic scale this is the time when increasing numbers of elderly couples find it necessary to go live with their children.

It is during this period of later maturity that death dissolves a significant number of couples, leaving, in a majority of cases, a widow with problems of readjustment that often make her housing problems more acute than those of a spinster of the same age.

Early old age

By the time couples reach the period in their lives which can be called "early old age," they are at the point of the cycle with which most of the writers on the housing problems of the aging begin their studies. By now retirement is almost universal. A portion of them, perhaps one in five, are in a sufficiently comfortable financial position to readily readjust their housing arrangements to meet current needs or to maintain present satisfactory quarters.

A growing number of those home owners who elected to stay where they were, however, are beginning to pay the price for their decision. These are the people who, having neither the physical strength nor the money, are unable to cope with the problems of maintenance of a big house and have let it run down or who have failed to recognize signs of neighborhood deterioration until blight and decay have undermined much of the value which the property once could have commanded. By now a growing share of those who have been renters find the quarters they are able to afford ill-suited to their current needs. It is to try to meet the needs of these groups that many of the present efforts in the elderly housing field are being directed.

Late old age

The last phase in the cycle comes as a sharply curtailed number of couples reach "late old age." By this time physical infirmities are great. Because thus far the medical profession has been more successful in extending the span of life than it has been in maintaining physical strength and mental alertness, a growing share of couples as they advance through late old age need more than mere shelter. As the years progress more and more need some type of sheltered care. Ultimately all but a favored few will require at least nursing care if not active medical care in the terminal phases of life.

PHASES OF AGING AS THEY RELATE TO HOUSING NEEDS OF SINGLE PERSONS

Among single men and women who are predominantly renters rather than owners, housing does not generally become identifiable as a problem before they reach later maturity. Then, faced with retirement and its attendant curtailment of income, along with increasing physical disabilities which limit activity, the need for the provision of more suitable quarters becomes more apparent.

The women and men who are widowed sometime during the aging cycle are frequently forced to face up to a readjustment in their living arrangements more quickly than is true of their counterparts among the couples.

Most single people, whether unwed or widowed, find the lack of a partner a serious deterrent to continued maintenance of a house or an apartment when physical disability seriously limits activity. Whereas couples can wait upon one another, single individuals have to look to others for this sort of care and assistance. This is why it is among this class of aging people that there is the greatest interest in some kind of special housing and the least resistance to moving. This is especially true as single individuals move on into early and late old age.

The housing problems of single persons, especially women, are accentuated as they grow old by their generally low standing on the economic scale. As a result, they have greater difficulty in securing and maintaining satisfactory living conditions as they grow older, and need progressively more assistance in their day-to-day living. Hence, while the single individuals among the aging are far outnumbered by the couples, their plight is far more pressing. An example of the urgency of the situation, in the United States at least, is to be found in the experience at a recently completed housing project in Hartford, Connecticut. Designed to accommodate 12 single persons and 8 couples, the management was hard put to find 3 eligible couples, yet had a waiting list of single women after admitting 17.

SCOPE OF PROBLEM

If the scope of the problem is regarded in its broadest dimensions, then it becomes immediately apparent that our need for knowledge of how best to cope with it is vast. It is not only a question of how best to deal with the obvious problems of aged infirm and destitute spinsters and of recently retired couples. Rather it is a question of how we can best attack the problem in its broadest dimensions. What can we do to anticipate the onset of shelter needs of an aging population so as to minimize its impact?

The U.S. Congress passed legislation giving the President the authority to convene a White House Conference on the Aging. The President did this, setting the date for January, 1961. An Advisory Committee was established to explore various aspects of the problem. In the field of housing a background paper was issued which stated in part:

Our knowledge of the environment in which middle-aged and older people live is fragmentary. Most of it is based upon personal observation of a limited number of cases—in both the independent and the group setting. The basic data which are available are far too scant to make many of the broad assumptions which are necessary for effective action. [White House Conference on Aging, 1960*a*, p. 72]

CHANGING CHARACTER OF THE PROBLEM

In the United States there is, in addition to the tendency to focus too much attention upon an initial meeting of the housing needs of the 65-year-olds, an unfortunate inclination to make long-range plans on the basis of the immediate needs of our present elderly population. In other words, there is a tendency to generalize that because elderly people today have certain characteristics, physically, economically, and culturally, so will their successors.

It is important to keep in mind that significant changes are arising which affect the characteristics of successive cohorts in the population as they age. Among the elderly in this country, it is most important for those considering future shelter needs of the aging to keep in mind that those who are now 65 years of age or older were faced during their potentially most productive years with several most unusual circumstances. One was the Great Depression of the 1930s which seriously affected their earning power for a substantial span of years. As a result, many were unable to save for their years of retirement. In addition, our social security program did not become available until late in the working years of many members of our present elderly population and few of them had the benefit of present-day, private, industry pension plans. As a result, many members of our present elderly population find themselves with less than adequate incomes on which to live. The nature of the housing assistance necesa definitive analysis of the extent and character of the entire range of shelter needs of the elderly, linked with an evaluation of the various ways in which these needs can be most effectively and economically met.

This is not to say that significant strides in research are not now being made. Important work has been done; more is under way.

PRESENT RESEARCH EFFORTS
IN THE UNITED STATES

In the United States a major contribution is being made by the Ford Foundation, which has made several grants to colleges to finance studies of various aspects of the elderly housing problem. The largest grant, for $160,000, has gone to Cornell University's Housing Research Center for a detailed study of the economic, sociological, and psychological aspects of the housing of older persons. This study is being integrated with others financed by the New York State Division of Housing, which have to do with the development of planning and design guides for apartments for the elderly.

Another large Ford grant, for $126,000, went to Western Reserve University which, in cooperation with the Welfare Federation of Cleveland, has embarked on a 5-year study that will include the establishment of: (a) criteria for admission or rejection of elderly applicants for elderly housing projects; (b) what social, psychological, and medical aids are required to extend the span of independent living by the elderly; (c) criteria for identifying aging persons no longer capable of independent living in noninstitutional projects for the elderly.

The University of North Carolina has received a $9,000 Ford grant to study the attitude of elderly citizens toward the community in which they live or would like to live.

New York, through its Division of Housing, has sponsored several studies of special facets of the housing program including such questions as: (a) home care and the housing needs of the aged and (b) housing problems and preferences of aging persons in certain relocation sites in New York.

As part of a study in which 12 midwestern states will be involved, Kansas State College has undertaken a survey of housing requirements and retirement patterns of aging persons in rural areas in southwestern Kansas.

THE NEED FOR A COMPREHENSIVE
RESEARCH PROGRAM

While we are fully mindful of the important contributions that are being made to our research in the field of housing for our elderly population here in the United States, the problem still must be regarded in its broadest dimensions and a comprehensive, definitive, and objective evaluation of the situation is greatly needed.

As has already been pointed out, the housing needs of the elderly are complex, various, and many-sided. In the United States less than 5 percent of those over 65 now live in institutions. Over 95 percent live independently in the community in various types of accommodations and in various types of households (single-family homes, apartments, hotels, rooming houses) alone, as couples, with children, and with friends. If the housing needs of the elderly are varied, they are also dynamic and constantly changing. For any individual or couple in the older population, housing facilities which are adequate today may not be so next year or 5 years from now. Loss of a spouse may change housing requirements suddenly. Loss of strength and health will certainly change them gradually over time. Housing requirements may change with a new generation of old people. The housing requirements of the present older generation are related to the health and lifespan of this generation; they are also related to the economic, social, and psychological experiences which conditioned it. The next generation of oldsters will probably have different conditioning experiences; it will certainly have better health and longer life expectancy, better and more stable income, and more experience in the use of leisure time. All of these factors will affect the housing requirements of the next older generation.

If the spectrum of the housing needs of older people is wide and varied, the types of shelter which will satisfy these needs are equally diverse. They are diverse in physical character, in location and services, in methods of production, types of tenure, financing, and management.

As we have noted, efforts in the United States to date have been largely focused on the institutional end of the need spectrum. This has been true with regard to actions aimed at meeting the housing needs of older people. It has been equally true of the limited research which is going on in the field.

Just as our national effort has to be extended and broadened to

It is urgent that the national data of the decennial Censuses of Population and Housing be tabulated in such a way that they give us reasonably conclusive knowledge of the conditions and situations in which older people live—at least to the extent that they are available for the population as a whole. It is equally necessary that this information be extended to include group settings—both institutional and non-institutional. Specifically, these should encompass:

Tabulations of the housing and living arrangements, not only of those elderly persons who are heads of households, but also of those older people who live in the households of other individuals, including younger families.

Tabulations of the 1960 Census data (and those of subsequent years) of the general type provided in the HHFA-financed, special tabulations of 1950 data.

Tabulations of data which provide age distribution for older individuals by five-year increments (as is now done below the age of 65). [White House Conference on Aging, 1960*a*, pp. 72–73]

In addition to data on how older people now live, we should have need-demand studies not only of present generations, but also of future generations of older individuals—individuals who have experienced higher standards of living and increasing amounts of leisure time. We need to know how much of the present and future needs consist of families and individuals who can live alone without assistance and what kinds of living units they want and can afford. Estimates should be made of how many older people could continue for a longer period to live in their own houses if nursing care, meals on wheels, and other collateral services were provided. We need estimates of the number of present and future elderly who require group housing with the provision of some central services and some degree of custodial care. We need to know how many will require full custodial care. How much of the present and future needs will consist of individuals who will require the services of chronic disease hospitals? Equally important to know is the number of older people now occupying hospitals and mental institutions who could be moved to nursing homes or other facilities for the care of the elderly if such facilities were available.

The urgency of the need for this type of information here in the United States is clearly illustrated by a situation which has developed in our Pacific Northwest. Operating on the assumption that because so little has been done to date, a great need must exist, three religious organizations laid plans for separate housing projects for the elderly, all to be located in or near a single large population center. To the amazement of their respective sponsors, not one of these projects has succeeded in getting enough applicants to fill it, even after the bars had been lowered with respect to religious affiliation of the applicants.

Obviously, these three projects were not geared to meet the type of need that exists in the Pacific Northwest. Adequate data on need-demand conditions in the area would have been invaluable to the sponsors of these three projects. As we move ahead here in this country with more and more efforts being made to provide special housing for the elderly, the need for comprehensive data on the size and character of the market will become increasingly imperative.

The economics of elderly housing requirements

Data and analyses of the economics of housing present and future generations of the elderly are also a necessary part of any comprehensive study of the housing requirements of the elderly. We need to know more of the incomes and liquid assets of various segments of the elderly population and their capacity and willingness to draw from income and assets to pay for shelter. Currently, many of the decisions as to the rent-paying ability of older people are being based upon experience with younger families with children. Even the most cursory examination of the situation makes it obvious that budgets of retired people differ from those of their younger counterparts. Savings are no longer a factor. Educational expenses for children are not in the picture. On the other hand, medical expenses mount and there is an increasing need to have things done by others which younger persons can do for themselves. Just what the proper balance of housing expense to total outlay is under these circumstances needs more study. The outcome of such study can play a vital role in determining at what rent and sales price levels our major housing efforts for the elderly are concentrated.

We need to know much more than we now do about the costs of providing various types of housing accommodations for the elderly. What part of the need can reasonably be served in the private market by private entrepreneurs? What part of the need can be served by nonprofit sponsors such as church, fraternal, and other groups? What part of the need will require some form of public subsidy, federal, state, or local? We need study and experimentation on the internal economics of various types of elderly housing developments and projects. What are proper ratios of land, construction, and financing costs? What about the costs of maintenance, management, and corol-

of private construction of new houses. Nearly all of the over one million annual output of new homes are built in suburban developments which are designed almost entirely for younger families of childbearing age. If this is true of the new houses themselves, it is equally true of the neighborhoods in which they are placed. To a lesser degree the younger-family bias characterizes private apartment-house construction, also. Much of this, too, takes place in the suburbs and is aimed at younger families, often at the prechildbearing stage. Downtown apartment construction, it is true, being less oriented to families with children, results in living units which, by space standards at least, are suitable for older couples or individuals. Even outlying apartment construction, because it tends to be aimed at families in the early years of marriage, produces units of a size which are suitable for the older generation. Yet very little new construction in the United States, either homes or apartments, is explicitly designed for the elderly housing market either in terms of physical characteristics or rent level.

Research is greatly needed which will illuminate, for the guidance of the private building industry, the physical needs and the economic capacity of the elderly population as a market for new house and apartment construction. This should include design criteria and income, cost and demand considerations, applying to new house and apartment construction aimed at both younger and older families and individuals (in many instances the demand and supply characteristics of very young families are identical or could be made identical with those of old families). It should also include design and economic considerations of new house and apartment construction intended to be marketed exclusively to the growing number of older people.

Because of the fixed nature and long life of housing construction, annual increments of new construction must always represent a very small percentage of the total existing supply of housing. Thus, at any given time, a far larger proportion of the population is served by old housing than by new housing. Facilities for financing the turnover and resale of existing housing make possible an adaptation of the existing supply to the changing needs and desires of individual families in the market. Upgrading, rehabilitation, and modification of existing dwelling units also facilitate the adaptation of the present housing inventory to changing needs.

Research is needed in this area, too. Such research should be directed to a better understanding of the market processes through which changing housing needs are served by the exchange of existing dwelling units, and particularly to discovering ways in which this process can be modified to better serve the housing needs of older families and individuals. Equally essential is research on the engineering, architectural, and economic implications of remodeling existing dwelling units to meet the needs and fit the pocketbooks of the older population.

Housing for group living

A small but significant proportion of the elderly population, particularly the single and widowed members, seek group living in apartment houses, hotels, rooming houses, residence clubs, and similar facilities. For the most part, older people who live in such arrangements still maintain their physical independence and, to a great degree, their social independence as well.

It is becoming increasingly apparent that this type of group living arrangement, which has developed more or less spontaneously, is serving a real and distinct shelter need. Yet such independent group living arrangements have been studied and evaluated very little. How adequate are these arrangements for the physical needs of older people? What do they cost and how do they relate to the incomes of the older people for whom they are an appropriate solution? How well do they meet the social and psychological requirements of older people? How could this type of living arrangement be improved? Should the creation of more facilities of this type be encouraged as a matter of public policy? How? What type of sponsorship and financing is most appropriate?

Institutional housing

Although serving a relatively small segment of the elderly population, institutional housing is, nevertheless, a significant and vital aspect of the need. It will undoubtedly continue to be important and the focus of greatest attention if only because it serves that segment of the elderly population which is most dramatically in need of help. Institutional housing is now being provided by church and fraternal groups, by public and private convalescent and rest homes, and by proprietary and nonprofit nursing homes. Institutional housing for many older people is also being provided by mental and chronic disease hospitals.

While this is the aspect of housing for older people which has received the greatest attention in the United States, there are still many unanswered questions. We need to know much more than we now do about how well present institutional arrangements are serving the

the world around their dwelling is conditioned decisively by the character of the neighborhood and the facilities it provides. Does the neighborhood provide access by foot or public transportation to stores, entertainment, cultural centers, and other facilities? Do the various facilities exist at all? Do they in any way reflect the needs and tastes of the older generation? What are the opportunities for social exchange with neighbors? What kind of neighbors are there? Are they all old or all young, or is there a cross section of ages, incomes, and social characteristics?

Neighborhood characteristics and urban patterns are the subject of much study among city planners and others concerned with urban development and redevelopment. But very little, if any, of this study gives attention to the special needs and characteristics of a rapidly growing elderly segment of the population. Research is greatly needed in city and neighborhood planning and replanning which recognizes and reflects the special economic, physical, social, and psychological characteristics of older people. This research should produce guide lines which are understood and observed by builders, architects, planners, road builders, and those responsible for the construction of public and private community facilities of all types.

Older people, especially those of low income, frequently live in houses or rooms in rundown areas in our central cities. Urban renewal programs which aim at the rehabilitation or clearance of such areas frequently uproot these elderly families or individuals. Both because of their age and their economic status older people find it more difficult to adjust to displacement from urban renewal. The special problems of older persons displaced by city rebuilding need study. Such studies may well lead to changed public policies which will ameliorate these difficulties.

NEED FOR MORE CROSS-NATIONAL RESEARCH

Because their competence is concentrated upon conditions as they exist in the United States, the authors have limited their discussion to the research needs in this country. It would be presumptuous, without a full knowledge of what is being done in other parts of the world, to describe what further should be done there. In fact, in trying to evaluate our total progress the world over, anyone working in this field cannot help but be impressed with the lack of adequate international dissemination of research findings in the aging field, especially as they relate to housing. *Excerpta Medica,* published by the International Abstracting Service of Amsterdam, is filling a gap in this field, but much remains to be done. In Merano, at the last International Gerontological Congress, Donahue and Ashley (1959) emphasized the need for "cross-national studies of the adjustment of residents to matched types of dwellings in different countries." They went on to urge that:

An international committee on housing for the elderly, working under the sponsorship of the Social Science Committee of the International Gerontological Association, could select one or more areas of investigation and could be ready to report its findings to the next International Gerontological Congress in 1960. [p. 154]

Progress along this line, if any, is still distressingly slow. It is still in order again to urge activity in time for the Sixth International Congress in 1963.

The need on the international front is for a sharing of experiences and their rationalization rather than simply uncritical collections of photographs by foreign travelers of what housing projects look like in other lands.

This is not to minimize the importance of understanding what the physical facilities of successful elderly housing developments look like. It is important. Of far greater importance, however, is an understanding of how and why the projects have been successful. It is also essential that effective solutions be evaluated in the light of the economic, social, and cultural background of the clientele they serve. An approach which has proven outstandingly successful in the United States will not necessarily be well received in France or, conversely, will methods used in Scandinavia necessarily be equally successful here in this country.

To get this kind of critical evaluation of ways of meeting the housing needs of the elderly around the world, there must be more technical exchange among nations. There must be more individual visits by architects, by social scientists, by students, and by administrators of elderly housing projects. We could profitably use many more international fellowships, something akin to our Fulbright Fellowships, to permit more specialists to spend time learning more about how nations other than their own successfully deal with the shelter needs of their elderly. Trying to obtain cultural exchange of this sort is a cause the International Gerontological Association could most profitably espouse.

REFERENCES

Ashley, E. E., III. 1956. Better housing for our older citizens. Washington, D.C.: Housing and Home Finance Agency.

Corson, J. J., and McConnell, J. W. 1956. Economic needs of older people. New York: Twentieth Century Fund.

Donahue, Wilma, and Ashley, E. E., III. 1959. Housing and the social health of older people in the United States. *In* C. Tibbitts (ed.), Aging and social health in the United States and Europe, pp. 141–54. Ann Arbor: University of Michigan, Division of Gerontology.

Federal Security Agency. 1951. Man and his years. Raleigh, North Carolina: Health Publications Institute, Inc.

Frieden, Elaine. 1960. Social differences and their consequences for housing the aged. J. Am. Institute Planners, 26: 119–24.

Hunter, W. W., and Maurice, Helen. 1953. Older people tell their story. Ann Arbor: University of Michigan, Division of Gerontology.

White House Conference on Aging. 1960*a*. Background paper on housing. Washington, D.C.: Government Printing Office.

———— 1960*b*. Background paper on research in gerontology: psychological and social sciences. Washington, D.C.: Government Printing Office.

Retirement Housing and Social Integration

IRVING ROSOW

A MAJOR change occurring in later years is the contraction of the social world, a process hastened by failing health and income. There is an atrophy of social roles and a shrinkage of primary groups. This attrition of membership groups reduces their customary support and may result in social alienation of the aged. Spouses, relatives, and friends retire or get sick and die. Children, friends, and neighbors migrate and move away. As people age, they simply spend more and more time attending funerals and saying goodbye to those who were once close to them. As the most meaningful people in their lives disappear, their social integration is undermined and the risk of alienation, isolation, and demoralization increases. Elsewhere it has been reported by Lowenthal that hospitalized mentally ill old people experience a more significant loss of major social supports than the aged in the community.

However, such effects are not uniform. Only a minority of old people is lonely, varying up to one-third of different groups (Tréanton, 1959), depending on the particular sample and how the loneliness figure is derived. However, it is a sizable minority. Significantly, Townsend (1957) found the most loneliness among those with the most disrupted lives—the widowed, the infirm, and those living alone. In the same vein, he also found that people with moderate social isolation were lonelier than the most isolated, which presumably included the recluse and the voluntarily withdrawn. Hence, shrinking primary groups apparently intensify alienation and produce old people who are vulnerable to growing dependency and frustrated social needs.

THE PROBLEM

This presents a twofold problem for those who may become alienated. (1) What substitutes exist for their shrinking primary groups? (2) How can retirement housing figure in their social reintegration?

The work on which this paper is based is supported by a grant from the Ford Foundation whose aid is gratefully acknowledged.

Clearly, only a minority of older people has a housing problem, even though it may be acute when it does occur. Seldom do even 5 percent spontaneously mention housing as a problem in various surveys, and only up to 15 percent say they are not satisfied with their living arrangements when asked about this directly. Therefore, we are not here considering the bulk of the aged.

But the problem of housing old people who need it is typically seen in a narrow, architectural perspective, mainly as a problem of physical design for safety, comfort, and convenience. This architectural bias may be a serious error because the physical aspects of housing seem strictly secondary (Arnett, 1956). The Yonkers Housing Authority finds that its old tenants generally manage nearly as well as the young in ordinary apartments without special provision (Anonymous, 1955). An eminent houser points out that occasionally many so-called housing standards for old people are simply good housing standards as such for all age groups, even though they may help the old a bit more than the young (Churchill, 1952; McFarland, 1959). Further, while special design features are desirable, most of them are quite simple and straightforward and pose no problem beyond that of additional cost (Massachusetts State Housing Board, 1954; McGuire, 1957). Thus, if no substandard housing is involved, the physical aspects of housing are important but are certainly not the problematic issue. When we have the economic resources, design problems are easily solved.

For the alienated aged, the crucial issue is the social consequence of different living arrangements, the social patterns which they breed or sustain, and the social networks which they engender (Dean, 1958).

When housers consider social consequences, they tend to regard housing as a direct physical means to certain social ends, and to assume that changes in housing produce specified social changes. But research clearly shows that housing seldom structures social life directly. It may modify the physical environment. But the physical setting is merely a stage on which the normal social forces which affect individual integration, family life, generational relationships, and community structure play themselves out. Thereby, the environment may set limits on emerging social patterns or favor some at the expense of others. While certain social changes may follow new housing arrangements, their causes lie in the familiar social forces which have free play in the new physical setting. In other words, in housing we may manipulate the conditions but not the determinates of social life.

In this sense, the most problematic variable in housing the alienated aged is their immediate social environment—particularly, the aged composition of the local neighborhood.

ALTERNATIVE AGE STRUCTURES

The age structure of old people's neighborhoods is one of three basic types: (1) normal or integrated, (2) isolated, and (3) segregated. The *normal* is the typical urban area of all age groups, with old people scattered through it almost randomly in numbers proportional to their part of the total population. The *isolated,* exemplified by institutions in the country or true retirement villages, are self-contained, completely separate settlements made up exclusively of older people. The *segregated* is the intermediate type, with disproportionate concentrations of older people in enclaves embedded in a large community. Thus, the isolated pattern concentrates old people together and separates them physically from any surrounding social life. The segregated also concentrates them, to a lesser degree, but insulates rather than separates them from a large community environment.[1]

HOUSING IDEOLOGY

Gerontologists have firm ideological convictions about the relative merits of normal, segregated, and isolated neighborhoods. They dislike segregated and isolated patterns because these seem undemocratic, invidious, and demoralizing. Presumably they intensify the alienation process without mobilizing any counterforces. On the other hand, they like age-integrated neighborhoods and want to keep old people in their normal, familiar surroundings as long as possible (Robbins, 1955) because this maintains continuity in their lives. But they like age integration particularly for the alienated with disrupted lives. They assume that different age groups in normal neighborhoods will develop social intercourse and mutual support. More formally stated, they believe that residential integration will maximize social integration (Mumford, 1956). This is the critical premise.

However, after this orthodox ideology is stated, we are confronted with a paradox. Ensuing discussions of model retirement housing are

[1] These three types can be abstracted from the patterned variation of two variables: (1) concentration or dispersion of older people, and (2) their physical separation or nonseparation from younger people and/or a surrounding community.

almost invariably based on age-segregated examples. These models embrace a familiar catalogue—the retirement villages of Ryderwood, Washington, and Salhaven, Moosehaven, or Kissimee, Florida; Tompkins Square House in New York City; Cobb's Hill Village in Rochester, New York; the Omaha Teachers Cooperative Apartment; Senior Center in Santa Barbara, California; Carmel Hall or Presbyterian Village in Detroit; Cedar Apartment in Cleveland; the Florida trailer courts or the various Lavin hotels, etc. The gerontologist's commitment to normal neighborhoods in principle and to age-segregated models in fact, poses an irony in which the right hand does not know what the left hand is doing.

This implies that our uncritical ideological position may not be appropriate to the alienated aged. Therefore, we propose to examine here the social effects of these neighborhood types in the light of existing information and research.

SOCIAL CONSEQUENCES
OF NEIGHBORHOOD AGE COMPOSITION
Isolation

These arrangements display mixed results. Presumably, true retirement villages, such as Ryderwood, Moosehaven, or Youngtown, Arizona, arouse the enthusiasm of their sponsors, residents, and visitors alike. Studies in Moosehaven, for example, show that residents have a high sense of security and morale (Kleemeier, 1954). Almost 30 percent of the couples got married after meeting each other there, and the evidence is conclusive that married older people are better adjusted than the widowed. But other places which are virtually isolated homes or relatively inaccessible institutions, often in the country, give a picture of lower morale and other correlates of adjustment.

The critical factor in morale is apparently whether an isolated setting is a full-fledged, self-contained community. To the extent that it approximates a community with all of a community's facilities, then it seems to support a thriving social life and to integrate its members (Burgess, 1954).

Segregation

Segregated arrangements seem to have few of the consequences feared by detractors. Reports about Tompkins Square House in New

York, Senior Center in California, Carmel Hall in Detroit, the Lavin Hotels, etc., portray, if not an idyllic, at least an active social process engaging and involving their members. This is equally true of the Florida trailer courts in which activities are withdrawn from the surrounding community and focused on the trailer court itself (Hoyt, 1954).

Also, where special facilities are provided in segregated settings, the local aged use them disproportionately for the total age group. For example, only very small proportions of the age group over 65 patronize "golden age" centers or their local equivalents anywhere. In New York City, the figure is about 1.3 percent (Kutner *et al.,* 1956); in a Syracuse sample, less than 5 percent (Downing, 1957); and the highest proportion reported anywhere in the literature for normal areas is 12 percent in a borough of East London (Townsend, 1957). Seldom do as many as 5 percent of the age group participate. In Cleveland, however, in a public housing retirement apartment with a substantial "golden age" facility, one-third of the residents are members, and fully one-half of all members are drawn from the retirement apartment or the adjacent public housing units. Similar results are reported for a Chicago public housing project with a somewhat smaller proportion of elderly persons (Aukes, 1956). Such findings indicate that segregation favors the use of services which would otherwise be uneconomical and perhaps unsupportable (Monroe, 1951).

Furthermore, Hoyt (1954) shows that a high order of mutual aid appears in a trailer park during illnesses which leave isolated old people in normal neighborhoods vulnerable (Hutchinson, 1954; Townsend, 1957). Informal groups in other segregated settings similarly become mutual aid groups (Aldridge, 1959).

We have very little evidence about prior attitudes toward segregated neighborhoods, although we know that people generally do not accurately predict their response to novel housing conditions until they experience them. In the State of Washington, Stone and Slocum (1957) found that only 10 percent of a rural and small-town sample were even tentatively interested in segregated living arrangements, possibly reflecting a low level of housing need. But, when we turn to more problematic, needy groups, the proportions rise significantly. In two aged samples of public housing applicants in New York City, about one-third of each group preferred segregated arrangements (New York State Division of Housing, 1958*a, b*). A survey of older clients of five social agencies in Schenectady showed that of those in need of rehousing, 60 percent did not want to live in a neighborhood with young children (Community Welfare Council of Schenectady

Country, 1957). These expressed preferences may bear no relation to subsequent responses. But experience indicates that, regardless of original preferences, when either public or private segregated housing promises to solve old people's housing problems economically, there is no dearth of applicants. People apparently accept and adapt to improved housing of any type, even though they may prefer alternatives. This is seen in a recent British housing study in which most people did not get their preferred choice of several different housing types (Hole and Madge, 1958): "As time went on, tenants tended to become identified with the [dwelling unit] type that they were occupying, and the majority of them came to claim that theirs was the best type in the scheme."

This principle is reflected in the only available data on reactions to segregated living. Hoyt (1954) reports that 88 percent of his trailer park sample preferred "to live in a community such as this where everyone is retired" rather than in one of employed people. In another study of 125 people in four segregated facilities and 175 in several normal public housing projects, Steinle and associates (1958) found that roughly 65 percent of each group preferred the type of neighborhood that it was currently occupying.

For those in substandard quarters or with any housing problem, any new housing as such seems more determinate of their reaction than the particular type of facility they are offered. Thus, after they had experienced it, 62 percent of the residents preferred a segregated neighborhood to one of normal age composition. Furthermore, the segregated residents in good health made this choice almost as often as those in poor health (57 percent versus 69 percent). But the difference in preference according to health was much sharper in the normal integrated projects where the sick indicated a preference for segregated settings three times as frequently as the healthy (65 percent versus 22 percent) (Steinle and associates, 1958).

Residents of some retirement communities, like the Florida trailer parks, may be self-selected (Hoyt, 1954; Michelon, 1954), but those of other segregated settings, as in Steinle's samples, are not. Self-selection might account for the high level of approval of segregation in the trailer parks, but it would not account for almost two-thirds of Steinle's segregated group preferring this neighborhood type. If some variables of self-selection may affect social integration, these still must be specified in terms of types of people who can adapt to this environment.

Our data are limited. But those we have indicate that for people with housing problems, rehousing itself is the primary determinate of their reaction; that old people respond favorably to segregated settings regardless of their health; and that as the health of those in normal neighborhoods declines, their choice approximates that of segregated residents of comparable health.

However, although the evidence is fairly clear that segregated neighborhoods may effectively integrate their members, few gerontologists have even questioned the assumption that segregation is inimical to old people (Kleemeier, 1956).

Integration

Clearly, the overriding consideration to be remembered about normal neighborhoods is that they have produced the bulk of our problematic group, the alienated aged; therefore, they offer old people no assurance of effective social contact with others (Townsend, 1957).

We can postulate perhaps four conditions under which the aged may be socially integrated into normal neighborhoods. Old people may be integrated to the extent that: (1) they are long-term residents; (2) they are in a relatively stable, unchanging neighborhood; (3) their neighborhood is socially homogeneous, especially for social class and racial, religious, and ethnic minorities; and (4) the person's local primary groups of family, relatives, friends, and neighbors are still reasonably intact. But to the extent that these conditions are not met —and people are recent arrivals, the neighborhood changes or is socially heterogeneous, and their primary group supports melt away —then their chances of becoming alienated from the social environment increase. It is clear that the alienating forces of residential mobility and neighborhood change are accelerating in urban areas.

If the effect of these independent trends is to alienate, then the crucial problem is the social integration that may result from the residential mixture of different age groups. Specifically, what kinds of social relationships develop between them? We will shortly review some compelling, if provisional and unpleasant evidence, especially for people living alone—about 24 percent of those over 65 in 1950 in the United States (Sheldon, 1958).

It has been argued that the urban residential community is not a viable basis for social integration (Warren, 1957), and this might be peculiarly applicable to the aged, especially after retirement. It is certainly axiomatic among gerontologists that older people have more difficulty in making friends than young people. This is probably intensified by the social distance and negative attitudes toward the aged maintained by other age groups. Younger people's indifference toward the rejection of the old is stated simply in Joyce Cary's (1949) novel, *To Be a Pilgrim:*

Love is a delusion to the old, for who can love an old man. He is a nuisance, he has no place in the world. The old are surrounded by treachery for no one tells them truth. Either it is thought necessary to deceive them, for their own good, or nobody can take the trouble to give explanation or understanding to those who will carry both so soon into a grave. They must not complain of what is inevitable; they must not think evil. It is unjust to blame the rock for its hardness, the stream for its inconstancy and its flight, the young for the strength and the jewel brightness of their passage. An old man's loneliness is nobody's fault. He is like an old fashioned hat which seems absurd and incomprehensible to the young, who never admired and wore such a hat. [p. 114]

It is consistent with this that the aged have been trenchantly analyzed as a quasi-minority group in America (Barron, 1953), one viewed in stereotypes by others (Ginzberg, 1952; Tuckman and Lorge, 1952), suffering from discrimination (Sheppard, 1960), and from their own defensive reactions in the fashion of other minority groups (Barron, 1953). And, like other minority groups, they accept many of the stereotypes about themselves developed by those around them. Indeed, for all practical purposes, young and old people have the same images of the aged (Havighurst and Albrecht, 1953; Hutchinson, 1954; Tuckman and Lorge, 1952; Tuckman *et al.*, 1953).

But where residential integration can destroy the social distance and negative images held by dominant groups about racial, religious, or other minorities, this apparently does not apply to old people. A study by Drake (1957) shows that younger people's attitudes do not vary according to their experience with or exposure to the aged, as measured by their living with older people at any time, or their frequency and intimacy of contact with them. In other words, stereotypes about the aged seem resistant to change by exposure.

Such inflexible images fit in with the patterns of association between generations. Aukes (1956) reports that the relations of younger adults and children to old people in a Chicago housing project "was fraught with the usual prejudices and lack of mutual interest and understanding." Similarly, in a Florida retirement community which was also occupied by young and middle-aged people, friendships and informal groups developed almost exclusively *within* age groups (Aldridge, 1959). This echoes the findings of an unpublished study in a retirement public housing apartment in which one-third of the units were specifically reserved for younger families in order to stimulate their association with the old. Out of the 88 friendships reported by a sample of both age groups, only one crossed the age barrier. A more recent pilot study with a 50 percent sample of the aged in this same apartment checked this point again and showed that of all the old people's friendships with neighbors, only 4 percent were with young neighbors. By the same token, Terreberry (1958) found that old people living alone in an integrated Detroit housing project were socially isolated and had almost no significant contact with their young and middle-aged neighbors.

Such evidence is fragmentary, but, pending further research, it is clear and consistent. Except under conditions previously noted, in modern urban settings, viable friendships do not spontaneously develop between age groups, but are confined almost exclusively within them. There is apparently an effective social barrier between the old and the young or middle-aged.

As unpleasant as this may be, it is not surprising, since it reflects the age-grading of the larger social order. In a mass industrial society, friendship groups are peer groups—people with basically similar social status, occupational rank, education, stage in the family cycle, values, problems, and life styles. These guides to selective social groups also become the mechanisms of age-grading. The symbols and stigmata of age ranks are increasingly externalized, formalized, and shared through numerous institutions: the educational system, adolescent or youth culture, career stages, suburbia, forced retirement, and the like. In a mass society, informal age-grading reduces the social bonds between age groups which may still survive where community membership remains a major social tie, where mobility and bureaucratization have not seriously weakened local identification. There is probably a growing trend of age-grading which links and binds people by characteristics which are highly correlated with age and which reduces the common problems and shared experiences of people of different generations.

Both the life cycle and societal trends weaken intergenerational relations. The attrition of occupational and familial roles, of health and income, and technological, scientific, and general social changes all combine to intensify the differences between generations, to limit the reciprocity of their relations to each other, and to weaken the basis of their association. The result is that a common social frame of reference exists primarily with one's own age peers. This is a bitter pill in America precisely because the larger society is youth-oriented and rejects old age, honoring it on occasion with perfunctory rituals. Therefore, to accept old age is to document one's social obsolescence and marginality—unless effective social insulation is established.

Because the dramatic increase in the number of older people has been so recent, old age is still a new social problem for which America has developed few definitions. Whether a clearer age role and re-evaluation of older people will crystallize to transform their future position in society is a moot problem which will not be resolved for another 10 to 20 years.

But we have been concerned with their current situation, and some major social class differences also enter the picture. Bell's studies show that the major differences in anomie occur between social classes rather than between age groups per se. In his samples, the old were not significantly more anomic than the young within the same social class (Meier and Bell, 1959). The relative importance of determinates of anomie proved to be: social class factors, social isola-tion, and, finally, age. Significant for the alienated aged, social isola-tion was inversely related to family activity (Bell and Boat, 1957), although highly intensive contact with children generally depresses morale, especially of the middle-class aged (Kutner *et al.*, 1956). In addition, the working class is much more dependent on neighbors as a source of friends than is the middle class (Bell and Boat, 1957; Smith *et al.*, 1954). Indeed, the middle-class aged may actively avoid the formation of friendships and entangling ties with neighbors (United Community Services of Metropolitan Boston, 1957*a*, *b*). Further, residential isolation is tantamount to social isolation and anomie for the working class, but not for the middle class (Bell, 1957; Kutner *et al.*, 1956; Townsend, 1957). Thus, the middle classes apparently have more personal resources or interests which make them considerably more self-sufficient than the working class and less de-pendent on the immediate social environment for their support, morale, and social integration.

If this is the case, if our society remains informally age-graded, and if the working class (to which the bulk of our aged belong) is strongly dependent on neighbors for its associates, then normal neighborhoods may be excellent instruments for ensuring the isolation and demoraliza-tion of alienated old people. With the attrition of family, friends, and other former ties, the dispersal of their age peers in a normal neigh-borhood reduces the number of potential new associates around them. The field of eligible new friends is thin and scattered, and the effects of this are intensified by any decline in health or mobility. Except under special conditions, then, normal neighborhoods may attenuate the pos-sible axes of social integration of older people.

This may be basically why segregated retirement communities are successful—they concentrate rather than diffuse the field of potential friends and support, thereby maximizing the conditions of social integration. This is not to suggest that new friendships necessarily attain the meaning, intensity, or intimacy of the old relationships. As people age, affection becomes less important in life and they consequently reduce their emotional investments (Rosen and Neugarten, 1960). In other words, their emotional relations become more superficial. But, under these conditions, even superficial friendships may be adequate to sustain the alienated.

Thus, there are grounds for reappraising the suitability of age-integrated and segregated environments for alienated old people. We hypothesize that the segregated neighborhood will integrate them socially more effectively than the integrated neighborhood.

POSSIBLE FUNCTIONS OF AGE-SEGREGATION

What, then, are some possible consequences of a heavy residential concentration of older people?

First, significant *economic* gains are feasible in the volume of both housing and special services which might be provided. It is much cheaper to build a large number of dwelling units in one place than an equal number of scattered units. Similarly, one can provide various services more economically and effectively to a concentrated than to a dispersed market.

Second, major *social* gains may be realized from new group memberships. The concentration of people with common status and problems, with similar life experience and perspectives, maximizes the opportunity for new friendships. By the same token, the high exposure to a field of eligibles maximizes the opportunity for remarriage. Further, new group memberships afford new identifications and psychological support as well as mutual aid (Hoyt, 1954). The sheer undermining of isolation may be an important barrier to demoralization, especially in the working class (Kutner *et al.,* 1956).

The reintegration of older people into new groups may facilitate their transition to a new aged role, especially when there has been confusion about this. Age peers provide role models on which a person may pattern himself. The older group can also generate new activities which crystallize new role dimensions. By clarifying expectations and appropriate behavior, especially in dealing with the leisure of retirement, older people provide each other with new norms. In legitimizing these norms, age peers may aid the acceptance of older self-conceptions and hedge this in with supports which are presently lacking, to the apparent detriment of adjustment. Indeed, if older people can accept their age peers as a new reference group, as a source of standards for themselves, then their chances of developing clear, acceptable new roles to which they can make some satisfactory adjustment may decidedly improve. They may no longer need to cling to youthful standards which they cannot meet and for which the necessary life conditions have withered away.

Two conditions will favor these effects of residential segregation. The most important is that residents be of basically homogeneous social composition, of broadly similar background, social class, and life experience, whether the mechanism of selection be the market, self-selection, or tenant-selection policy. Sharing similar values, interests, and problems can preserve a basic continuity in their lives and stimulate social intercourse. The second condition is that the context of segregation be insulating rather than invidious or stigmatizing. Segregation must impinge on residents in socially acceptable terms rather than in terms of devaluation, marginality, and loss of status. This, however, is not simply a problem of management and administration, but one of the larger social order.

REFERENCES

Aldridge, G. J. 1959. Informal social relationships in a retirement community. Marriage and Family Living, 21: 70–72.
Anonymous. 1955. Housing for aged. J. Housing, 12: 407, 418.
Arnett, W. T. 1956. Housing Florida's older people. *In* I. L. Webber (ed.), Aging: a current appraisal, pp. 142–51. Gainsville: University of Florida Press.
Aukes, Iva. 1956. Community services for older people at Prairie Avenue Courts. Chicago: Welfare Council of Metropolitan Chicago. (Mimeographed.)
Barron, M. L. 1953. Minority group characteristics of the aged in American society. J. Gerontol., 8: 477–82.
Bell, W. 1957. Anomie, social isolation, and the class structure. Sociometry, 20: 105–16.
Bell, W., and Boat, M. D. 1957. Urban neighborhoods and informal social relations. Am. J. Sociology, 62: 391–98.
Burgess, E. W. 1954. Social relations, activities, and personal adjustment. Am. J. Sociology, 59: 352–60.
Cary, Joyce, 1949. To be a pilgrim. New York: Harper and Brothers.
Churchill, H. S. 1952. Some random thoughts on housing for the aged. *In* T. L. Smith (ed.), Living in the later years, pp. 37–49. Gainesville: University of Florida Press.
Community Welfare Council of Schenectady County. 1957. A place to live. Schenectady: The Council. (Mimeographed.)
Dean, J. 1958. The neighborhood and social relations. *In* Forum on

neighborhoods. Philadelphia: Philadelphia Housing Association. (Mimeographed.)

Downing, J. 1957. Factors affecting the selective use of a social club for the aged. J. Gerontol., 12: 81–84.

Drake, J. T. 1957. Some factors influencing students' attitudes toward older people. Social Forces, 35: 266–71.

Ginzberg, R. 1952. The negative attitude toward the elderly. Geriatrics, 7: 297–302.

Havighurst, R. J., and Albrecht, Ruth. 1953. Older people. New York: Longmans, Green & Co.

Hole, V., and Madge, J. 1958. A case study of tenant experiences in some new Scottish houses. (British) Architects' J., 127: 539–46.

Hoyt, G. C. 1954. The life of the retired in a trailer park. Am. J. Sociology, 59: 361–70.

Hutchinson, B. 1954. Old people in a modern Australian community. Melbourne: Melbourne University Press.

Kleemeier, R. W. 1954. Moosehaven: congregate living in a community of the retired. Am. J. Sociology, 59: 347–51.

———— 1956. An analysis of patterns for group living for older people. *In* I. L. Webber (ed.), Aging: a current appraisal, pp. 167–79. Gainesville: University of Florida Press.

Kutner, B., Fanshel, D., Togo, Alice M., and Langner, T. S. 1956. Five hundred over sixty: a community survey on aging. New York: Russell Sage Foundation.

Massachusetts State Housing Board. 1954. Standards of design: housing for the elderly. Boston: The Board.

McFarland, M. C. 1959. Housing our senior citizens. Pub. Health News, 40: 267–71.

McGuire, Marie C. 1957. Housing for the aged. San Antonio: San Antonio Housing Authority. (Mimeographed.)

Meier, Dorothy, and Bell, W. 1959. Anomie and differential access to the achievement of life goals. Amer. Sociological Rev., 24: 189–202.

Michelon, L. C. 1954. The new leisure class. Am. J. Sociology, 59: 371–78.

Monroe, R. T. 1951. Diseases in old age. Cambridge, Mass.: Harvard University Press.

Mumford, L. 1956. For older people—not segregation but integration. Architectural Rec., 119: 191–94.

New York State Division of Housing. 1958a. Housing problems and preferences of aged applicants ineligible for public housing in New York City. New York: The Division. (Mimeographed.)

———— 1958b. Housing problems and preferences of aging persons on the site of Borgia Butler Houses. New York: The Division. (Mimeographed.)

Robbins, I. S. 1955. Housing for the aging. *In* Charter for the aging, pp. 300–32. Albany: Governor's Conference on Problems of the Aging, 1955.

Rosen, Jacqueline L., and Neugarten, Bernice L. 1960. Ego functions in the middle and later years. J. Gerontol., 15: 62–67.

Sheldon, H. D. 1958. The older population of the United States. New York: John Wiley & Sons.

Sheppard, H. 1960. Unemployment experiences of older workers. Geriatrics, 15: 430–33.

Smith, J., Form, W. H., and Stone, G. P. 1954. Local intimacy in a middle-sized city. Am. J. Sociology, 60: 276–84.

Steinle, J. and Associates. 1958. Home care and housing needs of the aged. New York: New York State Division of Housing. (Mimeographed.)

Stone, Carol, and Slocum, W. 1957. A look at Thurston County's older people. (Agric. Exper. Sta. Res. Bull. 573.) Pullman: State College of Washington.

Terreberry, Shirley. 1958. Survey of the health, welfare and recreation needs of the aging in Herman Gardens Housing Project. Detroit: Neighborhood Service Organization and United Community Services of Metropolitan Detroit. (Mimeographed.)

Townsend, P. 1957. The family life of old people. London: Routledge & Kegan Paul, Ltd.

Tréanton, J. R. 1959. Adjustment of older people to urban life in France. *In* C. Tibbitts (ed.), Aging and social health in the United States and Europe, pp. 167–73. Ann Arbor: University of Michigan, Division of Gerontology.

Tuckman, J., and Lorge, I. 1952. Attitudes toward older workers. J. Appl. Psychol., 36: 149–53.

——— 1953. Attitudes toward old people. J. Social Psychol., 37: 249–60.

Tuckman, J., Lorge, I., and Spooner, G. A. 1953. The effect of family environment on attitudes toward old people and the older worker. J. Social Psychol., 38: 207–18.

United Community Services of Metropolitan Boston. 1957a. Follow-up study: housing preferences of older people. Boston: The Services. (Mimeographed.)

——— 1957b. Housing preferences of older people: a case study of forty-seven evictions from a residential hotel. Boston: The Services. (Mimeographed.)

Warren, V. R. L. 1957. Eine sozialpsychologische analyse der buergerschaftlichen taetigkeiten in Stuttgart. (A social psychological analysis of community participation in Stuttgart.) Koelner Zeitschrift fuer Soziologie und Sozialpsychologie, 9: 619–42.

Housing Preferences and Social Patterns

WILFRED S. LAKE

THIS is a report on two studies of the housing preferences of older people in an urban area. Two sharply contrasting groups of individuals, forced to seek new housing as a result of the demolition of the buildings in which they lived, were interviewed. One group consisted of single or widowed individuals living alone in an old residential hotel which was being razed for business purposes, while the other was comprised of couples living alone in low-rent apartments which were being torn down for an urban redevelopment project. In both instances, the studies suggested that a basic consideration in housing needs of such people seemed to be housing which would enable independent older people to preserve and continue their established social patterns.

THE HOTEL BRUNSWICK STUDY

The Hotel Brunswick, an historic old hotel, was located in the Copley Square area of Boston. In this area were famous churches, the public library, art galleries, restaurants of all types, and many small shops. Only a block or two away was a fashionable shopping district adjacent to the Public Garden. The hotel itself, although old and faded, retained an aura of elegance from former days when it had been patronized by many celebrities. It presented a comfortable residence (United Community Services of Boston, 1957a, 1957b).

After World War II, the character of the hotel changed and it became more of a residential hotel for elderly people. The hotel management was unusual in exhibiting an active interest in the welfare of the permanent residents. The residents appreciated this interest and welcomed the hotel's sympathetic attitude and willingness to help with personal problems. This tolerance was indicated by the hotel's allowing one very deaf resident to keep some 50 parakeets in his room.

When the hotel was sold in late 1957 to make way for a modern office building and the residents had been given eviction notices, the Committee on Aging of the Division of Social Services to Families and Individuals of the United Community Services of Metropolitan Boston asked the Research Division to take advantage of the opportunity to make a study of the housing preferences of this special group. A schedule was drawn up to guide the interviewers who conducted informal interviews of about an hour in length. In addition to specific questions about the housing desired, a number of more general questions sought information about activities and relationships with families, friends, neighbors, and institutions. As much as possible of the basic data was obtained from the hotel manager who had a fairly intimate knowledge of the residents.

The group interviewed consisted of 47 individuals of whom 3 were men, single or widowed, of urban American background, mainly over 65 years of age. They had lived alone in the hotel from 1 to 10 years. Generally they were in fair health since they were able to climb stairs, including a steep flight of steps from the street to the lobby. Eleven of the group were employed, 18 had private incomes, and 18 received old age assistance. In the judgment of the hotel staff, 21 seemed to be fairly comfortable on a limited income, while the remainder were clearly at a minimal level.

All but 3 of the group had single rooms with rents ranging from $37 to $69 a month. Although the rents were modest, the Brunswick provided the usual hotel services. The rooms were furnished, there was a 24-hour elevator service and desk service in the lobby, and maid service was supplied. Most rooms contained a washbowl, but no private bath. In addition, hot plates and refrigerators could be rented for low monthly fees. However, most of the residents relied upon restaurants nearby for their main meals.

The retired group led relatively solitary lives with a great deal of time spent in their rooms. Reading, sewing, writing letters, and listening to the radio occupied a large share of their time. Outside the hotel their activities included: going to restaurants for meals, going to the library, attending church, strolling about Copley Square and the downtown area, occasionally visiting friends, window shopping, and observing those who were shopping. Much time was spent in sitting and watching the bustling activity of the area. Contacts with family, even for the small group with children or relatives, were almost nonexistent. Some expressed the belief that children should lead private lives away from their parents and that parents should not interfere with the lives of their children. Association with neighbors in the hotel was also limited; they preferred to see old friends.

All were questioned about their attitudes toward the various types of housing arrangements available to them such as: living with relatives, living in a nursing or boarding home, living with a friend, living in a public housing project, and living with people of their own age group. The consensus was negative. One common theme ran through their responses: they definitely wished to live completely private, independent lives without interference from any source. Public housing projects did not appeal to them because of the neighborhoods in which they were located, the lack of status of such residences, and the lack of the hotel service to which they were accustomed.

What did they want to find in housing? As a group they wanted essentially what they had at the Hotel Brunswick. The typical requirement was one furnished room, since few had furniture of their own, a washbowl, cleaning service, light cooking facilities, elevator service, and a location similar to that of the Brunswick. All were concerned about high rents, regardless of the amount they were actually willing to pay; over half wished to pay rents within the $50–79 a month range.

The attitudes of the group toward the Hotel Brunswick emphasized their housing preferences. The rank order of the responses to the questions of what they liked about the hotel was: nearness to shopping center, ability to cook some meals in the room, the friendly staff, the "homey" atmosphere, freedom of movement, reasonable rents, and privacy. The area and the hotel combined to give them the security they wanted and the ability to remain independent.

The next summer, after the hotel had been razed, a follow-up study was made to discover how successful the group had been in obtaining the kind of housing they desired. Thirty-three of the original group were available to be interviewed again. With few exceptions, they had found approximately the type of housing which they had sought. Most of them had single, "reasonably priced," furnished rooms in or close to Copley Square or the downtown area. The majority were in other old hotels with comparable physical accommodations. Most were at least comparatively satisfied with their new housing, and only a few were dissatisfied enough to wish to move.

Since this group chose their housing in terms of a life pattern largely free from any group entanglement, they probably do not represent a large proportion of the entire older population; yet they may represent a substantial segment of the older population in many cities. Fuller information is needed about the relative importance of this group in order to determine what consideration should be given to it in providing housing for the older person.

THE WEST END STUDY

In 1958 the Research Division, again at the request of the Committee on Aging, undertook a second case study of the housing
preferences of a distinct group of older people (United Community
Services of Boston, 1959). The opportunity for this group study arose
from an extensive urban redevelopment project in the West End of
Boston, a section immediately west of the central city, involving the
tearing down of old apartment buildings containing some 2200 housing units and their replacement with modern apartment structures.
Preliminary eviction notices were sent out by the Redevelopment
Authority during the period of the interviewing.

Physically, this redevelopment area appeared to be a distinct unit.
The streets were narrow and winding, while the boundaries were two
wide main commercial streets and the Charles River. It was within
walking distance of the downtown area, the Boston Common, Public
Garden, and the Charles River Esplanade. It included many health,
welfare, recreational, and religious institutions.

For over a century, the West End had been a port of entry for different groups of immigrants. At the time of the study the major cultural
groupings were: southern Italian, Jewish, Polish, and Ukrainian.
Although the West End immigrants lived next to neighbors of different
backgrounds, they tended to preserve their ethnic identity; thus, the
area contained separate communities which were closely knit among
themselves, mingling casually but not mixing.

The group chosen for the study consisted of all the couples living
alone in which there was a husband 65 years of age or over and a
wife of 60 or over. Couples with children in the home were excluded
since their problems were different. All but 3 of the 104 couples
meeting this requirement were interviewed; 3 refused. The median age
for the men was 73, and for the women, 69. Almost half the women
and about a third of the men had some health problem.

This group formed a very stable population, three-quarters of them
having come directly to the West End from small towns and villages in
southern and eastern Europe. Only one-sixth had moved into their
present apartments since 1951; about the same number had lived in
their present apartments since 1920 or earlier.

Rents for the apartments were very low, with a median figure of
$37 a month and a maximum of $65. None of the buildings had
elevators; hence, these people were accustomed to climbing flights of
stairs: three-quarters of the group had to climb from two to four

flights. Only 38 of the couples had apartments with central heating; the remainder relied upon coal or oil stoves which is not surprising because most of the buildings were built before central heating became commonplace. Most of the families had private bathrooms but 19 had to share one with an adjacent apartment. Incomes were also low, ranging from $100 to $179 a month with a median of $138. The majority, aside from the 19 families in which the man was employed, received their income from social security or old age assistance.

One of the basic questions in the study concerned the people and institutions which were important to these couples. All of the ethnic groups were characterized by fairly closely-knit family structures and fairly frequent contact with others of their own group, either informally while shopping or in clubs, societies, or churches. These contacts constituted a vital part of the lives of these couples. Not only did they provide companionship, but they afforded security in time of illness or other trouble.

Family relationships were especially significant for the 84 couples with children. Most of the families had regular contact with their children, most frequently over the weekend, indicating a strong sense of responsibility on the part of the children for the parents, and not infrequently involving a feeling of companionship between parents and children, although there were differences among the ethnic groups. The relationships between the couples and their relatives were similar, but not as strong. Of the group, three-fourths had relatives living in this country and about half had frequent contact.

Friends and friendship, again mainly from their own ethnic group, were as important in the lives of the couples as their children, and in many instances, more important than relatives. Most of the women's contact with friends consisted of casual, chance meetings while shopping or at church. The men relied less upon casual contact and took the initiative in visiting their friends in their homes, stores, barber shops, or bars. In maintaining contact with children, relatives, and friends, location is important, although not the sole factor. The impact was greatest with friends who were about the same age and thus tended to be less mobile. It is essential that the less mobile people have near them the individuals and institutions which are important to them.

What kind of housing did these couples want? With respect to location, nearness to their children was not imperative provided that the distance was not too great to permit weekend visits. Location of relatives of the same age range was more significant since they tended to be as immobile as the couples; hence, there tended to be a sharp break in contact if distance was great. Of prime importance was the proximity of friends and institutions. These couples needed companionship with people of their own background who "understood them" and whom "they could talk to." Since both tend to be immobile, distance can sever almost all contact. When the number of friends and meeting places in the neighborhood were small, the extent of activities declined sharply.

Although a slight majority expressed a desire to live near people of their own age range, they meant others of the same age and culture group. However, a substantial number did not care, and some did not wish to be grouped by age.

There was no antagonism toward public housing projects as such; the objection to them arose from the fact that the available projects, with one notable exception, were located in areas which were not suited to their needs; that is, they were out of the areas where others of their ethnic group lived. Some concern was voiced over the undesirability of those projects where juvenile delinquency had been a problem.

The nearness of institutions which would enable these people to participate in meaningful activity and to meet others of their own background was very important. Those who did not rely upon institutions to maintain personal contacts did depend upon them heavily for formal facilities to keep them busy.

Generally, the men appeared to be less concerned than the women with location. Those who were religious had to be near a church; otherwise, they were able and willing to seek out old places of business or other meeting places. They did want to be near enough to other men of their group to find a common meeting place without difficulty.

The social life of the West Enders influenced their desired housing arrangements as much as the location. Most wanted an apartment but did not insist upon an elevator; many had a strong aversion to self-service elevators. Many wanted a large kitchen since they had always thought of the kitchen as the main room of the house. Most wanted a four-room apartment, even though they knew that public housing projects ordinarily allot three rooms to a couple without children. Those with close family groups wanted a fourth room to provide for the visits of their children or grandchildren.

SOME IMPLICATIONS OF THE STUDIES

These two studies suggest that care be exercised in relying upon the expressed preferences of older people for types of housing. The reasons behind the preferences, arising from their patterns of life, must be obtained. For instance, the West End group expressed a desire to be with their own age group, but they actually meant their own age and ethnic group. Both groups objected to public housing projects, but an examination of their patterns of life indicated that certain types of public housing, or public housing with some modifications, would be wholly satisfactory, with the exception of the Brunswick group who would not find an outlying location acceptable. Consequently, housing arrangements completely contrary to expressed wants could be satisfactory if they satisfied the basic social needs.

While certain physical requirements of housing are important, these features were overshadowed by intangible needs and by their desire to preserve and maintain their customary patterns of life. Independence was desired by both groups, but each had important security needs which could be satisfied in different ways: by being near enough to their children for the West End group, and by the presence of a resident manager or supervisor for the Brunswick group.

These studies suggest that any housing program that claims to meet the needs of older people needs qualification. "Older people" are not a homogeneous group; they turn out to be many smaller cultural groups with some common needs, but with marked differences in types of housing arrangements and locations desired, and with special problems for those belonging to minority cultural groups. We need a variety of housing programs for older people who have had varying life patterns and relationships with their environment (Frieden, 1960).

REFERENCES

Frieden, Elaine. 1960. Social differences and their consequences for housing the aged. J. Am. Institute Planners, 26: 119–24.
United Community Services of Metropolitan Boston. 1957a. Housing preferences of older people: a case study of forty-seven evictions from a residential hotel. Boston: The Services. (Mimeographed.)
———— 1957b. Follow-up study: housing preferences of older people: a case study of forty-seven evictions from a residential hotel. Boston: The Services. (Mimeographed.)
———— 1959. Housing preferences of older people, study number 2. Boston: The Services.

Living Arrangements, Attitudes, and Preferences of Older Persons

GLENN H. BEYER

MANY professional and popular writings on the housing situation of the aged have implied that the aged represent a somewhat homogeneous group. For example, we have read that the aged have small households and large houses; that they usually own their own homes and that these homes are generally of low value and frequently of poor quality; that they have low incomes; and the like.

It is probably quite natural that we have this oversimplified image since, after all, most of our facts have been limited in large part to the relatively sparse data made available by the 1950 U.S. Housing Census.

Today, however, some new research efforts in this area are reaching their conclusion and some more detailed factual information is coming to light.

One of these research efforts is the project which has been undertaken since 1958 through the Cornell University Housing Research Center, sponsored in large part by the Ford Foundation. One phase of that project represented the collection of some new information from a total of 5200 individuals over the age of 65, based on 5 statistical samples representing universes totaling approximately 670,000 older persons. The sections of the nation represented by the samples and the number of interviews completed in each are as follows: 18-country upstate New York area, 1577 cases; Rochester, New York, metropolitan area, 1062 cases; Los Angeles County, California, 906 cases; St. Louis, Missouri, metropolitan area, 842 cases; and Cook County, Illinois, 815 cases. The samples represented the total population of this age group in these areas, excepting only individuals in certain occupational groups and those living in institutions.

For many of the characteristics and other factors to be discussed in this paper, there were no significant differences between findings of the various samples. Therefore, in order to simplify this presentation, a composite picture will be described combining the data from the different regions. The final report will deal in detail with any regional differences that may appear.

The purpose of this survey was broad, delving into economic, sociological, and architectural factors. After analysis of the data collected, a final report was expected to be completed late in 1961 (Cornell University Housing Research Center, 1958). A mimeographed report entitled "Housing Requirements of the Aged—A Study of Design Criteria," issued in November, 1958, as a part of this project, summarized results of early research and other literature in this area. The findings, concerning just a few of the selected items that have been investigated, include occupancy status, value and rent, size, quality and age of house or apartment, period of occupancy, future plans of the occupant, amount of social interaction in present location, and the kind of living arrangements preferred.

Steiner and Dorfman have proposed that neither the traditional terminology of the "family" nor the "individual" is appropriate in a discussion of this group. They defined and based much of their report, *The Economic Status of the Aged* (Steiner and Dorfman, 1957), on three kinds of aged economic units: (1) the couple, (2) the unrelated female, and (3) the unrelated male. By definition, a couple was comprised of man and wife living together, either with or without the presence of other persons in the household. Unrelated females and unrelated males were unmarried females and unmarried males, i.e., they were single, widowed, divorced, etc., either living alone or with someone else in the household.

This presentation will follow the same concept but will substitute the term "unmarried" for "unrelated."

Among the 5200 persons interviewed in this study, 46 percent were married couples, 39 percent were unmarried females, and 15 percent were unmarried males. Nearly all of the married couples (97 percent) were living in their own households. Of the unmarried males and females, approximately 70 percent were living in their own households, and the balance of 30 percent were not living in their own households.

SURVEY DATA
Household relationships of older persons

A number of important aspects can be seen in an analysis of the household relationships of older persons. There were significant differences between individuals living in their own households and those living in households of others, and also between married couples and unmarried males and females.

Looking first at those aged living in their own households, 77 percent of the married couples but only 60 percent of the unmarried males and 65 percent of the unmarried females lived alone. A higher percentage of unmarried males had relatives (other than children) and nonrelatives living with them than did unmarried females. Only a small proportion of married couples had other relatives or nonrelatives living with them.

The majority of those aged living in the households of others lived with their children. However, the unmarried males showed less tendency to live with their children than did unmarried females and married couples (although it may be recalled that the total number of married couples living in the households of others was found to be small) (see Table 1).

Table 1. Household relationships of older persons, by living arrangements, percentage distribution

	OWN HOUSEHOLD			NOT OWN HOUSEHOLD		
Living arrangement	*Married couples* ($N = 2302$)	*Unmarried women* ($N = 1396$)	*Unmarried men* ($N = 511$)	*Married couples* ($N = 73$)	*Unmarried women* ($N = 608$)	*Unmarried men* ($N = 231$)
Alone		65	60			
With spouse only	77					
With children	15	16	18	82	63	55
With others	8	19	22	18	37	45

Occupancy status

As may have been expected, there was a higher proportion of owner occupancy among married couples living in their own households than among unmarried individuals. Three out of 4 houses of the married couples were owner-occupied. This was true for 3 out of 5 of the unmarried males and for 57 percent of the unmarried females. Most of the balance were renters, since only 2 percent of the married couples, 5 percent of the unmarried males, and 4 percent of the unmarried females living in their own households lived in rent-free quarters.

Among the married couples living in their own households, a slightly higher percentage of renters than of owners (85 percent compared with 75 percent) lived alone. However, among unmarried males and females the differences between renters and owners were much greater. In addition, about 1 out of every 4 of the home owners had children living with them and approximately the same proportion had others living with them (Table 2).

Table 2. Occupancy status of dwelling units of older persons living in their own household, percentage distribution

Living arrangement	MARRIED COUPLES			UNMARRIED WOMEN			UNMARRIED MEN		
	Owners (N = 1794)	*Renters (N = 463)*	*Rent-free (N = 45)*	*Owners (N = 796)*	*Renters (N = 547)*	*Rent-free (N = 53)*	*Owners (N = 309)*	*Renters (N = 179)*	*Rent-free (N = 23)*
Alone				55	78	81	48	78	87
With spouse only	75	85	87						
With children	17	10	7	21	9	3	26	7	
With others	8	5	6	24	13	16	26	15	13

A somewhat frequent characteristic of the housing arrangements of the aged individuals who own their own accommodations is the proportion of dwelling units or structures containing rented rooms or apartments. Of the married couples who were owners, 23 percent rented rooms or apartments. The percentage for unmarried females was 33 percent and for unmarried males, 20 percent. It is interesting to note the larger proportion of unmarried females who rented rooms and apartments in the light of the earlier finding that a smaller percentage of these females than married couples or unmarried males owned and occupied their own homes. It might be hypothesized that the renting of rooms or apartments assists them in maintaining their ownership status.

Among the owners of single-family dwelling units, only 12 percent of the married couples had a mortgage on their house. Among unmarried females and unmarried males, the proportion was even lower —9 percent and 5 percent, respectively. In all three instances, however, the proportions were higher when those households having children present were considered (16 percent, 15 percent, and 14 percent, respectively, for the three groups).

Value and rent

In comparing the estimated present value of the single-family dwelling unit structures covered in this study with earlier statistics available from other sources, especially the 1950 U.S. Census, it is evident that the value of housing owned by the aged has followed the pattern of housing in general, increasing significantly in value in the last few years. The median value of units occupied by married couples living alone was $12,000 when this field survey was undertaken in

Table 3. Value and gross monthly rent of dwelling units of older persons living in their own households, percentage distribution

	MARRIED COUPLES			UNMARRIED WOMEN			UNMARRIED MEN		
Owners	With spouse	With children	With others	Alone	With children	With others	Alone	With children	With others
Value of one-dwelling-unit structures (in dollars)									
Less than 5000	7	4	7	12	3	7	30	6	9
5000–7499	9	10	8	12	11	12	13	16	11
7500–9999	11	12	11	18	17	12	13	18	9
10,000–12,499	23	31	20	24	21	29	16	16	28
12,500–14,999	11	10	8	9	7	9	5	4	5
15,000–17,499	15	14	13	10	17	16	10	6	12
17,500–19,999	6	5	5	4	7	4	5	6	2
20,000–24,999	10	8	15	6	10	6	5	18	14
25,000–34,999	5	4	6	3	4	4	2	8	5
35,000 or more	3	2	7	2	3	1	1	2	5
Number of cases	898	213	99	280	115	135	103	50	57
Median value (in dollars)	12,000	12,000	14,000	10,000	12,000	12,000	8000	12,000	12,000
Renters									
Gross monthly rent (in dollars)									
Under 30	1	3	5	5		3	16		11
30–39	6	5	14	10	10	9	26		15
40–49	10	5	5	23	10	8	17		4
50–59	15	18	24	23	10	14	17		22
60–69	18	5	9	13	18	20	9		11
70–79	12	15	5	10	20	13	7		
80–89	14	15	19	7	20	11	3		11
90–99	9	8	5	4	2	3	1		
100 and over	15	26	14	5	10	19	4		26
Number of cases	355	39	21	397	40	64	134	13[a]	27
Median rent (in dollars)	69	78	66	54	72	68	43	86	55

1958–1959. Unmarried females living alone occupied units valued approximately $2000 lower (i.e., median $10,000) and unmarried males, $4000 lower (i.e., median $8000). If there were children in the household, the median value of units occupied by unmarried males or unmarried females increased to $12,000 (Table 3). These differences in value levels reflect the different levels of quality of housing discussed later.

In reviewing the gross monthly rent figures, we again see a pattern of married couples living alone at the highest level, unmarried females at the middle level, and unmarried males at the lowest rent level. The median gross monthly rents for these three groups, when there were no children or other relatives or nonrelatives living with them, were $69, $54, and $43, respectively. It is interesting to note that these figures increased appreciably in each instance if there were children in the household. The important effect of the presence of children in the household is one of the significant early findings of this study. There was some reason to believe that in this particular instance the higher median rents might have been attributable more to contributions made by children than to increased household size, because when there were household members other than children present we did not find the same high level of rents.

Size of house

The median size of house occupied by aged individuals living in their own households was 6 rooms. However, when persons were living alone or with spouse only, the median was 5 rooms for married couples, 4 rooms for unmarried females, and 3 rooms for unmarried males. When there were children or others living with the aged persons, the median was 6 rooms for each of the three groups (Table 4).

When the respondents living in their own households were asked how they felt about the number of rooms in their house or apartment, between two-thirds and three-fourths said they had the right number. Among married couples and unmarried individuals living alone, only about one-fourth said they had more rooms than they needed. A low percentage of the various groups indicated they had fewer rooms than they needed.

These figures would tend to indicate that the size of the average house or apartment does not exceed actual need to the extent heretofore assumed.

Table 4. Number of rooms in dwelling units of older persons, percentage distribution

Number of rooms	MARRIED COUPLES			UNMARRIED WOMEN			UNMARRIED MEN		
	With spouse	*With children*	*With others*	*Alone*	*With children*	*With others*	*Alone*	*With children*	*With others*
Own household									
One	1	a		4		1	16	1	1
Two	2	1	1	14	8	2	21	2	1
Three	12	8	3	26	13	6	16	9	5
Four	18	21	10	20	25	11	15	20	15
Five	24	33	22	14	20	21	12	24	23
Six	19	16	26	10	14	24	7	13	14
Seven	12	21	14	5	20	11	6	31	19
Eight or more	12		23	7	a	23	7		22
Not reported	a		1	a		1			
Number of cases	1780	356	166	911	220	265	307	93	111
Median number of rooms	5	6	6	4	6	6	3	6	6
Not own household									
One				a	a	1			2
Two			1		1	5		1	3
Three		9	3		3	14		3	5
Four		23	10		10	21		25	25
Five		22	22		22	19		25	22
Six		20	26		26	13		21	10
Seven		23	20		20	23		21	21
Eight or more		3	14		17	4		4	12
Not reported			1		1				
Number of cases		60	13 b		386	222		126	105
Median number of rooms		6	5		5	6		6	6

a Less than 1 percent.
b Too few cases reported to make percentages meaningful.

Housing quality

In this study a quality of housing scale was developed, using as its basis items on structure, facilities, and equipment similar to the U.S. Census of Housing, but also incorporating a set of planning questions. These questions asked whether the bathroom was on the same floor as the bedroom, whether it was possible to reach the bathroom without passing through some other room, whether there was a clothes closet in the bedroom, and whether there were handrails on all stairs that were regularly used in the house. If there were no major deficiencies or no significant minor deficiencies, a house was classed as being of good quality. If there were no major deficiencies but one or more significant minor deficiencies, it was rated as fair quality. If it had any major deficiencies or a combination of serious minor deficiencies, it was rated as poor quality.

The housing occupied by married couples living in their own households was of appreciably better quality than that occupied by unmarried females; and the housing of unmarried females was, in turn, generally of better quality than that occupied by unmarried males. For example, approximately 3 out of every 4 units occupied by married couples were of good quality and the balance of 25 percent was distributed quite evenly between fair and poor quality. No significant difference was noted in quality, whether the married couple lived alone or with others.

Among unmarried females living alone, 64 percent occupied housing of good quality, 15 percent fair quality, and 20 percent poor quality. It is interesting to note that if others, such as children, other relatives, or nonrelatives, were living with the unmarried females, the percentage of units of good quality approached 3 out of every 4, similar to the proportion found among married couples. Among unmarried males living alone in their own household only 45 percent occupied housing of good quality and 40 percent lived in housing rated as being of poor quality, with the balance of 15 percent being rated as fair quality. Here again, however, the percentage of unmarried males living in housing of good quality increased if children were living with them. In such instances, the percentage of good quality housing increased to 64 percent, while 16 percent of the units were listed as being of fair quality and 19 percent as poor quality (Table 5).

No significant differences were found in the quality of housing occupied by married couples as the age of those couples increased. However, we see a picture of housing deterioration once the couple is

Table 5. *Quality of housing of older persons, percentage distribution*

	MARRIED COUPLES			UNMARRIED WOMEN			UNMARRIED MEN		
Housing quality	With spouse	With children	With others	Alone	With children	With others	Alone	With children	With others
Own household									
Good	75	71	76	64	70	73	45	64	58
Fair	13	15	11	15	16	13	15	16	18
Poor	12	13	13	20	13	13	40	19	23
Not reported	a	1	a	1	1	1		1	1
Number of cases	1780	356	166	911	220	265	307	93	111
Not own household									
Good		90			81	77		79	68
Fair		7			11	16		10	24
Poor					8	6		11	8
Not reported		3			a	1			
Number of cases		60	13[b]		386	222		126	105

[a] Less than 1 percent.
[b] Too few cases reported to make percentages meaningful.

broken up. This may mean either that the same house deteriorated or that the surviving individual moved into a poorer quality unit.

All in all, the quality of housing occupied by the aged covered by this study is similar to that reflected by the data obtained from the 1950 U.S. Housing Census. For some groups, however, especially for the unmarried males, the quality is poorer than represented in the general statistics heretofore available.

Age of dwelling units

Closely related to the matter of housing quality is the age of the dwelling units occupied by those individuals living in their own households. A total of 44 percent of the unmarried males were found to be living in units 50 years old or older, compared with only 38 percent of the unmarried females and 35 percent of the married couples. There was little change in this picture among unmarried males, whether they were under the age of 70 or over the age of 80. There was a change, however, with respect to couples and unmarried females. In both instances the age of the housing occupied tended to increase with the age of the individual or couple. For example, among married couples where the respondent was under the age of 65,[1] 22 percent of the dwelling units occupied were 50 years old or older, but where the respondent was 80 years of age or older, this percentage increased to 40. Among unmarried females, the percentages increased from 38 to 46 over this age span (Table 6).

Period of occupancy of present place and future plans

It seemed apparent, from the data collected, that a low proportion of the aged had lived in the same house all of their lives. In fact, for the total group living in their own household, less than 5 percent had lived in their present place 50 years or more, which would indicate that the remaining 95 percent had lived in at least one other place. On the other hand, roughly a third had lived in their present place from 25 to 50 years and another third from 10 to 25 years.

There did not appear to be any significant differences between married couples and unmarried individuals, for the groups as wholes, but differences did occur when attention was focused on whether these couples or individuals lived alone, with children, or with others. In

[1] While the survey generally focused on people over the age of 65, in a few instances wives under the age of 65 were interviewed if their husbands were over that age.

Table 6. *Time period in which dwelling structures of older persons were built, by age of respondent, percentage distribution* [a]

When structure was built	MARRIED COUPLES					UNMARRIED WOMEN					UNMARRIED MEN			
	Under 65	65–69	70–74	75–79	80 and over	Under 65	65–69	70–74	75–79	80 and over	65–69	70–74	75–79	80 and over
Since World War II	20	13	12	11	11	19	13	13	15	7	13	11	10	12
Between 1933 and 1945	10	8	8	11	5	50	9	9	8	4	11	5	10	6
Between 1909 and 1932	46	40	42	36	39	31	35	35	33	36	23	28	32	36
Before 1909	22	35	35	39	40		38	36	39	46	43	47	42	42
Not reported	2	4	3	3	5		5	7	5	7	10	9	6	4
Number of cases	178	873	780	368	178	32	692	664	411	214	147	262	219	173

[a] Based on total number of aged sampled.

Table 7. *Length of occupancy of present dwelling unit of older persons living in their own household, percentage distribution*

Length of occupancy (in years)	MARRIED COUPLES				UNMARRIED WOMEN			UNMARRIED MEN	
	With spouse (N = 1780)	With children (N = 356)	With others (N = 166)	Alone (N = 911)	With children (N = 220)	With others (N = 265)	Alone (N = 307)	With children (N = 93)	With others (N = 111)
Under 1	2	3	2	5	3	1	5	1	1
1–4	16	12	8	21	10	16	21	6	13
5–9	15	12	19	16	11	12	17	12	12
10–24	31	26	37	27	30	27	30	25	33
25–49	31	42	31	24	40	31	19	49	24
50 and over	3	4	2	3	5	12	5	6	13
Not reported	2	1	1	4	1	1	3	1	4

each instance, they had lived in their present place longer if there were children living with them than if they were living alone or had others living with them. (Among unmarried males and females, there was a distinct tendency for those having children living with them to have been living in their present place longer than if others were living with them, and also a tendency, if others were living with them, to have been living in their present place longer than if they were living alone.) (See Table 7.)

Most of the aged expected to stay in their present place indefinitely. At least 4 out of 5 of the married couples expressed this opinion and the proportion was only slightly smaller among unmarried individuals. Among the balance, practically none indicated that they would be moving—they simply did not know at the time of the interview what they would be doing.

This expectation to remain in their present place undoubtedly could have been anticipated, since most of the couples and individuals seemed quite satisfied where they were. They were asked about their desire to live closer to children, other relatives, friends, church, doctor, grocery store, movies, parks, and the like, and only a small proportion indicated such a desire. Closer proximity to children, other relatives, and church were indicated by some, but even here less than 20 percent expressed this desire. Parks, libraries, and movies were at the bottom of the list, with 5 percent or less indicating an interest in closer proximity to these (Table 8).

Amount of social interaction in present place

The amount of social contact, if it can be measured by such factors as having relatives and guests in for meals or to stay overnight, appeared to be greater among married couples than unmarried females, and greater among unmarried females than unmarried males. For example, 27 percent of the couples living alone in their own households had friends or family members come to eat with them at least once a week, compared with 21 percent of the unmarried females living alone and only 9 percent of the unmarried males living alone. Each of the groups served guest meals more frequently than this if there were children in the household. (As may have been expected, the frequency of entertaining was lower among those aged individuals who did not live in their own households.) (See Table 9.)

Approximately 40 percent of the married couples and unmarried females living in their own households sometimes had friends or relatives (other than children) stay overnight. In contrast, less than

Table 8. Preferences of older persons for living closer to selected groups and services, percent choosing given items

Group or service	MARRIED COUPLES			UNMARRIED WOMEN			UNMARRIED MEN		
	With spouse	With children	With others	Alone	With children	With others	Alone	With children	With others
Own household									
Grocery store	13	9	13	14	14	16	7	3	7
Relatives	13	7	13	17	12	15	8	6	7
Children	17	12	15	18	12	11	9	8	5
Bus service	11	8	7	12	14	11	6	6	4
Doctor	11	11	5	10	14	11	7	2	7
Hospital	8	8	6	7	11	8	5	3	4
Church	14	11	15	18	20	20	7	4	5
Friends	11	8	10	13	13	9	7	7	4
Parks	5	3	4	5	6	6	4	3	1
Libraries	4	2	2	4	4	4	2	1	1
Movies	3	2	3	4	2	5	1	1	3
Number of cases	1780	356	166	911	220	265	307	93	111
Not own household									
Grocery store		13			12	15		4	1
Relatives		8			13	11		11	7
Children		12			13	12		9	6
Bus service		10			12	14		12	1
Doctor		8			12	11		6	4
Hospital		5			8	7		5	4
Church		8			20	18		10	7
Friends		17			20	18		14	10
Parks		2			5	5		4	4
Libraries					3	3		2	
Movies		2			3	3		2	2
Number of cases		60	13[a]		386	222		126	105

[a] Too few cases reported to make percentages meaningful.

Table 9. *Frequency of serving regular meals to friends or family by older persons, percentage distribution*

Frequency	MARRIED COUPLES			UNMARRIED WOMEN			UNMARRIED MEN		
	With spouse	With children	With others	Alone	With children	With others	Alone	With children	With others
Own household									
Two or more times a week	9	8	12	8	10	9	3	6	10
Once a week	18	19	13	13	16	18	6	15	11
Once or twice a month	27	30	31	24	24	20	8	22	17
Less than once a month	43	41	40	47	45	49	61	53	57
Never	2	1	3	7	4	3	21	2	3
Not reported	1	1	1	1	1	1	1	2	2
Number of cases	1780	356	166	911	220	265	307	93	111
Not own household									
Two or more times a week		8			8	6		14	4
Once a week		18			11	10		15	6
Once or twice a month		22			26	17		23	11
Less than once a month		44			51	55		40	56
Never		3			2	7		4	22
Not reported		5			2	5		4	1
Number of cases		60	13ᵃ		386	222		126	105

ᵃ Too few cases reported to make percentages meaningful.

20 percent of the unmarried males living alone ever had such guests stay overnight. When the unmarried males had children living with them, however, there was an increase to 31 percent. (Among couples and unmarried individuals not living in their own households, approximately 3 out of 4 never had anyone come to stay overnight.) (See Table 10.) In considering these figures, it should be pointed out that about half of the respondents indicated that most of their friends lived in the neighborhood.

We also measured the extent to which the aged visited with younger people living in the neighborhood. Among unmarried males living alone in their own households, 52 percent rarely or never visited with younger people. For unmarried females living alone, the figure was 45 percent, and for couples living alone, 42 percent. Where there were children living in the households of couples and unmarried females, the amount of social contact of this type decreased slightly, but in the households of unmarried males, with children present, it increased. Among unmarried males and females living in the households of others, the percentage of aged rarely or never visiting with younger people in the neighborhood was even greater (Table 11).

It may be interesting to note here that among both the unmarried males and females living alone, approximately 4 out of every 5 had someone in the same building or within the city block who would give them immediate help in any emergency. Among 77 percent of the unmarried females and 59 percent of the unmarried males, someone stopped by the house or apartment regularly. In many instances, among approximately 70 percent of the unmarried females and 43 percent of the unmarried males, someone telephoned regularly.

Kind of living arrangements preferred

The respondents were asked what kind of living arrangement they thought would be best for people over 65 who could take care of themselves. The choices were (1) live with their families, (2) live by themselves but near their relatives, (3) live by themselves away from their relatives, or (4) some other arrangement. Very different responses were given among married couples, unmarried males, and unmarried females, although the majority in each group, among those living in their own households, preferred not to be living with their families. Sixty percent of the married couples and the unmarried females living alone preferred to live by themselves but near their relatives, and almost all of the remaining group preferred to live by themselves away from relatives. On the other hand, only 38 percent

Table 10. Older persons having friends and relatives staying overnight, percentage distribution

Have friends and relatives staying overnight	MARRIED COUPLES			UNMARRIED WOMEN			UNMARRIED MEN		
	With spouse	*With children*	*With others*	*Alone*	*With children*	*With others*	*Alone*	*With children*	*With others*
Own household									
Yes	41	36	40	39	36	44	17	31	31
No	58	63	60	60	64	56	82	68	68
Not reported	1	1	a	1	a		1	1	1
Number of cases	1780	356	166	911	220	265	307	93	111
Not own household									
Yes		23			26	28		24	10
No		77			73	71		75	89
Not reported					1	1		1	1
Number of cases		60	13[b]		386	222		126	105

[a] Less than 1 percent.
[b] Too few cases reported to make percentages meaningful.

Table 11. Frequency of visits with young people in neighborhood, percentage distribution

Frequency of visits	MARRIED COUPLES			UNMARRIED WOMEN			UNMARRIED MEN		
	With spouse	With children	With others	Alone	With children	With others	Alone	With children	With others
Own household									
Three or more times a week	25	25	25	25	22	24	26	37	30
One or two times a week	31	27	32	28	29	30	21	25	20
Never or rarely	42	48	42	45	48	45	52	37	49
Not reported	2	a	1	2	1	1	1	1	1
Number of cases	1780	356	166	911	220	265	307	93	111
Not own household									
Three or more times a week		22			16	13		23	22
One or two times a week		32			31	21		30	21
Never or rarely		41			52	65		46	55
Not reported		5			1	1		1	2
Number of cases		60	13[b]		386	222		126	105

a Less than 1 percent.
b Too few cases reported to make percentages meaningful.

of the unmarried males preferred to live by themselves but near relatives, while 50 percent preferred to live alone away from their relatives. In other words, there was a greater preference expressed among the married couples and unmarried females than among the unmarried males for living near relatives. In instances where the couples or unmarried individuals had children living with them, the proportion who felt they should live with their families increased very significantly (Table 12).

Another question was asked about where an elderly person should live when he or she was no longer able to take care of himself or herself. The choices were (1) in own home with nursing care, (2) with family, (3) with relatives, (4) in a nursing home, or (5) some other arrangement. Here again there were some significant differences among married couples or individuals living alone and those with children or other relatives living with them. The two predominant preferences among couples living alone and unmarried males and females living alone were for their own home with nursing care and for a nursing home. Between these two choices where married couples were concerned, the preference was for their own home with nursing care, but among the unmarried males and females there was a greater preference for nursing homes. Where there were children living in the households of the elderly couples and unmarried individuals, living with the family became an important preference. In fact, in households headed by unmarried males, 42 percent preferred this arrangement. Among those couples and individuals living in the households of their children, 38 percent to 44 percent expressed a preference for living with their families. The range preferring to live in a nursing home was from 23 to 32 percent, and the range preferring to live in their own home with nursing care was from 12 to 25 percent (Table 13).

SUMMARY

It has been demonstrated in this presentation that there are some significant differences in the living arrangements, attitudes, and preferences of older people depending upon whether they live in their own households or in the households of others, whether the spouse is still living or they are single, widowed, or divorced, and whether they are living alone or have children or other relatives or nonrelatives living with them.

The highest proportion of the aged, as has been previously known, live in their own households. Apparently they prefer to preserve this arrangement. This does not mean, however, that they desire isolation. Most of them prefer to live by themselves, but near their relatives. Among those covered by this study who were not living in their own households, the highest proportion lived with their children. Perhaps one of the most significant characteristics of this living arrangement, where the aged person is not the head of his or her household, is the obvious reduction in the amount of social contact outside of the household.

Couples and individuals living alone generally were found to be living in smaller housing accommodations than those having children or others living with them. If there were children living with them, the dwelling unit was usually larger and it frequently was of better quality and there was more likelihood, among owner-occupied units, that there was a mortgage on the house (although, even in these instances, only about 15 percent of such owners had mortgages).

Perhaps one of the most significant findings of this research, thus far, is the difference in value, age, and quality of housing accommodations occupied by married couples as compared with unmarried females and unmarried males. The highest percent of owner occupancy was found among married couples. Their units carried the highest market value and highest rentals and were of the best quality. Conversely, among unmarried males, the units had a market value appreciably lower and the proportion of poor quality housing increased significantly.

The nature of the household was found to have a significant influence on how the housing accommodations were used. In this paper, several items measuring social interaction between members of the household and relatives and friends were analyzed and it was found that larger households, especially those including children, were involved in more entertaining than the smaller household, especially where the couple or individual lived alone. In fact, a significant difference was found even between the sexes, with unmarried males living alone having significantly less social contact than their female counterparts.

In summary, then, we find that we cannot speak of aged individuals as being a very homogeneous group. Rather, we must attempt to break down the total group into its natural and meaningful classes and determine what the important variables are within those classes. This paper has touched upon only two or three of the major classes and a few of the important variables which need to be explored if we are to gain a more systematic knowledge concerning the aging individual and the aging process, as well as social changes and adaptations brought about by aging populations. The final report on this over-all research effort will delve into other important classes and important variables in greater detail in order to provide an analysis as definitive as possible of the extent and character of the entire range of shelter needs of the elderly, and an evaluation of how those needs can be effectively met.

REFERENCES

Cornell University Housing Research Center. 1958. Housing requirements of the aged: a study of design criteria. Ithaca: Cornell University. (Mimeographed.)

Steiner, P. O., and Dorfman, R. 1957. The economic status of the aged. Berkeley: University of California Press.

treatment with the object of effecting their rehabilitation. These are persons who do not need hospital care.

A home for the mentally infirm aged provides accommodations, care, nursing, and treatment for those who, owing to dementia or other mental or characterological complaints, can no longer look after themselves, but whose mental condition does not necessarily warrant admission to a mental hospital.

A recent report (Querido, 1960) proposes an alternate scheme for the use of nursing homes in which the task of the nursing home would be a more limited one. They would be used only for chronic patients in need of nursing care for the rest of their lives. Rehabilitation would be limited to helping patients maintain the level of function attained before admission to the nursing home. The report explicitly states that research, diagnosis, therapy, and rehabilitation should be kept together. Rehabilitation is seen as being the task of the hospital or of a rehabilitation center with a specialized staff.

On the basis of several studies it is estimated that 85 to 90 percent of those aged 65 years and over need no specialized living arrangements, that 4 to 10 percent need a hostel plan, and that 2.4 to 4.2 percent need nursing homes for the physically infirm or mentally infirm (Schreuder, 1957; van Zonneveld, 1956).

It is difficult to estimate the actual extent of the need for old people's dwellings. Owing to the postwar rent policy there is still a considerable gap between rents of prewar and postwar houses. As a result, the demand for postwar special old people's dwellings has been relatively small.

During the period between the end of World War II (May, 1945) and January, 1959, about 11,000 special dwellings for old people and 177 en-pension homes with a capacity of nearly 15,000 beds have been erected. In a few instances, the projects were combinations of en-pension homes and nursing homes. Only two nursing homes for mentally deficient old people have been completed. One large geriatric department has been developed by a hospital near Amsterdam. There is a striking contrast between the number of hostels being built and the slow progress made in providing nursing homes. The result is that bedridden patients have to stay in an en-pension home where they cannot receive adequate treatment, or, if they go to a nursing home, it is an inadequate one. Also, much of the value of the new en-pension homes has been lost because often the well-to-do who do not strictly require care have been admitted to these homes in places of persons of small means who absolutely require care.

The delay in building nursing homes may be attributed to a number of circumstances. For example, the lack of agreement in medical circles concerning possibilities for rehabilitation in nursing homes may have delayed to some extent the erection of this type of home. Other influential factors which have been deterrents to building are those of financing the building, special accommodations, and of educating the local authorities and other important groups with regard to the nature and extent of the need.

The economic problem

To live in an acceptable way in a special old people's dwelling, an aged couple in the Netherlands needs a yearly income of about 2700 guilders ($714), and a single man or woman needs an annual income of 1830 guilders ($484).

Since 1957, the Netherlands has had a compulsory old age pension scheme. The pensions under this system, however, are not meant to cover even the minimum cost of living. The idea is that people should provide for additional income, either on an individual basis or on an industrial basis. The 1958 statistics (Table 2) on the distribution of

Table 2. Distribution of income among the aged,
The Netherlands (in guilders)

Source of income	Married couples	Single men	Widows	Single women formerly employed
Pension	1533	942	942	942
Other	309	309	187	258
Total	1842	1251	1129	1200

income among the elderly show that approximately 50 percent of the aged do not have sufficient income to make it possible for them to obtain specially designed accommodations.

The picture becomes even worse when we calculate that the yearly cost of living in en-pension homes is 5000 guilders ($1452) for a couple and about 2900 guilders ($766) for a single person. Operating expenses of a first-class nursing home can be estimated at 12 to 15 guilders ($3 to $4) per patient per day. If the personal expenses of the patients are included, costs would amount to from 4800 to 5800 guilders ($1280–$1534) yearly. It is sometimes more economical to give people additional help in their own homes than to admit them to a home.

For about 75 percent of the population in the Netherlands, those with incomes up to 7450 guilders ($1971), there exists a nonprofit health insurance system, mainly on a compulsory basis. Practically no provisions have been made for payments for en-pension home and nursing home care, but there are indications that steps will soon be taken to bring nursing home care under the health insurance system.

At present, old people in need of en-pension or nursing home care without adequate means to pay for it can receive financial aid under the Poor Law Act through the Municipal Social Work Agencies. But this is a charity program and people often feel degraded when they have to accept this kind of financial aid. Under the Poor Law, the children are obliged to pay part of the necessary financial assistance for their parents. This often deters aged parents from moving into a hostel or nursing home. Local authorities are reluctant to build nursing homes because they will have to pay what the patients and their children cannot afford to pay.

A further factor contributing to the building of hostels almost to the exclusion of nursing homes is that the concept of the hostel is easily understood and accepted by most people, while, on the other hand, the concept of the modern nursing home providing rehabilitation services to persons usually considered beyond hope of recovery is a new and complicated notion.

There is a danger in the complacency of those who cherish the idea that the nicely built new hostels in the Netherlands are proof of how much has been done for the benefit of the aged. However, they overlook the fact, stated earlier, that the hostels are frequently occupied by elderly people other than those for whom they were meant. My personal recommendation to the central government and to private foundations is that grants be made for the building of institutions for the elderly only if a combined en-pension and nursing home plan is followed. To do so makes it possible to avoid the situation which occurs when the health of occupants of en-pension homes deteriorates, and it becomes necessary to choose between keeping the person in the hostel without adequate care or transferring him to a completely different institution.

The basic question is, of course, that of whether the country can afford to provide the kinds and numbers of accommodations needed by the aged. In order to get an answer to this question it is necessary to examine the various sources of revenue available in comparison with the costs of the necessary accommodations.

First, a calculation may be made of the effect of raising pensions paid in the Netherlands under the compulsory General Old Age Pension Scheme to a level securing income for all those whose additional incomes are too low to enable them to live at an acceptable minimum standard. On the basis of statistical data for 1958, it was found that this would have required 1.4 percent of the net national income of that year.

Second, to widen the scope of the health insurance system to cover all the aged in need of en-pension or nursing home arrangements would require 0.99 percent of the net national income.[1]

Third, to make up during the next 10 years for the lag in providing accommodations for the aging, consideration must be given not only to increasing the number of nursing homes, but also to the fact that most prewar homes for the aged should be replaced, that considerable investment in en-pension homes is still needed, that nursing homes for the mentally frail are required, and that there is a yearly increase in the number of old people needing care. To accomplish these goals would require an expenditure of another 0.47 percent of the net national income.

Altogether this would mean an additional yearly expenditure of 2.9 percent of the net national income. After a 10-year period, when the lag would have been overcome, the burden on the national economy would be diminishing since at that point the annual investment need only cover the increase in demand caused by the increase in the number of the aged. Thus the 2.9 percent of the net national income needed now could be lowered to 2.4 percent after 10 years. If the recently proposed policy (Querido, 1960) is followed, with the result that more hospital beds and fewer nursing home beds are provided, yearly expenditures may reach 3.5 percent of net national income. This higher cost figure is due to the fact that it is more expensive to provide hospital than nursing home beds.

There is, however, one other matter of cost to be considered: the need for more nurses and other personnel. If more and better nursing homes are to be created, or more hospital facilities for the aged provided, there will be a marked increase in the already short supply of nurses. In order to attract more personnel, wages should be augmented. This cost cannot be exactly calculated because data are lacking. As an example, however, an increase of 20 percent for nurses and other workers in all institutions and hospitals would mean an extra expenditure of about 0.2 percent of the (1957) net national income. From the national economic point of view this means a yearly expenditure of 2.9 percent, perhaps 3.5 percent, or even 3.7 percent of the net national income in The Netherlands.

[1] This estimate was based on statistical data for 1957. Calculations were based on the average of the highest and lowest estimates of need (7 percent for en-pension homes, 2.4 percent for nursing homes for the physically frail, and 1.0 percent for nursing homes for the mentally ill).

Can The Netherlands economy afford this cost? According to the Central Bureau of Statistics from 1953 to the close of 1957, the real income per capita increased by 18 percent, a yearly increase of 3.6 percent (The Netherlands Central Bureau of Statistics, 1959). It is predicted that real consumption per capita will increase from 1954 to 1980 by 58 percent or an average yearly increase of 2.3 percent (Delfgauw and Masizzo, 1955). In the light of these figures, it can be stated that the cardinal question is not whether we are *able* to spend a good part of our increasing wealth for the benefit of the aged, but whether we are *willing* to do so, assuming, of course, that the process of increasing expenditure takes place over a period of several years.

There are some peculiar difficulties to be considered. The longer a country postpones action on the required scale, the further in arrears it will be, the more difficult it becomes to make up the lag, and the more painfully the process of readaptation will be felt. Second, there is a point beyond which expenditures on behalf of the aged give no benefits from a purely economic point of view. If one country is spending an appropriate part of its national income for the benefit of the aged while a competing country is not pursuing a similar policy, but is making a higher level of industrial investment instead, the first-mentioned country will become economically weaker. Therefore, international cooperation, as through the channels of the International Labor Organization at Geneva, must be strongly recommended.

George Lawton (1943) once said: "Let us remind ourselves that the basic social question with which economics, political science, and sociology are concerned may be formulated in terms of 'who shall be sacrificed for whom?' " The implications of this sentence, as far as Western countries are concerned, need not worry us excessively. The problem of the aged as encountered in Western societies is, in a way, a by-product of modern industrial development. But it is just this same development that enables us to give all the aged better material accommodations than ever before in history without putting too heavy a burden upon the younger generation. We have the economic possibilities; we must decide whether we want to invest them on the behalf of older people.

REFERENCES

Bouwcentrum. 1955. Huisvesting van Bejaarden: Verpleegtehuizen. Rotterdam: Bouwcentrum. (English text.)
———— 1958. Huisvesting van Bejaarden: Verpleegtehuizen voor Geeste-

lijk Bejaarden (Nursing homes for mentally infirm old people.) A5.0 Rotterdam: Bouwcentrum. (English text.)

———— 1959. Huisvesting van Bejaarden Zelfstandige woningen en pensiontehuizen. (Housing of the aged—special old people's dwellings and en-pension homes.)

Delfgauw, J. S. M., and Masizzo, A. J. V. 1955. Naar een nieuwe gauden eeuw. (Towards a new golden age.) Utrecht, Antwerpen: Het Spectrum.

Lawton, G. 1943. New goals for old age. New York: Columbia University Press.

The Netherlands Central Bureau of Statistics. 1959. Jaarcÿfers voor Nederland, 1957–1958. Amsterdam: The Bureau.

Querido, A. 1960. Rapport Verpleegtehuizen. Amsterdam.

Schreuder, J. T. R. 1957. De Verpleging van Chronisch Zieke Bejaarden. The Netherlands: The Hague.

Zonneveld, R. J., van. 1956. Socio-medical surveys. *In* The need for cross-national surveys of old age, pp. 62–75. Ann Arbor: University of Michigan, Division of Gerontology.

The Purpose of the Institution

PETER TOWNSEND

SINCE the war there have been two important developments in Britain's approach toward institutional care. The first has been to encourage a change in the atmosphere and character of the institution by introducing a number of features of home and community life. The second has been to place greater emphasis on domiciliary and housing services so that there may be an effective alternative to institutional care. Whenever possible, it is argued, people should be looked after in their own homes. These changes affect parentless children, young adults who are physically handicapped, and mentally ill and sub-normal people as well as the chronic sick and aged. They appear to be taking place in several other Western countries.

In this paper I shall try to describe these changes and some of the reasons for them and go on to pose the dilemma with which I believe we are now confronted. While rejecting the social philosophy of the nineteenth century we have yet to find an adequate philosophy to put in its place. Fundamentally we are torn between the desire to segregate persons according to their physical or social condition and the desire to give them the advantages of living in a "normal" community. My main thesis is that if society advances in prosperity and if it becomes increasingly sensitive to the complex needs of the individual, the family, and the community, its justification for retaining more than a few highly specialized institutions will gradually disappear.

Britain's philosophy was built on the principle that housing large numbers of social casualties in custodial institutions seemed to be the only means both of saving them from destitution, neglect, and indolence and of protecting society itself from moral degradation and embarrassment. For several centuries the chief provision was a build-

The research on which this paper is based was carried out in conjunction with a survey of residential institutions for the aged in England and Wales, financed by a generous grant from the Nuffield Foundation. A short version of the paper was broadcast in the Third Programme of the B.B.C. and published in the *Listener*, June 23, 1960.

ing in which the young and the old, the sick, the infirm, the blind, the mentally ill, the homeless, and the destitute were all given asylum.[1] Although the Royal Commission on the Poor Law had advocated, in its Report of 1834, the abolition of this general mixed "workhouse," their other recommendations led largely to its retention. They did not think through to a rational conclusion their vague plea for a classification of institutions according to types of inmates, and they were obsessed with the problem of the able-bodied poor. They failed to consider in any detail the needs of children, the sick, the infirm, and the aged, and were partly responsible for the fact that their principle of less eligibility was applied indiscriminately to these persons as well as to young able-bodied adults.[2] The result was the perpetuation of a system admitted to be evil.

In their impressive history of the English Poor Law, Sidney and Beatrice Webb frequently expressed exasperation at the resilience of the general mixed workhouse (Webb and Webb, 1929). They showed that its defects were as profound in the first decade of this century as in the 1830s. But even though their vision and scrupulous empiricism still command admiration, it seems doubtful whether they fully appreciated the administrative and social pressures which kept it in being.[3] To the Victorians there seemed little alternative to the rather bleak institution. Community and medical services were few and far between, there were practically no trained workers to follow specialized roles, and the mixed institution afforded the neatest and most economical way of dealing with dire need. Conditions there had to be

[1] The Poor Law Commission of 1834 found that in the great majority of parishes the workhouse was "occupied by sixty or eighty paupers, made up of a dozen or more neglected children (under the care, perhaps, of a pauper), about twenty or thirty able-bodied adult paupers of both sexes, and probably an equal number of aged and impotent persons, proper objects of relief. Amidst these, the mother of bastard children and prostitutes live without shame and associate freely with the youth, who have also the examples and conversation of the frequent inmates of the county gaol, the poacher, the vagrant, the decayed beggar, and other characters of the worst description. To these may often be added a solitary blind person, one or two idiots, and not infrequently are heard, from among the rest, the incessant ravings of some neglected lunatic. In such receptacles the sick poor are often immured." (Anonymous, 1834, p. 303.)

[2] "The first and most essential of all conditions, a principle which we find universally admitted, even by those whose practice is at variance with it, is, that [the pauper's] situation on the whole shall not be made really or apparently so eligible as the situation of the independent labourer of the lowest class." (Anonymous, 1834, p. 228.)

[3] This is indicated by the fact that their proposals for reform were not all elaborated. It is difficult to see, for example, how the degree of classification they advocated could be put into effect by counties and county boroughs, which they favored for administering institutional services.

bleak because a large proportion of the population lived in poverty. If the staff had been kindly and sympathetic rather than repressive and if the food, amenities, and services had been better, more people would have applied for admission or would have been inclined to stay there longer than necessary. Low institutional standards were an inevitable consequence of low wage rates and the absence of social insurance and pension schemes. The fact that they took such a harsh form must be largely attributed to the Victorian attitude toward poverty and illness, which was compounded of ignorance, fear, superstition, and authoritarianism. People with mental disorders were regarded as "lunatics" who had to be protected from society as well as themselves, some of them in prisonlike asylums with up to 2000 or 3000 beds, but many in the workhouses. The poverty or destitution of other people was felt to be due in large part to their own misconduct or to the irresponsibility of their families. The "deterrent discipline" of the workhouse was felt to be necessary even for the aged, partly as an awful warning to the children of relatives living outside and partly as a penalty for an improvident or dissolute life. The strait jacket and the cell, the exercise yard, the ration of bread, and the serge uniform all symbolized public attitudes which prevailed well into the twentieth century. Even in the writings of enlightened reformers, such as the Webbs and Charles Booth, there are traces of moral values which we would be hard put to justify today.

As time passed and living standards improved, new social services were introduced. Sharper distinctions were made between different groups of the population experiencing adversity. The long-established claims for classification gradually came to be realized. A rudimentary hospital service developed in the workhouses and philanthropy guided the development of voluntary hospitals for the poor. More of the mentally ill entered mental hospitals rather than poor-law institutions. Separate homes for children, for the aged, and for some groups of handicapped persons began to appear, and a variety of hospitals for special types of diseases was created. Reform in administration began to give uniformity to policies followed in different parts of the country. The growth of the professions, of voluntary associations, and of local government produced small armies of physicians, officials, and social workers trained to treat special classes of the population in need. The process was slow and even today there are a number of hospitals and local authority institutions housing a medley of patients or residents. But, broadly speaking, the long battle for classification and specialization had been won by the end of World War II. In 1948 the Poor Law was abandoned in name and to a large extent in practice, and the various hospital and other institutional services were rationalized. The history of the institution entered a new phase.

RECENT CHANGES IN INSTITUTIONAL CARE

In the hospital services increasing emphasis has been placed, not on bigger and more numerous hospitals with more beds, but on the more efficient use of the beds they already have. New hospitals are seen as replacing the old, rather than adding to them. In the last 10 years, waiting lists in England and Wales have diminished and more people have been treated as inpatients. Yet the number of beds occupied has grown by only 5 percent (all of this increase occurring in the first 5 years). Periods of hospital stay have shortened and more importance has been given to outpatient treatment. Outpatient attendance, for example, has increased by 11 percent and courses of outpatient treatment by 13 percent. The numbers of "day-patients" and of day hospitals, though small, have increased quickly in the last few years, and visits paid by the domiciliary specialist service have more than doubled (Great Britain, Ministry of Health, 1959*b*).

Changes of an even more dramatic kind seem likely to take place if a number of new developments and experiments are repeated on a large scale. Hospitals are being built according to an entirely new design with small, intimate rooms for 2, 4, or 6 patients, grouped in special treatment wards. There are experimental consultative health centers (Anderson and Cowan, 1955) and pediatric home-care services (Lightwood *et al.,* 1957). In some hospitals mothers are being allowed to stay with their children and care for them during the day. Unrestricted visiting is more often allowed and encouraged. In various ways, patients are being treated more like human beings. A number of authorities foresee a great expansion of outpatient and domiciliary services (Anonymous, 1958*a*; World Health Organization, 1959), sometimes interpreted as meaning that inpatient services should be confined to those in the acute stages of illness (Stallworthy, 1960) and often at least that the life of the hospital will merge imperceptibly with the life of the community. "The distant chateau-hospital fortified against intrusion belongs to the past." (Bluestone, 1958.) As long ago as 1860, Florence Nightingale wrote a letter to William Rathbone in which she said, "Hospitals are, after all, but an intermediate stage of civilization. While devoting my whole life to hospital work, to this conclusion I have always come, viz., that hospitals are not the best place for the sick poor, except for severe surgical cases."

Some of the biggest changes are those affecting the psychiatric hospitals. Attempts are being made to break up the largest ones into smaller units with partitioned wards, more furniture and better amenities, social clubs, workshops, and facilities for working both inside and outside the hospital precincts (Baker, 1958; Sherrett, 1958; Collins *et al.,* 1959). Special "day centers" have been attached to the hospitals (Hemphill, 1960). Fewer wards are locked during the day and many patients are experiencing a wider measure of freedom. The restraint of patients is giving way to greater tolerance of their behavior. Superintendents and psychiatrists recognize many of the problems they are facing in modernizing buildings[4]; in changing the attitudes of staff; in extending the scope for far wider devolution of responsibility; in deciding what kind of balance should be struck between coercion, restraint, and freedom; and in making sure that after-care services are available for discharged patients.[5] They may be getting little guidance and help; but they cannot ignore the trend of public and professional opinion which has gained fresh stimulus from new legislation on mental health. There are pioneering mental health services at Nottingham (Macmillan, 1956), Oldham (Freeman, 1960), Worthing (Carse and Panton, 1958), and elsewhere (for a review of a number of schemes in Britain and abroad see Clein, 1960), on the experience of which general policies may be reformulated. At Worthing, for example, psychiatrists visit the homes of patients on the recommendation of family doctors or see them at outpatient clinics; social workers deal with family problems; and physiotherapy and other treatment may be given at home, in the day clinics, or in the parent hospital. Four in five patients are treated as outpatients. In the words of *The Lancet,* reviewing some of these developments, "The large self-contained mental hospital has had its day: modern demands have made it as obsolete as the Maginot Line." (Anonymous, 1958*b*.)

Such trends are not confined to the health services. The Curtis Report of 1946, followed by the Children Act of 1948, produced a new conception of how children deprived of a normal home life should be treated. The legislation led to a gradual decrease in the number of large institutions for boys or girls only and an increase in the number

[4] "Existing mental hospitals . . . embody in their architecture an obsolete conception of the psychiatric patients which acts as a positive obstacle to modern treatment." (Anonymous, 1958*c*.)

[5] It has been suggested that earlier discharge of patients may involve hardship for some relatives and that after-care services should be intensified (Brown *et al.,* 1958; Brown, 1959*a*). "Our findings demonstrate that . . . the scope for community action in the case of elderly psychiatric patients is frighteningly large." (Colwell and Post, 1959, p. 217.)

of small "family" type homes for children of both sexes, in which a small group of six to twelve children are placed under the charge of a housemother. A new impetus was given to boarding out. In 1949, 35 percent of the children in the care of the local authorities in England and Wales were boarded out; by 1959, 47 percent.

For the infirm aged some of the trends have been in the same direction. Fewer of them are cared for in the large local authority institutions, and more in residential homes for between 20 and 60 persons. Amenities and furnishings have been improved. But, as with children, successive governments have regarded institutional care as second best, in principle at least, to maintaining old people in their own homes for as long as possible through the further expansion of domiciliary services. In some areas, such as Exeter, Plymouth, Dorset, Kent, and Hampshire, experiments have been undertaken in boarding out and in providing special groups of bungalows and flatlets with a warden or housekeeper in charge, as a partial alternative to admission to residential homes. (See, for example, Ruck, 1960a and b; Richardson et al., 1960 a and b; Great Britain, National Corporation for the Care of Old People, 1959a and b.)

The speed and extent of all these changes should not be exaggerated. There are still many ugly institutions in which conditions are grim and administrative routines remain largely untouched by modern principles of human management. For example, out-of-date buildings with cavernous dormitories containing from 30 to 100 iron framed beds and little else are retained, where visiting is severely restricted and patients have few opportunities for passing the day except by sitting in huge dayrooms. Again, some local authorities and voluntary bodies cling to large institutions for children and make little use of boarding out; in 1959 only 19 percent of children in voluntary accommodations were boarded out (Great Britain, Home Office, 1959).

The resistance to new developments and the danger of acclaiming them before their worth is proved should not be underestimated. Yet there is no doubt that these general changes are taking place in the social services, and seem to be gathering momentum—that there has been a transformation of the institution itself and a shift toward caring for people in the community.

REASONS FOR CHANGE

How do we account for these changes? To give a full explanation would involve a detailed study of many different forces, educational, social, and economic, but we may refer briefly to a few of the major influences upon present trends: the inevitable consequences that had to be drawn from recent reforms in administration, the increasing cost of caring for individual patients and residents, and an awakened scientific and administrative interest in the reactions of individuals to institutional life.

Much of the postwar social legislation was motivated by a desire to treat all citizens equally, to establish national minimum standards of treatment, and to smooth out inequalities between different areas of the country and sections of the population by making the biggest social services comprehensive. Thus, the principles of the Beveridge Report on social insurance and the proposals for a national health service with free access to medical care and a new residential service for the handicapped and aged fired public imagination and gained universal acceptance. To take one small but revealing example, in his speech on the second reading of the National Assistance bill in Parliament at the end of 1947 the Minister of Health, Aneurin Bevan, said, "The workhouse is going. Although many people have tried to humanize it, it was in many respects a very evil institution. . . . Bigness is the enemy of humanity." He went on to describe the new residential homes for 25–30 persons which were to be created "so that any old persons who wish may go there in exactly the same way as many well-to-do people have been accustomed to go into residential hotels." It is difficult to find in such statements of intention any trace of the doctrine of less eligibility.

The consequences of recent administrative reforms could be pursued in many directions and I choose to draw attention to only a few of the consequences of a change in the administration of hospitals. New problems were posed. The advent of the national health service in 1948 brought with it a reclassification of voluntary and municipal hospitals and of former poor-law institutions. The new Regional Hospital Boards found themselves administering establishments of widely varying quality and kind. The voluntary hospitals had previously possessed a near monopoly of the better specialists and of medical and nursing training. They had attracted most of the inventive skills of medicine and as they were mostly hospitals for the acute sick, their functions had not been seriously questioned. (It was their financial stability which had been chiefly in doubt.) The public system had been left to provide medical and nursing care for the great majority of the aged infirm and chronically ill, especially mental patients. It had been the neglected backwater of hospital provision. Now leading members of the medical profession and central government administrators began to face up to the responsibilities for what went on in the institutional relics of the Poor Law. They were shocked by ill-equipped surgeries and operating theaters and by the miserable amenities and staffing standards. If they themselves were inclined to make the best of a bad job, they were often aroused from complacency by reminders from middle-class patients that the hospitals were not intended for the poor alone.

The reorganization of hospital services, therefore, brought with it new demands for better standards of treatment. These were not concerned simply with "leveling up" medical facilities and amenities in buildings which had been neglected. Doctors, administrators, and the public became aware that certain sections of the population had enjoyed social as well as medical privileges in the former system which had been denied to others. They also realized that higher standards of living compelled review of institutional standards and practices. A society which has established a new code of individual rights and which is advancing in prosperity is bound to concede claims for greater privacy and respect for individuals in the management of its institutional services. In the last 10 years it has been found necessary to search for new principles in dealing with a whole range of social needs and problems which had previously been largely ignored. Detailed recommendations for the reception and treatment of the patient in hospital have been made, even to the extent of describing what kind of information should be given to him about the hospital; how telephoned and written inquiries from relatives should be handled; what role should be played by chaplains, almoners, psychiatric workers, and nurses; how books, newspapers, and radio and television sets should be provided; how food should be served; and how unnecessary noise should be eliminated (Great Britain. Minister of Health, 1953). For children in hospitals a series of principles has been laid down which would have the effect of showing more respect for the parents and for the social needs of the individual child (Great Britain, Ministry of Health, 1959a). Some of the recommendations have even been put into practice.

It may seem strange that such matters are only now being considered, but as one authority has said, "The present system of medical qualification discharges into the world of general medical practice doctors who have only the vaguest idea of the needs of a patient confined to bed, and of the many conditions which contribute to his welfare and comfort, and hence in many cases to his recovery." (Kennaway, 1957.) Doctors and administrators have recently displayed signs of embarrassment about their comparative ignorance of the social needs of patients and of the importance of social provisions, and seem to be searching for a new interpretation of the doctor-patient and hospital-patient relationship. "Medical theory increasingly recognizes the influence of non-medical factors on the patient's medical condition and the necessity from this point of view for treating the patient as a whole." Patients do not "cease to be people with personalities, needs, and interests of their own and become merely bodies." They must not be identified, for example, as "the duodenal in the first bed on the left." (Great Britain, Ministry of Health, 1953.)

There was another consequence of the rationalization of the hospital services at a time when standards of living and medical techniques were rapidly improving. Responsibility for all hospitals in a large region caused physicians, geriatricians, hospital secretaries, and medical superintendents to look afresh at the functions of each hospital and particularly at the problems of overcrowding and large waiting lists. The so-called "acute" hospitals contained large proportions of beds for the chronic sick. There, as well as in hospitals for the mentally ill and the chronic sick, patients had been allowed to linger on in bed for 6 months, 2 years, and more, when it was quite evident that the imaginative application of techniques of rehabilitation could have put many of them on their feet again and led to their early discharge. A number of studies have shown that a substantial proportion of patients do not require skilled medical and nursing services in hospital or at least could be discharged earlier (Farrer-Brown, 1959; Forsyth and Logan, 1960; Thomson et al., 1951; McKeown, 1958).

To the problem of overcrowding and the apparent misuse of beds must be added the growing cost of maintaining hospitals and the lack of new buildings. The cost of maintaining a person in hospital can now range from £7 to well over £30 a week, a consequence not only of the rise in national living standards but also of the impact of scientific and technological change upon medicine, making expensive new drugs, equipment, and forms of therapy available for the first time. And although the building of new hospitals is now beginning to increase, it should not be forgotten that no new hospital was built in Britain for over 10 years after the war.

In this situation it is not surprising that many hospital authorities have sought means of reducing the length of stay. In this they have partly succeeded. It remains uncertain how far they have acted in the best interests of the patients concerned, because from the start their motives have been mixed and research has not yet been carried out to establish the distribution of medical and social needs in the population and the ideal distribution and shape of inpatient, outpatient, residential, and domiciliary services if these needs are to be met. Some authorities have looked no further than their accounts of inpatient costs in order to justify measures for keeping some people out of hospital or for sending them home at the earliest opportunity. Others have made a virtue of earlier discharge without showing, or finding out, what has happened to the patients concerned. Experiments and changes of policy must be looked at carefully before they can be considered successful. This seems to be particularly true of recent events in the field of mental health. Earlier discharge may be justifiable on grounds of hospital overcrowding or lack of treatment and stimulus for the patient, but if no adequate system of after-care services exists he may suffer. His home may not have reasonable amenities, he may have no relatives to support him, and the local nursing, home-help, and psychiatric services may be inadequate. Again, frequent admissions may be preferable to chronicity, but longer periods in hospital might lessen the risk of relapse. The subtleties of the various alternatives remain to be investigated. But even if new policies are sometimes adopted for the most superficial of motives, they may prove to be right in the long run. It is significant that the doctor primarily responsible for an experimental mental health scheme at Worthing admitted that although the service was started largely to deal with hospital overcrowding, experience has shown that the benefit to the patients is in itself sufficient reason for starting such a service. He felt that during 30 years' work he had lost sight of the inevitable defects of institutional life and their effect on the patient.[6]

There is then some uncertainty of purpose behind recent changes of policy, which have followed administrative reform. Physicians, geriatricians, and psychiatrists have shown that modern methods of treatment can sometimes do marvelous things for chronic patients.[7] Research workers have shown that, using purely medical criteria, substantial

[6] "In the very early days of the Worthing Experiment I learned somewhat to my consternation that the man or woman I saw in hospital bore little resemblance to that same man or woman at home. At home, even though he was a sick man, he retained his identity and the sense of belonging: he was with his family and he felt secure because he was still in the community which he knew and which he understood. In hospital, the patient is an enforced member of a group living in an entirely artificial environment bearing no resemblance to anything approaching ordinary home life, but where everything is strange and often frightening. . . . I cannot believe that it is helpful in treatment for our patients to be compelled to live as a member of a large group of strangers, all of whom are sick people, to be completely deprived of privacy and to have to submit to the segregation of the sexes." (Carse, 1959.)

[7] For a vivid example of what a short period of active treatment can achieve even for patients who have been hospitalized for 20 years, see Bayne and Warren (1955).

numbers of persons in the hospital population need not be there. But these things alone do not justify pushing many more patients back into the community. Responsibility does not end at the hospital gate. Policy cannot be framed solely on the basis of revised medical or psychiatric criteria for admission and need for administrative efficiency. It can only proceed from an awareness of the alternatives available to the patient, of the social life he expects to lead, and of the services present in the community. A more rigorous medical test for hospital stay, together with an administrative policy which took no account of developments elsewhere in society, would isolate the hospital further from the community.

What we have to seek out is the most appropriate and cooperative role for the hospital to play in the total process of preventing and treating ill-health. Approached in this light and not simply in terms of institutional and custodial care as an end in itself, it is possible to see the center of gravity in hospital work shifting from inpatient treatment to community service. . . . In brief, less hospitalized sickness and shorter periods of institutional care mean more social service to support the family and the community. [Abel-Smith and Titmuss, 1956]

THE EFFECTS OF INSTITUTIONS ON INDIVIDUALS

I have suggested some of the reasons why a change in policy has occurred and now want to consider one which is of particular importance. Through systematic and descriptive research we are discovering that many institutionalized persons have unsuspected potentialities and capacities and that the environment in which they live may have harmful effects upon them, particularly when they have been exposed to it for some months or years.

This research mainly refers to mental hospitals and institutions for children and handicapped adults, but many documentary accounts of general hospitals, residential homes for the aged, approved schools, prisons, and even camps for refugees and prisoners of war suggest that the conclusions to be drawn about the effects on individuals of different institutional environments may often be similar. I believe that the general picture that emerges can be expressed as follows: In the institution people live communally with a minimum of privacy, and yet their relationships with each other are slender. Many subsist in a kind of defensive shell of isolation. Their mobility is restricted, and they have little access to general society. Their social experiences are limited, and the staff leads a rather separate existence from them. They are subtly oriented toward a system in which they submit to orderly routine and lack creative occupation, and cannot exercise much self-determination. They are deprived of intimate family relationships and can rarely find substitutes which are more than a pale imitation of those enjoyed by most people in the general community. The result for the individual seems to be a gradual process of depersonalization. He may become resigned and depressed and may display no interest in the future or in things not immediately personal. He sometimes becomes apathetic, talks little, and lacks initiative. His personal and toilet habits may deteriorate. Occasionally he seems to withdraw into a private world of fantasy. In a recent study of "Institutional Neurosis," Dr. Russell Barton suggested that the mental patient even adopts in time a characteristic posture, "the hands held across the body or tucked behind an apron, the shoulders drooped, and the head held forward." The gait also has a "shuffling quality" (Barton, 1959). In some of the smaller and more humanely administered institutions these various characteristics seem to be less marked, but can still be found. Clinical pictures of children in institutions are broadly the same. Compared with those outside the institution, babies are less vocal, they smile less, they show diminished interest and reactivity, they are impassive, and more of them develop psychiatric disturbances (Bowlby, 1951; Brodbeck and Irwin, 1946; Gesell and Amatruda, 1947; Bakwin, 1949; Spitz and Wolf, 1946). Several studies develop the picture for the second and later years of life, drawing attention to backwardness in speech and in mental development (Goldfarb, 1945). Even in institutions with high staffing standards and liberal routines the children seem to be significantly different from those living in their own or in foster homes (Rheingold, 1943; Levy, 1947; Bowlby, 1951). Similar effects have been noted for mentally retarded children and adults (Kirman, 1957; Ellis, 1958; Tizard, 1960).

In turning to work on mental hospitals we find that for many years observers have described what has been variously called "prison stupor" or "psychosis" (Myerson, 1939); "institutionalization" (Martin, 1955); "institutional neurosis" (Barton, 1959); or just "apathy reaction" (Anonymous, 1960). Research workers and others felt impelled to ask what caused these alleged effects, or more generally to investigate the institution as a social system. They also took more interest in finding out how institutional populations differed in their social characteristics from the ordinary population. In concentrating on what distinguished long-stay from short-stay patients, some have shown that lack of visitors is sometimes associated with chronicity (Brown, 1959b; Sommer, 1959a). Others have described the relation-

ships between patients. One study of schizophrenic patients emphasized their isolation from each other (Slotkin, 1942), while another,
not necessarily contradicting this finding, suggested that informal associations between patients were more therapeutic than anything provided by formal treatment (Bateman and Dunham, 1948).

Others began to ask what features of the hospital environment and
administration were associated with these characteristics. Long-stay
patients tended to get left to themselves (e.g. Garratt *et al.,* 1957;
Garratt, 1958*a* and *b*); their case files were often inadequate; the
turnover in medical and nursing staff meant that continuing relationships were not possible (Sommer, 1959*b;* Belknap, 1956; Stanton and
Schwartz, 1954); the staff underestimated the capacities of patients to
communicate with them intelligibly (Sommer, 1959*b*); inactivity
on the wards and institutional routine sometimes resulted in incontinence (Thomson *et al.,* 1951); many normal skills fell into disuse
(Sommer, 1960). In short, there was a real risk of loss of identity
and of "desocialization" (Stanton and Schwartz, 1954; Greenblatt,
1957).

Still others have looked at the whole question of the staff hierarchy
and regulations adopted. It has been shown how the formal staff
hierarchy can break down into a series of informal, often clandestine,
friendship patterns (Rowland, 1939), but also how the hierarchy
tends to keep patients "in their place" (Bateman and Dunham, 1948).
One study showed how authoritarianism causes the breakdown in
personal relations that is so fatal to a "therapeutic" community (Tetlow, 1957).

In discussing these various studies, the difficulties of exploring the
effects of institutionalization upon patients must not be underrated.
In analysis of the behavior of one group of patients three causal
processes must be distinguished. First of all, their behavior may be
attributable to their previous social history and environment; thus
persons may have been "apathetic," "resigned," or "withdrawn" even
before their admission to an institution. Second, their behavior may
be attributable to the kind and degree of their illness; some symptoms
of "institutionalization" are displayed by patients with certain kinds
of mental illness whether or not they actually reside in an institution,
where others show a remarkable resilience despite many years in
institutions. Third, their behavior may be attributable to their exposure to the conditions prevailing in the institution. Speculation on
cause and effect is still rife (Wing, 1960), but it is highly unlikely that
individual reactions can be ascribed wholly to factors other than the
institutional environment in more than just a few cases. To an increas-

ing extent, therefore, recent work has been interpreted as justifying efforts both to improve the quality of life in institutions and to find other provision for people wherever possible.

THE FAMILY AND THE COMMUNITY
OF THREE GENERATIONS

Few studies have yet been made of the association between the behavior of individuals in hospitals or residential homes and the absence of family or three-generation relationships, except in children's institutions. Even here many of the research findings have been suggestive rather than conclusive. Dr. John Bowlby has vividly described evidence of the differences between young institutionalized children and those living in their own homes (Bowlby, 1951). The results of various experiments and research exercises have drawn attention to the importance of the family group. One classic study reported on a Hampstead nursery and its attempt to create "artificial families." When cared for indiscriminately by all the attendants, the children showed signs of retarded development. Family groups consisting of four children and one "mother" were formed. The mother alone bathed and dressed her group, was responsible for their clothes, and supervised them throughout each day. At first the innovation seemed to produce nothing but jealousies and disputes, but after a few weeks the "state of frenzy" gave way to a "quieter, more stable and comforting attachment." The children began to develop in "leaps and bounds"; their vocabularies grew, and some recalcitrants started to use the pot regularly and effectively (Freud and Burlingham, 1943).

The research studies on children's institutions, and the experiments carried out there, seem to have stressed the child's need for dependable love within a family. I suspect that if this is understood in the wider sense of the need to give as well as receive affection and to perform reciprocal services within a family or quasi-family group, the same need may exist for individuals of all ages. Recent sociological studies in Western society (following on from anthropological studies elsewhere) have begun to deepen our awareness of the importance to the individual of the family at all stages of his life. Within an organic unit of three generations, largely preserving its identity and independence on the basis of the recognition of biological attachment, the individual achieves a large measure of self-fulfillment, and can satisfy many psychological and social needs; first as a child, and later as adolescent, husband or wife, parent, and grandparent. In an important sociological study in Israel, Talmon-Garber (1956) showed that when an attempt was made to subordinate the relationships of the family to the collective values of the community in some of the early settlements, it was only a matter of time before the family reasserted itself as the basic unit of society, albeit in a modified form.[8]

To a sociologist the absence of close relationships between the three generations is perhaps the most distinctive feature of institutional populations. The institutional community is one which is relatively closed and artificial. It is closed in that it tends to be set apart from the rest of the community as a more or less self-contained unit in buildings of an identifiable kind; and it is artificial in that it is not a representative cross-section of the general community; it does not consist of people of both sexes and all ages, or of people held together by a network of family, occupational, and neighborhood ties. People who are usually strangers to each other are admitted from a wide area, and their relatives have long distances to travel just to spend a few minutes conversing quietly with them in a public room. Although casual relationships may of course arise, they are usually restricted to the very small circle of people living in a particular ward or building. They are usually fragile because, unlike relationships between neighbors or members of a family, they may not last long and cannot be based securely on the reciprocation of services.

In a three-generation family living in the outside community a grandmother may prepare meals and look after her grandchildren while her daughter may do all the heavy washing and shopping. There are many complex arrangements of this kind (Sheldon, 1948; Young and Willmott, 1957; Townsend, 1957 and 1959). In an institution people

---

[8] Thus, in the early stages many of the settlements were avowedly run on the basis of subordinating family interest to the common good. Sex differences in role were denied and women shared equally in every type of work; couples lived together without marrying and married only to legitimize the children; their roles were not differentiated; wider kinship ties were disrupted and any tendency to stay away and build up a segregated family life was strongly condemned. Private property was discouraged and emphasis was placed on communal activities and shared facilities. There were few family celebrations and little entertaining and visiting. Children lived apart from their parents and slept, ate, and later on studied in special children's houses. In time, however, these things have largely changed. "The family constitutes a basic and important social unit and should be accorded independence and privacy." The parent-child relationship was intensified. Women's roles became less stubbornly "masculine." Marriage now preceded the establishment of a family. Many parents craved for, and secured, closer contacts with their children. Wider kinship ties were renewed and strengthened. "Old parents used to live concentrated in separate blocks of dwellings but it is becoming more customary to set them up in rooms adjoining their children's flats." Family celebrations became important (Talmon-Garber, 1956).

often have the same disabilities, so they cannot do very much for each other even if they are encouraged to do so. Their behavior is necessarily overlaid by formal organization and routine while the scope for self-management is limited. Even when they have the capacity to do many of the things ordinarily undertaken in the course of home life— such as cooking, arranging furniture, repairing clothes, and gardening —institutionalized persons have little or no opportunity to exercise such skills. One American study found that a group of women mental patients had not cooked a meal for an average of 21 years (Sommer, 1960).[9]

Many authorities believe, following the policies of previous decades, that most of the problems posed by the shortcomings of institutional care can be met by two continuing reforms: by classifying institutions more rigorously according to the different types of inmates, and by creating better opportunities for occupational and social fulfillment as well as better physical facilities and material comforts. Thus they would carry even further the present practice of placing children, young adults, the aged, and persons suffering from certain diseases or handicaps in separate types of institutions, sometimes subdividing them also according to sex. Although this approach may be clinically appropriate or administratively convenient, since specialists and trained personnel are scarce and equipment is expensive, it may not assist the creation of real communities and may make the patients or residents psychologically more insecure. To pursue one aim may, in short, make the other impossible to achieve.

Whatever its defects, the old Victorian workhouse reproduced a number of the characteristics of the normal community. There were persons of all ages in all conditions. Some of the children, at least, were able to remain with their parents when they were sick; orphans might find a maternal widow to take an interest in them; and a destitute but not infirm woman could be accepted into the same building as her imbecile sister. I do not want to overstate this argument. The Victorian mixed institution was a scandal in a civilized society. People lived in miserable conditions on a poor diet, cross-infection was rife, and the same rules were often appled indiscriminately to both the

---

[9] "When a patient enters hospital . . . he has to give up personal control over even the simplest everyday functions. The time to get up, the time to go to sleep, what he will eat and when, with whom he will associate, whether the windows will be open or closed—these and other minutiae of daily living are no longer determined altogether by his own likes and dislikes or habits built up in the course of a lifetime. Instead they are now determined by an outside authority and have to be submitted to without question and without regard to personal preferences." (Field, 1958, p. 56; see also Bluestone, 1958.)

infirm and the work-shy. I merely wish to suggest that it may have taken so long to die because it possessed some of the social and psychological advantages to the individual of the general community of three or four generations. Now that we have set it firmly behind us we find ourselves posed with a fundamental dilemma.

SEEKING AN ANSWER TO A DILEMMA

How can we reconcile the medical or administrative argument for the specialized institution with the need of people to live in family groups within a community composed of individuals of both sexes and all ages? In a sense this dilemma has existed, if largely unrecognized, throughout history. But only now has it come to the forefront in a society which has the means and, thanks partly to some of the recent work of psychologists and sociologists, a greater inclination to act more tolerantly towards the victims of adversity.

How is it possible to meet individual and social needs in the institution? In the first place, we are a long way from possessing adequate knowledge of the potentialities and capacities of individuals who stay in institutions for longer than a few weeks. Some surprising results have been produced by recent research. The authors of one study carried out in a large English city, for example, considered that 25 percent of the mental patients were fit for productive work and a further 42 percent fit for light work or occupational therapy (Garratt *et al.,* 1957; Garratt, 1958*a* and *b;* see also Miller, 1957). Again, several studies have even drawn attention to the occupational and social potentialities of mentally subnormal children and adults (Gordon *et al.,* 1955; O'Connor and Tizard, 1956; Walton and Begg, 1955; Kirman, 1957; and Tizard, 1960), some of them arguing that a high proportion could be fitted into paid employment.[10] But the evidence, though growing, is still rather imprecise and some of it is open to question. We are badly in need of scientific measurement of the capacities of institutionalized individuals and of controlled experiments directed to showing how these capacities may be released.

[10] After a careful analysis of the prevalence of mental defect in one region (primary amentias, mongols, cerebral palsy and so on) the authors of one study concluded, "It is only necessary to write off 20 per cent of *bona fide* mental defectives as useless members of society; whereas 30 per cent will probably fit into community life permanently and contentedly employed under sheltered conditions in the humblest types of employment and without possessing any academic attainments; and 50 percent will be capable of employment requiring some degree of skill and will have their lives enhanced by the use of some academic knowledge." (Jones, *et al.,* 1959, p. 283.)

In the second place, we need to know a good deal about the composition of institutional populations and how they function as communities. Under what conditions do friendships and intimate relationships prosper? Can patients undertake modest administrative duties? Are there some situations in which their family relationships can be largely preserved? When is it possible for them to embark spontaneously on activities of their own choosing? Can they secure privacy when they seek it? How far is some degree of authoritarianism on the part of the staff unavoidable? What are the social, as well as the medical and administrative, advantages and disadvantages of mixing residents of different age and sex?

Finally, we need to know much more about the alternatives and potential alternatives to institutional care. In what conditions can the chronic sick, the mentally ill, and the infirm aged safely live in homes of their own? What are the costs, not only economic, but in terms of emotional strain upon relatives and neighbors, of administrative organization, and mental and physical health? How far is it practicable to take services to individuals rather than individuals to institutions?

Only when we can answer such questions with more confidence will it be possible to begin to decide the purpose and future role of the institution in society. We do not yet realize how difficult it is to meet some of the diverse psychological, social, occupational, and educational needs of individuals in institutions as we know and define them, or how much more difficult it is to meet them there than in the community. As one writer has stated, "It is only realistic to recognize the impossibility of making a home of an institution, and to avoid any pretense of so doing" (Hopkirk, 1944). Already there are signs that no more than lip service can be paid to some good intentions. Administrators agree, for example, that occupational therapy is desirable in residential homes for the aged and handicapped. Yet such therapy can rarely be organized successfully for more than a tiny proportion of residents, largely because their interests, talents, and capacities are too diverse to conform to a single scheme.

The means of resolving our dilemma may lie in two directions. The first might be to restrict hospital provision to general "accident" or "acute" hospitals with highly specialized treatment wards and adjoining "recovery" and outpatient annexes, breaking down the present separation between "general," "chronic sick," and "mental hospitals." [11] These would be for people staying for brief periods who

[11] For an interesting discussion of the need for reorganization of hospitals see McKeown (1958 and 1959).

require surgery and other forms of treatment which cannot be given in their own homes. The second means might be to gradually abandon most other types of institution, as we know them, by creating special types of housing and day clinics and by providing a much richer variety of home and welfare services. Those institutions that remain would have the purpose of assisting individuals through a transition from adversity or dependence to an independent home life. To me such a policy seems to follow logically from a projection of the trends we are now witnessing in our social services. It would take a long time to achieve and would involve immense difficulties. But once we accept the principle that no advanced democratic society should deny the individual the right to a normal home and family life, it does not seem that any other course is open to us.

Acknowledgments. I gained much help from Richard Titmuss and also from John Wing and George Brown of the Maudsley Hospital, and I owe a continuing debt to my colleagues on the full research project: June Vernon, Ruth Townsend, Robert Pinker, and Brian Rees.

REFERENCES

Abel-Smith, B., and Titmuss, R. M. 1956. The cost of the National Health Service in England and Wales. Cambridge: Cambridge University Press.
Anderson, W. F., and Cowan, N. R. 1955. A consultative health centre for older people: The Rutherglen experiment. Lancet, 2: 239–40.
Anonymous. 1834. Report from His Majesty's Commissioners for inquiring into the administration and practical operation of the poor laws. London: Fellows.
——— 1958a. The outpatient department. Lancet, 1: 1007–08.
——— 1958b. Child psychiatry. Lancet, 2: 1108–09.
——— 1958c. Falls in the elderly. Brit. Med. J., 2: 313–14.
——— 1960. Institutionalisation. Lancet, 1: 585.
Baker, A. A. 1958. Breaking up the mental hospital. Lancet, 2: 253–54.
Bakwin, H. 1949. Emotional deprivation in infants. J. Pediatrics, 35: 512–21.
Barton, R. 1959. Institutional neurosis. Bristol: Wright.
Bateman, J. F., and Dunham, H. W. 1948. The state mental hospital as a specialized community experience. Am. J. Psychiat., 105: 445–48.
Bayne, J. R. D., and Warren, M. 1955. Disposal of the chronic case. Lancet, 1: 1317.
Belknap, I. 1959. Human problems of a state mental hospital. New York: McGraw-Hill Book Co.
Bluestone, E. M. 1958. Fear in hospital practice: some advantages of home care. Lancet, 1: 1083–84.
Bowlby, J. 1951. Maternal care and mental health. Geneva: World Health Organization.

Brodbeck, A. J., and Irwin, O. C. 1946. The speech behaviour of infants without families. Child Development, 17: 145–56.

Brown, G. W. 1959a. Experiences of discharged chronic schizophrenic patients in various types of living group. Milbank Memorial Fund Quart., 37: 105–31.

——— 1959b. Social factors influencing length of hospital stay of schizophrenic patients. Brit. Med. J., 2: 1300–02.

Brown, G. W., Carstairs, G. M., and Topping, G. 1958. Post-hospital adjustment of chronic mental patients. Lancet, 2: 685–88.

Carse, J. 1959. Report to the South West Metropolitan Regional Hospital Board. London: The Board.

Carse, J., and Panton, Nydia. 1958. A district mental health service. Lancet, 1: 39–41.

Clein, L. 1960. Care of the mentally ill in the community. Med. Off., 104: 35–38.

Collins, S. D., Fynn, S.J., Manners, F., and Morgan, R. 1959. Factory in a ward. Lancet, 2: 609–11.

Colwell, C., and Post, F. 1959. Community needs of elderly psychiatric patients. Brit. Med. J., 2: 214–17.

Ellis, E. 1958. Responsibilities in cerebral palsy. Lancet, 1: 784–86.

Farrer-Brown, L. 1959. Hospitals for today and tomorrow. Brit. Med. J., 1 (Supplement): 118–22.

Field, Minna. 1958. Patients are people: a medical-social approach to prolonged illness. New York: Columbia University Press.

Forsyth, G., and Logan, R. 1960. The demand for medical care. London: Oxford University Press.

Freeman, H. L. 1960. Oldham and district psychiatric service. Lancet, 1: 218–21.

Freud, Anna, and Burlingham, Dorothy. 1943. War and children. New York: International Universities Press.

Garratt, F. N., Lowe, C. R., and McKeown, T. 1957. An investigation of the medical and social needs of patients in mental hospitals. I. Classification of patients according to the type of institutions required for their care. Brit. J. Preventive Soc. Med., II: 165–73.

——— 1958a. An investigation of the medical and social needs of patients in mental hospitals. II. Types of accommodation and staff required. Brit. J. Preventive Soc. Med., 12: 23–41.

———1958b. Institutional care of the mentally ill. Lancet, 1: 682–84.

Gesell, A., and Amatruda, C. 1947. Developmental diagnosis: normal and abnormal child development, clinical methods and pediatric applications. New York: P. B. Hoeber, Inc.

Goldfarb, W. 1945. Effects of psychological deprivation in infancy and subsequent stimulation. Am. J. Psychiat., 102: 18–33.

Gordon, S., O'Connor, N., and Tizard, J. 1955. Some effects of incentives on the performance of imbeciles on a repetitive task. Am. J. Ment. Deficiency, 60: 371–77.

Great Britain. Home Office. 1959. Children in care in England and Wales, March. Cmnd. 914. London: H. M. Stationery Office.

Great Britain. Ministry of Health. 1953. Central Health Services Council. The reception and welfare of in-patients in hospital. London: H. M. Stationery Office.

―――― 1959a. Report of the Committee on the Welfare of Children in Hospital. London: H. M. Stationery Office.

―――― 1959b. Report for the year ended 31st December, 1958. Cmnd. 806. London: H. M. Stationery Office.

Great Britain. National Corporation for the Care of Old People. 1959a. Boarding out old people. London: The Corporation.

―――1959b. Twelfth Annual Report, 1959. London: The Corporation.

Greenblatt, M. 1957. Implications for psychiatry and hospital practice: the movement from custodial hospital to therapeutic community. *In* The patient and the mental hospital, pp. 611–19. Glencoe, Ill.: The Free Press.

Hemphill, R. E. 1960. Psychiatric halfway hostel. Lancet, 1: 703–04.

Hopkirk, H. W. 1944. Institutions serving children. New York: Russell Sage Foundation.

Jones, G. C., Cochrane-Dyet, E. M., and Fuller, A. M. 1959. The preventive approach to mental retardation. Med. Off., 102: 277–83.

Kennaway, Sir E. 1957. Some notes on nursing from a patient's point of view. Brit. Med. J., 2: 1485.

Kirman, B. H. 1957. Research and mental deficiency. Lancet, 2: 1221–23.

Levy, Ruth J. 1947. The effects of institutional versus boarding home care on a group of infants. J. Personality, 15: 233–41.

Lightwood, R., Brimblecombe, F. S. W., Reinhold, J. D. L., Burnard, E. D., and Davis, J. A. 1957. A London trial of home care for sick children. Lancet, 1: 313–17.

Macmillan, D. 1956. An integrated mental health service: Nottingham experience. Lancet, 2: 1094–95.

Martin, D. 1955. Institutionalisation. Lancet, 2: 1188–90.

McKeown, T. 1958. The concept of a balanced hospital community. Lancet, 1: 701–04.

―――― 1959. Fundamental problems in hospital planning. Brit. Med. J., 1 (Supplement): 122–24.

Miller, M. I. B. 1957. Employment of chronic mental patients. Lancet, 2: 87.

Myerson, A. 1939. Theory and principles of the "total push" method in the treatment of chronic schizophrenia. Am. J. Psychiat., 95: 1197–1204.

O'Connor, N., and Tizard, J. 1956. The social problem of mental deficiency. New York: Permagon Press.

Reingold, H. L. 1943. Mental and social development of infants in relation to the number of other infants in the boarding home. Am. J. Orthopsychiat., 13: 41–44.

Richardson, I. M., Klopper, K. M., and Lynch, G. W. 1960a. Special housing for older people: a study of eighty households in Aberdeen. Med. Off., 103: 219–24.

―――― 1960b. Special housing for older people: a study of eighty households in Aberdeen. Med. Off. 103: 235–38.

Rowland, H. 1939. Friendship patterns in the state mental hospital. Psychiatry, 2: 363–73.

Ruck, S. K. 1960a. Housing the old: a reconnaissance. The Builder, March, 468–73.

——— 1960b. A policy for old age. Political Quart., 31: 120–31.

Sheldon, J. H. 1948. The social medicine of old age. London: Oxford University Press.

Sherrett, D. 1958. Impact of new methods of treatment in a provincial mental hospital. Brit. Med. J., 1: 994–96.

Slotkin, J. S. 1942. The nature and effects of social interaction in schizophrenia. J. Abnorm. & Social Psychol., 37: 345–68.

Sommer, R. 1959a. Visitors to mental hospitals: a fertile field for research. Ment. Hygiene, 43: 8–15.

———1959b. Patients who grow old in a mental hospital. Geriatrics, 14: 581–90.

——— 1960. Cooking skills of geriatric patients. J. Am. Geriatrics Soc., 7: 343–48.

Spitz, R. A., and Wolf, Katherine M. 1946. Anaclitic depression: an inquiry into the genesis of psychiatric conditions in early childhood. II. Psychoanal. Studies of the Child, 2: 313–42.

Stallworthy, J. A. 1960. Hotels or hospitals. Lancet, 1: 103–06.

Stanton, A. H., and Schwartz, M. S. 1954. The mental hospital. New York: Basic Books.

Talmon-Garber, Yonina. 1956. The family in collective settlements. *In* Transactions of the Third World Congress of Sociology, Vol. 4, pp. 116–26. London: International Sociological Association.

Tetlow, C. 1957. Medical administration in mental hospitals. Lancet, 1: 89–91.

Thomson, A. P., Lowe, C. R., and McKeown, T. 1951. The care of the ageing and chronic sick. Edinburgh: E & S Livingstone.

Tizard, J. 1960. Residential care of mentally handicapped children. Brit. Med. J., 1: 1041–46.

Townsend, P. 1957. The family life of old people: an inquiry in East London. London: Routledge and Kegan Paul, Ltd.

——— 1959. Social surveys of old age in Great Britain, 1945–1958. Bull. World Health Organization, 21: 583–91.

Walton, D., and Begg, T. L. 1955. Adult imbeciles. Lancet, 2: 616–17.

Webb, S., and Webb, Beatrice. 1929. English Poor Law history: Part II. The last hundred years. London: Longmans, Green and Co.

Wing, J. K. 1960. The problem of "institutionalism" in mental hospitals. London: Maudsley Hospital.

World Health Organization. 1959. Organisation of medical care. ("Technical Report Series," No. 176.) Geneva: The Organization.

Young, M., and Willmott, P. 1957. Family and kinship in East London. London: Routledge and Kegan Paul, Ltd.

A Brief Report on the Rehabilitation

of Long-Term Aged Patients

WILMA DONAHUE

A DEMONSTRATION-RESEARCH project on the care and rehabilitation of chronically ill aged persons has been undertaken by the Division of Gerontology and the Medical School of The University of Michigan to determine what the application of modern medical and social science techniques can do to ameliorate the physical and mental ills of older people and, in so doing, improve social health and decrease the financial drain upon society.

PLAN OF THE STUDY

Following a survey of 39 county (tax-supported) medical care facilities and their 2065 patients aged 45 and over, three facilities were selected which were matched for such patient characteristics as age, sex ratio, average length of stay, patterns of chronic illness, and disabilities of patients, and for such institutional variables as number of beds, patient cost per day, staffing patterns, and medical services. One of the three institutions was used as a control, while the other two constituted experimental units; later the control was to become an experimental hospital also.

THE STUDY POPULATION

The project was limited to patients 45 years of age and older. However, only 2 patients out of the 75 from the two hospitals included in the study population were under 50 years of age, while 58 were

The full text of this paper will be published in Wilma Donahue, C. Tibbitts, and R. H. Williams (eds.), *Psychological and Social Processes of Aging: An International Research Seminar* (to be published).

over 60. The median age of the experimental population at Jackson was 73 years, at Washtenaw it was 76 years.

OUTLINE OF PROCEDURE

The first phase of the study was the assessment of the physical, functional, psychosocial, and vocational status and potential of patients aged 45 years and over in all three hospitals. On the basis of the data collected, an evaluation of the potential of each patient was made and a "prescription" for medical treatment and psychosocial therapy was determined.

The second phase of the project consisted of instituting an experimental program which provided socioenvironmental and medical treatment according to the prescribed needs of the patients. In approximately 9 months, a second assessment of patients similar to the first one was made in all three hospitals to determine whether the program had resulted in measurable changes.

Finally, the third facility became an experimental hospital, also, when the physical rehabilitation and activity programs were introduced. After a period of demonstration (which is just now in progress) equivalent to that followed in the other two hospitals, a final assessment of the patients will be made. Thus "before" and "after" data, using the third hospital as its own control, will be available for comparison.

The psychological and social data were collected by means of personal interview; the Chicago Attitudes Scale (Cavan *et al.*, 1949); a patient schedule specially designed for the project; and the morale scale used by Kutner *et al.* (1956). Intelligence was tested with the WAIS, and in selected cases some projective tests were administered. A sociometric test was used to measure changes in social interaction. Other records included a nurse evaluation patient improvement scale and participation ratings of patients in various activities.

THE REHABILITATION PROGRAM

The rehabilitation program was conceived in terms of the activity theory. It sought to provide opportunities for the patients to engage intensively in a variety of activities, to establish and express interpersonal relationships, to take clear-cut roles similar to those of younger and noninstitutionalized people, and to expand the perception of their life space to include economic and social aspects of the community. In short, the program was designed to put forth every effort to restore (and reengage) the patients functionally and to increase their self-dependence and effective social interaction.

To achieve these goals four major therapeutic programs were selected: sheltered workshop, craft training, social-recreational programs (both intra- and extramural) and friendly visiting. Physical restorative procedures were carried out with the disabled to increase their functional independence and mobility. Training of the staff in the philosophy and techniques of physical and social therapy was also a major part of therapeutic programs from which patients benefited.

SOME RESULTS

Results of the initial assessment of patients which have already been published (Smith et al., 1960), (Donahue et al., 1960), (Currier, 1960), (Brandt and Tupper, 1960) indicate that county hospital patients have a high degree of pathology, especially neurological disorders, and that almost all were judged to be in need of some training to improve their health status and their mental and social well-being.

The results reported briefly in this resumé will be found in greater detail in another publication (Donahue, to be published), but they will serve to indicate the nature of some of the findings.

Nurse evaluation patient improvement scale

The day nurses who knew the patients best made independent ratings on each patient on eleven items of possible change. The ratings of the several nurses were pooled to obtain an improvement index in each area rated. On the basis of the nurses' ratings, slightly less than 30 percent of the study population at one of the hospitals was judged to have improved; there was little difference between men and women. At the other hospital, the percentage of those showing improvment was 63 percent for men and 100 percent for women.

At both hospitals greater patient improvement was judged to have taken place in those categories related to psychological behavior—participation in hospital life, cooperativeness, sociability, and morale —than in those more clearly related to health status—appetite, complaints about health, etc.

Sociometric studies

The sociometric test consisted of two questions: (1) Among the patients, whom do you like to visit with most? and (2) Among the patients, who is it that makes you the maddest? Patients were encouraged to make as many choices as they wished.

Comparing results before and after the activity program, it was found that changes occurred in the expected direction. The differences were of a magnitude to be statistically significant at Washtenaw hospital in three out of four categories: the total number of choices made, the number of patients who made one or more choices, and the number who chose each other. Considering the groups as a whole there were increases in group expansiveness, group integration, and group cohesion in both hospitals.

Results indicate that participation of patients in rehabilitation activities produced a more highly structured and socialized hospital community, and afforded them an opportunity to take roles which improved their status, positive expansiveness, and close mutual relationship—all characteristics considered to be associated with good personal adjustment.

The Chicago attitude scale of adjustment

As might be expected, the hospital populations showed low-average adjustment when rated on norms established for a normal noninstitutionalized population. When the attitude scores made at the time of the first testing period are compared with those made 9 months later at the close of the active rehabilitation period, it is found that a few of the patients in each of the two hospitals improved in adjustment, a few others worsened, while most remained in the same range with a slight shift toward better adjustment.

Levels of rehabilitation

Of the 75 patients who were members of the two hospital populations, three-fourths achieved higher levels of independence and self-sufficiency as a result of the physical restoration program. Fourteen percent were improved to a point at which they could maintain themselves completely and could be considered for employment outside of the hospital. Another 30 percent were made capable of living in the community with only minimal supervision and assistance. These persons could also undertake some work on a limited scale if available to them.

CONCLUSION

A program was based on the assumption that a full-scale approach to the physical and psychological restoration of chronically ill and disabled elderly patients will result in sufficient improvement to make possible the discharge of a significant proportion of the patients to other than hospital settings. Of those who must remain in the hospital, the level of personal independence can be increased to the point where most can care for themselves, and can also participate with benefit to their social and personal adjustment in meaningful activities carried on within the hospital setting.

REFERENCES

Brandt, R. L., and Tupper, C. J. 1960. Medical appraisal of elderly county hospital patients. Geriatrics, 15: 233–53.
Cavan, Ruth S., Burgess, E. W., Havighurst, R. J., and Goldhamer, H. 1949. Personal adjustment in old age. Chicago: Science Research Associates.
Currier, R. D. 1960. Neurologic findings in county hospital patients. Geriatrics, 15: 254–62.
Donahue, Wilma. Rehabilitation of long-term aged patients. *In* Wilma Donahue, C. Tibbitts, R. H. Williams (eds.), Psychological and social processes of aging: an international research seminar. To be published.
Donahue, Wilma, Hunter, W. W., Coons, Dorothy, and Maurice, Helen. 1960. Rehabilitation of geriatric patients in county hospitals. Geriatrics, 15: 263–74.
Kutner, B., Fanshel, D., Togo, Alice M., and Langner, T. S. 1956. Five hundred over sixty: a community survey of aging. New York: Russell Sage Foundation.
Smith, E. M., Brandt, R. L., and Currier, R. D. 1960. Medical care needs and rehabilitation potential. Geriatrics, 15: 296–305.

Changing Family Relationships of Older People in the United States during the Last Fifty Years

M. F. NIMKOFF

THE family relationships of older people have a number of facets: (1) the marital relationship; (2) the relationship of the aged and their children; (3) the relationship of the aged and their grandchildren; and (4) the relationship of the aged and their siblings and other kinfolk. Although a comprehensive review of the topic should encompass all of these facets, the paucity of available data does not permit this.

THE MARITAL RELATIONSHIP

There are now relatively more males and females in the United States of 65 years of age and over who have never married than there were in 1900 (Table 1). We do not know the family context of these

Table 1. Marital status of the population, 65 years of age and over, United States, 1900 and 1958, percentage distribution[a]

	MALE				FEMALE			
Year	Single	Married	Widowed	Divorced	Single	Married	Widowed	Divorced
1900	6.0	67.1	26.4	0.5	6.2	34.2	59.3	0.3
1958	6.7	69.4	22.6	1.3	7.5	36.0	55.3	1.2

[a] Sources: U.S. Bureau of the Census, Twelfth Census of the United States, 1900, Vol. II, Population, Part II, Government Printing Office, Washington, D.C., Table 49; Statistical Abstract of the United States: 1959, Government Printing Office, Washington, D.C., 80th ed., Table 39, p. 40

single persons but we probably can assume that the increase in their number means more aloneness, if not more loneliness. Our assumption derives from the fact that in 1900 somewhat better than one in two of the older population lived on farms as compared to one in seven in 1950, a very radical reduction. The chances that an unmarried person will live in a household with relatives are greater on the farm than in the town or city. The reduction in the number of farms is of course linked to the increase in celibacy. In an urban-industrial environment there is less social pressure to marry and the alternative to marriage is less unattractive than in a rural setting.

There are also relatively more married males and females, and relatively fewer widowed and divorced persons among the aged now than in 1900 (Table 1). This has been caused mainly by longer length of life and higher rates of remarriage in middle and old age. The latter reflects a more favorable, more permissive public attitude toward the remarriage of divorced and widowed persons.

In the last half century one of the more significant changes in the marital relationship has been the lengthening thereof. Both sexes marry earlier and stay married longer. On the average, the gain is about 10 years of married life. Modern couples have fewer children and the last child marries sooner. In 1890 the last child married, on the average, 2 years after the death of one of his parents, whereas in 1950 the last child married from 13 to 14 years before the death of one of his parents (Glick, 1957). This is an increase of from 15 to 16 years in the length of marriage without unmarried children living at home. Since married children now seldom live with their parents, whereas they often did in 1900, the result is an appreciable increase in the length of married life without children at home. The marital component has expanded and the parental component has shrunk.

The quality, as well as the quantity, of marriage has changed. The change is in the direction of equalitarianism. In 1900 the division of labor between the sexes was sharper than it is today, and more was made of the distinction between men's work and women's work. The home was more exclusively the woman's domain, and the man had his job. Since then, the trend has been for wives to take jobs away from home, and for husbands to share more in household duties. So far, to be sure, only token integration in domestic roles has been achieved, since the husband's help is often only symbolic and minor. But the prejudice against domesticity for men has broken down, and those who will may engage in housekeeping without public disapproval. Retirement of the breadwinner provides the occasion for stepping up his domestic role.[1] On the farm, the male's occupational role was continuous, with adjustments made as health and age required. Now, with compulsory retirement, the occupational role of the male is discontinuous. The adjustment of males in retirement is, then, facilitated

[1] Research on changes in role allocations on retirement has been undertaken by Alan Kerckhoff of Duke University and Aaron Lipman of the University of Miami.

by the availability of a socially approved domestic role to compensate for the loss of the occupational role.

THE RELATIONSHIP OF THE AGED AND THEIR CHILDREN

So far as children are concerned, two crucial variables are number and location. One of the more important changes, already mentioned, is that families are smaller, which means that there are fewer children to look after the parents in their old age. "Looking after" has an economic aspect and a sentimental one. If there are many children, the probability that they will collectively be able to support their aged parents is greater than if there are few children. This is the rationale that one very commonly finds in old agricultural societies like India, where the large joint or extended family exists. If you ask why they prefer the large family, they will tell you that it provides more protection in old age. This rationale may be reasonable in a static agricultural society but in a dynamic industrial society like the United States, with a rising standard of living, having fewer children may mean that the parents can accumulate more capital and be less dependent on their children in old age.

Where the children of the aged live is important for both economic and sentimental reasons. We have the data for recent years on the living arrangements of old people. If aged couples, unrelated males, and unrelated females are combined, then in April, 1952, a little over half of them (53.5 percent) lived alone; about one in six (17.6 percent) were heads of households and had children 21 years old and over living with them; an additional one in six (17.6 percent) lived with their children (Steiner and Dorfman, 1957). This picture, then, is primarily one of the aged in our time living alone, apart from their children or other relatives.

In this paper we are interested not just in the present situation but in how it compares with the situation of half a century ago. Unfortunately there are no data on living arrangements by age groups for this earlier period. But from our knowledge that better than 50 percent of the aged lived on farms in 1900 it is probably safe to make certain inferences. One is that there was less independent housing for the aged than now and more of a tendency to live with relatives. Another is that the aged parent, usually the father, was more often the head of the household, and that the arrangement of aged parents living in the household of a married child was more rare than it is now. Lacking census data, we cannot measure the extent of the change but the knowledge we do have disposes us to think that the changes are appreciable.

Separation of children from parents

One reason for thinking in this way is the considerable increase in physical mobility which has the effect of separating members of families from one another. In 1900 there were only 8000 registered automobiles and 144 miles of paved road in the United States, compared to 52,000,000 cars and over 2,300,000 miles of surfaced roads in 1955 (U.S. Bureau of the Census, 1957).

A recent study reports that 65 percent of the aged expect their children to live nearby (Streib, 1958). We do not have comparable data for 1900, but it seems safe to assume that a larger percentage had such an expectation at the turn of the century. Where children are separated from their parents, the expectation is that children will write to their parents. It would be interesting to know whether, when separated, children write as often as they used to visit. It is unlikely that they do, since daily visits are common when one lives nearby, while daily correspondence is not so common. In addition, a letter is rarely as satisfying as a visit in person.

One result of the greater physical separation is an increase in what may perhaps be called "routine visiting." Many oldsters are modern circuit-riders, visiting their married children in turn. The visits are usually short because living space is limited, and the visits, if protracted, are hard on both young and old. The perodic visit is a compromise on the part of the aged who wish to keep their independence and separate residence and yet maintain personal ties with their married children. The children may reciprocate by paying visits to the parental homestead, but this is usually less frequent than the converse because the children are less free. In fact, a not so minor purpose of the children's visits may be to deposit the grandchildren for safe keeping while the children take off on an unfettered vacation.

Modification of status

The changes involve a radical modification in the status of aged parents and their children. In a farming economy the young married sons were more often than not dependent upon their father for support. As unpaid family labor, at least one of the sons might remain with his parents after his marriage, with a view eventually to taking over the farm. Other sons might settle nearby on land provided by the father, or be given a cash settlement and migrate to town in search of jobs. The situation is very different in our industrial society where nonfamily employment is the rule and wages are in money, a highly individualizing commodity. Moreover, a father and son on the land are engaged in a common occupation, and the son is likely to respect his father for his knowledge of farming which comes with long experience.

Now things are very different. Ours is a time of great change. The proliferation of new occupations and new knowledge creates gaps between the generations. It creates different universes of discourse so that the generations cannot communicate with each other in these fields. To see how modern changes favor the young, one has only to see how young are the leading contemporary physicists of the United States. These are the authorities in the new space age.

The aged recognize this change. It may be one reason why they overwhelmingly prefer to maintain independent households. They were household heads in 1900 and want to remain so. In 1900 they did not object to having their married children in the household; indeed, they preferred it. With industrialization the norm has gained favor that married children should have households of their own and should not live with their parents or in-laws, if they can help it. This norm is now respected by the aged. They do not want their children to live with them, although they would like to have them nearby. Nor do they want to live with their married children, if they can help it. The spatial separation is a concomitant of the social distance between the generations.

Parenthetically, an interesting point in this connection is that in an agricultural society a married son often remained with his parents, and a married daughter seldom did, if she were living with her husband. Today, however, if an old parent lives with his or her relatives, the chances are 55 to 45 that it will be with a daughter rather than with a son (Glick, 1957). Apparently if an aged parent has to be dependent, it is safer to be dependent on a daughter than on a son. Or, to state it differently, since the woman usually sets the tone of the home, and has the major responsibility for the management of the home, it is more satisfactory to be dependent on a daughter than on a daughter-in-law.

In comparing residential arrangements of 1900 with those of 1950, we probably err if we place too much emphasis on living together, as opposed to not living together. In 1900, when a married couple lived with the husband's parents, a separate addition was often built onto the house for the newlyweds; or the parents might occupy the new addition. The point is that the two conjugal units often had separate, although adjacent, dwelling space. The residential arrangement is less important than the functional arrangement, although place of residence is not without bearing on function. What matters most in any case is the functional unity of the group. In the past, the extended family was a more highly integrated economic unit, with the aged parent as head. Now the economic integration of the family is much less, even when children contribute to the support of their aged parents. Further, the demand upon children to help with this support is lessened by programs of social security in industry and government.

Litwak has recently sought to establish the idea of the "modified extended family" in the contemporary United States (1960). He thinks it is a mistake to believe that the American family is organized on a nuclear or conjugal basis. He has tried to show that although the conjugal units are no longer characterized by propinquity, occupational similarity, and control, they are still tied together by mutual aid. We may note, however, that in using the phrase "modified extended family," he acknowledges the fact of change. The scientific question is: Precisely how much modification has occurred in the extended family since 1900? It would be unrealistic to ignore the ties that bind together the members of the extended family. The nuclear family seldom, if ever, operates in complete independence of kin. But if one is interested in the direction of social change in our time, it would be equally unrealistic to ignore the increasing individualism which expresses itself in attenuation of the ties of kinship and, for that matter, even in greater separation of the members of the conjugal family itself.

THE RELATIONSHIP OF THE AGED AND THEIR GRANDCHILDREN

The grandparents of 1960 have fewer living grandchildren than the grandparents of 1900, but the grandchildren of 1900 had fewer living grandparents than the grandchildren of 1960. The reason for the former is, of course, the lower birth rate; and the reason for the latter is the increase in the span of life.

Since grandparents now have fewer grandchildren, it may be that the grandchildren are more precious than they used to be, on the basis of the law of supply and demand. But we do not know this to be true. Another conjecture is that since grandchildren are fewer, each gets more attention than formerly. We have had many studies of the only child who is the recipient of undivided parental attention, but we should have some studies of the only grandchild. However, grand-parents in 1900 were more likely to live near their grandchildren, and it is difficult to have an intimate relationship at a distance.

One thing is clear. More grandchildren now have some association with a grandparent than was true in 1900. This association should have the effect of giving the children more of a sense of family tradi-tion. Grandparents are characteristically chroniclers of the past and help to keep the family history alive. This may offset somewhat the loss of interest in things familial which is the result of the increased individualism of our time.

When grandparents live with or near their grandchildren, the grand-parents take over some parental functions. In a recent study, 50 percent reported baby-sitting and child care (Streib, 1958). We do not know what percentage of grandparents performed these functions in 1900 but we surmise that the number was low. Recreation and social life away from home have greatly increased in recent decades, while the term "baby-sitter" did not come into our vocabulary until rather recently. In 1900 only one in twenty-five married women had a paying job outside the home, whereas at present the ratio is nearly one in three, and is expected to increase further (Ogburn and Nimkoff, 1955). The number of employed mothers is, of course, lower than the number of employed wives, but this too has increased. If the grand-mother is nearby and not infirm, she may assist her daughter with the responsibilities of child care, and the grandfather who has retired is pressed into service as a baby-sitter. The parental roles of grand-parents have accordingly been strengthened.

The family status of grandparents in 1960 is lower than it was in 1900 as they are rarely heads of the households in which the grand-children live, and do not have the authority that goes with economic control. Also, owing to accelerated change, the cultural gap between grandparents and grandchildren has widened even more than that between parents and children, because the new generation is the principal vehicle of change.

Grandparents in 1960 in the United States have the reputation of being highly permissive with their grandchildren. The arguments usually advanced here are that the old people have mellowed, that they have learned to put first things first, and that they are relaxed in dealing with their grandchildren because they are not principally responsible for them. As these are all more or less constant factors, we should expect to find them in 1900 also. But the relationship of grand-parents to grandchildren was not so permissive then; in fact, it was quite authoritative. Henry Seidel Canby (1934), in his illuminating memoir *The Age of Confidence,* describes his boyhood in his home in Wilmington, Delaware, around the turn of the century. He mentions particularly the thimbled finger with which his grandmother would rap him when she thought he needed disciplining. The children went about on tiptoe for fear of disturbing the peace and quiet of their elders, always addressed them as "sir" or "ma'am," and never contradicted them.

If the grandparents were more authoritative in 1900 than they are now, it was because they had more authority. "It was the grandparents you had to watch out for," because the family home belonged to the grandparents. The sprawling house was only one part of the family property which is so important a key to an understanding of the extended family. Now the big sprawling house is largely a thing of the past, and the less ample house of today more often belongs to the parents, not the grandparents. The greater permissiveness of grandparents in 1960 reflects their decline in status within the family.

We have said that the home now usually belongs to the parents. Why, then, do the children not show the deference to their parents that they showed to both parents and grandparents in 1900? Canby says that in those days children showed deference to their parents and grandparents even when they profoundly disagreed. His explanation is that the children showed more respect for authority because it was a responsible authority. The parents were held to account for their children's behavior and expected to be. They, in turn, expected to hold their children responsible. Now there is more shrugging off of the family responsibility, because this is shared by the school bus driver, the teacher, the playground director, the Boy Scout leader, the Sunday School teacher, the music teacher, the librarian, the doctor, the nurse, the employer, the sitter, and others *in loco parentis.*

THE RELATIONSHIP OF THE AGED AND THEIR SIBLINGS AND OTHER KIN

This paper would not be complete without some discussion of the relationship of old people and their siblings and other relatives. Unfortunately, students of the family have given little attention to these relationships, perhaps because they are more removed than those already considered.

The relationship of siblings, especially that of brothers, is generally more unstable than that of parent and child. Experience in India is instructive on this point. There the traditional joint family, when organized around the household of the head and two or more married sons and their families, often breaks down when the father dies. The estate is divided up, contrary to the ideal of the joint family. Basically, this is caused by competition or jealousy existing among the brothers. It is easier to maintain the joint family when it is organized vertically, in terms of three or more generations, than when it is organized horizontally, in terms of siblings. In the towns and cities, the vertical joint family is taking the place of the horizontal joint family of the village. It is easier to maintain the unity of the group when the members have a clear-cut relationship of superordination and subordination than when the members have a relationship of equality. In a joint family of brothers, the elder brother has authority over the younger, but the fact that they are all brothers makes their status more nearly equal than in the case of father and son. Whatever the explanation, the fact seems to be that parents and children usually live more harmoniously than siblings.

In the light of the foregoing, it seems reasonable to conclude that the relationship of siblings of aged persons, especially the relationship of brothers, would have changed more since 1900 than the relationship of parent and child. The parent-child relationship has become attenuated and we surmise, therefore, that the sibling relationship has been weakened even more.

We conclude with an observation on the changing relationship of the aged and other kin, such as uncles, aunts, nephews, nieces, and cousins. The increased individualism and physical mobility of the last half century have increased the social distance between kin. One important manifestation of this change is that the limits of responsibility have been modified. In 1900 there was more willingness to assume financial and psychological responsibility for cousins than there is today. The limits of acknowledged responsibility are now being drawn more closely. The effect of this on the aged is that the web of effective or functional relationships is not as wide and complex as it used to be. There are fewer relatives on whose support—material and psychological—the elders can count.

CONCLUSION

In 1900, in an era still agricultural, the aged were generally persons of considerable power in the family because they controlled property and occupations, and they were greatly respected for their knowledge and ability. Since then, with the growth of our industrial society, property and jobs have moved away from family control. Increased physical mobility separates the aged more often from their children and other kin. The relationship of aged husband and wife has been strengthened by its prolongation and its more equalitarian nature; but the older people now depend less on kin and more on government, industry, and philanthropy. The loss by the aged of economic power, authority, and deference within the family is probably the most important change in their family situation during the past half century. This loss is being offset by growing public benefits for the aged resulting from their increasing political power which, in turn, flows from their proportional increase in the population.

REFERENCES

Canby, H. S. 1934. The age of confidence. New York: Farrar and Rinehart.

Glick, P. C. 1957. American families. New York: John Wiley & Sons, Inc.

Litwak, E. 1960. Occupational mobility and extended family cohesion. Am. Sociological Rev., 25: 385–94.

Ogburn, W. F., and Nimkoff, M. F. 1955. Technology and the changing family. Boston: Houghton Mifflin Co.

Steiner, P. O., and Dorfman, R. 1957. The economic status of the aged. Berkeley: University of California Press.

Streib, G. F. 1958. Family patterns in retirement. J. Social Issues, 14: No. 2, 46–60.

U.S. Bureau of the Census. 1957. Statistical abstract of the United States: 1957. (78th ed.) Washington, D.C.: Government Printing Office.

Changes in the Family and the Position of Older Persons in Germany

GERHARD BAUMERT

A COMPARISON of empirical knowledge about modern society with the picture of social life that we derive from literary sources of the past reveals basic changes in the structure of the family. This comparison also reveals basic changes in the role and status of the old. It appears that these two tendencies are strongly interrelated: the changes in the role and status of the old affect the structure of the family and the changes in the family in turn affect the position of the old.

Our focus will be upon the changes in the family as far as they affect the old. However, at least passing consideration should be given to some changes in the relative positions of the young and the old in our society. In preindustrial civilizations in which economic and social conditions remained almost unchanged from one generation to the other, experience was most important for the functioning of the society. Since experience accumulates with increasing age, older persons were accorded positions of high prestige and respect. By contrast, in modern industrial societies, characterized by rapid technological progress, experience has lost much of its value. It is adaptation that is now of ever increasing importance for the maintenance of the social system. The loss of status and respect for the old as a consequence of the decreasing value of experience is accentuated by the difficulty old people have in preserving adaptability with increasing age.

Observations in Germany show that this tendency toward a loss of status of older persons has gained momentum during the last 50 years in accordance with the acceleration of economic development; there is evidence that it was stronger than ever in the last decade. The changing position of the old finds its most obvious expression in the present labor market situation: younger applicants are consistently preferred over older ones, and older persons are forced into early retirement. A similar trend to younger candidates can be observed in the sphere of politics.

These fundamental changes in the relative positions of the young and the old in our society should be kept in mind when we analyze the changes in the family as they affect the older persons. Some of the changes we observe within the family are undoubtedly influenced by general changes in the position of older persons in modern society.

TRENDS IN THE GERMAN FAMILY AND THE EFFECT OF THE WAR

According to studies on the development of the family as a group of related persons living together in one household, we find in Germany a distinct trend toward the smaller family consisting of the married couple and their minor children. We also observe the emergence of new relationships between family members. The majority of the families in Germany is still characterized by a more or less intense predominance of the husband (Baumert, 1954). However, there is little resemblance to the former authoritarian position occupied by the father in the older bourgeois and patriarchal type of family prevailing in the last centuries. The trend is toward an equalitarian partnership type of family in which family life is no longer centered around the figure of the father; rather, husband and wife consider each other as equal partners who jointly decide family issues (König, 1957). Thus, the observations fit into the general trend of modern family development as it is found in the Western societies and in some of the Eastern societies as well—a development which Ernest W. Burgess described about 15 years ago. Again, as far as Germany is concerned, there is evidence of an acceleration of the changes in family structure and family life during the last 5 decades, and an especially strong stimulation by the events of World War II.

Different views were held by German scholars in recent years about the influence of the specific situation in Germany during the war and postwar period. In the first investigations after the war, it was observed that the number of persons making up a family household had increased. Sociological studies found evidence of stronger cohesion among family members (Schelsky, 1953). Young couples or widows having turned into evacuees and refugees, moved into the houses of their parents; the older persons moved in with their middle-aged children. Often the extended family was felt to be the last remnant of stability in a world of destruction. The family reestablished social funcions which it had at least partly lost to other institutions long ago, among these care of the old. While on the one hand the war had intensified tendencies toward family disorganization, expressed by the frequency of separation and disruption, it may be concluded from these observations that it had also intensified tendencies toward family cohesion, especially among members of the extended family including the older parents and their middle-aged children. Some scholars expected the development of new conceptions regarding family life. A detached view, however, permitted by increasing distance from these events, proves that many of the effects are short-range adjustments to unusual living conditions. In so far as there have been any lasting influences, they appear to have strengthened and accelerated evolutionary tendencies already observed for many decades. We find neither a reversal of trends nor entirely new conceptions. It must be stated that war and postwar events have been of secondary significance for the basic changes in family structure and relationships, as well as for the changes in the status and the role of the old.

THE CHANGING ROLE OF THE CHILD

The position of the old is strongly determined by the relationships between parents and children. No other changes in German family life have affected the older persons as much as those which concern the role and the position of the child in the family. In summarizing the present position of the child in a few general statements the following tendencies should be emphasized: the child of today has become more liberal and independent. As education is increasingly aimed at the development of the child's personality, his individuality is more and more respected. The relationships between the child and the parents are more informal. The older children are attaining a companionlike position and begin to carry more weight in decisions within the family. We know that these are evolutionary tendencies in accordance with the trend from the authoritarian-patriarchal type of family to the equalitarian-partnership type. On the other hand, considerations that are based on symptoms reflecting a general trend do not take into account the influence of traditional views concerning the parent-child relationships which are still strong in Germany, nor do they reckon with differentiations regarding the role of children in families of different social standing.

Comparisons of recent survey findings with literary sources from the last century are sufficient to demonstrate that parents today perceive the role of their children quite differently from what parents did 50 or 100 years ago. These differences in views are partly caused by changes in economic and social conditions. For many families in the upper social classes the importance of the children was based on their function as future heirs of the family property and family tradition. The children were educated with respect to maintaining the continuity of the family. But the size of inheritances is shrinking and, as a consequence, the role of the child as the perpetuator of the family heritage becomes increasingly insignificant. The maintenance of family tradition—which, in any case, is difficult if the nuclear family is considered the central unit of the family—loses its original sense; the idea of family tradition tends to vanish. Simultaneously, the view of the role of the children changes in the lower social classes. For many families in these classes the children's importance rested on the expectation that they could soon contribute to the family income and support the parents when they were too old to work. Education was directed toward preparation for this role. Today relief and support of aged parents has become more and more a matter of governmental and private social welfare institutions, and less a concern of the family and the children. The aged parents become increasingly independent of the economic support of their children. In Germany this development was encouraged by the first social legislation in the Bismarck era; it reached a new height in the recent old age security laws of the Adenauer administration.

If we state that the child in the upper classes loses his function as the heir of family possession and family tradition, and the child in the lower classes his function as the supporter of the old, it must be added that at the same time in Germany these tendencies are accompanied by an increasing inclination of the parents to identify themselves as individuals with the child and his future. The emphasis on the child's advancement in social rank, connected with efforts to provide good schooling and professional training—so evident in the findings of postwar studies in Germany (Wurzbacher, 1958; Baumert, 1952)—indicates the character of the prevailing parent-child relationships.

It seems likely that the relationship between parents and children is also influenced by the spread of birth control which means that more and more parents have a limited and planned number of children (Freedman et al., 1959). All these developments have brought about a basic change in the parents' attitudes toward the child. Psychologically, the position of the parents becomes ever weaker, and the child increasingly dominates the family. It may well be that the change in the relationship of gainfully employed children with their working-class parents is characteristic of the attitude of German parents toward their children: in earlier times it was usual for children to turn their earnings over to their parents. Today many children surrender only a minor share for food received at home, or (as is frequently found) they live in the household of their parents but keep their earnings. While in former times in Germany one sometimes spoke of an exploitation of the children by their working-class parents, it seems more justified today to speak of an increasing exploitation of the parents by their children.

The new aspects of the role of the children and the new parent-child relationships, which emerge in connection with development toward a companionship family, lead to a weakening of the institutional ties between aged parents and their middle-aged children. Parents and children are no longer bound together by their common interest in the position and future of their family. The education of the children is no longer strongly directed toward their moral obligation to the tradition of the extended family and specifically toward their obligation to support aging parents. As a result, the relationships between aging parents and their middle-aged children are today less determined by an institutional code of conduct. The children are still legally obliged to take care of their parents in case of need. But with the old age insurance system reaching all groups of the population, even the farmers, such support is needed only in extreme cases. Thus relationships and decisions about living arrangements are increasingly determined by individual affection or by rational considerations concerning the income of the old and their possible functions in the family household.

FAMILY CONTRACTION AND THE EXCLUSION OF THE OLDER PERSONS

Had living arrangements and social norms remained unchanged, the probability of a family household including aged parents would be twice as great today as at the turn of the century. The proportion of persons 65 years of age and older has more than doubled; the percentages of the West German population in this age group was: about 4 percent in 1900, 7 percent in 1939, and 10 percent in 1955. On the other hand, the statistical figures show a persistent decline in the size of households during the last hundred years. In 1871 the average size of private households was 4.6; in 1950, 3.1. We know that several factors contribute to this reduction; but there is evidence that it largely reflects an increasing tendency toward exclusion of aging parents from the families of their married children. The general trend has reached different stages in different areas. There is a marked difference between urban and rural families. The trend toward the smaller family and the exclusion of aged parents has proceeded less far in rural areas, and has gone furthest in metropolitan areas. Data collected in the Darmstadt Community Survey reflect this situation for Germany in general. As the data show, the size of the family household decreases with increasing distance from agricultural life: family size is highest for the families of farmers, and it is lowest for families in the city. In between are the values for the intermediate types of family: the part-time farm family and the nonfarm family in the rural area. A comparison of these various types of families according to the number of generations living together in one household reveals the following differences: the extended family with three or more generations in coresidence occurs in 42 percent of the full-time farm families, in 16 percent of the part-time farm families, but in only 9 percent of the nonfarm units living in rural communities and in

Table 1. *Number of generations living together in urban and rural families in a West German city and its hinterland, percentage distribution*[a]

	Urban families (N = 387)	Rural Families			
Number of generations		Total (N = 434)	Nonfarm	Part-time farm	Full-time farm
One	36	25	27	35	7
Two	59	62	64	49	51
Three	5	12	9	15	37
Four		1		1	5

[a] Source: Darmstadt Community Survey, 1950.

merely 5 percent of the families in the city (Baumert, 1954) (see Table 1).

LIVING ARRANGEMENTS AND FAMILY CONTACTS

The present state of the evolutionary process finds its reflection in the living arrangements of older persons. The West German Census of 1950 reported that 17 percent of the population 65 years of age and over lived alone. A more recent representative survey of the living

arrangements of the aging found that 23 percent of the older persons
in West Germany were living in one-person households. Thirty-five
percent were living with spouse, 12 percent with spouse and children,
and 20 percent with children only.[1] This means that roughly one-third
of the older persons in West Germany are living with children while
two-thirds are not living with children but with spouse only, with
other persons, or alone (see Table 2).

*Table 2. Living arrangements of persons 65 years of age and over
in West Germany, percentage distribution*[a]

Living arrangements	Male (N = 338)	Female (N = 483)	Total (N = 821)
Alone	13	30	23
With spouse	49	25	35
With spouse and children	17	8	12
With children	14	25	20
With others or no information	7	12	10

[a] Source: Survey of the DIVO Institute, 1958.

A breakdown of the data by community size clearly indicates a
tendency toward exclusion of the old with increasing size of community. In small rural communities (up to 2000 inhabitants) we find
47 percent of the older persons living with their children; in larger
cities (more than 100,000 inhabitants) the figure is 22 percent. While
coresidence of aged parents with their middle-aged children seems
more and more to become the exception in the cities, it is still the
prevailing family form among farmers. Of persons 65 years and older
classified as farm population, 71 percent live in a household with
children, while only 2 percent were found to live alone.

In appraising the evolutionary process it is interesting to note that
the proportion of older persons living with children is higher in the
middle classes than it is in the lower classes. It appears that the exclusion of the old from the families of their middle-aged children has
proceeded less far in the classes in which families still have some
possessions to pass on to the next generation, and where a relatively
larger number still have a family business. We may assume that the
possession of a house is a decisive factor in the living arrangements
of the old. In fact a survey in Nordrhein-Westfalia, West Germany's
most populous state, shows a marked difference in that 51 percent of
those who live in a house owned by the family are living with their
children, as against 34 percent of those who live in a rented house or

[1] Survey of the DIVO-Institute, 1958, probability sample, West German
population 65 years of age and over, 821 cases.

dwelling.[2] Taking personal visits as an index of the contact between parents and children, we find that more than half of the older persons who have surviving children but do not live with them in one household have frequent and regular contact with their children: 7 percent state that they see their children less than once a year, 18 percent see them at least once a year, and 20 percent at least once a month; however, 55 percent see their children at least once a week.

If we try to summarize the findings on living arrangements of older persons in West Germany we arrive at the following general statement: about 30 percent of persons 65 years of age and older are living with their children in one household; 25 percent are living nearby with frequent contacts, at least once a week; another 25 percent also maintain family relationships with their children but do not see them very often, in some cases only once a year or even less; 20 percent have no surviving children.

STATUS AND ROLE OF THE OLD IN THE FAMILY

There are two situations which may lead to a joint household of aged parents and their children. One is the older form in which the children do not leave the home at all. In the modern form of coresidence of young and old, they move and establish their own home and then invite the parents, mostly the widowed, to join the new household. In the first case the old person is the owner of the house or dwelling and head of the household; in the second, the young usually have the dominant positions.

In Germany the old form still prevails over the modern form. Sixty-five percent of older persons living with children designate themselves or their spouse as head of the household. Only 35 percent live in a household with the child or his spouse being the head. Even in some of these cases the young live in the home of the old: according to the traditional view of the dominance of the man, which still survives in this respect, the son or the son-in-law will be declared as the head of household if the young couple lives in the home of the aged mother.

Many of the younger couples living with their parents wish to move, but are forced to stay with the old because of the housing shortage and the high rent they would have to pay for a dwelling in one of the new housing projects. In view of the strong tendency toward separation of the young and the old, which can be observed increasingly not

[2] Survey of the DIVO Institute, 1959, probability sample, Nordrhein-Westfalia population 65 years of age and over, 1248 cases.

only in cities but in rural areas as well, it seems safe to conclude that the proportion of common households of younger and older generations will decline rapidly with decreasing housing shortage. Indicative are the findings of a representative survey of workers and employees in West Germany concerning their old age expectancies: 79 percent voiced the opinion that aged parents should not live with their grown-up children, only 11 percent answered in favor of living together, and 10 percent were undecided (Friedeburg and Weltz, 1958). With the young neither forced to join a household with their parents by an institutionalized code of conduct, which is already the case in Germany, nor compelled by such unusual conditions as a housing shortage, which will soon be the case, the decision about living together will be based increasingly on the dominating factors of modern family life, on affection and economic partnership. In former times one of the children and his spouse had to live with the old parents in order to take care of them, possibly with the common support of all the children, and this was done quite independently of the ability of an old person to fulfill certain roles in the family. Today, expectations of both the old and the young concerning the ability of an old person to fulfill certain roles and economic considerations will become more and more decisive in plans to invite the aged parents.

With regard to economic considerations, the position of older persons will be strengthened with the increasing amount of old age pensions. If they wish to be admitted to the younger couple's home, they can point out that they will not be a burden on the family budget but may even contribute to the family income. Ignoring the influence of affection, a very simple relationship can be observed between the income of the old parent and the desire of the children to have him in the home: that is the desire grows with the proportion of pension which exceeds the expected living costs of the old.

The changes in the family are affecting both the aging father and the aging mother, but apparently the older man so far has been affected more fundamentally. His position is weakened not only by changes in the social position of the young and the old in general, but also by the decline of the father's and grandfather's authority once exercised in the older family system. Often in present-day Germany the aged parents play an essential role in those families which are making strong efforts to gain or to regain a higher social status. The parents and grandparents jointly aim at the social advancement of the children, transferring their own personal hopes to their children. Economically, the grandmother plays the more important role as she is the one who runs the household and cares for the children, thus enabling the wife to seek gainful employment. The increasing occupational activities of married women in Germany seems to be one of the few factors which presently work against the further loosening of the ties between the aged parents and their middle-aged children.

SUMMARY

In Germany the distinct trend toward the smaller family has been accompanied by a steady decline in patriarchal sentiment and the emergence of new relationships between family members. Statistical data show the increasing tendency toward exclusion of aging parents from the families of their married children. The general development from the three-generation family of the patriarchal type to the two generation companionship type of family has proceeded least far in rural areas and has reached its strongest expression in metropolitan areas.

The intensified cohesion between family members of different generations, which was observed in some families during the years of the postwar period, did not bring about a return to the older family system. It proved to be a temporary adjustment and did not affect the long-run position of the old.

The changing role of the child, which is related to the decline in size and importance of inherited property, and the taking over of care for the aged by other institutions, lead to new relationships between aged parents and their middle-aged children. Many older persons still live with their children, but there is a trend toward a separation of the young and the old. Since the increase in occupational activities of married women is partly dependent on the role of the aged mother, this is a factor which works against the further separation of aged parents and the families of their children.

Acknowledgment. The author wishes to thank D. Erwin K. Scheuch of the Sociological Department of the University of Cologne for his helpful suggestions and advice.

REFERENCES

Baumert, G. 1952. Jugend der Nachkriegszeit. Darmstadt: E. Roether Verlag.
———— 1954. Deutsche Familien nach dem Kriege. Darmstadt: Roether Verlag.

Aging in Collective Settlements in Isr

dependence. Elderly and old people a
insecurity and isolation, the futile inact
tailed in aging.

Yet in spite of the many safeguards a
by no means a smooth process in the
level it is experienced as a difficult, sad
orientation. It engenders quite severe int
cannot be overcome without carefully pl
zation.[1]

Freedman, R., Baumert, G., and Bolte, M. 1959. Expected family size values in West Germany. Population Studies, No. 2, 13: 130–50.

Friedeburg, L. von, and Weltz, F. 1958. Altersbild und Altersvorsorge der Arbeiter und Angestellten, Frankfurt am Main: Europäische Verlagsanstalt.

König, R. 1957. Family and authority: the German father in 1955. Sociological Rev., 5: 107–27.

Schelsky, H. 1953. Wandlungen der deutschen Familie in der Gegenwart. 3d ed. Stuttgart: Ferdinand Enke Verlag.

Wurzbacher, G. 1958. Leitbilder deutschen Familienlebens. 3d ed. Stuttgart: Ferdinand Enke Verlag.

FOCI OF STRAIN
Position of the aged

The ambivalent position of old age in a
centered (Kluckhohn, 1953) society is on
strain entailed in aging in the collectives. 7
closely related to evaluation of tradition a
between present and past. The collectiv
revolutionary movement. The founders h
from Jewish traditional life and had rebell
their elders. Most members were trained
youth movements. The values and patter
these youth movements have had a decisive
communal life. The original revolutionary i
a formative personal experience of rebellio
youth as full of potentialities, free, and cre
continuity.

The appearance of the second generation
of emphasis from disruption of intergenera
As mentioned before, children are expected
founded by their parents, and to continue th
family of orientation is no longer considere
influence. The continuity of the collective
tional continuity. The second generation is c
responsibility of maintaining and developing
generation (Talmon-Garber, 1959b).

This new ideology of continuity is just be
is of only secondary importance, because the c

[1] This paper is based on a research project carri
sample of the collectives affiliated with one of the
collectives.

Aging in Collectiv

YONINA TALMON-GAR

THIS paper is an analysi
and planned society. T.
(Kvutzot or Kibbutzim)
for a few personal belongi
tion and consumption. N
munal institutions on an (
common treasury and eac
allowance for personal ex
economic unit and as a
independent jobs. Main n
In most collectives, child
looked after by members
hours every day with their
their birth they sleep, eat, a
age group leads its own lif(
settlement is governed by
vened once a week, by a se
collective is affiliated with (

The collectives have sol
problems of aging. Aging
Communal services care f(
Retirement from work is g
complete break from work
from community life. Soc
avenue of activity and pr(
many cases it compensates
competence and status in th
portant of all, grown-up c
munity founded by their pa
and constant relations witl

This paper is based on a pro
Sociology Department of the H

not rely only on natural increase but is constantly seeking reinforce-
ment from the youth movements. As long as the collectives continue
to recruit new members from external sources, they have to rely on the
appeal of a youth-centered ideology and continue to preach rebellion
and discontinuity. Since this youth-centered ideology predominates,
aging is held to be a process of steady decline, a gradual fall from
grace.

The central position accorded to work and the exceptionally high
evaluation of productivity lead in the same direction. The founders
of the collectives have undergone a process of voluntary deurbaniza-
tion and proletarization which reversed the traditional Jewish occupational prestige hierarchy. Retraining for hard physical labor and
settlement on the land were imperative for survival in the difficul
conditions of settlement. Strenuous work was a dire economic necessity, but it has become much more than that. It has been endowed
with deep meaning and dignity and invested with a quasi-religiou
seriousness. Labor has come to be regarded as a uniquely creativ
act, an important instrument for the realization of social and nationa
ideals as well as an ultimate value in itself. The idealized figure of
farmer-pioneer tilling the soil has become one of the main symbols c
personal redemption and of national revival. The high evaluation c
work is a core element in the collective system of values.

Emphasis on productivity

The importance attached to work and productivity is generall
accepted in all collectives. It has become a compelling drive. Absenc
from work even for a legitimate reason engenders a feeling of di
comfort and a sense of guilt. An individual who shirks his wor
responsibilities is severely criticized. The position of a lazy or incom
petent worker is very precarious, irrespective of his other accom
plishments and achievements. The position of any member in th
collective is determined primarily by his devotion to his work ar
the excellence of his performance. Those engaged in physical lab
in agriculture enjoy the most prestige.

With a gradual retirement from work aging members are not su
denly deprived of their major social function, but they do undergo
steady and cumulative decline of their occupational status. Inevitab
they lose their capacity for hard work and find it increasingly difficu
to excel in their tasks. They gradually become part-time worke
Eventually they are transferred to lighter tasks, either in the same fie
or in a less arduous nonagricultural occupation. If an aging memb

happens to hold a managerial position, he relinquishes it in due time. Most work branches require a full-time manager and cannot be run on a part-time basis. Many aging members lose their permanent jobs. They wander from one work assignment to another, doing odd jobs here and there.

As the productivity of aging members declines and they gradually cease to be self-supporting, they simultaneously become much more dependent on communal institutions and require more services. In spite of the fact that most of them have earned this upkeep through many years of hard and devoted work, they cannot accept it without misgivings. The constant emphasis on productivity and self-maintenance discourages any easy adjustment to growing dependence. Moreover, unlike dependence on a state pension or on an old age insurance scheme, dependence on the collective is not neutral and anonymous. The aging member sometimes experiences it as a direct personal dependence on his fellow members. No wonder then that many refuse to make use of their right to part-time work and continue to work full-time as long as they possibly can.

Another factor accentuates the disadvantage of this emphasis on productivity. The constantly changing rationalized and mechanized economy of the collectives puts a premium on up-to-date specialized training. Long experience gained during many years of practical work cannot, in many cases, compete with systematic training. Inasmuch as long experience engenders rigid adherence to fixed routines and hampers adjustment to new techniques, it becomes a liability. Elderly people are thus severely handicapped. Younger people are stronger and more flexible, often better trained, and more up-to-date. The fear of losing one's position in the occupational sphere is a major source of insecurity of aging members in the collective. It is the cause of much anxiety and discontent.

The pattern of full retirement at a fixed age entails the total loss of one's major social function, but it has one advantage over the pattern of gradual retirement (Friedmann and Havighurst, 1954). It constitutes a clear-cut break from the occupational sphere. Gradual retirement spares the worker the major crisis of total retirement but at the same time it subjects him to a series of difficult and recurring changes. It is a long, drawn-out process of continuous reorientation and readjustment.

into the family and does not disrupt its unity. Moreover, it is mainly within the family that both parents and children have intimate relations which are unpatterned by their position in the community, and it is here that they are free from routine duties. It is only in the family that they get love and care which they do not have to share with many others.

The gradual withdrawal from the occupational sphere enhances the importance of the family. Curtailment of outside activities brings about a concomitant decline in the number and intensity of outside contacts (Homans, 1950). Elderly members seek solace and emotional security in their relationships with their children. Grandchildren become a major preoccupation, especially with aging women.

Elderly people render their children many small but important services. Although children are looked after primarily by communal institutions, the need for aid is not abolished. Children come to their parents' flat after work hours. The parents look after them during the afternoon. They take them to the children's houses at night and put them to bed. Being very tired after a day's work they find it difficult to cope with their children without some rest. Parents who have a number of young children often find the afternoon noisy and hectic. Consequently, grandparents can be a great help. They take their grandchildren for walks and help with older children after the birth of a new baby. They take over the care of children when their parents go on vacation. Whenever either of the parents is absent from the collective attending refresher courses for specialized training or seminars of advanced studies, the grandparents compensate the children for the temporary separation. They help regularly, but do so especially during emergencies.

Grandparents' needs are provided for by communal institutions. But they, too, often need help, especially when they are incapacitated or very old. Children visit their parents regularly, participate in nursing during illness, and often help in attending to their small flats. They will bring in food from the communal kitchen to their parents' flats whenever the parents are unable or disinclined to eat in the communal dining hall. Again, it sometimes becomes necessary to carry the parents' clothes to and from the communal laundry. These small domestic and personal services grow very important when the parents are very old or permanently infirm. They are indispensable when there is only one widowed and very old parent left. As long as both parents are alive they can help each other. When one of them dies the remaining spouse needs more help and more company.

It should be stressed that the services that children render to their parents are on the whole not very irksome or time-consuming. The children perform only auxiliary functions. The old parents' primary needs are provided for by the collective. The parents retain, to the very last, a basic semi-independence. The children are not overburdened with the full support and care of aged relatives. They only supplement collective institutions. Their obligations and duties are limited and do not, in most cases, interfere too much with their normal life routines. The curtailment and limitation of obligations seems to reinforce rather than weaken the family relationship. In most cases it does not undermine the sense of responsibility toward old parents, since the children can help spontaneously and generously because they are not under too many obligations. The relationship is free of the feeling of resentment and sense of guilt engendered by too heavy responsibilities. Moreover, the ties between aging parents and children are firmly based on reciprocal services, on a constant give and take of small but significant and continuous services. During the first and middle stages of aging the services flow mainly from parents to children. Children are helped by their aging parents during these stages much more than they in turn can help. It is only during the last stages of aging that the direction of the main flow of services is reversed. The asymmetrical exchange is reversed at this stage in favor of the parents, but it seldom becomes completely one-sided. It is only in cases of persistent infirmity and in cases of an early onset of incontinence or senility that aged parents impose a severe strain on their families.

The importance of the interrelation between parents and children can be clearly demonstrated by examining the problems of aging of unmarried and childless members on the one hand, and of parents whose children have left the collective on the other hand. Needless to say, we do not find here the extreme isolation and bitter loneliness found elsewhere (Townsend, 1957). Old people remain full members of a cohesive community and continue to participate in its life. Their diminishing participation in the occupational sphere may be partly counterbalanced by enhanced participation in communal affairs. They are surrounded by friends and neighbors. Yet, in spite of all these benefits and substitute functions, most members who have no children living in the same collective feel very lonely and discouraged, especially if they have no other relatives in the collective.

Increasing age enhances the importance of geographical proximity and daily face-to-face contact (Litwak, 1960). Aging people find it increasingly difficult to get about and visit their relatives who live elsewhere. They need daily care and company. Periodic visits by

very often find it difficult to get used to its way of life. But as they do not set their hopes too high, they are quite satisfied. They are able to enjoy many of the amenities of aging in the collective without suffering from concomitant strains. Many of them describe old age in the collective in glowing terms. By contrast, aging members are much more aware of the disadvantages. Their praise of the collective is very guarded and qualified, and they will always point out the need for further planning and reorganization.

REDEFINITION OF POLICY

The increasing number of aging members in long-established collectives has slowly brought about a growing awareness of the problems of aging. The collective movement is now beginning to develop supplementary institutional mechanisms which cope, to some extent, with the inherent difficulties of aging in the collectives. Some of these mechanisms develop as spontaneous adaptations to a changing situation. Some of them evolve as indirect and unintended consequences of planning in other fields. In addition there crop up proposals and definite plans which deal directly with the rights and duties of aging members.

As indicated in the analysis above, tension mostly develops in the occupational sphere. Consequently reorganization efforts are directed mainly toward a careful reassessment of the policy of gradual retirement.

The main issues are concerned with: (1) norms of retirement, (2) systematic increase of suitable employment opportunities, and (3) training and retraining programs.

Norms of retirement

This involves the establishment of norms with regard to age of retirement and progressive reduction of work hours. These norms aim at abolishing the present situation in which each collective deals with the problem of retirement in its own way. Since there are no clear standards, individual variation is the rule in any given collective. The rights and duties being undefined, aging members are hesitant to apply for partial retirement even when they need it badly. The proposed norms now put up for ratification in the federation fix more definite and uniform standards, without aiming at complete uniformity. The individual collective is to be allowed some variation within the accepted framework, with a view to its special conditions and the special needs of each of its aging members.

Systematic increase of suitable employment opportunities

Reorganization of existing work branches. The federation has engaged a research institute to undertake a thorough job analysis in all its work branches. This research scheme sets out to identify required skills, knowledge, and abilities entailed in each job and to sort out the jobs that, after certain modifications, can be successfully filled by aging members. An increase of possibilities for employment and a considerable improvement of the position of aging members can be achieved by dividing some of the work branches into subunits and entrusting elderly workers with responsibility in some of these semi-independent units. Aging members resent being gradually deprived of initiative and authority and find it difficult to work under the supervision of a much younger worker. The discrepancy between distribution of age and distribution of authority and the differences of opinion concerning work methods engender disagreement and disputes. The pattern of subdivision gives elderly workers some responsibility and independence. The partial segregation of elderly and young workers restricts the areas of potential conflicts. Not all branches are amenable to such a subdivision but many efforts are made to give the aging workers as much independence as possible. Quite a number of old members work on their own. Bedridden and house-bound members get outside work which they can perform whenever they feel like it. Placement of aging members is slowly becoming more selective and personal.

Development of new work branches. Many collectives have developed light industries. This has widened the possible employment opportunities of old people.

Reemployment in jobs outside the community. The occupational opportunities of aging members are not restricted to jobs available in the collective. Quite a number of aging members find suitable employment in local and countrywide organizations. They come home every day or every weekend. They spend part of their salary on their personal needs, but a large part of it goes to the collective.

The collective movement has lately developed a system whereby each established collective adopts a new one and sends a number of its members as social and agricultural instructors. Quite a number of elderly members volunteer for this job. The period of service in a young collective gives them a new lease on life. The young and in-

The other attempt to solve the collective's problems involved the development of suitable old age institutions for cases of severe mental and physical deterioration. The collectives turn to the institutional solution mainly in cases of complete loss of self-care ability which cannot be taken care of within the framework of the community.

The collective movement is now seriously considering the development of an intercollective old age insurance scheme which will pay each member a regular pension on retirement. The pensions are to go to the collective and contribute toward the maintenance of aging members. The scheme will enable retired workers to continue to be at least partially self-supporting and will enhance their feeling of security and independence. It is hoped that the collectives will be able to put aside part of the money obtained through this scheme and use it for development of comprehensive old age services.

Underlying the institutional reorganization is an ideological reorientation. There is a growing awareness that the basic difficulties inherent in aging in the collectives are directly related to the overemphasis on youth, on work, and on productivity. There are some signs of the emergence of a more balanced, more flexible, and developmental view of life.

Acknowledgments. Mrs. R. Bar-Joseph took an active part in the initial planning. Mr. A. Etzioni assisted me in direction of the project in its first stage. The other main research assistants were: Mr. E. Ron, Mr. M. Sarell, and Mr. J. Sheffer. Mr. M. Sarell and Mr. E. Cohen took over from Mr. Etzioni in the second stage. The main research assistants were Mr. U. Avner, Miss B. Bonne, Mr. U. Hurwitz, and Miss Z. Stup. Special thanks are due to Mrs. R. Gutman-Shaki who assisted me in preparing this paper for publication. I wish to thank Mr. E. Cohen for his comments. Our sincere gratitude is due to Professor R. Baki and Dr. R. Gabriel for their advice on statistical problems.

REFERENCES

Friedman, E. A., and Havighurst, R. J. 1954. The meaning of work and retirement. Chicago: University of Chicago Press.

Gluckman, M. 1956. Custom and conflict in Africa. Glencoe, Ill.: Free Press.

Homans, G. C. 1950. The human group. New York: Harcourt, Brace and Co.

Kluckhohn, Florence R. 1953. Dominant and variant value orientations.

In C. Kluckhohn, H. A. Murray, and D. M. Schneider (eds.), Personality, pp. 342–57. New York: Alfred A. Knopf.

Litwak, E. 1960. Occupational mobility and family cohesion. Am Sociological Rev., 25: 385–94.

Talmon-Garber, Yonina. 1956. The family in collective settlements. *In* Transactions of the Third World Congress of Sociology, Vol. *4.,* pp. 116–26. London: International Sociological Association.

—— 1959*a*. Sex-role differentiation in an equalitarian society. The author. (Mimeographed.)

—— 1959*b*. Social structure and family size. Human Relations, 12: 121–46.

Townsend, P. 1957. The family life of old people. Glencoe, Ill.: Free Press.

Aging in Underdeveloped Asian Countries

P. M. YAP

THE populations of underdeveloped countries are typically "youthful." Different measures can be employed to measure population "agedness," but the most usual one is to estimate the proportionate size of the group aged 60 and over. The most important factor in population aging is a decline in fertility or birth rates (United Nations, 1954). If this decline is permanent and a low level maintained, the population ages totally, i.e., the aged group is proportionately increased in the total population, whichever measure of aging is utilized. It takes about a century for the population to stabilize itself with a more aged structure. A temporary decline in fertility leads only to partial aging (aging only according to some measures), and some decades later partial rejuvenation takes place.

In contrast to fertility, a decline in mortality has only a slight effect on population structure, and, moreover, this may take the direction of either partial aging or rejuvenation. This aspect of the subject is important in view of the notable strides being made in reduction of mortality in many underdeveloped countries by the application of medical science. In Ceylon, for example, the death rate dropped from 20.3 in 1946 to 14.3 in 1947, and in 1953 it dropped further to 10.9, largely because of the use of DDT in antimalarial work after the war (Huyck, 1954). In Hong Kong the rate fell from 8.5 in 1954 to 7.1 in 1959 (Hong Kong Government, 1959). While the West has brought about a decrease in mortality mostly in infants rather than the aged, different social values may cause Asian countries to show some other pattern of decrease. The possibility exists that unlike the West, where mortality is already quite low, underdeveloped countries with further reduction of their high mortality may even find their populations partially rejuvenating.

Thus it is the spread of Malthusianism rather than the application of modern medicine, a fall in fertility rather than a decline in mortality, that will in the long run add to the burden of aged dependency in underdeveloped countries (if we ignore for the present purpose the factor of transmigration of people). It is a decline in fertility that is of essential importance: "In those parts of the world where birthrates have hitherto remained at a high level, no appreciable aging is to be expected, irrespective of the extent or rapidity of the decline in death rates. Marked aging can occur only after the onset of a decline in fertility. For most parts of the world, the emergence of such a trend cannot yet be foreseen." (United Nations, 1954.) A country may, of course, develop in the direction of having a greater percentage of both the young and old at the same time (as in the United States). The absolute increase in the number of aged must always be a serious problem for poor countries; aging does not have to be "marked" and total to make the old a special burden for peoples subjected to rapid culture change, along with breakdown of the extended family and urbanization with all its implications.

The question of fertility is so important that it deserves more detailed examination in the light of prevailing social and cultural values. Skinner (1956) has devoted considerable attention to this, and discusses various cultural elements that tend to increase or decrease fertility (and therefore in the long run influence population aging).

In cultures where there is a decided preference for children of one sex, this preference has the effect of increasing the birth rate; a family with three daughters in a row, for example, will still endeavor to have another child hoping it will be a boy, if boys are greatly desired. Chinese culture, as well as others historically influenced by it, gives much prestige to women who have borne children, so that motherhood is prized. A high marriage rate also increases fertility, and in agricultural societies there are so few alternative roles for women outside that of a spouse that most marry. A very few may become nuns, but in Buddhist society these have little social prestige. The same applies to monks, although in Japan and Korea they do not remain celibate and in Thailand and Burma they may at some time or other return to secular life. In Chinese culture, monks are celibate but they are given little social approval, so few are attracted to monkhood on a voluntary basis. Widow remarriage is no problem in Moslem and Christian cultures, but among the Chinese it is disapproved of; however, such marriages do take place among persons of lower social class especially when the woman is young, has not borne children, or is poor. Most cultures know about contraception but the methods employed are seldom efficacious. In premodern Japan abortion and infanticide were traditionally enjoined upon the samurai to keep up their standard of living; in China these were resorted to as a rule only in extreme circumstances of poverty occasioned by natural disasters. The practice of contraception along modern lines, of course, depends for its success on the attainment of a minimal level of income and education. It is also to be noted that the expectation of life is influenced by social organization and customs: where there is widespread poverty, strong intralineage obligation to help stricken relatives, and the custom of adoption, may permit survival of children who otherwise might die.

Other customs and practices serve to decrease fertility and hasten population aging. Almost all Asian societies enforce premarital chastity, and this without at the same time lowering the age of marriage. This shortens the age span for childbearing. The practice of concubinage is a common minority pattern and provided young adult women in the population do not outnumber men (as in Chinese communities), provided men take concubines only when they are themselves aged, and provided they do not go away to leave them behind, concubinage will lower the birth rate. There is, however, the possibility that births and the number of the young may in certain circumstances be increased because the number of spinsters is reduced and the children of concubines taken into rich homes have a better chance of survival. Chao (1940) after examining this question concluded that in China (traditional) concubinage, associated with widespread prostitution, probably had the effect of lowering fertility. Where divorce is relatively easy, as in Moslem lands, and in China where divorce by mutual consent is allowed, the result will be an increase in fertility, although the factor of family instability may reverse this effect. A rise in the status of women allows more widows and divorcees to remarry and this may temporarily raise the birth rate; but it is probable that in the long run the rate will fall with women being able to initiate and insist on family limitation. This matter is complex, for other factors are involved also. Thus sex equality will not encourage further childbearing if, for example, a family has already three girls and there is no compelling desire to have a boy. On the other hand it will allow more girls to survive to childbearing age by inducing parents to give them more care and attention.

URBANIZATION AND OVERURBANIZATION

The complex process of urbanization has multiple facets, each with relevance for inquiries into population change as well as the mental health of the old. In south and southeast Asia, apart from

Singapore and Hong Kong which are virtually city-states, the percentage of the total population living in urban areas (areas with more than 20,000 people gathered therein) only averages just over 10 percent. Malaya, for geographical as well as historical reasons, has 22 percent, but this is still well below that for industrialized Western countries. The increase in urban populations is, however, proceeding rapidly, and we find, for example, that in India as well as Malaya the percentage has nearly tripled over the past half a century or so (Smith, 1960).

In the past there have of course been large concentrations of population in Asian cities. But contemporary urbanization in Asia is characterized by the adoption of the individualistic values of industrialized Western culture, of the factory system, and of modern international commerce, the whole process being compressed into a very short span of time compared with the many decades of Western evolution. The change has been rapid, on the one hand because of rural distress causing many to migrate to the towns, and, on the other, the attraction of powerful economic forces generated by a wage economy based on manufacturing and overseas trade closely integrated with that of a highly industrialized West. Many consider that underdeveloped countries are overurbanized, the population in cities being too large in relation to the degree of economic development of the country as a whole and to their small nonagricultural labor force. The cities then do not fulfill their function of facilitating the progress of the country by raising productive efficiency. The result is that migrants from the countryside stream steadily into the cities, lose touch with their kin, are thrown onto the labor market and are at the mercy of economic pressures that they cannot understand. Above all, they are desperately in need of elementary housing.

It is true that urbanization has not progressed to the same extent in different countries. If we take the proportion of wage earners in the whole working population of all countries in south and southeast Asia, only Singapore shows as high a percentage as 75 percent (Smith, 1960). In Hong Kong it is 78 percent (Maunder and Szczepanik, 1957). Proportions of this size approach those of developed Western countries. But in other countries there are far fewer persons dependent on wages, and many more of them are self-employed or run small family businesses of the handicraft kind, or are in the sphere of trading and distribution. To the extent that this is so, much of the unhappy effect of an individualistic, impersonal, mechanized, and standardized industrial ethos can be avoided. Yet it is a matter of common ob-

reverence are centered in the ancestral hall, which is the focus of mutual help within the clan. Traditionally, after ritual ceremonies the food from the communion feast is distributed, and clan members over 60 receive a larger portion.

To varying degrees the above pattern of familism is breaking down with increasing agnosticism, secularization, and social mobility. But familism has been so dominant in Chinese culture that it has served as the model for other social institutions standing apart from the clan and family.

Familistic patterns of organization and the welfare of the aged

Of considerable importance for the welfare of aged persons outside the clan are the ancient institutions known as the vegetarian halls (*Chai T'ang*) which are found not only in Hong Kong and Taiwan but also among overseas Chinese in southeast Asia. They are residential places of worship with traditions derived from the Chen (Zen) sect of Chinese Buddhism or from a syncretic salvationist religion called the Hsien Tien Ta Tao. The most complete study of these was that by Topley (1958). They arose as a result of lay demands for the opportunity to practice self-cultivation. In return for contributions which vary according to age, or for labor offered, these halls receive persons who are usually of the older age groups. These men (and women) undertake to keep to a vegetarian diet, abstain from sex, and in return are given food and lodging. They engage in corporate worship and the more adept practice meditation or other similar exercises. When a member dies his or her burial is provided by the hall and fellow members form the body of mourners. After death the soul tablet is kept in the hall, and is tended ritually by surviving members.

These institutions are significant since they provide a substitute family for their members, and with this, roles and statuses that are to be found only within the social complex of patriarchalism and filial piety. Aged members thereby receive help, fellowship, and honor, and, since they are usually given work within their limitations even if it is only tending the altars, they retain their self-respect. Members are given generation names according to the lineage system and they trace their own lineage from a line of ancestors going back to a historical "master," the soul tablets of all these persons being kept in the hall itself. In everyday life the members address each other in kinship terms borrowed from the family. Interestingly enough, when a woman is head of a hall (confined to the female sex), she is addressed by her "family" in terms appropriate for a male patriarch.

Most of these halls cater to women who are spinsters, widows without children, or divorcees; for in the traditional society there was no secure place for them—they were in the "penumbra" to use Hsu's term. In south China and among the overseas Chinese in southeast Asia, there is a special group of women from the Shun Tak area of Kwangtung Province who, partly for economic reasons, have entered into sworn sisterhoods to remain unmarried; as a rule these women join the halls as they approach old age. Female halls are more common than male because of the vulnerability of women in traditional Chinese society. Many of the halls are attached to nunneries and monasteries and there is an intimate association between the inmates of the halls and the professional clergy of the latter. From time immemorial monks and nuns have been drawn largely from among persons who, because of poverty, death, or psychological complications, have become alienated and dislodged from their families. It is held that a religious or quasi-religious life is especially well suited to women of later age who have never married, since they are virgins.

While most vegetarian halls are organized along particularist lines, drawing their members from the same part of China or sometimes from the same lineage, there are other institutions providing for the welfare of the old (as well as the not so old) that are not particularist. Such, for example, is the long life association (*Jen Shou Hui*) which, among other things, provides for the recreational and religious activities of its members, burial rituals, establishment of soul tablets in temples which they may own, and death benefits. Especially for the older generation still attached to ancestral reverence, they are clearly a source of psychological security. Generally speaking, a certain amount of welfare work for those of declining years in the cities is performed by neighborhood associations (*Chieh Fang Hui*), and some guilds and lodges associated with particular trades or vocations (clan associations are an interesting outgrowth of the ancestral temple into the cities, although their functions in the process have become much broadened).

Institutions such as these have existed for centuries and they provide a welfare system outside the family group with little or no aid from the state. The comprehensive nature of the sustenance given by the vegetarian halls, economic, social, and spiritual, is especially notable. In Hong Kong a survey of the six existing old age homes run by private bodies and two infirmaries partly subsidized by the government shows that there are not more than about 1200 aged persons under care. This does not mean that the aged present a small problem of dependency, but undoubtedly there would be more destitution than at present exists were it not for the vegetarian halls. One of these indeed appears on the lists of the Hong Kong Council of Social Service as a home for the aged. However, many of these halls have financial difficulties. Topley (1958) also reports this in the case of the halls which she studied in Singapore. No doubt they will gradually be drawn into the nexus of "modern" social welfare organizations. The question is whether in the long run they can retain their original form.

Clearly, the same processes that accentuate the problem of dependency in the aged also tend to weaken these institutions. The spread of education, the possibilities of economic independence for women in cities, and the rise of the agnostic spirit are all inimical to their continued existence. And yet the vegetarian halls provide such a complete and sensible solution to the problem of isolated old folk that it would be an error for modern lay or governmental welfare agencies to ignore the contributions that, with modifications, they may continue to make.

Traditional forms of adoption

We have seen how the ideology of familism, by emphasizing the high status of the patriarch and buttressing itself with the quasi-religious practice of ancestral reverence, has enhanced the welfare of the old. Not only has the family served as the model for social organization, but customs of adoption have been evolved which, while serving the demands of ancestor reverence, have also the effect of ensuring the security of the old. A man without a son to perform the rites of reverence after he is dead may adopt one who is his nephew from the same lineage, so that boys and girls may become the adopted children of parents not related to them in any way (*chi* adoption). Many Cantonese spinsters, or women otherwise sworn to spinsterhood, adopt in this way young girls whom they try to indoctrinate against marriage so that they may be looked after by these girls in their declining years. The adopted child has certain economic and ritual obligations toward the support of the adopted parent, but sometimes adoption takes place without any economic motives involved, e.g., for sentimental reasons, or perhaps superstitious reasons based on belief in horoscopes.

Again we see that there are widespread customs that help to recreate the familistic pattern of relationships even when biological, social, or chance factors operate to prevent the continuation of the family or hinder its full growth. While spinsterhood declines and superstition weakens, there will for a long time be many in the penumbra of Chinese familism who will turn to adoption, in anticipation of their old age.

Attitudes toward death

Little attention has been given to the psychological significance of attitudes toward death in present-day discussions of the mental hygiene of the senium. This curious oversight needs to be corrected when we take a cross-cultural perspective, although none will deny the intricacy of this topic. In Asian societies where a secular orientation is as yet not prominent, philosophies of death and the afterlife couched in religious terms have more meaning and are taken more seriously than in the largely agnostic West. Most Chinese derive a strong sense of the continuity of family life from the ideology of ancestor reverence, which links the living and the dead; some who are Buddhists also believe in reincarnation on this earth; and both the less intellectual forms of Chinese Buddhism as well as of Taoism tell of a paradise. The traditional Chinese attitude toward death has been, and is, remarkably different from the Western. On approaching old age men will buy themselves coffins and funeral clothing and prepare their graves; after their husbands' death women will do the same. After the funeral the family will join together at a feast, even Christian Chinese retaining this custom. Death is regarded as opening the door to another life and is faced without fear if the man's responsibilities to his family have been discharged. This does not mean that longevity is not sought, and indeed many educated people in middle and later life engage in what Weber terms "macrobiotic" exercise and meditation, derived from Taoism and Zen Buddhism. It remains to be seen how much of this will be retained with intellectual currents flowing so strongly from the West.

PROSPECTS

The economic, social, and cultural changes that now affect so many peoples in Asia are all part of a composite historical process that is not easily disentangled. In so far as it is founded on industrialization and urbanization as a reaction away from age-old poverty, it need not be regretted. Many of the social and economic consequences that have resulted from similar changes in the West will be repeated, and the implications of these for mental health in old age will be the same. However, we must not forget that cultural traditions do diverge, and that underdeveloped Asian countries are not simply to be put alongside the premodern West. In Europe, for example, there has for centuries been a tradition of monogamy with more or less stable family organization, whereas this would be a new development in many parts of Asia. On the other hand, the broad traditions of India and China have long given high status to the aged, whereas in medieval Europe the old were given less regard, perhaps even less than today, if we can draw any conclusions from the persecution of old women as witches so graphically described by Archbishop Harsnett and the lawyer Roger North (Burstein, 1949). We have to guard ourselves against making false analogies. Undoubtedly contemporary social change has increased mental ill-health in ways already familiar against a Western background (if we may take our Hong Kong findings as representative); but it is a matter for conjecture whether or not the same course will be followed as in the West, because the tenacity, influence, and fate of ideological patterns are difficult to judge.

There is, finally, the question of national wealth. It is probable that many underdeveloped and overpopulated Asian countries have a lower national income than Western countries in the past at comparables stages of industrialization. If poor health in old age is directly related to poverty, then this factor must be clearly discerned, and we must avoid the tendency to regard old people as socially and psychologically incapable and maladjusted when in fact they are merely submerged in poverty. It will be important for practical purposes to confront this question.

REFERENCES

Burstein, S. R. 1949. Aspects of the psychopathology of old age: revealed in witchcraft cases of the sixteenth and seventeenth centuries. Brit. Med. Bull., 6: 63–71.

Chao Ching-hsin. 1940. Familism as a factor in the Chinese population balance. The Yenching J. of Soc. Studies, 3: 1–21.

Durand, J. D. 1953. Population structure as a factor in manpower and dependency problems of underdeveloped countries. Pop. Bull. of U.N., December, 1–16.

Fei Hsiao-tung. 1939. Peasant life in China. New York: E. P. Dutton and Co.

Hong Kong Government. 1959. Annual report. Hong Kong: Government Printer.

Hsu, F. L. K. 1949. Under the ancestors' shadow. London: Routledge & Kegan Paul, Ltd.

Huyck, L. 1954. Differential fertility in Ceylon. Pop. Bull. of U.N., December, 21–29.

Lang, O. 1946. Chinese family and society. New Haven: Yale University Press.

Levy, M. J., Jr. 1949. The family revolution in modern China. Cambridge: Harvard University Press.

Lin, T. Y. 1960. Reality and vision. Manila: Bureau of Printing.

Maunder, W. F., and Szczepanik, E. F. 1957. Hong Kong housing survey, 1957. Hong Kong: University of Hong Kong. (Mimeographed.)

Skinner, G. W. 1956. Cultural values, social structure, and population growth. Pop. Bull. of U.N., July, 5–12.

Smith, T. E. 1960. Population characteristics in South and Southeast Asia. *In* Men and women in southeast Asia. Paris: UNESCO.

Topley, M. D. 1958. The organization and social function of Chinese women's Chai T'ang in Singapore. (Unpublished Ph.D. dissertation.) London: University of London.

United Nations, Population Division. 1954. The cause of the ageing of populations: declining mortality or declining fertility? Pop. Bull. of U.N., December, 30–38.

Changing Family Relationships of Older People in Japan during the Last Fifty Years

YUZURU OKADA

FOR a long time in Japan the most important factor which determined family relationships was the members' role in maintaining the family property and carrying out the family occupation.

The Japanese family has long been regarded as an element of a solid kinship organization, rather than as an independent group which directly contributes to making up a large society. The Japanese kinship group is composed of a main family and its branch families which are connected with one another by patrilineal kinship. In the simplest case, the main faimly is the family which is succeeded to by the eldest son. Branch families are those which are established by the second and third sons. Japanese sociologists call such a patrilineal kinship group by a general name, *Dōzoku,* although it is given various names according to districts.

Families composing a kinship group help each other. The main family is regarded as a protector of its branch families and is expected to help them out of their social and economic difficulties. The branch families are expected, in turn, to serve their main family; for instance, they should assist the main family with weddings, funerals, and farming.

One of the reasons why the kinship organization has long been maintained among the Japanese people is that it has functioned well as a kind of social security system for its members, while state or community systems were weak and insufficient.

The family as well as the kinship group strives to exist beyond its members' existence. The continued existence of a family is guaranteed by its unbroken succession of male descendants (real or adopted). This succession consists of the inheritance of family property, succession of patriarchate, and maintenance of family occupation and family traditions (customs, religion, etc.).

STATUS OF OLDER PEOPLE

The duty of the patriarch, head of the family, is to maintain and increase the family property, to maintain and develop the family occupation, and to train his successor for patriarchate. As long as he fulfills this duty, he holds high status and prestige in his family.

The head of the family finds some difficulty in performing his duty as he becomes old. He hands over the patriarchate to his eldest son by the so-called institution of retirement from headship (*Inkyo*). After the retirement he and his wife usually live with their eldest son's family as advisers. Sometimes in farming villages they move out of the eldest son's house to establish a branch family with their second son. In each case they have latent power as advisers whose opinions are asked by the new head of the family whenever he must make a decision about family matters. Housekeeping is carried out by the wife of the family head and this role is symbolized by the keeping of a large wooden spoon for distribution of rice. The transfer of her role to the wife of her eldest son is also symbolized by the handing over of the wooden spoon. Scarcely any decision about housekeeping is made by the new housewife without consulting her predecessor.

Thus the older people's status in the family is high as long as the family property and family occupation are controlled by them. The most usual family occupation in Japan is farming and the percentage of farming population from among the total working population was 58.2 in 1900, 52.2 in 1920, and 41.7 in 1955. This means that many people are engaged in their family occupations.

MEANS OF MAINTAINING TRADITION

Even if there is no family occupation which unites the members, the family is for most people an everlasting group beyond individual member's existence. Such a family keeps its own tradition, the continuance of which is the concern of the head of the family. The head of the family controls and trains other family members so that this tradition continues smoothly through generations.

There are two most effective means of assuring the continued existence of the family and its tradition. One is to live with and train the eldest son, the successor, even after the latter's marriage. The other when there is no son to succeed the head of the family, is to adopt a man and have him marry one of the daughters.

The first case is generally expressed in statistics as the existence of three-generation households. Professor Toda shows in his study of the Japanese family, based on the census of 1920, that 29.6 percent of Japanese families (households) include three generations in each family. This is 70 percent of the families which might be expected to maintain three generations according to estimates based on the Japanese people's age of first marriage, birth rate, and length of life. This means that the tendency to observe the tradition of family concern and lineage respect was comparatively strong in 1920, in spite of the individualization of occupation brought about by the rapid industrialization since 1868.

The family tradition is also continued through the married-in, adopted son. If there is no son in the family, it is necessary to adopt a man who marries a daughter of the family. He is usually the second or third son of another family who could not afford to start a branch family. After marriage he moves to the home of his wife's family and works for them, changing his family name to hers.

The status of a married-in, adopted son in a family is usually very low. His opinion is not expressed to the parents directly, but through his wife. The parents scarcely ask his consent. He is not allowed to represent the family in making contracts with others while the father is alive. He has no right to the family property. The ownership of the family property is handed over from father to grandson, passing over the married-in, adopted son who is the father of this grandson.

CHANGES IN FAMILY RELATIONSHIPS

However, family development in the direction of modernization, especially since World War II, was given impetus by the reform of the civil code in 1948. Even in the farming villages, because of increased occupational mobility and mechanization of agriculture, family relationships are becoming more favorable to the younger generation.

Several families from a farming village in southwestern Japan, which were studied intensively by the author in connection with the mechanization of agriculture there, have been selected to show the character of and changes in the family relationships of older people.

Of 24 families (households) of the village, 16 include 1 or more old persons over 60 years of age and all but 1 are three-generation families. In 9 of the 16 above-mentioned families, the status of older people has been almost unchanged. In 6 families older persons have been losing their authority over the younger ones.

The families in which older people are enjoying high status can be divided into two types: those in which old persons are male and either are maintaining or have retired from the headship, and those in which old persons are the widows of the previous heads of the family.

If the old person is male, he controls other members in farming, in spending money, in choosing mates, and in all other spheres of life. There were 34 marriages in this village whose method of arrangement is known. Twenty of these were arranged by parents, particularly by fathers, 7 were arranged by go-betweens, 2 were unions between relatives, and only 4 were love matches.

A family head is concerned about the marriage of his heir because the prosperity of his family occupation, farming, depends on the ability and character of the heir's mate. Her loyalty to the husband's parents is regarded as very necessary for the latter's comfortable old age.

Rigid control by a family head over other members is illustrated by the following: the father, head of the family, controls every activity of his wife, son, and son's wife; holds the purse of the family; decides the schedule of farming and the selling of products of the farm; and even keeps the entire salary earned by his son who works at a rice mill in a neighboring town.

When the old person is the widow of the former family head, she continues to carry out the housekeeping without leaving any power to her son's wife. She also has much authority, through influence over her son, in the disposal of property and in the farming. If she has no grandson, but only a granddaughter, who will succeed the father with her married-in husband, the decision power on domestic matters passes from the grandmother to the granddaughter, passing over the mother. The mother and the husband of the granddaughter are powerless and have lower status.

In a family of this village, a 79-year-old widow lives with her son's family. Even when her husband was alive she had great power and, since her son is a good natured man, she has decided everything, neglecting him and his wife. In her old age she is handing over the decision power, not to her son's wife, but to her granddaughter who has had two children by her married-in husband. He is powerless, even though the household is much dependent on his outside day-labor wages.

Various reasons can be given for the older persons' loss of authority to the younger ones, but the chief cause is the mechanization of agriculture.

In one family, until recently, the 67-year-old father and the 66-year-old mother regulated the farming and controlled domestic matters, .

while the 41-year-old daughter and her 44-year-old husband followed their parents' directions. For instance, the father led an ox attached to a plow and assigned supplementary work to others. This means that the father was the leader with regard to farming. But after the introduction of a cultivating machine, the father had to withdraw from the essential part of farming because he did not know how to handle machines. The daughter's husband took the father's place in farming and the daughter now helps him as an assistant; thus the decision power is moving from the older couple to the younger couple, although not smoothly. Tensions have arisen between the two couples.

In another family the 66-year-old father has little voice on property because he is the married-in husband of a daughter born to the family and all the more powerless since the late former head of the family gave the family property to two grandsons (sons of the married-in husband), passing over their father. The 62-year-old mother is controlling all domestic matters. The 40-year-old son is a central figure of this family, not only because he is a full-fledged successor to headship, but also because he learned to use farm machinery and has expanded the farming to include greenhouse fruit culture.

A third family is becoming more dependent on the wages of the 33-year-old son who works at the National Railway Corporation, rather than on the farm income earned by the 65-year-old father. Another reason for the shift of authority to the son is that he is able to participate in cultivation which can be completed by machine on Sunday when he is free from his job.

In a fourth family, the 78-year-old father was for a long time a tyrant who decided everything without consulting his second wife (66 years old) and son-in-law (husband of his daughter). His daughter controlled the housekeeping. The daughter's husband had no voice in farming because he had been a teacher at an elementary school. Mechanization made it possible for him to farm and he became the representative of his family at an association set up to install mechanization. This helped him and his wife to get power. The father is withdrawing from the leading position and the younger couple is taking his place.

In a fifth family, the older couple, 65 and 56 years old, returned home from town after the war, so that they have no experience in farming. The farming has been carried out solely by their eldest son who is 32 years old; he has the decision power in farming. Housekeeping is controlled by the 56-year-old mother.

Living Arrangements of Older People in the United States

ETHEL SHANAS

OLDER people in the United States now tend to form their own households apart from those of their adult children. This development is a result of many factors, among which are increased urbanization, increased national mobility, and, most important, cultural values which stress independent living for the older person as long as is possible, and independent living for adult children as they mature and marry (Sheldon, 1958). Despite popular beliefs to the contrary, the fact that most older people in the United States live apart from their children does not mean that most older people in this country are isolated from their children. Indeed, findings from a national survey indicate that in the United States most older people with living children are in close physical proximity to at least one child and see him often.

The data which will be reported here are from a broad study of the health needs of older people made by the National Opinion Research Center of the University of Chicago under a grant from the Health Information Foundation. Interviews with a nationwide representative sample of persons aged 65 and older living outside of institutions were conducted in the spring of 1957. The sample design used was comparable to that employed by the United States Census Bureau. In this design every older person living outside of an institution had an equal chance of being located and interviewed. The general characteristics of the sample have been reported elsewhere (Shanas, 1959).[1] In Table 1 comparisons are made between some typical living arrangements of older persons in the general population as found in the National Opinion Research Center sample and the estimates of the Census Bureau for the same arrangements. As may be seen in Table 1, the simple

[1] James S. Coleman, formerly of the National Opinion Research Center and the Department of Sociology, University of Chicago, was responsible for the sample design. Dr. Coleman is now at Johns Hopkins University.

Table 1. Comparison of selected living arrangements of all persons aged 65 and over, U.S. Census and National Opinion Research Center Survey, 1957, percentage distribution

Characteristics	U.S. Census	National Opinion Research Center
Relatives present	77.2[a]	74.7
Parent or head of household	16.0[b]	11.2
Other	5.6[b]	6.1
No relatives present	22.8[a]	25.3
Married couple in own household	48.9[c]	51.8
Other in own household	27.8[c]	30.6

[a] Source: U.S. Bureau of the Census, "Marital Status and Family Status: March, 1956," *Current Population Reports,* Series P-20, No. 72, Government Printing Office, Washington, D.C. Computed from Table 5. The institutional population has been excluded from the population base.

[b] Source: These are 1950 data, therefore, the degree of agreement with the 1957 National Opinion Research Center sample might be expected to be less than that found in the 1956 comparisons. Computed from Henry D. Sheldon, *The Older Population of the United States,* John Wiley & Sons, Inc., 1958, Table E-3. The institutional population has been excluded from the population base.

[c] Source: Computed from Table 6 of work cited in footnote a. The institutional population has been excluded from the population base.

data for living arrangements are in good agreement with the independent Census Bureau estimates for 1956.

Table 2 reports the living arrangements of all older persons in the United States in 1957 and the living arrangements of those older persons who had living children. From Table 2 it can be seen that among all older people in the United States living outside of institutions, 2 of every 10 lived alone, 1 of every 10 was single or widowed and lived in a household with persons who were not his children, about 4 of every 10 were part of a married couple living alone, and about 3 of every 10 lived in a household with their children. Less than half of all older persons who lived with their children were married; the remainder were widowed or divorced. In numerical approximation, of the roughly 14,250,000 noninstitutionalized older people in 1957, 2,864,250 lived alone, 1,596,000 were single or widowed and lived in a household with persons who were not their children, 5,742,750 were part of a married couple living alone or with persons who were not their children, and 4,018,500 lived in a household with their children.

The living arrangements of aged men differed greatly from those of aged women. Women outlive men; they are much more likely to be widows than men are to be widowers. About 7 of every 10 older men were married and living with their wives; less than 4 of every 10 older women were married and living with their husbands. As a result,

Table 2. *Living arrangements of all persons aged 65 and over, and of persons aged 65 and over who report living children or no living children, percentage distribution*[a,b]

Living arrangements	ALL PERSONS			PERSONS WITH LIVING CHILDREN			PERSONS WITH NO LIVING CHILDREN		
	Total (N=1734)	Men (N=801)	Women (N=933)	Total (N=1350)	Men (N=637)	Women (N=713)	Total (N=384)	Men (N=164)	Women (N=220)
Alone	20.1	14.4	25.1	16.8	10.8	22.2	31.8	28.0	34.5
Married couple	52.6	69.5	38.1	57.0	74.2	41.5	37.2	51.2	26.8
With spouse alone	36.9	47.7	27.7	38.1	48.2	29.0	32.8	45.7	23.2
With spouse and children	12.3	17.6	7.7	15.8	22.1	10.1			
As head of household	11.5	16.7	7.0	14.8	21.0	9.1			
Not head of household	0.8	0.9	0.7	1.0	1.1	1.0			
With spouse and others, as head of household	3.4	4.2	2.7	3.1	3.9	2.4	4.4	5.5	3.6
Single parent with children	15.9	8.0	22.7	20.4	10.1	29.7			
As head of household	5.5	3.0	7.7	7.1	3.8	10.1			
Not head of household	10.4	5.0	15.0	13.3	6.3	19.6			
Older person with others	11.2	7.8	14.0	5.6	4.4	6.6	30.7	20.7	38.2
As head of household	5.0	2.9	6.7	3.2	1.6	4.6	11.2	7.9	13.6
Not head of household	6.2	4.9	7.3	2.4	2.8	2.0	19.5	12.8	24.6
No answer	0.2	0.4	0.1	0.2	0.5		0.3		0.5

[a] Source: U.S. Bureau of the Census, "Marital Status and Family Status: March 1956," *Current Population Reports*, Series P-20, No. 72, Government Printing Office, Washington, D.C.
[b] Noninstitutional population only.

men were much more likely than women to be part of a married couple, either alone in their own households or living with children and grandchildren; and men were far less likely than women to be living alone, or with persons who were not their children, or as a widowed parent in the home of a child. As Table 2 shows, 25 percent of all aged women, compared to 14 percent of all men, lived alone; 14 percent of all women, compared to 8 percent of all men, lived as widows or single persons in the same household with people who were not their children; and 23 percent of all aged women, compared to 8 percent of the men, were widowed parents living in the same household as their children.

These reports on living arrangements for all older people in the United States obscure the real differences between living arrangements of older people who had living children and those who were childless. Four of every 5 of the noninstitutionalized aged (78 percent) reported living children. Only 17 percent of older people with children compared to 32 percent of childless persons lived alone. Only 6 percent of older people with children compared to 31 percent of childless persons lived in a household with people who were neither spouse nor child. Among older people with children, then, only 23 percent were living alone or in a household with persons other than spouse or child. This is in striking contrast to the 63 percent of childless older persons who lived alone or in a household with persons other than their spouse.

Table 3. Location of nearest child of all persons aged 65 and over who report living children, percentage distribution[a,b]

Location of nearest child	Total (N = 1350)	Men (N = 637)	Women (N = 713)
Total sample	77.9	79.5	76.4
All children in household	5.9	4.6	7.2
Some children in household	30.2	27.6	32.5
In same block	11.6	11.8	11.5
Within walking distance	12.1	13.5	10.9
A short ride away	25.0	25.3	24.7
Within a day's travel or more	14.6	16.6	12.8
No answer	0.5	0.6	0.4

[a] Source: U.S. Bureau of the Census, "Marital Status and Family Status: March 1956," *Current Population Reports*, Series P-20, No. 72, Government Printing Office, Washington, D.C.

[b] Noninstitutional population only. Data subject to sampling variation

Table 3 gives the location of the nearest child of those older persons who had children. As has been indicated, 36 percent of all persons with children lived in a household with at least 1 child; an additional

24 percent, while they lived apart from their children, had at least 1 child who lived on the same block as they did, or within walking distance. Six of every 10 older persons with children, then, lived with at least 1 child, or within walking distance of at least 1 child. An additional 25 percent of the older population with children reported that their nearest child was a short ride away. In only 15 percent of all cases was the nearest child of older people with children as far from them as a day's travel or more.

As might be expected from these data, since most older people with children are physically close to at least 1 child, almost 9 of every 10 older people in the United States who had children, had seen at least one child within the week preceding the National Opinion Research Center interview.

The National Opinion Research Center data clearly indicate that although the three-generation household, all living under the same roof, may now be less important than it has been on the American scene, older people are not physically isolated from their children. For the great majority of the aged with children, at least 1 child is in the same household, within walking distance, or only a short ride away.

A new pattern of three-generation living may well be developing in the United States as a result of those demographic changes associated with urbanization. There is no evidence, present or past, that residence under a common roof means a united three-generation family. Wherever careful studies of older people have been made, however, there is considerable evidence that traditional family feeling about the aged continues to flourish despite the development of new patterns of living arrangements among older people (World Health Organization, 1959).

REFERENCES

Shanas, Ethel. 1959. Financial resources of the aging: reported resources available to those aged 65 and over in meeting medical costs up to $500. (Research series No. 10.) New York: Health Information Foundation.
Sheldon, H. D. 1958. The older population of the United States. New York: John Wiley & Sons, Inc.
U.S. Bureau of the Census. 1956. Marital status and family status: March 1956. *In* Current population reports: population characteristics. (Series P-20, No. 72.) Washington, D.C.: Government Printing Office.
World Health Organization. 1959. Mental health problems of aging and the aged. (WHO Technical Report, Series No. 171.) Geneva: World Health Organization.

Family Relations of the Aging
in Three-Generation Households

ARTHUR J. ROBINS

SHOULD aging parents live with their married children? Rose has suggested that where aging parents should live be based on a consideration of limiting factors: income, physical vigor, the relations between parents and children, the type of housing available in the vicinity, and personal choice (Rose, 1960).

The trend in our culture has been toward segregation of the aged from satisfying participation in important social institutions. The United States, according to Parsons (1942), assumes an extreme position in this type of isolation. This pattern also seems to have pervaded social welfare programs, designed to promote the well-being of the aged. In other words, the treatment of problems arising from tenuous parent-child relationships has some of the characteristics of the disease.[1] For example, old age assistance programs, operating under restrictions imposed by limited appropriations, have sometimes been administered in ways that have placed a premium on the aged applicant's living apart from his children. We see also the development of retirement colonies located beyond easy visiting range of children, i.e., the proliferation of homes for the aged. More recently, we see the development of foster or boarding homes for the aged, even when the latter have children, recommended as a desirable alternative to living with the children (Randall, 1954).

The parallel of the evolution of aged welfare programs to that of child welfare programs is interesting. The latter moved progressively through the following stages: "farming out," indenture, care in alms-houses, orphan asylums or "children's homes," foster homes, and

Research supported by a grant of the Research Council, University of Missouri.
[1] The author sees further evidence of the "contamination of treatment" in employment programs for the aged which rest on, and perpetuate, the troublesome notion of work as the only means of achieving self-respect.

boarding homes, to the present emphasis on keeping children with their natural parents while providing individualized services aimed at remedying the economic or emotional inadequacies of the parents (Witmer, 1942). Modern child welfare programs rest on the belief that the parent-child relationship has values for which there are no more desirable substitutes.

This belief does not underlie social welfare institutions for the aged who are facing problems in maintaining their independent living arrangements. Our culture values mutual independence of the aged and their married children. When grandchildren are involved, three-generational living arrangements are widely viewed as a last resort. Both popular and professional literature have supported that view. The physician writer of a syndicated newspaper column has warned:

Under [average] conditions . . . the presence of three generations at one table three times daily, including Sundays and holidays, is an invitation for a conflict, a serious threat to marital disharmony and a fertile soil for the development of all sorts of nervous and mental disorders. [Hyman, 1960]

A psychiatrist has unequivocally deplored the "extraordinarily pernicious influence" inevitably exerted by grandmothers on their grandchildren (Vollmer, 1937). On the other hand, we find nostalgic descriptions of life in three-generation households which caste doubt on the nursing-home solution to old age (Ruth, 1959). Mead claims that the modern family has lost not its moral fiber, but its grandmother (Mead, 1947).

Enough has been said to illustrate opposing views on aspects of three-generation living arrangements. Will welfare programs for the aging follow the history of child welfare programs? More appropriately, should services be developed toward facilitating three-generation living? What should be the content of such services?

The general question which current research was expected to illuminate was posed 20 years ago by Folsom:

Are we to continue the attitude indicated so clearly even in the thinking of up-state New Yorkers born before 1860, namely, the high valuation of "independence" of the aged from their families and relatives? Must old persons necessarily be an annoyance to younger persons who wish to live their lives in their own way? Is there not opportunity here for the creation of new patterns of living by which the aged can live with the young and have certain personal independence without mutual annoyance? Perhaps we have gone too far in the separation of ages and the creation of several family units; and we could wisely move in the direction of larger households and closer associations between age and youth. [Folsom, 1940, p. 37]

Descriptive studies of three-generation families have been made. Smith, Britton, and Britton (1958) have published the most recent of these, presenting a concise statement of the demographic aspects of the problem and a review, albeit uncritical, of the research literature. Demographic data on the prevalence of three-generation households are based mainly on estimates. The number of instances in which all three generations are alive is increasing. Although relatively uncommon in the United States, the three-generation household is perhaps more frequent than at any time in our past, according to data presented by Friedmann (1960). Research dealing specifically with such households has been even more limited than research on family relationships of the aging. Smith and associates hoped to describe the nature of three-generation families and attitudes and opinions of each generation concerning aspects of the living arrangement. The study also was directed toward determining the relationship between those characteristics and membership in first, second, or third generation; rural or urban residence; and the adjustment of the older person.

Time does not permit a review of the methodology of the Smith study. It may suffice to report that the investigation recognized the need for "more definitive answers to questions concerning relationships within three-generation families." The present research represented an effort to collect comparable data on these families, to measure different dimensions of family relationships, and to use different measures of dimensions that had been previously examined by others.

THE CRITERION

The primary interest of the investigator was to determine what variables were associated with successful three-generation living. The first set of tasks involved defining the criterion of success, finding an appropriate measure of it, and selecting variables potentially facilitating or hampering success and appropriate measures of those variables.

Previous studies have used a criterion of adjustment of the older person, measured by means of the Burgess-Cavan-Havighurst Attitude Inventory (Cavan *et al.*, 1949). That criterion focuses on the older person, whereas a measure of the total functioning of the three generations would seem to be more appropriate. A living arrangement which involves all three cannot effectively be evaluated in terms of the outcome for one. Further, the Burgess scale, while a good quantitative descriptive tool, had the disadvantage of incorporating some of the variables with which it was to be correlated. Correlations obtained by comparing a whole with one of its parts would be questionable. A measure was desired that would primarily reflect relevant intergenerational adjustment, would not be contaminated with independent variables such as health and economic status, and would have reasonable reliability and validity.

Reported satisfaction and conflict measures were believed to be too undisguised to be useful, although data of this nature were obtained in an effort to substantiate the criterion measure chosen. Criterion measures based on the continuation or termination of the arrangement may testify only to the unavailability of alternatives. Further they would require comparison with a group who had terminated the arrangement. The stability of interviewer ratings of satisfaction was also questionable. The criterion decided upon for the present investigation was a component of Farber's index of marital integration (Farber, 1957) which he later extended as a measure of family integration in a study of the mentally retarded child and his family. Farber defined family integration as a combination of consensus of the members as to domestic values and a lack of interpersonal role tension among family members. The effectiveness with which a family performs its several institutional functions depends upon the effective coordination of roles to achieve these shared values. The interpersonal tension measure was obtained by asking family members to rate themselves and each other on the degree to which each had certain traits.

For the present investigation, the tension rating alone served as the criterion. Consensus on values, measured not by Farber's ranking of domestic values but by means of the traditional family ideology scale (Levinson and Huffman, 1955) was used as one of the independent variables. It did not seem necessary to incorporate a measure of value consensus into the criterion since value discrepancies do not necessarily constitute an unhappy situation. The important question is whether the discrepancy would be manifested in conflict; hence, success of the three-generation arrangement was measured in terms of the interpersonal tension that was inferred from the ratings. Unfortunately ratings by the third generation were not obtained because of time limitations.

QUESTIONS AND HYPOTHESES

Data were obtained in order to describe the three-generation (3-G) family and to analyze the relationship of each variable to the tension criterion. To minimize repetition the hypotheses have not been made explicit.

What are the characteristics of the household with respect to: blood relationships of G-1 and G-2, age of each member, religion, education, occupation, ownership of the home, total family income, number of rooms per person, and health of G-1 and G-2, rated from excellent to very poor.

What was the history of the 3-G plan? How long has it been in effect? How long married? What gave rise to its adoption? Who proposed it and what were the initial reactions to it? What agreements were made, and have they been kept?

How helpful is G-1 with the maternal and housekeeping tasks of the G-2 mother? How much does G-2 expect of G-1? (A task inventory was used for this item.)

What are the stereotypes, positive or negative, that G-2 has of old people in general? The Tuckman-Lorge Scale of Stereotypes of aging (Tuckman and Lorge, 1953) was used.

What is the family value orientation of G-1 and G-2? What discrepancy is there between them? The Levinson-Huffman TFI scale, referred to earlier, was used.

How much communication is there among the generations on important and unimportant matters? The measure was adapted from a scale developed by William R. Morrow and the author for use in other research in progress. To what extent is there more talk between G-2 spouses than there is between G-1 and G-2?

What is the general morale of G-1 and G-2? The Rundquist-Sletto morale scale (Rundquist and Sletto, 1936) was used.

What do G-2 and G-1 each think should be the obligation of children toward their aging parents? A number of case situations were presented which involved some conflict from G-2 and which had to be resolved in favor of G-1 or G-2. Two of the case situations were borrowed from a National Opinion Research Center Study (Shanas, 1959).

What is the extent of formal social participation of G-1 and G-2? Chapin's scale was used (Chapin, 1952). A measure of informal social participation was discarded in order to reduce the length of each interview.

Were factors suggested by Sussman (Sussman, 1951) as being associated with family continuity also related to tension? Only one of Sussman's determinants was examined: type of courtship and marriage ceremony.

How satisfied with their marriage were G-2? A modified version of items drawn from the Burgess-Wallen scale (Burgess and Wallin, 1953) was used.

How supportive or undermining of G-1 were G-2 in common social situations, as reported by G-1?

THE STUDY DESIGN

Personal visits to area samples of homes in order to solicit information regarding the whereabouts of any three-generation households were discontinued since they were too time-consuming. A telephone survey based on regular-interval sampling of the directory was surprisingly fruitful, yielding 120 three-generation households representing 1.6 percent of the estimated 7500 occupied dwelling units of Columbia, Missouri. Since the percentage of three-generation families in other communities varies from 1.9 percent to 8.4 percent, comparison with them was not necessarily corroborative. The 120 families were reduced to 40 after subsequent contact. Fifty-seven were temporary arrangements; 5 refused; 2 had terminated by reason of death of the G-1; and 11 Negro households were excluded in which the G-1 member was in middle years and the G-2 was an unmarried mother.

Data-gathering procedures

Pairs of interviewers had simultaneous, but separate, interviews with the G-1 and the G-2 women. The former was the only G-1 member in the home in most instances; the latter was assumed to have had increased contact, in contrast to the G-2 male, with G-1. Further, if we assume that the wife is in a mediating role between husband and children (Farber, 1957), then we might expect that she is called on to perform this role for the G-2 husband and the G-1 female, particularly when the latter is the husband's mother-in-law. It was also assumed that the greater possibility of intergenerational role conflict between adults of the same sex gave greater importance to interviewing the G-2 female whose relationship to G-1 was more crucial to the success of the three-generational arrangement. For the purpose of description and analysis of tension and its correlates, the families were grouped into categories of socio-economic status, the most general variable which might have tended to obscure the other relationships being investigated. The Minnesota Scale for Paternal Occupations[2] was used to give a measure of socio-economic status.

Findings

Typically, the 3-G family consisted of a widow living in the home of her daughter and son-in-law. The 3-G arrangement had been suggested by G-2, usually because of G-1's poor health, inadequate means of support, or some combination of reasons which indicated that the arrangement was primarily adopted to solve a G-1 problem. In only a negligible number of cases was some kind of agreement, even informal, made. Almost every family had two G-3 members.

In the upper-class family the arrangement, instituted 13 years after the G-2 marriage, had been in effect for 8 years; in the middle-class, instituted 10 years after marriage and in effect for 10 years; in the lower-class, 9 years after marriage and for 7 years. The G-2 marriages commonly had followed traditional patterns of courtship, long engagement, marriage with parental approval, and church wedding attended by both families. There were a few Catholic families in the study, one Jewish family, and no preponderance of any Protestant denomination.

All classes reported more communication on important matters between G-2 spouses than between G-1 and G-2. There was no difference, either among classes or between generations, with respect to unimportant matters.

For all classes the morale of G-1 was lower than G-2, the former being "undecided" on most items, a response which itself reflects lowered morale.

Data on other characteristics are presented in Table 1.

The correlation of each of the independent variables with the tension criterion was measured, when appropriate, by means of the Kendall rank correlation coefficient (Siegel, 1956). The Fisher test (Tuckman and Lorge, 1953) was used with data which did not lend itself to ranking. The probability of obtaining each coefficient under the null hypothesis was computed. Only those correlations significant at a level equal to or less than .05 are given in Table 2.

Correlations do not imply cause and effect, but we frequently have no better basis on which to act in our effort to control the outcome of any given phenomenon. Unfortunately none of the significant varia-

[2] *The Minnesota Scale for Paternal Occupations,* University of Minnesota, Institute of Child Welfare, Minneapolis, Minnesota.

Table 1. Selected characteristics of 3-G families, by class[a]

Characteristic	G-1			G-2			G-3		
	Upper	Middle	Lower	Upper	Middle	Lower	Upper	Middle	Lower
Household composition, percentage of families with									
Male only	0	0	11	0	7	0			
Female only	96	93	67	15	20	22			
Couple	4	7	22	85	73	78			
Children									
Under 13							34	44	60
13–20							51	50	35
21 and over							15	6	5
Health	poor	fair	fair	good	good	good			
Education (in years)	10	6	9						
Age	78	77	69						
Income (in dollars)	730	775	1180	8500	6225	4075			
Rooms per person									
Before 3-G				1.9	1.3	1.4			
After 3-G				1.6	1.3	1.1			
Tuckman-Lorge stereotype scale									
Total score				48	48	60			
Negative attitude items only				34	33	41			
Traditional family ideology	5	5	5	4	4.5	5			

[a] This sample included 26 upper-class, 15 middle-class, and 10 lower-class families. There were 47 children in the upper-class families, 34 in the middle-class, and 19 in the lower-class.

Table 2. Variables significantly related to role tension

Variable	Nature of relationship	Class to which applicable
Helpfulness with housekeeping	High helpfulness = low tension	Upper
Health of G-1	Poor health = high tension	Upper
Negative attitude toward aging	Negative attitude = high tension	Upper and middle
Morale of G-1	Low morale = high tension	Upper
Morale of G-2	Low morale = high tension	Upper and lower
Social participation of G-2 woman	High participation = high tension	Upper
Marital satisfaction	High satisfaction = low tension	Upper and middle
Supportiveness		Upper and middle

bles is easily manipulatable. In this study the temptation to impute causality to the independent variable must be regretfully resisted inasmuch as it is logical to presume that some of the independent variables, e.g., morale, marital satisfaction, and negative attitudes toward older people, are functions of tension.

Tuckman and Lorge interpreted responses to their scale as obviously indicating that: "Old people are living in a social climate which is not conducive to feeling of adequacy. . . ." (Tuckman and Lorge, 1953, p. 260.) Intergenerational tension might explain the negative attitudes.

High social participation of the G-2 woman might lead to tension if she feels handicapped by her responsibilities in relation to G-1.

The writer sensed from the data available that the 3-G families studied had not progressed appreciably toward meeting Simmons' challenge that our culture create a "brave new climate in which to grow older" (Simmons, 1958). At the same time the accomplishment of these families is of great consequence, particularly in view of the lack of support given by our culture to this type of family institution. The factors responsible for some living together with a minimum of tension are still elusive. The three-generation living pattern seemed to be a response to situational pressures that probably would not have been made in the absence of such pressures. Why some people make the response and others do not is an engaging question, the answer to which would probably require data from people who have avoided three-generational living arrangements, and more subtle and sensitive measures than have been used in this study. The answer is worth seeking if we accept the importance of the following principle: "Whenever a society and the families, with support of the prevailing culture, can create and sustain mutually supportive relationships between its youth and its elders, old age security rests on its firmest foundations." (White House Conference on Aging, 1960, p. 14.)

The mutually supportive aspects of the families studied were not readily apparent beyond the housekeeping assistance rendered by G-1 and the occasional household in which the G-2 female was freed for employment. Perhaps there were subtle complementary needs which the three-generation arrangements were meeting. The overwhelming weight of our cultural norms is against the arrangement. Although neither supported nor refuted by the study, the author feels strongly that service programs should not ignore the minority who have undertaken the task of providing a home for their aging parents. We need to seek ways of maximizing the capacity of these families to be mutually supportive, and ways of minimizing intergenerational conflicts.

Acknowledgments. The author gratefully acknowledges the assistance of the Research Council, University of Missouri, and the help of the following in the collection and processing of data: Robert Blachly, Paul Brandt, Marvin Combs, Larry Schwartz, Bertha Short, and Joan Simon.

REFERENCES

Burgess, E. W., and Wallin, P. 1953. Engagement and marriage. Philadelphia: J. B. Lippincott Co.

Cavan, Ruth S., Burgess, E. W., Havighurst, R. J., and Goldhamer, H. 1949. Personal adjustment in old age. Chicago: Science Research Associates.

Chapin, F. S. 1952. Social participation scale. Minneapolis: University of Minnesota Press.

Farber, B. 1957. An index of marital integration. Sociometry, 20: 117–34.

Folsom, J. K. 1940. Old age as a sociological problem. Am. J. Orthopsychiat., 10: 30–39.

Friedmann, E. A. 1960. The impact of aging on the social structure. *In* C. Tibbitts (ed.), Handbook of social gerontology, pp. 130–44. Chicago: University of Chicago Press.

Hyman, H. T. 1960. The doctor says. Columbia Missourian, February 8.

Levinson, D. J., and Huffman, Phyllis E. 1955. Traditional family ideology and its relation to personality. J. Personality, 23: 251–73.

Mead, Margaret. 1947. What is happening to the American family. J. Social Casework, 28: 323–30.

Parsons, T. 1942. Age and sex in the social structure of the United States. Am. Sociological Rev., 7: 604–16.

Randall, Ollie A. 1954. The older person in the modern family structure.

In Growing with the years, pp. 81–84. (Leg. Doc. 32.) Albany, N.Y.: New York State Joint Legislative Committee on Problems of the Aging.

Rose, A. M. 1960. Spanning the generations. New York: National Council of Jewish Women, Inc. (Mimeographed.)

Rundquist, E. A., and Sletto, R. F. 1936. Personality in the depression: a study in the measurement of attitudes. Minneapolis: University of Minnesota Press.

Ruth, Mary C. 1959. Fond memories of life with grandmother. St. Louis Post-Dispatch, March 24.

Shanas, Ethel. 1959. Some sociological research findings about older people pertinent to social work. *In* Toward better understanding of the aging, pp. 49–58. New York: Council of Social Work Education.

Siegel, S. 1956. The Kendall rank correlation coefficient. *In* Nonparametric statistics for the behavioral sciences, pp. 213–23. New York: McGraw-Hill Book Co., Inc.

Simmons, L. W. 1958. Aging in modern society. *In* Toward better understanding of the aging, proceedings of the seminar on aging, pp. 1–8. New York: Council on Social Work Education.

Smith, W. M., Jr., Britton, J. H., and Britton, Jean O. 1958. Relationships within three-generation families. (Res. Publ. 155.) University Park: Pennsylvania State University, College of Home Economics.

Sussman, M. B. 1951. Family continuity: a study of factors which affect relationships between families at generational levels. (Unpublished Ph.D. thesis.) New Haven: Yale University.

Tuckman, J., and Lorge, I. 1953. Attitudes toward old people. J. Social Psychol., 37: 249–60.

Vollmer, H. 1937. The grandmother: a problem in child rearing. Am. J. Orthopsychiat., 7: 378–82.

White House Conference on Aging. 1960. Background paper on family life, family relationships, and friends. Washington, D.C.: U.S. Department of Health, Education, and Welfare.

Witmer, Helen L. 1942. Social work: an analysis of a social institution. New York: Farrar and Rinehart.

Role Conceptions of Couples in Retirement

AARON LIPMAN

RETIREMENT of the male from the occupational system represents a major crisis in marital adjustment. Like divorce, or the advent of children, it demands a new set of role conceptions, based on an altered mode of existence for the married pair. The principal orientation of scholars interested in retirement as a social and personal problem has been psychological and physiological; the present study attempts a more sociological approach. Taking the conjugal pair as a unit, the author has investigated the effects of retirement on the conceptions that each partner has as to his own role and that of his spouse. Specifically, this paper will examine preretirement role orientations, present evidence of new role conceptions emerging as a direct result of retirement, and, finally, relate the morale of retired men and women with the degree to which they relinquish old role conceptions and adopt an altered postretirement viewpoint.

During that range of years when he is considered young and vigorous, the male in our society plays social roles that are sharply differentiated from those of women of similar age and health. In particular, the American adult male has his primary roles and acquires his primary conceptions of himself in two institutional systems: the occupational, where he is a worker, and the familial, where he is husband and father. These two systems are sharply separated both geographically and temporally; life on the job is normally quite distinct from life in the household and involves different actors, different goals, and different status. Nonetheless, there is a profound interdependence and interpenetration of the two because the "success" of the male in his familial roles (husband, father) is defined, partially, in terms of his achievement in his occupational role (worker). One bit of evidence helping to establish the social reality of this conception of the adult masculine role is contained in the responses of a national sample of women to the question, "What do you consider the most important

This research has been supported by a National Institutes of Health grant (M 1625) to the Geriatric Clinic of the University of Miami.

quality of a good husband?" Forty-two percent of the married respondents selected the answer, "Being a good provider," which refers, not to the familial role of the male, but to his abilities in the occupational system (Strunk, 1948). An instrumental role is thus clearly institutionalized for the male (Zelditch, 1955).[1] As Parsons states, "It is fundamentally by virtue of the importance of his occupational role as a component of his familial role that in our society we can unequivocally designate the husband-father as the 'instrumental leader' of the family as a system" (Parsons and Bales, 1955, p. 13).

The role of the American female is sharply differentiated from that of the male; while his major focus is in the occupational system, her role is centered in the internal affairs of the family, where she is manager of household and familial activities (Parsons and Bales, 1955). Cavan points out that, "Just as the chief and most absorbing role of the husband is that of good provider, so the chief role of the wife is that of home-maker" (Cavan, 1959, p. 337). Most men conceive of female role patterns in the same fashion; thus, the most frequent response of a national sample of married men to the question, "What would you consider the most important quality of a good wife?" was "Good homemaker, good housekeeper, etc." (Strunk, 1948). And, in a more recent study of marital role expectations of predominantly unmarried adolescents, it was found that the majority of girls saw housekeeping as their responsibility, while the majority of boys expected earning a living to be theirs: "In these areas both boys and girls are reluctant to give up their own traditional roles, or to recognize a change in the spouse's role" (Dunn, 1960, p. 101).

Retirement of the aged male from the occupational sphere has a decided effect on these differentiated role patterns. For the husband, the role of wage earner, which he had conceived as his primary role, is suddenly withdrawn; structurally, he is isolated from the occupational system, and this shock often has grave effects upon his entire existence. If the married male is to adjust to retirement, he must necessarily redefine his social function and his familial role.

[1] Zelditch (1955) differentiates between instrumental and expressive leadership in this way:

Ego . . . will be considered *instrumental* leader of the nuclear family if . . . 1. Ego is boss-manager of the farm: leader of the hunt, etc. Ego is the final court of appeals, final judge and executor of punishment, discipline, and control over the children of the family.

Ego will be considered *expressive* leader of the nuclear family if . . . 2. Ego is the mediator, concilator, of the family; ego soothes over disputes, resolves hostilities in the family. Ego is affectionate, solicitous, warm, emotional to the children of the family; ego is the "comforter," the "consoler," is relatively indulgent, relatively unpunishing. [p. 318]

One aim of this research was to investigate the conceptions that retired men have of their marital roles and to relate this to their patterns of adjustment. I suggested in a previous paper (Lipman, 1960) that the retired male's adjustment would be influenced by the degree to which he had internalized the instrumental values so that they had become an integral part of his marital role conceptions. My hypothesis in this research has been that the retired male who still viewed himself primarily in an instrumental fashion, i.e., being a good economic provider for his family, would have the poorest adjustment, since he would envision himself enacting a role that was functionally related to participation in the occupational system, but maladapted to a denial of this occupational participation.

If the male is no longer to view himself in an instrumental fashion, what new orientation is he to adopt, in order to achieve a good adjustment to his new situation? A further aim of this research, then, was to determine whether adaptive mechanisms evolved which would mitigate the strain of retirement by providing the male with substitute roles and role conceptions consistent with feelings of self-respect and self-worth.

A final aim of this study was to investigate the commonly accepted assumption that the female undergoes no major qualitative alterations in role or role conceptions on the retirement of her husband, but merely retains her traditional role of housewife intact.

A sample of one hundred retired couples over 60 years of age residing in metropolitan Miami was interviewed. In order to maximize variability, they were selected from almost all the census tract areas of Dade County. Their salient characteristics are as follows: over 80 percent were migrants from other states, predominantly the north and northeast; the median number of years resident in the Miami area was 7; median and mean age of the wife was 64 years; median and mean age of the husband was 69; median number of years married was 39½. The group was heavily represented in the upper educational and upper occupational levels. (Other studies have indicated that this is characteristic of aged Florida migrants.)

The study consisted of a battery of questions, among which were scattered seven items (which were later reduced to six), from which the morale scale was constructed. This morale scale was utilized as an index of adjustment. It consisted of the following six items, as adapted by Kutner from the Guttman scale used in the Elmira Study of Aging (Kutner *et al.*, 1956):

1. How often do you feel there's just no point in living?
2. Things just keep getting worse and worse for me as I get older.

3. How much do you regret the chances you missed during your life to do a better job of living?
4. All in all, how much unhappiness would you say you find in life today?
5. On the whole, how satisfied would you say you are with your way of life today?
6. As you get older, would you say things seem to get better or worse than you thought they would be?

Scores of one point each were assigned for the following response categories.

Question	Scored response	Other responses
No point in living	Hardly ever	Often; sometimes
Things get worse and worse	Disagree	Agree
Regret chances missed	Not at all	Somewhat; a good deal
How much unhappiness	Almost none	Some, but not very much; a good deal
How satisfied with life today	Very satisfied	Fairly satisfied; not very satisfied
Things seem better or worse	Better	Same; worse

The distribution of scores was similar for both males and females. For analytical purposes, the respondents were grouped into three categories representing high, medium, and low morale; those with high morale had scores of 5–6; medium, 3–4; low, 0–2. The coefficient of reproducibility for this morale scale reached the 90 percent level (Table 1).

Table 1. Morale rankings by sex, percentage distribution

Morale rankings	Male	Female
Low (0–2)	26	29
Medium (3–4)	43	43
High (5–6)	31	28

In the previously cited national survey (Strunk, 1948), husbands were asked what they considered to be the most important quality of a good wife, and wives were questioned as to the most important quality of a good husband. In this study, the following pair of questions was asked separately both of husband and wife: "What would you say is the most important quality of a good husband who is past sixty years of age?" "What would you say is the most important quality of a good wife who is past sixty years of age?" Each spouse was thus required to present his conception of a proper and desirable role orientation for both himself and his partner.

The joint responses from both spouses concerning the male may be grouped into the following four categories, concerning qualities of (1) love, understanding; (2) companionship and compatibility; (3)

helps wife; and (4) being a good economic provider. Categories (1) and (2) comprised over half of all responses, from both men and women. This would indicate that, in contrast to his preretirement role, the role of the older male is viewed as primarily an expressive one, i.e., involved in giving emotional support in some fashion.

To test the adequacy of these role conceptions for the retired male, these four categories were tabulated against his morale scores. The relatively few males who selected an instrumental conception of the husband's role [response category (4) above] makes analysis tenuous. The contrast between expressive and instrumental role conceptions provides suggestive insights rather than definitive conclusions. Apparently, the retired person who views himself as a good economic provider is twice as likely to have low moral as the male who views his marital role as expressive. Although not statistically significant $(.3 > P > .2)$, of the males who considered the instrumental quality of the older husband as most important, 42 percent had low morale, and this was exactly twice the proportion of those who considered the expressive as his most important quality (Table 2).

Table 2. Male conceptions of good husband and low morale, percentage distribution

Morale	Instrumental[a] (N = 12)	Expressive[b] (N = 57)
Low	42	21
Not low	58	79

[a] Category (4): being a good economic provider.
[b] Category (2): companionship and compatibility.

In Table 3 we can interpret this tendency by pointing out that for the retired male adherence to a role conception structured primarily in relationship to an occupation system must be personally dysfunc-

Table 3. Morale rankings by male conception of good husband, percentage distribution[a]

Morale	Instrumental[b] (N = 12)	Expressive[c] (N = 57)	Quasi-instrumental[d] (N = 15)	Miscellaneous and don't know (N = 23)	Total (N = 107)[e]
Low	42	21	20	26	24
Medium	33	47	40	48	45
High	25	32	40	26	31

[a] $.8 > P > .7$. [b] Category (4): being a good economic provider.
[c] Categories (1) and (2): companionship and personality characteristics.
[d] Category (3): helps wife.
[e] Total exceeds 100 because some respondents mentioned more than one quality.

tional; it denies the objective reality of his role discontinuity from wage earner to retiree.

This role discontinuity obviously necessitates a male marital adjustment; the majority of respondents recognized this consciously and agreed with the statement, "After retirement, the husband has more of an adjustment to make in marriage than the wife." Seventy-three percent of the men and 67 percent of the women responded affirmatively.

A feeling of greater inactivity is one reflection of the male's more difficult marital adjustment. For example, in response to the question, "Do you feel that you have plenty to do every day?" more women (91 percent) said "yes" than men (78 percent). And in response to the question, "Do you feel that your husband (wife) has plenty to do every day?" there were more women who felt that their husbands did *not* have enough to occupy their time (24 percent) than there were men who felt that their wives did not have enough activities (5 percent).

This feeling of greater male inactivity is further seen in response to the question, "Has your husband (wife) urged you to start any new activities?" Almost twice as many men (29 percent) said "yes" to this question as women (16 percent). The husband's greater inactivity might create a certain tension in the marital relations. It is important to note, however, that this inactivity is great only in relation to that of the women; the majority of both men and women felt that they had plenty to do every day.

What are these activities? Presumably, those of the female remain substantially the same before and after retirement. In what kinds of new activities, then, does the male participate? Besides an increase in joint recreational activities (both passive and active), it was found that one of the adaptive mechanisms for the retired male was the creation of a new meaningful and functional role to replace the occupational one. There was a deliberate acceptance of a substitute, quasi-instrumental role that was also inadvertently expressive in relation to the wife. This new role involved the performance of many household chores, especially those requiring little specialized skill and knowledge, and which could be participated in jointly. According to the wives, three-quarters of the husbands did completely or helped with the shopping, while over half cleared the breakfast table, wiped the dishes, and picked up and put away the clothes (Table 4). When the women in the sample were asked, "What does your husband do when you do your housework?" almost half (41 percent) replied that their husbands helped.

Table 4. Male household activities, percentage distribution

Activity	Participating
Take care of the garbage and trash	80
Go grocery shopping	75
Pick up and put away the clothes	68
Wipe the dishes	60
Clear the breakfast table	55
Wash the dishes	43
Make the breakfast	41
Set the table for the day's main meal	34
Hang up the laundry	29
Clean and dust	26
Do the laundry	22
Make the beds	21

The noncompetitive, rather compassionate nature of this new shared role can be discerned by the male responses to the question, "How do you feel about doing these things?" (household chores). Only 4 percent of the responses could be viewed as truly negative; most men did not mind getting involved with household activities. They did them voluntarily, with attitudes ranging from a feeling of obligation to a sense of real satisfaction and pleasure in helping with or performing the household chores. The range of responses varied:

"I enjoy doing these things, it lightens my wife's load."
"I'm glad to help. It gives me something to do."
"I feel I should help. I like to do my share."
"I don't mind. It's okay."
"It's woman's work, and I don't like housework, but I help so the wife is through sooner."
"I don't like to do these things, but I have to do something to keep busy."

If we think of roles as expectations which individuals have concerning behavior in a particular position, we notice that participation in household activities is actually defined as a role for the retired male by most men and women. Sixty-two percent of the women and 58 percent of the men agreed with the statement, "Once a man retires, a wife has a definite right to expect her husband to share in household activities." Although not statistically significant ($.7 > P > .5$), the men who disagreed with this statement had a somewhat greater percentage of poor morale than those who agreed with it (Table 5).

Before retirement, one effect of the husband's active involvement in the occupational system had been to "narrow the range in which the sharing of common interests can play a large part" (Parsons, 1949, p. 228). This acquisition of household duties after retirement adds a new dimension of common interests for the husband and wife, solidifies emotional bonds, and is therefore functionally related both to the

Table 5. Male morale and agreement with household involvement,
percentage distribution

Morale	Agree (N = 58)	Disagree (N = 41)	Total (N = 99)
Low	22	32	26
Medium[a]	47	39	44
High	31	29	30

[a] There was one "don't know" response that had medium morale.

aged male's emphasis on expressive roles and his marital adjustment.
The majority of men (52 percent) and 47 percent of the women felt
that their marriages had become more satisfactory since retirement
(Table 6).

Table 6. Marital satisfaction of men and women,
percentage distribution

Marriage after husband's retirement	Men (N = 100)	Women (N = 100)
More satisfactory	52	47
Less satisfactory, but still good	26	29
Same	19	22
Unsatisfactory	0	0
No answer, don't know	3	2

Although not statistically significant ($.5 > P > .3$), the males who
accepted their involvement in household chores (as reflected in the
agreement with the statement, "Once a man retires, a wife has a
definite right to expect her husband to share in household activities")
had a somewhat greater proportion of more satisfactory marriages
(57 percent) than those who disagreed with the statement (46 percent) (see Table 7).

Table 7. Male marital satisfaction and agreement
with household involvement, percentage distribution

Marriage after retirement	Agree (N = 58)	Disagree (N = 41)	Total (N = 99)
More satisfactory	57	46	53
Less satisfactory, but still good	26	27	26
Same; don't know[a]	17	27	21

[a] There was one "don't know" response whose marriage was the same.

Unlike that of the male, the female role conception after retirement
has commonly been assumed to remain the same as her preretirement
orientation. She undergoes no dramatic alteration of role; her center
of gravity remains in the home both before and after the retirement of

her husband. As one author puts it: "Married women seem to adjust more quickly to retirement than do married men, apparently because they need make no abrupt transition from everyday life. The usual responsibility of caring for the family is not much changed, except as to pace. . . ." For most married women, therefore, there is a continuum from working life to retirement.

Although it might appear that no discontinuity exists in the female domestic role, nevertheless, the present study suggests that a wife does not retain her self-same role conceptions after the retirement of her husband. The role remains, but its emphasis undergoes a distinct shift. The emergent new male roles relating to housework are responsible for this shift. Since any change in the behavior of one spouse also alters the reciprocal behavior of the other, the wife is forced to adjust to her readjusting husband. With his involvement in household activities, her instrumental orientation "good housewife and homemaker" can no longer be the major distinction between the role of the wife and her retired mate. Can women then still think of themselves primarily as housewives, and make good adjustments to their husbands' retirement?

This research found that women who did not alter this instrumental role conception for themselves did not make good adjustments as measured by the morale scale.

Women's responses to the question, "What would you say is the most important quality of a good wife who is past sixty years of age?" could be grouped into three main categories: qualities of (1) love and understanding; (2) companionship and compatibility; and (3) being a good housewife, cook, etc. By far the greatest concentration (73 percent) was in categories (1) and (2), which emphasized the giving and receiving of affection, love, and companionship. Comparing their category of response to this question with their score on the morale scale, we discover that those wives who adhered to the traditional sentiment of the woman's role [category (3)] manifested the greatest percentage of low morale. Almost two-thirds (63 percent) of the women who gave this instrumental role conception had low morale. This was significantly greater ($.02 > P > .01$) than the percentage of low morale among women who considered companionship and personality characteristics to be most important (Tables 8 and 9). Adherence to a preretirement role conception appears to be dysfunctional for the female personality system.

We see, then, that retirement brings a definite change in the traditional activities of the male, which alters the preretirement division of male and female roles. Prior to retirement there is a role differentiation

Table 8. *Female conceptions of good wife and low morale,*
percentage distribution[a]

Morale	Instrumental[b] (N = 16)	Expressive[c] (N = 61)
Low	63	26
Not low	37	74

[a] .2 > P > .01.   [b] Category (3): being a good homemaker.
[c] Category (2): companionship and compatibility.

Table 9. *Morale rankings by female conception of good wife,*
percentage distribution[a]

Morale	Instrumental[b] (N = 16)	Expressive[c] (N = 61)	Miscellaneous and don't know (N = 25)	Total (N = 102)
Low	63	26	36	29
Medium	12	46	52	43
High	25	28	12	30
Total	100	100	100	102[d]

[a] .05 > P > .02.   [b] Category (3): being a good homemaker.
[c] Categories (1) and (2): companionship and personality characteristics.
[d] Some respondents mentioned more than one quality; the total therefore exceeds 100.

on the basis of sex, with the male's occupational role strongly separated from the domestic role. In retirement, since the man can no longer attain the work and achievement goals, striving for them and adherence to them is associated with poor adjustment. A feeling of usefulness and purposefulness is achieved by the male increasingly through assistance with household activities, and emphasizing expressive qualities such as giving of love, affection, and companionship to his wife. A new and meaningful functional role is thus created that aids in individual adjustment. Apparently, role differentiation by sex is reduced with increased age and retirement.[2]

The increasing preemption of household activities by the male retiree has definite repercussions on the role of the woman and on her conception of her role. Since her husband's new activities have blurred the traditional distinction between the male and female roles, the woman can no longer view her major role primarily as good housekeeper and homemaker. Both men and women who had clearly and rigidly defined their preretirement role in a predominantly instrumental fashion that strongly differentiated husband's and wife's activities, now

[2] Dr. Murray Wax has pointed out to the author that this phenomenon of decreasing role differentiation by sex in old age is also frequent in primitive societies.

move toward a common area of identity in role activities—an area that emphasizes sharing and cooperation, where similar expressive qualities such as love, understanding, companionship, and compatibility become the most important things they can both give in marriage. These non-sex-differentiated supportive roles that demand expressive, rather than instrumental, qualities appear well adapted for the personality system of both the husband and wife in retirement.

REFERENCES

Cavan, Ruth S. 1959. American marriage: a way of life. New York: Thomas Y. Crowell Co.

Dunn, Marie S. 1960. Marriage role expectations of adolescents. Marriage and Family Living, 22: 99–111.

Kutner, B., Fanshel, D., Togo, Alice M., and Langner, T. S. 1956. Five hundred over sixty: a community survey on aging. New York: Russell Sage Foundation.

Lipman, A. 1960. Marital roles of the retired aged. Merrill-Palmer Quart. Behavior & Development, 6: 192–95.

Parsons, T. 1949. Essays in sociological theory, pure and applied. Glencoe, Ill.: Free Press.

Parsons, T., and Bales, R. F. (eds.) 1955. Family socialization and interaction process. Glencoe, Ill.: Free Press.

Strunk, Mildred. 1948. Compilers, "the quarter's polls." Pub. Opinion Quart., 12: (Summer) 357–58.

Zelditch, M., Jr. 1955. Role differentiation in the nuclear family: a comparative study. *In* T. Parsons and R. F. Bales (eds.), Family, socialization, and interaction process, pp. 307–52. Glencoe, Ill.: Free Press.

The Role of Older People in Family Rituals

RUTH ALBRECHT

ONE dimension of aging is the continuance of family rituals that have been going on for years and which take on special meaning for all participants. The loss of these may leave people feeling alone, outcast, and bereft. This study was made to learn to what extent older people continue to participate in family rituals and what roles they play in them.

THE SAMPLE

The data were obtained by interviewing members of the family groups represented. One reporter often described rituals for a single generation such as husband and wife, for two, three, and even four generations. Of the 252 such family groups, 240 reported from one to fifteen different rituals but about 5 percent had only what would be called family routines. These are not included here. A total of 601 rituals were described and of these 233, or over one-third, included older members of the family. An analysis of the family structure showed that most families with older members included them in their rituals. Illness or distance accounted for most noninclusion in these particular family functions.

An additional group of 45 older people was interviewed to verify practices and to elicit personal expression of the meaning of rituals and the reaction toward loss of members.

Members of the middle class were selected for study because they are apt to have more variation than the upper class whose rituals are patterned within the status group and kinship structure. On the other hand, the mode of life of those with lower status does not make allowances for coordinated time, leisure, space, and other factors that help develop rituals.

THE MEANING OF FAMILY RITUALS

Ritual is used here to mean "a pattern of prescribed formal behavior, pertaining to some specific event, occasion, or situation, which tends to be repeated over and over again" (Bossard and Boll, 1950). Certain family group activities are repeated until they follow a definite pattern. Members of the family often have a path of action or specific roles in these rituals and, as they repeat their activities, develop a sense of "rightness" about them.

What is done is not important in itself, but the meaning associated with the activities is vital. Certain routines can be just that, an expedient way of getting things done, but the rituals studied here take on deeper meaning and seem to contribute to the deepening of family relationships, to the development of feelings of closeness to other family members, and to family loyalty. A few examples will show what is meant.

On Christmas Eve our family goes to my great-aunt's home. She is my great-grandmother's sister and we have gone there for years. All of the relatives gather and place their presents under the tree. We have a big dinner, then sing carols. Someone, usually one of the men, reads the Christmas story. After that, someone is chosen to be Santa Claus and hands out the gifts one at a time. Everyone watches the recipient open his or her gift and joins in the exclamation of pleasure. When all of the gifts have been opened it is time for coffee and special Christmas cakes. Small children are put to bed early and have their celebration in the morning but the older people stay up late and visit. They tell stories of the days when they were young and all of us enjoy this. The next day we go to father's mother's home for the morning and noon meal, then spend the evening with my maternal grandparents. We used to bring presents for everyone but now we draw names and give one gift to an adult or child but every member of the family brings a gift to our great-aunt and to each of our grandparents.

The mother of two young children remembered this from her own childhood:

My grandmother was quite a psychologist when it came to dealing with us. When my sister and I visited her she did not tell us what to do as our mother did. For example, she had an old-time Seth Thomas clock that had to be wound every night. First she wound the right side with a key, then took another key to wind the side that made it strike. We always watched her and as soon as this was done we knew it was bedtime. She never told us, but we knew and did not beg to stay up longer as we did at home.

A 26-year-old man told this:

Every year at Christmas my family and I went to my grandfather's house. From year to year we could tell what was going to take place. We usually arrived two or three days before Christmas. Just as soon as my mother and I got out of the car my grandfather would take us to the woods to look for a Christmas tree. He never had one cut because he seemed to know how much we enjoyed picking the tree we wanted. This was the big moment for us! The next day grandfather brought it into the house and put it up. All of us decorated it. We followed this pattern every year until grandfather died, but we still associate the tree-finding ritual with him.

These family rituals are secular rather than strictly religious even if they occur on, or are somehow associated with, religious holidays. Some of those reported in this study were at least 50 years old and continued after the instigators had passed. This ritual shows the forces that can keep a ritual alive:

The largest family ritual of which I am a part is a dinner in memory of my great-grandfather. This began when he was about 60 years old and lasted until he died at the age of 92. He had two wives during his lifetime; the first wife died after her twelfth child was born. He married again and had seven more children. With this big family he naturally had many grandchildren and great-grandchildren. They decided to have a big out-door dinner in his honor each year on the Sunday nearest his birthday, which was the third of June. Since great-grandfather died the family continued the observances but the number of relatives attending decreased from between four and five hundred to about one hundred and fifty to two hundred. Many members are too far away now, but last year one cousin came from California (about 3000 miles away) to be with us.

All of these rituals have been condensed to concentrate on a few highlights. It is obvious that the rituals described are more meaningful due to frequent or at least annual repetition, are social in nature, and have a certain amount of emotional coloring. Special occasions stimulating rituals are Christmas, birthdays, Sundays, reunions, Thanksgiving, and Easter. Mother's Day and Father's Day seem generally to be rituals of the immediate family.

THE ROLES OF OLDER PEOPLE

Before we move to the specific roles of older people, emphasis should be given to the fact that there seemed to be no preference for either the paternal or maternal side of the family. It did not really matter whether the aged person was male or female. Older couples were more apt to be the center of rituals than were the lone persons.

When a spouse died the locus of rituals might be changed but the ritual often continued in some form similar to the one used before. We found that really advanced age, illness, infirmity, and widowhood were the main causes of shifting the locus of a ritual involving a large kinship group. When only two or three generations were involved, the family of one child tended to bring the older member into the home, and also protected this person, if necessary, by reducing both the number of people who came in at one time and the length of time spent on a ritual.

The older people started to plan for certain rituals like Christmas or the visits of grandchildren months ahead of time and spent much time reminiscing after they were over. They planned much of their time to include these activities. For example, trains are crowded with elderly people going South after the December holidays because they want to participate in the family functions. The religious celebrations took place in other parts of the country but as several said, "It isn't Christmas without the children."

Three distinct patterns of roles emerged in this study and they are listed here without any attempt to show importance or precedence.

First are rituals with younger children, usually grandchildren. Whether these were described by young people as part of the memory of grandparents or by the older people, they left pleasant feelings. It is possible that unpleasant intergeneration experiences were not repeated to the point of ritualization.

Second are rituals that older people started many years ago and continued because they were meaningful to the family members. These were often strong enough to outlive the loss of originating elders but continued with the next generation of oldsters stepping into the vacated roles.

Third are rituals initiated and carried on by the younger generation, but centered around their elders as a way of honoring them and showing respect and love for them.

Symbols of various kinds were mentioned frequently and were associated with persons or past incidents that were called to mind. An example of this was the family in which each member had his own Christmas tree ornament. He placed it on the tree himself but if he could not be there it was used and identified as his.

EPISODES OF CHANGE

Certain episodes within the family brought about changes in the rituals or in the people participating in them. The older people identified them as follows:

Adolescent youngsters frequently wanted to be excused from participation because they had peer group plans. Grandparents understood this better than parents and frequently took the initiative in releasing them. After they reached their twenties, they enjoyed the rituals on a more adult level.

Marriage required adjustment to and by the newlyweds, especially during periods when both sides of the family observed rituals. They either started separate celebrations or had to decide which side of the family would be favored unless distance made this unnecessary. Parents and grandparents helped here and frequently changed the time or location of an observance so that the young people could be with each side of the family part of the time.

Infants were absorbed into the group quite readily.

Death of a member changed the locus of a ritual in about one-half of the cases described. Husband-wife rituals of older people were stopped if one spouse died. Most of the families, however, continued their rituals and gave due recognition to the lost member. In some cases it was a matter of recalling the long prayer, recognition of a story or a symbol of the roles played, or some other memory factor stimulated by the ritual.

While family rituals can serve as stabilizers they can also serve to restrict family members. We need more information about the attitudes of older people toward present and past rituals. How do the couples who move to retirement homes feel about their current role in family rituals? What do they mean to the people now living in homes for the aged? Also, would a family Christmas with strangers fill the need for rituals? Even if the home for the aged has mainly people of one faith it may use the ceremony and symbols of an important occasion and still fail to fill the emotional void left by the memory of the days when family rituals were associated with the same occasion.

SUMMARY

Older family members served as hosts to later generations for holidays, special family gatherings, and visits by individuals. They were recipients of gifts, especially at Christmas when other family members drew names or had discontinued exchanging gifts. They were usually the nucleus of the whole group and received attention even when the center of activity shifted to the home of a son, daughter, or other relative. They frequently developed rituals that formed a bond between themselves and grandchildren or other members of younger generations.

With more people reaching advanced age, families had to adjust rituals to absorb and accommodate new members, especially when new families were formed by marriage, but we did not find any evidence of jealousy in this respect. In fact, in one young family the grandparents from both sides of the family joined in several rituals a year because the grandfathers enjoyed each other's company so much.

REFERENCE

Bossard, J. H. S., and Boll, Eleanor S. 1950. Ritual in family living. Philadelphia: University of Pennsylvania Press.

Family Relations and Social Contacts
of the Aged in Vienna

LEOPOLD ROSENMAYR AND EVA KÖCKEIS

THE Social Science Research Center at Vienna University has so far been able to conduct two gerontological studies mainly concerned with housing problems and family relations. These projects were designed to fulfill a double purpose. First, they had to meet a request of the City Planning Department which wanted to find out whether the special types of dwellings being built for the aged in the preceding 7 or 8 years had been positively received by the inhabitants for which they had been designed and constructed. Second, our research was directed toward the construction of a cumulative theory aiming at an empirically based "sociology of the aged" which we hope will be the outcome of continued cross-national social gerontological research.

SELECTED DEMOGRAPHIC DATA
ON THE AGED IN VIENNA

Before discussing the details of our research it may be useful to present and discuss some demographic data on the aged population of Vienna. Gerontological research is particularly urgent in Vienna because 216,000 or 13 percent of the 1,600,000 inhabitants are aged 65 or over (census of 1951).[1] This is, as far as we know, a proportion not yet reached in any other European city. It is due not only to the developments observed in all industrialized countries (Rosenmayr, 1957) but also to an especially low birth rate (Rosenmayr, 1959a). Another demographic particularity is the distribution of the aged with regard to sex: 174 women to 100 men. Furthermore, over 70 percent of the women in this age group are without spouse as compared with 25 percent of the men. A comparison of the number of widowed men

[1] If, in the course of our paper, we speak of "the aged" we always refer to the age group of 65 and over.

and women shows that more than 80 percent of the widowed are women. The distribution of the aged in various types of private households is not included in the census data, but on the basis of the sample of study A (Table 1), we are able to calculate an estimate.

Table 1. *Living arrangements of persons 65 and over in private households, study A, 1957, percentage distribution*

Living arrangements	Men (N = 326)	Women (N = 335)	Total (N = 661)
Not married			
Alone	12	37	28
With relatives	12	30	24
With nonrelatives	3	7	6
With spouse	54	21	32
With spouse and relatives	17	4	9
Married			
With spouse and nonrelatives	1	1	1
With relatives and nonrelatives	1		

We see from Table 1 that one-third of aged persons live with relatives, whereas nearly double that number, namely 63 percent, have children still living. (The term "relative" is used here for any individual belonging to the extended family other than husband or wife.) The great majority of those living with relatives are persons widowed or otherwise without spouse. Only 9 percent of the aged live with their spouses *and* with relatives. Briefly stated, nearly half of the widowed and single live with relatives (this applies equally to men and women), but only just over a quarter of the married live with relatives.

Approximately 5 percent of aged Viennese (12,000) are accommodated in traditional old age homes (or in the hospital wards attached to them). Some of these homes have hundreds, some even thousands of inmates, and many of them sleep in public dormitories. The number who stay in small private old age homes could not be exactly ascertained but it is considered to be very low. The only other special accommodations for the aged are the old age apartments which the city government has started to establish in recent years. These old age apartments (Altersheimstätten) are self-contained small flats consisting of a bed-sitting-room, kitchen, hall, and closet, with a bathroom, and in the later types, a glassed-in porch. Twenty to forty such apartments are arranged as a unit in various ways as shown in Figs. 1–4. These buildings for the aged are set in courts and gardens between blocks of flats or one-family houses; such one-family houses, intended for the population in general, at the same time are built to

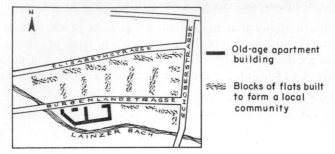

Fig. 1. *Plan of public housing development with an old age apart-ment building in Vienna, Austria*

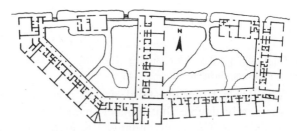

Fig. 2. *Floor plan of old age apartment building*

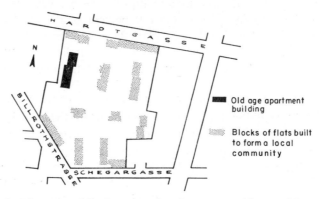

Fig. 3. *Plan of public housing development with an old age apart-ment building in Vienna, Austria*

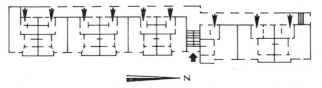

Fig. 4. *Floor plan of old age apartment building*

form a residential community. So far no provision has been made for any special community services for the inhabitants of the old age apartments. On 18 sites a total of 400 such flats housing some 700 persons have already been established and 150 more are in construction (Stadtbauamt der Stadt Wien, 1956).

THE THEMATIC AND METHODOLOGICAL FRAME OF OUR STUDY

We have carried out two studies: one in 1957 which we termed "study A" and one in 1960 which we termed "study B." The four main topics of our two studies were: (1) the dwelling, its utilities, and its furnishings as viewed by the inhabitants; (2) the environment of the dwelling: its esthetic and social aspects and the availability of public transportation and other municipal services; (3) formal and informal aid in case of need (problems of social work concerning the aged); (4) social contacts and family relationships (extent and intensity).

Study A was conducted on three groups of aged people (Rosenmayr, 1958, 1958a, and 1959b (1) a stratified sample of the inhabitants of Vienna aged 65 and over and living in private households (326 men or 41 percent, and 335 women or 25 percent), systematically selected from files covering all inhabitants of Vienna (Personenstandserhebung, December, 1955); (2) a sample of 85 men and 85 women selected from the inhabitants of traditional homes for the aged; (3) eighty-one men and 120 women, practically all the inhabitants of the special apartments for the aged which had been erected by the city government before 1957.

The second survey, in scope hardly more than a pilot study, was begun in March, 1960; only some preliminary results will be presented here. It was conducted in three groups of the special old age apartments inhabited by a total of 113 persons, and covered 92 persons. Both study A and study B were carried out through interviews.

In reporting the various standpoints of our paper we will first discuss the results of study A, and we will then show how these results were used as points of departure for hypotheses to be tested by the more elaborate investigation, study B. We will, of course, be forced to select only certain areas of our results, and we will concentrate mainly on social contacts. We have already mentioned in connection with Table 1 that one-third of the aged in Vienna live with relatives; and we have observed that single people tend to live with their relatives, whereas the married are more likely to live with their spouses only.

RESULTS OF STUDIES
Family relationships of the aged

Let us now turn to the attitude of the elderly toward living with relatives. This was explored in study A with the rather impersonally phrased question: "Do you consider it agreeable to live in the household with one's adult children?" The percentage distribution of the answers was: In favor, 29; not in favor, 50; no reply, 21. Of those actually living with their children, the percentage "not in favor" was a little lower, but still amounted to one-third. It might, therefore, be surmised that present housing difficulties in Vienna raise rather than diminish the number of old parents actually living with their children. This conclusion was quite contrary to the frequently expressed view in Vienna that the present-day housing policy of building predominantly small flats separates aged parents from their children against their will.

Typical comments received from persons not in favor of living with adult children were: "The young ought to be by themselves," "Views and aims are too different," "Old people require a quiet life." A desire to avoid quarrels and to preserve one's independence was also mentioned.

Considered by themselves, these results might induce one to jump to conclusions about the disruption of the multigeneration family as such. But our studies provide ample evidence that in Vienna, as elsewhere, the desire to have a separate household is combined with strong family ties with the aged. Answers, for instance, to the question: "To whom would you apply if you were in need of help or support?" prove that family relationships are by no means disrupted, because "the family" was the reply of about half of the respondents with children. The aged parent is quite confident that he can easily obtain help and support from his own family in case of need.

We also investigated the frequency with which old people were regularly visited. We found the expected correlation between the number of social contacts of the old people with the number of their adult children.

The attitude toward living with adult children was explored more fully in study B. This time we used a more direct and at the same time more differentiated approach as is shown in Table 2.

Table 2. *Attitudes of 92 aged persons toward living with adult children, study B, 1960, percentage distribution, N = 92*

("*Would you like to live with your adult children and their families . . .*")	*In favor*	*Not in favor*	*No reply*
In the same household?	12	58	30
In the same house but in another flat?	38	27	35
In the vicinity of their dwelling?	48	15	37

The large percentage of "no replies" is due to the fact that the question was put to all persons interviewed. Nearly half had no living children. It is to be expected that the affirmative replies on all three levels would have been more numerous had the questions been put to aged inhabitants of ordinary dwellings. Table 2, then, brings out very clearly the desire to live near, but not with their children. We were led to the notion of an intimacy "par distance," to typify ideal family contacts as old people in Vienna desire them. This is just the attitude which Sheldon in 1954 called "independent propinquity" (Sheldon, 1954, p. 151) or, as Townsend (1957, p. 204) says, "a 'supported' independence."

Actual contacts with children and grandchildren, though, do not seem to be quite as frequent in Vienna as Townsend finds them in Bethnal Green. For instance, the number of contacts with grandchildren as revealed by persons interviewed in ordinary dwellings showed that of those having grandchildren but not living with them in the same dwelling only 10 percent saw them daily, while another 24 percent saw them at least once a week.

In the special case of the old age apartments it was found in study B that nearly half the inhabitants with children had regular (at least monthly) contact with their children. But this varies considerably according to the number of children; for those with two or more children it was reduced to 10 percent. This result will rather have to be considered as an indication of the difficulties involved in any large-scale planned housing policy, for among the 19 persons with at least one child within 2 miles' distance, there was only one without regular contact.

In this connection it is interesting to note that in study A the main reason given by inhabitants for discontent with the old age apartments was that the distance from their families was too great. Accordingly we find that the discontent varies greatly between the various sites, ranging from 66 percent discontented on a rather outlying estate with poor public transport facilities to 12 percent on an estate in a fairly high-class suburb within easy reach of underground and tram.

Social contacts and local environment

The local environment itself presents quite a number of special problems. The planners had believed to some extent that the people in the old age apartments would establish close contacts with young children and their parents living on the same estate, so that the latter would act as substitutes for family contacts. This was one of the reasons for locating the aged right in the middle of the housing estate. Study B reveals, however, that only 11 percent had any contacts with people on the estate not living in old age apartments. These contacts, on closer inspection, frequently turned out to be with acquaintances known before moving into the estate.

Some old people mentioned that they liked to watch small children at play but that they strongly disliked the intrusion of children and youths into the special arrangement of garden benches provided in front of each group of old age apartments. Tenants told us that they wanted this place to be fenced in and definitely reserved for them and their visitors. On the other hand, they do not want to be completely shut off from their surroundings, as is proven by the resentment against the opaque plastic shades which have been put up on some sites as a weather protection (Massachusetts State Housing Board, 1954).

Such results lead us to the hypothesis that not only in relation to their families but also for environmental factors the "intimacy par distance" theory may be applied. Those interviewed declared a vivid interest in observing even minor and trivial happenings in the vicinity. They did not want, however, to be involved and were very sensitive to the presence of children and youths as mentioned above. It may be said: "They desire an unlimited view but resent interference."

This hypothesis is borne out by yet another result: the more recent old age apartments are in one-storied buildings,[2] and we had rather suspected that many tenants would resent the first floor. Quite to the contrary, 26 of the 29 interviewed living in old age apartments on the first floor said they preferred it to the ground floor. The main reasons given implied that they felt more secure there (less fear that somebody might climb through the window, the window could be left open at night, etc.). Another reason why those questioned seemed to favor the first floor may well be rooted in their preference for an "unlimited view."

[2] It should be borne in mind that a one-storied building in most European countries corresponds to the American two-storied structure. The "ground floor" and "first floor" in this paper are equivalent to the first and second floors, respectively, in buildings in the United States.

The first floor preference, considered in conjunction with the fact that, although not accustomed to them, 62 percent of the persons in study B said they did not mind using elevators seems a strong indication that apartment houses with more than two stories might not inconvenience the aged as long as the necessary utilities were provided.

Help in case of need

In considering the sources of help we discovered an astonishing fact: although contacts with persons living in the blocks surrounding the old age apartments were so rare, the old persons living in the same old age apartment building played very important roles as friends and companions, and particularly as support in emergencies. Thus, only 5 percent replied that they knew none of their neighbors. Sixty-two percent had more than casual contacts with at least one other person among the aged, i.e., they visited neighbors regularly. Among the women, this quota rose to 68 percent and among the widowed and single women even to 74 percent. If we include contacts with friends and with relatives other than children, in addition to relations already mentioned, it seems to a large extent due to these neighborly contacts that there was among the 92 interviewed in study B only one single person with no regular social contacts at all.

But even if some kind of regular social contact is maintained, this does not by any means imply that every aged person, when ill, can get the help and care required from relatives, friends, or neighbors. The following figures obtained in study B illustrate the problem quite well (see Table 3).

Table 3. Where 92 aged persons expect to get help and care in case of illness, study B, 1960, percentage distribution, N = 92

("In case of illness, who would . . .")	Spouse	Neighbor	Relative	Others	Nobody	No reply
Call the doctor	24	52	8	3	13	
Do the shopping	23	41	14	4	17	1
Do the housekeeping	22	19	23	4	29	3
Do the nursing	24	8	24	4	36	4

It can be seen from Table 3 that neighbors are in most cases expected to be willing to call the doctor if need be. They might even do the shopping as far as they are themselves able to do so. Few, of course, are in a position to do more. Relatives, on the other hand, are expected to help to an increasing extent as the illness grows more serious. Yet, simultaneously, the number of those who believe there would be nobody to perform the services required rises. Over one-third expect that nobody would nurse them if it were needed.

We can clearly distinguish two different "networks" of social relations responding to two different types of needs and expectations of the aged: the neighbors and the relatives.

These results show very clearly how closely are intertwined the problems of care, housing, and family relations of the aged. Therefore, although gerontological research will have to become still more differentiated and specialized, we must not lose sight of the interconnections among the various social problems of the aged. This general view also has many practical consequences with regard to the necessary coordination of help provided by the family with assistance given by formal institutions.

REFERENCES

Massachusetts State Housing Board. 1954. Standards of design: housing for the elderly. Boston: The Board.

Rosenmayr, L. 1957. Altersstruktur und gesellschaftsform. Internat. J. of Prophylactic Med. and Social Hygiene, 1: (September) 1 ff.

———— 1958. Der alte mensch in der sozialen umwelt von heute. Kol. Z. Soziol. Soz.-psychologie, 10: 642–57.

———— 1959a. Der Weiner geburtenrückgang im lichte soziologischer forschung. *In* International Population Conference, pp. 317–28. Vienna: The conference.

———— 1959b. Values and roles in Viennese family life: some research examples to demonstrate the inner connection between "pure" and "applied" research. (Report to the 4th World Congress of Sociology.) Vienna: Milan-Stresa. (Mimeographed.)

Sheldon, J. H. 1954. The social philosophy of old age. Lancet, 2: 151–55.

Stadtbauamt der Stadt Wien. 1956. Heimstätten für alte Menschen. (Mimeographed.)

Townsend, P. 1957. The family life of old people. London: Routledge & Kegan Paul, Ltd.

The Aged in the Rural Netherlands

GERRIT A. KOOY

MANY aspects of sociocultural life have received ample attention from Dutch sociologists. It is, therefore, surprising that so far they have hardly dealt with the aged, even though The Netherlands has a rapidly aging population. As a result, Dutch social gerontology, as a theory leaning on empirical investigation and as a complex of empirical research based on theory does not exist. In fact, to date, Diederich (1958) has published the only study of the life circumstances of the aged in small- and medium-sized Dutch communities.

DEMOGRAPHIC FACTS

The Central Bureau of Statistics in The Hague also publishes data which can be used in comparative studies of the aging. Figures from the Bureau show the marked growth, both absolutely and relatively, of the aged part of the Dutch population during the last 100 years (see Table 1).

After World War II the percentage of aged persons in The Netherlands increased rapidly; however, the percentage is still low in comparison with that in other western European countries. As against the 8 percent in The Netherlands one finds, for instance, about 10 percent in Great Britain and 12 percent in France (Durand, 1955). An explanation for this difference cannot be found in the mortality rate in The Netherlands. Everyone who wants to prolong his life should settle down in the Rhine delta and nowhere else. The Dutchman has the longest life-span in the whole world. The explanation for the relatively low percentage of aged people in The Netherlands is to be found in the birth rate. The exceedingly high probability of survival in The Netherlands is coupled with a marriage fertility no longer existing elsewhere in Europe. The economically active part of the Dutch population, therefore, carries the same economic burden or an even higher

Table 1. Growth of the aged part of the population
of The Netherlands, 1849–1958[a]

Year	Number 65 years and over	Total population	INDEX		Aged as percentage of total population
			Aged	Total population	
1849	145,079	3,056,879	100	100	4.7
1859	161,512	3,309,128	111	108	4.9
1869	197,223	3,579,529	136	117	5.5
1879	218,552	4,012,693	151	131	5.4
1889	270,875	4,511,415	187	148	6.0
1899	306,541	5,104,137	211	167	6.0
1909	358,527	5,858,175	247	192	6.1
1920	404,000	6,865,314	278	225	5.9
1930	491,918	7,935,565	339	260	6.2
1947	683,139	9,625,499	471	315	7.1
1954	889,971	10,680,023	614	349	8.3
1955	912,498	10,821,700	629	354	8.4
1956	936,066	10,957,000	645	358	8.5
1957	960,372	11,095,700	662	363	8.7
1958	991,064	11,278,000	683	369	8.8

[a] Source: Central Bureau of Statistics, The Hague.

one than does the same part of the population in other western countries.

As in other countries, women outnumber men among the Dutch
aged (Table 2). A tendency toward leveling is now perceptible in the
sex ratio.

Table 2. Sex ratio in the Dutch population, 1955[a]

Age	Aged women per 100 aged men
65–69	109
70–74	109
75–79	111
80–84	115
85 and over	129

[a] Source: Central Bureau of Statistics, The Hague.

Cities have a lower proportion of aged people than the countryside
(Table 3). The higher proportion of old people in the rural population is easily explained. The limited economic possibilities in rural
areas cause many a country dweller to migrate to the city. It is self-
evident that the aged do not predominate among those migrating for
economic reasons. This is also the case when other reasons are the
cause of migration.

The percentage of the aged in the total population differs considerably from municipality to municipality. Several factors account
for the difference. One of these is the formation, mostly in the years

Table 3. *Percentage of total and aged population by size of municipality, May 31, 1947*[a]

Size of municipality	Percentage of total population	Percentage of persons 65 and over	Index of concentration of aged persons
Less than 1000	0.89	1.10	124
1000–2000	2.69	3.06	114
2000–5000	12.15	13.35	110
5000–10,000	13.85	14.00	101
10,000–20,000	15.69	15.37	98
20,000–50,000	13.86	13.61	98
50,000–100,000	10.54	10.14	96
100,000 and over	30.33	29.37	97

[a] Source: Central Bureau of Statistics, The Hague.

after World War II, of regional centers for aged people. It is evident, however, that this factor is not the main one. A more forceful influence is the religious composition of the population on which the size of the nuclear family appears to be strongly dependent. The Netherlands' high birth rate is primarily due to the procreational orientation of the Roman Catholics and the Calvinists. In these municipalities and in regions where the percentage of Roman Catholics is relatively high, the percentage of aged is normally relatively low. For example, the province of Groningen with its 6 percent Roman Catholics had 8.3 percent aged people, while the province of Limburg with its 94.5 percent Roman Catholics had, on the same data, 5.7 percent aged people. Of course, there are other factors and their common influence can be, and in several cases appears to be, greater than that of both factors mentioned above.

While, as has been mentioned, aged women outnumber aged men in The Netherlands, the contrary situation is found in the Dutch countryside. In general the number of male aged increases relatively with an increase in the agricultural character of the municipality (see Table 4). The difference in sex ratio which exists in other countries as well as in The Netherlands has not yet been fully explained.

Table 4. *Sex ratio in municipalities of different sizes, May 31, 1947*[a]

Size of municipality	Aged women per 100 aged men
0–1000	89
1000–2000	92
2000–5000	95
5000–10,000	97
10,000–20,000	102
20,000–50,000	114
50,000–100,000	121
100,000 and over	127

[a] Source: Central Bureau of Statistics, The Hague.

The composition of the rural aged according to marital status is not available. The Central Bureau of Statistics does possess rather recent data on the marital status composition of all Dutch aged, as well as of those aged living in the big cities of Amsterdam, The Hague, Rotterdam, and Utrecht. A comparison of these data leads to the impression that the number of married male aged is relatively smaller in the countryside than in the cities, while the reverse holds for the female aged (Table 5).

Table 5. Marital status of the aged population, December 31, 1947, percentage distribution[a]

Marital status	All Aged		All Aged Excepting 4 Large Cities[b]	
	Male	Female	Male	Female
Married	61.5	41.3	60.3	42.4
Single	9.0	13.2	9.9	13.3
Widowed	28.4	44.1	29.1	43.4
Divorced	1.1	1.4	0.7	0.9

[a] Source: Central Bureau of Statistics, The Hague.
[b] Amsterdam, The Hague, Rotterdam, and Utrecht.

If the impression is right, the explanation can possibly be found in the stronger hereditary bond with the rural environment which males have. In a rural environment, as is well known, chances for marriage are relatively slight. In the cities, as well as in the countryside, the number of married male aged is relatively higher than the number of married female aged. There are several reasons for this, such as the surplus of women, the better chance of remarrying for widowed and divorced men, and the age difference between the marriage partners. (Many aged men are married to women who are not yet aged.)

The marital status of the aged gives an insufficient indication of the measure to which the aged are self-dependent in everyday life. Those who remain unmarried, widowed, or divorced do not always live alone. Some of them live with relatives, married children, and cousins. Table 6 shows the extent to which the aged live together with related families in the cities and in the countryside.

We are able, in one of our own studies, to show considerable differences in the types of residence among aged in different rural regions. While in one district many older persons live in the same household with their married children, in another district they normally live apart (see Table 7).

To summarize, then, the statistical data yield the following results: (1) the number of aged people is relatively larger in rural areas than

Table 6. *Type of residence of the aged, June 30, 1956*[a]

Residence	Amsterdam, Rotterdam, The Hague		Rest of The Netherlands	
	Number	Percent	Number	Percent
Dwellings	188,338	96.1	628,769	92.9
In nuclear family	126,782	64.6	429,883	63.5
In relative's household	12,167	6.2	82,579	12.2
With nonrelatives	4,806	2.5	16,621	2.5
Alone	44,583	22.8	99,686	14.7
Institutions	7,603	3.9	48,132	7.1
Total	195,941	100.0	676,901	100.0

[a] Source: Central Bureau of Statistics, The Hague.

in cities; (2) men form the majority of the aged population in the countryside; in the cities, however, women outnumber men; (3) the number of married men among the aged is presumably lower in the countryside than in the cities, but the number of married women among the aged is probably higher in the countryside than in the cities; (4) between rural areas considerable differences exist in the proportion of the aged in the total population; (5) substantial differences exist between rural regions as to the percentage of aged people living with their kin.

Table 7. *Composition of all farmers' households in three rural regions*

Household composition	Achterhoek	Nort West Veluwe	Tielerwaard
One nuclear family or single person			
Alone	5366	2587	730
Plus brother of husband	268	34	23
Plus sister of husband	104	21	5
Plus brother of wife	54	20	7
Plus sister of wife	45	21	1
Plus father of husband	439	82	9
Plus mother of husband	633	92	27
Plus father of wife	113	33	3
Plus mother of wife	91	29	8
Plus distant relatives	221	68	27
Two nuclear families of successive generations			
Related by husbands	1677	205	39
Related by wife	563	95	12
Two nuclear families of same generation			
Related by husband	5	6	7
Related by wife	2	5	1
All other situations	443	64	16
Total	10,024	3362	910

STATUS AND ROLE OF THE RURAL
AND URBAN AGED

Of course, these differences do not offer the slightest certainty about the differences in status and role between the urban and rural aged or between the aged in diverse rural regions. They give rise, however, to certain presumptions about the part played by the aged in different societal contexts and coincide with our experiences gained during field work in several parts of Holland. We have to keep in mind, of course, that the differences in the status and role of the aged are also a result of social class. The results of Diederich's investigation, for instance, show that considerable status and role differences can exist among the aged in different social classes in the same sociogeographical environment. As much as possible, however, we will avoid the differences resulting from membership in different social classes. So far as neglect of social stratification is possible and permitted, we dare to state then that the status of the rural aged is generally higher than that of the urban aged, and that the former's role in the community is also more important than that of the latter. As important as the difference in status and role between the rural and urban aged is, that between the aged in different rural areas must also be considered. In the eastern sand area of Holland the status of older people is substantially higher and the role played by the aged is more important than in the alluvial coastal region of the west.

The basic sociological question is why these differences in status and role exist between urban and rural aged, as well as between rural aged in diverse regions. In our approach to this, we refer to a very concise and particularly clear observation of Ernest Burgess (1955). This well-known sociologist enumerates at least five factors which contribute to the degradation of the American aged: the trend from the rural to the urban way of life; the trend from self-employed to employee; the decline of self-assured economic security; the transition from cultural homogeneity to cultural diversity; and the shift from the primary to the secondary significance of human relations. All these factors, Burgess states, enter into the framework of the transition of a rural into an urban society. In The Netherlands, too, the status of the aged decreases as urbanization advances. Incidentally it should be mentioned that urbanization proceeded rather quickly in The Netherlands during the twentieth century: in 1899 more than 51 percent of the Dutch population lived in municipalities having less than

10,000 inhabitants; in 1958 only 25 percent of the total population still lived in such municipalities.

If urbanization leads to a lowering of the aged's status, then it is clear why the status of the urban aged is lower than that of the rural aged in The Netherlands. When, as already established, the status of the aged in the one rural area is obviously lower than that of the aged in another rural area, the question arises as to whether this difference can be explained on the basis of a difference in the degree of urbanization between the two areas. An affirmative answer to this question cannot be given in all cases. If the status of the aged is considered in neighboring rural municipalities or groups of municipalities, then we find that generally in the more urbanized areas the status of the aged is indeed lower. Comparing the status of the rural aged in Holland proper and that of the rural aged in the eastern sand area, the conclusion has to be drawn that the established connection between urbanization and lowering of status is not perceptible in this case. While the status of the rural aged in the west is considerably lower than that of the rural aged in the east, the urbanization of the western countryside surely does not surpass that of the rural east. In our opinion, the status difference last mentioned has to be explained by taking into account the differing historical developments of both parts of The Netherlands.

In an historical-sociological approach it is immediately obvious that these regions have a very different history. The western countryside has been "open" for many years and experiences the direct influence of having been economically and mentally taken up in a circle whose focus is the neighboring cities of Amsterdam, Leyden, Utrecht, etc. Thus, it lies in the stream leading to the existence of a republic once feared all over the world, the Republic of the Seven United Netherlands. This countryside of the west was an urbanized area early in history. How different is the development in the eastern sandy regions! The poor fertility of the soil and a far-reaching isolation have hardly led to evolution. In a local community of some hundreds of people, the population is mentally enclosed. One does not live in terms of a promising future, but is constantly referring to the past. Mental attitudes and circumstances combine to prevent the advance of urbanization. The foregoing explains why, in the second half of the nineteenth century, the status of the aged in the western countryside was considerably lower than in the eastern sand area. The emancipation of the nuclear family was already well advanced in the west in that period. It was normal there that a young couple lead an autonomous existence by keeping an independent household. This phenomenon is one of the clearest indications of the relatively low status and the relatively restricted role of the aged. On the eastern sand area, to the contrary, a nuclear family individualism was still completely lacking by the second half of the last century. The nuclear family is fully integrated in a broader family group and nobody makes any noticeable objection to this integration. The household as an economic unit commonly embraces the members of three succeeding generations, and the pattern of life in and outside the household is in nearly all aspects determined by the representatives of the oldest generation.

Toward the end of the nineteenth century the eastern sand area lost its static sociocultural character as the result of the coincidence of several factors. The process of cumulative change which took place in the area is quite impressive. A region traditionally characterized by backwardness has worked off its economic and technical arrears in an astonishingly short time; its social structure has changed substantially; the education of the native population has improved considerably. What happened can be characterized as urbanization at high speed. Notwithstanding the quick evolution—an evolution also based on the wishes of the inhabitants themselves—the population insists on the preservation of the traditional basic structure of the local society. So persistent is this that the rural society of the eastern sand area, although at this moment at least as modern as that of the west in several respects, is still based in the last instance on the social norms developed during its long era of excessive isolation. Primarily due to these norms the status and the role of the aged have lost substantially less of their importance than one might have expected. The number of households embracing grandparents, parents, and children, for instance, is still abnormally high, if compared with the rest of The Netherlands. The oldest generation still dominates within these households and also in enterprises conducted by all household members.

In our opinion everything appears to point to a gradual disappearance with time of the status and role differences between the rural and urban aged in The Netherlands. In stating this, we only extend a visible trend. From an intensive investigation in the field we learned that the high status of the aged in the east has been seriously undermined in recent years. Nuclear family individualism did not come to a standstill at the boundaries of the eastern sand area. It also finally penetrated into the mind of a population which wanted to share in the advantages of modern civilization and to preserve its specific social relationships at the same time. Because of this penetration the main support of the aged's important status and role, namely, their great authority and prestige inside the extended family, has dropped from under them. There is enough reason, indeed, to presume that the problem of the status and role of the Dutch rural aged as such will have lost nearly all its actuality within a measurable space of time.

REFERENCES

Burgess, E. W. 1955. Human aspects of social policy. *In* International Association of Gerontology, Old age in the modern world, pp. 49–58. Edinburgh: E. and S. Livingstone.

Diederich, J. 1958. Levensomstandigheden van bejaarden in kleinere en middelgrote gemeenten van Nederland (Life circumstances of aged people in smaller and medium sized Dutch municipalities). The Hague: Nationale Raad voor Maatschappelijk Werk.

Durand, J. D. 1955. Demographic background in developed and under-developed countries. *In* International Association of Gerontology, Old age in the modern world, pp. 32–36. Edinburgh: E. and S. Livingstone.

The Social Life of the Aged Homeless Man on Skid Row

KEITH A. LOVALD

THE community of the homeless man has been largely ignored since Nels Anderson (1923) studied "hobohemia" in 1923. The present discussion is based on a study of such a community—the Gateway district of Minneapolis, Minnesota—carried out by the writer between June, 1958, and May, 1960 (Caplow *et al.*, 1958; Lovald, 1960). The findings of this study indicate that, among other important changes, the Gateway's population has aged considerably since the community's origin before the turn of the century. In 1910 the median age of the Gateway's inhabitants was 34 years (Solenberger, 1911). Thirty years later (1940) the median age was 53 years. By 1950 the median age had increased to 57 years and in 1958 it was 60 years. A special census in that year showed that 60 percent of the total population of approximately 3000 inhabitants was 60 years of age or more. All but 27 of these were men (Lovald, 1960).

While the trend toward an aging population is not peculiar to the community of the homeless man, we find its elderly members resolving the problems of aging in a different manner from the elderly members of other communities. Some of these differences occur as a result of the particular circumstances of the aged homeless man. Equally important, however, is the fact that on skid row—the term used to describe the contemporary form—the individual is prepared for aging and its problems in ways which are in contrast to those found in most American communities. To a great degree, this is because skid row contains unique institutions which substitute for those of the larger community. Most of these institutions have been inherited from a previous era when the community performed such highly specialized functions as the recruiting and supplying of migratory-casual workers. Hobohemia's institutions were, for the most part, appropriate to the needs of young unattached transients, most of whom were extremely mobile and had few commitments to organized community life in the usual sense of the word.

The Great Depression brought an end to the hobohemian phase. During the 1930s the community of the homeless man became associated with the poverty of mass relief, when the "shelter house" and the "bread line" were its most notable features. Elements from both of these periods can be found in the present-day community. These elements constitute vital parts of the social life of skid row's aged homeless men. This paper is a brief description of these elements. The material which follows derives from a variety of sources, including interviews with a random sample of the Gateway's homeless men, observation over a period of approximately one and a half years, and analyses of records of private and governmental agencies.

THE ECONOMIC SITUATION OF THE GATEWAY'S ELDERLY HOMELESS MEN

Like a slum, skid row is an area of the city where poverty prevails. Most of its buildings are falling apart; accumulations of filth and refuse are common; and few of its inhabitants possess clothing other than that which can be purchased at rummage sales, secondhand clothing stores, or is given away by the Salvation Army and other charitable organizations. In 1958, the median annual income for the total population of the Gateway was $960. For the employed (including the partly employed) it was $1440. For the unemployed (including the retired) it was $920 or $77 per month. Approximately 67 percent of the Gateway's inhabitants received income from sources other than employment, with social security pensions and old age assistance making up the largest portion (40 percent of the total). More than 80 percent of the Gateway's elderly inhabitants (i.e., those 65 years of age or more) received monthly incomes of $115 or less (Caplow *et al.,* 1958).

Despite the fact that the cost of living in the Gateway is the cheapest in the city—for example, in the summer of 1958 one could buy a meal of salt pork and beans for 40 cents and rent sleeping quarters for 50 cents a night—it frequently becomes necessary for those living on retirement and assistance incomes to find other ways of maintaining themselves. In the hobohemian tradition these may include holding part-time jobs, taking an occasional casual job, peddling, panhandling, mooching, and the mission bread line.

A few of the Gateway's elderly men engage in various kinds of employment. Some have permanent part-time jobs, such as sweeping out a store for a few hours each day, while others attempt to secure casual employment in what is called the "slave market."

The Gateway's slave market resembles the one of the 1920s in that jobs may be secured on a formal basis through the Minnesota State Employment Service or, informally, on the street outside this office. Because the market value of older men is less than that of younger ones, most make use of the informal facilities of the street. The procedure is simplicity itself. A nearby farmer or a local enterpriser in need of extra help drives up to the curb in front of the waiting men, makes his requirements known, and, after deliberation on the merits of the would-be workers, selects the ones he likes. Higgling over wages and conditions of employment is common; older men, however, will take jobs the younger men have turned down. Most of the jobs are of the general maintenance variety, fill-ins in industry for short periods of time and farm-labor jobs. Handbill distributors also seek temporary employees in the Gateway's slave market. A large share of these jobs are taken by elderly men.

A few of the Gateway's elders feature peddling as a principal source of income, while others will peddle from time to time in order to make up a deficit in their income. Most of the peddling done in the Gateway is without benefit of a license. These men peddle a miscellany of articles, usually small things of nominal value; often they sell flowers. The flower sellers do business in the bars during the evening and their clientele is usually composed of men who are accompanied by women. Clothing is ordinarily peddled on the main streets of the Gateway. The market for used clothing (particularly overcoats) is best in the fall, but it is in the spring when such peddlers are found in greatest number.

There are few professional beggars in the Gateway. Panhandling, however, is quite common. Despite the fact that the panhandler enjoys little esteem in the community, a considerable number of its inhabitants are forced to turn to this form of begging. Panhandlers are more apt to be middle-aged, though older men will resort to it when necessary.

Mooching in bars likewise is ordinarily done by younger men. A much more respectable form of mooching, however, is a common end-of-the-month practice of the long-time resident. This is called "coffee-ans." The practice is exactly the same as was utilized by hobohemians: with a minimum of a dime a man asks for a cup of coffee and something to go with it. Depending upon the particular restaurant, this may include a sandwich, a roll or doughnut, a piece of pie, or just a piece of bread. In most instances the extra free fare is usually several days old and has been set aside for this purpose. A few restaurants do a fairly substantial business in "coffee-ans." Others tolerate it because they do not want to embarrass an old customer who is temporarily without funds. Some restaurants will even provide a second cup of coffee if requested. In order to get added nourishment, the practitioner will sometimes drink about half of the coffee and then load the cup up with sugar and milk.

Finally, one alternative to a desperate economic situation is to visit a rescue mission. The Gateway's Protestant missions adhere to the hobohemian tradition of holding nightly services, after which the participants are invited to remain for something to eat. Several of the missions also provide free beds. Most of the Gateway's residents express distaste for the missions' policy of "soup, soap, and salvation," and the man who makes a habit of "getting saved" is called a "mission stiff," a hobohemian term still often heard in the Gateway.

LIVING ARRANGEMENTS IN THE GATEWAY

The Gateway has inherited, with very little modification, the types of housing characteristic of hobohemia. The flop house has disappeared (although some missions will make their floors available for a free "flop") but the lodging house with "cage" (or "cubicle") sleeping quarters is still common. Cages are partitioned areas averaging, in size, about five by seven feet. They are arranged in rows separated by narrow corridors. The partitions around each cage are usually made of corrugated steel or wall board about seven or eight feet in height. Most are covered with chicken wire. Each cage contains a narrow bed; some include a chair and chest. Most of them rent for 60 cents a night.

Approximately one-half of the Gateway's elderly men live in such cages. Many of them have radically transformed the original intention of the cage's designers. Since the cage does not include storage space, possessions are conspicuously displayed, with clothing ordinarily hung on nails behind the door and on convenient two-by-fours. Articles other than wearing apparel are usually stored in boxes placed under the bed and in corners. Many of the older men are avid collectors of oddments—some of which they purchase at rummage sales in the community. One lodging house operator ruefully describes these collectors as "pack rats" and finds it necessary to make occasional raids, in the tenant's absence, to clear the cage of the excess.

Many of the Gateway's older men prepare meals in their quarters and the smell of cooking often permeates the already overburdened atmosphere of several of the hotels and lodging houses. Since this is against the law, electric hotplates and cans of soup, coffee, and beans are surreptitiously stored under beds or in boxes.

The question has often been raised as to why there are so few major fires in the area. None of the hotels and lodging houses have adequate fire-fighting equipment. Combined with overloaded electrical circuits and the ever-present "drunk," it would seem that these places invite catastrophe. Most of the residents are very much aware of the danger—a major reason why the habitual drinker is disesteemed—and, as a result, they maintain a more or less continuous alert for fire. When queried on the subject, some of the residents, particularly the older men, indicated their preference for the open-cage facilities because a fire in them can be detected more readily than it can in closed private rooms.

LEISURE AND RECREATIONAL ACTIVITIES OF THE GATEWAY'S ELDERLY HOMELESS MEN

Unless it is very hot, the older man spends the largest share of his waking hours in the hotel or lodging house. While in his sleeping quarters he may alternately nap or sit by his bed, read, or listen to the radio. A few even have television. In the hotels without lobbies several men may get together in a larger room for an afternoon or evening of drinking. The drinking that takes place is usually well controlled and only under the most unusual circumstances is there apt to be trouble.

The lobby performs a number of functions. Its principal one is to supply a setting for certain leisure-time activities, the most popular of which are cardplaying, visiting, and reading. Newspapers constitute the bulk of the community's reading material, and local papers are the most popular. All but a few of the Gateway's restaurants sell the morning paper, and it is a common practice for older men to read part of the paper while eating and then return to the lobby to finish it. By 10:00 A.M. the average lobby contains a number of papers, and these are available to anyone who failed to get up in time to purchase one, or who prefers to spend his money on other things. Such magazines as *Time, Life,* and *Newsweek,* plus mystery, detective, and sports varieties are the most popular. Book readers prefer popular fiction such as western stories. Most of the men read in silence, but in some lobbies it is common to hear mutual exchanges of information,

A striking change has occurred in the homeless man's intellectual interests. Hobohemians were avid readers of left-wing publications, such as the *Hobo News*. If there are any old-time hobos still around the Gateway, their presence was not detected by an enumeration of the community's reading habits.

A feature of life on skid row which increases in importance for the older man is walking and park sitting. Many of the Gateway's elders, and younger men as well, embark each morning during favorable weather for one of Minneapolis' parks to remain there for a large part of the day. While parks within the Gateway accommodate the greatest number of men, it is not uncommon for a man to make the 2-mile journey to one of several parks south of the main business district. Walking is a regular part of the daily itinerary of all but a few of the elderly men. While many combine a stroll with a visit to a park or some other public place, others set out each morning with no particular route in mind. A construction or clearance project attracts many of the Gateway's inhabitants—a spectacle which has been largely substituted for the soapbox gatherings of the previous era. A nearby "jungle" is visited by a limited number of the residents, especially during the summer months. Here, among other activities, it is possible to indulge in undisturbed drinking.

DRINKING IN THE GATEWAY

The prevailing conception of skid row is that it is inhabited primarily by drunks and alcoholics in the final stages of dissipation. While intoxicated men are a common sight, it would be a mistake to conclude that all of skid row's inhabitants make drinking their sole objective in life. The Gateway's drinkers comprise two distinctly different kinds of groups, with the age of the drinker and length of his residence in the community of critical importance. One type of group is called the "bottle gang." Bottle-gang members do most of their drinking outside; cheap wine, often fortified with various substances, is the favored drink. Most bottle gangs are made up of younger men, although occasionally elderly men may be seen assembled with the others in alleyways and behind buildings. If they do drink, the Gateway's elders are more apt to fall into a second type, that of beer drinkers; most beer drinking is done in the community's bars and saloons. The regular consumption of beer is the most reliable indicator that a man is not an alcoholic unless, of course, he is a teetotaler. Several of the Gateway's bars allow regular customers to charge drinks and many pensioners take advantage of this convenience—especially toward the end of the month. For many of them, the bar is a substitute for the hotel lobby. During the afternoon, when they are not crowded, some of the bars permit men to congregate in the booths without buying. Thus situated, the spectator is often treated to such interesting sights as a prostitute "on the make," a fight, and various kinds of police activities.

Older men are much less apt to get into difficulty with the police than are the younger men. In 1957, for example, there were 6372 arrests (nearly all were for drunkenness) in the Gateway. Of these, 3678 were arrests of members of the community. The median age of this aggregate was 48. More than half (54.7 percent) were 49 years or less. Slightly less than 19 percent of the older men (i.e., those 60 years of age or more) were involved in any difficulty with the police. Their offence rate was less than one-fourth as great as that of the younger residents (Lovald 1960). There are several reasons which explain this differential. Older men do not drink as heavily, most of their drinking is done inside, and they are more apt to benefit from the Gateway's informal system of police control. Regarding the latter, if an old-timer suspects that an evening of drinking will lead to severe intoxication, he makes this belief known to his favorite cop. He indicates where he will be at a certain hour and, so that he does not forget, he asks to be given a reminder to go home when the policeman makes his rounds. In some instances the policeman even helps the man get to his quarters.

CONCLUSION

Little can be concluded from such a brief description as this, except that it provides contrasting materials for a more general consideration of the community life of older persons. The elderly unattached man on skid row differs from his counterpart elsewhere in that the community in which he lives enables him to resolve many of the problems of aging in ways not found in other communities.

REFERENCES

Anderson, N. 1923. The hobo: the sociology of the homeless man. Chicago: University of Chicago Press.
Caplow, T., Lovald, K. A., and Wallace, S. E. 1958. A general report on the problem of relocating the population of the lower loop redevelop-

ment area. Minneapolis: Minneapolis Housing and Redevelopment Authority.

Lovald, K. A. 1960. From hobohemia to skid row: the changing community of the homeless man. (Unpublished Ph.D. thesis.) University of Minnesota.

Solenberger, Alice W. 1911. One thousand homeless men. New York: Charities Publication Committee.

Social Isolation in Destitution *

ANGELO PAGANI

THE term *destitution* is used instead of *poverty* because the incomes of the aged included in this study were far below any possible subsistence level, and because the state of want produced by old age is essentially irreversible since it does not offer those perspectives of solutions that are usually associated with the notion of poverty.

The purpose of the study was to examine the impact of irregularity of earning and consequent destitution on the system of social relationships of the elderly in destitution, especially to determine which kinds of relationships are retained when the elderly are obliged to remain for a long time in a situation of this kind.

Four aspects of the problem were investigated: leisure-time activities, friendly relationships, family relationships, and loneliness. Information was collected on (1) the usual patterns of life of the subjects—leisure activities in which they usually engaged; frequency, type, and occasion of social relations; origin and significance of the common relations formed in the neighborhood, at work, with youth, etc.; and on (2) frequency and type of relations maintained with relatives not living in the household; activities and services exchange; relevance of family contacts for the care of the elderly; opinions with regard to amount of solitude experienced; and degree of social isolation.

THE STUDY SAMPLE

The subjects for the study were 86 men and 203 women drawn from the list of recipients of monthly relief in the city of Milan. Age and sex distribution of the sample is shown in Table 1.

The approximately equal proportions of the major age groups in the sample encourage the assumption of age as an independent variable.

Marital status is important because it influences the availability of

Table 1. *Age groups in the study sample, percentage distribution*

Age groups	Men (N = 86)	Women (N = 203)	Both sexes (N = 289)
65–70	23.3	29.1	27.4
71–75	30.2	29.1	29.4
76–80	30.2	22.7	24.9
81–85	15.1	16.3	15.9
86–90	1.2	2.0	1.7
91 and over		1.0	0.7

family relations. Among men the prevailing group is that of married persons with a surviving spouse; among women the widowed group is largest. The high percentage of persons widowed more than 20 years indicates that conjugal loneliness is firmly established as a life pattern (Table 2).

Table 2. *Marital status of the study sample, percentage distribution*

Marital status	Men (N = 86)	Women (N = 203)	Both sexes (N = 289)
Single	12.8	28.0	23.5
Married	66.3	0.5	20.1
Separated	3.5	4.4	4.2
Widowed	17.4	67.1	52.2
Over 20 years	2.3	25.1	18.3
11–20 years	4.6	17.2	13.5
6–10 years	4.6	11.3	9.3
Under 5 years	5.8	13.3	11.1

The most striking fact that emerged from a study of the living arrangements of the group was the high number of old people living alone. Among the women, 85 percent lived alone. Thus, social isolation, even as crudely defined, has become the general life pattern of the destitute aged, owing to their separation from the family context.

In terms of size of household, 69 percent consisted of one person, and another 25 percent consisted of two persons (usually a man and his spouse). Only 6 percent consisted of more than two persons.

RESULTS

Because of space limitations, results are presented here for only two parts of the study—friendly relationships and loneliness. Data regarding leisure activity and family relationship are available from the author.

It should be kept in mind that the restriction of the sample to the destitute aged and the lack of control groups from other populations limit the applicability of the results to the general population or to relevant portions of it.

Friendly relationship

Social isolation in old age is often attributed to the biological survival of a few members of a cohort among a few pairs or relatives already eliminated. The main biological fact could not produce definitive effects if it was not associated with the social immobility typical of old age. The old do not have the physical ability of youth to promote social contacts. The objective fact of the breakdown of old friendly relationships is therefore associated with a psychological lessening of interest in people. The rate of this process of isolation is influenced by the effective degree of physical mobility of the elderly, and by the level of economic means available to them. When the elderly are bound to a life of mere subsistence or destitution, the possibility of keeping or gaining new social contacts is heavily reduced.

The general hypothesis of a reduction in friendly relations as a basic phase of the process of aging has been clearly defined by our results as shown in Table 3.

Table 3. Maintenance and sources of friendship relations, percentage distribution

Maintenance of friendships	Men (N = 86)	Women (N = 203)	Both sexes (N = 289)
Previous friendships kept			
Without acquiring new ones	19.8	20.2	20.1
Acquiring new ones	18.6	13.3	14.9
Old friendships lost			
Without acquiring new ones	45.3	49.7	48.4
Acquiring new ones	12.8	13.8	13.5
No answer	3.5	3.0	3.1
Closest friends are			
Schoolmates	2.3	1.0	1.4
Fellow soldiers	2.3		0.7
Playmates of youth	7.0	9.3	8.7
Fellow workers	15.1	5.9	8.7
Neighbors	17.5	52.2	41.8
New friends	15.1	2.5	6.2
Have no friends	13.9	8.9	10.4
No answer	26.8	20.2	22.1

Almost 62 percent of the old people in the sample claimed to have lost old friends, and only 28.4 percent reported having made new friendships. Of the approximately 140 who lost old friendships, only 39 or about 28 percent acquired new ones. Of those who kept their old friendships, 14.9 percent made new friends.

The term *friendship relations* covers situations which are socially very different. The impact of friendship on social life differs according to the elements of affinity that formed the companionship.

The highest proportion of the subjects indicated that their neighbors were their closest friends. Table 3 shows that the trend was more marked for women than men, perhaps because the men had a wider range from which to choose. The preeminence of the neighbor relationship can be explained by the long residence of old people in the same house; 62.2 percent had lived in the same flat for more than 20 years. This fact also explains the persistence of old friendships and scarcity of new ones.

The frequency of friendship contacts is shown in Table 4. It is probable that the old people recognized as friendship contacts only those which were of a formalized type, for example, a visit paid to or received from a friend.

Table 4. Frequency and place of friendship contacts, percentage distribution

Friendship contacts	Men (N = 86)	Women (N = 203)	Both sexes (N = 289)
Frequency			
Several times daily	12.8	20.2	18.0
Once a day	23.3	28.6	27.0
Once a week	23.2	23.1	23.1
No answer	40.7	28.1	31.9
Place			
Home	19.7	63.5	50.5
Public House	21.0	1.0	6.9
Street	18.6	7.4	10.7
No answer	40.7	28.1	31.9

Women had almost two-thirds of their friendly contacts in homes, theirs or their neighbors, while men had about an equal number in homes, public houses, and on the street. Age did not seem to influence where friendly meetings occurred; nearly the same proportion in every age group met friends in the home. Neither did the meeting place influence the frequency of friendly contacts—the highest proportion of cases fell within the class frequency of "once a day" for all meeting places.

Examination of the content of friendly contact shows that talking was almost the only activity in which either men or women engaged. Among men, 47.6 percent declared they spent their friendship time talking, 7 percent indicated that they played cards, and 3.5 percent drank. Almost half—41.9 percent—of the men failed to give any response. Among the women, 64.5 percent said they talked, 2 percent played cards, 3 percent drank, 2 percent did other things, and 28.5 percent failed to reply. It is felt that the question was somewhat resented in view of the unusually high number of persons failing to reply.

Where personal and holiday festivities are held is important since aloneness on days that ought to be happy is surely a sad experience. Table 5 shows that for 73 percent of the sample, personal festivities

Table 5. Locations of personal festivities, percentage distribution

Location of festivities	Men (N = 86)	Women (N = 203)	Both sexes (N = 289)
Homes of friends	3.5	2.5	2.8
Own homes	65.1	76.3	73.0
Have no friends	4.7	3 5	3.8
No answer	26.7	17.7	20.4

were usually held in their own homes; only 2.8 percent said that they usually were guests of friends on such occasions; another 3.8 percent escaped the question by declaring not to be in touch with friends.

Aloneness on occasions of personal festivity assumes a different meaning for old people living alone and for those living with spouse or sons. A separate consideration of those who declared they were alone for personal festivities according to the composition of the household, showed that the proportion of those obliged to hold their festivities alone decreased from 74.8 percent for those who lived alone, to 69.5 percent for those living with spouse, to 68.7 percent for those living with sons.

The lack of friendly or family relations on occasions culturally recognized as times of close contact (Christmas, etc.) can be accepted as a proof of the lack of social integration. For the destitute aged this situation predominates for both men and women. Approximately 52.5 percent of the group spend major holidays at home and alone. Of the remaining group, 32.5 percent can rely on an invitation from friends and sons, and 6.5 percent, even if remaining in their own homes, are visited by friends or sons. Actually the participation of sons, as guests or hosts, outnumbers that of friends by 22.1 percent and 16.9 percent, respectively.

Table 6 shows that when the old people lived with sons they were less likely to be invited by other sons but were more likely to be visited by sons than when living alone or with spouse only. The participation of friends, as guests or hosts, was also more frequent in households in which sons were present.

Table 6. *Where holiday celebrations are held, by type of living arrangements, percentage distribution*

		Living arrangement		
Where holiday celebrations are spent	Alone	With spouse	With spouse and son	With sons
At home	53.5	71.2	55.6	57.2
Receiving son (other son) at home	1.0	10.1	22.2	
Invited to son's (other son) home	20.7	11.9	11.1	7.1
Receiving friends at home	3.1			7.1
Invited to friend's home	18.6	3.4		21.5
No answer	3.1	3.4	11.1	7.1

Loneliness

Following the lead of other researchers, loneliness of the destitute old people constituting the sample was studied from two points of view—the empirical situation and the personal attitude toward it. *Social isolation* was used to define the objective situation while *solitude* was used to indicate the personal attitude, in the sense of self-judgment, toward the situation experienced.

The measures of loneliness included attitude of respondents toward their situations, future perspectives as viewed by the respondents, and values attached to some of the commonly proposed solutions.

About half the group indicated that they felt lonely during the day. A smaller proportion of the men (35 percent) than of the women (57.2 percent) reported themselves as lonely during the day. A higher proportion of the old people living alone (56.5 percent) reported loneliness, while among those living with spouse and sons only 22.2 percent felt that they were lonely.

About 60 percent of the men and about 50 percent of the women said they would not like to have more social contacts. Apparently accustomed to living alone, they showed little readiness to label their situation as loneliness. Even among those who reported feeling alone, more than a fourth declared that they were not interested in an increase of social contacts.

The different attitude toward increasing contacts can derive from a different attitude toward the future. Old people who believed that their situation was likely to be changed saw the usefulness of social contacts. Age is directly related to optimistic attitudes toward the future as shown in Table 7. These findings are compatible with the objective situation in that betterment of the situation, through an increase of social contacts, is more probable and feasible when persons

Table 7. *Age and attitudes toward future improvement of situation,*
percentage distribution

| | Age group | | | |
Attitude toward future situation	65–70	71–75	76–80	81–85
Can be improved	65.0	56.3	58.3	47.8
Will remain unchanged	28.6	36.8	37.5	41.3
No answer	6.4	6.9	4.2	10.9

are relatively younger, that is, when they are better able to cope with
the new social order.

Two solutions were presented for stimulating social contacts—organization of clubs for old people and planning of domestic visits.
Equal proportions (50 percent) of the male and female groups expressed the belief that their social situation would be improved by
both of these measures. About one-third of the men recognized only
the usefulness of clubs, and one-third of the women felt the same way
about domestic visits. The different attitude of the two sexes toward
the problem of social contacts reflects men's greater interest in outside experiences and, therefore, greater appreciation of the solution
that increases the sphere of external contacts. On the contrary,
women, accustomed to living inside the home, are more interested in
solutions which can extend the sphere of domestic contacts.

The type of household in which the old person lives conditions his
attitude toward the two solutions offered. Those who live alone prefer
to rely on an increase in visits; those who live with a spouse expect
improvement in their situation from new contacts fostered by clubs.
Even those who live with sons prefer the club solution.

The sense of loneliness can be fostered by the incapacity of relatives to cope with the needs and wishes of old people. The effective
roles performed by family members in the support and care of the
elderly persons can determine the situation of isolation as subjectively
judged by the older persons. When asked whether they were satisfied
with what their relatives had done to help them, the majority said
they were satisfied with the help received.

There was a marked difference between those who lived with a
spouse and those who lived with sons only with regard to satisfaction
with what had been done to relieve the sense of loneliness. In the
former instance, 52.5 percent said they were satisfied, while in the
latter instance only 5.9 percent were satisfied and 58.9 percent were
dissatisfied. Obviously the companionship of sons did not guarantee
the kind of help expected by the elderly.

Destitution which characterized all members of the study group was presumed to have an influence on the subjective attitudes expressed. About one-third of the group believed that the solution of their economic problem would not be effective in improving their social relationships. But nearly two-thirds expressed the opposite opinion.

The two circumstances which the elderly felt would be helped by a solution of their economic troubles were "the wish to move about" and "more money to go and see relatives." Surprisingly the wish to move about seemed to be more important for persons relatively more aged, while availability of money for visits to friends and relations seemed to be considered most desirable by less aged persons.

CONCLUSIONS

It can be concluded from the study that destitution which results in social isolation without sufficient financial resources to extend activities or to decrease dependency on neighbors and family members for social satisfaction is associated with feelings of loneliness and deprivation. There is a need for an analytical approach devoted to the interpretation of opinions of the elderly in order to state (a) the range of correspondence of solitude as feelings expressed by the elderly and the objective situation of isolation, and (b) the causal assessment of social isolation in order to differentiate between the effects of old age and those of financial need.

The Aged in Rural and Urban Japan

YUZURU OKADA

THE Japanese family has long been regarded as an element of a kinship organization and as a unit group existing beyond its constituent individuals. The continued existence of a family is guaranteed by the unbroken succession of male descendants (real or adopted). This succession consists of the inheritance of family property, succession of patriarchate, and maintenance of family occupation and family traditions (customs, religion, etc.).

The head of the family has the duty of training his successor, that is, his eldest son, for patriarchate. For this purpose it is most effective to keep the eldest son in his home, even after the latter's marriage, to share occupation, tradition, and property with him. This living together also benefits the head of the family since it makes his old age secure.

The Japanese people are preserving the custom of living with children in spite of the reform since the war of the civil code which emphasized the nuclear family. According to the author's study of a village (1956–1959) in southwestern Japan, old people over 60 years of age are, without exception, living with their children.

A research study done by the National Research Institute on Public Opinion in 1953 of 500 old people over 60 years of age showed that 81 percent of old persons in city areas and 79 percent of those in rural areas are living with their children, and mostly with eldest sons and their families (National Research Institute on Public Opinion, 1954).

Although there seems to be no real difference between rural and urban areas as to living with children, there is some as to attitude. Research by the same institute on 2000 persons 20–59 years of age pointed up this difference.

To the question, "Do you think it is better for married children to live with their parents or live separately?" there was the following percentage distribution of answers by urban and rural areas.

	Together	Separately	Other
Urban	44	44	12
Rural	70	22	8

But if the question was asked as pertaining to their own case, the difference between urban and rural residents became small.

To the question, "Do you wish to live with your children and grandchildren if you get old or do you think you need not do so?" the following percentage distribution of answers was obtained.

	Together	Separately	Other
Urban	73	22	5
Rural	89	9	2

Thus there is greater discrepancy between attitude and real life of urban people than of rural people. The reasons for this are more individualization, more rapid disappearance of family occupation, and more youths who are sensitive to the change of social life in city areas than in rural areas.

It is interesting that, in spite of the individualization in Japanese cities, there was no mention of preference for their own and other's privacy and independence, except fear of troubles which might necessitate living separately. This is the difference from the Western societies described by Professor Townsend (1957).

The status of persons in the family has been determined by their role is dealing with the family property and occupation. Since farming, the dominant occupation in the rural area, is a family occupation, the older people enjoy high status in their family so long as they control farming and property.

In city areas, small-scale commerce and industry have been regarded as semi-family occupations and those engaged in them have enjoyed stable status. But workers, white and blue collar, are increasing rapidly. Their occupations are not hereditary and they are not able to work when they reach old age.

Table 1. Occupational status of 500 older persons, by age group, Japan, 1953, percentage distribution[a]

Age group	Farmers	Merchants and small factory owners	Management	Clerical employees	Laborers	Professionals	Other	Not working
60–64	24	9	1	5	5	3	2	51
65–69	28	9	2	1	7	1	1	51
70–74	12	9		9	1	4	1	64
75–79	6	2				2		90
80–84	10							90
85–89								100

[a] Source: National Research Institute on Public Opinion and Ministry of Postal Service, Post Office Life Insurance Bureau, *Public Opinion Research on Old Age Life*, The Institute, Tokyo, Japan, 1954.

Of the 500 old people studied by the National Research Institute on Public Opinion (1954), more worked at farming and small-scale commerce and industry than at any other occupation. Table 1 shows the distribution by occupation.

The old people living in cities who have not been engaged in such semi-family occupations do not have as stable a status in the family as do the farmers in villages.

REFERENCES

National Research Institute on Public Opinion and Ministry of Postal Service, Post Office Life Insurance Bureau. 1954. Public opinion research on old age life. (In Japanese.) Tokyo: The Institute.

Townsend, P. 1957. The family life of old people. London: Routledge and Kegan Paul, Ltd.

American Culture and the Phenomenon of Friendship in the Aged

MALCOLM J. ARTH

THIS paper represents the perspective of an anthropologist looking at one aspect of the culture of the United States often neglected by social scientists, namely, the nature of close friendship. In particular, it is concerned with the depth of such relationships. This paper does not use proximity or frequency of contact as measures of friendship. It focuses rather on feelings, and views close friendship as a relationship between two non-kin involving deep feelings of personal liking, trust, confidence, and dependability in time of crisis.

There have been several significant investigations touching upon the topic of friendship in the aged, though it was not a major focus. Such studies include work in the area of personal adjustment by Cavan *et al.* (1949), the recent investigation of Kutner *et al.* (1946) and also that of Townsend (1957), the latter treating the topic with more intensity than the others. However, these studies are not primarily concerned with exploring the limits or the depth of close friendship.

In this paper, data from three separate studies by the author are reported. Table 1 briefly categorizes each of these, and is intended merely to help the reader in keeping them distinct.

Table 1. Some characteristics of study samples

| | | Number | | |
	Source	Male	Female	Average age
Community group A	Volunteers from city-sponsored golden age club	3	12	65–88
Hospital group	Random sample of newly admitted patients to a state psychiatric hospital serving Boston	13	27	60–90
Community group B	Randomly selected homes in a middle-class Boston suburb	6	8	40–50 (3 male, 4 female) 60–70 (3 male, 4 female)

Some of the differences among the three groups are immediately apparent, and these will be discussed. Note that the three investigations do not represent a total research design conceived in terms of cross-checks. Each does contain data relevant to the general topic; but the investigations were carried out at different times and, except for the last, were largely independent of each other. All three studies collected data through interviewing informants. In the hospital group, these were supplemented with interviews with family members and other persons. Both open-ended and semi-structured interviewing techniques were used. The establishment of an intimate field relationship with informants was seen as crucial, and some subjects were interviewed as much as 10 hours each, none for less than 2 hours. A brief description of each of the three studies follows, after which some implications are discussed.

COMMUNITY GROUP A

Community group A consists of 15 volunteer subjects from a city library golden age group, who were interviewed in 1955. These 15 subjects were quite heterogeneous; there were married, widowed, and single persons, several ethnic and religious affiliations, as well as several social class levels. Despite this heterogeneity, several basic patterns emerged from the interviews. These included (1) a general mistrust of others, and (2) a dearth of close relationships with others. The following responses illustrate these patterns.

Miss Green relates, "The people in my life have all had other interests and other friends than me. If I had someone from childhood who I knew and liked, and saw all the way growing up, that would be a best friend. No one is. I have no best friend."

Mrs. Lyons says, "Hardly anyone's worthy of secrets. The minute you displease them they gossip and tell what you disclosed and more besides. . . . I make friends and leave them all the time. Some stay on but that's because they want to, not because I want them. I could leave any one of them at any time."

Mr. Moore says, "It takes a long time to be sure of a person. You have to know 'em winter and summer, many years, to be sure they're a real friend, and you can't be sure then. . . . Even your folks and nearest relatives can do you out of things."

These excerpts are not isolated remarks taken from otherwise pleasantly toned interviews. The theme of mistrust and the dearth of close friends characterized the interview sessions of most of these community volunteers.

HOSPITAL GROUP

In contrast, the hospital group is a random sample of 40 patients newly admitted to the state psychiatric hospital which serves the city of Boston.[1]

A mistrust of others and a lack of close friendships similar to that encountered in community group A is also found in the hospital group. This is perhaps not unexpected since mental illness often implies an inability to relate well to others. However, many of the patients lived quite normal lives until their later years and even in these cases, with very few exceptions, close friendships were not found in spite of a considerable amount of social involvement.

In regard to the limits of close friendship, it is interesting to note that friends played a minimal role in the sequence of events leading to hospitalization. The issue of hospitalization seems to call more for family involvement. Family interest was extremely strong in the hospital group and also in community group B. In light of recent discussions of changes in the American family, this has importance. In all three studies, the role of the family, particularly at times of crisis, is clear. This is not to be identified with living arrangements, since not many subjects lived with children. It may be that studies concerned with proximity or living arrangement as primary measures of family interest are neglecting an important consideration, namely, feelings.

The author at first assumed that the phenomena observed in the two investigations described above (i.e., dearth of close friendships and general mistrust) were primarily a function of the subjects' age. The question was then asked, however, whether these subjects might be reflecting an underlying American cultural pattern rather than a pattern peculiar to old age. Perhaps there was a "friendless American." What, then, in American society, culture, and national character might account for such a phenomenon?

The author assumes that the nature of interpersonal relationships within a society is markedly influenced by its institutions, values, and

[1] Geriatric Hospitalization Project located at Boston State Hospital, Boston, Massachusetts. Sponsored by the National Institute of Mental Health, June, 1958–June, 1961.

national character. Thus, writings concerned with the alienation of the individual are viewed as important in explaining the shallowness of friendships. The "anomie" described by Durkeim (1951) and the "spurious culture" outlined by Sapir (1949) seem particularly relevant. Fromm (1941) also comments on the alienation of the individual within the mass society, and Riesman's (Riesman *et al.*, 1953) analysis of the "other-oriented" character structure is likewise pertinent. By and large these writers have not been concerned with friendship as such, but their comments on the nature of Western society, America in particular, seemed consistent with the findings from the two studies described previously. It was hypothesized that the United States, with its competitive institutions, its system of cultural values emphasizing achievement and status, and its fostering of an "other-oriented" national character, might well produce a spirit *not* conductive to the formation of close friendships. Moreover, these are still other mechanisms in the culture which sometimes function to inhibit the formation of close friendships. These include: the extensive geographic mobility pattern, social class mobility, and, particularly for the aged, physcal infirmity. A third study was begun to explore this hypothesis, and is reported below.

COMMUNITY GROUP B

Community group B, currently being studied, was to consist of 10 men and women between the ages of 40 and 50, and 10 men and women between the ages of 60 and 70. In this ongoing investigation, the expectations and limits of close friendship are explored in depth. Contrasts with closeness to kin are made, and informants compare their contemporary experiences with those earlier in life. At the time of this writing, the work with this group has not been completed, and the present paper reports only the trends of data thus far collected.

First of all, the dearth of friendship and general mistrust of others is not as marked in these subjects, regardless of age, as it was in the two earlier studies. Some informants from both age groups do have close friends, though these informants acknowledge that it is a rare phenomenon. In this regard, there are some differences between the sexes. Men seem to have fewer close friendships than women. There is even a tendency for men somewhat jokingly to name their wives as their "best friends," though wives seldom so designate their husbands.

The tendency for the males not to have close friendships may be related to their relatively greater involvement in the competitive occupational structure. Also the culture's strong negative sanctions regarding male homosexuality may be pertinent. A close friendship involving strong positive feelings might produce anxiety on an unconscious level and would thus tend to inhibit the formation of such relationships between men in the United States. Gorer (1948) and others have commented on this aspect.

The role of the American wife as a "friend" is intriguing, because in the husband-wife relationships many of the factors cited as inhibitors of friendship are removed. Spouses do not ordinarily compete in the occupational sphere, or for class position. Geographic mobility as a dividing force is not potentially present, and the culture positively sanctions the stability, trust, and confidence basic to close friendship. The American love-marriage may thus provide a functional solution for a system which undoubtedly creates strong needs for affective response from others, yet surrounds the individual with institutions not conducive to that end.

The differences between the volunteer subjects and the randomly selected ones have important methodological implications. It is not argued here that the randomly selected subjects of community group B are "typical" even of the suburb from which they come. They are too few in number, and in one sense they too were volunteers, since only half of the people approached agreed to cooperate. It is suggested, however, that the marked difference between these subjects and the volunteers strongly indicates a need for some type of systematic sampling, particularly when dealing with a research topic that might tend to draw "lonely" volunteers.

SUMMARY

In summary, then, it is suggested that the term "friend" is a gross one in need of refinement and definition. Evidence has been offered to suggest that volunteer subjects may be a poor choice for research, particularly in this topical area. Differences between men and women in regard to the existence of close friendships have been cited, and interpretations of underlying reasons for this have been made. Finally, the general hypothesis that Americans, in spite of an outgoing informal nature, do not have close friends, was not completely supported. In spite of institutional, value, and personality impediments, such relationships apparently do occur with some frequency, particularly between women.

The author is aware that the groups described are small in number and that it is presumptuous to talk about "American" patterns from these data. Variation doubtless occurs within the culture. Indeed, variations are found within these very data. Nevertheless the data are offered as suggestive of possibly widespread cultural patterns. This topic would profit greatly from more extensive research not only within the United States, but also in other societies, both literate and illiterate. The interdependence of personality, values, and social institutions in the creation and maintenance of such interpersonal relationships offer intriguing research possibilities.

The close friend might be viewed even as a linking role combining attributes of the primary institution of the family, on the one hand, and secondary affiliations on the other. As a linking role in the social system, it seems worth further examination.

Acknowledgments. A dept of gratitude to Professor Cora DuBois and to Dr. Florence C. Shelton who have contributed substantially to the author's thinking in regard to this problem is happily acknowledged.

REFERENCES

Cavan, Ruth S., Burgess, E. W., Havighurst, R. J., and Goldhamer, H. 1949. Personal adjustment in old age. Chicago: Science Research Associates, Inc.

Durkheim, E. 1951. Suicide, a study in sociology. Glencoe, Ill.: Free Press.

Fromm, E. 1941. Escape from Freedom. New York: Farrar and Rinehart.

Gorer, G. 1948. The American people: a study in national character. New York: W. W. Norton & Co.

Kutner, B., Fanshel, D., Togo, Alice M., and Langner, T. S. 1956. Five hundred over sixty: a community survey on aging. New York: Russell Sage Foundation.

Riesman, D., Glazer, N., and Denney, R. 1953. The lonely crowd. New York: Doubleday & Co.

Sapir, E. 1949. Culture, genuine and spurious. *In* D. G. Mandelbaum (ed.), Selected writings of Edward Sapir in language, culture and personality, pp. 308–31. Berkeley: University of California Press.

Townsend, P. 1957. The family life of old people. Glencoe, Ill.: Free Press.

MENTAL HEALTH and

REHABILITATION

Organized by
RICHARD H. WILLIAMS
National Institute of Mental Health, Bethesda, Maryland
MARTIN ROTH
University of Durham, Newcastle upon Tyne, England

A Comparative Analysis of Employment Patterns of Older Psychiatric Male Patients and Men in the Community

HELEN M. JAMBOR

IN a work-oriented culture, such as exists in the United States, value is placed upon employment and its rewards. Financial rewards largely determine the mode of life adopted and position in the community. Other rewards, such as feelings of achievement and identification with the work group, may also be derived from employment. Participation in the occupational community indicates one's ability to function at a more or less normal level in the nonaged world (Friedmann and Havighurst, 1954; Havighurst and Albrecht, 1953; Lipset and Bendix, 1959). Accordingly, factors connected with occupational participation might be expected to discriminate between persons who become mentally ill in later years and other older persons.

This paper is concerned with a preliminary analysis of work histories of older men hospitalized for psychiatric reasons and of a sample of men in the community. A subsequent analysis of the occupational histories of women is planned. The purpose has been to determine whether certain variables pertaining to occupation differentiate the two groups. Did the hospitalized men work at lower occupational levels during most of their productive years? Did they retire at a younger age and for different reasons than did the rest of the community population?

Six occupational characteristics were chosen as particularly important in shedding some light on the relationship of the individual to the occupational realm: present occupation, main gainful occupation, age when last employed in main gainful occupation and total time

This is one of a group of five papers based upon preliminary findings from a 5-year interdisciplinary study of geriatric mental illness, conducted at the Langley Porter Neuropsychiatric Institute, San Francisco, and sponsored by the National Institute of Mental Health and the California Department of Mental Hygiene.

spent therein, time since leaving last regular job, and reasons for leaving last regular job.

The data used in this analysis were based upon work histories of two groups of men in San Francisco. The hospitalized group was composed of 246 male patients 60 years of age and older who were admitted to the psychiatric ward of San Francisco General Hospital during the calendar year of 1959, excluding those previously hospitalized for mental illness or alcoholism and those who had not been residents of San Francisco for at least 1 year. This hospital serves the city and county of San Francisco. Virtually all persons hospitalized for psychiatric disorders spend a brief period there prior to disposition to a state mental hospital, a nursing home, or release. The men in this sample were interviewed at the hospital shortly after admission.

The community sample, consisting of 300 men 60 years and over, was drawn from the 18 San Francisco census tracts in which the highest proportion of persons 60 years and over resided in 1950. They were interviewed in their own dwellings in the community.

Ages in the two groups ranged from 60 to 95 years. Since occupational differences might be obscured by differences due to age over this 35-year span, comparisons were made by two age groups: those 60 through 69, and whose 70 and over. The younger and older age groups are reported on separately wherever significant differences were found. Otherwise, ages have been combined in the report of findings. Totals vary depending on the availability of information on each variable. The unemployed have been grouped with the retired in this paper since the likelihood of securing employment, once men become unemployed and are over 60, is relatively slight. Eighteen percent of the hospital and 11 percent of the community samples were unemployed. To facilitate reporting, the two groups will be referred to as the "hospital men" and the "community men."

FINDINGS

The most critical fact to be known about the occupation of an older person is his current employment status; that is, whether he is employed or retired.

There were striking differences between the community and hospital samples in regard to current employment status. Two-fifths of all community, as contrasted to one-twentieth of all hospital men, were currently employed. Put another way, 59 percent of the community, as contrasted to 95 percent of the hospital group, had retired (Table

Table 1. *Present occupational status of all men, community and hospital samples, percentage distribution*

Occupational status	Community (N = 298)	Hospital (N = 246)
Employed[a]	41	5
Retired[a]	59	95

[a] Denotes a significant difference between the hospital and community samples.

1). Since one might expect a sizable proportion of retirees among men 70 and over, the two samples were compared by age groups. Over half of the 60 to 69-year-old community men, as compared to one-tenth of the hospital sample in the same age group, were employed. Similarly, over one-fourth of the older community men, as compared to a very small fraction (only two men) of the older hospital group, were still working (Table 2).

Table 2. *Present occupational status of all men by two age groups, community and hospital samples, percentage distribution*

Occupational status	Community	Hospital
60–69		
Employed[a]	54	10
Retired[a]	46	90
Number sampled	154	95
70 and over		
Employed[a]	27	1
Retired[a]	72	99
Number sampled	144	151

[a] Denotes a significant difference between hospital and community samples.

Consideration was given to the possibility that the employed in the community sample might have come from a higher socioeconomic status prior to their productive years. Educational achievement was used to give a rough idea of preemployment socioeconomic status. Almost half of the employed community men, as contrasted with about one-fourth of the retired in both the community and hospital sample, had completed high school. Further, almost one-fourth of the employed community men had attended college, as contrasted with about one-tenth of the retired in both the community and hospital sample (Table 3). These findings would suggest the better educated tend to continue to work at a later age.

The striking differences in the proportion of employed and retired in the two samples led to the decision to compare only the retired men in the remainder of this analysis. The problem was restated as follows:

Table 3. Educational achievement of all men by current occupational status, community and hospital samples, percentage distribution

Education (in years)	Community		Hospital[a] (N = 178)
	Retired (N = 174)	Employed (N = 121)	
7 or less	38[b]	23	28
8 through 11[c]	37	30	49
Completed high school	13[b]	25	16
1 or more of college[c]	12[b]	22	7

  [a] This includes 12 employed hospital men.
  [b] Denotes significant differences between groups within the community sample.
  [c] Denotes a significant difference between hospital and community groups.

What factors pertaining to work histories differentiate older retired men who require hospitalization for psychiatric reasons from other retired men in the community? Were there, for example, differences between them in regard to the level achieved or the length of time spent in their main occupation; that is, the occupation in which they worked longest? In this analysis, professional-managerial work was considered as the highest level, white collar next, and blue collar as the lowest level of occupation.

Significant differences were found between the older retired men as to level of main gainful occupation. One-third of the older community men, as compared to about one-eighth of the older hospital men, had as their main gainful occupation professional and managerial work. Almost half of the older community men, as contrasted with about two-thirds of the older hospital men, had worked longest in blue-collar occupations. Thus, the older retired men in the community tended to have achieved a higher occupational status than did their hospitalized contemporaries during their productive years. No such differences, however, were found between the younger men in the two samples as to level of main gainful occupation. Almost two-thirds had been blue-collar workers, roughly one-fourth had been white-collar workers, and a little over one-tenth had been professional managerial (Table 4).

The findings suggest that the older hospital men resembled the younger men in both samples, but were differentiated from the older community men as to level of main gainful occupation. Why should level of main gainful occupation distinguish the older, but not the younger men? Perhaps analysis of other factors regarding occupation might provide some clues.

One factor might be greater mobility from occupation to occupation among the hospitalized. The total times worked in the main gainful occupation were, therefore, compared. No important dif-

Table 4. Level of main gainful occupation of retired men by two age groups, community and hospital samples, percentage distribution

Occupational status	Community	Hospital
60-69		
Professional, managerial, officials, and proprietors	13	11
White collar	29	23
Blue collar	58	66
Number sampled	68	80
70 and over		
Professional, managerial, officials, and proprietors[a]	33	15
White collar	22	22
Blue collar[a]	45	63
Number sampled	97	135

[a] Denotes a significant difference between hospital and community samples.

ferences were found. About three-fifths of both samples had worked in their main gainful occupations for 30 years or more. The older men in both groups tended to have worked longer than the younger men in their main gainful occupation, but not much longer (Table 5).

Table 5. Total time in main gainful occupation of retired men, community subsample and hospital sample, percentage distribution

Time in occupation (in years)	Community (N = 49)	Hospital (N = 172)
1 through 19	10	13
20 through 29	31	26
30 or more	59	61

Perhaps the hospital men left their main gainful occupations at an earlier age either to enter another occupation or to retire. Such a shift from main gainful occupation might constitute a major life change, and the ages at which such shifts occur might provide clues as to reasons for the malfunctioning of the hospital group. Only small differences were found between the older retired men in both samples in regard to the age when they had last worked in their main gainful occupations. One-fifth of the older community men and a little over one-fifth of the older hospital men left their main gainful occupations prior to age 60. Slightly less than half of the older community men and slightly over half of the older hospital men left their main gainful occupations during their sixties; and roughly one-third of the older community and one-fourth of the older hospital men left their main gainful occupations at 70 or over.

These findings would indicate that of the older hospital men, the majority (two-thirds) had left their main gainful occupation at an age that is considered customary for retirement. In this respect they were not differentiated from the older community men.

The younger men of both community and hospital groups tended to leave their main gainful occupations at an earlier age than did the older men of both samples.

Significant differences were also found regarding ages at which the younger men of both samples last worked in their main gainful occupations. Less than half of the younger community men, as compared to two-thirds of the younger hospital men, were less than 60 years of age when they last worked in their main gainful occupations. Since no differences were found in regard to total time in main gainful occupation the younger hospital men may have started working in their main gainful occupation earlier and therefore probably left at an earlier age (Table 6).

Table 6. Age last worked in main gainful occupation of retired men by two age groups, community and hospital sample, percentage distribution

Age last worked	Community	Hospital
60–69		
Under 60[a]	44	64
60 through 69	56	36
Number sampled	71	66
70 and over		
Under 60	20	23
60 through 69	45	53
70 and over	35	24
Number sampled	104	119

[a] Denotes a significant difference between hospital and community samples.

This was the first variable which differentiated the younger men in the two groups. Could it be that the younger hospital men retired from the employment realm when they left their main gainful occupation? Or did they change to other occupations prior to retirement? In an attempt to answer these questions a further comparison was made of the two samples as to period of time since they left their last regular job. No significant differences were found between the retired of the two samples for either age group. It is interesting that a higher proportion of the younger community men (about one-sixth), as compared to the younger hospital men (roughly one-fourteenth), had not worked for 10 or more years at a regular job (Table 7).

Attitudes toward retirement have been reported as affecting the

Table 7. *Time since leaving last regular job for retired men by two age groups, community and hospital samples, percentage distribution*

Time since leaving last job (in years)	Community	Hospital
60–69		
Within past 2	34	43
2 through 4	32	26
5 through 9	18	24
10 and over	16	7
Number sampled	71	76
70 and over		
Within past 2	12	13
2 through 4	12	17
5 through 9	30	31
10 and over	46	39
Number sampled	105	124

individual's adjustment in retirement (Crook and Heinstein, 1958; Thompson and Streib, 1958; Thompson *et al.,* 1960). Other things being equal, one might anticipate that individuals who retire voluntarily would adapt themselves to retirement status, whereas those who are forced to retire might have more difficulty in functioning in retirement. We were interested in determining the reasons for retirement which might distinguish the two groups.

Slightly over one-third of the older men in both samples retired voluntarily. Contrary to what might be anticipated, a higher proportion of the older community men than of the older hospital men was forced to retire because of ill health. A higher proportion of the older hospital men than of the older community men was forced to leave their last regular job for such reasons as employer's policy, being laid off, or dissolution of business.

In contrast, no significant difference was found as to the reason for retirement for the younger men in the two samples. Slightly over half of the younger men in both groups left their last regular jobs because of ill health or inability to do the work. Almost one-third of the younger community men, as compared with one-fifth of the younger hospital men, was forced to retire for reasons other than ill health. Only a small percentage of both samples in the younger age group retired voluntarily (17 percent of the community men and 12 percent of the hospital men). Further analysis is clearly required concerning the association between attitudes toward and reasons for retirement (Table 8).

Table 8. Reason for leaving last regular job for retired men by two age groups, community and hospital samples, percentage distribution

Reason for leaving job	Community	Hospital
60–69		
Voluntary: Retired	17	12
Forced: Employer policy, laid off		
or business dissolved	31	21
Ill health or inability to		
do the work	52	54
Other	0	13
Number sampled	71	68
70 and over		
Voluntary: Retired	37	34
Forced: Employer policy, laid off		
or business dissolved[a]	25	43
Ill health or inability to		
do the work[a]	34	16
Other	4	7
Number sampled	105	95

[a] Denotes a significant difference between hospital and community samples.

DISCUSSION AND SUMMARY

Malfunctioning in later years, as reflected by hospitalization for psychiatric disorders, appears to be associated with retired status; that is, a much higher proportion of the hospital group than the community group had retired from employment. Relatively late retirement tends to be associated with higher educational achievement and a higher occupational level. One might speculate that continued employment in later years provides a positive use of time and additional income, which may be important for maintaining a high functioning level. These ramifications are beyond the scope of this paper, but will be explored in further analysis of our data.

Among the retired, some men continue to function in the community, whereas others have psychiatric disorders severe enough to warrant hospitalization. Yet it is interesting that the level of occupation did not differentiate the hospitalized group from younger retired men in the community.

Early retirement appears to be associated with ill health for both the hospital and community men. A detailed analysis has not yet been made of the types of ill health which resulted in forced retirement. However, a brief review of the cases of younger hospital men revealed that alcoholism and affective disorders were prominent among their diagnoses. It may be that such disorders interfered with their ability to continue in the labor force.

It would appear that admission to a mental hospital reflects a more rapid decline in functioning ability of some men in their sixties than might be true of the general male population. But further exploration may reveal that the younger community men have environmental supports, such as higher income, presence of family and friends, etc., which help them to function in the community. Additional examination of our data will deal with these alternative explanations.

Although they differed in many respects, in some respects the younger retired men in both samples were more alike than were the younger and older men within each sample; for instance, in regard to main gainful occupation, age at last work therein, and reason for leaving last regular job. One might therefore speculate that there is an association between historical events, such as the depression of the thirties and World War II, and occupational change and age. Further, it is possible that technological changes from craft to machine, emergence of retirement programs, and changing attitudes toward work from one generation to the next may account for age differences. Again, this is an area for further exploration.

It appears from our findings that the later retirement occurs, the less important do occupational factors become. For example, differences in levels of main gainful occupations among the older men did not appear to affect age at which they retired, and a sizable percentage of older men of both samples retired after reaching 70 years of age. Apparently the development of psychiatric disorders among those who retired at a later age may be due to factors other than those which are associated with occupation. In preliminary analyses of some other social factors, we found that differences between the hospitalized and nonhospitalized tend to decrease with advancing age.

Differences between the older men and the younger men in the hospital sample provoke one more speculation. It may be that the cohorts of the older hospital men who died in their sixties or seventies were more like the younger hospital men with regard to physical, mental, and sociological variables. As we follow up these younger hospital men, we may find that few of them reach an older age group.

Further analysis of our data is necessary for an understanding of the effect of occupation upon style of life during productive years and the development of psychiatric disorders in later years.

Acknowledgments. Acknowledgment is given to the assistant research sociologists under the supervision of the author: Mrs. Karen Many, Mrs. Patricia Gumrukcu, Mrs. Alide Eberhard, Miss Audrey Thaman, and Mr. Robert Mielke.

REFERENCES

Crook, G. H., and Heinstein, M. 1958. The older worker in industry. Berkeley: University of California, Institute of Industrial Relations.
Friedmann, E. A., and Havighurst, R. J. 1954. The meaning of work and retirement. Chicago: The University of Chicago Press.
Havighurst, R. J., and Albrecht, Ruth. 1953. Older people. New York: Longmans, Green & Co.
Lipset, S. M., and Bendix, R. 1959. Social mobility in industrial society. Berkeley: University of California Press.
Thompson, W. E., and Streib, G. F. 1958. Situational determinants: health and economic deprivation in retirement. J. Social Issues, 14: No. 2, 18–34.
Thompson, W. E., Streib, G. F., and Kosa, J. 1960. The effect of retirement on personal adjustment: a panel analysis. J. Gerontol., 15: 165–69.

Psychosocial Reasons for Geriatric Hospitalization

DAVID BLAU, MALCOLM J. ARTH, MARJORIE E. KETTELL,
J. WEST, AND D. J. OPPENHEIM

THE increasing number of people 60 years of age and older being admitted to mental institutions each year has been a cause of growing concern. There has been much speculation about the reasons for this increase in admissions. A recent report by the Group for the Advancement of Psychiatry (1950) states, "It may be said that whenever an aged patient cannot care for himself and has no one to care for him, he eventually goes to the state hospital although many of the aged presently admitted for care in a mental hospital show nothing more important than memory impairment, confusion, and physical infirmity." This implies that such individuals are not emotionally ill. In order to test such hypotheses as these, Boston University received a 2-year research grant from the National Institute of Mental Health to study the reasons for admission of patients 60 years of age and older to the Boston State Hospital. Two major questions guided the research: (1) What are the relative roles of social, economic, physical, and psychological factors in precipitating hospitalization, and (2) What are the general characteristics of these elderly patients?

DESIGN AND METHODS

The Boston State Hospital has an annual admission rate of about 500 geriatric patients. The hospital serves residents of the city of Boston. Admission can be accomplished by the signature of one physician, who certifies that a patient is "emotionally ill," but does not have to state that the patient is "psychotic." Patients must have 12 consecutive years of residence in Boston prior to their current hospitalization to remain at this institution.

Thus far, 40 newly admitted patients, randomly selected from

The investigation was supported by a research grant OM-69 (C2) from the National Institute of Mental Health, Public Health Service.

approximately 1 year's admissions, have been studied intensively. "Newly admitted" means the patients either were completely discharged from any previous admission, or had no previous admissions. As a check on the typicality of the 40 patients, as well as to collect certain additional data, a survey was conducted of 300 consecutive admissions. A comparison of this group of 300 patients on a number of variables shows that the sample of 40 is by and large representative of geriatric admissions.

The full-time project staff consists of a psychiatrist, who is the project director, psychiatric social worker, clinical psychologist, and social anthropologist. An internist has been employed part time to do a physical evaluation of each patient. Methods have included intensive interviews and psychological tests. A larger sample was sacrificed in favor of an exhaustive exploration of each individual, his family, and other persons such as physicians, police, nursing home operators, friends, and clergymen.

FINDINGS
Demographic characteristics

Of the 40 intensively studied patients there are 27 females and 13 males ranging in age from 60 to 92 with a mean age of 73. Thirty-five of the individuals are Caucasian and 5 Negro. There are 23 Roman Catholics, 12 Protestants, and 5 Jews. Currently, 13 patients are married, 13 widowed, 9 single, 4 separated, and 1 divorced.

Economics

Over 80 percent of the sample are from the working class, fewer than 20 percent being from lower segments of the middle class. The sources of income are as follows: 13 patients are supported by public welfare, 14 patients are supported by social security or private pensions, and 9 by their families, including spouses. Only 4 patients were working.

In general public resources are available to provide the basic necessities for these patients. Only the 4 working patients expressed any concern about money, since they were unable to work at the time of hospitalization. It did not seem that any of the patients were admitted to a psychiatric institution as a result of inadequate funds. However, it is certainly likely that public rather than private psychiatric hospitalization is selected for this group because of their income level.

Social Characteristics

Here we were concerned with three questions: (1) Where do the patients live; (2) How interested are their families; (3) Did isolation or family rejection contribute heavily toward bringing the patient to the hospital?

Twenty-one of the 40 patients were living with relatives (including spouse) at the time of hospitalization, 9 were living in nursing homes, and 10 were living alone. Fourteen of the 19 patients not living with kin had relatives living in the same city within a radius of 4 miles. Only 5 patients had relatives who were living farther away than 4 miles. There were no cases for whom some blood kin could not be contacted by the project staff.

Having thus established that kin are available, let us consider how involved they were with the patients. In 27 cases interest and concern of the relatives were rated as strong. Criteria for this high degree of interest and concern included families making efforts to care for the patient, having the patient live with them, attempting alternatives to placement in the state hospital, visiting in the hospital, and other more subtle ways of demonstrating genuine involvement with the patient.

In 11 cases the relatives' concern was rated as moderate, that is, the relationship with the patient was positive, but the relative was not as involved with the patient's problems or daily life prior to hospitalization. In only 2 cases the relatives had no contact with the patients and patients were completely rejected. Thus, a vast majority of our patients had available family, most of whom displayed a high degree of involvement with the patients.

It is worth pointing out that interested and concerned families are not always willing or able to take care of patients who require full-time supervision and care. It is equally true that at least 4 patients rejected alternative solutions to hospitalization which were proposed by their friends or families.

Isolation or family rejection played a contributing role in bringing the patient to the hospital in only 5 cases. However, it was not the crucial factor even then, nor should it be inferred that these 5 cases were inappropriate referrals to the hospital.

Physical status

Two aspects of the physical condition of the patients at the time of admission were evaluated: (1) the presence of physical illness; and

(2) the degree of physical disability. The question was whether patients might have been hospitalized for physical illness or inability to take care of themselves.

The most prevalent physical abnormalities included defects of vision, nutritional deficiency states, and cardiac disorders. Four of the patients were discovered to have serious physical disorders that were undetected prior to admission, including leukemia, carcinoma of the rectum, congenital cyst of the third ventricle, and an undiagnosed cerebro-vascular accident. Further, 11 of the 40 patients had moderate to severe debilitation which interfered with their ability to take care of themselves. The fact that patients suffered from physical illness or debilitation, however, does not account for their admission to the state mental hospital. For, in addition to physical factors, these patients displayed emotional or behavioral disturbances, which were more important in precipitating hospitalization.

Psychological factors

The first approach to classifying the emotional problems of the 40 patients was to ask how many of them were psychotic and how many were not psychotic? The term "psychotic" was defined as severe impairment of reality testing, presence of delusions and/or hallucinations, regressed behavior, and personality disorganization. Thirty-four of the patients were psychotic and 6 were not psychotic. Table 1 shows the distribution of patients in the various diagnostic categories. The categories employed are recommended by the American Psychiatric Association (1952).

Many of the diagnostic terms used above are quite restrictive and are inadequate in cases where there is a mixture of functional and organic symptoms. Classifying the group on the dimension of organic impairment shows 26 patients with moderate to severe impairment, and 14 with little or none.

The group of 40 patients contains 18 individuals with a history of previous psychiatric hospitalization, with 10 of these first hospitalized before the age of 60. The clinical history gives support to the view that the patients hospitalized before age 60 have mainly functional disorders. In general, those patients without previous hospitalization were the gradually deteriorating organics.

Considering the emotional problems of the entire group, certain concerns cut across diagnostic categories. Incapability, vulnerability, and helplessness were a common reaction of the group to any new task. These feelings were related to being older and to an attitude of de-

Table 1

Diagnosis	Number of patients
Psychotic (85 percent)	
Chronic brain syndrome associated with senile brain disease	8
Chronic brain syndrome associated with cerebral arteriosclerosis	6
Chronic brain syndrome associated with intoxication (Korsakoff's psychosis)	2
Acute brain syndrome, alcohol intoxication	1
Acute brain syndrome of unknown cause	1
Manic depressive reaction, manic type	1
Manic depressive reaction, depressive type	1
Involutional psychotic reaction	5
Psychotic depressive reaction	1
Schizophrenic reaction, undifferentiated type (chronic)	1
Schizophrenic reaction, paranoid type	6
Paranoia	1
Total	34
Not psychotic (15 percent)	
Depressive reaction	3
Acute brain syndrome, barbiturate intoxication	1
Chronic brain syndrome associated with cerebral arteriosclerosis	1
Chronic brain syndrome associated with intoxication and central nervous system syphilis	1
Total	6

creasing worth. At a deeper level, many patients were distressed by a strong wish to be taken care of. Patients usually defended themselves against this regressive wish by massive denial or projection. In a few cases, these wishes became dramatically clear when people verbalized a literal fear of abandonment. In light of their weakened capacity for adaptation, such anxiety is understandable. About half the patients were overwhelmed with depression and guilt, often associated with ideas about death. It appeared that some of these patients were attempting to prepare for death, but rather than experiencing pride from past accomplishments, they were preoccupied with past sins and shortcomings.

DISCUSSION

It has become clear that in spite of obvious psychological and physical impairment, other factors must be considered to understand why a patient is hospitalized at a particular time. The important factor seems to be the patient's behavior just prior to hospitalization and how that behavior affects the people around him. There are several types of behavior which create problems for the community. There were 14 patients who were management problems. This group made themselves objectionable to others by being noisy or assaultive.

Self-care problems formed another large group, one-fourth of our sample. They were confused and got lost or were incapable of caring for their physical needs. Most of these people had been living alone, but in actuality needed full-time custodial care.

A third group consisted of 14 patients admitted because of their psychotic ideation or severe depression. The depressed patients were a suicidal risk in the community.

Although the type of behavior displayed is crucial in the decision to hospitalize, it should be emphasized that many patients demonstrated some kind of symptoms for long periods before their hospitalization. Thus the time at which hospitalization is initiated requires another factor, the intolerance of certain types of behavior.

In this reciprocal balance between behavior and community tolerance, it seemed that in some cases the behavior became much worse while in other cases the environment shifted. For example, the person who had been caring for a patient might have become too old and feeble to continue.

In view of the duration and abnormal quality of patient behavior, hospitalization seems often an appropriate step. The mental hospital has positive contributions to make in terms of placement, evaluation, diagnosis, and treatment. These positive contributions, however, are lost sight of because many persons, even professionals, continue to maintain the stereotype of the mental hospital as a last resort for dealing with mental illness.

Acknowledgments. The authors wish to acknowledge the assistance of the principal investigators Dr. Walter Barton, Dr. Ruth Ehrenberg, and Dr. Roy Hoskins.

REFERENCES

American Psychiatric Association. 1952. Diagnostic and statistical manual for mental disorders. Committee of Nomenclature and Statistics. Washington, D.C.: American Psychiatric Association, Mental Hospital Service.

Group for the Advancement of Psychiatry. 1950. Committee on Hospitals. The problem of the aged patient in the public psychiatric hospital. Report No. 14. Topeka: The Committee.

Some Social Dimensions of Psychiatric Disorders in Old Age

MARJORIE FISKE

THIS paper summarizes the social differences found among 1134 older San Franciscans, about half of them comprising a probability sample of 18 census tracts, stratified by age, sex, and living arrangements, the other half having been admitted to the psychiatric screening wards of the public hospital in 1959. While the hospitalized sample is in considerably worse socioeconomic straits at the present time, this is as much the result of a downward shift since prime of life as it is of the fact that persons sampled in a public hospital are likely to come from the lower socioeconomic strata to begin with.

As might be expected, the hospitalized are more likely to have experienced "insults of aging" than the nonhospitalized, but while this is true in the areas of physical health and retirement, it is not true of widowhood. Furthermore, regardless of the nature of such life changes, the hospitalized are scarcely more likely than the nonhospitalized to have undergone them recently. In fact, more changes took place 10 or more years ago than during the year prior to hospitalization.

Other rather unexpected findings include evidence that residential (i.e., within city) mobility is far more frequent among the hospitalized, while in terms of geographic mobility (length of residence in San Francisco, for example) the hospitalized look very much like the nonhospitalized. The data also indicate that loneliness is not always associated with social isolation, nor are the socially isolated always lonely; the subjective feeling of loneliness, furthermore, seems to be of varying significance at successive age levels beyond 60. Preliminary analysis of other age variations suggests that (1) different patterns of stress and disability prevail at successive age levels; (2) conducements and

The full text of this paper is published in Wilma Donahue, C. Tibbitts, and R. H. Williams (eds.), *Psychological and Social Processes of Aging: an International Research Seminar* (to be published).

deterrents to mental hospitalization may vary with age accordingly; (3) on many counts, especially those reflecting withdrawal from social contacts and accustomed activities, the youngest among the hospitalized resemble the oldest in the community, raising the question whether persons hospitalized for psychiatric reasons may not be undergoing a more rapid pace of aging; (4) at the same time, the degree of difference between hospitalized and nonhospitalized decreases with each advancing age group, with the oldest in both samples looking much more alike in respect to a number of social factors—emphasizing once more the importance of taking survival factors into account in studying patterns of aging.

The Intellectual Functioning of Aged Patients and Nonpatients

GUY HAMILTON CROOK AND LAWRENCE KATZ

THE general purposes of this research are to ascertain what factors are associated with the mental hospitalization of aged individuals and to study the course of geriatric mental illness.

The research staff studied every individual aged 60 or more admitted to the psychiatric receiving wards of San Francisco General Hospital during 1959, who was a resident of San Francisco and had not been hospitalized in a psychiatric ward before the age of 60. There were 534 such patients. Project personnel also studied 600 persons over age 60 who were residents of the San Francisco community at the time they were seen during the latter part of 1959 and early 1960.

After pretesting several instruments, psychologists on the staff decided to use a brief battery of four verbal subtests of the Wechsler Adult Intelligence Scale as the principal means of investigating the intellectual functions of the hospital group. The four subtests chosen were Information, Comprehension, Arithmetic, and Digit Span.

Only four verbal subtests were given instead of all six because of time limitations. The ones selected were chosen because they had the combined characteristics of being relatively brief, of differing from one another in content, and of being highly correlated with over-all WAIS verbal scores (Wechsler, 1955; Doppelt and Wallace, 1955). Experimentation with the Performance subtests indicated that Picture Completion and Digit Symbol were the most promising for use with our group under the existing testing conditions. The attempted administration of these subtests to several hundred patients, however, indicated that even these were not feasible, primarily because of

This report is one of a series growing out of a 5-year multidisciplinary research project on geriatric mental illness, conducted at the Langley Porter Neuropsychiatric Institute under grants from the National Institute of Mental Health (Grant 3M-9145) and the State of California Department of Mental Hygiene.

widespread sensory and motor handicaps, and they were eventually abandoned.

It was desired to have some gross estimate of the intellectual functioning of the community sample as well. With this in mind, the Kent E-G-Y (Kent, 1946) was administered to over 200 consecutive testable patients in our hospital sample to determine whether scores on the Kent were comparable to scores on the four WAIS subtests. A correlation of .83 was obtained between the Kent and the WAIS, and it was decided that the Kent could be used for a gross measure of functioning in the community. Accordingly, the Kent was administered to the 600 subjects in the community group. It was possible also to administer the very brief WAIS Digit Span subtest. In addition, an unselected group of 97 subjects in the community sample was given the WAIS Information, Comprehension, and Arithmetic subtests.

Because it was believed that available intelligence tests are not wholly satisfactory for measuring functional ability in older persons, particularly at lower levels, we are developing and using a new test specifically for this age range. We call it the Practical Functioning Scale; it consists of sections on memory and orientation, information, arithmetic, and practical judgment. This scale shows considerable promise at this point, but because our data on it are only partially analyzed we shall reserve further discussion of it for a later paper. Some personality testing was also carried out with both patient and nonpatient groups, but, again, discussion of findings from these must be deferred to some time in the future. The present paper is confined to the results of the Kent and the WAIS subtests, particularly the latter.

The actual number of subjects completing the Kent and the four WAIS subtests is indicated in Table 1. In the community, a small

Table 1. Number of subjects completing Kent E-G-Y and four WAIS *subtests*

Test	Hospital	Community
Kent E-G-Y	231	534
WAIS, 4 subtests	359	95
WAIS Digit Span only	372	528

number of subjects refused to perform on psychological tests or were otherwise untestable. The proportion of untestable patients in the hospital sample was much larger.

COMMUNITY SAMPLE FINDINGS

The rationale and procedures for selecting our community sample are described elsewhere.[1] Suffice it to say here that this sample consists of 600 persons aged 60 or over, who were selected from 18 San Francisco census tracts, by categories of age, sex, and living arrangements.

The community subjects performed at a generally high level on both the WAIS and the Kent E-G-Y. The mean combined WAIS weighted score for the 95 subjects who completed the four WAIS verbal subtests was 38.3, almost what one would expect from a large group of young adults, and significantly higher than the expected average score for individuals of advanced age.

Although there is some decline in WAIS score with age ($r = -.21$) in this group, this is due entirely to the decrease beyond the age of 75. There is no decline in average test score from age 60 to age 74; in fact, the average score for the 70–74 age group in this sample is as high as that of the average 20- or 30-year-old in the WAIS standardization group (Wechsler, 1955). The average scores and prorated verbal IQ's by age groups are given in Table 2.

Table 2. Mean combined WAIS *verbal weighted score and prorated verbal IQ of each of five age groups, community sample*

Age group	Number sampled	Mean weighted score	Prorated IQ
60–64	20	39.8	104
65–69	21	40.7	107
70–74	20	40.8	113
75–79	17	32.3 ⎰	108
80 plus	17	36.7 ⎱	
Total	95		

The mean Kent E-G-Y and Digit Span scores of these 95 persons are almost identical with those of the other 500 individuals in our community sample, which suggest that the 95 subjects completing the WAIS subtests are representative of the total group of 600.

Two findings in this community group are of special interest: (1) the fact that the scores tend to be higher than those in the WAIS standardization study, and (2) the absence of any decline in score

[1] Community sampling is discussed somewhat by Marjorie Fiske, "Some Social Dimensions of Psychiatric Disorders in Old Age," in this volume. A detailed presentation of the sampling procedure used in our community project may be found in the unpublished manuscript "Geriatrics Research Project Community Survey Field Report," June, 1960; copies of which are available upon request.

until age 75. One explanation for the first finding is that our group may not be representative of the older residents of San Francisco. There is some reason to believe that this is true, although it can be neither verified nor refuted until the 1960 census data become available. Two other possible explanations merit some consideration. One of these is that the WAIS standardization figures for the verbal subtests are too low; the other is that older San Franciscans are actually brighter than aged residents elsewhere.

If the third alternative should prove true—that among noninstitutionalized older persons San Franciscans are brighter than those in certain other parts of the country—our data suggest that this cannot be attributed to the superiority of native-born San Franciscans. In our sample people who had recently arrived in San Francisco had significantly higher WAIS scores than did those who have lived here for 20 years or more.

Concerning the failure of our group to decline with age, several possibilities again exist. For example, it may be that norms for aged individuals include two rather distinct groups: a group of intact individuals who are functioning as well as they ever have, and a group of organically impaired individuals who, while they have not been hospitalized, nevertheless are performing considerably below their past peak. The average for these two groups would then show some decline with age. In San Francisco, the processes of selection may have operated in such a manner that the aged in this community are to an unusually great extent well-functioning individuals. The fact that our hospital group, composed largely of individuals with brain damage, did show a significant decline with age, may offer some indirect support for this hypothesis.

An alternative explanation for the lack of decline in test score among our community subjects is that this is a superior group to begin with and that persons with superior ability do not decline as much or as rapidly as do those with average or inferior ability. This may well be true, but it is interesting to note in passing that Wechsler's norms do not show such a differential decline in this age range.

The average score of 534 community subjects on the Kent E-G-Y was 24.5. Unfortunately, there is no aged standardization group available against which to compare this score. There is a sex difference on Kent performance, the men performing significantly higher than the women. (There is no such sex difference in the WAIS scores.) There is again very little decline in average score with age, the correlation between Kent Scores and age being only $-.09$. The mean scores are almost exactly the same for each age interval from age 60 through age 79, with a small decrease in the 80–84 group, and a larger one in the 85 plus group. In the community sample the Kent and WAIS correlate .64.

The two measures of intellectual functioning were found to correlate significantly with several other variables upon which data were available in the community sample. The following are a few of these relationships.

Educational level correlated .56 with WAIS scores, but only .05 with Kent E-G-Y scores. This may be due in part to the relatively small spread of E-G-Y scores, most of which clustered at the upper levels, or it may be due to differences in content of the two tests.

There were significant but small correlations between measures of intellectual functioning and income during the previous year: .23 with the WAIS, and .29 with the Kent.

Various measures of the extent of social activity (e.g., amount of reading time per day and activity in organizations) were generally related positively to these measures of intellectual functioning.

HOSPITAL SAMPLE FINDINGS

The analysis of intellectual functioning in the hospital sample is also centered around the Kent and WAIS results, primarily the latter. In interpreting these data, several limitations should be kept in mind. For one thing, a large number of patients were not tested. The receiving wards of San Francisco General Hospital are screening wards; patients are usually not kept more than 5 days and sometimes are discharged within 24 hours of their admission. Thirty-six patients were not seen at all by the psychologists because of scheduling problems or rapid patient discharge. An additional 94 subjects were judged to be completely untestable, because of severe confusion and disorientation, gross sensory or motor handicaps, or acute emotional disturbances. This large proportion of untestable individuals (19 percent of all patients seen) is indicative of the very serious testing problems encountered in this group of patients.[2] In addition to these factors, the Digit Span subtest was not given early in the year, hence, there was only a total of 359 subjects out of a possible 534 who received a WAIS verbal weighted score on all four subtests. The

[2] The very complicated problem of testability will be further explored in another paper.

intellectual functioning of the 359 tested patients can be assumed to be better than that of the total group of 534, but the extent of the difference is at present unknown.

Further, there are problems of interpretation of test scores for those patients who were tested. Many patients who were tested had physical or psychological impairments which were not so severe as to make testing impossible, but which tended to hamper their performance, and probably lower their test scores. Only 162 patients (about 45 percent of the tested group) were considered to be completely free of any problem which might tend to result in spuriously low test scores. In addition, patients were typically tested at their bedsides, in noisy and crowded wards, subject to frequent distractions and interruptions. These poor testing conditions would probably also tend to lower test scores.

With these problems and limitations stated, some findings of this group follow.

In contrast with the community group, the WAIS performance of the hospital sample was quite poor. The average combined WAIS weighted score, on the four subtests, was only 21.9 with an average prorated verbal IQ of 84. More than one-fourth of the hospital group had prorated verbal IQ's below 75, and only about 30 percent of the group scored IQ's in the average range or better. More than 90 percent of these patients earned WAIS weighted scores lower than that which could be expected from the average 30-year-old in the WAIS standardization population.

The low level of functioning extends across both sexes, and all age groups. Nevertheless, there are some sex and age differences in WAIS score among the patients. The males score significantly higher than the females at almost all age levels (an average over-all weighted score of 24 points versus 20 points). Inasmuch as a sex difference in WAIS scores does not exist in the community group, it may be that males are hospitalized with relatively less intellectual impairment than females.

The correlation between age and WAIS score in the hospital group is −.31. There is a steady gradual decline from age group to age group among the males; and, while the decline among females is more irregular, it tends to follow the same trend. The average WAIS verbal weighted score and prorated verbal IQ for each age group of patients is given in Table 3.

The average score of 231 patients on the Kent E-G-Y was 14.9. In general, the results from the Kent are very similar to those from the WAIS. There are again major sex and age differences in score.

Table 3. Mean WAIS *weighted score and prorated verbal IQ for each of six age groups, hospital sample*

Age group	Number sampled	Mean weighted score	Prorated IQ
60–64	49	31.0	90
65–69	70	23.7	83
70–74	73	22.4	87
75–79	76	18.1 ⎫	
80–84	53	18.5 ⎬	83
85 plus	38	18.3 ⎭	
Total	359		

Males again score significantly higher than females (17.3 points versus 12.1 points), and the correlation between age and Kent score is —.18. The average Kent E-G-Y score for each age group of patients is given in Table 4.

Table 4. Mean Kent E-G-Y score for each of five age groups, hospital sample

Age group	Number sampled	Mean Kent score
60–64	34	18.9
65–69	47	16.5
70–74	40	14.8
75–79	45	11.5
80 plus	65	13.5
Total	231	

Each patient was evaluated by a project psychiatrist, and diagnoses were made. These diagnoses are discussed in detail elsewhere (Simon and Neal, in press). All patients received a "primary diagnosis," which was intended to indicate that condition most immediately responsible for a patient's admission to San Francisco General Hospital. There are significant differences in WAIS score among the various primary diagnostic groups, at the .001 level, as indicated by an analysis of variance. The average WAIS score for each primary diagnostic group is given in Table 5.

In addition to "primary diagnosis," many patients were given "secondary" and "tertiary" diagnoses to indicate significant psychiatric conditions in addition to those most immediately responsible for hospitalization. Thus, for example, many patients admitted because of an acute brain syndrome were found also to have an underlying chronic brain syndrome of some duration.

When the secondary and tertiary diagnoses are considered together with primary diagnosis, the intellectual picture presented is not greatly different from that for primary diagnosis alone. Thus patients with no

Table 5. Mean WAIS *weighted score by primary diagnosis, hospital sample only*

Diagnostic group	Number sampled	Mean weighted score
Problem drinkers	6	32.2
Affective disorders	37	28.1
Schizoid disorders	18	27.5
Personality disorders	10	22.6
Acute brain syndromes	199	22.1
Arteriosclerotic brain disorders	24	18.1
Senile brain disorders	45	16.1
Chronic brain disease, other (primarily alcoholic)	17	14.6
Total	356	

organic diagnoses show an average WAIS weighted score of 29.7; all those with acute brain syndromes (with or without chronic brain disease) show an average of 22.2, whereas all those with chronic brain syndromes (with or without acute brain syndromes or functional disorders) show an average score of 19.0.

Historical information was gathered which enabled project psychiatrists to make some estimate of the duration of any diagnosed disorder. This is of particular interest in those patients with chronic brain syndromes. The relationship between WAIS score and duration of CBS is indicated in Table 6.

Table 6. Mean WAIS *weighted scores of patients with chronic brain syndromes of varying duration*

Duration of CBS (in years)	Number sampled	Mean weighted score
Less than 1	126	21.1
1–2	39	16.0
2–3	30	19.3
3–5	39	16.7
Over 5	36	17.4
Total	270	

Table 6 suggests that the deterioration after 1 year is negligible. Considering a weighted score of 30–35 as the average expectancy for a normal person in our age group, we may compare this with an average of 21.1 for those in our sample with chronic brain syndromes of less than 1 year's duration, and an average of 17.2 for those with duration of 1 year or more. Although there is a large drop in test score in the first year, there is no consistent decline thereafter. Further information on this point will be collected in follow-up studies which are now being carried out on these patients.

Disposition from the hospital was also found to be associated with

WAIS weighted score. A decision was made about the disposition of each patient from the psychiatric receiving ward, based upon an evaluation by the regular hospital staff, and, in most cases, a court hearing.

Most patients were committed to state mental hospitals but some were discharged, either to the care of a relative or to their own care; and small groups of patients were sent to public or private nursing homes, to San Francisco General Hospital psychiatric treatment wards, or to San Francisco General Hospital medical or surgical treatment wards. The mean WAIS score of each disposition group is indicated in Table 7.

Table 7. Mean WAIS *weighted score by disposition from SFGH psychiatric ward*

Disposition	Number sampled	Mean weighted score
Discharge to self	21	30.7
SFGH treatment ward	13	29.4
Discharge to family	26	24.0
Committed to state hospital	239	20.5
SFGH medical wards	24	19.0
Nursing homes	10	14.2
Total	333	

Here it is interesting to note that the patients discharged to their own care score materially higher on the WAIS than do those discharged to family members, while these in turn score higher than the large number of patients committed to state hospitals.

Ratings of the degree of over-all psychological and social impairment of each patient were made by psychiatrists who evaluated them. These ratings are significantly related to WAIS score, patients rated as less severely impaired scoring higher than patients rated more severely impaired. Patients were also rated on the degree of impairment of specific psychological functions, and these ratings are also significantly correlated with WAIS scores. Specifically, ratings made by psychiatrists about patients' orientation, memory, and quality of thought correlate quite highly with WAIS scores.

Other findings regarding intellectual functioning in the hospital sample include the following.

Test intercorrelations are generally high; either relative to our community group, or to groups described in the WAIS standardization. Specific WAIS subtests tend to intercorrelate highly, and the correlation between Kent and WAIS is higher than in either our own community group or in previously reported research on the Kent and

Wechsler-Bellevue (Wright *et al.,* 1949; Delp, 1953). It may be that the inclusion of a number of severely impaired patients in this group, who did very poorly on all tests and subtests, contributes materially to these correlations. Parenthetically it may be noted that many of our patients with chronic brain disease do not demonstrate the widely scattered test scores that one often encounters in younger individuals with brain damage.

WAIS scores correlate significantly with such factors as education ($r = .39$), and income during the previous year ($r = .13$). These correlations, however, are smaller than similar correlations in the community group. This may be due to the direct effects of mental illness on the WAIS scores. For example, a college graduate with a severe chronic brain syndrome may obtain a low score on the WAIS, and even an individual functioning effectively enough to have earned a fair income during the past year may have recently suffered some form of acute brain syndrome, and consequently obtained a low WAIS score.

Indices of activity and social participation again correlated significantly with WAIS scores, for some variables very highly. For example, those individuals who spend more than 5 hours a day reading obtained WAIS scores just about twice as high as those who do no reading at all (an average of 34.1 points versus 17.4 points). With older individuals, probably more than with younger, the extent of participation in various kinds of activity seems to be a good index of remaining intellectual ability; and this seems even more strongly true of older impaired individuals than of well-functioning ones.

COMPARISON OF HOSPITAL AND COMMUNITY SAMPLES

The community sample as a whole is not strictly comparable with the hospital sample. The sex ratios are different, and the community sample tends to be both younger and of a higher socioeconomic status than the hospital sample. For this reason, a special community subsample was drawn, to allow a direct comparison of intellectual functioning between hospitalized and nonhospitalized aged persons. This special subsample consisted of 260 individuals matched with the hospital group for age and main lifetime occupation within each sex. Individuals were selected at random within these categories from the original 600 subjects in the community group. Of the 260 individuals so selected, 48 had completed the four WAIS subtests, and 226 had completed the Kent E-G-Y.

The mean WAIS verbal weighted score for these 48 subjects was 36.4, not significantly different from the mean score obtained by the entire group of 95 subjects. The mean Kent E-G-Y score was 23.6, slightly lower than for the total group, the women again being significantly poorer than the men. The special community subsample is compared with the total hospital group in Table 8. In this table, cut-off

Table 8. *Comparison of hospital group
with matched community sample*

	Hospital		Community	
	Number	Percent	Number	Percent
WAIS weighted score				
28 plus	112	31.2	40	83.3
0–27	247	68.6	8	16.7
Total	359		48	
Kent E-G-Y score				
20 plus	72	31.4	164	72.6
0–19	157	68.6	62	27.4
Total	229		226	

points on the WAIS and Kent were selected so that a below-average score would be in one category, and average or better in the other. The cut-off score on the Kent was selected by examining the scatter plot of Kent and WAIS scores, and picking a point which seemed equivalent to the lower limit of average WAIS scores. This procedure is rather arbitrary, but inasmuch as no external adult norms are available, any designation of "average" can only be made arbitrarily. With both the Kent and the WAIS about two-thirds of the hospital sample falls into the lower category; while only one-sixth of the community group is in this category on the WAIS and about one-fourth on the Kent. Simply knowing a person's WAIS weighted verbal score would enable one to place him correctly in either the hospital or community group, in about 70 percent of all our cases.

SUMMARY

Perhaps our major finding is the very poor intellectual performance of our hospital group, in comparison with either existing test norms or the performance of our own community subjects. For many of our patients the very low level of intellectual functioning suggests that hospitalization, or at least some kind of external aid, was quite necessary at the time of testing. In particular, older patients with brain disease almost always obtained very low test scores. Younger patients appeared to function somewhat better than older, and patients who were hospitalized for "functional" disorders performed relatively quite well.

Other findings indicate correspondence between measures of intellectual functioning and some estimates of social competence. Patients who reported a fairly good level of social activity obtain higher scores than those who reported restrictions of activity. In general, patients who were committed to state mental institutions are more severely impaired intellectually than those discharged to the community.

The community group generally functions at a high level, few subjects showing any significant intellectual deficit, and few subjects reporting major difficulties in maintaining themselves independently in the community.

Almost all of the above findings seem to "make sense," or to have been predictable in terms of what one thinks about mental illness and intellectual impairment. Many of the findings suggest, in fact, that there are few "mysteries" about geriatric mental illness—the typical person with geriatric mental disease is markedly impaired, and so is sent to a local hospital for evaluation, and then on to a state mental hospital. With relatively little overlap in test scores between hospital and community groups it seems likely that, regardless of the possible relevance of other variables, intellectual functioning is of great importance in determining whether an individual will be able to maintain himself in the community or require institutionalization.

These findings are straightforward and predictable. Nevertheless, there are some provocative questions implied by some of our results. For one thing, there are atypical individuals, patients who are functioning relatively well intellectually yet are hospitalized, and individuals in the community whose intellectual performance is poor. These atypical individuals will provide an interesting area for further investigation. Then, too, questions may be raised about the age and sex differences in test scores found in the hospital, and the absence of an age difference in test scores in the community. Why are women in our hospital group significantly more impaired than men? Is the typical course of mental illness different among men than among women? And what is the typical course of some of these disorders? Is it true, as our data suggest, that individuals with chronic brain disease may not show further deterioration beyond a certain point? And why do our normal subjects show no decline at all until after the age of 75? In spite of the pedestrian nature of many of our findings, there do seem to be areas open for further study, with many significant questions still unanswered.

REFERENCES

Delp, H. A. 1953. Correlations between the Kent E-G-Y and the Wechsler batteries. J. Clin. Psychol., 9: 73–75.

Doppelt, J. E., and Wallace, W. L. 1955. Standardization of the Wechsler Adult Intelligence Scale for older persons. J. Abnorm. & Social Psychol., 51: 312–30.

Kent, Grace A. 1946. Series of emergency scales manual. New York: The Psychological Corporation.

Simon, A., and Neal, M. W. Patterns of geriatric mental illness: II. Diagnosis and classification. (In press.)

Wechsler, D. 1955. Manual for Wechsler Adult Intelligence Scale. New York: The Psychological Corporation.

Wright, H. F., McPhee, H. M., and Cummings, S. B., Jr. 1949. The relationship between the Kent E-G-Y and the Bellevue Verbal Scale. J. Abnorm. & Social Psychol., 44: 223–30.

Predicting the Psychiatric Problems of Older Persons: A Follow-Up Study

JAMES M. A. WEISS, BARBARA BARNEY WILLIS,

J. MARCIA JONES, K. WARNER SCHAIE,

ARTHUR J. ROBINS, AND GENE L. FIELDS

THE psychiatric problems of the aging and the aged members of the population constitute a critical area in any mental health survey of present-day society. Busse, Dovenmuehle, and Brown (1960) and the New York State Mental Health Research Unit (1959a, b, in press) cite good evidence that many of the noninstitutionalized older persons still remaining in the community are suffering from some degree of psychiatric disorder, but it seems clear that there is still a great need for better information and understanding of the dynamic psychological problems associated with aging before definite therapies can be formulated (Weiss et al., 1958).

For the past several years, therefore, the authors and other coworkers have been conducting a series of studies designed to investigate and analyze the nature and type of the mental health problems of older persons, with an ultimate aim of providing fundamental data to be used in planning rational programs of prevention, treatment, and rehabilitation. The basic assumptions underlying our studies are: (1) that all patients referred to a psychiatric outpatient clinic have some sort of individual problems which are likely to be of clinical significance, and (2) that the symptoms and complaints of the patients are significant manifestations of psychiatric disorder or, at least, have important psychological significance. (These assumptions have been

This paper is one of a series reporting a larger study of mental health problems of older persons attending the Malcolm Bliss Psychiatric Clinic, St. Louis, Missouri. These investigations were supported by the Malcolm Bliss Mental Health Center and the Department of Psychiatry and Neurology, Washington University School of Medicine, St. Louis, Missouri, by a grant from the Missouri State Division of Health, and by Research Grant M-1252 from the National Institute of Mental Health, U.S. Public Health Service.

discussed in prior reports by the authors, and also by Busse *et al.,* 1954; Magraw and Dulit, 1958; and Whitehorn, 1956.) The purpose of this paper is to report an investigation of the ability of the Psychiatric Evaluation Index, a new and original assessment instrument for gerontological research, to predict the psychiatric problems of older persons.

PROCEDURE

The PEI is a balanced 70-item sample of empirically derived, representative psychiatric symptoms, signs, and complaints. Each subject is asked to distribute the 70 items along a continuum of applicability. All items can be classified quantitatively and qualitatively on a two-dimensional schedule also empirically derived. The first dimension, the determinant, identifies the dominant or major characteristic of the complaint items; the second dimension, the referent, identifies any situational factor which the subject relates in any way to the determinant.

Completed studies and investigations in progress indicate that the PEI has a high degree of internal consistency and is both meaningful and useful in differentiating various kinds and degrees of psychiatric problems in older persons, in relating such problems to concurrent variables, and in formulating new theoretical concepts relative to the assessment of behavioral dysfunction associated with aging and the aging process (Weiss *et al.,* 1961; Schaie *et al.,* 1959; Weiss *et al.,* 1959).

As part of an earlier study performed in 1957, twenty-five patients, ranging in age from 45 to 78 years of age and of both sexes, were evaluated in consecutive order on their first visits to a metropolitan psychiatric outpatient clinic. The PEI was utilized as part of a thorough psychiatric evaluation (including psychological testing and social history) obtained for each patient. Definite age-linked differences in the kinds of problems affecting such patients were found (Weiss *et al.,* 1961). Explicit in the original study of 1957 was a suggestion that there be a follow-up study on the same group of subjects. This was planned to delineate any changes occurring with time in the nature of the complaints, and also to assess the possibility of predicting subsequent adjustment from the results found in the original study. Specifically, the objective of the present study was to establish the predictability (if any) of the patients' present social functioning in relation to the 1957 PEI scores.

It was planned to use the same twenty-five subjects that we used in the original study. However, there was a loss of twelve subjects: eight had changed their place of residence and either moved out of the state or left no forwarding address, three refused to participate, and one had been killed in an automobile accident. Therefore, only the remaining thirteen subjects of the initial investigation were available for follow-up study.

In order to measure the social functioning of the subjects, certain criteria had to be established so that categorization of the follow-up interview data might be organized to permit comparison with the PEI material. Ten criteria were available on which the group of subjects were divided approximately evenly, so that comparison was feasible. These criteria were:

1. Reported physical illness originating since 1957
2. Utilization of medical services (regardless of the presence of actual somatic disease) since 1957
3. Reported mental illness since 1957
4. Economic self-sufficiency
5. Church activity
6. Attitude toward own mental health (i.e., whether patient reported verbally that his mental health complaints had become more or less disabling)
7. Attitude toward employment (whether patient indicated willingness or unwillingness to accept employment if feasible and/or available)
8. Attitude toward social activity (whether or not the patient was making attempts to expand his range of social activities)
9. Attitude toward present functioning (whether or not the patient felt satisfied with his present adjustment)
10. Attitude toward the psychiatric clinic (whether or not the patient felt that his clinic contact had been helpful).

Each subject was then assigned a rating of positive or negative with respect to each of the above ten categories. The PEI mean scores were further rated as high or low depending upon their position with respect to the mean for the total 1957 sample. Using the above procedure, it was possible to test respective cell frequencies by means of Fisher's exact probability test. Because of the small number of subjects, we decided not to specify conventional probability levels, but rather to consider probabilities under $P = .10$ as most likely predictive of trends, and those between the .10 and .20 points as hinting toward possibilities worthy of further investigation.

RESULTS: CRITERIA OF SOCIAL FUNCTIONING

Analysis along the above lines of the ability of the 1957 PEI scores to predict current levels of social functioning demonstrated the following patterns:

1. Reported physical illness was predicted by a high number of "anxietal" complaints (P = .08), a low number of "reality distortional" complaints (P = .09), and a low number of "economic-occupational" complaints (P = .10).

2. Utilization of medical services was not predicted by any PEI score.

3. Reported mental illness was predicted by a high number of "reality distortional" complaints (P = .18) and a low number of "somatic" complaints (P = .12).

4. Economic self-sufficiency was predicted by a high number of "nonspecific" complaints (P = .10), "reality distortional" complaints (P = .09), and "behavioral" complaints (P = .18), as well as by a low number of "somatic" complaints (P = .10).

5. Church activity (as expressed by degree of participation) was predicted by a low number of "interpersonal" complaints (P = .18) and a high number of "social welfare" complaints (P = .08).

6. Reported decrease in disability due to mental health problems was predicted by a high number of "anxietal" complaints (P = .18).

7. Willingness to accept employment was not predicted by any PEI score.

8. Eagerness and definite attempts to expand the patient's social activities were predicted by a high number of "effective" complaints (P = .15) and a low number of "mentational" complaints (P = .18).

9. Dissatisfaction with the patient's present level of functioning was predicted by a high number of "anxietal" complaints (P = .15), "behavioral" complaints (P = .15), and "mentational" complaints (P = .18), as well as by a low number of "affective" complaints (P = .15).

10. The patient's statement that he felt he had been helped by attendance at the psychiatric clinic was predicted by a high number of "physical health" complaints (P = .12) and "mentational" complaints (P = .12).

RESULTS: PEI REPLICATION

A considerably less ambiguous step in the follow-up procedure than that of attempting to establish objective criteria of social functioning (as above) was the simple testing of hypothesized changes in the patients' complaint behavior on the PEI. For this purpose scores on the PEI for the 1957 and the 1959 follow-up administrations were compared by means of the analysis of variance. Table 1 presents the results of this analysis. Our principal interest was in the terms involving variance associated with "occasions" (i.e., the repeated administrations of the PEI). The interactions between occasions and *referents,* as well as between occasions and *determinants,* did not reach significance, suggesting that there were no changes for the group as a whole in the patterns of endorsement of the referent and determinant dimensions. The triple interaction between patients, occasions, and *determinants* was similarly nonsignificant. However, the triple interaction between patients, occasions, and *referents* reached significance at the 5 percent level of confidence. This latter finding means that some of the individual patients changed their pattern of endorsement of referents over the 2-year interval. Such changes, however, were not in any direction which was significantly systematic for the group as a whole.

On the other hand, the main effects were highly significant at or beyond the 1 percent level, as in earlier reported investigations. The "physical health" and "economic-occupational" referents were significantly higher than the "nonspecific" and "mental health" referents, all of which in turn received significantly greater endorsement than did the "interpersonal" referent. Among the determinants, highest endorsement was given to the "somatic" complaints, with "anxietal," "affective," "mentational," and "behavioral" complaints following in that order. All these determinants received significantly higher endorsement than did "welfare" and "reality distortional" complaints. Significant F ratios at the 1 percent level were found also for the interaction between referents and determinants, and for the interactions between patients, referents, and determinants; while the interactions between patients and referents, and patients and determinants, were significant at the 5 percent level of confidence.

Within the over-all pattern of profile stability there were two shifts in means which were significant at the 5 percent level of confidence. These shifts were an increase in the average number of "somatic" complaints and a decrease in the average number of "anxietal" complaints.

Table 1. Analysis of variance for the repeated administrations of the Psychiatric Evaluation Index

Identification[a]	Source of variation	SS	df	MS	Error term	F ratio
a	Patients	0	12			
B	Occasions	0	1			
C	Referents	433.88	4	108.47	aC	13.33[b]
D	Determinants	557.25	6	92.88	aD	11.74[b]
aB	Patients × occasions	0	12			
aC	Patients × referents	393.83	48	8.20	aBC	1.61[c]
aD	Patients × determinants	569.65	72	7.91	aCD	1.65[c]
BC	Occasions × referents	7.24	4	1.81	aBC	1.38
BD	Occasions × determinants	31.84	6	5.31	aBD	
CD	Referents × determinants	562.60	24	23.44	aCD	4.88[b]
aBC	Patients × occasions × referents	243.62	48	5.08	aBCD	1.54[c]
aBD	Patients × occasions × determinants	277.26	72	3.85	aBCD	1.17
aCD	Patients × referents × determinants	1381.79	288	4.80	aBCD	1.45[b]
BCD	Occasions × referents × determinants	82.42	24	3.43	aBCD	1.04
aBCD	Patients × occasions × referents × determinants	950.62	288	3.30	e	
e	Within cells	4180.00	910	4.59		
	Total variance	9672.00	1819			

[a] Capital letters denote fixed constants; small letters denote random variates.
[b] Significant at the 1 percent level of confidence.
[c] Significant at the 5 percent level of confidence.

These findings may point to an increasing tendency of older psychiatric patients to reduce subjective discomfort by somatization.

To gain further insight into the frames of reference utilized in the patients' complaint sorting, a factor analysis was conducted of the correlations among all 26 PEI sorts (both the 1957 and 1959 administrations). This analysis was done to identify the various sorting patterns utilized by members of our sample. The centroid analysis resulted in the extraction of ten factors. However, the last five of these seemed to be specifics and contained little variance, so that rotation and attempt at interpretation was confined to the first five factors.

Factor I was identified as "anxious concern with economic well-being." The twelve sorts which had substantial loadings on this factor seemed to be characterized by heavy emphasis on the "economic-occupational" referent and the "anxietal" determinant. These patients then were primarily demanding services designed to reduce their anxiety by modification of their financial or occupational situations.

Factor II was identified as "loss of intellectual controls attributed to decline in physical health." The ten sorts with substantial loadings on this factor emphasized the "physical health" referent, but the resulting problem specifics emphasized first of all mentational complaints, and only secondarily those with a somatic component. These patients then were most aware of loss of intellectual function, but saw as their preferred remedy the modification of their physical health status.

Factor III can best be described as "neurotic turmoil." The sortings loading on this factor were characterized by emphasis on both "anxietal" and "somatic" complaints which were related to some extent to "physical health," "mental health," and "economic-occupational" referents. This particular pattern would seem to reflect a more diffuse state of disturbance and a demand for multiple services directed toward clarification and amelioration of the patients' problems.

Factor IV was identified as "mood disturbance related to concern about economic well-being." It seems to be quite similar to Factor I, in that the patients' loading on this factor emphasized modification of their economic environment as basic to the relief of their problems. However, the symptomatic manifestation of their problems here appeared as mood disturbance (primarily as feelings of inadequacy and depression) rather than as nonfocalized anxiety.

Factor V may be described as "somatic symptoms attributed to physical causes." The patients loading on this factor emphasized the "somatic" determinant and the "physical health" referent, asserting in essence that their problems are primarily of a medical instead of a psychiatric nature, but (despite such protestations) secondary elevations on the "anxietal" and "affective" components suggest that their physical complaints are probably related to emotional difficulties.

Only four patients loaded on just one of these factors, while the more typical pattern was that of loadings on two factors, indicating the complex nature of the frame of reference utilized by patients in considering the relative priority of their complaints. When the factor patterns for the individual patients over both sets of PEI sortings were compared, it became evident that all but one of the subjects retained at least one of the original sorting dimensions. Four of the patients added another dimension, while five of the patients shifted one sorting dimension to another. Of these nine changes or additions, five involved Factor IV. That is, when change in the use of sorting dimensions over a 2-year period occurred, the modal change was towards emphasis of "mood disturbance related to concern about economic well-being."

DISCUSSION AND SUMMARY

The Psychiatric Evaluation Index (PEI) was administered to a group of 13 psychiatric clinic outpatients 2 years after it had first been given. Patients were also interviewed and rated with respect to a number of criteria of social functioning. The pattern of PEI complaints remained stable over the two administrations with the exception of a trend toward lessening of anxiety and increased somatization. A factor analysis resulted in the extraction of five sorting patterns. Modal changes of preferred patterns from the original to the follow-up study were toward increased emphasis on "mood disturbance related to concern about economic well-being." Patients' scores on the original PEI administration were related to and able to predict a number of criteria of current social functioning.

Interpretation and generalization from these results are limited by several technical factors pertaining to experimental method and analysis. The subjects represented a rather small and fairly homogeneous group. Both these limitations tend to conceal important factors or patterns. There is also some question as to whether the length of the interval between the original and follow-up studies (2 years) was optimal. A longer interval, perhaps 5 years or more, might produce quite different results. And, unfortunately, the social histories taken from the original sample of patients and those taken on the follow-up interview were not entirely comparable. Finally, our criteria of social functioning may well have been too specific, and may have omitted certain crucial variables.

It seems clear from this study, however, that both at the original and the follow-up interviews, problems attributed to physical health and economic factors were seen as primary by these older patients. Emotional reactions to these perceived causations, as expressed in specific complaint determinants, were most often in the area of non-focalized anxiety and mood disturbance, or in resort to somatization, or in experienced deficit of intellectual functioning. It seems probable that patients with the first group of symptoms are likely to benefit from psychiatric and social services, while patients with the latter groups of symptoms are less likely to be amenable to psychotherapeutic intervention, and may require primarily medical and/or custodial treatment.

While our findings are limited by the nature and size of our sample, they do suggest that the PEI is useful as a predictor of future social functioning and as a relatively simple and clear-cut data language for the longitudinal study of complaint behavior. This pilot study can therefore serve as a point of departure for major investigations attacking the same problems, with the goal of providing basic data to be used in planning programs of prevention, treatment, and rehabilitation.

REFERENCES

Busse, E. W., Barnes, R. H., Silverman, A. J., Shy, G. M., Thaler, Margaret, and Frost, L. L. 1954. Studies of the process of aging: factors that influenced the psyche of elderly persons. Am. J. Psychiat., 110: 897–903.

Busse, E. W., Dovenmuehle, R. H., and Brown, R. G. 1960. Psychoneurotic reactions of the aged. Geriatrics, 15: 97–105.

Magraw, R. M., and Dulit, E. P. 1958. The patient's presenting complaint—signpost or goal? Univ. Minn. Med. Bull., 29: 329–40.

New York State Mental Health Research Unit. 1959a. A mental health survey of older people. I. Psychiat. Quart., 33 (Suppl.): 45–99.

——— 1959b. A mental health survey of older people. II. Psychiat. Quart., 33 (Suppl.): 252–300.

——— A mental health survey of older people. III. Psychiat. Quart., 34: (in press).

Schaie, K. W., Rommel, L. A., and Weiss, J. M. A. 1959. Judging the relative severity of psychiatric outpatient complaints. J. Clin. Psychol., 15: 380–88.

Weiss, J. M. A., Chatham, L. R., and Schaie, K. W. 1961. Symptom formation associated with aging: dynamic pattern. A. M. A. Arch. Genet. Psychiat., 44: 22–29.

Weiss, J. M. A., Gildea, E. F., Davis, D., and Mensh, I. N. 1958. Psychiatric problems of later life: I. Nature and scope. Am. Practit. Digest. Treatment, 9: 1955–59.

Weiss, J. M. A., Rommel, L. A., and Schaie, O. W. 1959. The presenting problems of older patients referred to a psychiatric clinic. J. Gerontol., 14: 477–83.

Whitehorn, J. C. 1956. Strategy and tactics in psychiatric therapy. *In* Theory and treatment of the psychoses: some newer aspects, pp. 47–58. St. Louis: Washington University Studies.

The Objective Measurement of Psychobiologic Decline: A Preliminary Report

DAVID B. VINSON AND CHARLES M. GAITZ

THIS study was undertaken in order to test the following hypotheses: (1) it is possible, on the basis of performance on certain objective psychological techniques, to detect an acceleration of the rate of aging; (2) there is a positive correlation between the clinical and psychological assessment of an annual decline of performance in geriatric patients.

SUBJECTS

During the period 1958–1959, a battery of psychological tests was administered to twenty-nine geriatric patients at the Jewish Home for the Aged, Houston, Texas. One year later only twenty of these patients could be retested. Of these, twelve were female. Ten were foreign born. One had completed 2 years of college, five had completed high school, twelve had completed elementary school, while two had not received formal education. The educational level of those born in the United States was at the ninth grade. In the main, the patients came from the lower middle and middle socioeconomic strata; the males had worked as salesmen or merchants, while the females were predominately housewives.

Ten of the patients demonstrated symptomatology diagnostic of diabetes mellitus. The patients were considered, by the medical staff, to be relatively cooperative, to be in touch with reality, and to be making a satisfactory adjustment to the home. The mean age of the geriatric patients was 76 years, with a standard deviation of 2.0 years.

Financial assistance is acknowledged in the presentation of this study from the Texas Academy for the Advancement of Life Sciences.

METHOD OF STUDY

Clinical assessment of the geriatric patient was carried out by one of us (CMG). Patients were assessed as to memory, somatic complaints, rigidity, empathy, and capacity for testing reality. The psychological assessment of the geriatric patient was based on performance with regard to certain objective psychological techniques. The clinical assessment of an annual decline of performance was correlated with the psychological assessments of an annual decline of performance.

TESTS

Certain objective psychological tests, reported to discriminate between normal controls and patients with known structural and/or physiologic changes in the brain make up the psychological examination. In addition to the usual characteristics of validity and reliability, these tests appear to be relatively free of cultural bias, are easily administered, and do not penalize the individual who, in his normal affairs, seldom writes. Further, these tests do not arouse, in the anxious patient, a sense of failure.

Memory and/or learning is assessed by the Modified Learning Test (MLT). Walton and Black (1957) report this test capable of differentiating organics with general cortical damage from functionals and normals with a negligible degree of misclassification. Rigidity is assessed by the S test, described by Eysenck (1952). In this test the patient is required to shift rapidly from one visual-motor pattern to another. Coordination is assessed by the Partington's Pathways Test (P) (Partington and Leiter, 1949). In this test the subject is required to serially connect 25 printed numbers. The capacity for testing reality and the ability to identify oneself with the group is assessed by the Objective Rorschach Score (ORS), described by Vinson (1960). Empathy is assessed by the Reitman Pin-Man Test (Ra), (Reitman and Robertson, 1950). Somatic complaints are assessed by the Complaint Scale (C), using items taken from the Mental Examiner's Handbook (Wells and Ruesch, 1945) and the Maudsley Medical Questionnaire (Eysenck, 1952).

FINDINGS

The null hypothesis that any agreement between test and retest performance, on these objective psychological techniques, is no better than chance was tested by calculating t. The t values for the several tests are shown in Table 1.

Table 1. t Values for each test

Test	t
Wechsler-Bellevue (W-B)	2.03
Modified Learning (MLT)	1.24
Rigidity (S$_2$)	0.21
Pathways (P)	0.40
Complaint (C)	1.48
Objective Rorschach (ORS)	1.05
Reitman Pin-Man (Ra)	2.05

The null hypothesis that the performance of geriatric patients with diabetes mellitus does not differ significantly from geriatric patients without diabetes was tested by calculating t (t was found to be 1.25).

The null hypothesis that the clinical and psychological assessment of annual decline in performance in the geriatric patient agrees to an extent no greater than chance was tested by calculating the coefficient of colligation. The covalues for the several tests are shown in Table 2.

Table 2. Coefficients of colligation for each test

Test	w value	P
Rigidity (S$_2$)	0.67	0.001
Capacity for Testing Reality (ORS)	0.51	0.050
Memory and/or Learning (MLT)	0.44	0.050
Somatic Complaints (C)	0.43	0.050
Coordination (P)	0.15	n. s.
Empathy (Ra)	0.11	n. s.

The geriatric population studied here complains of dizziness, difficulty in getting to sleep, difficulty in staying asleep, and frequent waking between the hours of 2 and 4 A.M. Memory is described as failing; they are troubled with constipation and frequency of urination, and have attacks of shaking and trembling. They tend to be nervous and excitable, find it difficult to keep their balance when walking, and have some degree of paralysis.

Based on the generally accepted interpretation of certain categories of the Rorschach test, the thinking, feeling, and behavior of the population studied here may be described as emotionally labile and stimulus-bound. Blocking and perseveration of the associative process is demonstrated. Affect is appropriate, and there is no loss of capacity for testing reality. These patients appeared surprisingly free from conflicts, able to identify themselves with the group, and to be relatively uncritical of others. They seldom perceived the environment as threatening, and only rarely projected their guilt.

CONCLUSIONS

There is essential agreement between the clinical and psychological assessment of the geriatric patient.

A statistically significant annual decline of performance on certain objective psychological techniques is not demonstrated.

A tendency toward acceleration of the rate of decline associated with diabetes mellitus is suggested.

COMMENTS

It would be important to better understand why the geriatric patients studied were relatively without conflict. For this reason alone, the study should be repeated in many settings.

Since it has been observed, clinically, that patients who develop diabetes late in life appear older than their chronologic age, it would be important to compare these patients with diabetic patients who developed diabetes at an early age, and who have been treated with insulin for a number of years.

The history of science is the history of objective measurement. The psychological techniques described here present a higher order of scientific description than is found in observational methods. The use of certain objective psychological techniques, therefore, makes prediction of past or future levels of performance, and reproducible findings possible.

SUMMARY

In order to test the hypothesis that it is possible, on the basis of the performance on certain objective psychological techniques, to detect an acceleration of the rate of aging, twenty geriatric patients were studied. The findings lead to the following conclusions: (1) a definite relationship exists between the clinical and psychological assessment of the geriatric patient; (2) a statistically significant annual decline of performance on certain objective psychological techniques is not demonstrated; and (3) a tendency for an acceleration of the rate of decline associated with diabetes mellitus is suggested.

REFERENCES

Eysenck, H. J. 1952. The scientific study of personality. London: Routledge & Kegan Paul, Ltd.

Partington, J. E., and Leiter, R. G. 1949. Partington's Pathways Test. Psychol. Serv. Center Bull., 1: 11–20.

Reitman, F., and Robertson, J. P. S. 1950. Reitman's Pin-Man Test: a means of disclosing impaired conceptual thinking. J. Nerv. & Ment. Dis., 112: 498–510.

Vinson, D. B. 1960. Responses to the Rorschach test that identify schizophrenic thinking, feeling and behavior. J. Clin. & Exper. Psychopathol., 30: 34–40.

Walton, D., and Black, D. A. 1957. The validity of a psychological test of brain damage. Brit. J. Med. Psychiat., 30: 270–79.

Wells, F. L., and Ruesch, J. 1945. Mental examiners' handbook. New York: The Psychological Corporation.

An Evaluation of Community Care:

Some Findings on the Aged

PETER SAINSBURY AND JACQUELINE GRAD

THE WORTHING EXPERIMENT

THE emphasis in treatment of the mentally ill has been shifting in recent years from hospital to community care. The Worthing Experiment, a domiciliary and day-hospital service, is one of a number of schemes that represent this change (Carse *et al.,* 1958). The object of this experiment, to quote Dr. Carse, was "to discover whether the provision of large-scale psychiatric treatment on an out-patient basis could materially affect the great annual increase of admissions to the mental hospital." (Carse, 1959.)

The experiment originated from Graylingwell Hospital, the county mental hospital for West Sussex. This is a predominantly rural county which has a population of approximately 370,000 and includes nine towns, the largest of which is Worthing, a seaside resort with a population of approximately 72,000. Chichester, with a population of 19,000, is the county town and administrative center, and it is in Chichester that Graylingwell Hospital is situated. There are no other private or state psychiatric hospitals in this county, and indeed no private psychiatrists practice in the area. All psychiatric services for adult patients are provided by the National Health Service and are centered in Graylingwell. It will be noted, therefore, that this community-care experiment is essentially a hospital-centered project.

For the purpose of convenient administration of West Sussex, the catchment area of Graylingwell is divided into three, and psychiatric out-patient clinics are held at the general hospitals in the main town in each area—Chichester, Worthing, and Horsham. The mental health services of each area are administered separately by one of the staff consultant psychiatrists of Graylingwell and each area has its team of junior psychiatrists and psychiatric social workers (PSWs) who work both in the local outpatient clinics and with the patients admitted to Graylingwell Hospital from their area.

The community-care scheme was started in the Worthing area in January, 1957 by converting The Acre, a large private house in the center of the town, into a day hospital and a treatment, occupation, and administrative center for all patients from Worthing and district. All the medical practitioners and representatives of the local health services were approached at this time. The purpose of the experiment was explained and their cooperation sought, so that from then on they referred all their psychiatric patients directly to The Acre. The team at The Acre decided whether to visit the patient in his own home or examine him at the center. This is in marked contrast to the previous and traditional process whereby the general practitioner or local authority contacted the parent hospital directly to inveigle them into finding a bed for their patient. About one-third of the new referrals are now seen at their homes, a third at the day hospital, and a third at the outpatient department.

Cooperation with the local practitioners and the local authority mental welfare officers has been maintained by arranging periodic meetings with them to discuss problems as they arise. In fact, an extremely high level of cooperation has been maintained ever since the inception of the service. The local health authority has provided a hospital car service without which many patients who have been treated at the day hospital would have had to be admitted to hospital. The general practitioners have come to have an extremely good personal relationship with the service psychiatrists which has enabled rapid referral and handling of patients.

Effect of the experiment on admission rates

There is no doubt that the Worthing Experiment has been outstandingly successful in achieving what it set out to do. Admissions to Graylingwell from the experimental area in 1957 decreased by 56 percent when compared with the admissions from this area in 1956; whereas admissions from the rest of the catchment area (the Chichester and Horsham districts) in which the service did not operate at that time, increased by 4 percent during the same period. Admissions from Worthing continued to decrease—by 62 percent in the second year and 58 percent in the third year as compared with the pre-experiment year of 1956 (Carse, 1960). This decrease in admissions, it has been said (Parnell and Skottowe, 1958), may reflect no more than the reduction of an exceptionally high admission rate to that of the national average. Certainly there was a high level of admissions to Graylingwell before the introduction of the community service, but, compared with many other mental hospitals, Graylingwell has for some years enjoyed a good reputation locally. Once a hospital becomes accepted by the community it will attract the admission of those who previously shunned the lunatic asylum. Hence, an overcrowding problem develops in the hospital, and long waiting lists force us to consider who will benefit most from admission and who may more suitably be treated by day hospitals and by domiciliary and outpatient care.

The crucial point, therefore, in evaluating a hospital's community-care program is not how the level of, or decrease in, admissions compares with a national average, but whether the decrease occurs over the whole range of clinical groups referred, not just in those which in other areas would not ordinarily be admitted; and whether the most appropriate service is being provided to patients both within and without the hospital.

THE CHICHESTER SERVICE

In January, 1958, this experiment was extended to Chichester. The Chichester and district psychiatric service serves the western half of the county of West Sussex which again has a mainly rural population of approximately 112,000. The only large towns in the area are Chichester and Bognor with a combined population of some 44,000. The organization of domiciliary and day-hospital treatment closely follows that of the original scheme in Worthing. The aim of the service was to find out whether results similar to those obtained during the previous year in Worthing could be achieved (a) by other workers, (b) in a more scattered and more rural area, and (c) by a medical staff which had to spend at least half of its time on inpatient work.

Evaluating the community service

When the Chichester service had been established for one year the Medical Research Council's Clinical Psychiatry Research Unit began to investigate a number of factors associated with this type of community care. We knew from the Worthing Experiment that admissions to a mental hospital could be reduced by a community psychiatric service. This experiment had not, however, shown what the comparative therapeutic values of the community and traditional types of treatment were or what benefits or burdens this type of service had brought to the community, particularly to the families of the patients who had been treated at home; and it had not shown which clinical and social considerations favored community care and which favored hospital care.

The community service and the elderly

One of the problem groups with which we were particularly concerned was the elderly. The admission of geriatric patients is becoming an increasing problem in England and particularly in the area of West Sussex which has a higher proportion of elderly people than any other part of the country. It is of interest, therefore, to note how the reduction in admissions from Worthing affected the later age groups (Carse, 1960). In 1959 as compared with 1956, the year preceding the introduction of the service, a decrease of 42 percent was achieved in the age group 65–74, but the admission of those aged 75 and over was reduced only by 24 percent. This discrepancy is even more marked when admissions from the Chichester service are considered. In 1959 as compared with 1957, the year preceding the introduction of the service in Chichester, there was a decrease of 41 percent in the admission of patients aged 65–74, but there was an increase of 14 percent in admissions of patients aged 75 and over.

It is clear, then, that age is a factor which is related to whether or not the patient is admitted to hospital. It might, we thought, be possible that other factors, not necessarily related to diagnosis, also influenced whether a mentally ill patient is treated at home or in hospital. For example, if two clinically similar patients with a depressive illness of moderate severity are referred, whether they are treated at home or in hospital is likely to be determined by such factors as whether they are living alone, the type of job they have, or the number of their family responsibilities.

The primary aim of our research into the Chichester and District Psychiatric Service, therefore, was to study the clinical, social, and environmental factors which determine whether a mentally ill patient is treated at home or in hospital.

The preliminary study

The relation of these factors to disposal was explored in a preliminary study in which the effect of the service on admissions in various groups was examined (Morrissey and Sainsbury, 1959). Admissions from this area to Graylingwell Hospital in 1957 were compared with those in 1958, the year in which the community service was introduced. We found a proportionately and significantly greater reduction in certain vital, social, and clinical groups in 1958.

During the first year (1958) 842 new patients were seen. This gave a referral rate for the area of West Sussex served by the Chichester service at 7.5 per 1000 population. The referral rate for the previous year for the same area was 6.8 per 1000 population. It seems probable, therefore, that the existence of a service of this kind means that more people are referred to the psychiatrist by general practitioners. Six-hundred and fourteen, or 73 percent of the patients referred, were treated as outpatients, in the day hospital or at home. In 1957 there were 463 admissions from the area covered by the Chichester scheme. The number of admissions from this area in 1958 was 228, which gives a reduction of 51 percent. We therefore next asked which clinical, social, or other groups contributed most to this reduction in admission following the introduction of the community service.

Reasons given for admitting patients. In each new case we recorded the main factor that the psychiatrist believed determined his decision to admit the patient (Table 1). In 158 patients admission to

Table 1. Reasons given for admitting patients to hospital, Chichester, 1958

Clinical reasons	Number of cases	Social reasons	Number of cases
Disturbed behavior	107	Request of relatives	20
Poor physical state	16	To give relatives a rest	17
Suicidal risk	13	Living alone	16
Patient uncooperative	11	Direct request of patient	
For investigation	9	or general practitioner	4
Stabilization of epileptic fits	2	Distance from hospital	2
Total	158	Bad home conditions	1
		Condition of residence	
		(Magistrate)	1
		Total	61
Transfer from Summersdale Hospital to Graylingwell Hospital	9		
Total admissions	228		

hospital was decided primarily on clinical grounds, but in 61 patients admission was arranged because of the home circumstances or the attitude of the patient or the relative.

Age and sex. In order to inquire further into the factors determining admission in these 228 patients it was decided to compare the admissions over the 6-month period April to September, 1958, with the admissions during the same 6 months in 1957. Table 2 shows that

Table 2. Number of admissions, by age, from Chichester in 1957 and 1958[a]

Number of admissions

Age	Apr.-Sept. 1957	Apr.-Sept. 1958	Percentage change
0–24	8	7	−12.5
25–44	38	18	−52.6
45–64	73	24	−67.1
65–74	40	26	−35.0
75 plus	21	27	+28.6
Total	180	102	−43.3

[a] $X^2 = 15.11$; $P < 0.01$.

there were significant changes in the age distribution of admissions in 1958. There was an over-all decrease of 43 percent. There was a proportionately greater decrease in ages 25–44 and 45–64, but there was an increase (29 percent) in those aged 75 and over.

There was a significantly greater decrease in male than in female admissions, the percentage changes being 52 percent and 40 percent, respectively.

Distance from hospital. Distance from the hospital was also a factor in determining admission. For those living in Chichester and in the Chichester Rural District Area, which extends some 8–10 miles from the hospital, the decrease was 55 percent, and for those living in the rest of the area the decrease was only 14 percent.

Marital status. There was a significant change in the categories of civil status during the two periods under review (Table 3). The

Table 3. Numbers of admissions, by marital status, from Chichester in 1957 and 1958[a]

Marital status	1957 (N = 181)	1958 (N = 101)	Percentage change
Single	53	29	−45.3
Married	93	37	−60.2
Widowed	26	30	+15.4
Separated	9	3	−44.4

[a] $X^2 = 10.75$; $P < 0.05$.

decrease in the proportion of married was greater than that of single and separated, and there was an increase in the admission of widows.

Social class. The social class to which the patients belong also plays a part in determining admission. The percentage decreases in the different social classes of the two groups were: classes 1 and 2, 45 percent; class 3, 49 percent; classes 4 and 5, 32 percent. There is therefore a proportionately smaller decrease in classes 4 and 5, but these differences are not significant.

Table 4. Numbers of admissions, by mode of living, from Chichester in 1957 and 1958

Mode of living	1957 (N = 169)	1958 (N = 102)	Percentage change
With family	84	48	−42.9
With parents	23	13	−43.5
With other relatives	18	11	−38.9
Alone	44	30	−31.8

Mode of living. Table 4 shows the effect of the mode of living. The decrease in admission in those living with parents and marital family was greater than in those living with other relatives. The least change (32 percent) occurred in those living alone. These differences, however, were not statistically significant.

Diagnosis. There were also changes in the admission rates in the different diagnostic categories (Table 5). There was a highly sig-

Table 5. Numbers of admissions, by diagnosis, from Chichester in 1957 and 1958[a]

Diagnosis[a]	1957 (N = 178)	1958 (N = 102)	Percentage decrease or increase 1958/1957
Schizophrenia	27	17	−37
Affective psychoses	82	46	−44
Neuroses	32	5	−84
Senile psychoses	18	26	+44
Other	19	8	−58

[a] $X^2 = 18.7$; $P < 0.001$.

nificant difference in the patterns of admissions in the different groups in the 2 years. The greatest decrease was in the neuroses. The affective psychoses and schizophrenia also decreased considerably, but there was an increase in the cases of senile psychoses—an unexpected finding. It is possible that, because of the facilities provided by this service, more senile patients were referred to us. Nearly all of this increase occurred during the first 6 months of 1958.

Previous admissions. Table 6 shows the percentage change in admissions in 1958 as compared to 1957 (a) when there had been a previous admission to Graylingwell or any other hospital, and (b) in the cases in which the only previous admission had been to Graylingwell. There was a significantly greater decrease in patients with a history of a previous admission to any mental hospital, and this de-

Table 6. *Numbers of admissions in 1957 and 1958, by first and previous admissions to Graylingwell and other hospitals*

Admission status	Any hospital[a]			Graylingwell[b]		
	1957 ($N=158$)	1958 ($N=95$)	Percentage change	1957 ($N=148$)	1958 ($N=81$)	Percentage change
Previous admission	116	54	−53.4	106	40	−62.3
First admission	42	41	−2.4	42	41	−2.4

[a] $X^2 = 7.38$.
[b] $X^2 = 11.20$; $P < 0.001$.

crease was even more marked in patients with a history of a previous admission to Graylingwell Hospital.

It might be expected that with the decrease in the admission of patients suffering from neurosis and uncomplicated affective illness and with the increased admission of senile psychotics, the duration of stay of the patients admitted in 1958 would be increased. In 1957 the mean stay in weeks was 8.6 and in 1958 it was 10: this increase is not significant.

In summing up the experiences of the psychiatrists working in the community service Dr. Morrissey wrote:

We were impressed by the flexibility of approach which this service allowed. A decision could be made on clinical and on social grounds to treat the patient in hospital, in the day hospital, in the out-patient department, or in his own home. Each psychiatrist worked in all these fields and he could provide a continuity of treatment when the patient required admission to hospital. Similarly, on discharge the follow-up was carried on by the psychiatrist who had seen the patient in the first instance.

The current study to evaluate the community-care service

We thought that these findings of the preliminary study justified a more detailed investigation and therefore predicted those factors we believed more likely to favor treatment at home and those likely to favor treatment by admission. We planned to assess and compare these in two areas which resembled one another closely except that in one, Chichester, the domiciliary service obtained; whereas in the other, Salisbury, there was a more usual and conservative policy of admission to the mental hospital. We chose Salisbury as our control area because it had a hospital of similar size to that of Graylingwell and it had a demographically similar catchment area.

Our method of comparison was to arrange for the clinical data on every patient in both areas to be systematically recorded on a prepared item sheet. This is completed by the psychiatrist at his initial interview with the patient. The clinical details so recorded are: family and previous history, duration of illness, the principal symptoms (for which the item sheet gives a check list), diagnosis, treatment and disposal. In the Chichester area the psychiatrist also records on a prepared list his clinical and social reasons for admitting or not admitting the patient.

In addition to the item sheet, a detailed social schedule is completed by our PSWs on a visit to the home of every third new patient. Data on the following social and familial factors believed to determine disposal are obtained: the patient's mode of living and composition of his household (this includes the age of members of the household, their relationship to the patient, and the number of people in the home); next, his social and economic status; his employment situation; certain characteristics of his housing and locality; the health of other members of his family and the cooperation obtained from friends and neighbors; then, the attitude of household members to the patient and to his admission; and, finally, the effects of specified symptoms and of their duration on the household.

A second aim of this study was to find out what effect caring for a mentally ill person at home has on his family and household.

Our method of doing this is to arrange for the following factors to be recorded in the schedule by the PSWs when they visit the patient's family: the effects of the patient's illness on the employment of household members, on domestic routine, and on the children's schooling; also recorded are the effects on the social and leisure activities, on the family's income, on the mental and physical health of household members, and on their relations with neighbors. In this way each informant's appraisal of the advantages and disadvantages to his family of admission or domiciliary care is tabulated or rated.

This research is in its early stages; however, two pilot studies have been completed. Their purpose was, first, to measure the reliability of the doctors' item sheet and the PSW's schedules, and, second, to find out whether these two questionnaires are, in fact, able to discern the differences or effects with which we are concerned.

Reliability studies

To assess the reliability of the item sheet, two psychiatrists independently completed it for 90 patients and their agreements were recorded. The extent to which agreement on diagnosis is determined by that on symptoms, on the duration of the illness, on the previous history of illness, etc., has been calculated. These results show that agreement on broad diagnostic categories was 79 percent; but for organic illness in the elderly it was higher, 85 percent. For the psychoses it was 71 percent, for the neuroses 52 percent, and for all other conditions it was 33 percent. Agreement on diagnoses was found to be significantly related to the level of agreement on previous illness. It was not related to agreement on symptoms. The percentage agreement on symptoms of the kind found in old age was consistently high.

To assess the reliability of the interviewing schedule, three PSWs visited the households of 60 patients in pairs and completed separate schedules for each joint interview (Grad *et al.,* to be published). The percent agreement between them on the 72 items in their schedule was assessed and showed an agreement of at least 85 percent on 63 items. With this information obtained from the pilot study, unreliable questions were redefined or omitted from the schedule which is being used for the major inquiry.

Other pilot study results

The pilot study findings also indicate that interesting material both on factors determining disposal of patients and on the effects of caring for a mentally ill person at home is likely to emerge. For example, as well as bearing out the preliminary inquiry's findings that admission was related to age and diagnosis, it also indicated that there was a trend for admission to hospital to be related to household size, to social class, and to the patient's financial status.

Our tentative conclusions from a preliminary analysis of the problems that these 60 patients were causing their family at the time of referral were that in 36 percent of the families social activities had been restricted; that in 25 percent the job of a family member had been affected; and that 40 percent of the cases presented some problems of management (in 20 percent this was severe). The health of the informant was affected psychologically in 32 percent and physically in 36 percent; the health of other family members was affected in 44 percent of households. Family income was diminished on account of the patient's illness in 33 percent of the households (severely in 20 percent). These figures were higher in the families of those patients whom it was decided to admit. Following admission, however, the effects on the families of the inpatient group were numerically less than on the families of those who remained at home.

It will be a year before we have collected all the clinical and social data on patients referred in both districts. Only then will it be possible to analyze and compare the findings in the two services, and to begin a follow-up study to compare outcome in each of them according to the type of treatment given and by clinical categories. We hope to assess outcome in terms of the changes in the patient's clinical symptoms, in the effects reported by the family, or in his altered social and economic position.

Findings on the elderly

We would like briefly to present some preliminary data relating to the 60 elderly people seen in the Chichester area so far as these are available. The findings at this stage of the study can only broadly indicate some of the factors affecting the disposal of elderly patients and some effects on the households in which they live. More definitive statements will be possible only when comparable data have also been obtained from the control area.

Of these 60 patients 18 were male and 42 female; 32 were diagnosed as suffering from an organic psychosis and 28 from an affective disorder. After the initial interview 21 of the 60 patients were admitted to Graylingwell, 5 were admitted to other institutions, and 34 were treated at home.

Can we show that any factors were related to these differences in disposal? And can we describe the effect that the care of these patients has had on their families?

Age and diagnosis. Seventeen (61 percent) of the 28 patients aged 75 plus were admitted as compared with only 9 (28 percent) of the 32 aged 60–74 (Table 7).

Table 7. Disposal of 60 elderly patients, by age[a]

Age	In Graylingwell or other hospital	At home
60–69	4	19
70 plus	22	15
Total	26	34

[a] $X^2 = 8.58$; $P < 0.01$.

The association found between diagnosis and age in this small sample was as follows. Eighty-two percent of those over 75 had an organic psychosis, as compared with 28 percent in the age group 60–74 (Table 8). Moreover, 56 percent of the organic cases were admitted to Graylingwell as compared with only 29 percent of the patients with affective disorders (Table 9). In considering the effects

Table 8. Diagnosis and age in 60 elderly patients[a]

Age	Organic	Affective
60–74	9	23
75 plus	23	5
Total	32	28

[a] $X^2 = 15.4$; $P < 0.001$.

on the family it should be borne in mind that whereas an organic diagnosis and an age of 75 years or more were associated with in-patient care, yet there were still 11 (39 percent) persons aged 75 plus, and 14 (44 percent) with organic diagnoses, who remained in the community.

Elderly people in our community—which is a favored retirement area for persons of superior or aspiring social status—tend to live apart from the younger generation of their own families. Usually our patients are one of an elderly couple, or a widow or a spinster living in a boarding house where other elderly people have retired to live in quiet gentility, or one of a pair of siblings or friends who have set up home together or remained in the parental home. Thus the other people in the patient's environment are usually elderly and quite often infirm. It is rare for a young or middle-aged family to have their aged relative live with them, unless that relative is seriously physically infirm and bereft of other support. When this sheltering of the elderly becomes necessary it is often a considerable burden to the young family. Partly because the physical demands made are then great, and partly because the elderly person is not a real member of the household with a useful role to play, he becomes and feels himself to be a nuisance.

Family composition. With these considerations in mind we looked at the age and composition of the family household and its attitude toward hospital care for the elderly patient to see if these factors could be related to the type of care that the Chichester service provided.

The patient who was living with a spouse had the most chance of remaining at home while being treated. Twenty-five percent of those who lived with spouses were admitted, but of those who lived

Table 9. Disposal of 60 elderly patients, by diagnosis[a]

Disposal	Organic	Affective
Graylingwell or other hospital	18	8
At home	14	20
Total	32	28

[a] $X^2 = 3.60$ N. S.; $P < 0.05$.

with any other person 62 percent were admitted, a significant difference (Table 10). This influence of the spouse is slightly outweighed

Table 10. Disposal of 60 elderly patients, by mode of living[a]

Disposal	Alone	With spouse	With others
Graylingwell or other hospital	7	6	13
At home	8	18	8
Total	15	24	21

[a] $X^2 = 6.31$; $P < 0.05$.

when he or she is also aged, but, even so, 71 percent of those patients whose spouses were aged 65 or more years were able to remain out of hospital.

It is interesting and surprising to see that, in contrast to the general trend of admissions in *all* age groups, the elderly are not more likely to be admitted if they live alone; in fact, they are less likely to be admitted if they live alone than if they live with any person other than the spouse (Table 10). This may be because those who are still living alone when they come to the psychiatrist's attention have been managing tolerably well. They have not demanded the continuous physical care of younger relatives, and unless their mental condition now precipitates this, they are able to remain as domiciliary or outpatients.

Family attitudes. This difference found between those who live with a spouse and those who live with any other person leads us on to consider the family's attitude toward hospital care for their mentally sick elderly relative. We found this to be very significantly related to disposal (Table 11).

Table 11. Disposal of 55 elderly patients, by attitude of family toward mental hospital care[a,b]

Disposal	Not wanted but accepted as necessary	Preferred	Strongly wanted or it was a great relief
Graylingwell or other hospital	7	8	9
At home	24	4	3
Total	31	12	12

[a] $X^2 = 12.97$; $P < 0.01$.
[b] In 5 cases there was no family.

Seventy-one percent of the relatives of *inpatients* were in favor of hospital care. To 37 percent it had indeed been a great relief. Twenty-nine percent, however, would have preferred to have their patient at home. Of the relatives of *outpatients,* etc., 23 percent would have preferred hospital care. The probable bias in this finding is undoubtedly an over-reporting of preference for home care. There is no doubt that admission to a mental hospital or even a nursing home bears the stigma of "putting the old person away." We may therefore consider that this 23 percent is an underestimation of the number of families who would have preferred hospital care.

When the attitude to admission of outpatients was considered further, it was found that only 18 percent of spouses favored or desired hospital care, but 31 percent of relatives and others living with the patient would have preferred it. This may go some way toward helping to explain the finding that those living with any other relative are more likely to be admitted than those living alone.

Family's competence. To move from the realm of attitudes to some more tangible aspects of the patient's social environment, our figures seem to show that not only the person with whom the patient lives, but the ability of the family to cope with the patient, is related to admission.

From the general history and description of the family composition, of housing, health, attitudes, occupation, etc., the PSWs made an assessment in each case of the family's ability to look after the patient at home. When there was no family, or when the family refused to have the patient, or when the family was physically or mentally incapable of managing, or when they found their own family life or peace of mind seriously threatened by the patient's presence, this was rated as "poor." Similar but less severe problems were given a middle rating of "some difficulty." All other families were rated as "able." We then found that 88 percent of the inpatients' families and 44 percent of the home-care families had difficulties in coping with the patient; in 65 percent of the "inpatients'" families and in 26 percent of the "home-care" families, these difficulties were severe (Table 12). When health alone was considered a similar trend appeared. The health of the family was rated as "poor" in 25 percent of those admitted to hospital, but in only 10 percent of the home group.

Table 12. Disposal of 60 elderly patients, by ability of family to cope with the patients[a]

	Ability to cope with patients			
Disposal	*Good*	*Some difficulty*	*Poor*	*No family*
Graylingwell or other hospital	3	6	15	2
At home	19	6	5	4
Total	22	12	20	6

[a] $X^2 = 16.51$; $P < 0.001$.

Effects on family. A separate assessment was made of the effect that the patient's presence had on the family. Such measurable factors as effect on income, leisure activities, and household routine were considered along with the informant's self-ratings of poor health, exhaustion, disturbed nights, anxiety, irritability, etc., due to the patient. We found (Table 13) that more than two-thirds of those who were

Table 13. Disposal of 55 elderly patients, by effect on the family[a,b]

Disposal	No burden	Some burden	Severe burden
Graylingwell or other hospital	2	9	13
At home	13	12	6
Total	15	21	19

[a] $X^2 = 10.37$; $P < 0.01$.
[b] In 5 cases there was no family.

rated as being a "severe burden" had been admitted to Graylingwell, but that 6 (19 percent) of the 31 outpatients were also a severe burden to their families, and that an additional 12 (38 percent) were some burden. Thus, while problems of the family in managing the patient are clearly associated with inpatient care, yet there are many families who, despite similar problems, continue to support the burden of caring for their mentally ill aged relatives.

CONCLUSIONS

It would be premature to draw any firm conclusions from these somewhat sketchy interim data. We believe, however, that the evidence we have collected so far points to the need for careful consideration of the problems that families have to cope with when the only alternative to looking after a senile or depressed elderly patient at home is admission to a mental hospital. It has been the impression of our investigators during the course of their visits that most families have an extremely positive and helpful attitude toward their handicapped elderly member. However, the effort involved in caring for them is, by the time they have come to the notice of the psychiatric service, considerable. We would consider some method of providing earlier help and advice and some alternative institutional provision to be of paramount importance.

Acknowledgments. These studies could not have been carried out without the generous help and cooperation of Dr. Carse, Medical Superintendent of Graylingwell, and Dr. Morrissey, Consultant in charge of the Chichester Service, and their colleagues; and Dr. Galbraith,

Medical Superintendent of the Knowle Group of Hospitals and his staff at the Old Manor, Salisbury.

REFERENCES

Carse, J. 1959. The Worthing Experiment: a report on the first two years of the Worthing and district mental health service, 1957–1958. Chichester, England: Graylingwell Hospital.
———— 1960. The community services of Graylingwell Hospital, Chichester, January 1, 1957 to December 31, 1959. Chichester, England: Graylingwell Hospital.
Carse, J., Panton, N. E., and Watt, A. 1958. A district mental health service: the Worthing Experiment. Lancet, 1: 39–41.
Grad, J. C., Collins, J., and Stamp, S. The reliability of social assessments. (To be published.)
Morrissey, J., and Sainsbury, P. 1959. Observations on the Chichester and district mental health service. Proc. Roy. Soc. Med., 52: 1061–63.
Parnell, R. W., and Skottowe, I. 1958. A district mental health service. Lancet, 1: 319.

Factors in Selection of Psychiatric Treatment for Institutionalized Aged Persons

ROBERT L. KAHN, ALVIN I. GOLDFARB, MAX POLLACK,

AND ARTHUR PECK

RECENT investigations have shown that not only the type of illness but also sociopsychological factors influence the type of psychiatric treatment a patient receives. As shown by Hollingshead and Redlich (1958), persons from the upper social classes, as defined by education, occupation, and place of residence, are more likely to be selected for psychotherapy, while somatic treatment or custodial care is more common among the lower social groups. Rosenthal and Frank (1958) reported an almost straight-line relationship between education level and frequency of referral for psychotherapy in an outpatient clinic. In another clinic, Myers and Schaffer (1954) found that the higher a person's social class the more likely he was to be accepted for psychotherapy and treated intensively by highly trained personnel over a long period of time. In a study of a private, nonprofit, mental hospital, Kahn, Pollack, and Fink (1957) found that better educated, native-born, and younger patients were most likely to receive psychotherapy as their sole form of treatment, while EST and psychotherapy were more frequently prescribed for the older, foreign-born, and more poorly educated patients.

This paper reports on a preplanned investigation of the relation of specific characteristics in residents of a home for the aged to the selection of psychotherapy, other forms of psychiatric treatment, or no psychiatric treatment.

METHOD

The population studied was a random sample of 160 persons, 65 years of age and over, residing in the Home for Aged and Infirm Hebrews of New York.

A psychiatrist who was a member of the staff of the home examined each patient for psychiatric disorder and entered his observations in a standard way on a precoded form. The psychiatrist noted the presence or absence of chronic brain syndrome or other psychiatric disorder, the degree of the disorder, an opinion as to the need or indication for psychiatric treatment, and the type of treatment indicated.

In addition each patient was given two brief psychological tests of mental status. These were a ten-item questionnaire testing orientation, memory and general information, and the "face-hand test," measuring ability to perceive two tactile stimuli simultaneously applied to the face and hand (Kahn *et al.,* in press).

The relationship of the recommendations for psychotherapy, "other" psychiatric treatment, or no treatment to specific characteristics and performance of the patient was correlated.

RESULTS
Recommendation for psychiatric treatment

In the psychiatrist's opinion, 84 percent of the total number of 160 persons needed psychiatric treatment. Psychotherapy was the type of treatment recommended for 26 percent of the whole group; a recommendation for "other treatment" such as milieu therapy or drugs was made for 58 percent of the group; 16 percent were not considered to be in need of any psychiatric care.

Education

The relation between the type of psychiatric treatment recommended and educational background of the patient is shown in Table 1. Patients recommended for psychotherapy had a mean educational

Table 1. *Psychiatric treatment recommendation and education*

Treatment recommended	Number of cases	Mean education	Difference	t
Psychotherapy	42	8.7	1.5	2.32[a]
Other	71	7.2		
None	21	8.1		
Total	134	7.8		

[a] Significant at .05 level.

level of 8.7 years, whereas those recommended for other forms of treatment had a mean of only 7.2 years. The difference between these groups was significant at the 5 percent level. Patients for whom no psychiatric treatment was recommended had an educational level of 8.1 years, between the other two groups.

Age

As shown in Table 2, the patients recommended for psychotherapy

Table 2. *Psychiatric treatment recommendation and age*

Treatment recommended	Number of cases	Mean age	Difference	t
Psychotherapy	42	79.4	2.8	N.S.
Other	88	82.2		
None	23	78.7		
Total	153	80.9		

were, on the average, almost 3 years younger than patients recommended for "other kinds" of psychiatric treatment, although the difference is not statistically significant. The group for whom no psychiatric treatment was recommended was slightly younger than the psychotherapy group.

Sex

The sample was predominantly female, accurately reflecting the population of the home (Table 3). Males, who contributed 27 percent

Table 3. *Psychiatric treatment recommendation and sex, percentage distribution*

Treatment recommended	Male	Female	Number of cases
Psychotherapy	21	79	42
Other	28	72	93
None	32	68	25
Total	27	73	160

of the sample, constituted 2.1 percent of those for whom psychotherapy was recommended, 28 percent of those for "other treatment," and 32 percent of the group for whom no treatment was recommended. These differences fall short of statistical significance.

Chronic brain syndrome

The relation of treatment recommendation to the evaluation of chronic brain syndrome is shown in Table 4. There was very little

*Table 4. Psychiatric treatment recommendation and evaluation
of severity of chronic brain syndrome, percentage distribution*

| | Chronic brain syndrome | | |
Treatment recommended	None or mild	Moderate or severe	Number of cases
Psychotherapy	64	36	42
Other	57	43	93
None	80	20	25
Total	63	37	160

difference between the group recommended for psychotherapy and the
"other-treatment" group with respect to the presence or severity of
chronic brain syndrome. Sixty-four percent of the psychotherapy referrals were rated as having no or mild CBS as compared to 57 percent
of the "other-treatment" group. In contrast, 80 percent of the no-
treatment group was so rated.

Mental status questionnaire

A marked difference between the psychotherapy and other treatment
groups was shown for number of errors on the mental status questionnaire (MSQ) (see Table 5). Eighty-six percent of the "psycho-

*Table 5. Psychiatric treatment recommendation and
MSQ error score, percentage distribution*

| | MSQ errors | | |
Treatment recommended	0–2	3–10	Number of cases
Psychotherapy	86	14	42
Other treatment	63	37	93
No treatment	76	24	25
Total	72	28	160

therapy" group made fewer than three errors, but only 63 percent of
the "other-treatment" group did as well, a difference significant at the
1 percent level of confidence. The "no-treatment" group fell in between with 76 percent making so few errors.

Face-hand test

Of the persons recommended for psychotherapy 77 percent were
negative on the face-hand test, compared to only 44 percent of those
recommended for other treatments (Table 6), a difference significant

Table 6. *Psychiatric treatment recommendation and response to the face-hand test, percentage distribution*

Treatment recommended	Negative	Positive	Number of cases
Psychotherapy	77	23	42
Other	44	56	93
None	68	32	25
Total	63	37	160

at the 2 percent level. The "no-treatment" group fell in between, with 68 percent negative.

DISCUSSION

In general, psychiatric values and sorting methods have tended to restrict the use of psychotherapy to young adults. In recent years more interest has been shown in treating older persons by such methods. The selection of patients for psychotherapy, however, still appears to be influenced by a number of social factors which tend to eliminate older persons. The high percentage of persons recommended for psychotherapy in The Home for Aged and Infirm Hebrews is notable especially because almost all the residents were foreign born and many had difficulty in speaking English. These are factors which militate against referral for psychotherapy in our society. The Home for Aged and Infirm Hebrews, however, has pioneered in the use of psychiatric treatment, including psychotherapy, with the aged (Goldfarb, 1956). The psychiatrists doing the evaluations for this study, who are members of the staff of the Home, were undoubtedly more ready to recommend persons for psychotherapy than is customary. Nevertheless, our study has shown that even in this institution referral for psychotherapy is influenced by social and cultural characteristics of the patient. Referral for psychotherapy is more likely to be made in persons who are better educated, who are more alert, and who are operating at higher levels of intellectual functioning. There is also a slight tendency for psychotherapy to be recommended more often for females, younger persons, and those without chronic brain syndrome, but these differences fall short of statistical significance. In general, then, the selective factors evidently affecting their recommendations for psychotherapy are still comparable to those noted in studies of other populations.

The most common interpretation advanced to account for the relationship of sociopsychological factors to selection of psychiatric treatment is that psychiatrists tend to select for psychotherapy persons who are most like themselves in terms of their social characteristics.

Kahn *et al.* (1957) have emphasized that the critical factor in selecting patients for psychotherapy may be the possible communicative interaction between therapist and patient. From this point of view it is understandable that those persons who are better educated, functioning at a superior intellectual level as measured by the mental-status questionnaire, and more alert as measured by the face-hand test would be more appealing to the psychiatrists as possibilities for psychotherapy.

These findings are of importance because they appear to illustrate that psychiatrists believe that a psychotherapeutic relationship requires discriminatory capacity, conversational ability, good memory, and interest in establishing and maintaining a patient-doctor relationship. This psychiatric attitude is contrary to what is often actually discovered in medical and psychiatric practice. Experience with aged ill patients has revealed that brain-damaged, poorly educated persons with disturbance of orientation and memory desire and can make use of supportive personal relationships. They can benefit from a controlled patient-doctor relationship in which the development of insight is not an aim. It is possible that the very characteristics which provoke their rejection as candidates for psychotherapy may be indications rather than contraindications for such teratment. As has been pointed out (Goldfarb, 1956) the helplessness of the brain-damaged person who has limited intellectual resources on account of early social and educational deprivation may be more amenable to personal-treatment techniques which involve implicit suggestion and are contingent upon his rapid and complete delegation of special powers to the physician.

CONCLUSION

The selection of aged patients for psychotherapy appears to follow the same sociopsychological trends as in younger persons. This manner of selection may tend to weed out the most helpless, anxious, and most psychotherapeutically malleable candidates for psychiatric care.

Acknowledgment. We are grateful for the cooperation of Frederick D. Zeman, M.D., Director of Medical Services of The Home for Aged and Infirm Hebrews of New York.

REFERENCES

Goldfarb, A. I. 1956. Psychotherapy of the aged: the use and value of an adaptational frame of reference. Psychoanal. Rev., 43: 68–81.

Hollingshead, A. B., and Redlich, F. C. 1958. Social class and mental illness: a community study. New York: John Wiley & Sons.

Kahn, R. L., Goldfarb, A. I., Pollack, M., and Peck, A. Brief objective measures for the determination of mental status in the aged. Am. J. Psychiat. (In press.)

Kahn, R. L., Pollack, M., and Fink, M. 1957. Social factors in the selection of therapy in a voluntary mental hospital. J. Hillside Hosp., 6: 216–28.

Myers, J. K., and Schaffer, L. 1954. Social stratification and psychiatric practice: a study of out-patient clinic. Am. Sociological Rev., 19: 307–13.

Rosenthal, D., and Frank, J. 1958. The fate of psychiatric clinic out-patients assigned to psychotherapy. J. Nerv. Ment. Dis., 127: 330–43.

Social Factors and Mental Illness in the Institutionalized Aged Person: Role of Education

MAX POLLACK, ALVIN I. GOLDFARB,

AND ROBERT L. KAHN

THIS study is part of a survey of the institutionalized aged in New York City being conducted by the Office of the Consultant on Services for the Aged of the New York State Department of Mental Hygiene.

A major emphasis in the survey is the determination of factors related to individual differences in mental functioning of the aged. The study has shown that in institutionalized aged subjects factors other than age, e.g., physical functional state, are more highly correlated with mental functioning than chronological age (Kahn et al., 1960). This report focuses on the relation of social level, as measured by the amount of formal education, to mental status. Years of formal education appears to be an excellent index for the measurement of social status (Ginzberg et al., 1959).

In persons first institutionalized during old age, psychiatric illnesses are most frequently associated with brain damage. In our survey (Goldfarb, 1959b), chronic or acute brain syndromes were detected in 83 percent of the subjects by the interviewing psychiatrist. Behavior disorder diagnosed as psychosis, and judged as certifiable for admission to a psychiatric institution, was significantly higher in patients with severe chronic brain syndromes. The findings are similar to those of other investigators (Darvill and Jones, 1958; Simon et al., 1960), who have surveyed the diagnoses of aged persons admitted to the psychiatric service of a general hospital or state mental hospital.

Since the diagnosis of brain damage is made largely on impairment in intellectual functioning, e.g., disorientation, memory defects, etc., an investigation of the relation of social factors to intellectual organization would have importance for the study of mental illness in the aged. In this paper education and increasing age as factors related to mental functioning are compared.

SUBJECTS

The population sampled consisted of 1105 persons residing in homes for the aged, nursing homes, and state mental hospitals located in New York City. The subjects included were those who were 65 years of age or over at the time of first admission to the institution, and in residence as of a given month during the survey period of March to November, 1958.

Both the institutions chosen for study and the persons tested within each institution were selected by random sampling. All three state hospitals in New York City were sampled, with a total of 169 patients examined. Of the 102 proprietary nursing homes registered by the Department of Hospitals in January, 1956, samples were drawn from 13, and 426 persons were examined. Nine of the 49 homes for the aged within the metropolitan limits, listed by the Community Council of New York City in 1957, were sampled, with 482 residents examined.

The subjects ranged in age from 65 to 96 years with a mean of 79 years, the majority were foreign born, and there were twice as many women as men.

PROCEDURE

Two psychological tests were used in this study, the mental-status questionnaire (MSQ), and the face-hand test. These have been described elsewhere (Kahn *et al.,* in press; Pollack *et al.,* 1958) and will therefore be reviewed briefly.

The mental-status questionnaire

The mental-status questionnaire consisted of a series of 31 questions covering such areas as orientation, memory, calculation, and general and personal information. These questions were drawn partly from standard mental-status-examination procedures, and partly from recent special investigations of patterns of altered behavior with cerebral dysfunction (Weinstein and Kahn, 1955).

From the total questionnaire, ten items were selected as the most discriminating and used for the quantitative determination of mental status. These items were: (1) What is the name of this place? (2) Where is it located (address)? (3) What is today's date? (4) What is the month now? (5) What is the year? (6) How old are you? (7) When were you born (month)? (8) When were you born (year)? (9) Who is the President of the United States? (10) Who was the President before him?

While these questions themselves are familiar enough, our procedure ensured that the same questions, worded in the identical fashion, and in the same order, would be asked of everybody. Second, by obtaining a score based on the number of errors in response to these ten questions, a quantitative index of mental functioning was provided.

The face-hand test

The second psychological procedure used was the face-hand test. This test was first described by Fink, Green, and Bender (1952) as a diagnostic procedure for brain damage; and studied in aged persons by Green and Bender (1953). The test consists of touching the patient simultaneously on the cheek and on the dorsum of the hand, and asking him to indicate where he was touched. Ten trials are given: eight face-hand combinations divided between four contralateral (e.g., right cheek and left hand) and four ipsilateral (e.g., right cheek and right hand) stimuli, and two interspersed symmetric combinations of face-face and hand-hand. After the second trial, if the patient reports only one stimulus, he is asked, "Were you touched any place else?," in order to give him the concept of twoness. If the patient fails consistently to locate both stimuli correctly within the ten trials, he is classed as positive. The main types of errors are extinction, in which only one stimulus is indicated (almost always the face), and displacement, in which two stimuli are indicated but one of them, generally the hand stimulus, is displaced to another part of the body (e.g., if the person indicates both cheeks when the face and hand were actually touched). A patient is rated negative if he is consistently correct within the ten trials. Frequently he might make an error on the first four trials (the ipsilateral stimuli), but would be consistently correct after perceiving the two symmetric stimuli.

The face-hand test was first given with the eyes closed and then if the subject's test was positive it was repeated with the eyes open. Since it was found that in nearly 90 percent of the cases the responses under both condition were identical, the response with eyes open has been used in our analysis of data.

The face-hand test was considered a desirable procedure for this survey, not only because of its established value as a test for cerebral dysfunction, but also because it is relatively "culture free," being an unlearned perceptual task. It has the further advantage of being usable with patients who do not speak English well or present some other problem in verbal communication.

RESULTS
Age

The relation of mental-status questionnaire (MSQ) errors to age is presented in Table 1. As shown, there was a slight tendency for

Table 1. Relation of mental-status and face-hand test performance to age, percentage distribution

MSQ error score	65–74 (N = 290)	75–84 (N = 555)	85 or more (N = 260)
0	13.7	13.8	6.9
1	10.3	9.1	7.3
2	10.3	6.4	6.5
3	4.4	8.6	3.8
4	6.5	4.6	6.9
5	6.5	4.8	4.2
6	4.4	5.5	5.7
7	4.1	5.9	4.2
8	6.8	5.0	5.0
9	5.8	5.7	9.2
10	26.5	30.5	40.0
Face-hand test positive	57.2	61.3	71.5

younger persons, in the 65–74 age group, to be over-represented in the groups with the best mental functioning (fewer MSQ errors or negative face-hand test), and for the older patients, 85 or more, to be disproportionately represented in the poor mental-status groups. The differences between groups are nevertheless statistically significant at the .001 level (Chi-square test) for MSQ errors and age, and at the .01 for face-hand test performance and age.

Education

In contrast to the small group differences between test performance and age, there was a more marked difference between these tests and years of education (Table 2). The relationship to education for both MSQ and face-hand test is significant at the .001 level of confidence. The group differences are not truly reflected in the results. Accurate information on years of education was lacking for almost five hundred subjects. Judging from other data, e.g., occupation and birthplace, nearly all of these subjects could be classified as having less than 8 years of formal education: this procedure would, for example, increase by more than 20 percent the incidence of positive face-hand test performance in this group. Excluding this group, the incidence of positive face-hand tests is almost twice as high in the 0-to-7-year group as compared with the 9-years-or-over group (Table 2).

Table 2. Relation of mental-status and face-hand test performance to education, percentage distribution

MSQ error score	Years of schooling		
	0–7 (N = 319)	8 (N = 149)	9 or more (N = 137)
0	9.7	22.8	39.4
1	10.9	18.7	16.0
2	8.1	10.0	9.4
3	6.5	8.0	12.4
4	8.7	8.7	2.9
5	6.5	5.3	5.8
6	7.2	6.6	3.6
7	7.5	5.3	3.6
8	6.2	4.0	0.7
9	8.7	3.3	1.4
10	19.4	6.6	4.3
Face-hand test positive	59.1	44.4	31.2

Contingency coefficients were determined to show the comparative relationship of the MSQ scores to age and education. With education the correlation is +.33; the contingency coefficient of MSQ and age, however, is only +.18. This difference is paralleled in the correlation between the face-hand test and age (+.10), as compared with education (+.24).

While the findings clearly indicate that education was a more crucial factor than increasing age in a population of institutionalized persons over the age of 65 years, it is important to note that there were marked differences between institutions sampled. Thus, of the subjects with no years of formal education, approximately twice as many errors on the MSQ were made by residents of nursing homes and state mental hospitals as compared with those in homes for the aged.

DISCUSSION

The question may arise as to whether the tests employed in this study measure factors associated with school learning. We have found, however, that performance on the face-hand test correlates highly with the MSQ (Kahn *et al.,* in press; Pollack *et al.,* 1958). We have also examined a large group of aged persons living in the community and attending day centers for aged persons, whose age and educational level were comparable to our institutionalized population. Of the 71 persons in this sample only two subjects made more than three errors with the MSQ procedure, and only five had positive face-hand test results. There was in this population a consistent but nonsignificant trend for error scores to be correlated with educational and vocational attainment, a finding that corroborates the earlier studies of van Zonneveld (1958).

In one of the institutions we sampled, a majority of the subjects had no formal education; however, they showed little impairment on these psychological tasks. This institution was a home for aged trade union members, almost all of whom were literate, self-assertive, cultured, and self-educated. Our findings indicate that there was a marked interrelation between the social level of the patients and the type of institutional care, particularly the training and professional experience of the staff.

In institutions where almost all the residents were positive on the face-hand test and made persistent MSQ errors, there was an atmosphere of despair and futility. The residents were frequently apathetic, lethargic, withdrawn, and inattentive. Although many had been living in the same institution for years, they were unable to give its name or address. Few of these residents read newspapers or books or even listened to the radio. It would appear that, at least in part, the residents were responding to the expectations and the social philosophy of the institution.

A high correlation exists between a subject's alertness and his responses on these tests (Jaffe and Bender, 1951). Seemingly, alertness in old age is best maintained by persons who have stressed intellectual achievement all their lives. Furthermore, attentiveness is a reflection of the environmental milieu; institutions that foster intellectual stimulation facilitate the alertness of their residents. Geriatric psychiatrists such as Goldfarb (1959a) and Post (1958) have been keenly aware of the influence of social factors in the pattern of psychiatric illness in aged persons. Post (1958) refers to "the mutual interdependence of 'social' and 'psychiatric' as applied to elderly people."

Our findings concerning the importance of educational background in regard to mental functioning in the aged is consistent with previous observations on the relation of premorbid characteristics to behavioral changes with altered brain function. In their studies of patients with acute brain damage associated with tumors or vascular pathology, Weinstein and Kahn (1955) demonstrated that behavior changes were nonspecific for location of lesion, but were dependent on pre-morbid modes of adaptation. In a series of studies of induced altered brain function associated with convulsive therapy, Fink, Kahn, and Pollack (1959) found marked variations in behavior even with comparable degrees of cerebral dysfunction. They showed that these differences were related to such factors as premorbid personality, social background, and mode of communication.

Recent experimental studies of cortical ablation demonstrate results that are consistent with our observation. Animals that have been overtrained, i.e., beyond the usual learning criteria, do not show sensory (Benjamin, 1959) and perceptual (Chow and Survis, 1958) defects following removal of tissues that supposedly subserve these functions.

The relation of social factors to the alterations in psychological performance in the presence of deteriorating brain function is analogous to that of the developing child. Knobloch and Pasamanick have reported evidence that in infancy "Social factors affect the psychological level of integration primarily through biological mechanisms" (Knobloch and Pasamanick, 1960). In attempting to explain individual differences they claim that the precise role of genetic variation (in our study, the aging factor) cannot be assessed until the noxious effects of adverse socioeconomic conditions are removed.

The cultural influence is further demonstrated in the parallel between preschool children and the aged in their performance of simultaneous tactile stimuli. Pollack and Goldfarb (1957a; 1957b) have reported that children from middle and upper social classes made fewer errors than children from socially deprived families. The children in this latter group were poorly oriented for time, calendar organization, and such personal referrents as age and birth date. As in the aged, there was a significant relationship between orientation, intellectual functioning, and the face-hand test.

Our findings, we believe, have many public health implications. The educational level of the population is increasing markedly with each generation, a factor which we suggest may be more critical in determining behavioral differences than age alone. Even when controlling for the actual number of years of education, the quality of the education received in the past decade, or in a foreign country, as was true of much of our sampled population, may be quite different from an equivalent amount received in the United States today.

The general increase in educational level, as well as improvements in medical care, would also seem to forecast a decrease in the proportionate degree of mental impairment to be found in our aged population of the future.

SUMMARY

Years of schooling, as an index of social status, was compared with increasing age, as factors associated with mental functioning in a random sample of 1105 persons 65 years or older residing in homes for the aged, nursing homes, and state mental hospitals located in New York City. Since in this population psychiatric illnesses were associated with brain damage in over 80 percent of the group, two tests of intellectual functioning, the mental-status questionnaire, consisting of ten questions examining orientation and recent and remote memory, and the face-hand test, a test of cutaneous perception, were employed as indices of mental status.

Education was more highly correlated with performance in these tests than increasing age. Patients with less than public school education made approximately twice as many errors as those who attended high school. In contrast, persons living in communities of equivalent age and education showed little impairment in mental status as measured by these tasks.

The interaction of social factors and brain damage as factors related to behavior disorder in aged persons is discussed.

REFERENCES

Benjamin, R. M. 1959. Absence of deficits in taste discrimination following cortical lesions as a function of the amount of preoperative practice. J. Comp. Physiol. & Psychol., 52: 255–58.

Chow, K. L., and Survis, J. 1958. Retention of overlearned visual habit after temporal cortical ablation in monkey. A.M.A. Arch. Neurol. Psychiat., 79: 640–46.

Darvill, F. T., Jr., and Jones, C. H. 1958. Evaluation of a medical admission ward for old patients in a psychiatric hospital. Geriatrics, 13: 587–93.

Fink, M., Green, M., and Bender, M. B. 1952. The face-hand test as a diagnostic sign of organic mental syndrome. Neurology, 2: 46–58.

Fink, M., Kahn, R. L., and Pollack, M. 1959. Psychological factors affecting individual differences in behavioral response to convulsive therapy. J. Nerv. & Ment. Dis., 128: 243–48.

Ginzberg, E., *et al.* 1959. The ineffective soldier. New York: Columbia University Press.

Goldfarb, A. I. 1959*a*. Depression, brain damage, and chronic illness of the aged: psychiatric diagnosis and treatment. J. Chronic Dis., 9: 220–33.

—— 1959*b*. Summarization of activities for the year 1959. From the Office of the Consultant on Services for the Aged, New York State Department of Mental Hygiene. (Mimeographed.)

Green, M. A., and Bender, M. B. 1953. Cutaneous perception in the aged. Arch. Neurol. Psychiat., 69: 577–81.

Jaffe, J., and Bender, M. B. 1951. Perceptual patterns during recovery from general anesthesia. J. Neurol. Neurosurg. & Psychiat., 14: 316–21.

Kahn, R. L., Goldfarb, A. I., Pollack, M., and Gerber, I. E. 1960. The relationship between mental and physical status in institutionalized aged persons. Am. J. Psychiat., 117: 120–24.

Kahn, R. L., Pollack, M., and Goldfarb, A. I. Factors related to individual differences in mental status of institutionalized aged. *In* P. Hoch and J. Zubin (eds.), Psychopathology of the senium. New York: Grune and Stratton. (In press.)

Knobloch, H., and Pasamanick, B. 1960. Environmental factors affecting human development before and after birth. Pediatrics, 26: 210–18.

Pollack, M., and Goldfarb, W. 1957*a*. The face-hand test in schizophrenic children. A.M.A. Arch. Neurol. & Psychiat., 77: 635–42.

—— 1957*b*. Patterns of orientation in childhood in residential treatment for severe behavior disorder. Am. J. Orthopsychiat., 27: 538–52.

Pollack, M., Kahn, R. L., and Goldfarb, A. I. 1958. Factors related to individual differences in perception in institutionalized aged subjects. J. Gerontol., 13: 192–97.

Post, F. 1958. Social factors in old age psychiatry. Geriatrics, 13: 576–80.

Simon, A., Fiske, Marjorie, and Neal, M. W. 1960. Preliminary report on studies in geriatric mental illness. Newsletter (Gerontol. Soc.), 7: 17–26.

Weinstein, E. A., and Kahn, R. L. 1955. Denial of illness. Springfield, Ill.: Charles C. Thomas.

Zonneveld, R. J., van. 1958. An orientation study of the memory of old people. Geriatrics, 13: 532–34.

Aging and Adequacy in Communication

ATWOOD HUDSON

REGARDLESS of his age, man's ability to control his environment, or to adapt to his environment, depends upon his ability to communicate. An impairment of communication skills, either perceptual or motor, may be one of the most serious problems faced by the geriatric patient. A recent study (Bloomer, 1960) reports that 45 percent of the elderly people at a county hospital for the aged had speech or language disabilities, whereas such problems in the average adult population do not exceed 2 percent.

Serious deficiencies in understanding and expression found among the aged are: aphasia, dysarthria of central or peripheral nervous system origin, dysphonia due to serious neuro-pathologies, loss of voice resulting from surgical removal of the larynx, and hearing loss.

Since there is a body of research on hearing, that will be considered first. The National Health Survey, reported by Beasley (1940), established that there is an increasing decrement in hearing acuity with increasing age. More recent studies, both here and abroad, reported by Weiss (1959) corroborate the early results, for they show a consistent loss in hearing acuity with aging for frequencies above 500. The well-known study of Pestalozza and Shore (1955) reports that even though pure-tone testing may show only a mild loss, elderly people have poor discrimination for speech. An investigation by Pell (1957) found that older workers suffered greater loss of hearing from occupational noise than did younger ones. The hearing function, as a matter of fact, has been rather widely explored in the course of studying the sensory systems in aging. So far as intervention and treatment are concerned, however, there are only a few reports in the literature. Lederer and Marcus (1952) described a hearing rehabilitation program which included a group of patients over 60. A hearing survey at a home for the aged in Chicago is described by Grossman (1955). And there is a recent report of a hearing rehabilitation program at the Montefiore Home in Cleveland (Heffler, 1960).

It is generally agreed that the first step in intervention should be otological examination. The patient may be quite unaware, for example, of impacted cerumen and yet its removal may improve hearing function as much as 30 decibels. There should follow comprehensive audiological procedures including pure-tone and speech audiometry and then hearing-aid evaluation. Kleemeier (1959) points out the important service rendered by hearing-aid evaluation centers —an individual seeking a hearing aid can only be confused by the multiplicity of clever advertisements. All the reports stress the importance of a program of auditory training, whether the person is to have a hearing aid or not. It has long been a practice in the training of children with a hearing loss to provide a program of auditory training before the child is allowed to use an individual aid; and this program is continued to teach use and care of the instrument. And, yet, the elderly person, who has become accustomed to a world where environmental noises do not impinge upon his consciousness, is often given a powerful hearing aid with no training in its nature or use. It is only to be expected that the aid soon will be discarded. The investigators further agree that in many cases the elderly person regards the necessity to wear a hearing aid as a final indignity, and he therefore needs to be prepared both physically and psychologically for its use. Another compensatory measure is training in speech reading which complements the use of amplified sound. There is an outstanding need for more comprehensive hearing programs of the type described by Lederer and Marcus (1952) where a multidisciplinary approach provides complete otological examination, audiological study, hearing aid evaluation, and a program of instruction which includes lip reading and auditory training.

Turning now to a consideration of aphasia and other communication problems of neuro-pathological origin, the few studies reported also stress the necessity of a multidisciplinary approach to rehabilitation because speech and language disorders accompany varying degrees of paralysis and other neuromuscular disabilities. Marks, Taylor, and Rusk (1957) reported a 4-year study at Bellevue Rehabilitation Center which used such an approach. They concluded that service should be extended to a larger group of aphasic patients "despite the handicaps of age, disease, or relatively long duration of symptoms." Le Fevre (1957), speech consultant at Highland View Hospital, Cleveland, wrote of speech and language instruction as part of a comprehensive rehabilitation program for the geriatric patient and stated that many patients could profit from treatment at ages which once would have excluded them from rehabilitation. She concluded that age per se is not a determining factor. Although no mention of age was made in

Morley's (1955) article, he discusses dysarthria and voice problems resulting from Parkinsonism, multiple sclerosis, and chronic bulbar palsy. In his opinion, "A prognosis for stabilization or recovery of speech function must be extremely limited," although control of rate and phrasing may be improved. Furthermore, the clinician may re-assure the patient who is reluctant to speak because his speech is "too different" by pointing out that he still is able to communicate and thus encourage him to continue to speak. That is, the speech pathologist intervenes to encourage as much social adequacy as the patient's residuum of ability will allow.

An especially significant 4-year study was described by Mitchell (1958), speech specialist at the Geriatric Unit of the Oxford Hospitals. This program was limited to older patients with serious problems of aphasia and dysarthria. Of the 55 patients in this study, only 19 failed to improve in communication skills. Since the publication of this report, Miss Mitchell has had experience with 45 additional cases. On the basis of her experience with 100 elderly individuals, Miss Mitchell, in a personal communication, questions the wisdom of think-ing in absolutes about both the goals and the success of communica-tion training with the aged. Perhaps the intervention will not be in terms of language training per se; perhaps it will be in the realm of family understanding; perhaps it will be in the sphere of assistance to coworkers to prevent confusion of aims in planning for rehabilitation. That is, the role of the specialist in communication may be one of direct effort in evaluation and in administration of training for im-provement and support, or it may be indirect in an attempt to modify the patient's environment to better meet his needs.

Time allows consideration of one more rapidly increasing type of disability, that of loss of voice due to surgical removal of the larynx because of cancer. Currently, a survey is being made by the American Cancer Society to establish more accurate information on incidence. According to a personal communication from J. L. Ranney, the society statisticians estimate there are between 12,000 and 15,000 living laryngectomees in the United States. There are approximately 4400 new cases of cancer of the larynx annually and this figure is said to be increasing by 4 percent each year. Men outnumber women 10 to 1. The average age of persons who have a laryngectomy is between 55 and 60. Consequently, because the survival rate is high, many laryn-gectomees are in the 65-and-over age group.

The reports on the success of voice training are few, they do not agree and none is limited to the older patient. J. L. Waldrop, in a personal communication, stated that approximately 90 percent of the laryngectomees referred to the St. Luke's Clinic over a 2-year period mastered satisfactory esophageal speech; the ages of this population were not given. Heaver and his associates (1955) reported that the 274 laryngectomees admitted for voice training in their program ranged in age from 15 to 85 years with a median age of 59. Of the 274, 152 achieved "facility in the use of esophageal voice." Almost half those admitted were reported to have discontinued treatment against advice. Lueders (1957) stresses the importance of discovering what psychological, medical, or other factors are responsible for the rejection of voice training by the laryngectomized. As a matter of fact, considering the communication-handicapped aged group as a whole, more is being done for laryngectomees than for individuals with other types of problems because of the interest of the American Cancer Society and because they have their own organization, the International Association of Laryngectomees.

Obviously the field of communication offers rich, challenging, and relatively untouched areas for research. There are, for example, no statistics on the incidence of aphasia in the ever-increasing number of those who have sustained cerebral vascular accidents. Little is known concerning the responses of elderly persons to the use of hearing aids. There is no satisfactory explanation of why some accept aids and others reject them although their use would provide more adequate personal adjustment and reduce frustration on the part of those responsible for the care of the aged. The research results on aging in other fields are indisputably significant to audiology and speech pathology both in evaluation and in planning treatment (Hudson, 1960). Especially significant are the delayed response, slowness in perception, uneven decrement of the sensory modalities, and environmental exclusion, to mention only a few. Similarly, research studies in communication problems are needed because of the contribution they may make to the general study of aging.

The ability of the aged individual to understand and to be understood is important in his medical treatment, economic adequacy, home or institution management, and personal adjustment. The rationale for intervention and treatment in communication was aptly stated by Gerard (1959): "To maintain life without health is tragic, to maintain life and health at the animal level without the capacity for interpersonal human behavior is only less so."

REFERENCES

Beasley, W. C. 1940. The general problem of deafness in the population. Laryngoscope, 50: 856–905.

Bloomer, H. H. 1960. Communication problems among aged county hospital patients. Geriatrics, 15: 291–95.

Gerard, R. W. 1959. Aging and organization. *In* J. E. Birren (ed.), Handbook of aging and the individual, pp. 264–75. Chicago: University of Chicago Press.

Grossman, B. 1955. Hard of hearing persons in a home for the aged. Hearing News, 23: 11–20.

Heaver, L., White, W., and Goldstein, Nona. 1955. Clinical experience in restoring oral communication to 274 laryngectomized patients by esophageal voice. J. Am. Geriatrics Soc., 3: 687–90.

Heffler, A. J. 1960. The Montefiore Home hearing conservation program. Geriatrics, 15: 180–86.

Hudson, A. 1960. Communication problems of the geriatric patient. J. Speech & Hearing Disorders, 25: 238–48.

Kleemeier, R. W. 1959. Behavior and the organization of the bodily and the external environment. *In* J. E. Birren (ed.), Handbook of aging and the individual, pp. 400–51. Chicago: University of Chicago Press.

Lederer, F. L., and Marcus, R. R. 1952. The adult and his hearing problems. Annals Otolaryng., 61: 126–43.

Le Fevre, Margaret C. 1957. Speech therapy for the geriatric patient. Geriatrics, 12: 691–95.

Lueders, O. W. 1957. Evaluation of postlaryngectomy rehabilitation programs. Arch. Otolaryng., 65: 572–74.

Marks, M., Taylor, M., and Rusk, H. 1957. Rehabilitation of the aphasic patient. Neurology, 7: 837–43.

Mitchell, J. 1958. Speech and language impairment in the older patient. Geriatrics, 13: 467–76.

Morley, D. E. 1955. The rehabilitation of adults with dysarthric speech. J. Speech and Hearing Disorders, 20: 58–64.

Pell, S. 1957. The relation of occupational noise exposure to loss of hearing acuity. Arch. Otolaryng., 66: 79–92.

Pestalozza, G., and Shore, I. 1955. Clinical evaluation of presbycusis on the basis of different tests of auditory function. Laryngoscope, 65: 1136–63.

Weiss, A. D. 1959. Sensory functions. *In* J. E. Birren (ed.), Handbook of aging and the individual, pp. 503–42. Chicago: University of Chicago Press.

PERSONALITY THEORY, ATTITUDES, ROLES, AND ADJUSTMENT

Organized by
BERNICE L. NEUGARTEN,
The University of Chicago, Chicago, Illinois
JEAN-RENÉ TRÉANTON,
University of Lille, Lille, France

A Further Contribution to the Study of Adjustment in Old Age

MARCELLO CESA-BIANCHI AND GIANCARIO TRENTINI

FOR 10 years the authors and their assistants have been studying the problem of psychological functioning and adjustment in old age. For this purpose it seemed necessary to restrict observations to a sample which was comparatively homogeneous from the social, educational, and psychological points of view. In this way, the influence of a number of variables related to the subject's present and past life is lessened. The authors have long been aware of all the methodological difficulties that appear in undertaking to study mental activity in old age, and not merely the mental activity of this old man or of that old woman. The introduction of statistical methods is certainly of great advantage but we have also to remember the limitations of such methods. In the psychology of old age we find, increased in number and intensity, some of the difficulties encountered in studying infancy, childhood, and adolescence; but we have some other difficulties that are typical of this period of life. In this field more than in others we must keep in mind the danger of extending the results obtained from a particular sample to the whole aged population. On the basis of these considerations we want to emphasize that our conclusions apply only to the sample we have examined.

In all our research the samples have consisted of physically and psychically healthy subjects aged 70 or more, living in an institution for old people in Milan. From data obtained from psychological examinations (interviews and test performance on the Wechsler-Bellevue Intelligence Scale, Form A, and on the Rorschach), from direct observation of the male subjects, and from information obtained from institution personnel, we have found (Cesa-Bianchi, 1951a, b, 1952, 1955; Gemelli and Cesa-Bianchi, 1952):

A regular decrease, after 70, in psychological functioning. This decrease was more rapid for those mental activities that had been less utilized by the subject during his past life;

A maladjustment to old age that appears between 73–74 and 77–78 years of age; this maladjustment is both subjective and objective, according to the meaning that Stieglitz (1958) and Havighurst (in press) have given these terms;

A following phase of readjustment.

THE SAMPLE AND THE DATA

The principal aim of the present study was to examine sex differences in maladjustment in old age. Twenty-six men and 26 women, physically and psychically healthy, aged 70 or more, and inmates of the same institution, were examined by means of a semi-structured interview and the Rosenzweig Picture-Frustration Study (Rosenzweig, 1950a, b). Other data for each subject were obtained by observing his behavior in the institution and by interviews with his physicians, assistants, supervisors, and other personnel of the institution.

Characteristics of the sample were as follows: mean age for the men, 77.5, for the women, 78.3; mean length of stay in the institution, 42.7 months for men, 52.1 for women; mean number of children born, 3.4 for men, 3.5 for women; number of children still living, 2.5 for men, 1.5 for women. Educational level, main occupation before retirement, and socioeconomic level were generally equivalent for both groups. A higher number of men than women had been born in the south of Italy and had moved to Milan later in life.

The data obtained from the interviews included:

The subjects' attitudes toward their past and present, and the ways in which different aspects of their experiences were subjectively evaluated;

Diagnostic evaluations made by the examiner of the various aspects of psychological functioning, using the ten psychological variables indicated by Cattel (1950) and Ancona (1957, 1959). For both types of interview data, the subjects were rated on each variable on a five-step scale. The results of the Rosenzweig test were treated in terms of Rosenzweig's variables.

RESULTS

First of all, men generally showed more favorable attitudes than women. This appeared in the subjects' attitudes toward their mothers, brothers and sisters, own infancy and adolescence, present and past physical status, spouses, and living children. Attitudes for men and women were on the whole equivalent toward the father (favorable), dead children (indifferent), the institution (more resigned than negative), the capacity for making new friends (poor). Women's attitudes were more positive only in regard to a tendency to maintain old friendships and the better opportunity of doing some active work in the institution.

There was no significant difference between men and women in regard to the motivation for their marriages (in almost every case sentimental reasons were given), or in regard to the motivation regarding their admission to the institution (mostly voluntary for men, but not for women; and for both groups due, in a high percentage, to economic difficulties, to solitude, to disagreement with children, to the wish for autonomy). It should be pointed out that women actually worked in the institution more than the men.

In relation to diagnostic evaluations, men and women were similar, on the whole, as regards memory and affectivity; adjustment was very low in both groups, but especially in women. Furthermore, women were more efficient in intellectual abilities, less dominant, and more autonomous than the men.

The data of Rosenzweig's test were compared with those of the French standardization (Pichot and Danjon, 1951) and expressed in T scores. They showed some statistically significant differences between the two groups. The men had lower ratings than women on group-conformity, were low on ego-defense, high on internal strength, and low on obstacle-dominance. The latter, together with high ratings on need persistence, indicated the males' efficiency in resisting and overcoming psychological stress.

The women, on the other hand, were high on extrapunitiveness, low on impunibility, higher on obstacle-dominance and ego-defense, and low on need-persistence.

In short, while the "directivity" of the reaction was not substantially different for the two groups, there were significant differences related to the ways in which the two sexes reacted.

CONCLUSIONS AND DISCUSSION

Comparing all the results obtained and referring to statistically significant differences, we may say that the psychological functioning of old men who are inmates of an institution varies substantially from that of old women in the same cultural and educational level living in the same institution.

According to Pollak (1948), old age is "the age of maladjustment" which may appear as a consequence of various physical and psychological changes in the personality and of various changes in family and social environment. It is from this point of view—that there are many facets of "adjustment"—that the two groups reported here seem to be substantially different. In the women, who show a rather normal level of objective adjustment, there is the tendency to project onto others and onto external events any responsibility for their own primarily subjective maladjustment: they show a less favorable attitude toward their past and present life. In the men, on the contrary, there is an evident objective maladjustment, but generally positive attitudes toward past and present, and relatively little subjective maladjustment.

In men, therefore, maladjustment appears to be primarily objective; in women, subjective. This finding cannot be discussed only in terms of intellectual ability and affectivity; we have also to consider the importance of social variables and, particularly for the present sample, the age at which retirement occurred. Retirement, which in preceding research we have found to be the main factor in subjective and objective maladjustment in men, occurs at a younger age for women. In women, too, retirement probably determines (through a mechanism now being analyzed in a new study) a similar maladjustment.

When a woman is admitted to an institution, a number of years have generally passed since her retirement, and she has had time to readjust. In fact we must remember that almost all Italian women, even if they spend most of their time in an outside job, are daily occupied with domestic work. This domestic work has only to be quantitatively increased to fill the empty time created by the interruption of the outside job. Furthermore, because in the greatest part of Italian society the man always has a role of higher prestige and responsibility, he suffers more than the woman from the ending of his work activity. When the woman goes into the institution, the generally forced separation from her home and family, the loss of her family role, may act as the major frustration and may be the obstacle in her acceptance of the role of inmate of an institution. For a man the entrance to an institution may occur during the phase of maladjustment following retirement and is perhaps considered a simple variation, perhaps initially well accepted, of a troubled situation.

We may therefore conclude that maladjustment in old age seems in men to be primarily related to the changes connected with aging itself;

living in an institution does not appear to be an important factor. In the women, however, the admission to an institution appears to be the main factor responsible for maladjustment, even though the maladjustment does not reach very low levels.

REFERENCES

Anacona, L. 1957. I fondamenti psicologici del colloquio e la sua utilizzazione in psicologia. Arch. Psicol. Neurol. Psichiat., 18: 215–59.

—— 1959. Il colloquio come strumento di indagine in psicologia sociale e clinica. Contrib. Lab. Psicol. dell'Univ. Catt., 23: 59–73.

Cattel, R. B. 1950. Personality. New York: McGraw-Hill Book Co.

Cesa-Bianchi, M. 1951a. L'applicazione dei reattivi mentali nello studio dell'invecchiamento. Arch. Psicol. Neurol. Psichiat., 12: 390–93.

—— 1951b. Ricerche sull'attività psichica nell'età senile. Acta Gerontol., 1: 3–32.

—— 1952. Il reattivo Wechsler-Bellevue applicato all'età involutiva. Contrib. Lab. Psicol. dell'Univ. Catt., 16: 140–45.

—— 1955. Contributo allo studio delle modificazioni psichiche in rapporto con l'età. Contrib. Lab. Psicol. dell'Univ. Catt., 19:127–89.

Gemelli, A., and Cesa-Bianchi, M. 1952. Disadattamento del vecchio alla vita individuale, familiare e sociale. Riv. Gerontol. Geriat., 2: 113–21.

Havighurst, R. J. 1961. The measurement of successful aging. In Wilma Donahue, C. Tibbitts, and R. H. Williams (eds.), Psychological and social processes of aging: an international research seminar. (In press.)

Pichot, P., and Danjon, S. 1951. Le test de frustration de Rosenzweig. Rev. Psychol. Appl., 1: 147–225.

Pollak, O. 1948. Social adjustment in old age. Bull. 59. New York: Social Science Research Council.

Rosenzweig, S. 1950a. Revised norms for the adult form of the Rosenzweig Picture-Frustration Study. J. Personality, 18: 344–46.

—— 1950b. Some problems relating to research on the Rosenzweig Picture-Frustration Study. J. Personality, 18: 303–5.

Stieglitz, E. J. 1958. Medicina geriatrica. Note Terap., 3: 4, 2.

Analysis of the Mental Health
of Older Women in Australia

GEORGE VERNON DAVIES

IN spite of a comparatively small population, Australia is sharing with other Western democracies the problem of preserving the mental health of its older people. The fact that a mere ten million people are occupying a whole continent is offset by the large majority of these who are town dwellers, with about three and a half million living in the two largest cities. As in the United States and Britain, the proportion of geriatric admissions to mental hospitals has increased in recent years. Twelve percent of the population are over 60 years of age, and are supplying 30 percent of our total admissions to these hospitals.

In 1957, at a mental hospital in Melbourne, a pilot study was made of fifty consecutive admissions of patients over 60 years of age. An attempt was made to assess the relative importance of various etiological factors in the mental breakdown of persons in this age group. Some pointers of possible value appeared to emerge. These were:

The importance of chronic alcoholism as a causative factor in mental disorders in older men

The greater degree of brain damage in males in this age group, by the time they are admitted to mental hospitals

The greater influence of noncerebral disease and of poor family adjustments on mental ill health of the women.

Because alcoholism and arteriosclerosis, apart from their influence in geriatric psychiatry, are already subjects of widespread research, the decision was made to begin a survey of females.

THE SAMPLES

The present project was planned to comprise an examination of three groups of women over 60 years of age in the state of Victoria,

SUMMARY

It has been suggested that interviews with disaster victims indicate that older persons tend to react to their experiences with a high sense of deprivation more frequently than do younger persons. The inversion of a current explanation of the tendency of disaster victims generally to depreciate their deprivations suggests the dynamics involved in such behavior and fits into an emerging theory of personality development in the aged. Since the hypothesis can be stated in a form adapted to statistical test, it is obvious that further research is desirable. If such research should support the hypothesis, it would be of importance not only to students of disaster but to students of personality theory as well, for it would demonstrate the applicability and adequacy of a general theory of personality to an area which many believe to require a special conceptual framework.

Acknowledgments. The author is indebted to Dr. Harry E. Moore of the University of Texas for the use of the interviews with Waco and San Angelo victims and to the Faculty Research Committee of North Texas State College for assistance in the preparation of this paper.

REFERENCES

Fritz, C. E., and Williams, H. B. 1957. The human being in disasters: a research perspective. Ann. Amer. Acad. Pol. Soc. Science. 309: 42–51.

Henry, W. E. 1956. Affective complexity and role perceptions: some suggestions for conceptual framework for the study of adult personality. *In* J. E. Anderson (ed.), Psychological aspects of aging, pp. 30–41. Washington, D.C.: American Psychological Association.

———— and Cumming, Elaine. 1959. Personality development in adulthood and old age. J. Proj. Tech., 23: 383–90.

Kuhlen, R. G. 1956. Changing personal adjustment during the adult years. *In* J. E. Anderson (ed.), Psychological aspects of aging, pp. 21–29. Washington, D.C.: American Psychological Association.

Marks, E. S., and Fritz, C. E. 1954. Human reactions in disaster situations. (Unpublished manuscript.) University of Chicago, National Opinion Research Center.

Merton, R. K., and Kitt, Alice S. 1950. Contributions to the theory of reference group behavior. *In* R. K. Merton and P. F. Lazarsfeld (eds.), Continuities in social research: studies in the scope and method of "The American Soldier." Glencoe, Illinois: Free Press.

Moore, H. E. 1958. Tornadoes over Texas. Austin, Texas: University of Texas Press.

Powell, J. W., Rayner, Jeanette, and Finesinger, J. 1953. Responses to disaster in American cultural groups. *In* Symposium on stress. Washington, D.C.: Army Medical Service Graduate School.

Prince, S. H. 1920. Catastrophe and social change. New York: Columbia University Press.

Rosen, Jacqueline L., and Neugarten, Bernice L. 1960. Ego functions in the middle and later years; a thematic apperception study of normal adults. J. Gerontol., 15: 62–67.

Wallace, A. F. C. 1956. Tornado in Worcester. Washington, D.C.: National Academy of Sciences—National Research Council Publication.

Wolfenstein, Martha. 1957. Disaster. Glencoe, Illinois: Free Press.

Rorschach Indicators of Senility
in Geriatric Patients

MARJORIE E. KETTELL

THE investigation reported here was part of a multidisciplinary research project carried out at the Boston State Hospital in Boston, Massachusetts, to find out (1) what kinds of old people are admitted to a state mental hospital, and (2) what factors, both intrapsychic and environmental, contribute to their hospitalization. The social anthropologist and the psychiatric social worker are responsible for evaluating environmental factors, while the psychiatrist and clinical psychologist evaluate the patient.

An intensive investigation has used as its primary methods clinical interviewing and psychological tests with forty patients randomly selected from incoming admissions. A larger sample had to be sacrificed in favor of an exhaustive study of each individual and his environment. The generalizability of our results is expanded to some degree by matching demographic and commitment statements for the forty against 300 consecutive admissions. On the whole, the small sample is representative of the larger one.

Psychological tests administered to the sample include the Wechsler Adult Intelligence Scale, Thematic Apperception Test, Bender-Gestalt, Wechsler Memory Scale, and tests of vision, as well as the Rorschach. In spite of warnings that it would be extremely difficult to use traditional tests from the clinician's repertoire, it was felt that using them might allow comparison with other age groups. It is true that testing elderly patients can be a tedious and time-consuming task. Their attention span is short, and their usual reaction is a feeling of being threatened or bothered by tasks which appear meaningless and childish to them. As in testing children, the examiner had to be warmly reassuring, without being patronizing. Because motivation, attention, and memory were sometimes attenuated in administration of the

This investigation was supported by a research grant OM-(C2) from the National Institute of Mental Health.

Rorschach, the inquiry immediately followed the patient's free association.

Indicators of senility discussed in this report are drawn from the Rorschach, and the indicators themselves from the work of Louise Bates Ames *et al.* (1952, 1954, 1959), who has devoted considerable energy to collecting normative data for children, adolescents, and old people. The current study attempts to overcome two methodological limitations of Ames' work; namely, the lack of a random sample and the lack of external criteria (other than the Rorschach) for differentiating her total group into senile and nonsenile.

We asked: Are there patterns of response which seem typical of geriatric patients? In what ways do they perceive and cope with their world? What can be inferred about their level of ego organization, particularly in reference to regression?

The group being described consists of 33 patients. Of the 40 patients in the random sample, 6 were not tested because of blindness, disorientation, or assaultiveness. The patients' ages range from 60 through 91; mean, 71. Twelve are male; 21, female. The group is primarily working class. The homogeneity of their socioeconomic status led the author to assume no significant differences in Rorschach patterns attributable to this variable. Diagnostically, 85 percent of the patients are psychotic and two-thirds of the total group have moderate to severe organic impairment.

In trying to classify the perceptions and behavioral reactions of the group, we turned to Ames' work, and predicted that patients with moderate to severe senility would give protocols that were limited in scope (content categories of four or less), meager in number of responses ($R = 15$ or less), and visualized in ways that did not conform to the shape of the blots ($F+\% = 80$ or below). We also expected patients to ignore color, shading, and the possibility of imbuing the blots with movement. These determinants, in addition to the behavioral reactions of complaining that the task is too difficult and expressing insecurity about responses, have led to the image of the senile patient as a constricted, insecure, egocentric person preoccupied with his own thoughts to the point of perseveration, and having little emotion available to invest in his surroundings. Because of his inner demands, the senile is not always able to attend to reality or to discriminate it clearly.

The *entire* group is considered at this point in relation to the senile indices. In terms of group means, 15 responses are given which fall into 4 content categories. Form as a determinant greatly outweighs the use of color, shading, or movement. In fact, the experience balance is extremely coarctated, the ratio of M : Sum C being .8 : .9. Response locations are concentrated in large details as opposed to wholes, and small details are almost nonexistent. Thus the entire group displays a predicted senile pattern, with the exception of low $F+\%$. The form level is below 80 percent but is close to the $F\%$ of 71; hence there is not a great discrepancy between form and goodness of form. These indices were also found by Dörken and Kral (1951) in a group of patients classified as senile dementia cases.

Because there might be differences within the group which could be related to sex, intelligence, age, or degree of organic impairment, these variables were used to subdivide the 33 patients. Data were analyzed with the chi-square formula which includes Yates' correction for small samples. Results at the .05 probability level or better are given here with a few additional trends that do not quite reach this level of significance.

Of the indices considered, only one behavioral response was significantly different when the 12 men were compared to the 21 women. A greater proportion of men gave physical excuses for what they perceived as their poor performance on the test.

Differences in response pattern do not appear to be attributable to differences in intelligence. (Intelligence groupings were "average" and above versus "dull normal" and below; and only the verbal IQ from the WAIS was used.)

When the group is subdivided along other dimensions, however, significant differences occur. Age differences are of particular interest to us because Ames concluded that for her sample, "Sheer chronological aging had virtually no effect on Rorschach performance." (Ames *et al.,* 1954, p. 119.) She did find two effects with age: the total R decreased, and the percentage of human content increased.

Our patients fall into three age groups. Twelve patients are 60–69, nine are 70–79, and twelve are 80 or over. The oldest group manifests poorly delineated percepts that do not conform to the shape of the inkblots (low $F+\%$). Their range of associations is narrow, usually including many animal and vague object responses. They do not use color or shading in describing their responses, but rely upon form or some esoteric reason for having seen what they did, e.g., seeing plants because, "My daughter has plants at home." Added information from inquiry is almost nil in this group, most often there is the simple justification of a percept, "because it just looks like it."

The 70-year-olds, like the oldest group, tell their own experiences in preference to conforming with the examiner's directions. Also, few humans are seen, but the 70-year-olds have more affect available than the 60- or 80-year-olds. It is rather surprising that they would outdo younger people in color responses, but perhaps this is due to the fact that the younger patients were withdrawn because of depression or paranoid suspiciousness, two common syndromes in that group.

The youngest subjects perceive with better form, are less apt to perseverate, and have a wider variety of content. Color and movement are given as reasons for percepts, and shading appears, though not often. In spite of their objectively more adequate performance, the 60-year-olds express more feelings of insecurity than either of the other two groups.

Turning to the organic dimension, on the basis of psychiatric diagnosis, ability to adapt in the community, and estimates of organic impairment from tests other than the Rorschach, the patients were grouped as having "little," "moderate," or "severe" impairment. This dimension was chosen because an organic process is assumed to underlie the differences between normal senescence and pathological senility.

When these three groups are compared we find that the only distinguishing feature of the patients with "little" organicity is that they complain about the task being too difficult. However, the severe organics do this even more so. The only significant feature of the "moderate" organic group is that they have more human responses than either of the other two groups. Thus, they seem best able to tolerate the idea of interaction with people. The most significant indices of an organic process are the increase in form-determined percepts and the dramatic decrease in *good* form. The differences in $F+\%$ between the severe organics and the other two groups are significant at the .001 level, the only difference which reached this level of significance. In addition, there were tendencies toward a low R, paucity of movement, and meager shading.

The emotional withdrawal and cognitive leveling seen in these patients suggests a simplified level of ego functioning which might be understood as regression. Regression has been postulated as one defensive reaction to stress. There are two patterns of "regression" derived from this study. For the functional psychotics, this process involves overwhelming guilt, depression, or anxiety as attempts are made to cope with the stress of real or feared losses and separations. Many patients are attempting to reintegrate their past accomplishments and failures in preparation for death, but become inundated with painful recollections of their failures.

The stress for the primarily organic group seems more related to declining strength and capacities. Inner demands require more and more attention, while waning adaptive mechanisms make commerce with the environment less satisfactory. Appropriate to this point is Rapaport's formulation of a reciprocal relationship between autonomy from reality versus autonomy from psychic needs. As the demands of reality are lessened and inner needs are increased, ego energy is withdrawn from reality and reinvested in the self. The patterns observed in our geriatric sample may represent two manifestations of a more general process of regression—or autonomy from reality—in response to increased inner demands.

REFERENCES

Ames, Louise B., Learned, Janet, Métraux, Ruth W., and Walker, R. N. 1952. Child Rorschach responses; developmental trends from two to ten years. New York: Paul B. Hoeber, Inc.
——— 1954. Rorschach responses in old age. New York: Hoeber-Harper.
Ames, Louise B., Métraux, Ruth W., and Walker, R. N. 1959. Adolescent Rorschach responses. New York: Paul B. Hoeber, Inc.
Dörken, H., and Kral, V. A. 1951. Psychological investigation of senile dementia. Geriatrics, 6: 151–63.

A Conceptual Model for Rating Projective Test Responses from Aged Subjects: Relationships between Test Ratings, Health Status, and Certain Behavioral Features

MARGARET THALER SINGER

OVER a 2-year period a group of sixteen investigators at the National Institute of Mental Health studied a group of 47 normal men over 65 years of age who were admitted to the Clinical Center two at a time every 2 weeks for a 2-week study period (National Institute of Mental Health, 1961). The investigators asked the question: To what extent are physiological, mental, personal adjustment, and social adjustment factors interrelated in a group of normal, healthy aged men? During the 2-week study period, 500 individual measurements were obtained from each subject (cerebral metabolism, blood flow, psychiatric assessment, cognitive and perceptual functions, internal medicine, EEG, social psychology, sociology, social work, and personality factors were studied). Young comparison groups with a mean age of 25 years were also studied with certain of the tests.

The writer used eleven projective and related tests in assessing the men: the Rorschach, selected TAT pictures from the early Murray series, the Emotional Projection Test, the Adult Family Scene Picture, problem situations, a sentence completion test constructed for the aged by the writer, a homonyms test constructed to study the amount of inferred "information" in verbalizations, the Weigl Color-Form Sorting Test, the Draw a Person Test, proverbs, and a level of aspiration test.

This work was done in collaboration with the National Institute of Mental Health, Section on Aging, while the author was a research psychologist at the Walter Reed Army Institute of Research, Washington, D.C.

Formal aspects of communication

Projective tests are essentially a series of communication tasks. The subject is asked to interpret some sample situations. On the basis of what and how he communicates in responding, four aspects of his performance are rated: (1) his comprehension of and set toward the instructions, (2) his formal style of perceiving as well as the content of his apperceptions, (3) his reasoning, and (4) his communication as it reflects the foregoing components of the interaction process with the materials, instructions, and the examiner. These tasks, items, and material are regarded as sample situations, and interpretive inferences are made predicting a subject's adequacy in handling similar *actual* situations. The rating procedures later described were designed specifically to assess how well a man "programs" or plans his thinking and behavior in relation to the test interaction. The ratings as they are presented here were derived from our own past experience with groups of aged, and from our early work with the group reported here.

It had been our impression from this previous work that well-functioning aged persons can handle test interactions in the same ways as do adequately functioning younger persons. It is possible that the great numbers of relatively unhealthy, possibly brain-damaged individuals included in large samples of aged persons are responsible for some of the cultural stereotypes in our society about what to expect of the aged (e.g. garrulousness or impoverished output, pointless ruminating in the past, poor memory). To what extent this is true is yet to be studied, but great numbers of aged persons appear to suffer from various infirmities, ailments, and debilitations which seem to color their entire behavior.

The performance of those aged persons who differed from younger normal persons seemed roughly analogous to ineffective performance by a computer. Various things seemed wrong with the programming of behavior. The input or reception of instructions, the subsequent memory search and response selection procedures, and the proper stopping or termination of performance, seemed to have inefficiencies or breakdowns at one or all stages. The response behavior of these more poorly performing aged persons suggested to us that breakdowns in the planning of performance or the programming of behavior (as they could be inferred from assessment of verbalized thought productions) differentiated them from persons demonstrating normal, adequately "planned" performances. For example, at an input level, instructions may not be clearly and properly received (only parts get in; or an incorrect level of meaning is assigned them, either a more literal or personal meaning than the one intended). Performance often begins well, but the purpose and goal of the performance blurs. The instructions seem to have become lost; and the focus of the memory search broadens or unduly constricts. "Drifting" is noted when the point of the memory search is lost, and the subject drifts from topic to topic. Perseveration may be blatant (as when an idea stays in the mind too long and is repeated, and the memory search seems obviously to bog down) or subtle and less readily recognized (as when there is a high redundancy in the ideas presented). The final characteristic of the inefficient programming of behavior is poor termination. The impaired aged subjects seem not to have programmed the proper point for stopping, either stopping their performance too soon, or going on until fortuitously stopped by an outside person or distracting event, thus seeming to forget to plan an end to a purposive performance. These conceptualizations of the test behavior of impaired aged subjects led us to formulate the ratings used.

Table 1. Graded features of the TAT descriptive groups

Interpretation versus card description	Perseveration versus nonperseveration and presence of drift	Misperceptions	Themes	Roles and identities
Interprets	No perseveration or repetitiveness	None	Variety	Clear
Interprets	Subtle repetition	None	Subtle repetition	Clear
Primarily card description	Mild repetitiveness, may serialize cards into running story	Mild	No particular theme, or mild repetition	Merely described
Barren card description	Obvious perseveration of words and themes	Moderate	No particular point to tale	Some shift
Pointless card description	Severe perseveration Cards seen as serial story	Marked	Pointless ˉor severe repetition	Gross shifts

Raters were given criteria such as those in Table 1 which were used in rating the TAT stories.

SUBJECTS

The group of men studied had been carefully screened medically and psychiatrically to ensure that an especially "healthy" group would be studied.

However, health criteria used in the course of the research itself divided the sample into two groups: Group I, a very healthy group of 27 men, and Group II, 20 men found to have asymptomatic or subclinical disease processes present. A second grouping based on psychiatric criteria split the group of 47 men into two: a group of 36 designated as "not senile quality," and 11 men designated as "senile quality," these designations based upon pooled impressions from all investigators.

Test scoring was done on a blind basis by experienced raters using criteria designed to secure over-all clinical judgments about total test performance.

RESULTS

Using 20 different measures obtained from the 11 personality tests mentioned earlier, comparisons were made between Groups I and II, and between "senile" and "not-senile quality." Analysis of the results indicated the following:

When the very healthy group (Group I) was compared with the group with subclinical or asymptomatic disease processes (Group II) the less healthy group consistently, although not at a statistically significant level, performed less adequately on the tests.

The "senile quality" group performed significantly more poorly than the "not-senile"; and in particular it appeared that the Group II (the less healthy) "senile quality" men contributed heavily to this finding.

A further division of the "senile quality" group, using cerebral blood flow (CBF) criteria, indicated that the most poorly functioning men had a "low oxygen uptake" apparently due to cerebral arteriosclerosis. A group having normal oxygen uptake on the CBS studies appeared to be a more "functionally" senile group whose senility perhaps related to psychosocial events and to personality factors. (Where young comparison groups were studied, there were no differences between Group I and the young adults.)

Various interrelationships between test performance and psychiatric ratings indicated that those individuals with obsessive-compulsive personality traits tended to be making better adaptation to their life situations and were functioning more adequately on tests than those rated as having hysteric-repression-avoidance coping mechanisms.

Formal test features were far more discriminating than were differences in test content in distinguishing the subgroups within the sample, as well as contrasting the subgroups with normal younger groups.

DISCUSSION

In terms of the conceptual model used, the performance of the very healthy subgroup can be characterized as follows: Verbal behavior and over-all ability to function within the context of the test situation were not noticeably different from that expected of younger adequately functioning persons; their programming or planning ability was adequate. At any input level, instructions appeared to be received clearly and properly. These men were able to wait until the total set of instructions was given; they seemed to receive and weigh properly the various parts of the instructions; to assign a level of meaning that was neither more literal nor more personal than the intent of the instructions. They neither broadened nor constricted the focus of the memory search, neither drifting pointlessly, nor bogging down into repetitiveness or redundance. Finally, they seemed able to plan or program a proper termination. Further, this group seemed to have a wide range of available and appropriate associations, and they seemed able to discuss nuances of ideas.

In contrast, the behavior of the "senile quality" men in Group II can serve as a prototype of those features usually considered "senile." The start of their performance was particularly poor. They tended to start too soon, on the basis of only partial understanding or because they had attended to only part of the instructions. (This tendency is worth noting because on most performance tasks similar groups are characterized as slow. Here, where verbal responses were elicited, a too hasty and impulsive beginning was noted.) Further, there was a tendency for these men to respond to directions on an incorrect "level," taking a more literal or personal connotation than was intended. The ability to sense or respond to the proper "intent" of instructions was impaired in this group. Thus, input seemed impaired, and the initiation of response was poorly controlled. There seemed to be a blurring and losing of the point or purpose of the act. It was as if the instructions which had not been too well received became even further deteriorated. These men drifted from one association to another, rather than seeming to direct their memory search according to a plan or goal. Both drifting and perseveration were often noted in some individuals. In some, whose perseveration was subtle (labeled here, high redundancy), there was superficial verbal facility, but impoverished thinking. There appeared to be a restricted range of associations, and a reduced skill at communicating nuances about most ideas. The verbal expressions of the "senile" seemed more stark, primitive, and gross than the "not-senile." The capacity of the "senile" to plan a proper termination to each performance was poor; some stopped after very brief and insufficient responses; others talked endlessly until the tester or an outside event interrupted.

It is suggested that the approach to assessment outlined here should be further explored and extended. It permits the analysis of verbal behavior on projective tests, and it can be easily transposed to clinical behavior ratings. Rating formal thought qualities enables the investigator to compare test performance at various ages without the content of responses beclouding the issues. Even though age-determined associative content was present, the formal characteristics of the test performances for the very healthy group did not seem to differ from those expected of younger well-functioning adults.

The present findings, combined with prior work with other groups of aged, give some indication that, in terms of the conceptual model used, one can roughly consider three groups among the aged: The first evidences patterns of thought processes similar to those grossly considered appropriate for young, adequately functioning adults. The second, a "transition" group, appears to be composed of individuals who, in test situations like these, are impulsive and overtalkative in responding, provide a low ratio of "information," and show a tendency to "drift" as they associate. One infers that "something is amiss" about the functioning of these individuals. At one level of inference this behavior may appear "self-centered" in the aged person, and may be attributed to personality or attitudes. Some of this behavior is even excused as a burst of talking from a somewhat lonely person who has just received positive attention from a receptive audience. However, the impression remains that impulsive test behavior, combined with marked, or obvious drift from topic to topic, and combined with moderate to obvious perseveration of ideas within the drift, is not an expected, necessary, or normal component of aging.

The third group, rarely represented in the present sample but prominent in institutional samples of aged, is characterized by slow responses, an impoverished range as well as a low output of expressed ideas, and perseveration within thought content.

These groups need further exploration. The problem of assessing and distinguishing depression, "brain damage indications," and psychoses occurs in test evaluations of the aged. Some of the formal features rated in the tests reported here combined with content analysis might help to elucidate the subgroups that exist within the three large groups described here.

REFERENCE

National Institute of Mental Health. 1961. Human aging: biological and behavioral aspects. Washington, D.C.: Government Printing Office.

A Study of Affective Expression among the Aged

MARTIN LAKIN AND CARL EISDORFER

THE focus of the present investigation is on affective expression among normal aged persons. The method derives from that traditionally used with projective techniques where an indirect measure of emotionality, i.e., the perception and verbal response modality, is employed. This indirect measure is admittedly limited in assessing such variables as emotionality potential, and is clearly dependent upon the subject's adequacy of perception and verbalization. Nevertheless, it is useful in studying expressive aspects of affect as they may be associated with age differences.

SUBJECTS

The identifying characteristics of the three samples are shown in Table 1. Group I was made up of young normals, and consisted of

Table 1. The samples

Group	N	Mean age	Male	Female	Negro	White	Other race
I	24	23.7[a]	11	13	0	24	0
II	55	73.2	25	30	13	42	0
III	28	39.6[a]	9	19	7	18	1

[a] Incomplete, age data for one S unavailable.

secretaries and ward attendants. Group II was composed of aged "normally adjusted" persons living in the local community who had volunteered to be subjects for the Duke University Geriatrics Project (a longitudinal, multidisciplinary research program involving over 350 subjects). Group III was composed of new patients of the Duke

This research was carried out by the Department of Psychiatry and the Center for the Study of Aging, Duke University, with the support of USPHS grants M-900, M-2109, and H-3582.

University Medical Center's Outpatient Clinic. These persons had come for examinations on the basis of presumed physical illness.

PROCEDURES

A set of twelve stick figures devised by Reitman was shown to each subject (Reitman and Robertson, 1950). These stick figures, because of posture of head and attitudes, body and limbs, suggest emotional states. Description of these figures is typically phrased in affective terms. The subjects were instructed as follows: "I am going to show you some stick figures. Tell me what sorts of feelings you get from looking at them. Give me as many as you can." Incidental comments were recorded.

Responses were scored as follows: (1) Number of discrete affects used in describing a figure; (2) intensity of affective expression as rated on a 4-point scale; (3) comments relating explicitly to the somatic state of the figure; (4) the attribution of activity to the figure (active, passive, none).

RESULTS

Table 2 lists the mean score obtained by the three groups on each of the four variables. For two variables, number of affects and activity,

Table 2. Mean scores obtained by subject groups for four variables

Group	Number of affects	Intensity of affect	Somatic comments	Activity
I	13.2	2.0	0.6	9.0
II	8.8	1.9	0.8	5.6
III	6.2	3.8	3.0	3.5

the performance of the three groups was analyzed with the use of a simple random analysis of variance design; in each case the F was significant at beyond the .01 confidence level. In order further to investigate the relationship between the scores of the various groups, t tests were performed.

Since a Bartlett test of homogeneity of variance had indicated differences between groups with respect to the variables of intensity and somatic comments, nonparametric techniques, the Kruskal-Wallis and Mann-Whitney tests, were used to test the significance of differences for these two variables.

For number of affects the three groups all differed from one another (t was $p < .01$). The second variable, intensity of affect, showed a statistical difference only between Groups II and III (Mann-Whitney u test, significant at the .05 level).

For the third variable, somatic comment, while Groups I and II do not differ from each other, both differ from Group III (Mann-Whitney u test, significant at the .01 level). In their expression of activity (variable four) all groups differ from one another (in every case t is significant at beyond the .01 level).

It may be seen from these results that the following distinctions can be drawn among the performances by the aged group (Group II), the somatically ill subjects (Group III), and the younger normal controls:

In the comparison between the elderly subjects and the medical outpatients, the older persons produced a greater number of affectively toned statements; they showed a higher level of activity (more active and more passive as contrasted with static quality) in their descriptions of the figures; they produced less somatic content. However, the intensity of affect in their descriptions was less than that of the outpatient group.

In the comparison between the aged and the normal younger group, the aged subjects were exceeded by younger normals in number of affective descriptions and in the activity levels (active and passive as contrasted with static quality) depicted for the figures. There were no differences with regard to somatic content and intensity level.

A qualitative analysis of the affective expressions suggests a descending order for the three groups, young normals, aged, and outpatients in terms of such factors as variety, presence of conflicting or alternate responses, and in what might be termed "degree of personal involvement" in the expressions.

DISCUSSION

The performance of the elderly subjects relative to the two other groups may illustrate the problem of the differential in affective expression among the aged. The finding of differences along several of the dimensions between young and old nonclinic groups conforms to the anticipation that the aging process will be associated with a decline in affective "energy," at least insofar as this is reflected in verbal material. A theoretical formulation which would emphasize the normative developmental decline in emotionality among the aged is that of Banham (1951). She emphasized the saliency of consolidation, constriction, and disintegration as sequential processes in emotional organization in later life. A limited number of emotional responses and their relative unchangeability are cited as characteristic of normal aged. The point is made that the emotions of older people are characterized by paucity rather than by abundance of affective energy. It is also pointed out— relevant to the mental health versus psychopathology issue—that there is psychologic economy in this relative constriction. The reduced affective sensitivity and changeability may actually be helpful factors in adjustment.

The views of Cumming *et al.,* as elaborated in their theory of disengagement, closely parallel this position, and the results of the present study would seem to lend support to the concept they express as the *appearance of deviance* in old age (Cumming *et al.,* 1959), i.e., the disengagement of the aged from life outside themselves. That diminished ability of older individuals to perceive action or affect on the part of others may contribute to the phenomenon of *mutual withdrawal* seems readily apparent. A qualitative approach to the material would appear consistent with this interpretation insofar as the aged show noticeably less personal involvement with the task than do the younger nonclinic subjects.

Preoccupation with bodily ailments and impairments has been widely assumed to affect the emotional responsiveness of the aged and the psychopathologic implications of this preoccupation have been emphasized in the categorization of the emotional traits and characteristics of the aged (Pollak, 1948). Consistent with this assumption would have been a finding of difference between old and young on the dimension of somatic content, and similarity of performance between old and sick with regard to this dimension. Our findings do not support this assumption. It would appear that, although their physical status is clearly important to the aged group (a powerful motivation for participation by normal elderly persons in the Duke University Geriatrics Research Program is the physical examination given each individual), somatic preoccupation has not grossly affected them in terms of their emotional expressiveness. In the case of the outpatients, their somatic concerns are explicit and are, of course, heightened at the time they come to the clinic for diagnosis and treatment. A similar psychological process may underlie the finding of greater intensity of affect expression for this group.

Decrement in reactivity potential in emotionality among the aged appears to be an empirical fact (Ames *et al.,* 1954; Banham, 1951). While comparison with a group of somatically ill individuals shows a higher level of reactivity for the aged sample (productivity, variety, activity) and fewer "regressive" features (bodily preoccupation), comparison with young normals seems to reveal the decrement. The issue with regard to primary etiological factors is yet to be resolved. In opposition to the genetic and sequential constriction hypothesis there is the viewpoint of Ross (1959) and Gitelson (1948) who emphasize the psychosocial as well as physical assaults on the aged to which the constricted emotionality is but an understandable response.

The present investigation has focused not upon etiological issues as such but has aimed at exploration of the dimensions of affective expression among the normal aged. Their performances in terms of productivity, activity level, and somatic emphasis by contrast with younger, somatically ill patients and with younger, normal controls accentuate the unique pattern of affect expressions among the aged. The question of etiology with regard to this pattern is complex and there is need for further study to examine the principal hypotheses.

REFERENCES

Ames, Louise B., Learned, Janet, Métraux, Ruth W., and Walker, R. N. 1954. Rorschach responses in old age. New York: Hoeber-Harper.

Banham, Katherine M. 1951. Senescence and the emotions: a genetic theory. J. Genet. Psychol., 78: 175–83.

Cumming, Elaine, Dean, L. R., Newell, D. S., and McCafferty, Isabel. 1959. Disengagement—a tentative theory of aging. Sociometry, 23: 23–35.

Gitelson, M. 1948. The emotional problems of elderly people. Geriatrics, 3: 135–50.

Pollak, O. 1948. Social adjustment in old age. Bull. 59. New York: Social Science Research Council.

Reitman, F., and Robertson, J. P. S. 1950. Reitman's Pin-Man Test: a means of disclosing impaired conceptual thinking. J. Nerv. and Ment. Dis., 112: 498–510.

Ross, M. 1959. A review of some treatment methods for elderly psychiatric patients. AMA Arch. Gen. Psychiat., 1: 578–91.

A Study of Introversion-Extraversion in the Aged

KAKUSHO TACHIBANA

THIS study reports the results of an introversion-extraversion test administered to 197 men and 147 women all aged 60 and over who are residing in an old age home named Yokufu-en.

The test, based upon Jung's introvert-extravert concept, was designed by Drs. Awaji and Okabe, Japanese psychologists. It consists of 50 items to be checked "yes" or "no"; items such as "Are you gloomy by nature?" "Are you often reckless in doing things?" "Are you talkative?" "Do you trust others more than you think you should?" While the test is usually based on self-evaluations, the evaluations were made in this case by the nurse who had been in intimate contact with the subjects.

A version quotient (V.Q.) was devised, whereby scores of 101 and over indicate extraversive tendencies; 99 and below, introversive.

RESULTS

The V.Q. scores obtained from the aged persons are presented in Table 1.

Table 1. V.Q. score by sex

Sex	Average V.Q. score	SD
Male	99.3	25.38
Female	104.5	30.40
Both	101.5	28.18

We see that the average V.Q. score for the female group is greater than that for the males, indicating that females are more extraversive. These scores were compared with those obtained in earlier studies of younger persons. The results are shown in Fig. 1. It should be pointed out that the SD's for the aged samples are much greater than those for

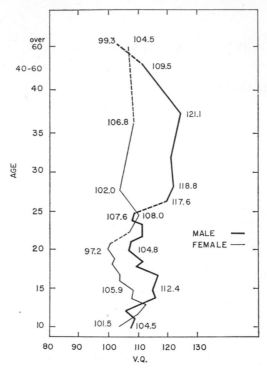

Fig. 1. Version quotient scores for males and females by age

younger samples, indicating greater individual differences in old age.

The male is found to be extraversive in adolescence, decreasingly so in later adolescence, increasingly so in maturity. Introversion increases gradually in later maturity and old age. The female is introversive in adolescence, slightly extraversive in later adolescence and maturity, and more extraversive than the male in later maturity and old age.

Finally it is possible to make the following conclusions regarding the personality traits of the aged as compared to younger persons:

Not so gloomy, and also not so reckless in doing things
Not so hot-headed, or so easily cooled down
Not so easily tempted by flattery
When they speak, they take into consideration the other person's ideas
Not so quick in making decisions
More stubborn
Do not act vigorously
Do not like to be secluded, but are not so socialized.

Thematic Analysis of Aging

HANS THOMAE

STUDIES like those of Buhler (1959), Erikson (1950), Peck (1956), and others have shown the importance of a thematic analysis of the aging process. The changes and the continuous adjustment patterns that are combined with this process can be revealed by a demonstration of the problems typical for certain age groups. These problems may consist of worries, stress or tension situations, or frustrations. Some of these arise out of the roles which society expects from the individual at different ages.

The dealing with these problems always forms a structuration of a typical "situation" within the individual's life space, and of a typical "need" or tendency. Therefore the criteria for the theme given by Murray (1938) are met in these problem situations.

The definitions of these themes or problems given by Erikson (1950) and Peck (1956) seem to be oriented toward the study of neurotic or unadjusted persons. The study to be reported here is based on interviews with normally adjusted persons. In one of these studies we included 150 male white collar employees aged 35 to 55 at the beginning of the study. They ranged in occupation from bookkeepers to engineers to vice-managers. About 70 percent of these men were followed and interviewed through a 3-year period; and 46 percent for 5 years. Because of the small number of cases, this research should be considered a pilot study.

In a supplementary study, a group of women of the same age were followed; in another, the relationship between psychosomatic symptoms and age was investigated. Other studies refer to more or less specialized adjustment problems.

The interviews were repeated three or four times in the first year, and once or twice during the following years. Four interviews included standardized open-end questions, the others were free interviews.

The content-analysis of this interview material shows that the differentiation and structure of life course of the individual as seen by the individual himself is determined by the major events of the biography.

Marriage, major changes in job and profession, war, time spent in a prisoner of war camp, reunion with family, and time before and after social and economic recovery are events which structure the life into different periods and stages. The same events are regarded, too, as origins of attitudinal and behavioral changes. Objective observation of the same cases known to the research team for a longer time show that these subjective impressions are not illusions but reflect the natural forms of structuration of the life course. In other words, the individual pattern of a life history seems to be more important than general developmental laws for the differentiation of "stages" of life.

Nevertheless there is evidence of typical sequences of major problems, of adjustments required by changes in the individual's life situation, and of restructurations of the main themes within personality.

OCCUPATIONAL SUCCESS

The first of these themes typical for the younger members of our employee group is that of aiming at success on the job, at expansion, and at promotion within a professional career. It is necessary to characterize these themes by different criteria, since none of them alone meets the central problem. We rated all statements referring to the question, "Do you expect in your obtained or desired position more change, expansion, and promotion? Or more security and stability?" There was a significant difference between those men who were 50 and over and those who were below 40. The older expect security; the younger, the chance for positive change, for satisfying activity, and for contact with other people. The difference between age groups was significant at the 1 percent level.

The age groups differ to the same degree if we rate the statements referring to security on the one hand, and to promotion on the other. There is no significant difference between the groups when statements regarding the longing for security are compared with statements regarding independence. The need for independence on the job is found even more in the older than in the younger group.

Apparently there is a change of the main theme in this personality area, within the decade of the forties, by which security becomes more important than change and progress. This can be shown, too, by a study of attitudes toward one's job, in a population representative of Western Germany as reported by Bergler (1961). The percentage of people satisfied with their jobs is around 55 to 58 percent until age 30 and after age 45. The percentage is higher at 50–60 years, lowest at 30–44 years.

The degree of dissatisfaction with job can be regarded as another index of the theme of professional progress, change, and expansion. According to these findings, this theme would be prevalent within the thirties and early forties, whereas a later tendency toward consolidation can be shown.

In our own study statements about attitudes toward job show the same trend but with no significant differences between the age groups.

MARRIAGE AND FAMILY

Another major theme expressed in the interviews is that of winning and maintaining happiness in family life. This theme certainly is basic for human life generally; but as already stated by Peck (1956) and Kuhlen (1956), we can find changes in the form and content of this theme. The importance of this theme is shown by the statements on problems and worries about family life, marriage, and on general dissatisfaction in this region of the life space. Thirty-three percent of our cases revealed major crises in family and marriage life; 42 percent revealed serious problems and crises. Thus, 75 percent of the cases have more or less serious problems in the marital and familial aspect of their lives. This result does not show a general dissolution of family life in the present society. It merely points to the fact that the problem of maintaining happiness and harmony within the family is an important aspect throughout the age span between the thirties and the sixties.

So far we have not found any significant differences between the age groups as far as this problem is concerned. There is, however, a tendency toward greater stress and tension in this area in the younger age group. They stress almost to the same degree the values of a nice home, of happiness under one's own roof and within one's own garden, and satisfaction from children. It should be mentioned here, too, that the younger men more than the older characterized the changes they had experienced within their own personalities during the last two years by statements like: "I have become more stable, calm, more of a homebody."

This is even more true for women as is shown in an ongoing study by Lehr (1960). According to her findings there is a long period of adjustment to marital life after the twenties, with changing attitudes toward the husband. There is a certain consolidation after age 50. This is especially shown by the worries and complaints expressed by women aged 30–40 as compared to those aged 50 and over. The number of these worries and complaints is significantly lower in the older group than in the younger.

ADJUSTMENT TO REALITY

A third major problem of the adult personality revealed in our interviews is that of a specific adjustment to reality. Changes in the patterns of reality adjustment during the life span have been described by many writers. The *problem of adjustment to reality* typical for our sample can be defined as that of dealing with imperfections and frustrations in life. Adolescents and young adults have more or less higher demands and expectations of life than older persons. This refers to problems of everyday life as well as to problems of ideology. In the forties, men more and more learn to make compromises; and this becomes increasingly the only adequate form of adjustment to reality for the aging personality. Aging in the sense of personality maturation begins when the unavoidable frustrations in everyday life as well as in general self-realization do not result in resentment, aggression, or resignation, but when the realization of many restrictions upon one's possibilities leads to the art of enjoying the situation as it presents itself.

Successful compromises of this kind could be evaluated in the interviews of 63 percent of our male group. The younger ones made less, the older more successful compromises of this kind. (This difference was not statistically significant.)

Indirect but even more impressive evidence for the statement that aging is correlated with the art of making positive compromises can be seen from our psychosomatic study now in progress. The case histories of 500 patients taken from psychosomatically oriented clinics showed that the disturbances began in 18 percent of the cases before the age of 20; in 36 percent, between the ages 20 to 30; in 30 percent, between 30 and 40; and in 16 percent, when they were over 40.

This means that 65 percent of the psychological problems resulting in functional disturbances began between the 20th and the 40th years of life. According to the classical theory of neurosis we can regard psychosomatic symptoms as consequences of nonsuccessful adjustment to reality. Hence the age distribution of the beginning of psychosomatic illness shows that the adjustment to reality in the sense used here becomes possible usually within the fifth decade of man's life.

We did not find significant differences between the age groups as far as the special field of the compromise was concerned. The areas of "job," "family," and "personal problems" were represented in the same proportion in all age groups with "job" as the most frequent and "personal sphere" as the least frequently mentioned.

In our women's group the area where compromises had most often to be made was the field of family, marriage, and similar personal relationships. (The difference between the men and women is significant at the .01 level.)

MONOTONY

A fourth problem of theme prevalent in our middle-aged group is that of monotony of life. In 48 percent of our men, and in 42 percent of our women, we found direct or indirect complaints about the monotony of job or of life generally. On the other hand the same cases could show fears about the stability of the present situation. The tendency to realize monotony in one's own life situation grows with increasing age.

The importance of this theme is even greater in other social groups if we recall that in many careers (like that of foreman) the top position is reached between 33–34 years. We do not yet know if this realization of monotony is a culturally patterned reaction toward family and job in middle-aged people, or if it is a general reaction.

The theme of adjustment to monotony in life is closely connected with the theme of adjustment to the realization that the present situation is a permanent one. So far this relationship can be shown only by case histories. The same is true for the combination of both themes with a third one which points in the opposite direction and which has been mentioned before: the theme of anxiety about the instability of the present situation.

This instability can be expected or feared with reference to job, or happiness and harmony in family life, or one's own health, or the health of other family members. Actually an intensive analysis of the autobiographies contained in our interviews showed that major changes occur in the lives of older people almost in the same degree as in the lives of younger people. Certainly health problems and major illness interfere more and more at the beginning of the sixth decade. Also, the job situation does not look very stable, even in a time of prosperity, for this group of successful and well-adjusted people. There are some promotions, there are demotions, there are ups and downs of different kinds.

The dynamics of the themes characterized as "longing for a change" and "fear of change" are shown by an evaluation of our material which tries to rate the general attitude of a person toward the future. For this purpose we compared the statements which, on the one hand, point to expected changes and to the approximation of a given goal, to those responses which, on the other hand, express a basic need for stability or a return to a previous stage. The attitude of the younger group differed from that of the older in the expected way ($P < .01\%$). In younger subjects, the attitude toward the future is determined by the expectation of or longing for a positive change. Older persons want stability or a return to a stage known as stable.

The dynamics mentioned before seem to be a major problem for the group 40 to 50 years old. This group showed an ambivalence regarding the future. They both longed for a change and were afraid of a change. The same dynamics are shown, too, in our finding that the evaluations of one's own physical and mental efficiency were even more optimistic in the older group than in the younger. The expectation of being able to change one's life by activity and efficiency is equally frequent in all age groups. If change is feared more and more after age 50 this may be explained by social factors or by the fact of decreasing health.

CONCLUSIONS

There may be more themes of the aging process if we study other social groups. There may also be more significant differences between the themes prevailing in different age groups if greater numbers of cases are included in a study. It would be wrong, however, to deduce a typical stage of life from the changes in the frequency of certain themes with changing age. The *longitudinal* analysis of our cases especially could show that the same person can work himself through the same theme again and again at different stages of his life. On the other hand we see from the permanence of some themes that it is scarcely possible to refer to old age as a closed psychological unity.

What is shown, too, in the longitudinal analysis of single cases is the variety of reactions of the same person toward the situation of getting older. This shows that despite all age trends found in this or in other studies, we must regard the aging process as the result of a specific biography with all its social implications. "Result" in this connection means a product of conditioning as well as canalization, especially, of an *active* adjustment of the personality toward typical demands and press situations as they arise in life. Therefore we might deduce from a thematic analysis of aging the hypothesis that aging is a typical sequence of reactions toward certain typical social and environmental changes rather than a mental or motivational unity.

REFERENCES

Bergler, R. 1961. Beiträge zur psychologie des erwachsenenalters. Bibliotheca Vita Humana. Basel-New York: S. Karger.

Buhler, C. 1959. Der menschliche lebenslauf als psychologisches problem. Göttingen: Hogrefe.

Erikson, E. H. 1950. Growth and crises of the "healthy personality." *In* M. J. E. Senn (ed.), Symposium on the healthy personality, pp. 91–146. New York: Josiah Macy, Jr., Foundation.

Kuhlen, R. G. 1956. Changing personal adjustment during the adult years. *In* J. E. Anderson (ed.), Psychological aspects of aging, pp. 21–29. Washington, D.C.: American Psychological Association.

Lehr, Ursula. 1960. Spezifische probleme in 4.–6. Lebensjahrzehnt der frau. Proceedings XVI. Internat. Congr. Psychol. Amsterdam: Nijnhoff.

Murray, H. A. 1938. Explorations in personality. New York: Oxford University Press.

Peck, R. 1956. Psychological developments in the second half of life. *In* J. E. Anderson (ed.), Psychological aspects of aging, pp. 42–53. Washington, D.C.: American Psychological Association.

The Measurement of Successful Aging

ROBERT J. HAVIGHURST

THE definition and measurement of successful aging is a crucial step in social gerontology. It is impossible to evaluate programs for and activities of older people unless one has a measure of successful "adjustment" to the aging process.

The measures used in the past have been self-reports or ratings by judges on social adjustment, or self-reports or ratings by judges on a personal subjective quality variously called personal adjustment, morale, or satisfaction. For both types of measure the problem of validity has not been satisfactorily solved. There is usually an element of circularity in the measuring and validating process.

This particular research has attempted to take a step forward through the following procedures:

Definition of successful aging as an inner state of satisfaction and happiness.

Operational definition of this state in terms of five interrelated variables which can be used as a basis for rating scales applied by judges when they read intensive interviews. This is called the *Satisfaction Rating*.

Validation against the Satisfaction Rating of two self-report instruments: a self-report attitude inventory, called the Satisfaction Index (A); and a set of open-ended questions, called the Satisfaction Index (B). These instruments overlap in content. They are slightly different ways of securing a self-report on items relevant to successful aging and of evaluating this self-report.

Results of this study are presented for a sample of people aged 45–80 in the Kansas City Study of Adult Life.

The full text of this paper is published in Wilma Donahue, C. Tibbitts, and R. H. Williams (eds.), *Psychological and Social Processes of Aging: An International Research Seminar* (to be published).

Some Sociological Considerations on the Problem of Adjustment in Older People

JEAN-RENÉ TRÉANTON

THE concept of "adjustment," inherited from the nineteenth century intellectual tradition, is becoming less frequently used in the social sciences. Like the concepts "personality" or "morale," it has an ambiguous meaning, even if "personal" is distinguished from "social" adjustment. When studying older people, it seems important to keep clearly separated: (1) the subject's verbal expression of *satisfaction;* and (2) the subject's *behavior* in work, leisure, and social areas of life. Some recent studies on industrial "morale," especially the studies done at the University of Michigan, show that there is a strong tie between morale on one hand and, on the other hand, the subject's expectations and the effective rewards provided by the environment. It may be that, in studying older people, too strong an emphasis has thus far been put upon social interaction.

Social roles, as defined and prescribed by the environment, do not necessarily affect the two preceding dimensions. It may be that the "desocialization" process, which occurs when externally defined social roles become less and less in accord with self-expectations, does not necessarily decrease the older person's level of satisfaction. Another question to keep in mind is this: To what degree is the old person *functionally* integrated in his close social environment? This is a different, objective meaning of the word "adjustment," and one which is more difficult to translate into precise measurements.

The full text of this paper is published in Wilma Donahue, C. Tibbitts, and R. H. Williams (eds.), *Psychological and Social Processes of Aging: An International Research Seminar* (to be published).

Personality and Adjustment to Aging

SUZANNE REICHARD

THE influence of personality upon reactions to aging and retirement is illustrated by the description of five personality types, each with a different pattern of adjustment.

The subjects of our study were a group of 87 older male workers aged 55–84 residing in the San Francisco Bay Area. Forty-two were retired and 45 were still employed. Workers who volunteered to participate in the study were invited to come to the University for a series of intensive interviews covering major facets of their life histories, social relationships, and personal concerns.

The interviews were evaluated by means of a group of 115 over-all ratings of mental functioning and personality characteristics derived from psychoanalysis and from general psychological theory. These ratings gave us personality profiles for each respondent.

Using happiness, life satisfaction, and freedom from anxiety and depression as criteria of successful aging, we rated the interviews on a five-point scale of adjustment to aging ranging from very well adjusted to minimal adjustment. This was a forced rating in which approximately 20 percent of the sample was assigned to each of the five points of the scale.

The patterns of adjustment to aging to be described here were identified empirically by means of two inverse cluster analyses of the intercorrelations of rating profiles, one of 40 persons who were rated high (4 or 5) and the other of 30 persons who were rated low (1 or 2) on adjustment to aging. An intermediate group of 17 persons who were rated 3 was not included in the two cluster analyses. These yielded five distinct personality types each with a particular pattern of adjustment to aging—three in the well-adjusted group and two in the poorly adjusted.

The first cluster identified among the well adjusted consisted of 14

The full text of this paper is published in Wilma Donahue, C. Tibbitts, and R. H. Williams (eds.), *Psychological and Social Processes of Aging: An International Research Seminar* (to be published).

persons whom we have called "the mature," because they take a constructive rather than an impulsive or a defensive approach to life. Their relative freedom from neurotic inhibitions and character defects permits them to enjoy life to the full. They are warm people. They readily assume family responsibilities and are affectionate husbands and good fathers. In some cases, their first marriages ended in divorce, but all eventually married happily. They enjoy seeing friends and belong to one or more organizations in which they participate actively. They are interested in hobbies. In outlook, they are realistic and flexible; they do not think in terms of "black and white" or try to oversimplify complex issues. Being adaptable, they adjust well to retirement. They may even look forward to retirement as allowing them to spend more time with their friends, and they occupy themselves happily with their hobbies. Although not rich, they have been financially prudent and can look forward to an old age free from financial worries. Most of the mature have adjusted well to life's crises and have glided smoothly into old age. Those whose life-course has been less smooth have, nevertheless, achieved some serenity in later years. All feel that their lives have been essentially worthwhile. Because their lives have been rich in satisfactions, the mature approach the end of life calmly and without despair.

The next cluster consisted of six persons designated as the "rocking-chair" group because of their characteristic need to lean on others and to take it easy. In psychoanalytic terminology, the rocking-chair group are oral characters. Their emotional needs find direct expression in the great importance they attach to eating, and some have a tendency to drink to excess. They tend to be impulsive and extravagant. Their need for external restraints leads them to marry domineering women who control the purse strings. They enjoy rest and relaxation and look forward to leisure time and holidays. They are not "joiners." They do not pursue social relationships and prefer to stay at home. Although their lives have been less rich in satisfactions than those of the mature, they too accept the past. Unambitious men who find little satisfaction in work, they are glad to take it easy when retirement comes. They adjust well to aging because, in old age, society grants them the permission to indulge their needs for passivity and dependence that it does not grant young people.

The third well-adjusted cluster consisted of seven persons who maintain a highly developed but smoothly functioning system of defenses against anxiety. We have called them "the armored." Unlike the rest of the groups, whose mean age falls in the low sixties, the mean age of the armored is close to 73. This was the only group in which retired predominated; six of the seven men in the group were retired. Resembling the mature group in their determination to remain active and independent, the armored manifest a compulsive quality not characteristic of the former. They do not look forward to retirement. Generally they do not plan for retirement, tending to put it out of mind. Therefore retirement often comes as an unpleasant surprise. Despite knowledge of company policy, they say they expected to go on working as long as they were able. Following retirement, they either seek part-time work or set up a daily schedule of activities. They try to counteract their fear of growing old by remaining active. Afraid of the physical and mental deterioration associated with aging, they are happy and well adjusted as long as they can keep busy because they cannot face the passivity and helplessness of old age.

Among those who were poorly adjusted to aging, the first and largest cluster is composed of 16 individuals whom we have called "the angry men." They are hostile and blame others for their frustrations and failures. They are constantly on the alert for hostility in others. Some feel so exploited that they are almost paranoid. They cannot bear doubt or uncertainty. Thus, they oversimplify issues in terms of good and bad, of "black and white." They are so rigidly set in their ways that they are unable to learn from experience or to adapt to change; they are at least realistic of all the groups. The angry men are even more strongly defended than the armored group, but the difference between the two is crucial: in the armored men the defenses work, in the angry men they do not. Of all the types of adjustment, the angry men least accept the fact of aging, and see growing old as a rapid decline of mental and physical powers, which leads to early death. Their defense is to remain active; they want to keep on working as long as they can. Death is an adversary to be defied. Unable to sublimate, they have no hobbies or interests to sustain them in old age. Retirement, for them, is the beginning of the end.

The second poorly adjusted cluster is made up of only four persons who deal with frustration and failure in an opposite manner from that of the angry men. They turn their anger on themselves and blame themselves for their misfortunes; hence, we have called them "the self-haters." They despise themselves. Seldom crediting themselves with any virtues, they belabor their weaknesses. Two of the four in this group were obviously depressed—one was suicidal. When asked: "If everything were to be the same, would you like to live your life over again?" the depressed men say no. All of the self-haters make many references to death, and the two depressed men openly wish to die. For the self-haters, death may be a longed-for release from an intolerable existence. Although less accepting of the fact of aging than the well-adjusted groups, they accept aging better than the angry men.

Thus, basic personality significantly determines the individual's style of adjustment to aging. Those who grow old successfully do so in different ways. Some find happiness in remaining active; others like to take it easy. There is no single formula for successful aging; each individual must find the formula that best fits his needs.

Personality and the Aging Process

BERNICE L. NEUGARTEN

THIS paper is a summary report and evaluation of the several studies of personality changes with age that have been carried out in connection with the Kansas City Studies of Adult Life. The Studies have been made by different investigators using various frames of reference; but all have drawn from the same pool of data. Interview and projective test responses have been analyzed for various subsamples of persons aged 40 to 80, all of whom are functioning members of the community. In all these studies, 100 or more cases were used.

In those studies which relied heavily upon interview data, chronological age has been found to be a relatively insignificant variable in accounting for differences between persons in the age range 40 to 70. In those studies, however, which relied upon projective data, consistent and significant age changes have been found.

These findings are discussed from two points of view: (1) problems of method; and (2) implications for a theory of personality change in adulthood and old age.

The full text of this paper is published in Wilma Donahue, C. Tibbitts, and R. H. Williams (eds.), *Psychological and Social Processes of Aging: An International Research Seminar* (to be published).

A Comparison of Interdisciplinary Findings of the Study of Objective Criteria of Aging

ERNEST W. BURGESS

THIS paper is based on the data of an interdisciplinary study of criteria of aging and the determinants of retirement. This project was begun in 1955 and concluded in 1959 with Robert K. Burns, chief investigator, and Leonard Z. Breen, director. It was financed by a grant from the National Institute of Mental Health.

The interdisciplinary nature of the study is indicated by the specialties represented by the investigators. Emmet B. Bay, M.D., is a biologist and physician, specializing in internal medicine; Ward C. Halstead, Ph.D., is a medical psychologist; Bertha Klien, M.D., is an ophthalmologist; Robert W. Kleemeier, Ph.D., is an experimental and industrial psychologist; Robert K. Burns, Ph.D., is an economist specializing in industrial relations; and Leonard Z. Breen, Ph.D., is a sociologist, specializing in social gerontology. The project was unusual in that it embraced personnel from both the social sciences and the biological sciences.

The data for the study were obtained through the cooperation of the management and employees of four companies in the Chicago area. The subjects of the study were male employees 40–44 years of age and 60–64 years of age, carefully matched on the following characteristics: race, sex, occupation, place of work, and a minimum of 3 years in the occupation for which pairing was made. All of the men studied were on individual incentive pay.

From the theoretical standpoint the investigators were interested in obtaining data upon three main questions:

Do changes in physical fitness, biological intelligence, arteries of the eye, psychomotor capacities, and social psychological traits take place with aging?

If so, to what extent are these changes associated with differences in the production records of matched pairs of workers employed on individual incentive pay?

Are these independent variables, or is there a statistically significant association between the variables indicating that they are not independent?

DIFFERENCES IN RESPONSES
BETWEEN YOUNGER AND OLDER WORKERS

It may be provisionally assumed that differences in responses of younger and older employees represent the effects of aging, since the individuals studied are matched to eliminate the influence of race, sex, and occupation.

A brief description of the tests discloses their wide range.

Physical fitness.   Emmet B. Bay, M.D., states that "Each examination involved an elaborate medical history, a complete physical examination including a neurological one, ordinary blood and urine tests, chest x-ray, and electro- and ballistocardiograms."

Condition of arteries in the eye.   Dr. Klien gave the subjects an ophthalmoscope examination of the eye to determine the increase with age of abnormalities of the retinal arteries, indicative of tendencies to arteriosclerotic-cardiovascular disease.

Psychomotor capacities.   Kleemeier's battery included the following tests: grip, bolt board, tracing, sorting, capsule, punch board, finger movement, and number board.

Biological intelligence.   Halstead states that the higher brain functions as measured by his tests include: (1) ability to make reflective decisions, (2) judgment in making sound decisions under the pressure of time, (3) mental power, (4) memory for over-all organization and form, and (5) memory for critical details.

Self-perception of age.   Breen gave the subjects of the study a card by which they could identify themselves as young, young adult, middle aged, elderly, old, or aged.

The degree to which the different tests are associated with aging is disclosed in Table 1.

It is clear that the order from lower to higher association between these different characteristics and aging is: physical fitness, biological intelligence, self-perception of aging, psychomotor capacity, and condition of the small arteries of the eye.

Two of the tests, the condition of the arteries of the eye and differences in psychomotor capacity, are very discriminating.

The tests for physical fitness are the least discriminating. It must be remembered, however, that these are tests of fitness to continue

Table 1. Test findings on younger and older workers,
percentage distribution

Characteristic	Younger workers	Older workers
Physical fitness (67 younger, 68 older workers)		
No obvious defect	54.0	46.0
Defects	41.7	58.3
Biological intelligence (67 younger, 64 older workers)		
Little or no brain damage	72.7	27.3
Moderate to much brain damage	35.5	64.5
Self-perception (67 younger, 64 older workers)		
Less than middle aged	82.8	17.2
Middle aged and older	35.4	64.6
Psychomotor capacity (61 younger, 41 older workers)		
High scores	80.3	19.7
Low scores	27.5	72.5
Condition of small arteries of the eye		
(44 younger, 42 older workers)		
Normal	84.4	15.6
Abnormal: A.B.C.	25.0	75.0

working at the job now held. The indication is that the large majority of older workers are physically capable of continued employment beyond 65.

The two other tests, self-perception of aging and biological intelligence, also discriminate rather markedly between the younger and the older workers.

On all the tests there is more or less overlapping. Individual differences are greater than differences between age groups. So far as physical and mental ability are measured by these tests it is evident that chronological age is not only an arbitrary criterion of aging but an unrealistic and unreliable one.

DIFFERENCES IN PRODUCTIVITY RECORDS BETWEEN YOUNGER AND OLDER WORKERS

No differences were found between younger and older workers in productivity. But there still remained the question: Are there variations in productivity between younger and older workers who were rated as normal or below normal on the five personal characteristics? The findings from these comparisons are given in Table 2.

Although none of the differences shown in Table 2 is statistically significant because of the small number of cases on which the comparison is based, it should be noted that in three out of five instances the normal younger workers exceed the older normal workers in productivity; in one instance they are equal, and in one instance they

Table 2. High productivity in relation to differential characteristics of younger and older workers, percentage distribution

	High productivity (above median)	
Characteristic	Normal rating	Below normal rating
Physical fitness		
Younger	54 (48)[a]	42 (19)[a]
Older	54 (39)	48 (25)
Retinal artery normality		
Younger	58 (38)	45 (11)
Older	71 (7)	53 (38)
Psychomotor capacity		
Younger	53 (30)	47 (34)
Older	52 (21)	40 (20)
Biological intelligence		
(absence of brain damage)		
Younger	58 (40)	41 (27)
Older	53 (15)	52 (46)
Perception of own age		
Younger	56 (25)	47 (43)
Older	50 (24)	50 (34)

[a] Number of cases on which percentages are based is in parentheses.

are lower. Of those employees rated as below normal on these characteristics, however, the older exceed the younger in productivity on all characteristics except psychomotor capacity.

When those employees who rate normal (whether younger or older) are compared with those who are rated below normal on the five characteristics, nine of ten comparisons show higher productivity in those rated as normal; and the tenth comparison shows equal productivity.

INDEPENDENT OR INTERCORRELATED VARIABLES

Table 3 gives the findings on the intercorrelation of variables for the younger and the older workers.

The only moderately high correlation is .46 between psychomotor capacity and biological intelligence. This association is not unexpected because the Halstead battery includes certain tests similar to those in the Kleemeier battery. But only 21 percent of the variance between the variables is accounted for by this correlation, leaving nearly 80 percent of variance due to other factors.

Neither the correlation of .23 between the Kleemeier psychomotor battery and the Klien tests of the arteries of the eye nor the correlation of .24 between the tests of physical fitness and the Klien tests is statistically significant because of the small number of cases examined by Klien.

Table 3. *Intercorrelations between characteristics*

Characteristic	Retinal arteries	Psychomotor capacity	Biological intelligence	Self-perception of age
Younger workers (40–44)				
Physical fitness	.24	.01	.02	.10
Retinal arteries		.23	−.05	−.06
Psychomotor capacity			.46	.10
Biological intelligence				.06
Older workers (60–64)				
Physical fitness	.48	.05	−.04	.07
Retinal arteries		.05	−.13	.06
Psychomotor capacity			.39	.41
Biological intelligence				−.22

The lack of intercorrelation on the other seven possibilities is much more interesting than the above three associations. Most important is the lack of any significant correlation between any four objective variables—physical fitness, condition of the eye arteries, psychomotor capacity, and biological intelligence—and the one subjective variable, self-perception of age. Evidently the perception by younger workers of their age has no relation to their physiological or psychological status, at least as measured by these tests.

For older workers among the objective factors there are only two statistically significant associations. One of these is .39 between the Halstead and Kleemeier batteries which, as was the case with the younger workers, is to be expected because of the similarities of certain tests in these batteries. The correlation is .48 between the results of the bay examination of physical fitness and the Klien examination of evidence of cardiovascular disease as indicated by the condition of the small arteries of the eye. This association tends to substantiate the physiological validity of both examinations since the two are very different from each other in data and in research method.

Even more revealing is the correlation of .41 between Kleemeier's findings on psychomotor capacity and self-perception of age by the older workers. This finding is all the more interesting because there is practically no correlation between self-perception of age and physical fitness, or between self-perception of age and the condition of the retinal arteries. In other words psychomotor capacity is the only objective criterion to show a moderate correlation with self-perception of old age.

Summarizing the analysis of the intercorrelation findings the following main points may be made:

The only objective tests that are intercorrelated are (1) those of Kleemeier on psychomotor capacity and Halstead on biological intelligence for both younger and older workers, and (2) those of Bay on physical fitness and Klien on tendency to cardiovascular disease as indicated by eye condition of the small arteries. The latter is statistically significant for older workers, and the chances are one out of ten that the association is significant for the younger workers.

There is no statistically significant association either for younger or for older workers between the findings on the tests of either Bay or Klien with either Halstead or Kleemeier. In other words psychomotor capacity and biological intelligence overlap with each other but not with physical fitness or condition of the small arteries of the eye. But the latter two overlap with each other for the older worker and perhaps for the younger worker.

Most revealing is the relation of the objective variables with the subjective variable of self-perception of aging. There exists no relation for the younger workers. But for the older workers self-conception of aging seems to be influenced by psychomotor capacity as measured by Kleemeier's battery with a correlation of .41, and to a lesser degree by the Halstead battery on biological intelligence.

SUMMARY

The findings of the comparisons presented in this paper may be briefly summarized.

The tests do discriminate by age, indicating probably a decline on the average in physical and mental capacity among workers in the 20- to 25-year period between 40 and 64.

The overlap in ratings of younger and older employees is significant, showing considerable individual differences in aging in the characteristics measured by the tests.

While there are no differences in productivity between younger and older workers as groups, there are great individual differences in both age groups.

There is some evidence that employees rated as normal on the tests tend to show higher productivity in the younger than in the older workers; but that for those graded as subnormal the older outperformed the younger.

The only statistically significant correlation among the tests for younger workers is between psychomotor capacity and biological intelligence. This association is to be expected since the two batteries contain similar tests.

For older workers this correlation of psychomotor capacity and biological intelligence reappears.

For older workers the ratings on condition of the retinal arteries are associated with the grading on physical fitness which may be said to validate the findings of the two examinations which are entirely different in method and in locus of examination.

Only two objective variables are correlated with self-perception of aging, namely, the psychomotor tests and biological intelligence.

Findings from the Duke Geriatrics Research Project on the Effects of Aging upon the Nervous System

EWALD W. BUSSE

THE Duke geriatrics research project is an interdisciplinary study of changes in the aging human nervous system and their relationship to the health and adjustment of the individual. Observations are made from the social, psychologic, and physiologic standpoints. Major attention has been given to elderly persons living in the community— volunteers 60 years of age or older who are making a satisfactory adjustment to community life. The observations made on this group of subjects are compared with observations of institutionalized elderly persons and other defined groups. Recent serial observations on the aged community subjects have underscored the importance of instituting a full-scale longitudinal study. Such a longitudinal program is the major objective of our present and future work.

SPECIFIC AIMS

The specific aims of the Duke geriatrics research project may be briefly stated as follows:

To identify social, psychologic, and physiologic factors influencing the behavior of elderly people, and to relate these changes to intellectual function, personality, and social competence.

To establish firmly an intensive longitudinal study of aging community subjects which will continue over a period of 10 years or more.

To extend our observations to groups of elderly people who have been subjected to specific psychic or physical stress, or who have distinctive patterns of living—for example, residents of homes for

This investigation was supported by NIH grants M-900, M-2109, and H-3582; and by a grant from Foundations' Fund for Research in Psychiatry.

the aged, hospitalized veterans, patients admitted for the first time to mental institutions, and inmates of facilities for the treatment of chronic diseases. Appropriate control groups of young persons have been and will be included as required.

To develop and improve techniques of observation and data analysis. Special emphasis is placed on the development of rating scales and methods for quantifying data.

To maintain a stimulating research atmosphere in order to attract young investigators into the field of aging. The participants in this project feel that it has provided them with a particularly rewarding experience in the fields of both geriatrics and mental health.

METHOD OF PROCEDURE

Some of the terms adopted by the investigators involved in this interdisciplinary effort may require definition here. The term *core study* refers to research activity which involves contributions from all members of the team in a manner previously agreed upon by the group. The core study forms the basis of the proposed longitudinal program. *Pilot studies* are exploratory projects used to determine the validity or feasibility of incorporating a new procedure into the core study and the longitudinal program. *Peripheral studies* are extensions of research ideas which stem from the core study. They frequently emerge as research efforts beyond the defined scope of the core investigation. These peripheral studies have provided an exciting source of new ideas.

The senior investigators who comprise the research team and are responsible for this work represent the following scientific areas and medical specialties: Psychiatry, Neurology, Psychology, Electroencephalography, Psychophysiology, Sociology, Social Work, Dermatology, Anatomy, Ophthalmology, Otology, Internal medicine, Cardiology, Statistics.

The investigators hold weekly seminars throughout the academic year. Research planning meetings are scheduled at least twice a year, and last a minimum of one full day. Meetings for administrative purposes are held as required.

The routine battery of tests used in the core study consisted of the following:

Medical history
Physical examination
Neurologic examination

Psychiatric evaluation

Dermatologic examination

Ophthalmologic examination, including visual fields, visual acuity, and color and depth perception

Fundus photography in color

Examination and photography of the microscopic vascular structure of the bulbar conjunctiva

Audiometry: pure tone and speech threshold

Electroencephalogram

Electrocardiogram

Ballistocardiogram

Chest roentgenogram

Laboratory studies: Urinalysis, morphologic blood studies, nonprotein nitrogen, fasting blood sugar, serologic test for syphilis, and blood cholesterol

Psychologic testing: Rorschach, Wechsler Adult Intelligence Scale (WAIS), Wechsler Memory Scale, simple and complex reaction time, and verbal

Social history and evaluation, including socioeconomic classification.

This routine battery of observations requires 2 full days of participation on the part of the subject. It is evident that such extensive observations are possible only as long as the subjects are in relatively good health and can be examined at the Duke University Medical Center. As longitudinal evaluations progress and some of the subjects become incapacitated, it will be necessary to examine them in their homes or elsewhere. In such cases, the evaluations will be appropriately modified.

Subjects and sampling

The community sample is composed of volunteer subjects 60 or above who, when initially screened and accepted into the study, appeared to be relatively free of disease and were functioning at an acceptable level in the community. The sample cannot be considered random or truly representative, since volunteering for such a study can be a biasing factor.

The community sample, as utilized for statistical purposes in the early part of this year, is composed of 260 individuals. This sample is being expanded. The age range of the group is 60 to 94 years, with a median age of 70. Race and sex distributions are as follows: Caucasian, 65 percent; Negro, 33 percent; men, 41 percent; women, 59 percent. These distributions are comparable to those in the total population of Durham. With regard to socioeconomic status, the sample is somewhat top-heavy, since 40 percent of the subjects or their spouses have been business executives or professional workers.

The remaining 60 percent came from lower socioeconomic groups, corresponding generally to the lower middle and lower classes in Warner's classification of social categories. We hope to correct this distortion as additions are made to the community sample.

The morale and cooperation of the subjects have been excellent. All have agreed to participate in a longitudinal study, and 173 of the subjects have also become members of what is referred to as a *permanent panel*. This panel is utilized for pilot and peripheral studies.

In addition to the community sample, we have already studied 116 elderly institutionalized subjects (78 psychiatric patients and 38 residents of a home for the aged). We will continue to study subjects from the Methodist Home for the Aged, which is adjacent to the Duke campus, and will utilize the patient populations of the Veterans Administration Hospital in Durham and of the Butner State Hospital nearby.

Longitudinal study

All available subjects in the community sample will participate in the longitudinal study. Approximately half of the 260 subjects have already been reexamined, and the remainder are scheduled for reexamination during the coming year. Because of death, incapacitating illness, change of address, or lack of cooperation we have lost approximately 20 percent of the original sample over a period of 3 to 4 years. New subjects will be recruited in an effort to broaden the base of the longitudinal study.

All procedures utilized in the core study will be repeated in the follow-up examinations made during the course of the longitudinal study. The procedures will be duplicated as closely as possible, although minor modifications will be dictated by experience. Interviews for the collection of historic data will be appreciably shorter than on the initial visit, since they need to cover only the interval between examinations. The time thus saved will be reserved for new procedures in the pursuit of important leads suggested by earlier work.

Treatment of data

The processing and analysis of data are facilitated by the use of IBM methods. Observations are entered in coded form on specially designed data sheets, from which standard IBM cards are punched. Each subject studied to date has a total of 18 cards of coded information, involving 827 variables from 21 different examinations. More than a quarter of these variables are continuous, quantitative measurements; a substantial number of those remaining are in the form of rating scales.

Preliminary analysis consists in obtaining a frequency distribution for each variable, and determining differences between groups divided according to age, sex, race, and social class. This preliminary analysis is accomplished by a counter-sorter. Interrelations between variables are explored by constructing contingency tables and running simple cross-sorts.

If trends become apparent, the data are entered into a 650 IBM computer for statistical evaluation. Computer programs are available for the following parametric statistics: mean, standard deviation, *t*-test, product-moment correlation, and biserial correlation. Nonparametric tests include chi-square, contingency coefficient, and rank-difference correlation. Additional programs are being developed as the need arises. To control unwanted sources of variation, matched group techniques are used when feasible. Matching is accomplished with the aid of collating and tabulating equipment. In special instances, analyses of variables have been performed on hand calculators.

FINDINGS

Limitations of time make it impossible to review all the important contributions from this project that have appeared in the literature, particularly those by former members of this research team. This report is limited to relatively recent publications and to articles which will be published in the near future.

WAIS performance of the aged

WAIS (Wechsler Adult Intelligence Scale) data on 239 elderly subjects above the age of 60 have been reported. No national norms for the WAIS are available for subjects above 65 years of age. Since data based on 352 elderly subjects from a Kansas City study have been suggested as tentative norms, it was of special interest to compare these data with the Duke statistics. Stable differences were found between the samples, with the Duke group showing superiority in the verbal subtests and lower achievement in the performance subtests. While no satisfactory explanation of these differences, other than the possibility of regional and socioeconomic influences, is offered, the need for establishing national norms on a national sample of the aged has been demonstrated (Eisdorfer *et al.*, 1959).

Effect of sensory impairment on the Rorschach developmental level

A study was performed to investigate the effects of visual and auditory defects on Rorschach performance in an aged population. The Rorschach test was administered to 48 senescent, community-adjusted volunteers divided into six groups on the basis of three visual and two auditory levels of functioning. The subjects were screened to eliminate those with demonstrable damage to the central nervous system and those with extremes of verbal IQ. Three dependent variables—Functional Integration score, Grace's Content (vocabulary) score, and the Index of Primitive Thought—were utilized in order to reflect various levels on a developmental continuum of Rorschach performance (Eisdorfer, 1960a, 1962).

The results were as follows:

Impaired hearing was associated with significantly lowered developmental performance as defined by vocabulary level and Functional Integration scores.

No differences appeared between subjects with normal vision and those with "impaired" vision, whether or not the impairment was corrected.

The performance of subjects with both visual and auditory decrements was not significantly worse than that of subjects with auditory decrement alone, although the performance of the former group was consistently the poorest of the subject population.

Changes in cognitive functioning on the Rorschach Test in relation to intellectual level in senescence

Recent findings have suggested a relationship between the intellectual level and the rate of decline in cognitive functioning with age. These findings have been based primarily upon structured intellectual examinations; it seemed valuable, therefore, to investigate this relationship in terms of performance on complex unstructured tasks (Eisdorfer, 1960b).

Total sum of responses, sum of human movement responses (M), vocabulary level score, and Functional Integration score on the Rorschach Test were analyzed and correlated with the intelligence quotient (IQ). While there was no significant decline with advancing age in the high IQ group, there appeared to be an age-related decline of performance in the middle IQ group and an even more striking decline in the low IQ group. The findings may be interpreted to support the concept that the rate of decline in cognitive functioning with age is related to the intellectual level.

Factors predisposing to psychic disturbances

Because of the limitations imposed by physical impairment, *physical functioning* was considered to be a factor of potential psychic importance in persons in this age range. Subjects were rated on physical functioning by the following scale: No diagnosis of illness; pathologic findings present, but no disability; up to 20 percent disability; up to 50 percent disability; up to 80 percent disability; up to 100 percent disability. When this rating was applied, no difference was found between neurotic and normal subjects. The number of individuals with some disability was significantly greater in the psychotic group than in the normal group, but there was no significant difference between the nonpsychotic subjects with mixed or pure organic mental signs and symptoms and the group of normal subjects. In a previous study it was found that the incidence of pathologic findings, but not of disability, was significantly greater in depressed persons than in normal subjects; and that the hypochondriac subjects, although they had many more symptoms than the total group, had no more limitations on physical functioning than did the subjects classified as "normal" from the psychic standpoint.

Subjects were questioned concerning memories of enuresis and nightmares in early childhood. Considering the fact that early childhood memories are apt to be deeply repressed in adults and that there is a great time span intervening in these elderly persons, it is not surprising that only 36 of the 222 subjects interviewed recalled having enuresis, and only 49 remembered nightmares. Thirty-six percent of the severely neurotic subjects and 22 percent of the "normal" subjects recalled having nightmares, while 35 percent of the former and 17 percent of the latter remembered enuresis. The fact that these differences are not statistically significant suggests that undue emphasis may be given this area of ordinary psychiatric work-up (Busse and Dovenmuehle, 1960).

Psychoneurotic reactions of the aged

Psychiatric diagnoses were based on specific signs and symptoms. Many of the diagnostic criteria were rated on a quantitative scale, with a cutoff point differentiating "normal" from pathologic. Of a total of 222 aged people, 89 (40 percent) were considered normal; 56 (25 percent) were psychoneurotic, and 25 of these had severe neurotic reactions; 21 (9 percent) demonstrated relatively mild, nonpsychotic organic changes; 42 (19 percent) had combined nonpsychotic and neurotic symptoms; and 14 (6 percent) presented evidence of psychosis (Busse *et al.*, 1960).

The psychoneurotic subjects were compared to the normal individuals in a number of parameters, including physical, psychologic, and social measurements. The psychoneurotic subjects were decidedly less social than were those in the normal group, and they were often hypochondriacal and depressed. Although their attitude toward friends was distorted, their attitude toward work was not strikingly different from that of the normal group. This acceptable attitude toward work may be one of the determinants that prevents emotionally disturbed people from becoming patients.

The factor distinguishing hypochondriac subjects in the community from the hospitalized hypochondriac patients was the absence of feelings of neglect and persecution; patients who sought medical attention because of abnormal concern about their health felt strongly that they were being mistreated.

This study presents evidence that many elderly people with psychoneurotic reactions of varying degrees are still able to maintain a reasonably acceptable adjustment in society. Recognition of the elements which permit a person to maintain such an adjustment will require much further investigation.

Temporal lobe electroencephalographic abnormalities

Electroencephalograms on 223 community volunteers confirmed the previously reported finding of a high incidence of temporal lobe foci in elderly people. Temporal slowing was present in 30 percent of the cases, and in a third of these was accompanied by severe abnormalities in the delta range. In a few subjects spikes were associated with the slow waves. Unilateral and bilateral disturbances were about equally represented. Approximately 80 percent of the foci, however, were predominantly or entirely left-sided. Voltages were maximum from the anterior temporal leads, with a gradient extending usually into the posterior temporal region but occasionally involving the frontal area. Relaxation and drowsiness favored the recording of these focal abnormalities, which frequently disappeared during sleep (Busse and Obrist, 1960; Obrist and Busse, 1959).

Relation of electroencephalographic findings to intellectual function

Two hundred and fifty-five community subjects from several socio-economic levels and 150 residents of a home for the aged were studied in an effort to determine whether electroencephalographic changes commonly found in senescence are correlated with early signs of mental deterioration, as indicated by psychologic tests. The tests employed included the Wechsler-Bellevue Intelligence Scale, Wechsler Adult Intelligence Scale, Wechsler Memory Scale, and paired associate learning and retention (Busse *et al.,* 1956; Barnes *et al.,* 1956).

Minor, but definite, EEG alterations were observed in relation to age. There was a shift of frequencies to the slow side, particularly in the alpha rhythm, and a relatively high incidence (30 percent) of temporal lobe abnormalities.

The degree of correlation between intellectual function and EEG changes associated with aging was low. A slow alpha rhythm was significantly related to impairment on intelligence, learning, and memory tests, but the correlation became less significant when age was controlled. Temporal lobe foci, on the other hand, were not related to intelligence test performance, although there was a tendency for such abnormalities to occur in people with deficient learning ability.

Although there appears to be little relationship between electroencephalographic and intellectual changes in normal senescence, the following study on aged psychiatric patients showed, in contrast, a high degree of correlation.

Electroencephalographic findings, blood pressure,
and cerebral arteriosclerosis

A total of 233 hospitalized psychiatric patients aged 60 or above and 261 mentally normal elderly subjects from the community were available for this study. Electroencephalograms were classified as normal, fast, focal slow, diffuse slow, and mixed slow (diffuse with focal accentuation). An average blood pressure was obtained by computing the geometric mean of the systolic and diastolic readings, as determined by routine physical examination. When several EEG categories are plotted separately against mean blood pressure in the hospitalized group, it is apparent that the incidence of normal electroencephalograms increases markedly as the blood pressure rises, while the number of diffusely slow and mixed electroencephalograms is maximum with the lower blood pressure readings. In contrast, the mentally normal subjects in the community showed no correlation between EEG abnormalities and blood pressure (Obrist *et al.,* 1960).

These findings suggest that a mild elevation of blood pressure (consistent with age) may tend to preserve a normal electroencephalographic pattern by maintaining adequate circulation to the brain, thus compensating for cerebral arteriosclerosis. The blood pressure level appears to be critical in psychiatric patients, who presumably have more arteriosclerosis, but does not seem to be an important factor in the electroencephalograms of normal old people.

Factors in age awareness

A study was made to discover factors which influence awareness of age in a group of Caucasian and Negro subjects 60 years of age and older, who were functioning at various levels in family and community life (Busse *et al.,* 1957).

The following variables were found to be significantly related to age awareness: chronologic age, race, and feeling of health.

Since there was a statistically reliable tendency for Negroes to consider themselves older than did White persons, the racial differences were investigated further. The following four factors varied significantly with race: physical status (based on functional capacity), feeling of financial security, listing of advantages and disadvantages of aging, and change in religious interest. Eighteen other variables in the areas of health, intelligence, environment, present activities, and attitudes were studied, but none of these gave statistically significant results in relation to age awareness.

Social isolation of older persons

An exploratory study on family structure and social isolation of older persons casts some doubt upon the generalizations commonly made about the older person and his family—generalizations such as the high spatial mobility of adult children, the physical isolation of elderly parents, and their feeling of being neglected by their families. Evidence that familistic patterns and dependent parent-child relationships are more prevalent in Durham than in the hypothetical midwestern community of Prairie City suggests the possibility of regional variations (Brown, 1960).

Although the extended family pattern appears to have disappeared in urban areas for the most part, we are unable to conclude that interdependence between the generations has been replaced by independence or by isolation and neglect for the majority of aged persons. Though physically separated in many instances, elderly parents and their children may maintain close ties based on mutual affection and some measure of dependence. This relationship may vary in different regions, however, and perhaps in different social classes, ethnic groups, and sizes and types of cities. Once again, we find that the aged population is not a homogeneous one—a fact which has important implications for social action programs and legislation. Finally, it would appear that the family relations of older people are in need of further careful investigation, with special emphasis upon the varying patterns to be found.

Dermatologic findings

Cherry angiomas were found in 47 percent of the group studied, senile keratoses in 23 percent, and seborrheic keratoses in 41 percent. The significance of the cherry angiomas in the aging process—particularly in relation to nutritional factors and liver function—should be studied more intensively. Careful studies of the keratoses should lead to a better understanding of their significance in malignancy and of the reason for their growth on old skin if they are of viral or bacterial origin. Plans are under way to study keratoses by the method of Toolan, that is, by transplant into the pouches of cortisonized hamsters.

Pruritus is being studied and correlated with psychologic features. The incidence of pruritus is high in a clinic sample, but low in the community subjects (Olansky *et al.,* 1959; Olansky, 1960).[1]

Vascular changes in the eye

Photographic observations of the blood and blood vessels visible on the bulbar conjunctiva substantiate previous findings of increased vascularity with aging, associated with numerous sacculated venules and a marked increase in tortuosity of the veins. Most of these subjects were observed before and after the administration of vasoconstrictive drugs, and it has been constantly found that both the sacculations and the "outsides" of the curves in the tortuous veins fail to respond to constrictive agents.[2]

[1] S. Olansky, unpublished observations.
[2] W. H. Knisely and R. Frayser, unpublished observations.

Sexual activity

A study of the sexual activity and attitudes of older people included both Caucasoid and Negroid men and women. Analysis of the data showed little correlation between sexual activity and age, but in this study Negroid subjects were more active sexually than Caucasoid, and men more active than women. The subjects also rated themselves on the strength of their sexual urge in youth and in old age, and comparisons of the two ratings showed a remarkable constancy in the relative strength of an individual's sexual drive throughout life. Although older people experience a decline in sexual activity and in the strength of the sexual drive, persons in reasonably good health, with partners who are also physically healthy, continue to be sexually active into their seventh, eighth, and ninth decades (Newman and Nichols, 1960).

CONCLUSION

The results of the Duke Geriatrics Research Project have been scientifically rewarding, and the project has given professional and personal satisfaction to the members of the interdisciplinary research team—in addition to the advantage of considerable experience as a working unit. It has proved to be an excellent resource for research training and experience, and several of the team's members have achieved considerable status as investigators and teachers.

REFERENCES

Barnes, R. H., Busse, E. W., and Friedman, E. L. 1956. Psychological functioning of aged individuals with normal and abnormal electroencephalograms. II. A study of hospitalized individuals. J. Nerv. & Ment. Dis., 124: 585–93.

Brown, R. G. 1960. Family structure and social isolation of older persons. J. Gerontol., 15: 170–74.

Busse, E. W., Barnes, R. H., Friedman, E. L., and Kelty, E. J. 1956. Psychological functioning of aged individuals with normal and abnormal electroencephalograms. I. A study of non-hospitalized community volunteers. J. Nerv. & Ment. Dis., 124: 135–41.

——— and Dovenmuehle, R. H. 1960. Neurotic symptoms and predisposition of aging people. J. Am. Geriatrics Soc., 8: 328–36.

———, Dovenmuehle, R. H., and Brown, R. G. 1960. Psychoneurotic reactions of the aged. Geriatrics, 15: 97–105.

————, Jeffers, F. C., and Obrist, W. D. 1957. Factors in age awareness. *In* Proceedings of the Fourth Congress, International Association of Gerontology, Merano, Italy, *3,* 349–57. Fidenza: Tipografia Tito Mattioli.

———— and Obrist, W. D. 1960. Temporal lobe abnormalities in the senescent electroencephalogram. (Paper presented at the Seventeenth Annual Meeting of the American Geriatrics Society, June, 1960, Miami.) Unpublished.

Eisdorfer, C. 1960*a.* Rorschach rigidity and sensory decrement in a senescent population. J. Gerontol., 15: 188–90.

———— 1960*b.* Developmental level and sensory impairment in the aged. J. Proj. Techn., 24: 164–70.

———— 1962. Changes in cognitive functioning in relation to intellectual level in senescence. *In* C. Tibbitts and Wilma Donahue (eds.), Aging around the world. Social and psychological aspects of aging, pp. 888–96. New York: Columbia University Press.

————, Busse, E. W., and Cohen, L. D. 1959. WAIS performance of an aged sample: the relationship between verbal and performance IQs. J. Gerontol., 14: 197–201.

Newman, G., and Nichols, C. R. 1960. Sexual activities and attitudes in older persons. J.A.M.A., 173: 33–35.

Obrist, W. D., and Busse, E. W. 1959. Temporal lobe EEG abnormalities in normal senescence. (Paper presented at the Thirteenth Annual Meeting of the American Electroencephalographic Society, June, 1959, Atlantic City.) Unpublished.

————, Henry, C. E., and Busse, E. W. 1960. Blood pressure and EEG abnormality in old age. (Paper presented at the Fourteenth Annual Meeting of the American Electroencephalographic Society, June, 1960, Cape Cod.) Unpublished.

Olansky, S. 1960. Dermatologic changes in the aging. *In* White House Conference on Aging, Background paper on research in gerontology: medical, pp. 42–53. Washington, D.C.: Department of Health, Education, and Welfare.

————, Tully, H. T., Jr., and Knisely, W. H. 1959. Growth of heterologous human tumors from aging individuals in hamster cheek pouches. J. Invest. Dermatol., 32: 117–25.

Age, Personality, and Health Correlates
of Death Concerns in Normal Aged Individuals

PAUL J. RHUDICK AND ANDREW S. DIBNER

WHILE the contemplation of one's death may be almost a universal concern, this area of psychology has received relatively little attention in terms of experimental study. There have been a number of speculations about the psychological processes involved, ranging from Freud's notions of the relationship of death concern to castration anxiety and repetition-compulsion, to theological systems which advocate transcendentalistic explanations. The status of investigations in this area has led Gardner Murphy (Feifel, 1959) to conclude, "I have also been impressed . . . with the cultural contradictions that lie even in the deepest scientific thinking about the whole matter."

Although there has been a paucity of systematic studies, some investigators have attempted to delineate the factors involved in concerns, awareness, and fears of death; frequently, however, reaching contradictory conclusions because of differing research methods. For example, in a developmental context, Wahl (1958) observed that thanatophobia (fear of death) occurs as early as the third year of life. This finding may be somewhat exceptional inasmuch as Nagy (1948) suggested that genuine acceptance of death does not occur until ages 9 or 10, or about the time the child develops his sense of causality and morality.

Feifel (1955) compared attitudes toward death of mentally ill patients and normal individuals and found that the degree of mental disturbance exerted little effect on thoughts about death. In another investigation, the same author (Feifel, 1959) reported that religious persons fear death more than nonreligious ones. However, Alexander and Adlerstein (1959) suggested, in their experimental study, that death anxiety was aroused more rapidly and with less direct stimuli in nonreligious persons.

This investigation was supported by a research grant (M-1833) from the National Institute of Mental Health, Public Health Service.

While the status of death attitudes is at best ambiguous in respect to the general population, there are even fewer systematic studies using gerontic populations. Does death concern increase in the later years? Is it related to the losses—interpersonal, vocational, or physical—which occur with advanced age? Or, is death concern to be considered a reflection of basic anxiety, present throughout life, and therefore, if present in the older person, to be seen more as a neurotic manifestation than as a result of events or processes accompanying aging? Swenson (1958), in a comprehensive investigation of death attitudes in an aged sample, found no relationship between age or sex of respondent and particular attitude toward death. His positive findings revolved around health factors, education, and religion. On the basis of his measuring techniques he found, in general, that death attitudes of a fearful or negative nature were not admitted by his gerontological sample.

It is apparent that research on the psychological factors in attitudes about death has not yet produced clear-cut findings. This is partly due to the fact that questionnaire techniques have primarily been employed. Both Swenson and Feifel admit that their results refer only to the conscious, "public" layers of personality structure. The observation by Swenson that fear of death in aged persons is virtually nonexistent may in large part reflect attitudes of denial in his sample. There is reason to believe that fear of death may well exist in an aged sample but is either not readily admitted to consciousness or not easily admitted through questionnaire responses. In any case, there is clearly a need for systematic explorations in this area, especially in the field of gerontology, for as Feifel (1959) pointed out, the adaptation of the older person to dying and death may be a crucial aspect in the aging process. A systematic study of death concerns must use techniques which are not likely to be nullified by ego-defensive maneuvers in eliciting death-relevant material.

THE PLAN OF THE STUDY
The problem

The aim of the present study is to investigate the relationship of death concerns in a normal aged group to various sociological, psychological, and health variables.

The specific hypotheses of this study are as follows: (1) Death concerns in an aged sample are related to personality factors rather than to demographic factors such as age, sex, marital status, and occupational status, in that high death concern in older persons is associated with neurotic tendencies; (2) death concerns in an aged sample are related to attitudes about health, in that older persons who are concerned about death are concerned about their own health.

Subjects

The sample was taken from the research population of the Age Center of New England which is located in Boston, Massachusetts. The 58 subjects can be described as healthy, well-motivated individuals who live independently in the community and who serve as voluntary participants in various research projects. The group includes both sexes, married and unmarried, working and nonworking. Table 1 presents characteristics of the sample in terms of age and education.

Table 1. Age and education of the sample

Group	Number of cases	Age		Years of education	
		Range	Mean	Range	Mean
I	20	60–69	65.9	9–20	13.7
II	28	70–79	74.8	5–20	13.4
III	10	80–86	82.6	6–18	13.0
Total	58	60–86	73.1	5–20	13.4

In this group there are 30 females and 28 males. Twenty of the subjects are married and 38 are unmarried, widowed, or divorced. Thirteen members are currently employed, while 45 are retired.

Method

Each subject completed the Minnesota Multiphasic Personality Inventory (MMPI) and the Cornell Medical Index (CMI) as a part of a "core program" of data collection at the Age Center of New England. These two questionnaires were used to assess personality factors and attitudes toward health.

Inasmuch as some investigators have alluded to the strong tendency of denial of death in questionnaire situations, the Thematic Appperception Test (TAT) was used to minimize the possibility of such defensive behavior. In this projective test the subject is presented with a series of moderately ambiguous picture cards and is asked to make up a story about each picture. The rationale for use of fantasy productions is that the more unconscious, not readily reportable aspects of personality can be more easily expressed in story constructions than in answers to direct questions.

Twelve standard cards from the TAT were administered in the manner recommended by Murray (1943). Both sexes received cards 1, 2, 3BM, 6BM, 6GF, 4, 10, 13MF, and 15. In addition, the females were shown cards 7GF, 12F, and 18GF; while the males were given cards 7BM, 8BM, and 12M. Inasmuch as statistical analysis revealed that there were no significant differences in death concerns reported between males and females as a result of the three additional cards for each sex, the findings reported in this study are based on analyses of all twelve TAT cards responded to by each subject.

In this study death concern operationally refers to the introduction of a death in the story-response to a TAT card. The reasoning is that mention of death as an integral part of the story production has some personal relevance to the respondent, and may serve as the basis for a measure of his death concern. Two judges agreed 90 percent in scoring for death content in a story, indicating the reliability of this measure.

It had been noted in a pilot study on a similar sample at the Age Center that certain cards frequently elicited death stories while others seldom did. It was therefore reasoned that mention of death in response to a card in which death is rarely associated must mean a greater concern with this topic than is the case where death is mentioned in response to a death-relevant card, and should be weighted accordingly. Utilizing the pilot data on 47 cases, it was determined that on cards 15, 3BM, 8BM, and 18GF death was a frequent theme or outcome. Cards 4, 6BM, and 10 elicited considerably fewer death references, while cards 1, 2, and 7BM rarely prompted such responses. Accordingly, a three-point scale was derived in which a rating of "1" was recorded if death was introduced on one of the first-named group of cards; and "2" and "3," respectively, for the second and third groups. The total score for a subject was simply the numerical sum of the weighted death references totaled for all twelve cards. On this basis, the lowest possible score was "0" and the maximum score was "24."

All TAT stories were rated without knowledge of the age, marital status, or occupational status of the subject. The only variable known to the rater was the sex of the respondent.

While measurement of the amount of death concern was the principal aim of the research, an additional judgment was made to indicate the extent of appearance of three types of affects in the TAT stories, viz., anxiety, guilt, and depression. These measures were rated simply on a two-point scale. A rating of one was recorded if the affect was mentioned; zero if it was not. The criteria used by the raters to evaluate these affect states were the commonly accepted manifest clinical indices used in clinical evaluation of TAT protocols. Correlations between two raters in scoring for affects were .81 for anxiety, .79 for guilt, and .77 for depression, all of which are statistically significant. Two scores on each affect dimension were determined for each individual, one the sum of affects across all cards presented to a subject, and the second the sum of affects only on those cards to which the subject responded with a story involving death. The first score is thus an indication of the general intensity of each affect for the individual, and the second score indicates which affect is associated with death concern for him.

RESULTS

Table 2 presents characteristics of the distribution of death concern scores for the three age groups. For the purpose of comparison of the

Table 2. Distribution of death concern scores

		Death score	
Group	*Range*	*Mean*	*Median*
I	1–10	4.9	4
II	1–12	4.2	4
III	1–8	3.6	4
Total	1–12	4.4	4

death scores with other variables, the median death score of "4" was used to separate the subjects into groups of high and low death concern.

Personality factors

The hypothesis relating to the importance of personality factors in relation to death concern was tested by comparing scores on certain selected scales of the MMPI with death concern scores by means of the chi-square test. The results appear in Table 3 and may be summarized as follows: (1) higher death concerns were exhibited by those subjects who also scored significantly higher on these MMPI dimensions: hypochondriasis, hysteria, dependency, and impulsivity; (2) a suggestive but not significant relationship appeared between high death concern and high score on the depression scale; and (3) no significant relationships appeared between death concern and any of the other MMPI

Table 3. Relationship of death concern to MMPI personality
measures, health attitudes, and affect states

Variable	N^a	Significant level of chi-square tests[b]
Demographic factors		
Age	58	N.S.
Sex	58	N.S.
Occupational status	58	N.S.
Marital status	58	N.S.
Education	58	N S
Personality factors (MMPI)		
Hypochondriasis	47	P < .01
Depression	52	P < .10 > .05
Hysteria	52	P < .05
Psychasthenia	52	N.S.
Paranoia	48	N.S.
Schizophrenia	47	N.S.
Hypomania	47	N.S.
Ego Strength (Barron)	47	N.S.
Social Introversion	47	N.S.
Anxiety (Welsh)	47	N.S.
Repression-Denial (Gough)	47	N.S.
Dependency (Navran)	47	P < .05
Impulsivity (Gough)	47	P < .05
Neuroticism (Winne)	47	N.S.
Health attitudes (CMI)		
Sections A–L (physical)	58	P <.005
Sections M–R (psychiatric)	58	P <.05
All sections (physical and psychiatric)	58	P <.025
Affect states		
Anxiety	58	N.S.
Guilt	58	N.S.
Depression	58	P <.05

[a] Not all subjects received all the MMPI scales because the population at the
time of study was utilized simultaneously for other research projects which precluded administration of all the scales.
[b] One-tailed.

scales. Thus high death concern seems to be related to certain neurotic
tendencies, but unrelated to the tested demographic variables.

Health attitudes

In order to test the hypothesis relating death concern to health
attitude, the death concern scores were compared with CMI scores by
means of the chi-square test. The scores on the CMI were the number
of "yeses" checked in each section. For sections A–L the median was
12; for sections M–R the median was 3; and for all sections, the
median was 19. (The median was used to differentiate high and low
scorers.) Results showed that: (1) those individuals who report a
multitude of physical symptoms (CMI sections A–L) exhibit sig-

nificantly more death concern than those who admit to fewer somatic complaints; (2) those subjects who list more psychiatric complaints (CMI sections M–R) manifest more death concerns than those who check few or no psychiatric symptoms; (3) those subjects who admit both to more physical and psychological disturbance show higher death concerns significantly more than those who list fewer such health complaints.

Affect states

Ratings of affects across all cards for a subject (general affect tendencies) were compared with affect ratings on only those cards in which the subject mentioned death. These sets of ratings were almost perfectly positively correlated. There were no statistically significant differences as to the kinds of affects that accompanied the TAT productions, whether or not a death was mentioned.

The type of affective state most frequently appearing was depression. Guilt and anxiety occurred approximately equally, and about half as frequently, on the average, as depression in that order. These proportions remained constant for the different age groups and for the two sexes.

Tests were then made of the relationship between death concern and affect. The findings are shown in Table 3. Concern about death in these older persons seems to be accompanied by depressive affect rather than by anxiety or guilt.

DISCUSSION

These findings tend to corroborate some of those of Swenson (1958) who reported no demonstrable relationship between type of death attitude and sex, age, and occupational status. On the other hand, the results of this study suggest some relationships to certain MMPI scales which Swenson's investigation did not. Further, while Swenson suggested that more educated aged individuals face death more readily than the less educated, this research reveals no significant differences in respect to education.

Some of the inconsistencies may be resolved by reference to the difference in measuring techniques. Swenson relied on responses to questionnaire items, while this study used ambiguous projective stimuli, i.e., TAT cards. The subjects in this study were uninformed as to the particular area being studied, while Swenson's subjects were confronted with direct questions about death. Certainly some defensive behavior can be expected in the latter situation.

The lack of demonstrable relationships between death concerns as operationally defined in this study and certain demographic variables requires comment. It might have been predicted, for instance, that females would express more death concern because they tend to be more expressive in fantasy than males (Lindzey and Goldberg, 1953). While this observation may apply to certain areas which carry special social restrictions for the females, e.g., sex, it apparently does not include the concerns over death.

When the findings in relation to personality variables are examined more closely, several important suggestions emerge. The high scorers on the dimensions of hypochondriasis (HS), hysteria (Hy), dependency (Dp), and impulsivity (Im) demonstrated significantly more death concerns than low scorers. At the same time, there were no significant relationships between death concern and the measures of hypomania, paranoia, schizophrenia, anxiety, and psychasthenia. The implication is that the profile of those subjects with high death concerns tends more to be like the neurotic than the psychotic. As May (1950) stated, "It may be that whenever concern about death arises, it is best to work first on the assumption that neurotic elements may be present. . . ."

The type of neurotic constellation suggested by these findings is that of preoccupation and withdrawal into body symptoms, dependence, affective liability, and depression. The lack of relationship of high death concern to anxiety and psychasthenia suggests that those who have preconscious death concern do not have anxiety of the free-floating or obsessive variety; rather, the anxiety tends to be attached to bodily symptoms. This statement seems to be partly corroborated by the finding on the CMI data, i.e., the more frequent the reporting of physical symptoms, the higher the death concern. It is important to note that the CMI elicits attitude toward health, not necessarily the actual physical status of the respondent. The strongest relationships are suggested by the subjects who admit to many physical symptoms on the CMI and also score high on the hypochondriasis scale of the MMPI.

The finding that those persons who report more psychiatric symptoms on the CMI evidence more death concern than those who check fewer symptoms, tends to be consistent with the neurotic pattern exhibited on the MMPI scales.

The examination of the data in relation to type of affect introduced tended to substantiate some previously reported work (Busse *et al.*,

1955). The most prominent affect, of the three measured, both in cards which had death as an outcome and in those which did not, was that of depression. The fact that anxiety occurred less frequently than depression points to several possibilities: (1) it corroborates, at the projective level, the relative lack of anxiety exhibited on the MMPI; (2) it indicates that death concerns do not necessarily mean the arousal of anxiety; rather, concern over it is accompanied by some somatizing and withdrawal tendencies.

The findings suggested no variation with age in predominant kind of affect. In part this may be due to the simplicity of the measuring device, for Busse and associates (1955) observed in their elderly subjects reported changes with age in the frequency and depth of depressive feelings.

The findings of this study are based on intragroup differences among a normal, apparently healthy, aged population. The amount and type of death concern can be inferred only from these comparisons. Further research should include a younger sample to test age differences in a longer time context than afforded by this study, perhaps aiming at some kind of developmental explanation. In addition, institutionalized aged samples might be studied because such a population could be expected to manifest different attitudes toward death, perhaps as a response to their institutional setting or as a reaction to more pathological health states. Finally, both young and old persons who are in the actual process of dying from terminal-type diseases might serve as a focus of study to assess the handling of death concerns as it is influenced by knowledge of impending death. Ideally, a study with strict controls for age, health, and mental status is needed to ferret out the kinds of complex interactive factors that contribute to death concern.

One comment should be made regarding the measuring technique used in this study: admittedly the TAT is a complex vehicle for expression of certain fantasy states. The scoring scheme used here, though leading to some quantifiable results, can be further refined and elaborated. For example, the circumstances under which the fantasied deaths occur in the TAT stories can be categorized; also, the death responses on the TAT can be studied in relation to autobiographical material such as actual experiences with death of loved ones. Both of these are logical next steps in the examination of factors that influence death concern.

SUMMARY

This study focused on certain anticipated correlates of death concerns among a sample of 58 normal aging individuals. Twelve TAT cards were used to elicit death concerns, and two questionnaires, the MMPI and CMI, were used to measure personality characteristics and health attitudes.

As predicted, there was no relationship of high death concern to such demographic variables as age, sex, occupational status (retired or working), marital status, or education; but high death concern was associated with high scores on the MMPI dimensions of hypochondriasis, hysteria, dependency, and impulsivity. This finding was interpreted to mean that concern over death involves neurotic preoccupation, particularly in relation to bodily symptoms. The interpretation tended to be confirmed by the relationship of high death concern to high scores on both the physical and psychiatric disturbance sections on the CMI.

REFERENCES

Alexander, I. E., and Adlerstein, A. M. 1959. Death and religion. *In* H. Feifel (ed.), The meaning of death, pp. 271–83. New York: McGraw-Hill Book Co.

Busse, E. W., Barnes, R. H., Silverman, A. J., Thaler, Margaret, and Frost, L. L. 1955. Studies of the processes of aging. X. The strengths and weaknesses of psychic functioning in the aged. Am. J. Psychiat., 111: 896–901.

Feifel, H. 1955. Attitudes of mentally ill patients toward death. J. Nerv. & Ment. Dis., 122: 375–80.

———— (ed.). 1959. The meaning of death. New York: McGraw-Hill Book Co.

Lindzey, G., and Goldberg, M. 1953. Motivational differences between male and female as measured by the Thematic Apperception Test. J. Personality, 22: 101–17.

May, R. 1950. The meaning of anxiety. New York: Ronald Press.

Murray, H. A. 1943. Manual of Thematic Apperception Test. Cambridge, Mass.: Harvard University.

Nagy, Maria. 1948. The child's theories concerning death. J. Genet. Psychol., 73: 3–27.

Swenson, W. M. 1958. A study of death attitudes in the gerontic population and their relationship to certain measurable physical and social characteristics. (Unpublished Ph.D. dissertation, University of Minnesota.)

Wahl, C. W. 1958. The fear of death. Bull. Menninger Clin., 22: 214–23.

Attitudes toward Death in an Aged Population

WENDELL M. SWENSON

WHAT are some of the characteristics of the "death contemplation"? Is it a construct that exists in all persons? If so, with what does it vary or to what does it relate? How do old people deal with the problem of death? As they grow less and less productive in our society, do they have less and less desire to live? The present investigation attempts to answer in part some of these provocative questions.

A search of the literature for psychologically oriented investigations of the death-attitude construct yields few reports, in spite of the fact that the published studies cover a span of more than 60 years.

In 1896, Scott published a paper entitled "Old Age and Death." Of 16 persons called "old people," whose mean age was 76 years, 94 percent said they would not care to live their lives over again. Seventy percent "longed to die," and 14 percent felt that life was "not worth living now." Scott concluded that most of the "dwelling upon death" takes place during adolescence (Scott, 1896).

Chandler (1950) later revised and brought up to date Scott and Hall's original questionnaire on death. In answer to the question, "Do you worry about dying or the hereafter more or less than formerly?" Chandler found that the great majority of the 950 professional men questioned denied entertaining any increased worry.

Klopfer (1947) studied attitudes toward death in the aged by analyzing responses to ten Thematic Apperception Test (TAT) cards, and concluded that fear of death among people in a home for the aged was significantly lessened when greater activity was possible for such persons.

Shrut (1955) studied attitudes toward death in older Hebrew women by means of clinical impressions of responses to the TAT and a sentence completion test. He found that: "Subjects residing in an environment more closely approximating their pre-institutional homes or domestic environment (apartment residence) revealed lesser fear of death. . . ."

More recently, Feifel (1956) interviewed 40 Caucasian male veterans of World War I who were either physically ill or otherwise unable to support themselves. He concluded that these men had two dominant outlooks: one group visualized death as the dissolution of bodily life and the doorway to a new life, and the other group looked at death with a "philosophic resignation," as "the end."

A recently published book edited by the same author (Feifel, 1959) yields no further studies specifically designed for the objective evaluation of attitudes toward death in elderly people. Feifel's own chapter in this book elaborates to some degree the study just mentioned.

THE SAMPLE

In the present investigation 210 persons were studied, all 60 years of age or more and all residents of Minnesota. They were contacted through homes for the aged, golden age clubs, and organizations and industries scattered throughout the state that employ persons more than 60 years old. It is estimated that approximately 65 percent of the attending members of the golden age clubs with whom contact was established cooperated in some part of the study, and that approximately 40 percent of the persons reached in rest homes cooperated. Although the point is more difficult to determine because of the method by which contact was made, approximately 75 percent of the employed persons solicited cooperated in the study.

The sample consisted of 152 females and 58 males. Table 1 gives a specific description of the sample in respect to age, education, work status, marital status, urban-rural residence, and religious activity. Certain sampling biases are obvious. The group is heavily loaded with females and there is a preponderance of Protestants in the group. A large majority of the group come from urban surroundings. There may be other more subtle biases, but they are not explicit in the data.

THE METHOD

Two separate methods of evaluating attitudes toward death were used. The first was a check list of death attitudes. Written essays describing attitudes toward death were obtained from 34 persons (not included in the final study) 50 years old or more. These essays were methodically examined by the investigator, and a check list was de-

Table 1. *Characteristics of the sample*

Chief characteristics	Male (N = 58)	Female (N = 152)
Age		
60–69	17	49
70–79	24	62
80+	17	41
Education		
Grade school	25	70
High school	15	49
College	17	32
Not stated	1	1
Work status		
Full time	15	16
Part time	6	12
Retired, no work	28	61
Physically unable to work	7	40
Housekeeping for husband	0	22
Not stated	2	1
Marital status		
Single	3	26
Separated	3	9
Married	31	25
Widowed	20	91
Not stated	1	1
Urban or nonurban		
Urban	42	108
Nonurban	15	42
Not stated	1	2
Religious activity[a]		
Regular	38	108
Some	18	38
None	1	4
Not stated	1	2

[a] Protestant: 75 percent, Catholic: 10 percent, no religious affiliation: 15 percent.

vised containing 35 descriptive statements as reproduced in the following:

We all think about death at some time or other. Below are a number of words or phrases that can be used in some way to describe *your* attitudes or feelings as you think of death. Go through the list quickly and put a mark (X) in front of any word or phrase that describes your *present* feelings about death. Don't spend too much time on any one, but be sure to check all those which describe your feelings. You can help most by being as frank and as truthful as you can. Remember, your name doesn't appear anywhere on these sheets.

1. Happiness

B 2. Don't think about it

A   3. Glorious happy life
     4. Pleasant
     5. Sadness
     6. The end of everything
     7. Fear leaving loved ones
A   8. It will be wonderful
A   9. All troubles will be over
    10. Something you face every day
    11. Promise of new and better life
    12. Terror overcomes me
    13. Very difficult to accept it
A   14. Most beautiful experience of all
B   15. I don't think about death
    16. Everyone's time is set
    17. I fear death
B   18. Don't dwell on it at my age
A   19. I look forward to death
A   20. Peaceful bliss
    21. Many more "living" things to think about
A   22. Enter into true Paradise
    23. Think of Hell's torments
B   24. Don't waste time thinking about it
B   25. Feel fine and no reason to think about it
    26. It disturbs me a great deal
A   27. It gladdens my heart
    28. Have nothing to do with the subject
    29. Deliverance from all this pain and difficulty
    30. All God's wonderful promises will come true
    31. No doubt a grim experience
B   32. Still a long way off
    33. Death is as sure as taxes
    34. Dread the thought of it
    35. All that I read in the Bible will come true

The 8 items marked A constitute cluster A; the 6 marked B constitute cluster B.

A second measuring instrument was a forced-choice rating scale on which the subject summarized his attitudes toward death as follows:

A wonderful experience to look forward to
Look forward to it
Just don't think about it
Think of it with some fear
Very fearful of it
None of these fit my feelings

There was also developed a 22-item check list on interests, hobbies, and activities. The recipients were asked to check any of the hobbies or activities in which they had taken part during the previous year and to check whether they engaged in these activities "often" or "sometimes." Some examples are: senior citizens' clubs; sewing, knitting, or other fancywork; listening to music; traveling; gardening or flower raising; and card playing, checkers, or chess.

The Minnesota Multiphasic Personality Inventory (MMPI) (Hathaway and McKinley, 1945) was employed primarily to obtain: (1) a measure of devotion to religion as defined by a "religiosity scale" previously developed by Cottrell [1] (this scale measured primarily the fundamentalist type of religious attitude with items such as "I believe in a life hereafter," "I go to church almost once a week," "I read the Bible several times a week"), and (2) a measure of latitude of interest by means of use of the "interest items" in the MMPI item pool. Of the 210 persons, 95 cooperated in completing the MMPI and provided valid profiles.

RESULTS

Determination of clusters of items on the death-attitude check list was done on an empirical basis. Tabulation of the frequency of checks for each of the items and for each of the respondents was made. The relationship or overlap between any two items in the check list was determined. A ratio was calculated between the expected and the actual frequencies of each pair of items. A table of these ratios was used for obtaining a basis of related items. When the relationship of these item pairs was compared, two distinct clusters evolved. The 8 items forming cluster A (items 3, 8, 9, 14, 19, 20, 22, and 27) seem to describe a positive or forward-looking attitude toward death, whereas the 6 items in cluster B (items 2, 15, 18, 24, 25, and 32) form what might be labeled an "actively evasive" attitude toward death.

Each of the 210 persons was given a score on cluster A and on cluster B. The group was then divided into three subgroups:

A: High in cluster A and low in cluster B (82 persons)
B: Low in cluster A and high in cluster B (71 persons)
C: Either zero or equal score in both clusters A and B (57 persons).

Group C could be best described as persons who were either very indecisive about their attitudes toward death or "passively evasive" about them. It is significant that the cluster analysis yielded no significant "fearful of death" cluster.

[1] Lilian Cottrell, "An MMPI Scale for the Measurement of Religiosity," unpublished.

The rating scale of attitudes toward death yielded four groups of subjects as shown in Table 2.

Table 2

Group	Composition	Label	Number of persons
1	Items 1 or 4	Positive	96
2	Item 2	Active-evasive	55
3	Items 3 or 5	Negative	21
4	Item 6 or no response	Passive-evasive	38

This rating scale of attitudes toward death elicited a "fearful of death" response from only 10 percent of the respondents.

The results from both the check list and the rating scale were checked against all the variables listed in Table 1. Results are based upon the construction of a series of contingency tables from which chi-square was derived to determine the statistical significance of the relationships. These chi-square calculations appear in Table 3.

Table 3. Relationships between attitudes toward death and various physical and social characteristics

Characteristic	Instrument	χ^2	p
Religious activity	rating	18.06	.01
Religious activity	check list	13.67	.01
MMPI rel score	check list	16.74	.01
Home living conditions	check list	15.23	.01
Level of education	rating	16.80	.01
Home living conditions	rating	14.95	.02
Marital status	check list	10.53	.04
MMPI interest score	check list	10.70	.04
Self-concept of health	check list	10.32	.04
Sex	check list	5.80	.06
MMPI rel score	rating	11.65	.07
Number of hobbies and activity	check list	8.71	.08
Level of education	check list	7.36	.11
Age	rating	9.96	.13
Source of income	check list	5.88	.19
MMPI interest score	rating	8.20	.23
Source of income	rating	10.22	.32
Sex	rating	3.34	.35
Marital status	rating	6.19	.40
Occupational status	rating	5.61	.50
Number of hobbies and activity	rating	4.68	.60
Age	check list	2.60	.60
Occupational status	check list	2.60	.75
Urban versus nonurban	check list	0.07	.79
Urban versus nonurban	rating	0.67	.88
Self-concept of health	rating	2.27	.90

A summary of some of the significant findings shown in Table 3 is as follows:

Both a check list and a rating scale can be used to measure attitudes toward death in older persons.

The check list shows significant relationships with other variables more than twice as frequently as does the rating scale, suggesting the greater sensitivity of the check list.

There is a significant relationship between religiosity and attitudes toward death as measured by both religious activity and the MMPI rel scale. Persons with more fundamental religious convictions and habits look forward to death more than do those with less fundamental convictions and less activity. Fearful attitudes toward death tend to be found in those persons with little religious activity.

There is a significant relationship between home living conditions and attitudes toward death. Persons residing in homes for the aged have a more positive, forward-looking attitude than do those who live alone, these latter persons tending actively to evade issues related to death. Fear of death is found more often in those living alone than in those living with relatives or in homes for the aged.

There is a tendency for less-educated persons to be evasive in regard to their attitudes toward death, whereas persons who have finished college express themselves more specifically, either looking forward to the experience positively or fearing it.

Three other characteristics show less clear, but still suggestive, relationship with attitudes toward death:

Marital status. Widowed persons passively evade the issue of death, whereas single, separated, and married persons tend to look forward to death.

Latitude of interest. Persons indicating that they have a large number of outside interests tend to be actively evasive concerning the subject of death, and those who report only a few activities refuse to commit themselves at all (passive-evasive) on the matter.

Health. Persons who reported good health were most often actively evasive in considering death. Those reporting poor health most often looked forward to death in a positive manner.

None of the other characteristics listed—age, sex, source of income, occupational status, or urban-rural location—manifested any significant relationship with attitudes toward death.

COMMENT

Within the framework of the specific observations just enumerated, a number of conclusions seem justified.

It is apparent that attitudes toward death can be measured by a structured psychometric device. Projective technics apparently are not the only tools that can be used to elicit specific information about contemplation of death.

It is apparent that the aged person does not often admit to a fear of death. In fact he either looks forward to death or tends to be evasive in his contemplation of the experience of death. Investigators postulating a relatively common "fear of death" in the persons they study probably have resorted to subjective or indirect inferences.

Religion apparently plays a very significant role in the aged person's attitude toward death. Since a large percentage of persons interrogated in this investigation identified themselves with some form of the Christian religion, it seems logical to infer that the eschatologically oriented person contemplates death in a positive manner.

People in homes for the aged look forward to death much more than do those living outside of institutions. The data suggested that solitary existence in old age is somewhat associated with a fearful contemplation of the experience of death.

The relationship between education and attitudes toward death is difficult to interpret. It is possible to infer that the experience of death is a very complex one to contemplate and that it is therefore directly considered (either with fear or with a forward-looking attitude) only by those persons of above-average intelligence.

Certainly, additional objective investigations conducted with the use of structured personality devices are indicated.

REFERENCES

Chandler, A. R. 1950. Attitudes of superior groups towards retirement and old age. J. Gerontol., 5: 254–61.

Feifel, H. 1956. Older persons look at death. Geriatrics, 11: 127–30.

———— (ed.) 1959. The meaning of death. New York: McGraw-Hill Book Co.

Hathaway, S. R., and McKinley, J. C. 1945. Manual for the Minnesota Multiphasic Personality Inventory. New York: Psychological Corp.

Klopfer, W. G. 1947. Attitudes toward death in the aged. (Unpublished Ph.D. dissertation.) City College of New York.

Scott, C. A. 1896. Old age and death. Am. J. Psychol., 8: 67–122.

Shrut, S. D. 1955. Old age and death attitudes. (Unpublished Ph.D. dissertation.) New York University.

Attitudes of Older Persons toward Death:
A Preliminary Study

FRANCES C. JEFFERS, CLAUDE R. NICHOLS,

AND CARL EISDORFER

SCHELER (1953) has said that death is viewed by mankind merely as the end point of aging. It may be, however, that attitudes toward death have a direct effect upon adjustment and upon attitudes toward life. The first step in research undertaken to test this hypothesis will necessarily be an exploration of methods to determine attitudes toward death; second, to see what these attitudes may be; and third, to investigate to what other factors these attitudes may be related.

A few earlier studies bear upon these points. Feifel (1956, 1959), for instance, studied Caucasian male veterans living at a Veteran's Administration domiciliary. When asked "What does death mean to you?" 40 percent expressed religious belief, with a new life expected after death; 10 percent thought death would mean relief and a peaceful sleep; 10 percent did not know. When asked, "What do you think happens to us after we die?" 25 percent said, "When you're dead, you're dead"; 60 percent had some religious orientation, with hope of a hereafter (15 percent of those who thought death was the end now asserted a belief in some kind of hereafter); 10 percent still did not known; and 5 percent thought it would mean a long sound sleep.

In another study on what age groups least and most fear death, 45 percent of Feifel's (1956) same older subjects thought that people most feared death in the seventies and beyond, "because you're close to it then; you're at the end of your rope"; 15 percent thought the most feared period was in the forties and 15 percent saw it as in the twenties. On the other hand, old age was singled out by 35 percent of the older subjects as the time most people *least* feared death because, "You accept and are resigned to it; you've lived your life." The inference was that certain people fear idleness and uselessness in old age more than they do death.

This investigation was performed with the support of the USPHS grants M-900, M-2109, and H-3582, Dr. E. W. Busse, principal investigator.

Feifel found that there was a religious outlook evident in those 48 percent who "occasionally" and those 20 percent who "frequently" thought about death, as distinguished from the 32 percent who "rarely" thought about it. He also reported that older persons who are religiously inclined give more thought to concepts about death than do those to whom death represents the inexorable end. Do the former master their anxiety about death by thinking of it as a precursor of a new life? It was interesting that 77 percent of this older age group viewed old age as "the end of the line," with only 15 percent seeing it as a time of leisure and contentment. In conclusion, Feifel pointed out that his data pertained to conscious and public attitudes of his respondees more than to the deeper layers of the personality.

Shrut (1958) compared attitudes toward death of a group of 30 ambulatory aged Causasian female residents in the apartment section of the Home for Aged and Infirm Hebrews in New York with those of 30 similar persons who lived in the larger and more institutionalized Central House of the same home. He used clinical impressions based on a sentence completion test and 10 TAT cards, plus three questionnaires on health, adjustment, and participation in activities. He found that the subjects living in the apartments, which were more like their previous living arrangements, showed less fear of or preoccupation with death; which might mean, he said, that they enjoyed better mental health. He reported that both groups of subjects revealed at least mild anxiety with regard to thoughts of death.

Bromberg and Schilder (1933) studied responses to a series of questions on death given by 70 normal adults of various ages and by mental patients in whom death thoughts were prominent (Schilder, 1942). They concluded that, "There seemed to be no essential difference as far as age of the subject was concerned. . . . It is possible to correlate closely the attitudes toward one's own death with attitudes toward death of other people."

Faunce and Fulton (1958) have reported that "emotional responses suggesting either fear of death or of the dead were more frequent among spiritually oriented than among temporally oriented individuals."

THE DATA

As part of a 2-day series of examinations involving a variety of disciplines, the bi-racial group of 260 community volunteers, 60 years of age and older, were asked, during the course of a 2-hour social history interview, "Are you afraid to die?" and "Do you believe in a life after death?"

Fear of death

Answers to the first question were distributed as shown in Table 1.

Table 1. Percentages of answers to "Are you afraid to die?" (N = 254)

Yes	10
No	35
Want to live as long as possible	13
Dread pain of dying	2
Mixed feelings (balanced ambivalence)	16
Don't want to be sick or dependent a long time	4
It's inevitable	17
Other elaboration	3

Fear of death was explored in relation to 52 other variables: demographic (race, age, sex, marital status, education); physical (functional rating, cardiac status, symptom count); psychological (taken from three WAIS and four Rorschach ratings); psychiatric (classification, subjective emotional reaction, hypochondriasis); and social (activities, attitudes, self health rating and concern, religious items, adjustment ratings). Analysis by chi-square yielded the statistically significant associations shown in Table 2.

Table 2. Fear of death in relation to other variables

Variable	χ^2 level of confidence
Less belief in life after death	.01
Less frequent Bible reading	.01
Feelings of rejection and depression	.05
Lower full-scale IQ	.05
Lower performance IQ	.001
Fewer number of Rorschach responses	.02
Fewer leisure activities	.10

Since many of the older subjects answered the question, "Are you afraid to die?" in religious terminology, an analysis of these answers yielded the following associations (chi-square significant at the .001 level). The *unqualified no* answers were associated with religious terminology. The answers suggesting *ambivalence* were associated with an absence of religious connotations. The answers *admitting fear of death* tended to have no religious connotation.

It therefore appears that the factors associated with *no* fear of death include a tendency to read the Bible often, more belief in a future life, reference to death with more religious connotations, fewer feelings of rejection and depression, higher scores on full-scale and performance IQ, and more responses on the Rorschach (with the suggestion also of more leisure activities).

Belief in afterlife

The inquiry on belief in life after death revealed that very few of the subjects denied such a belief outright. Only 2 percent said "No"; 21 percent said "Not sure"; and 77 percent said, "Yes, sure of it."

Belief in life after death was examined in relation to 37 demographic, physical, psychological, psychiatric, and social variables. Statistically significant associations were obtained for 10 of these variables (Table 3).

Table 3. Belief in afterlife in relation to other variables

Variables	χ^2 level of confidence
Less fear of death	.01
More frequent church attendance	.01
More frequent Bible reading	.001
Greater number of religious activities	.001
Stronger religious attitudes	.001
Feeling that religion is the most important thing in life	.001
Less depression (psychiatric rating)	.001
Lower scores on full-scale IQ	.02
Lower socioeconomic status	.05
More women than men	.05
Lower level of education	.10

Religious activities and attitudes appear to be the most important variables associated with belief in life after death, but depression, intelligence, and socioeconomic status are also probably associated.

CLINICAL IMPRESSIONS

The clinical impressions and experience of the present investigators, who have had extensive study and contact not only with the 260 community volunteer subjects in the present group but also with other groups of older persons during the past 6 years or more, may be useful in interpreting the empirical data.

As Schilder (1942) has suggested, there may be no common human idea of death, but it may be an extremely individualized concept. He hypothesized that individual experiences become the determining factor for the picture which one develops of death. Gardner Murphy, in his discussion of the contributions to Feifel's book (1959) concludes that, "It is apparent that fear of death is not psychologically homogeneous at all, even in a narrowly defined cultural group." (p. 335.)

The technique of direct questioning may be inappropriate for reaching the real feelings of the subject, even though in the present study the questions were asked near the end of a social history taken in an informal setting; and even though the interviewer was previously known to the subject and good rapport had been established. In addition, in all such inquiries, a semantic factor which needs clarification is that of differentiation between the words "death" and "dying."

Bearing in mind that the subjects were community volunteers living in their own homes and neighborhoods, and following Shrut's finding (1958) that those older persons having less institutionalized living arrangements show less fear of or preoccupation with death, it is perhaps to be anticipated that only a small proportion of the present sample should express fear of death.

Religion is a very great part of community life in the North Carolina region in which the study was carried out. Only 6 percent of these older subjects had no church membership. It is accordingly to be expected that most of them would think of death in religious terminology.

The distribution of responses to the question, "Are you afraid to die?" (Table 1) confirms the clinical impressions of the Duke geriatrics research group that denial is a very important mechanism for dealing with anxiety in old age. The mental mechanism of denial may be among the most common adaptive techniques employed in personality adjustment by persons beyond the fifth decade of life. Its use may be promoted chiefly by three factors: (1) perceptual distortions (as suggested by Linn, 1953) during the later period of life due to concomitant changes in cortical and receptor processes; (2) changes in body image with age and chronic disease; this parallels the frequent utilization of this same regressive maneuver by younger persons who have devastating chronic disease; (3) gradual deterioration of the central nervous system, which causes reversal of the mental processes toward those of early childhood, when the denial mechanism of unacceptable reality situations is quite universally utilized.

SUGGESTED TECHNIQUES FOR STUDYING ATTITUDES TOWARD DEATH

It is the feeling of the investigators that fear of death and illness plays an important part in the unconscious psychological life of the individual, but it is clearly evident that much further research is needed in this area. Several avenues are suggested for the further study of attitudes of older persons toward death.

Direct questioning has certain advantages, even though, as Feifel (1956) has noted, the answers to direct questions tap the conscious and public attitudes of the subjects rather than the deeper layers of the personality. Direct questioning on the topic of death may prove too threatening to aged or ill persons, and such affects need to be given careful consideration. We have, however, found a willingness on the part of older subjects to speak freely on the topic of death. This confirms the finding of Beard (1956) in her study of centenarians who, she said, have "no morbid fears about death or any special reticence in discussing it."

Clinical depth interviews, preferably repeated through time, would doubtless be the most valuable single method for determining an individual's attitudes toward death. Considerations of staff time and of the psychotherapy which might be involved necessarily limit the widespread utilization of this method.

Projective methods such as focused thematic pictures, sentence completions, and word association tests specifically designed to elicit responses to death and illness are fruitful methods. The sorting of TAT responses, as has been done by Neugarten and Gutmann (1958), and the utilization of sentence completion data for assessing attitudes, as by Golde and Kogan (1959) and their colleagues, provide possible models for dealing with such data.

The work of Osgood *et al.* (1957), Nunnally and Kittross (1958), and more recently that of Altrocchi and Eisdorfer (to be published) suggests that semantic differential procedures are useful for assessing attitudes toward such concepts as illness, death, and dependency.

It would also be useful to obtain psychophysiological correlates of the aged person's discussion of concepts involving death. Psychophysiological measurements could be studied either as a measure of the response to focused projective material or in conjunction with a series of interviews designed to elicit the aged individual's affects and his defensive techniques in dealing with feelings in this area.

Acknowledgment.   The authors wish to express their gratitude to Mrs. Dorothy Heyman for her assistance in this study.

REFERENCES

Altrocchi, J., and Eisdorfer, G. A comparison of attitudes toward old age, mental illness and other concepts. *In* Wilma Donahue, C. Tibbitts, and R. H. Williams (eds.), Psychological and social processes of aging: an international research seminar. To be published.

Beard, Belle B. 1956. Social adjustment in extreme old age. (Paper presented at the First Pan-American Congress on Gerontology, Mexico City).

Bromberg, W., and Schilder, P. 1933. Death and dying: a comparative study of attitudes and mental reactions toward death and dying. Psychoanal. Rev., 20: 133–85.

Faunce, W. A., and Fulton, R. L. 1958. The sociology of death: a neglected area of research. Social Forces, 3: 205–9.

Feifel, H. 1956. Older persons look at death. Geriatrics, 11: 127–30.

——— (ed.) 1959. The meaning of death. New York: McGraw-Hill Book Co.

Golde, Peggy, and Kogan, N. 1959. A sentence completion procedure for assessing attitudes toward old people. J. Gerontol., 14, 355–63.

Linn, L. 1953. The role of perception in the mechanism of denial. J. Am. Psychoanal. Assoc., 1: 690–705.

Neugarten, Bernice L., and Gutmann, D. L. 1958. Age-sex roles and personality in middle age: a thematic apperception study. Psychol. Monogr., 72: (470) No. 17, 1–33.

Nunnally, J., and Kittross, J. M. 1958. Public attitudes toward mental health professions. Am. Psychologist, 13: 589–94.

Osgood, C. E., Suci, G. J., and Tannenbaum, P. H. 1957. The measurement of meaning. Urbana, Ill.: University of Illinois Press.

Scheler, M. 1953. Tod und Fortleben. Schriften aus dem Nachlass, Berlin.

Schilder, P. 1942. Goals and desires of man. New York: Columbia University Press.

Shrut, S. D. 1958. Attitudes toward old age and death. Ment. Hygiene, 42: 259–66.

Attitudes toward Death among a Group
of Acute Geriatric Psychiatric Patients

ADOLPH E. CHRIST

CAN one broach the topic of death with a group of debilitated psychiatrically disturbed geriatric patients whose death is imminent? With the increased interest in the study of death (Ficarra, 1960; Guttentag, 1959; Natanson, 1959) and living man's relation to its inevitability, some systematic evaluation of how different population groups (Feifel, 1959) deal with this problem is useful to patients and physicians alike, and a prerequisite to the formulation of a thanatology (Eissler, 1955).

This is a pilot study to determine how a group of geriatric psychiatric patients felt about the topic of death. The data are based on interviews of 100 consecutive patients admitted during the last 3 months of 1959 to the psychiatric wards of the San Francisco General Hospital. Each patient in this group was 60 years or older, had lived in San Francisco for 1 or more years prior to his hospitalization, and had not required psychiatric treatment prior to the age of 60.

Of the 100 patients, 62 were questioned and were able to respond concerning their attitudes toward death. The death questions used are as follows:

Have you had any friends or relatives who have recently been in the hospital, and what happened to them?
How old do you wish to get, and how old do you expect to get?
How is your physical health?
Have you talked about death with anyone before? If not, why not? If yes, what was said?

This study was made in the course of work with the Studies in Geriatric Mental Illness, a multidisciplinary undertaking affiliated with the Langley Porter Neuropsychiatric Institute. The studies are under the direction of Dr. Alexander Simon, and are supported by Grant No. 3M–9145(C1S1) from the National Institute of Mental Health.

What is your feeling about death?

Have you made any plans for the future? Do you have a will, a burial plot, or any plans following your death? What are they?

How do you feel about capital punishment, about mercy killing?

If a patient is going to die soon, should the doctor tell him? Would you want to be told? Would you want . . . (nearest relative or friend) to be told if he were going to die soon?

If you had the choice of dying tomorrow or being bedridden for the next three years, which would you choose?

If you had the choice of dying tomorrow or being in severe pain for a year, but knew you would be O.K. at the end of that time, which would you choose?

How did you feel about our talk about death? Do you think doctors in general should talk about death with their patients?

With regard to the other 38 patients, the interviewer was at first fearful that a discussion of death would upset the more severely dis-oriented, disorganized, or delusional patients. As the study pro-gressed, however, it was found that those patients who could respond at all to the questions about death gave meaningful answers. There-fore, more and more seriously disturbed patients were drawn into the sample, until in the last half of the group only the deaf, aphasic, or comatose patients were excluded. None of the patients became so upset consequently that the hospital staff noticed an adverse behavioral change. To obtain more meaningful responses, the death questions were introduced in as personal and unstructured a way as possible during the course of a psychiatric and neurological examination. One-third of the patients, however, fell asleep, became delusional, became markedly irritable or angry, became more disoriented, or attempted to leave the interviewer, so that it was necessary to explain the re-search nature of the death questions before the examination was com-pleted.

While discussing the topic of death with this group of psychiatric patients, the interviewer wanted to gather data on the following four questions. What is the physician's subjective impression of patients' reactions to a discussion of death? Would a more objective test, such as the word association test, substantiate the interviewer's subjective impression? Are there any factors such as age, religion, schooling, etc., which may be associated with the patients' adjustment to the inevitability of his own death? What is the expressed opinion of these patients on various questions dealing directly and indirectly with death? The findings will be given as answers to these four questions.

FINDINGS
Physician's impressions

The interviewer felt that all but two of the patients were considerably upset about death and used denial, suppression, and repression as defenses. For example, a chronic alcoholic woman, whose husband had suddenly and unexpectedly died 5 days before her admission, required hospitalization because of severe intoxication. When asked her feelings about her husband's death, she seemed perplexed. She then spoke of the settlement of his estate. Although the interviewer attempted to bring out her feelings about the impact of her husband's death on her future, she could not discuss it. She stated that she had not thought or talked about death before this discussion. In contrast, a woman with a large fungating necrotic carcinoma of the breast spoke quite freely and with relief that she was in a situation where she could speak about death. She discussed the pros and cons of having a radical mastectomy, saying that she seriously wondered whether she should prolong her life—probably only to live in pain.

Since 55 of the 62 patients were judged to require supervision at least at night because of physical illness or incapacitation (although all had been hospitalized for psychiatric reasons), and because 5 of the 62 died within a few days of the examination, one can speculate that their psychiatric symptoms might in part have been an outgrowth of this marked conscious denial of death.

Word association test

Half the patients were asked to respond to the words: food, sleep, water, sickness, hospital, family, doctor, to leave, milk, dying. The interviewer postulated that longer association time to the death words than to the other words is correlated with greater anxiety about death. With these patients the association time to the word "dying" was longer than the association times to the other nine words. (Statistically, using the t test, the difference obtained could occur by chance alone less than five times out of one hundred.)

With the second half of the patients the word "grave" was substituted for "sickness," and "death" was substituted for "to leave." The average of the association times to the three death words was also longer than the average of the association times to the seven other words. (Again, this difference could occur by chance alone less than five times out of one hundred.) The associations to the death words were often more bizarre and produced more blocking. Also, these words were more often than the other words not heard by the patient. These findings would substantiate the subjective impression of the examiner that these patients were anxious about death.

Background factors

To determine whether there were any factors in the patients' backgrounds that might have decreased their anxiety about death, the patients were first grouped into those who were more and those who were less afraid of death. To do this, four clinicians (two psychiatrists and two clinical psychologists on the teaching staff of the Langley Porter Neuropsychiatric Institute) were asked to rate the death questions as to their validity as a test of fear of death, and a scale was devised as follows.

The patient has some plan following his death, such as a will: yes, rated 0; no, rated 1.

During the talk about death the patient made one or more spontaneous statements about death and showed appropriate affect, rated 0. If he made no spontaneous statement or treated the topic blandly, he is rated 1. If he gives one-word answers or shows anger or resentment at being questioned about death he is rated 2. If he becomes abusively angry or markedly suspicious he is rated 3.

In the word association test used with the first half of the patients, if the word "dying" was the longest of the ten, the patient is rated 2: if it was the second longest word, rated 1; otherwise, rated 0. With the second half of the patients where "death," "dying," and "grave" were used, if the average association time of these three words is longer than the average association time of the other seven words, rated 1. One additional point is given if one of the three death words was the longest association time of all the words. If neither of these is the case, the patient is rated 0.

The patient has talked about death or dying before this interview: yes, rated 0; no, rated 1.

The patient wants to be told of his own imminent death by a physician: yes, rated 0; no, rated 1.

The patient would want his relative or friend told if the relative (friend) were terminally ill: yes, rated 0; no, rated 1.

The patient is asked, "How is your physical health?" If he says good, and his health is judged by a physician as "can live alone or needs assistance only at night for physical reasons," rated 0. If he says good, but is judged by a physician as needing almost full-time assistance for physical reasons, rated 1. If he says good, but he is judged by a physician as needing full-time assistance for physical reasons, rated 2.

Scores were computed for 60 patients; and the group was then divided into those with "less fear of death" (N = 26) and those with "more fear of death" (N = 34).

A series of contingency tables were then constructed to investigate the relationship between fear of death and each of six variables, and the distributions tested for significance by use of the x^2 test. The variables were: (1) health (good versus poor); (2) age (60–69 versus 70 or more); (3) religion (Catholic versus Protestant); (4) religiosity (religiously staunch versus religiously indifferent or atheistic); (5) schooling (up to eighth grade versus high school or higher); and (6) sex (male versus female). Of the six variables, only the first proved to be significantly related to fear of death; those patients with better health were less afraid of death than those with poorer health. The negative findings with regard to the other five variables do not agree with the findings from other studies. For instance, Feifel (1959) states, "The religious person, when compared to the non-religious individual, is personally more afraid of death" (p. 121), but this was not borne out in the present study. Later Feifel states, "Women tend to think more frequently about death than do men" (although "We should not forget that there is no necessary relationship between thinking about death and fear of death") (p. 119). The present study indicates that in this group of geriatric psychiatric patients, men and women are equally afraid of death.

Patients' expressed opinions

Of the 62 patients, 54 had never talked to anyone about death or dying before this interview. This agrees with Feifel's statement (1959), "It is noteworthy that in all the groups, particularly that of mentally ill patients, some find thinking about death so anxiety provoking as to deny having any ideas at all about it." (p. 117.) This is particularly striking in the present study because most of the patients came from homes or hotels with a large population of older people; many had had friends or relatives who had recently died. One patient did state, "Oh, yes, but my family immediately say, 'Why do you have to talk about such a morbid topic? You should be grateful to be alive!' "

One-third of the patients stated that they had a will or some other plan for the disposal of their effects after their death. One-third had no interest in discussing this topic; and one-third stated, "The state will take care of that." Of 48 patients, 23 favored capital punishment, 4 were noncommital, the rest were against it. Ten patients favored mercy killing, about half of them making a restriction; one said, "Yes, but you should have a priest, a lawyer, the patient, and three doctors there at the time of decision." Most of those who were against euthenasia were markedly angry and agitated; for example, one said, "The doctor should be put to death!"

To the question, "If a patient is going to die soon should the doctor tell him?" 23 of 47 patients said yes, and all said they personally would want to be told. A few volunteered that they wanted to know only a few days or hours beforehand "so I could get myself ready, but not too long, or I would get too upset." Those who did not want to be told were often defensive; one said, "There are too many times when the doctor is wrong." This one question aroused the most anxiety, and with about 30 percent it was necessary to explain that the question was part of a research project and did not refer to them personally. When asked, "Would you want . . . (closest relative or friend) to be told if he were going to die soon?" 17 of 35 said no, 4 refused to commit themselves, the rest said yes.

When asked to choose between being bedridden for the next 3 years or dying tomorrow, 15 of 32 patients chose dying, 8 refused to say, and 10 chose living. When asked, "If you had a choice of dying tomorrow or being in severe pain for a year, but knew you would be O.K. at the end of that time," 14 of 32 chose living, 10 refused to commit themselves, and the rest chose dying.

When at the end of the interview it was explained that the questions were for research and had nothing to do with their specific situation, almost all the patients showed signs of decreased anxiety. Asked how they had felt about the questions on death, and whether doctors in general should discuss death with their patients, 17 of 57 stated they had enjoyed the discussion, or had been grateful or proud to have been asked these questions. Another 17 stated that they did not mind talking about it, or had accepted talking about it in a bland, emotionally uninvolved way; and 23 ranged from saying that they were fearful of the questions to stating that they disliked talking about death. A very few of these 23 became frankly suspicious or abusively hostile.

SUMMARY AND DISCUSSION

One hundred acute psychiatric geriatric patients consecutively admitted to the San Francisco General Hospital were examined in this pilot study. Sixty-two could give relevant answers to most of the questions on their attitudes toward death. The patients were fearful of death, but as a whole were willing, and in some cases were relieved to discuss it. Even some physically terminally ill patients with severe psychiatric symptoms were able to discuss the topic, at times with evident relief.

It has been said that the topic of death is as taboo today as the topic of sex was during the nineteenth century. Since the direct outcome of many diseases in this age group is death, it would appear that it is the physician's duty to acquaint his patients with this fact and to help them deal with the attendant fears. Eighty-nine percent of the patients in this study needed supervision at least at night because of physical illness, and 87 percent stated they had never talked about death or dying before. One can speculate that at least some of their psychiatric symptoms, which often included fear of being poisoned, killed or thrown out of their homes, as well as frank, somatic delusions, may be symptoms of marked denial of death. It would seem that with this marked denial of death it becomes incumbent on the physician to broach the topic with his patient, and not to wait for the patient to raise the question of his approaching death.

Acknowledgment. Dr. Lawrence Katz, Associate Research Psychologist with the Geriatrics Research Project, has given invaluable aid with the statistical analysis.

REFERENCES

Eissler, K. R. 1955. The psychiatrist and the dying patient. New York: International Universities Press.

Feifel, H. (ed.) 1959. The meaning of death. New York: McGraw-Hill Book Co.

Ficarra, B. J. 1960. Psychologic management of the aged surgical patient. J. Am. Geriatrics Soc., 8: 55–61.

Guttentag, O. E. 1959. The meaning of death in medical theory. Stanford Med. Bull., 17: 165–70.

Natanson, M. 1959. Death and situation. Am. Imago, 16: 447–57.

PSYCHOLOGY OF AGING:

EXPERIMENTAL STUDIES

Organized by

JAMES E. BIRREN

National Institute of Mental Health, Public Health Service,

Bethesda, Maryland

ALAN T. WELFORD

St. John's College, Cambridge University,

Cambridge, England

Age Changes in the Times Taken by Choice, Discrimination, and the Control of Movement

A. T. WELFORD

AN important advance in the study of sensory-motor performance was made when Hick (1952) showed choice reaction times to follow an information theory law. The subject in a choice reaction task can be regarded as gaining information, in the information theory sense, at a constant rate, and this rate can be regarded as a measure of his capacity for this kind of task. The same approach has been extended to discrimination tasks (Crossman, 1955; Welford, 1960) and to the control of movement (Fitts, 1954; Crossman, 1957). In each of these areas several sets of results, obtained under widely different conditions, confirm the general formulation, although in each area there are results which do not fit and so indicate that other factors have important effects in certain circumstances. A review and reappraisal of this work has recently been made by the present author (1960).

Hick's law may be stated as:

$$T = a + b \log N,$$

with meanings attached to the symbols as follows.

Choice reaction times. T = reaction time and N = the effective number of equiprobable choices open to the subject.

Reaction times for discriminating between two magnitudes. T = reaction time and N = the ratio of the larger of the two magnitudes to the difference between them. The subject can be conceived as having to "choose" the difference between the two magnitudes out of a total represented by the larger.

Time taken to make accurate movements to a target. T = movement time and N = the ratio between the distance from the starting

This paper is reprinted from *Gerontologia* by permission of the editor. Figure 1 is reproduced from Crossman and Szafran's (1956) paper by permission of the authors. Figures 3 and 4 are reproduced from the present author's paper (1960) by permission of the publishers.

point to the far edge of the target and the distance between the near and far edges of the target. The subject may be thought of as "choosing" the target width out of a total distance to the far edge of the target.

In all cases *a* and *b* are constants, and with normal subjects in their twenties *a* appears to be zero if care is taken to exclude from the measured reaction (or movement) time all elements which do not properly belong to it such as time lags in the experimental apparatus.

It is pertinent to ask whether age effects can be represented as an increase in *a* or in *b*. The latter would indicate a decrease in capacity for choice, discrimination, or movement control as the case might be. The former would imply the operation of some additional factor outside the process being studied. The question thus opens up an approach to the location and analysis of slowness of performance among older people.

It should be said at once that evidence regarding age effects in all three areas is conflicting. The purpose of this paper is to bring the evidence together and to suggest reasons why the discrepancies arise.

CHOICE TIMES

The first results obtained with a view to answering the present question were those of Crossman and Szafran (1956) who required their subjects to sort a pack of ordinary playing cards into red, black, the four suits, or the four suits separating court cards from the rest. The subjects thus performed a sorting task requiring in different trials two, four, or eight choices. The time per pack was taken by stopwatch and from this the average time per card was calculated. The time per card was conceived as consisting of two portions: first, a *movement* time, i.e., the time taken to turn up the card from the pack, which was held face down, and to place the card on its appropriate pile; second, a *choice* time, i.e., the time required to identify which class of card it was and on which pile it should go. An estimate of movement time was obtained by having the subjects place the cards on two piles alternately so that no choice was involved. Choice time was inferred by subtracting the movement time ascertained in this way from the time per card.

The results are shown in Fig. 1 in which times have been plotted against the logarithm of the number of classes into which the subject was sorting. The trends are quite clear: the times taken by the youngest subjects rise approximately linearly, in accordance with

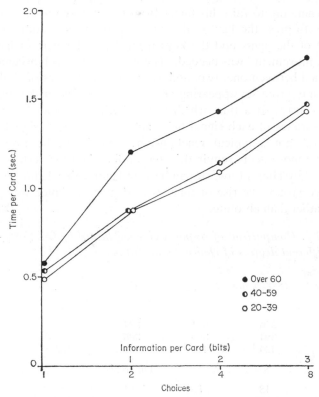

Fig. 1. Times taken to sort playing cards into various numbers of categories, in an experiment by Crossman and Szafran
There were 15 subjects in the youngest age range, 14 in the middle, and 19 in the oldest. The times are the averages for sorting three packs of 52 cards at each level of choice.

Hick's Law, from the time taken to place the cards alternately. The times for the older subjects at each degree of choice are longer by an approximately constant amount. This slowing with age cannot be accounted for by a lengthening of movement time since the times taken to place the cards alternately were closely similar at all ages. The slowing is therefore to be described as an increase of *a* in Eq. (1) due to some factor other than movement.

A different pattern of results is shown in an experiment which had previously been reported by Goldfarb (1941). The subject in this was confronted by a display of 5 lights arranged in a semicircle. By each light, and toward the center, was a key, and there was an additional key in the center of the semicircle. The subject's task was, when a light came on, to raise his finger from this last key and, as soon as possible, to press the key by the light which had just come on. The distance of the lights and the keys from the center was such that "a full arm movement" was needed. The number of possible signal lights was varied between one, two, and five in different series of trials, each light in any given set appearing at random. A click in the apparatus which occurred at a time which varied between 2 and 4 sec before the appearance of each signal light, acted as a "ready" signal. Goldfarb's was not a typical reaction-time experiment because of the large arm-movements required in responding, and the results are not well fitted by Hick's Law. It can be seen from Table 1, however, that in all age groups the rise of times with degree of choice was proportional rather than absolute.

Table 1. Comparison of response times obtained by Goldfarb for different degrees of choice, by age range

Number of signals	18–24 years	25–34 years	35–44 years	45–54 years	55–64 years
			Response times (in milliseconds)		
1	376	321	334	366	387
2	394	380	395	436	451
5	429	418	432	472	495
			Differences[a]		
2–1	18	59	61	70	64
5–1	53	97	98	106	108
5–2	35	38	37	36	44
			Proportions[a]		
1/2	.96	.85	.85	.84	.86
1/5	.88	.77	.77	.78	.78
2/5	.92	.91	.91	.92	.91

[a] The proportions are clearly more uniform from one age group to another than are the differences.

The same result was found with a somewhat similar task by Griew (1958, 1959). The apparatus consisted of eight light bulbs arranged in a semicircle of 5-in. radius. Close by each, toward the center, was a metal disk 1 in. in diameter. The subject's task was, when a light appeared, to raise a stylus from a center disk and to move it as fast as possible to the outer disk corresponding to the one on which the light was situated. The experiment was administered to different groups of subjects under two different conditions: one in which each signal was given separately about 2 sec after a warning

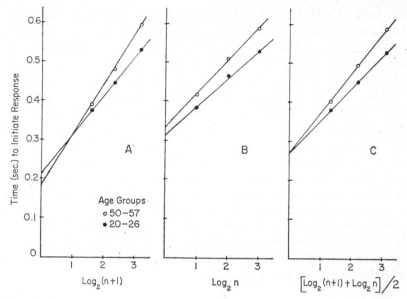

Fig. 2. Response times in relation to degree of choice, from an experiment by Griew

(a) Discontinuous presentation of signals; (b) continuous presentation; (c) means of A and B. Each point in (a) and (b) is the mean of 240 readings, 20 from each of 12 subjects, obtained after twice this amount of practice.

signal, and another in which a new signal came on at once when the subject returned his stylus to the center disk.

In different trials two, four, and eight possible lights were used with equal frequency. Two times were recorded: first, the time to raise the stylus from the center plate, and, second, the time between doing so and reaching the indicated disk. The second is a movement time and, as in Crossman and Szafran's experiment, differed little with age. The first time can be regarded as a reaction time, and results for the two age groups are shown in Fig. 2.

In the discontinuous condition, the subject does not know the precise moment at which the signal is coming and thus has to guard against premature or false reactions. This necessity can be conceived as adding one to the number of possible states he has to distinguish— instead of having to distinguish between states corresponding to signals $1, 2, 3, \ldots, n$, he must distinguish between states corresponding to signals $0, 1, 2, 3, \ldots, n$. Times are therefore plotted against log $(n + 1)$ with $n =$ the number of lights used. In the continuous condition the subject brought on the signals for himself and thus did not have to guard against premature or false reactions. The times have therefore been plotted against log n. Plotting the times from the discontinuous condition against log n or those from the continuous condition against log $(n + 1)$ did not give as good fits as those shown. The problem of when to use log n versus log $(n + 1)$ is discussed by Hick (1952) and by Welford (1960). For each condition the responses in half the trials were simply to touch the indicated disks, and in the other half to insert the stylus into a small hole in the indicated disk—a more accurate response. The points shown are the means for both types of trial taken together.

It can be seen that Hick's law fits reasonably well and that the times for the two age groups differ mainly by an amount which is not constant but proportional: such a constant difference as exists at the intercept is small and is in opposite directions for the two conditions. In other words, the age effect is shown not as a rise of a in Eq. (1), but as an increase in the slope constant b. There is here a clear conflict with the results of Crossman and Szafran.

DISCRIMINATION TIMES

In the experiments just reviewed, degree of choice was varied while the discriminability of signals was held above the level at which it might limit performance. Age effects with choice held constant and discriminability systematically varied have been studied in an experiment by Birren and Botwinick (1955). Pairs of lines were exposed side by side in a tachistoscope. The longer line was 80 mm and the shorter from 1 to 50 percent less. In half the exposures the longer line was on the right and in half it was on the left. The subject recorded his judgments by means of a voice key saying "right" or "left" according to which line he considered the longer. The lines were exposed for 2 sec so that with few exceptions they were on view until after the subject's judgment had been given.

The results are shown in Fig. 3 plotted in terms of Eq. (1) with $N = x_1/(x_1 - x_2)$ where x_1 is the longer and x_2 the shorter of the lines being compared. The figure of 1.32 percent given for the finest discrimination is the average for the two pairs of lines nominally 1 percent different, one of which was found to differ by rather more than the correct amount. It can be seen that the times within each age group for discriminations between 50 and 15 percent are approximately equal, and from this point to 1.32 percent they rise linearly. Regression lines were fitted to the points from 10 to 1.32 percent

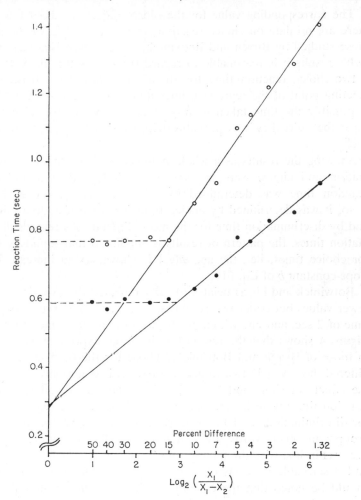

Fig. 3. Times taken to discriminate between lines of different lengths, in an experiment by Birren and Botwinick

Open circles: subjects aged 61–91; filled circles: subjects aged 19–36. Each point is the mean of the medians of 43 older or 30 younger subjects. The medians were each based on at least four readings.

by the method of least squares and those for the two different age groups were found to meet approximately at the zero information line. The difference between the point of their intersection and the time taken by the younger subjects for discriminations of 50 to 15 percent is about 0.3 sec which is about the value usually obtained for two-choice reaction times.

The corresponding value for the older subjects is about 0.5 sec—there are no data on choice reaction times for subjects of the age of those studied by Birren and Botwinick, but extrapolating from Goldfarb's results it is reasonable to regard 0.5 sec as the likely value of a two-choice reaction time for them. The difference between the meeting point of the regression lines and zero time (about 0.28 sec) is possibly the time taken to pronounce the word "right" or "left" since the voice key was probably tripped by the final "t" sound of each.

Viewing the results as a whole it looks as if the tasks of discrimination and choice were in some sense independent and that the reaction time was determined by whichever process took longer. If so, it was determined by choice time for the easier discrimination and by discrimination time for the more difficult. As regards discrimination times, the pattern of results is similar to that found by Griew for choice times, i.e., the age effect is shown as an increase in the slope constant b of Eq. (1).

Botwinick and his associates (1958) repeated the experiment using fewer values but under two conditions: one with the original exposure time of 2 sec, and one with a much shorter exposure time of 0.15 sec. Figure 4 shows that the results for the 2-sec exposures were similar to those of Birren and Botwinick. Those for the 0.15-sec exposures differed, however, in two respects. First, as is commonly found when the effects of short and long stimuli are compared, all the average reaction times were faster. Second, the slopes of the regression lines for discriminations of 10 to 1.32 percent were equal for the two age groups; in other words, the difference of discrimination time with age was in line with the findings of Crossman and Szafran for choice, and describable in terms of a rise in the constant a in Eq. (1). It should be noted that the equality of slope was not achieved by the older subjects at the expense of accuracy. Many errors were made by both age groups with the brief exposures, but the proportions of errors were about equal for older and younger.

There is thus again the conflict of evidence found for choice times, as to whether the age effect is in terms of a or b in Eq. (1), but this time it occurs between the results from two conditions of the same experiment.

The results of Botwinick et al. for brief exposures are also in line with those of two further experiments by Crossman and Szafran (1956); in one subjects sorted packs of cards according to numbers of spots on them, and in the other they sorted series of weights into "lighter" and "heavier." The main sense data in the latter experiment

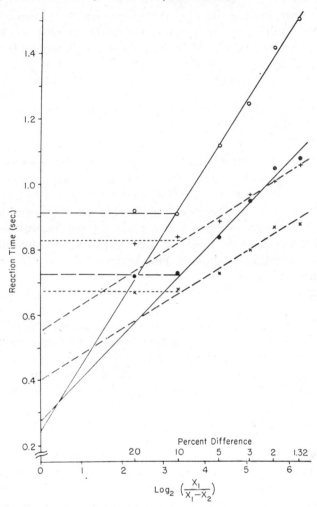

Fig. 4. Times taken to discriminate between lines of different lengths, in an experiment by Botwinick et al.

Results are indicated as follows. Age range 65–79: exposure time, 2.00 sec (open circle), 0.15 sec (plus sign); age range 18–35: exposure time, 2.00 sec (filled circle), 0.15 sec (multiplication sign). Each point is the mean of the medians of 34 older or 26 younger subjects. The medians were each based on eight readings.

are likely to have arisen from the initial lifting rather than from holding the weight in the hand once it had been raised, so that it is fair to regard the signals in this case as brief. The times taken to sort both cards and weights became longer as the differences between the classes became finer, but the rise of time with age was by an amount which tended to diminish rather than increase as the fineness of discrimination became greater. Certainly, it could not be described in terms of a proportional rise.

MOVEMENT TIMES

Evidence relating age systematically to the accuracy and speed of movement is extremely limited, and only one, somewhat preliminary experiment by A. T. Welford (see Welford, 1958) will be considered. The subject "tapped" rapidly back and forth with a stylus made of plastic rod ½ in. in diameter between two circular targets set either 1 ft or 2 ft between centers, in such a way that movements were made from side to side across the body. The targets were holes either 2 in. or 1 in. in diameter in Masonite board, immediately underneath which were other pieces of Masonite which when struck made electrical contacts and thus enabled the beginning and end of each "tap" to be recorded.

Preliminary examination of the results indicated that the times spent on the targets should be added to those spent moving from one to another when calculating the average "time per movement" and over-all rate of information transfer. The average times were plotted against log $(A + \frac{1}{2}w)/w$, with A taken as the distance between centers and w taken as the clearance between the stylus and the target holes. The quantity 2 was thus ½ in. with the 1-in. targets, and 1½ ins. with the 2-in. targets. An alternative way of expressing $(A + \frac{1}{2}w)/w$ is to write $d_1/(d_1 - d_2)$, with d_1 and d_2 as the distances to the far and near edges, respectively, of the "target," i.e., of the target hole less the diameter of the stylus. This alternative expression is clearly similar to that used for discrimination in Figs. 3 and 4.

The four points, one for each target size at each distance, for any one age group, did not fall upon a single line as they would be expected to do from Fitts' exposition—the times taken with the large targets were relatively longer than those taken with the small. This may indicate that some modification is required of the method of calculating $(d_1 - d_2)$, or else that for some reason the subjects were not making full use of the tolerances provided by the larger targets. As this result occurred with all age groups, however, it is not of concern in the present discussion.

Figure 5a shows that the points for a given target size at different

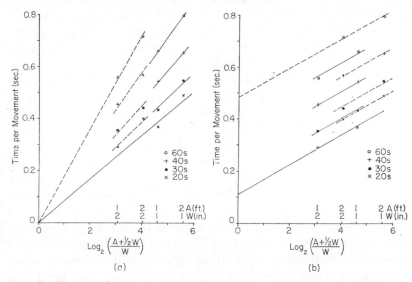

Fig. 5. Times taken for tapping between two targets
(a) At different distances with the same target size; (b) with different target sizes at the same distance. Each point is the mean of about 40 readings from each of 8 subjects.

distances fall roughly on a set of regression lines radiating from the origin and becoming steeper with age. The points for different target sizes at the same distance, however, fall roughly on a set of parallel lines, which cut the intercept at points which become progressively higher as age advances, as shown in Fig. 5b. The data points in Figs. 5a and 5b are of course the same so that there is here a conflict similar to that found before, but this time in the results of a single experiment. The regression for distance, holding target size constant, shows a proportional rise with age, i.e., of the slope *b* in Eq. (1). The regression for target size, holding distance constant, shows a rise with age of an absolute amount, i.e., of the constant *a* in Eq. (1).

DISCUSSION

The clearest relationship between this conflict and an experimental variable is in the results of Botwinick *et al.* (1958) on discrimination, and in seeking an explanation it seems best to start with these. Two questions arise: first, why should the difference of exposure time have so markedly changed the age effect, and, second, will an explanation of this case also fit the others?

With regard to the first question, results for short exposures indicate that the older subjects took longer to deal with *any* signal, however easy or difficult. The extra time cannot have been taken in the choice of response because if it had been it would have raised the time required for the easy discriminations which were limited by choice time but have left the more difficult unaffected. The slowing with age must therefore have occurred in some process of perception or of receiving the signal which preceded the discrimination of longer from shorter. The slowing may tentatively be attributed to "neural noise" early in the chain of perceptual mechanisms, as suggested by Crossman and Szafran (1956) in connection with their results and by Gregory (1959) to account for the higher differential thresholds he found to occur among older subjects.

The results of Botwinick and associates for short exposures further suggest that once a signal has been received, the actual process of discrimination can be achieved as rapidly by older subjects as by younger. Crossman and Szafran recognized the same point in relation to their results. If this is so, however, why should there be an age difference of slope with long exposures? It is obvious that once the exposure has ceased, continued inspection of the material is impossible and that no further data can be gathered. There may be some brief aftereffects or storage between the sense organ and the perceptual mechanism (Broadbent, 1958, Welford, to be published), but this will rapidly decay, so that the subject will gain little or nothing by delaying his reaction, and may indeed lose information.

With a brief exposure a subject is therefore likely to react quickly. When exposure is longer a subject will go on inspecting material until a stage is reached at which the data gathered are in some way "sufficient." If this process occurred at a conscious level, one would say that the subject gathered data until he was *confident* in his judgment, and that the results obtained by Botwinick and associates indicated that older people required relatively more data for confidence than for accuracy. Almost certainly the process is not conscious, or not always so, and in any case the term "confidence" is subjective. It is therefore preferable to say that there is some mechanism for stopping the intake of data when enough have been gathered, and that this mechanism becomes sluggish or impaired with age. Such an impairment would affect performance only with long exposures, since with short exposures, the intake of data would be stopped by the cessation of the signal. Some mechanism of this kind seems highly probable on general grounds, quite apart from the present results, although, so far as the writer is aware, evidence concerning it has not been systematically examined.

If this view is correct, reaction times for discrimination tasks will be limited either by the time taken to receive a signal, or by the time taken to terminate the reception of data, whichever is longer. This would mean that when long exposures were given, results for progressively more difficult discriminations would follow the regression line for *short* exposures until this cut the regression line for long exposures. Unfortunately it is not possible to see from the results of Botwinick and associates whether or not this was so, because the time taken for easier discriminations was limited by the time needed to make the required choice of responding action.

Can the other results which have been surveyed be explained in the same way? More specifically, with regard to choice times, can Crossman and Szafran's card-sorting tasks be regarded as having presented a short exposure and Goldfarb's and Griew's experiments as having given a long one? Observation of subjects in card-sorting experiments suggests that they normally take a brief look at each card and then transfer their attention to finding the pile on which the card is to go. The "signal" in the design on the card is therefore, in effect, exposed to the subject's view for only a short time. In Goldfarb's and Griew's apparatus the lights were immediately next to the corresponding keys or disks, and were thus in full view the whole time until the subject had completed the response. It is reasonable therefore, in these experiments, to regard the exposure as having been long.

If the same explanation is to cover the results for speed of movement, it is necessary to postulate that *distance* acted as a long signal and *target size* as a brief one. We may think of a movement of the duration under consideration here as aimed approximately at the target, and as subject to minor modifications during its progress and to a major modification near the end, the latter being made in order to achieve the final hit on the target. This much is a fair inference from detailed studies of movement (e.g. Vince, 1948) and from the fact that most of the difference in time taken by movements of different degrees of accuracy seems to occur in the final portion of the movement near the target (Annett *et al.*, 1958).

The subject can make slight modifications to the distance at which his movement is aimed, and can thus go on taking in data about distance, until quite late in the execution of a movement; in other words, he does not have to "close his sample" quickly. The distance aimed at can thus be reasonably regarded as producing a signal of long duration. The final adjustment made to hit the target, however, appears to involve a complex, fine modification of the movement which probably takes into account its velocity and the position the hand has arrived at a short time before the target is reached. Since the position of the hand is continually changing, the signal for the final modification is inevitably almost instantaneous unless some very complex integration of position in time can be made, or unless the movement is actually brought to a halt just before the target is reached.

These explanations are very much *post hoc,* and it is, of course, not *necessary* that one explanation should apply throughout discrimination, choice, and the control of movement. What is clear is that there are two very different types of age effect which recur in three rather distinct stages of sensory motor function. The attempt to explain these effects points to the need for a considerable amount of further study. This would almost certainly yield important knowledge about the sensory motor mechanisms in general, quite apart from an insight into changes that come with increasing age.

SUMMARY

Researches on sensory-motor performance not specifically related to aging have shown that speed of several kinds of performance can be described by a formula of the type:

$$T = a + b \log N.$$

These are: (1) Choice reaction times, where $T =$ reaction time and $N =$ the effective number of equiprobable choices open to the subject; (2) Reaction times for discriminating between two magnitudes, where T again equals reaction time and $N =$ the ratio of the larger of the two magnitudes to the difference between them. (3) Time taken to make accurate movements to a target, where $T =$ movement time and $N =$ the ratio between the distance from the starting point to the far edge of the target and the distance between the near and far edges of the target. In all cases a and b are constants.

Age effects are shown in some cases of each kind of performance as an increase in $a,$ and in others as an increase in $b.$ The reasons for the discrepancies between different results are not clear, but detailed examination of performances and inferences about the mechanisms underlying them suggests that the increase of a with age occurs when the signals for action are effectively brief, and an increase of *b* when their effective duration is longer.

REFERENCES

Annett, J., Golby, C. W., and Kay, H. 1958. The measurements of elements in an assembly task—the information output of the human motor system. Quart. J. Exper. Psychol., 10: 1–11.

Birren, J. E., and Botwinick, J. 1955. Speed of response as a function of perceptual difficulty and age. J. Gerontol., 10: 433–36.

Botwinick, J., Brinley, J. F., and Robbin, J. S. 1958. The interaction effects of perceptual difficulty and stimulus exposure time on age differences in speed and accuracy of response. Gerontologia, 2: 1–10.

Broadbent, D. E. 1958. Perception and communication. London: Pergamon Press.

Crossman, E. R. F. W. 1955. The measurement of discriminability. Quart. J. Exper. Psychol., 7: 176–95.

——— 1957. The speed and accuracy of simple hand movements. *In* E. R. F. W. Crossman and W. D. Deymour (eds.), The nature and acquisition of industrial skills.

———, and Szafran, J. 1956. Changes with age in the speed of information intake and discrimination. Experientia Supplementum, 4: 128–35.

Fitts, P. M. 1954. The information capacity of the human motor system in controlling the amplitude of movement. J. Exper. Psychol., 47: 381–91.

Goldfarb, W. 1941. An investigation of reaction time in older adults and its relationship to certain observed mental test patterns. ("Teachers College Contributions to Education" No. 831.) New York: Columbia University Press.

Gregory, R. L. 1959. Increase in "neurological noise" as a factor in ageing. *In* Proceedings of the Fourth Congress, International Association of Gerontology, Merano, Italy, 1, 314–24. Fidenza: Tipografia Tito Mattioli.

Griew, S. 1958. Some industrial and experimental studies of ageing. (Unpublished Ph.D. thesis, University of Bristol.)

——— 1959. Complexity of response and time of initiating responses in relation to age. Am. J. Psychol., 72: 83–88.

Hick, W. E. 1952. On the rate of gain of information. Quart. J. Exper. Psychol., 4: 11–26.

Vince, Margaret A. 1948. Corrective movements in a pursuit task. Quart. J. Exper. Psychol., 1: 85–103.

Welford, A. T. 1958. Ageing and human skill. London: Oxford University Press.

——— 1960. The measurement of sensory-motor performance: survey and reappraisal of twelve years' progress. Ergonomics, 3: 189–230.

——— Social, psychological, and physiological gerontology: an experimental psychologist's approach. *In* Wilma Donahue, C. Tibbitts, and R. H. Williams (eds.), Psychological and social processes of aging: an international research seminar. To be published.

Performance of Young and Elderly Persons on Embedded-Figure Tasks in Two Sensory Modalities

LOUIS D. COHEN AND SEYMOUR AXELROD

THERE is evidence that compared with younger subjects elderly subjects show poorer performance on tasks requiring the identification of ambiguous visual figures (Basowitz and Korchin, 1957), and on tasks involving embedded visual figures in which the subject is required to extract a simple two-dimensional figure from a complex one so designed as to embed the simple figure in a compelling and confusing ground (Gottschaldt, 1926; Thurstone, 1944; Crook et al., 1958).

These findings of deficit have been derived from visual tasks, and the question can be raised whether the results are modality-specific or whether there is cross-modality communality. Working with brain-damaged and control subjects Teuber and Weinstein (1956) have demonstrated deficits in the performance of brain-damaged subjects on visual embedded-figure tasks, the performance deficit being unrelated to the locus and extent of the lesion. While such deficits may be considered a consequence of specific central visual disturbance, Teuber and Weinstein (1956, p. 2) suggest as another possibility the view of Goldstein (1927) that "The deficit may . . . represent a basic disturbance which transcends the visual sense modality. . . ." Teuber and Weinstein speculated on the modality-generality of the deficit; however, lacking nonvisual analogues of the visual task they could not explore the question of transcendence.

The study to be described here undertakes to explore the performance of young and elderly subjects on both a visual and tactile version of an embedded-figure task. These questions will be asked: Are performances on the visual and tactile embedded-figure tasks related? To what extent do "lower-level" (threshold) sensory mechanisms relate to performances on the complex task; are they independent of

Acknowledgment is due for the support of the Center for the Study of Aging, Duke University, and to the National Institutes of Health, Grants M–2109 and H–3582.

each other or is deficit on the complex performances associated with heightened thresholds?

METHOD

There were two groups of subjects: 19 young men, ranging from 21–34 years of age (mean 27.8) with an educational range of 2–14 grades (mean 10.6), most recently employed in the local factories of Durham, North Carolina; and 30 men ranging from 62–78 years of age (mean 68.8) with an educational range of 2–17 grades (mean 7.5), and a varied work background similar to that of the younger group. All subjects were recruited from the Durham office of the North Carolina Employment Security Commission and were paid for their participation on an hourly basis. While the method of recruitment was planned to provide groups differing only in age, there were some additional differences that did not seem to be overcome easily. Differences in educational level seem in large part due to differences in educational customs at the times the groups were raised. The lower educational experience of the older group is evidently not an indication of lower intellectual ability, since on the WAIS vocabulary subscale the older group had a mean scaled score of 9.2 and the younger group had a mean scaled score of 9.4.

The older group seemed to be eager to find some employment, or at least some time-filling activity, and cooperated actively and seriously. Many of the younger group were recruited during slack periods of their regular employment and were less eager. This difference in their employment situation may account for the discrepancy in group size; there was a smaller pool of young clients at the Commission in the first instance, and less willingness on their part to participate.

In addition to providing interview information on age, occupation, and related material, subjects performed on five tasks.

Near vision was assessed using a test-card printed by the Pennsylvania Optometric Association. The card was placed before the seated subject, and he was permitted to view it from whatever distance he desired. If he wore glasses for near vision, he was asked to put them on. Score was the Jaeger index associated with the smallest size of type he could read.

Light-touch and two-point thresholds were obtained on the thumbs and palms of the two hands. For the former, a set of nylon monofilaments, graded for force exerted when the filament is bent against a surface, were employed. Two-point thresholds were measured by use of a General Hardware vernier caliper whose jaws were machined down to blunt points. Three ascending and three descending trials were given in each of the tactile threshold determinations, according to the method of limits.

The vocabulary subscale of the Wechsler Adult Intelligence Scale (WAIS, Wechsler, 1955) was administered in standard fashion.

A visual embedded-figures task of the Gottschaldt type (Thurstone, 1944) was administered. This task had five parts, each on a separate 8½ in. x 11 in. page. Part I consisted of 27 pairs of figures, the first member of each pair being the sample figure, and the second being a

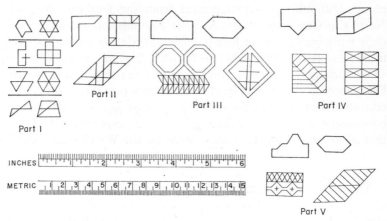

Fig. 1. Items from the visual embedded-figures task (from Thurstone, 1944; after Gottschaldt, 1926)

complex test figure in which the sample was embedded. Part II had a sample figure and seven test figures in each of which the same sample figure was embedded. Part III consisted of two sample figures and seven test figures, in each of which one, but not both, of the samples was embedded. Part IV again had two samples, but 10 test figures. Part V had two samples and 10 test figures. The subject was given a simple example and asked to mark the sample in the test figures. He was instructed to *attempt all items,* and told that there was no time limit, and that although the examiner was timing his performance, accuracy was the important factor. At 30-sec intervals, the examiner recorded the *number of correct items* so far. The subject was encouraged to return to items he had attempted but not marked. Figure 1 shows representative items from each part.

Tactile analogues of 14 of the visual figures were constructed by fixing strips of ⅛-in. balsa wood to enlarged projections of the figures drawn on ¼-in. plywood boards. Figure 2 shows three of these items. For each item, the following procedure was used. *Sample period:* the subject put his hands through an opaque curtain. The experimenter guided the subject's left forefinger twice over the sample, usually starting from the lower left-hand corner of the figure. The subject was then instructed to palpate the sample, with one or both hands, as desired, and to tell the experimenter when he felt he was completely familiar with it. *Test period:* the subject's right hand was then guided to the test figure, and he was required to trace the figure

Fig. 2. Items from the tactile embedded-figures task (the uppermost pair are the example)

corresponding to the sample in the test figure. He was told that he could refer back to the sample figure as often and for as long as he desired, that either or both hands could be used, and that he could palpate the sample and test figures simultaneously or successively. He was instructed to indicate verbally ("That's it") when he was satisfied that he had correctly traced out the sample in the test figure. Upon completion of the procedure with the example, the subject was shown the example board visually. For each item, the experimenter noted the elapsed time between the beginning and end of the test period, and the correctness or incorrectness of the response. In order for an item to be scored "correct," the subject had to trace out the sample figure without duplicating any lines.

RESULTS
Visual

The measure of visual acuity that was used here failed to provide a range of scores of visual sensitivity. All subjects were able to reach a Jaeger index level of J2; most scored at J1 (the best level), suggesting that the visual test served primarily as a screening device to establish minimal levels of visual acuity—all subjects were able to see the test figures clearly enough to perform the complex task.

However, since data were available for 11 of the young subjects and 11 of the elderly subjects on another series of visual tests of greater sensitivity—absolute and differential brightness thresholds—these latter data were examined for relationships between visual

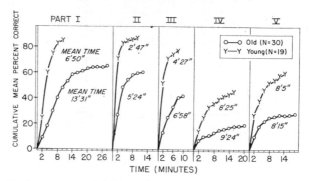

Fig. 3. Performance of old and young subjects on the visual embedded-figures task

acuity and the visual embedded-figures task. Comparisons between the young and old groups on the absolute brightness thresholds—stated in apparent foot candles for a 2-in. square 8 ft from the subject's eye—showed the young with a mean threshold of .000245 apparent foot candles, with the older group's mean threshold at .000627. This difference was reliable at less than the .05 level, but on differential brightness thresholds the young and old were not reliably different in these samples. Absolute brightness threshold was not related to the Gottschaldt performance for these groups: the r for the young group was .02, for the older group, .01.

Returning to the total sample, Fig. 3 shows the performance of the young and old groups on each of the five parts of the visual Gottschaldt task. The abscissa represents time spent at the task, with mean percent correct on the ordinate. The final ordinate in each curve represents the final mean percentage of items correctly identified; the slope indicates the rate at which items were correctly identified. The curves were continued as long as the means continued to rise. Since some subjects continued to work at the task, and to solve items longer than others, increases at various parts of the curves represent solutions of varying numbers of subjects. The differences between the young and old groups are graphically evident; the young were able to identify more items than the older group, and worked more rapidly. For each part of the Gottschaldt task the differences between the young and old in the number of items correctly identified are significant at the .025 level or better.

As may be noted, the mean time spent on each part of the test was longer for the older group—about twice as long for Parts I and II. As the test became more difficult, the time difference between the groups was reduced, and in the last part the total times were almost equal. However, since the young group identified about twice as many items in the latter parts of the test, the older group still required about twice as much time to identify each item.

We may conclude, confirming Crook *et al.* (1958), that the older subjects were slower and identified fewer visual embedded-figures than the young group. We can say further, that there is no relationship between visual acuity (as measured here) and performance on the visual embedded-figure task.

Tactile

As may be seen in Table 1, in all comparisons involving light-touch and two-point thresholds, the younger group was reliably more sensitive than the older group.

In Fig. 4 we have the results of the comparisons between young

Table 1. Comparisons between young and old groups on light-touch and two-point thresholds[a]

Age group	Right palm	Left palm	Right thumb	Left thumb
	Mean light touch (in log 0.1 mg)			
Young (N = 19)	3.14	2.95	2.77	2.51
Old (N = 30)	3.65	3.51	3.53	3.27
	Two-point threshold (in mm)			
Young (N = 19)	6.06	6.36	2.17	2.21
Old (N = 30)	7.33	8.32	3.85	4.04

[a] All differences between young and old were significant at less than the .01 level.

and old on the tactile embedded-figure task. The abscissa represents cumulative test-period time, with the ordinate giving the percentage of items solved. The graph may be understood in terms of assumed time limits. Thus, if the subjects had been allowed 1.5 minutes *per item,* the young group would have completed an average of 55 percent of the 14 items within this time limit, and 60.5 percent if the limit had been 2.5 minutes; the elderly group would have completed 21 percent of the items in less than 1.5 minutes each, and 27 percent in less than 2.5 minutes each. Again, the final ordinate represents the mean percent correct, and the slope represents rate of solution. It is graphically evident that the young group was superior to the old group in the total number of test items correctly completed, and that the young group

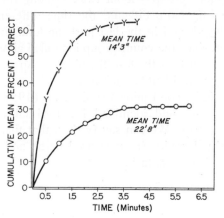

Fig. 4. *Performance of old and young subjects on the tactile embedded-figures task*

completed more figures within any given period of time. The young were also able to complete the total task in much less time. These differences between the young and old were reliable at the .001 level or better.

Table 2. *Correlations among the tactile measures*

	Young ($N = 19$)			Old ($N = 30$)		
Measure	1	2	3	1	2	3
1. Light-touch total		.514[a]	−.086		.213	−.141
2. Two-point total			−.474[a]			−.217
3. Tactile embedded figures (number correct)						

[a] $P < .05$ (one-tail).

In Table 2 are the correlations between the tactile sensitivity measures and scores on the tactile embedded-figure task. For the old group there was no significant relationship between tactile sensitivity (as measured here) and the complex performance, but for the young group the two-point threshold measures were significantly related to tactile embedded-figure scores.

We may conclude, as with the visual tasks, that the older subjects showed lower basic sensitivity, were slower, and identified fewer embedded figures than the younger group. The relationship found between the two-point threshold and the tactile embedded-figure performance in the young group suggested an analysis of covariance to test whether the difference in two-point threshold could account for the difference between the groups in the tactile embedded-figures task. This control of the two-point measure left unchanged the inference concerning group differences in tactile embedded-figure performances —the difference between the groups in tactile sensitivity did not entirely account for the difference in the tactile embedded-figure task.

Relationship between visual and tactile

The contributions to the embedded-figure task performances of the WAIS vocabulary subscale score, our index of intellectual level, were next examined. Table 3 presents these data. As may be noted in the table, there are reliable positive relationships between the WAIS scores and the embedded-figure scores.

Table 3. Correlation table for the young and old groups on the embedded-figures tasks and the WAIS Vocabulary Subscale Score[a]

Tests	Young (N = 19)			Old (N = 30)		
	1	2	3	1	2	3
1. Tactile embedded-figure task		.790[b]	.433[a]		.680[b]	.494[b]
2. Visual embedded-figure task			.530[b]			.410[a]
3. WAIS Vocabulary Subscale						

[a] $P < .05$ (one-tail).
[b] $P < .01$ (one-tail).

In order to control the effects of intelligence (WAIS Vocabulary) on the relationship between the embedded-figure scores, a partial correlation was computed with intelligence partialled out. The relationship between the visual and the tactile embedded-figure task for the young group with intelligence held constant changed from an r of .79 to an r of .73; for the older group it changed from an r of .68 to an r of .60. The partial correlations are still significant at the .01 level.

We may thus conclude that a reliable relationship exists between the visual and tactile embedded-figure tasks, for both young and old groups, independent of intelligence.

DISCUSSION

It is clear from these results that there was a high degree of association between the visual and tactile embedded-figure performances for both the young and old groups, and that the older group was markedly less accurate and slower than the young group on both tasks. Differences in sensory acuity and intelligence level, as measured here, did not account for the differences between the two groups in embedded-figure task performances. The data suggest a cross-modality function, relatively independent of sensory acuity and psychometric intelligence.

Teuber and Weinstein (1956) found not only that their brain-damaged patients were significantly poorer than their controls on the visual embedded-figure task, but that their aphasic patients were reliably poorer than the other brain-damaged patients. The deficit performance of the aphasics could not be attributed to intellectual defects or to specific losses of associations or engrams for linguistic patterns, and the investigators point rather to "a defective organization or selection of material (linguistic as well as nonlinguistic)" which is reflected by the failure in the embedded-figure task as well as in others.

Thurstone (1944), in a factor-analytic study of perceptual tasks, identified the cluster of tasks involving the visual Gottschaldt as requiring "the ability to perform a perceptual closure against some distraction." (p. 101.) Thurstone also noted high loadings in another factor, which he described as involving the manipulation of two configurations simultaneously or in succession. The two factors were related, and were seen to "transcend in significance the immediate perceptual content." (p. 119.) Thurstone appeared to be intrigued by the possibility that the perceptual tasks from which these relationships were secured might give a reliable index of the subject's facility for handling more complex tasks. Recently, Gardner et al. (1960), in a factor-analytic study of "cognitive controls," described the cluster of tasks including a visual embedded-figure task, as a "scanning" factor, representing "the degree of attention deployment to objects, object properties, and events." (p. 82.) This factor is said to involve "a) a tendency to narrow awareness and to keep experiences discrete; and b) a tendency to separate effect from idea." (p. 46.) Both Thurstone and Gardner *et al.* speculate on a broad meaning of the perceptual performance, and tend to link it to some cognitive, organizational function, whose nature is largely unspecified.

The complex functions tapped by visual embedded-figure tasks would thus seem not to be linked exclusively to visual processes. However, so far as our data are concerned, the absence of modality-specificity may be more apparent than real. Many subjects report that they visualize tactile figures; performance on the tactile task may then reflect the excellence of this translation. Performance on the tactile task may in fact depend upon visual processes (or vice versa), and a way of dissociating the contributions of the modalities would be useful. The old distinction between "good" and "poor" visualizers might be usefully explored in this respect; if tactile embedded-figure performance does involve visual processes, "good" should perform better than "poor" visualizers on this task.

SUMMARY

The generality of previous findings of deficit performance by the elderly in a visual embedded-figure task was examined by the use of a tactile analogue with a group of 19 young (mean age 27.8) and 30 older (mean age 68.8) subjects with similar work backgrounds and intelligence (WAIS Vocabulary) levels. The older group showed consistent deficits in the number of items correctly identified, and were consistently slower than the young, in both the visual and tactile embedded-figure tasks. While the older group had higher basic thresholds, these differences did not account for the embedded-figure deficits. Intelligence level and embedded-figure performances were associated. The data demonstrate a cross-modal commonality in the embedded-figures performances, but it is unclear whether the obtained association reflects a modality-transcending function or a more or less general tendency on the part of subjects to translate forms presented in one modality into schemata in another.

Acknowledgments. The help of Robert Canestrari, Mrs. Gail Bradley, and Peter Kohler is gratefully acknowledged.

REFERENCES

Basowitz, H., and Korchin, S. J. 1957. Age differences in the perception of closure. J. Abnorm. & Social Psychol., 54: 93–97.
Crook, M. N., Alexander, Edith A., Anderson, Edythe M. S., Coules, J.,

Hanson, H. A., and Jeffries, N. T., Jr. 1958. Age and form perception. Report 57–124. Randolph Air Force Base, Texas School of Aviation Medicine, USAF.

Gardner, R., Holtzman, P. S., Klein, G. S., Linton, H., and Spence, D. P. 1960. Cognitive control: a study of individual consistencies in cognitive behavior. Psychol. Issues, 1: (No. 4), Monogr. 4.

Goldstein, K. 1927. Die lokalization in der grosshirnrinde. *In* A. Bethe, J. V. Bergmann, G. Embden, and A. Ellinger (eds.), Handbuch der normalen und pathologischen physiologie.

Gottschaldt, K. 1926. Uben den einfluss der erfahrung auf die Wahrnehmung von figuren. Psychol. Forsch., 8: 261–317.

Teuber, H. L., and Weinstein, S. 1956. Ability to discover hidden figures after cerebral lesions. A. M. A. Arch. Neurol. & Psychiat., 76: 369–79.

Thurstone, L. L. 1944. A factorial study of perception. Chicago: University of Chicago Press.

Wechsler, D. 1955. Manual for the Wechsler Adult Intelligence Scale. New York: The Psychological Corporation.

Age Differences in Response Speed as a Function of Controlled Variations of Stimulus Conditions: Lights, Numbers, Letters, Colors, Syllables, Words, and Word Relationships

JAMES E. BIRREN AND KLAUS F. RIEGEL

PREVIOUS work has shown that with advancing age there are both incremental and decremental changes in intellectual performance. In language functions older adults show better performance, whereas measures involving psychomotor speed and perception frequently favor young adults. The problem has become one of determining the extent to which the incremental or decremental changes associated with advancing age are large or small, and whether they are general or particulate in nature.

The present study compares the performance of young and elderly adults on a series of tasks in which the symbolic content was varied while holding constant the manner of presenting stimuli and registering responses. The general purpose of this study involved two classes of determinants of age differences in intellectual performance: (1) changes which have a presumed origin in altered functioning of the nervous system, and (2) changes which result from experience and are expressed as habit patterns of responses. The first class of determinants would include hypothetical age changes in excitability of the nervous system and possible reduced inhibitory control over behavior. Most responses show some increase in latency with age although it is not known what the longer latencies imply for a neurophysiological basis or for intellectual activity. The slowing may primarily reflect processes associated with effecting responses although contrariwise the latency change may represent a general alteration in the nervous system such that no behavior could be expected to be independent of its influence.

In this vein the quality of—and the capacity for—intellectual

operations in thinking and reasoning might be limited by the speed
of the mediating processes, e.g., might result in a limitation in the
amount of information which can be received, made available for
simultaneous manipulation, and synthesized into categories to even-
tuate in appropriate responses. This might be illustrated by the task
of listening to a conversation wherein grasp of the issues depends upon
an adequate speed of perception and integration of the spoken words.

In addition to presumed biological antecedents, experiential antecedents may also result in age differences in response dispositions.
Thus, word associations may develop different habit strengths with
age as a consequence of selective use of word combinations. Individual differences in response characteristics presumably may arise from
protracted experience of a specialized sort. A preference for certain
words could arise from selective avoidance, and with age there is
very likely a unique pattern of word habits typical of a given individual. The individual may also share some general tendency in word
usage in common with most persons of his age group. Such phenomena may be largely limited to social relations but they might also have
consequences for thinking. That is, word choices not only represent
habit patterns in overt responses or modes of expression but also in
modes of thought. Interactions between the two groups of determinants are likely to occur. Thus avoidance of certain classes of words
would not necessarily reflect a pure experiential determinant, since
this may also be a compensation for increased cognitive strain incurred by attempts to grasp certain abstractions.

The apparatus used in this study, the Psychomet, was previously
developed as an instrument at the National Institute of Mental Health.
It consists of a subject's panel on which ten light and ten key associations are programmed and the speed and accuracy of the responses
are registered. The experimenter can pair any light with any key or
response button and also present the stimulus lights in any predetermined order. The time the subject takes to respond to the onset of
each light by pressing the appropriate button is recorded on 1/100-sec
electric timers. A total of 22 stimulus response conditions were
studied; each condition consisted of ten light-button pairings and each
series was presented twice.

EXPERIMENTAL CONDITIONS

All subjects went through the experimental conditions in the order
given below. Each condition was repeated as soon as the data were

recorded from the experimenter's panel; the two successive series of trials are designated as A and B. The specific instructions are available from the authors.

1. Simple movement time: The subject presses the buttons as fast as he can from left to right, turning off the lights in order.

Lights	1	2	3	4	5	6	7	8	9	0
Buttons	1	2	3	4	5	6	7	8	9	0

2. Serial, simple movement time: The subject presses the buttons and turns off the lights as above but begins a new cycle after completing the last response. Each trial consists of three cycles or a total of 30 responses.

3. Choice reaction time: Lights and buttons regularly paired but presented in a random order; light 5 first, 4 second, etc.

Lights	5	4	8	9	6	7	2	0	3	1
Buttons	5	4	8	9	6	7	2	0	3	1

4. Choice reaction time: Same as in number 3 but with a different random order; light 9 first, 1 second, etc.

Lights	9	1	8	5	7	4	3	6	0	2
Buttons	9	1	8	5	7	4	3	6	0	2

5. Numbers: The lights and buttons are numbered from 1 to 0. Buttons turn off lights with corresponding numbers. Lights are presented regularly from left to right but designated with numbers 1–0; buttons are ordered regularly from left to right.

Lights	2	5	7	1	6	0	9	4	3	8
Buttons	1	2	3	4	5	6	7	8	9	0

6. Numbers: Both lights and buttons are numbered from 1 to 0 as in 5 above, button designations as well as lights are randomized.

Lights	0	5	6	9	3	1	8	2	7	4
Buttons	2	4	7	0	9	3	8	6	5	1

7. Letters: Lights and buttons are designated with letters of the alphabet A through K except J which was an ambiguous letter in the letter style used. Lights were presented regularly from left to right but designations were randomized; buttons were in alphabetical order from left to right.

Lights	I	D	G	A	F	H	E	K	C	B
Buttons	A	B	C	D	E	F	G	H	I	K

8. Letters: Both light and button designations are randomized.

Lights	A	I	G	D	B	K	E	C	F	H
Buttons	H	F	I	K	B	D	A	C	E	G

9. Colors: Lights and keys are designated with colors, five with single colors, five with two colors each; lights were presented in random order, Y = yellow, G = green, R = red, B = blue, O = orange.

Order	7	10	2	3	9	6	8	1	4	5
Lights	Y	OG	B	GR	O	YR	G	BO	R	YB
Buttons	R	GR	O	B	BO	G	Y	YR	YB	OG

10. Colors and symbols: Lights and buttons are designated with one of two symbols X or O and with one of five colors. A correct response consists of the proper selection of both color and symbol.

Order	5	8	9	4	6	10	1	7	3	2
Lights	YO	RX	GO	OX	RO	YX	BX	GX	BO	OO
Buttons	RO	GX	BO	OX	YX	OO	YO	BX	GO	RX

11. Digit-symbol: Lights are designated with numbers 1 to 10; buttons are designated with symbols which had to be decoded by reference to a decoding card placed on the subject's panel; lights are presented regularly from left to right.

Lights		5	2	10	3	6	1	7	9	8	4
Buttons		ᗡ	ᔕ	ᖇ	⋗	⊃	⊂	⅄	⅂	⌐	ꓶ
Decoding card		1	2	3	4	5	6	7	8	9	10
		ᖇ	⌐	ᔕ	ꓶ	⊂	⋗	⊃	⅄	ᗡ	⅂

All the verbal relations stimuli (lights) are presented from left to right in regular sequence.

12. Syllable matching:

Lights	be	cor	ex	tab	ans	gard	den	sold	morn	im
Buttons	ex	gard	tab	morn	im	den	be	ans	sold	cor

13. Word matching:

Lights	short	cold	foot	girl	light	blue	head	joy	bed	salt
Buttons	bed	blue	foot	salt	cold	girl	short	joy	head	light

14. Word association: Button is pressed which has the word which goes best with the stimulus. Lights: table, man, slow, hard, eagle, bread, long, hammer, king, blossom; buttons: flower, woman, bird, soft, short, butter, fast, chair, queen, nail.

15. Word association: Lights: hand, whistle, wish, earth, memory, bath, child, lion, green, afraid; buttons: fear, mind, stop, grass, foot, tiger, baby, clean, want, round.

16–18. Word relations: The same stimulus words are used for response words of three kinds, coordinates, superordinates, and parts. Lights: scissors, fruit, baby, house, whiskey, moon, music, square, spider, bible; buttons (coordinates): adult, ant, beer, koran, earth, tongs, hotel, meat, poetry, rhombus; buttons (superordinates): animal, tool, edifice, liquid, art, person, planet, figure, scriptum, food; buttons (parts): page, tone, blade, feeler, angle, orbit, arm, peel, alcohol, walls.

19. Word completion: adjectives and adverbs. Lights: al, hap, rath, pleas, pret, sud, in, of, per, cru; buttons: haps, py, ant, ten, deed, el, er, most, ty, den.

20. Word completion: concrete nouns. Lights: val, win, mon, kitch, moun, farm, jour, bu, po, on; lights: en, tain, ley, nal, ion, ey, dow, ny, reau, er.

21. Word completion: verbs. Lights: ap, fol, ad, ar, ex, for, suf, dis, flat, main; buttons: ter, pear, fer, get, mit, turb, rive, low, tain, pect.

22. Word completion: abstract nouns. Lights: pow, sys, af, ef, man, meth, na, prob, spir, suc; buttons: ner, ces, er, fair, lem, tion, od, it, tem, fort.

Of the 22 experimental conditions, 21 consisted of 10 stimulus-response pairs. The remaining single condition consisted of three cycles of ten simple movement responses (Experimental Condition 2). Two measures were used for each subject under all conditions: the fastest time for any single response in a series and the median response time. Since each experimental condition was repeated, a total of four groups of data was gathered on each subject; fastest time and median time for series A and series B. Because of space limitations only selected portions of this data are presented here.

A total of 30 young adult subjects and 21 elderly subjects was studied. The young group consisted of 15 men and 15 women in the age range 18 to 33 years. Their mean education was 14.0 years. All were volunteers; 13 were religious volunteers for research in the Clinical Center of the National Institutes of Health; the remainder were volunteer employees.

The elderly group consisted of 9 women and 12 men in the age range 60 to 80 years. Their mean education was 12.9 years. These subjects were all volunteers and were either retired government employees or were the spouses of retired employees.

RESULTS

Under all experimental conditions the elderly subjects were slower in their responses than were the young subjects. In Table 1 are shown the mean values of the two groups of subjects. The differences in response time can be considered both in absolute and in relative terms. The smallest absolute age difference in the mean values occurs for the simple movement time series, about .14 sec. The differences in choice reaction times were .18 and .16 sec. The largest difference was for the superordinate word association, 2.03 sec. The largest absolute difference was not necessarily the largest in relative difference. Several of the word association measures did not show as large a relative age difference as some of the more simple tasks.

When the experimental conditions are ranked in terms of both relative and absolute difference (ranked from 1 to 22), five conditions had a combined rank of 38 or above out of a maximum possible of 44.

Table 1. Mean time of correct performance of young and elderly subjects on the Psychomet, first trial, median values for individuals. (Reported in hundredths of seconds, decimal point omitted)

Experimental conditions	Young			Elderly			Old-young	Percent difference
	Mean	σ	N	Mean	σ	N		
1. Movement time	32	9	30	46	18	21	14	44
2. Movement time, 3 cycles	70	12	30	105	34	21	35	50
3. Choice reaction time	64	8	30	82	10	21	18	28
4. Choice reaction time	58	6	30	74	10	21	16	28
5. Numbers	104	12	30	161	29	21	57	55
6. Numbers, random	142	27	30	220	51	21	78	55
7. Letters	105	11	30	162	31	21	57	54
8. Letters, random	151	27	30	228	47	20	77	51
9. Colors	174	40	30	336	160	21	162	93
10. Colors plus symbols	153	21	30	292	96	20	139	91
11. Digit-symbol	288	49	30	418	65	21	130	45
12. Syllable matching	129	22	30	190	41	21	61	47
13. Word matching	133	22	30	195	38	21	62	47
14. Word association	252	80	30	340	89	21	88	35
15. Word association	181	53	30	250	59	21	69	38
16. Word relations (superordinate)	250	82	29	453	136	21	203	81
17. Word relations (part)	223	65	30	408	124	21	185	83
18. Word relations (coordinate)	230	52	29	428	104	21	198	86
19. Word completion, adjectives and adverbs	389	23	29	428	205	21	39	10
20. Word completion, concrete nouns	442	251	25	516	256	20	74	17
21. Word completion, verbs	294	124	28	418	159	21	124	42
22. Word completion, abstract nouns	279	122	29	380	97	20	101	36

They are color matching, color and symbol matching, superordinate, coordinate, and part word associations. Showing least absolute and relative age difference were the choice reaction time measurements. In view of the fact that much work has been done to establish the fact that reaction times show significant differences with age, it is surprising that reaction time is not necessarily the task in which the largest age difference in speed appears, either absolutely or relatively. In a general way the age difference in speed appears to increase as the task is made more complex. These results might lead one to suspect that there was a common factor operating in these experimental conditions to produce such large differences. If this is so it is not readily apparent in the analysis of the data from the young group alone.

A principal component analysis of the data on the young group not reported in detail here shows a large common component found in all conditions except that for the first. Since the largest coefficient in the first component was found for the last experimental condition, abstract-noun association, there is a temptation to interpret this as indicating speed of abstract association. However, the common variable leading to the age differences need not appear at all in the data obtained from the young subjects. That is, the basis for the age difference lies in a variable not operating for young adults, hence the findings are not interpretable at present.

The effects of randomizing the response buttons can be examined by comparing the performance of the subjects on experimental conditions 5 and 6 (numbers), and 7 and 8 (letters). In both instances the essential difference between succeeding experimental conditions is a scrambled order of response buttons in contrast to a regularly numbered or alphabetically ordered series from left to right. In both instances the elderly subjects showed a somewhat greater difference in response time when responses were randomized in position, i.e., .38 versus .59 sec, and .46 versus .66 sec, respectively. In terms of percentage increase, however, both groups increased their response time by about 40 percent in the scrambled response order. This suggests that for both age groups the increased time required with increased complexity is proportionate to the time required in simple stimulus response associations, a point worthy of verification.

SUMMARY

The purpose of this study was to compare the speed of performance of young and elderly subjects in a standardized experimental context varying the nature of selected stimulus and response associations. The subject's task was to respond to one of ten signal lights by pressing one of ten buttons. There was always a predetermined association between lights and buttons. The subject turned off the ten lights serially as rapidly as possible by pressing the correct buttons. A total of 22 experimental conditions were used ranging from simple movement and reaction times through numbers, letters, colors, symbols, and word associations of a predetermined nature.

A total of 30 young subjects, age range 18 to 30 years, and 21 elderly subjects, 60 to 80 years, was studied. Under all experimental conditions the elderly subjects were slower than the young. The largest age differences both relative and absolute appeared for the superordinate, coordinate, and part word associations, and the color and color-symbol associations. The smallest differences were found for choice reaction time and adjective word associations.

It is apparent from these results that age differences in speed of response are not limited to the simple motor aspects of tasks but involve to an even greater extent the associative processes. Even if one were to dissociate the time required for simple reaction time from the response times for complex associations only about 10 to 15 percent of the age difference would be accounted for. Furthermore, it is not obvious that this is a justifiable computation since the age difference may involve processes common to any stimulus response association, excepting neither relatively simple choice reactions nor complex verbal associations.

The common variance involved in the age differences in speed of association requires further analysis along the lines described in this study.

Although the order of stimuli and responses was changed for each experimental condition, the 22 conditions were always performed in the same order. For this reason any adaptation to the experiment might result in somewhat better performance of the later conditions; the extent of any possible adaptation or learning requires a different kind of design than that employed in this study.

A Study of the "Psychological Refractory Phase" in Relation to Aging

JACEK SZAFRAN

THE refractory phase, as a feature of nervous function, has possibly a broader significance than that traditionally given to it in physiology. There are indications that it may apply to decision processes in continuous performance. Without necessarily implying one mechanism for all decisions at all levels, it has been shown that an increase in latency occurs when responding to a signal which closely follows another (Craik, 1948; Hick, 1948; Vince, 1948; Welford, 1952, 1959). The present communication refers to a series (as yet uncompleted) of experiments, in which the subject is required to deal simultaneously with two streams of signals, one a regular, highly probable input, and the other irregular, i.e., with high temporal uncertainty. Different rates of work are imposed (in the cases here reported, a response every 2 or 4½ sec in the former subtask), and details of the timing of performance are recorded in terms of intervals (in the cases here reported, 50, 150, 300, and 600 msec) between the nth signal and the beginning of response to the $(n-1)$th signal. Thus an estimate is obtained of the subject's capacity for receiving and acting upon information while dealing with a routine task.

The available data are still too few to warrant definite conclusions, but such trends (all statistically significant) as have been observed appear to be related to age in the sense that: (a) older adults show greater refractoriness, and (b) older adults are more influenced than the younger by changes in the rate of work in the regular subtask. It can be seen from Table 1 that the response latencies to the regular signal also decrease with the increase of rate, and that this is a feature of performance of all subjects. It will be seen, by comparing Figs. 1, 2 and 3, that their response latency to the occasional signal tends to decrease with increase in the frequency of background input, and

The work is supported by a grant from the Nuffield Foundation and carried out with the assistance of J. Brebner.

Table 1. *Mean response latency to irregular and regular signals (in milliseconds)*

Age group	Interval			
	50	*150*	*300*	*600*
Irregular signal at faster rate of the regular subtask				
20–39 (N = 11)	319	300	298	307
40–59 (N = 12)	320	306	292	310
60–80 (N = 11)	376	356	339	345
Irregular signal at slower rate of the regular subtask				
20–39 (N = 11)	329	295	299	317
40–59 (N = 12)	358	302	299	323
60–80 (N = 11)	419	374	364	374
Regular signal[a] at faster rate of the regular subtask				
20–39 (N = 11)	237	243	232	237
40–59 (N = 12)	242	245	244	242
60–80 (N = 11)	268	279	259	269
Regular signal at slower rate of the regular subtask				
20–39 (N = 11)	280	273	270	277
40–59 (N = 12)	276	282	282	280
60–80 (N = 11)	302	310	307	306

[a] Only responses immediately preceding the occurrence of the irregular signal have been recorded.

the refractoriness is shortened (there are indications that it is the "absolute refractory phase," rather than the "relative phase" which shows the decrease). These observations suggest the possibility that amplification of routine activity may serve, in the case of the aged, to improve selective responsiveness of central mechanisms to a high-information signal. If such an amplification increases the "gain" of mechanisms upon which the sensory inflow impinges (a change of this kind corresponding to an altered level of "vigilance" or "arousal") —presumably by influence via the reticular formation—it is conceivable that decision processes are enhanced (Magoun, 1954; Lindsley, 1958; Long, 1959).

Acknowledgments. A. C. Staniland helped to design and construct the apparatus, and D. J. Stone gave statistical advice.

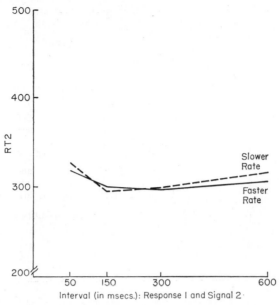

Fig. 1. *Mean response latency to the irregular signal for 11 subjects under 40 years of age*

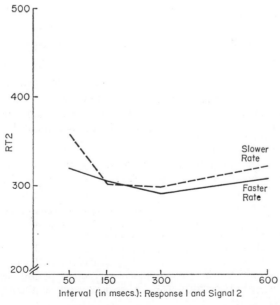

Fig. 2. *Mean response latency to the irregular signal for 12 subjects between 40 and 60 years of age*

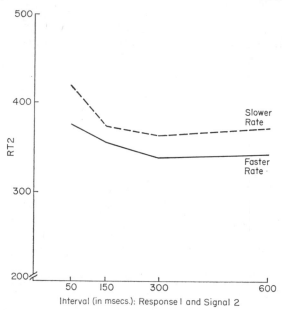

Fig. 3. Mean response latency to the irregular signal for 11 subjects over 60 years of age

REFERENCES

Craik, K. J. W. 1948. Theory of the human operator in control systems. II. Man as an element in a control system. Brit. J. Psychol., 38: 142–47.

Hick, W. E. 1948. The discontinuous functioning of the human operator in pursuit tasks. Quart. J. Exper. Psychol., 1: 36–51.

Lindsley, D. B. 1958. The reticular system and perceptual discrimination. *In* H. H. Jasper, L. D. Proctor, R. S. Knighton, W. C. Noshay, and R. T. Costello (eds.), Henry Ford Hospital International Symposium, pp. 513–34. Boston: Little, Brown & Co.

Long, R. G. 1959. Modification of sensory mechanisms by subcortical structures. J. Neurophysiol., 22: 412–27.

Magoun, H. W. 1954. The ascending reticular system and wakefulness. *In* E. D. Adrian, F. Bremer, and H. H. Jasper (eds.), a symposium of the Council for International Organization of Medical Sciences, pp. 1–20. Springfield, Ill.: Charles C. Thomas.

Vince, Margaret A. 1948. The intermittency of control movements and the psychological refractory period. Brit. J. Psychol., 38: 149–57.

Welford, A. T. 1952. The "psychological refractory period" and the timing of high-speed performance—a review and a theory. Brit. J. Psychol., 43: 2–19.

———— 1959. Evidence of a single-channel decision mechanism limiting performance in a serial reaction task. Quart. J. Exper. Psychol., 9: 193–210.

Variations in Conditions of Set in Relation to Age Differences in Reaction Time

JACK BOTWINICK AND JOSEPH F. BRINLEY

RESEARCH on reaction time suggests that set plays a role in at least two ways. First, the elderly are at a relative disadvantage in responding quickly when the situation involves long periods of waiting for the stimulus to arrive. This situation appears to involve ability to maintain attention. Second, the elderly are relatively slow on short-time intervals during which responses must be readied and executed at the appropriate instant. In this case, the situation may involve speed of programming responses as well as the correct timing of the stimulus.

Is the absolute or is the relative length of the preparatory interval the significant factor in set? Questions such as this may be answered by comparing reaction times associated with preparatory intervals varied in length, and in range and central tendency within a series. Are the two types of set independent? Are they associated with more than one sense modality? Are the answers similar for elderly and younger subjects?

The present study compares young and elderly adults in their reaction times to both visual and auditory stimulation with preparatory intervals of 0.5, 1, 3, 6, and 15 sec in both regular and irregular series. In addition, auditory reaction times were measured with an irregular series of 0.5, 1, 1.5, 2, and 3 sec intervals, and a second irregular series with intervals of 3, 6, 9, 12, and 15 sec. Thus each subject was given 30 preparatory interval conditions and each condition was given for 10 trials.

The full text of this paper is published in Wilma Donahue, C. Tibbitts, R. H. Williams (eds.), *Psychological and Social Processes of Aging: An International Research Seminar* (to be published).

The Learning of Statistical Structure: A Preliminary Study in Relation to Age

STEPHEN GRIEW

IT is unusual in everyday life for the cues that guide our behavior to be drawn from arrays of equiprobable signals. It is much more likely that one or two possible signals in any given situation will occur very frequently, while others will occur only rarely. This paper concerns the learning of such frequency unbalance, and reports an experiment preliminary to others which are to be concerned with the manner in which expectancies are built up on the basis of our understanding of the probabilities of occurrence of events.

The problem of frequency unbalance has intrigued psychologists for some years. Skinner (1942), for example, has demonstrated some of the effects on guessing behavior of subjects' ideas of chance, while Hake and Hyman (1953) have shown how an initial hypothesis that two alternative events will occur equiprobably will be modified to conform to their actual probability of occurrence. Senders and Sowards (1952) have studied the effect of instructions upon the type of initial hypothesis set up about the probabilities of occurrence of events and, at the same time, have demonstrated that ideas of frequency unbalance will affect judgments of material currently being presented as well as predictions of what is about to be presented. Weiss, Coleman, and Green (1955), Collier and Verplanck (1958), and others have shown that, as well as showing a tendency to learn the over-all probabilities of events, the human operator tends also to respond on the basis of sequential dependences which he perceives within series of events. Not only, for example, is the fact that event A will occur more frequently than event B taken into account, but the fact that B will follow the sequence B-A-A more frequently than it follows the sequence A-B-A will tend to be learned and to affect behavior. The whole subject of the perception of frequency unbalance and the development of expectancies has been discussed fully by Hake (1955).

In relation to aging, this topic is of particular interest, for two reasons. First, frequency unbalance to some extent alters the information conveyed by signals, and hence must rate as an aspect of task complexity worthy of study in relation to age. Second, if, as the statistical properties of series of signals are learned, hypotheses initially set up about these probabilities are rejected and new ones established which experience shows to be more adequate, then one might expect the lack of "flexibility" which is frequently said to be associated with aging to make the task more difficult for older than younger subjects. Parallel cases might be cited in Kay's (1951) report that errors made early in learning tend to persist in the performance of older subjects, and in the findings of Korchin and Basowitz (1956) and O'Doherty (as reported in Welford, 1958) that perceptual flexibility decreases with age, as measured by the ability of subjects to modify early interpretations attached to ambiguous drawings.

In order to test this prediction, changes in response latency have been studied in relation to the progressive learning of the statistical structure of a series of signals. In planning this study the view was taken that since more frequent signals would convey less information than less frequent ones, the reaction times associated with them would, once frequency unbalance was recognized, become shorter. Similarly, as learning takes place, reaction times to less frequent signals should become longer. The signals to which subjects had to respond were derived from two lights mounted above two brass targets. As soon as a signal appeared, the subject was required to move a stylus, initially held in contact with another brass disk, to whichever target was indicated by the signal, and back again to the third disk, as quickly as possible. This apparatus is a slight modification of that described fully elsewhere (Griew, 1959).

Signals were presented in sets of twelve, the less frequent occurring three times, and the more frequent, nine times in each of these sets. The order of presentation of signals was randomized. Ten sets, each different, were presented without break to subjects. Before responding to the 120 signals given in this manner, subjects responded to a random sequence of twelve equiprobable signals. This preceded the longer, unbalanced series without break, and was introduced to assist subjects, so to speak, in formulating an initial hypothesis in terms of equiprobability which was inadequate to the main task. The measure of reaction time employed was the interval between the appearance of the signal and the beginning of the response, that is, the moment the stylus first moved from its resting position. Signals were separated by intervals of three seconds.

In order to guard against the dangers of experimental error due to order and positional effects, two further controls were introduced into the design of the experiment. First, the younger and the older groups of subjects were each divided into two subgroups. One of these performed with the infrequently occurring signal to the left of the display, and the other with the infrequently occurring signal to the right of the display. This was to counteract any error due to signal position. Second, in order to guard against the possibility that, despite the precautions which were taken to ensure randomness within sets of signals, the 120 as planned in ten sets of twelve might contain properties liable to affect the results, half the subjects in each subgroup were given the signals in the originally arranged order, that is, sets 1 to 10, while the other half were given the sets in the order 6 to 10, first, and then 1 to 5.

Twenty subjects took part in the experiment. Ten below the age of 30 years were matched for intelligence, education, and occupational background with ten between the ages of 45 and 60 years.

Mean reaction times to frequently and infrequently occurring signals within sets are shown, for both younger and older subjects, in Fig. 1. The points at which mean reaction times to frequent and infrequent signals are significantly different are indicated with arrows, and the points at which these differences are first observed are considered as representing the stages at which the inadequate hypothesis of equiprobability is rejected. The tentative prediction based on the argument of "inflexibility" was that this stage would be reached earlier by younger subjects than by older ones. It will be seen that this prediction is not supported by the results which suggest that older subjects have rejected their initial hypothesis even more rapidly than the younger ones.

The number of errors made was very small, and was roughly the same in the two age groups. Although the majority of subjects in both age groups reported after the experiment that they became aware at some stage during the course of the experiment that signals had ceased occurring equiprobably, a surprisingly small proportion actually reported that they had engaged in "guessing" which signal was going to appear next.

As a final control, introduced in case these results had been partially an effect of the fairly extended practice involved which might have affected the two age groups differently, a second experiment was conducted, along identical lines to the first, but presenting ten sets of equiprobable signals. Six of each appeared in every set of twelve, again in random order. Eight younger and eight older subjects took part, and the results are shown in Fig. 2. It will be seen that, while a

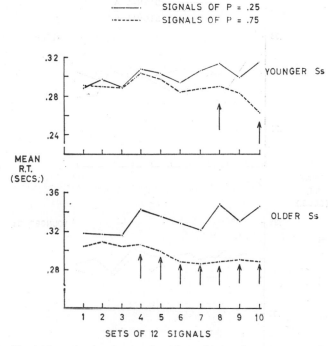

SIGNALS OF P = .25
SIGNALS OF P = .75

Fig. 1. Variations in mean reaction time during learning of unbalanced frequencies

small practice effect is noticeable in both groups of subjects, there is no significant difference at any stage between the mean reaction times to signals "A" and "B."

To draw many conclusions from so limited a study would be dangerous and premature. The various issues raised by the results require further, experimental elucidation. The important outcome is that it shows the efficiency of older subjects to be greater than that of younger subjects in adjusting to unequal probabilities of occurrence of signals presented in series. Two points of interest arise out of the results, however, which might be raised.

First, the apparently more efficient learning by older subjects of the statistical structure of the unbalanced series of signals may, in fact, be a function of their lower efficiency in learning the initial, inadequate hypothesis which the preliminary set of equiprobable signals was designed to reinforce. If this were so, and the younger subjects' learning of the structure of the preliminary set was more efficient, then this might result in a greater difficulty on the part of younger subjects in modifying their subsequent behavior.

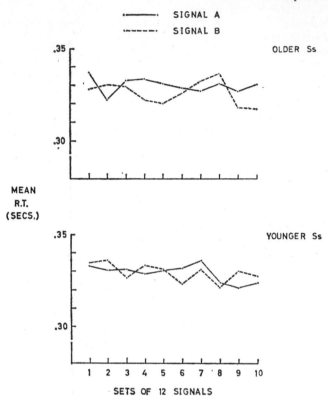

Fig. 2. Variations in mean reaction time during series of responses to equiprobable signals

Second, there is no evidence in this study of the "rigidity" which is frequently said to characterize the performance of older subjects. Examples of the rejection of hypotheses based upon the supposed increase in rigidity with age appear to be increasing in number, and the results presented here may be thought to be yet another example of the inadequacy of this type of interpretation of age changes in human performance.

REFERENCES

Collier, G., and Verplanck, W. S. 1958. Non-independence of successive responses at the visual threshold as a function of interpolated stimuli. J. Exper. Psychol., 55: 429–37.

Griew, S. 1959. Complexity of response and time of initiating responses in relation to age. Am. J. Psychol., 72: 83–88.

Hake, H. W. 1955. The perception of frequency of occurrence and the development of "expectancy" in human experimental subjects, pp. 257–77. *In* H. Quastler (ed.), Information theory in psychology: problems and methods. Glencoe, Ill.: The Free Press.

———— and Hyman, R. 1953. Perception of the statistical structure of a random series of binary symbols. J. Exper. Psychol., 45: 64–74.

Kay, H. 1951. Learning of a serial task by different age groups. Quart. J. Exper. Psychol., 3: 166–83.

Korchin, S. J., and Basowitz, H. 1956. The judgment of ambiguous stimuli as an index of cognitive functioning in aging. J. Personality, 25: 81–95.

Senders, Virginia L., and Sowards, Ann. 1952. Analysis of response sequences in the setting of a psychophysical experiment. Am. J. Psychol., 65: 358–74.

Skinner, B. F. 1942. The processes involved in the repeated guessing of alternatives. J. Exper. Psychol., 30: 495–503.

Weiss, B., Coleman, P. D., and Green, R. F. 1955. A stochastic model for time-ordered dependencies in continuous scale repetitive judgments. J. Exper. Psychol., 50: 237–44.

Welford, A. T. 1958. Ageing and human skill. London: Oxford University Press.

Interference in Short-Term Retention as a Function of Age

GEORGE J. SUCI, MELVIN D. DAVIDOFF,

AND JOHN C. BRAUN

WE were primarily interested in the study of age differences in the interference value of an intervening set of stimuli on learned discriminatory responses. The study was planned and set up in an anchoring type of paradigm.

The procedure may be outlined as having the subject learn to discriminate between the sizes of a set of five cardboard squares to a prescribed criterion of learning, then to present five larger cardboard squares a number of times, and finally to present the original set again until the criterion was once more met. A control group went through the same process except that irrelevant conversation was substituted for the interposed set of cards. The effects of presenting the larger squares could thus be compared with the effects of the mere passage of a similar length of time.

The sample was composed of 34 control and 62 experimental subjects divided almost evenly between those under and over 60 years of age. These groupings reflect an attempt to get essentially rectangular age distributions. The subjects were drawn from patients at the Infirmary of the Baltimore City Hospitals and the Veterans Administration Hospital at Fort Howard, Maryland. Seven (all from the City Hospitals) were women, three in the control group and four in the experimental group.

All subjects had less than a full high school education. This was a control in sampling adopted for the Veterans Administration Hospital subjects to make them comparable with the previously tested City Hospitals sample. The sample was restricted to people without

This paper is based on research carried out while the authors were members of the Gerontology Branch, National Institutes of Health, and Baltimore City Hospitals.

known history of central nervous system disease. All were also able to see and hear reasonably well.

The apparatus consisted of (a) two sets of grey cardboard squares, (b) a card on which was typed in large size, "very large," "large," "medium," "small," and "very small" (the names of the various size cards within a series), and (c) a large white cardboard set on a wooden frame which holds it upright on a table. This white cardboard served both to shield the experimenter when selecting cards to present, recording the data, and to remove possible background cues for judging the size of the squares.

PROCEDURE

Subjects judged the first set of cards until a criterion of learning was reached. The subjects in the experimental groups were then given 20 stimulus presentations of the other "interposed" set of cards to judge. The first or "standard" set was then given again and stimulus presentations continued until the same criterion was reached as in the first set of presentations. The control group went through the same process, except that a 5-minute interval was substituted for the interposed set of cards. This interval represents the average time taken in preliminary runs for judging the interposed set of cards. The order of presentation of the squares in each set was random with the limitation that within every ten presentations each of the five cards in the set was presented twice.

If the criterion was not reached within 90 stimuli in the first set of presentations, the subject was discontinued. If the criterion was reached in the first set within 90 presentations, but was not reached within 90 in the final set, the subject's score was recorded as 90+.

Performances of the control and experimental groups did not differ significantly as regards the first set of presentations, thus indicating no bias in the assignment of subjects to these groups. Performances in the first and the interpolated sets were not related in any significant manner, nor was performance in the first set related to age—a very surprising result. The numbers of trials taken to the criterion in the second presentation of the standard set of stimuli were tabulated, and the numbers of subjects below and above the median for the combined samples of young and old are shown in Table 1.

The nature of the data makes nonparametric tests advisable. The Mann-Whitney Test, while usable for the experimental group results, is not advisable for the control group results because of the presence

*Table 1. Number of subjects above or below median scores
of combined samples*

Group	Young	Old
Control: Above	8	9
Below	8	9
Experimental: Above	26	5
Below	5	26

of ties in rank in a small group. We, therefore, employed median tests. Comparing the young controls versus the old controls, Fisher's exact probability test yielded a *p* of 0.73, which is wholly consistent with the obvious apparent lack of difference between young and old.

The experimental group data were analyzed by a median test employing a chi-square test of significance. The null hypothesis was refuted far beyond the 0.001 level (χ^2 of 10.8 needed for *p* of 0.001 as compared to an obtained χ^2 of 25.8). Here, too, we are confirming a result that seems obvious from inspection of the data.

The only variable other than performance in the fixed set of presentations that was related to age was the number of squares judged correctly by the experimental group in the interpolated task. In this the older subject's accuracy was poorer. Scores for the interpolated and the fixed sets of presentations were, obviously, also related.

FURTHER STUDIES IN PROGRESS

Dr. Dave Arenberg, who has collaborated in these studies, expects to carry on this line of research in an attempt to seek out the extent of this phenomenon using different populations and types of stimuli. As a first step the present study is being repeated with a highly educated sample of scientists and other professional people. Preliminary trials revealed that the five cards were too easy for them. An increase to seven cards was made and it was too difficult—an interesting result indicating a remarkably small critical zone. We finally settled on six cards for the standard stimulus set and five for the interpolated set. The results so far indicate that the interpolated set has an *anchoring effect* on judgments, but that there are no age differences.

This would have made us very suspicious of the results of the first study, despite its overwhelming character, if we had not simultaneously initiated a similar study in which time intervals instead of card sizes were judged. After preliminary tryouts, a set of five intervals was used as a standard and four as an interpolated series. In this experiment age differences, although not as pronounced as in the original study, are holding up quite well so far.

Auditory Time-Error and Context Effects in the Aged

SEYMOUR AXELROD AND CARL EISDORFER

DEFICITS in the perceptual abilities of aged subjects have been well documented (*cf.* reviews by Braun, 1959; and Weiss, 1959). Of special interest are the senescence-related declines in ability to resolve repetitive stimuli. Lower visual critical flicker frequencies for aged than for young subjects have been reported by a number of workers (e.g., Coppinger, 1955). Semenovskaia and Verkhutina (1949, cited in Weiss, 1959) have demonstrated similar results using nonadequate (electrical) stimulation of the eye. In audition, Weiss and Birren (1957) obtained a (nonsignificant) difference favoring young subjects in the ability to discriminate two clicks from one. Vibration sensitivity, according to Rosenberg and Adams (1958) and others, similarly declines in senescence.

It seems possible to view these deficits in temporal resolving power as secondary to alterations in recovery of the aged nervous system from the short-term effects of stimulation. The particular alteration suggested by the work cited above is an increased persistence of the neural effects left by a brief stimulus, i.e., of the so-called "stimulus trace."

The finding of Bender and Green (1952), that double simultaneous tactile stimulation of face and hand gives rise to "extinction" (non-report) of the stimulus presented to the hand more persistently in elderly than in young adults, may be similarly interpretable: the afferent impulses generated by a touch on the face, reaching the CNS sooner than those from the hand, make access of the latter to the CNS more difficult.

An interesting physiological finding dealing with neural recovery function may be relevant here. Mundy-Castle (1953) has reported that afterdischarges following photic driving of the electroencephalo-gram (EEG) occurred "far more often" in elderly than in young

The work was supported by the Center for the Study of Aging, Duke University, USPHS grants M–900C, M–2109, and H–3582.

adults. It is as though the senescent CNS takes longer to return to a resting level of activity.

Köhler (1923) has proposed that time errors (TEs) in successive comparisons may be used as indicators of trace processes, and that the commonly obtained negative TE (overestimation of the second of two identical stimuli relative to the first) can be understood by positing a neural trace of the first which decays or fades spontaneously with time. In essence, the subject compares the second stimulus with the faded trace of the first. If increased trace-decay time does indeed occur as a correlate of advanced age, then in the successive-comparison situation one might expect systematic differences between young and elderly adults. Experiment 1 was undertaken to investigate the TEs of groups from these populations. Experiment 2 was designed as a test of an hypothesis arising out of the first experiment.

EXPERIMENT 1
Procedure

Thirty-five men aged 62–82 years (mean age 68.1) and 34 men aged 18–35 years (mean age 22.8) served in the experiment. The older group, Group O, included five community volunteers from the Duke Geriatrics Research Project, and 30 men recruited from the Durham office of the North Carolina Employment Security Commission who were paid for their participation. The younger group, Group Y, included 22 undergraduate students enrolled in the introductory psychology course at Duke who were fulfilling a course requirement by serving as subjects, and 12 men recruited from the Employment Security Commission. All subjects were naïve about psychophysics generally.

Pairs of 750-cps tones were recorded on magnetic tapes from two Heathkit AG-9A audio generators. The first tone (standard, *St*) of each pair was constant in intensity (5 v on the generator meter) and the second (variable, *V*) varied randomly from pair to pair in 0.5-v steps from 3.5 to 6.0 v (resulting in six *St-V* combinations). Since audiometry was not done on our subjects, rather intense stimuli were used. The loudness of *St* at the subject's ear was approximately 80 db as calibrated with a Maico audiometer (Model Hl-B). None of the subjects reported any discomfort due to the tones. All stimuli were supraliminal for all subjects. Each taped program consisted of 60 *St-V* pairs, with each *V* presented 10 times in random sequence according to the method of constant-stimulus differences. Stimuli lasted

0.5 sec, and the *St-V* intervals were 1, 2, 4, and 6 sec. Stimulus durations and *St-V* intervals were timed by Hunter decade timers; interpair periods were approximately 5 sec.

Subjects were run in groups of 2–6. Stimuli were presented diotically via earphones fed by a tape recorder. Each of the 4 programs (1, 2, 4, 6 sec) was presented to each subject, with the sequence of programs varied between groups of subjects to distribute possible order effects. Subjects indicated on protocol sheets whether the second member of a pair was *louder* or *softer* than the first. Each program was preceded by a sample program of 12 *St-V* pairs, each *V* being represented twice; this served to familiarize the subjects with the *St-V* interval, and to assure that subjects understood the instructions.

Results

The simplest index of the point of subjective equality (PSE)— that intensity of *V* which is judged equal to *St*—is the *number of times the subject reported the variable tone to be louder than the standard* (NL). If PSE = point of objective equality (POE), i.e., if TE = 0, then NL would be 25. If NL > 25, TE is negative; if NL < 25, TE is positive. Figure 1a presents data on NL for the 2 groups. Mean TEs are uniformly negative. The curve for the older Group (O) drops consistently as a function of interstimulus interval, while the Group Y curve levels off after 2 sec. The interaction is statistically significant ($p < .025$) as is the interval effect ($p < .001$), while the age effect is not significant ($F = 1.06$).

A more refined measure of TE may be obtained by fitting curves to the points determined by the probability of a response of "louder" for each variable intensity, computing PSE as the value of the variable at which "louder" and "softer" are equally likely, and taking TE = PSE − POE. Points of subjective equality were computed on the basis of straight lines of best fit (least-squares criterion) to the NL-*V* points. (The expected curve, when NL is plotted against intensity of *V,* is ogival. However, because of the small number [10] of judgments involving any *V*, the obtained individual curves were quite irregular, and straight lines appeared to fit the points as well as or better than ogives. The data of seven elderly and three young subjects whose curves for one or more *St-V* intervals showed radical departure from monotonicity were discarded as probably reflecting inability to perform the task, and are not included in this report.) Figure 1b presents these data. The curves are quite similar to those in Fig. 1a, and the statistical inferences are identical. Correlations between the number of

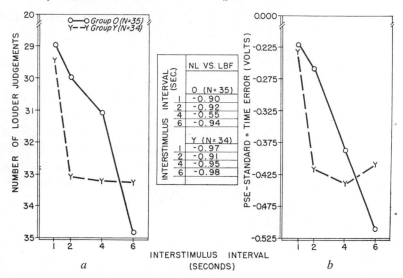

Fig. 1. *Mean time errors of young and elderly adults as a function of interstimulus interval*

The curves on the left were derived from the mean number of "louder" judgments (scores > 25 indicate negativity). The curves on the right were derived from lines of best fit to each subject's NL-V points. The inset gives the correlations between these measures.

"louder" judgments and PSEs determined by best-fit lines appear in the inset of Fig. 1; these are quite high. Figure 2 shows TE as a function of interstimulus interval when *group* TEs were computed from normal probability plots, and with log intensity used rather than voltage.

Discussion

The most interesting result is the interaction between the TE-interval curves for the two groups. If PSE does indeed represent the effective value or trace of *St,* then it appears that in the older group the trace continued to fade past the time when it reached a plateau in the younger group. It is tempting to think of the continued drop in PSE as somehow representing the persistence in the older group of a process of fading whose operation had ceased in the younger group at around 2 sec. Under this interpretation, one would predict that, if the interstimulus interval were extended, the curve for the older group would eventually level off.

Another possibility is that the older group was less susceptible to the so-called context (*series, central tendency*) effect. Extending Köhler's

(1923) line of reasoning, Lauenstein (1932) introduced the idea of *assimilation* of the trace to the background against which the stimuli are presented, and Koffka (1935) pointed out that the context effect is similarly interpretable. This effect (overestimation of weak standards and underestimation of strong ones when several standards are used in the same session, or underestimation of weak stimuli and overestimation of strong ones in the method of single stimuli) may be viewed as a shift in the standard against which a comparison stimulus is judged, from its tone value toward some central tendency of *all* the

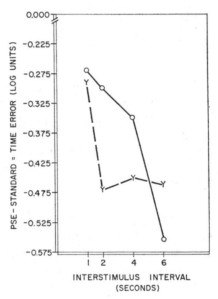

Fig. 2. Time errors as a function of interstimulus interval
The curves were derived from *group* normal probability plots.

stimuli previously encountered in the experiment. Needham (1935) reported that the effect increased with interstimulus interval in young adults: "As the time interval becomes longer, the various comparison stimuli are judged less upon the basis of [the standard] and more by reference to the total range of preceding stimulation." (p. 540.) The trace of the immediately preceding *St* becomes less salient as a reference magnitude, that of the combined averages more salient. The result would be the kind of nonmonotonicity seen in our Group Y. Needham (1934), employing interstimulus intervals of 1, 2, 4, and 8 sec, obtained, with naïve subjects, a slightly positive TE at 1 sec, becoming increasingly negative through 4 sec, and with a slight rise toward, but not to, zero, at 8 sec.

Under this interpretation, the monotonicity of the curve for Group O would imply that, in this group, the trace of the immediately preceding *St* remained more salient than the combined trace of the series for a longer time than in Group Y. If this is the case, then it should be possible to demonstrate directly a lesser susceptibility of older subjects to context effects. Experiment 2 was devised for this purpose.

EXPERIMENT 2
Procedure

Ten men aged 63–79 years (mean age 70 years) and 10 men aged 22–34 years (mean age 26 years) served in this experiment. The older subjects were recruited from the Employment Security Commission; 5 of the younger ones were students at Duke University and 5 were clients of the Commission. The method of constant stimulus differences was again used. Two standard intensity levels were employed, a "loud" one (approximately 70 db) and a "soft" one (approximately 60 db). A standard was followed by a *V* which was randomly 1 or 2 db above or below *St*, or identical to *St*. Loud and soft pairs were intermixed. The two intensity levels were presented in quasi-random sequence with the restriction that no more than three consecutive trials at either intensity level were permitted.

Each of the five *V* tones followed its *St* ten times; as there were two *Sts,* this made a total of 100 judgments per run. Two runs were executed, one at a 4-sec interstimulus interval, and one at a 6-sec interval, half the subjects getting the 4-sec interval first, and half the 6-sec interval first. Tones were presented diotically directly from a Heathkit AG-9A audio generator. A short rest period was interpolated between the runs.

Results and discussion

Figure 3 summarizes the data. As in Fig. 1, if NL > 25, then TE is negative; if NL < 25, then TE is positive. Context was strikingly effective; loud *Sts* tended to be "pulled down" during the interstimulus interval, and soft ones to be "pulled up." Each of the 20 subjects had a negative TE when judging loud pairs and a positive TE when judging soft pairs. There were no significant differences between the two interstimulus intervals.

Of primary interest is the absence of a significant age × intensity interaction. If the young subjects were more susceptible to context effects, then their TEs would have been more positive than those of the elderly subjects for soft pairs, and more negative than those of the elderly subjects for loud pairs. As it turned out, there were small mean differences in the other direction, but these did not approach significance ($F = 1.25$, $df = 1.18$). It would appear that the two age groups were equally susceptible to context, and that differential susceptibility cannot be invoked to explain the results of Experiment 1. It is possible that intensity differences between loud and soft pairs less

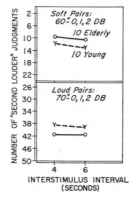

Fig. 3. Effects of context: time error as a function of interstimulus interval with "loud" and "soft" pairs intermixed
Ordinates > 25 indicate negativity of TE.

marked than the ones used here might have given rise to an interaction involving age; the present data offer no indication one way or the other on this possibility.

SUMMARY

In Experiment 1, time errors for 750-cps tones at interstimulus intervals of 1, 2, 4, and 6 sec were obtained for 35 elderly and 34 young adult males, all experimentally naïve. Time errors for both groups were uniformly negative. In the elderly group, TEs increased in negativity as a monotonic function of interstimulus interval; TEs in the young group increased in negativity from 1 to 2 sec and then leveled off.

In Experiment 2, the hypothesis was examined that these results were explainable on the basis of greater susceptibility of younger subjects to context effects. Ten elderly and 10 young adults were presented with intermixed loud and soft tone-pairs. No significant group differences in the effect of context upon time errors were obtained.

Acknowledgments. The advice and assistance of Dr. David Arenberg, Mrs. Elaine Crovitz, and Mr. Peter Kohler are gratefully acknowledged.

REFERENCES

Bender, M. B., and Green, M. A. 1952. Alterations in perception in the aged. J. Gerontol., 7: 473 (Abstract).

Braun, N. W. 1959. Perceptual processes. *In* J. E. Birren (ed.), Handbook of aging and the individual, pp. 543–61. Chicago: University of Chicago Press.

Coppinger, N. W. 1955. The relationship between critical flicker frequency and chronologic age for varying levels of stimulus brightness. J. Gerontol., 10: 48–52.

Koffka, K. 1935. Principles of Gestalt psychology. New York: Harcourt, Brace & Co.

Köhler, W. 1923. Zur theorie des sukzessivvergleichs und der zeitfehler. Psychol. Forsch., 4: 115–75.

Lauenstein, O. 1932. Ansatz zu einer physiologischen theorie des vergleichs und der zeitfehler. Psychol. Forsch., 17: 130–77.

Mundy-Castle, A. C. 1953. An analysis of central responses to photic stimulation in normal adults. E.E.G. Clin. Neurophysiol., 5: 1–22.

Needham, J. G. 1934. The time error as a function of continued experimentation. Am. J. Psychol., 46: 558–67.

———— 1935. The effect of the time interval upon the time error at different intensive levels. J. Exper. Psychol., 18: 530–43.

Rosenberg, G., and Adams, Anne. 1958. Effect of age on peripheral vibratory perception. J. Am. Geriatrics Soc., 6: 471–81.

Semenovskaia, E. N. and Verkhutina, A. I. 1949. (Age changes in the functional mobility [lability] of the visual analyzer.) Probl. Fiziol. Optiki, 7: 34–38.

Weiss, A. D. 1959. Sensory functions. *In* J. E. Birren (ed.), Handbook of aging and the individual, pp. 503–42. Chicago: University of Chicago Press.

———— and Birren, J. E. 1957. Age changes in click perception. Am. Psychologist, 12: 385 (Abstract).

Immediate Memory and Memory Disorder

JAMES INGLIS AND R. E. SANDERSON

IT seems paradoxical that while both clinical psychiatrists (Mayer-Gross *et al.,* 1954) and experimental psychologists (Welford, 1956) have attached a good deal of importance to that breakdown of "short-term retention" which seems to underlie at least some of the decrements of performance shown by both the normal and the abnormal aged, the kind of "test" of such ability most popularly used in the clinic (the digit-span test) does *not* seem to provide an adequate estimate of anything that could be called "immediate memory," even in cases where there may be quite evident impairment of learning ability.

For example, as part of one experiment with elderly psychiatric patients Inglis (1957) gave four different kinds of digit-span tests. Two groups of patients were tested, one group with memory disorder (and demonstrably impaired in their learning of paired associate material), the other group being matched with the latter for age, sex, and verbal intelligence but showing no memory disorder. The relevant tests involved the following material:

The first item was the Wechsler (1944) Digit Span (Forward) Test, which, of course, involves auditory presentation and verbal recall.

The second item (like the third and fourth) was an adaptation of the Knox Cube Test (Arthur, 1933). The examiner tapped out the digit series on four cubes, the subject being required to tap the same sequence back. This method, then, involved visual presentation and manipulative recall.

In the third subtest the cubes were numbered for the subjects from one to four. The digit series was then tapped out by the examiner and the same sequence had to be recalled verbally by the subject. This method therefore involved visual presentation and verbal recall.

Fourth, the examiner read out the series by number and the subject

The senior author was assisted in the preparation of this paper for the Fifth International Association of Gerontology by a Summer Research Associateship from Queen's University, Kingston, Ontario, Summer, 1960. The data were gathered in a series of investigations financed by the Canadian National Health Grants Administration, Mental Health Grant 605–5–285.

had to tap out his answering sequence on the cubes. This test involved auditory presentation and manipulative recall.

The means and standard deviations and the significance of the difference between the group means, estimated by Sandler's *A*-Test (1955), are shown in Table 1.

Table 1. Digit-span tests: differences between means of scores of experimental memory disorder and control nonmemory disorder groups

Digit-span tests	Administration	Recall	Experimental (N = 8)		Control (N = 8)		A	P
			Mean	S.D.	Mean	S.D.		
i	Auditory	Verbal	5.50	0.76	5.75	0.89	1.000	N.S.
ii	Visual	Manip.	4.38	0.92	4.25	0.46	9.000	N.S.
iii	Visual	Verbal	3.63	1.60	4.13	1.36	1.250	N.S.
iv	Auditory	Manip.	4.38	1.06	5.25	0.46	0.265	c.05

On the basis of these results it can be said that performance on this kind of test does not seem to be closely related to clinically apparent (and also otherwise experimentally demonstrable) differences in memory function in elderly psychiatric patients. In only one case does the difference between the groups approach significance.

A number of experiments reported by Broadbent (1958) and a "mechanical model" described by him (Broadbent, 1957a) seem, however, to go some way toward resolving the contradiction between the high degree of apparent validity and the low degree of actual usefulness of digit-span items as tests of immediate memory.

Broadbent (1958) has suggested that the capacity to deal with orthodoxly presented digit-span stimuli may involve only, or principally, a simple "perceptual" process. On the other hand when different *parts* of such spans are presented simultaneously to the subject through different sensory "channels" (e.g., both ears at once) then successful performance may require the participation of a simple "storage" system, which may itself provide the basis for short-term memory.

Thus, in one experiment, Broadbent (1954) showed that when digit-span stimuli were relayed to young, normal adult subjects so that one half of each span went to one ear and, simultaneously, the second half went to the other ear, then these subjects could reproduce the digit-series *sequentially*. Furthermore, in such reproduction, elements from one half-span were never alternated with elements from the other. He has suggested, therefore, that two processes may be involved in the reproduction of digit-series, depending partly on the mode of delivery of such material. One of these is concerned with passing information directly, the other is concerned with storing excess information arriving, for example, when the former phase is fully occupied in coping with information, say, from another channel.

Broadbent (1957a) has illustrated his theory by drawing out a "mechanical model" in the form of a Y-shaped tube, as illustrated in Fig. 1. The stalk of this Y-tube is narrow, the branches rather wider. Where the stem and branches join is a flap, so hinged that it can swing about its upper edge and seal off one or other of the branches.

Items of information entering this system, at the upper ends of the branches, can be represented by small round pellets, each bearing a distinctive identification mark. These are of about the same diameter as the stem of the Y-tube. The flap at the junction of stem and branches may be preset or it may be left free so that a ball dropped into one branch of the tube will push the flap aside (thus temporarily closing the other branch), then fall into the stem and out at the

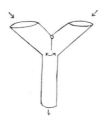

Fig. 1. Y-shaped tube, from Broadbent (1957a)

foot. This whole series of events constitutes a kind of "stimulus-response cycle."

Broadbent (1957a) has been able to show that such an ingeniously simple model can comprehend a large number of experimental observations concerned with the processing of information. For example the "distraction effect" sometimes seen in the simultaneous presentation of competing auditory stimuli (Poulton, 1953), may be likened to the simultaneous delivery of balls down each branch, so jamming the junction. Again, the advantages of intense over-weak stimuli (Berlyne, 1950) may be compared to the situation in which a ball forcibly delivered into one branch has an advantage over another less forcibly delivered through the alternative channel.

Broadbent has found it necessary to add further elements to this model to enable it to comprise other facts about immediate memory; only one of these additions need be mentioned here.

Suppose the branches of the Y-tube were lined with a substance

which, after some period of time, could corrode and eventually eliminate any of the pellets which happened to be "stored" there. If, on
any occasion both branches contain pellets, then, by hypothesis, the
functioning of the flap will tend to put one group of pellets into action
before the other (since a movement of the flap while a group was
passing would be likely to create a jam). All the pellets from one
branch, therefore, are likely to pass down the stem before the pellets
stored, in the meantime, in the other branch are allowed to do so.
These stored pellets would then show more evidence of corrosion
than would those which had not been stored. This, of course, is an
analogue in accord with what Broadbent (1957*b*) has shown does
happen in the case of responses to dichotic stimulation when information simultaneously delivered is sequentially reproduced. Under these
conditions performance is in fact better on the first half-set of digits
recalled than is performance on the second half-set recalled, as the
"corrosion" theory would predict.

How then, it might be asked, may this model be related to the
phenomena of memory disorder? Two notions have so far been
advanced and tested. It might be that the "corrosive material" in the
branches of the Y-tube is more powerful in the case of those suffering
from memory disorder. Material stored under those conditions might
then be eliminated more rapidly than usual.

This suggestion was investigated in the following way. Two groups
of subjects were tested. The experimental group consisted of 15
elderly psychiatric patients with memory disorder. The control group
comprised 15 similar patients, matched for age and orthodox digit-
span capacity with the experimental group.

The test material consisted of 4 half-spans of each length from one
to four digits, recorded in each channel of a stereophonic tape and
played back to the subjects through earphones. Thus the shortest
whole span consisted of two digits, both read out at the same time, the
first to one ear, and the second to the other ear. The longest span
consisted of eight digits, similarly presented two at a time, one to each
ear. No instructions were given to the subjects as to which half-set
of digits they were to recall first. Whichever half-span the subject reproduced first was labeled "dominant," whichever he produced second
was labeled "nondominant." Scores were obtained in terms of the
average number of correct responses made to the "dominant" and to
the "nondominant" half-spans; these results are shown in Table 2.

It can be seen that the differences between the groups in their
responses to such binaural stimulation are significant in the case of

Table 2. Dichotic stimulation digit-span tests: significance of differences between means of scores of experimental memory disorder and control nonmemory disorder groups, matched for orthodox digit-span capacity

Variable	Experimental (N = 15)		Control (N = 15)		t	p
	Mean	S.D.	Mean	S.D.		
Age	75.73	4.42	75.00	4.46	0.57	N.S.
Digit Span Forward	5.93	1.44	6.53	0.83	1.36	N.S.
Dichotic stimulation						
1 digit						
dominant	0.98	0.14	1.00	0.00	0.55	N.S.
nondominant	0.47	0.41	0.95	0.44	3.10	<.01
2 digits						
dominant	1.83	0.20	1.95	0.20	1.64	N.S.
nondominant	0.09	0.63	1.80	0.45	8.30	<.001
3 digits						
dominant	2.42	0.48	2.90	0.17	3.64	<.01
nondominant	0.05	0.14	2.15	0.67	11.86	<.001
4 digits						
dominant	2.82	1.06	3.63	0.45	2.72	<.02
nondominant	0.09	0.63	0.95	0.66	3.55	<.01

the "nondominant" (i.e., "stored") responses for all lengths of digit-series used. This result is, of course, in accord with the "corrosion" theory outlined.

Another kind of difficulty, however, could have been responsible for the higher incidence of error in the nondominant half-spans of the memory disordered group.[1] In terms of the Y-tube model a certain "rustiness" might impede the swing of the flap at the branch and stem junction; or, in other words, a slowness of shift of attention in the experimental group might have been responsible for the nondominant half-spans being in store longer. The longer this period, then, the more likely it would be that the stored information should exceed the critical time and be eliminated from the system, even if the hypothetical "corrosive substance" were no more powerful in the one group than in the other. This idea was examined in the following way.

Two groups of 11 elderly psychiatric patients were tested, again there was one group with clinical evidence of memory disorder and a matched group without.

The apparatus used in the previously described dichotic stimulation experiment was adapted so that the half-spans were no longer pre-

[1] The authors are indebted to Dr. Henry James, Queen's University, for this suggestion.

sented two digits at a time to both ears at once, but were instead so recorded as to be played to one ear after the other. In the case of the shortest two-item digit span, for example, the first digit would be presented to one ear and then, immediately following, the second digit would be presented to the other ear. In the longest, eight-item span, four digits would first be read into one ear, followed by the second half-span of four being read into the other ear. Both ears received equal and random apportionment of the first and second half-spans.

This procedure in fact required the subject to switch his attention from one channel to the other at the end of each first half-span. Any delay in effecting such a change in the case of the experimental group in terms of the hypothesis outlined should have resulted in a significant decrement in the adequacy of their reproductions of the second half-spans. The results of this experiment may be indicated very briefly in Table 3.

Table 3. Split-stimulation digit-span test: differences between means of scores of experimental memory disorder and control nonmemory disorder groups

Variable	Experimental (N = 11)		Control (N = 11)		t	p
	Mean	S.D.	Mean	S.D.		
Length of span (alternate ears)	5.636	1.5	6.000	0.82	1.09	N.S.

It can be seen that, in this case, the difference between the groups is not significant so that the notion that the differences observed in the case of dichotic stimulation may be due to some defect of "attention" rather than to some effect of "storage" is not confirmed.

In summary it may be said that the results of the experiments reported confirm that performance upon the orthodox digit-span test is probably *not* related to memory function. It has, however, been shown that clinically ascertained memory-disorder may be related to a defect of the storage system which has been adduced to account for some aspects of "immediate memory" in young, normal adult subjects, in particular their ability to make successive responses to simultaneous stimuli. Such breakdown in elderly patients is probably *not* due to any simple defect of attention.

REFERENCES

Arthur, Grace. 1933. A point scale of performance tests. II. The process of standardization. New York: Commonwealth Fund.

Berlyne, D. E. 1950. Stimulus intensity and attention in relation to learning theory. Quart. J. Exper. Psychol., 2: 71–75.

Broadbent, D. E. 1954. The role of auditory localization in attention and memory span. J. Exper. Psychol., 47: 191–96.

———— 1957a. A mechanical model for human attention and immediate memory. Psychol. Rev., 64: 205–15.

———— 1957b. Immediate memory and simultaneous stimuli. Quart. J. Exper. Psychol., 9: 1–11.

———— 1958. Perception and communication. London: Pergamon Press.

Inglis, J. 1957. An experimental study of learning and memory function in elderly psychiatric patients. J. Ment. Sci., 103: 796–803.

Mayer-Gross, W., Slater, E., and Roth, M. 1954. Clinical psychiatry. London: Cassell.

Poulton, E. C. 1953. Two-channel listening. J. Exper. Psychol., 46: 91–96.

Sandler, J. 1955. A test of the significance of the difference between the means of correlated measures based on a simplification of Student's t. Brit. J. Psychol., 46: 225–26.

Wechsler, D. 1944. The measurement of adult intelligence. Baltimore: Williams & Wilkins Co.

Welford, A. T. 1956. Age and learning: theory and needed research. *In* F. Verzar (ed.), Experimentelle Alternsforschung, pp. 136–43. Basel: Birkhäuser Verlag.

An Example of More Accurate Auditory Perception in the Aged

RICHARD M. WARREN

THIS study deals with an auditory illusion; that is, changes which seem to occur when a recording of a word is repeated again and again. The illusion was found through reasoning that an auditory analogue of the visual reversible figures might exist. The train of thought went as follows: In order to produce visual reversible figures, it is necessary to exclude cues, which normally operate when viewing real objects and which prevent ambiguity. When looking at real cubes or real staircases rather than ambiguous drawings, there is usually no doubt as to the correct identification and orientation of the object.

Now, in speech, ambiguity is usually avoided by the context provided by other words. If a single statement of a word is repeated over and over, without pause, this might be analogous to continued inspection of a visual reversible figure. Thus, repeating a word such as "tress" over and over without pausing might result in hearing first "tress" for a while, then "stress."

When this experiment was tried using a loop of recording tape, repeated clearly enunciated words did indeed seem to change with continued stimulation, but not quite in the way anticipated. Most changes involved more than just rearrangement or reinterpretation of the component speech sounds.

This illusion was recently studied by the author in England at the Medical Research Council Applied Psychology Research Unit at Cambridge using young subjects—British sailors. This study revealed some fundamental differences between this auditory illusion—which may be called the "verbal transformation effect"—and the visual reversible figures: (1) The visual illusion generally involves alternation between two forms, while the auditory illusion generally involves several forms for each subject. (2) The visual illusion is restrictd to a few special stimulus configurations, but the auditory illusion appears to be a general one found for all the two dozen or so stimuli employed: the stimuli varied in phonetic complexity from "see" having only two speech sounds up to sentences such as "Our side is right." (3) The visual illusion usually involves the same perceptual forms for different people, but the forms perceived for the auditory illusion differ for individuals. (4) The transitions of the visual illusion do not involve a significant distortion of the stimulus, but rather the selection of a plausible alternative interpretation; the auditory illusion, however, frequently involves transitions with considerable phonetic distortion. The distortions are especially great for the phonetically simple stimuli. With the single repeating word "see," responses included not only clearly related words such as "seed," "fee," and "tea," but also "base," "last train," and "three is the place."

The present study was designed to investigate possible age differences for the verbal transformation effect. The evidence concerning the effect of age on susceptibility to visual reversible figures is conflicting. Speakman (see Welford, 1958) found a clear decrease in susceptibility with age, while Miles (1934), on the other hand, found no age differences.

In the present study the young experimental group consisted of 16 men and 4 women, all junior college students, 18–25 years old. The older group had 16 men and 4 women, 62–86 years of age. Most subjects were retired professional men and their wives. Several men from the older group were staying at the Veterans Administration Center at Martinsburg, West Virginia, and their testing was made possible through the kind cooperation of Dr. Arnold Krugman.

The procedure employed was similar to that used in the earlier study with young sailors. The stimuli were prepared by recording the desired stimulus on tape. A loop of tape containing a single statement of the stimulus was prepared. When this loop was played, each repetition was thus identical. Since the loop was too fragile to withstand more than a few thousand repetitions, a rerecording was made from it onto a conventional reel of tape which was employed as the actual stimulus. The subject listened to this reel for 3 minutes through headphones, calling out what he heard as soon as he could, and then calling out any change as soon as it was perceived. The experimenter wrote down each response and the time it was made. As soon as the tape was stopped, the subject wrote down all of the words he could remember calling out, which the experimenter checked against his record.

Responses were scored in terms of numbers of transitions and numbers of different forms heard. These two measures are not related directly—a subject may hear only 2 forms and yet by alternating between them may hear as many as 100 changes in 3 minutes.

Table 1. Verbal transformations during 3-minute test (values are averages for 20 subjects in each age group)

	Transitions		Different forms	
Repeating stimulus[a]	*62–86 years*	*18–25 years*	*62–86 years*	*18–25 years*
1. Tress	4.3	22.8	2.3	5.5
2. See	4.7	35.8	2.2	5.4
3. Flime	6.6	32.4	3.5	7.9
4. Police	5.8	33.9	2.2	5.4
5. Trice	6.5	29.4	3.0	6.5
6. Our cider's ripe	1.8	11.6	1.7	2.7

[a] The order of presentation was as shown.

Table 1 shows the repeating stimuli used, and summarizes the responses of the two age groups. The younger group, on the average, reported five times (or more) as many changes as the older. The younger group also reported more different forms, more than twice as many with most stimuli. While not indicated by this table, there was also a rather marked difference in the way in which changes occurred for the two groups. Younger subjects typically heard abrupt changes from one stimulus repetition to the next. With older subjects, changes often took place gradually during several repetitions.

Figure 1 shows the distribution of scores for transitions heard during

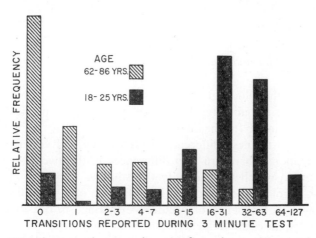

Fig. 1. Distribution of scores for number of transitions reported by older and younger groups

the 3-minute tests for the two age groups. Each interval along the abscissa is double the preceding one, so that the scale may be considered a logarithmic one. For almost half the stimuli presented to the older group, no changes at all were reported—subjects hearing the same word throughout the 3-minute test. It can be seen that the behavior of the younger group was different—the frequency of responses rose to a maximum for the interval representing 16 to 31 transitions in 3 minutes.

Figure 2 shows the distribution of scores for numbers of different forms. Again we see that for nearly half the stimuli presented to the older group no changes were reported, and so only one form was

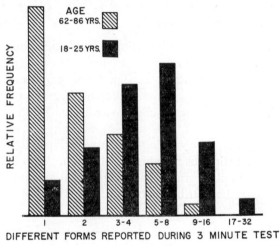

Fig. 2. Distribution of scores for the number of different word forms reported by older and younger age groups

heard. For the older group, the scores drop in frequency as we proceed along the abscissa, but for the younger group, the frequency rises to a maximum for the interval from 5 to 8.

In addition to these differences in frequency and variety of verbal transformations, there are also differences in the two age groups in the extent to which they identify the stimulus correctly. It appears that, for the older group, correct identification of a stimulus word is a function of its frequency of occurrence in English, but that younger people's responses are influenced much less by familiarity.

The left-hand column of Table 2 lists the single words employed as stimuli in order of frequency of usage based on the Thorndike and Lorge word count. From the third column it can be seen that all the

Table 2. *Frequency of usage and correct identification of stimulus word*

Word	Frequency of usage (per million words)	Percentage of subjects reporting correct word		Percentage of stimulation time spent hearing word correctly by subjects reporting it	
		62–86 years	18–25 years	62–86 years	18–25 years
See	1000	100	100	84	46
Police	70	100	100	74	45
Tress	2	90	95	77	50
Trice	1	75	100	66	46
Flime	0	30	85	52	29

older subjects identified the two most common words correctly, but that correct identification decreased with less familiar words. Only 30 percent of the older group heard the nonsense word correctly. Among younger subjects practically all managed to identify the real English words properly, and even with the nonsense word "flime," 85 percent identified it correctly.

The right-hand column of Table 2 shows the percentage of stimulation time spent hearing the word correctly by those subjects reporting it. We see that for each of the five stimuli, the older people kept with the correct word a higher percentage of the time than did the younger. With the older subjects, there appeared to be a general tendency for less familiar words to be heard a smaller percentage of the time. With the young group, on the other hand, all English words were heard correctly about half the total stimulation time—both the most common word "see" and the least common real word "trice" were heard 46 percent of the stimulation time: only in the case of the nonsense word "flime" was there a clear difference—a drop to 29 percent.

Another measure dealing with nonsense words is obtained if we list all verbal responses to the five tapes containing repeating words. Comparing the behavior of the two age groups on this measure, it was found that for the young group 48 percent of all the different forms reported involved nonsense words. The corresponding percentage for the older group was only 21.

These different measures all indicate that there is a probabilistic element differentiating the behavior of the two age groups: the older group tends to favor to a greater extent verbal organizations which have occurred frequently in the past.

The finding that frequency and variety of transitions are much fewer for the older group than for the younger group may seem to suggest, at first, an interpretation in terms of increased rigidity of response by the aged. However, since the term "rigidity" implies an unchanging response to changing conditions it does not seem applicable in the present study in which the stimulus is not changing. The stability of perceptual organization in the older subjects in the present study corresponds more closely to the reality of the stimulus situation. The instability exhibited by the young subjects and their considerable perceptual distortions represent highly inaccurate reports concerning the stimulus. It may be, however, that the mechanisms leading to such gross errors of the young subjects in the present study represent adaptive mechanisms which, when operating under normal conditions of speech perception, lead to greater accuracy of perception.

REFERENCES

Miles, W. R. 1934. Age and the kinephantom. J. Gen. Psychol., 10: 204–7.
Welford, A. T. 1958. Ageing and human skill. London: Oxford University Press.

A Psychomotor Learning Test: Influence of Age, Sex, and Intellectual Level

F. CLÉMENT

IT has often been assumed that advancing age was associated with lower learning abilities. However, such authors as Lorge, Wimer, Wigdor, Chen, Tachibana, and others have denied, if not a decrease in learning, at least the rate of decline. Contradiction might arise as a consequence of: (1) the few subjects upon which some investigations have been based, or (2) the way in which the subjects have been selected, according to their intellectual background, since learning abilities may decrease in various ways according to the intellectual background, or (3) the particular apparatus upon which learning has been practiced, or (4) concomitant learning, or immediately preceding activities. All these influences have already been investigated. Learning is as difficult as the extent to which it interferes in existing habits (more numerous for the older subject), since it requires an important reorganization.

In order to control misleading influences, we endeavored to: (1) define our subjects so that we might have maximum homogeneity in well-determined grades, (2) develop through research a test which might be simple and useful, however old the subject might be, and noninterfering in habits, knowledge, and previous acquirements.

In regard to the first point, the 297 men and 127 women subjects have been divided into six age groups. We have been able to show that age groups are comparable for socioeconomic levels, verbal-intellectual background, and sex. In regard to the second point, the selected test was a simple response—to press on a determined place either with a foot or a hand when shown a signal light.

The learning consisted in establishing and remembering the relations between stimuli and responses. There were four responses for four signals, that is to say, the task was extremely easy. The examination conditions and especially the directions and stimuli regulations had been standardized. Every transition between the four signals was

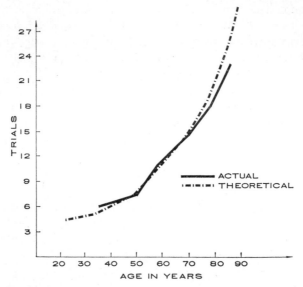

Fig. 1. Age differences in simple psychomotor learning: mean number of trials by age groups

The task required learning the correct response of four possible responses to each of four different light signals. The mean number of trials to reach the criterion of 12 consecutive correct responses is plotted for the different age groups. The solid line is the empirical curve of means; the dotted curve is a derived theoretical curve.

considered as a trial. The score was the number of trials necessary to establish automatic (correct) answers.

RESULTS

The mean values found for both men and women were identical: the general mean was 11.38 trials. Since we have said male and female groups were otherwise comparable, it may therefore be concluded that men and women do not differ in their psychomotor learning abilities. This allows us to combine the data from men and women and to get a more accurate number for the mean number specific to each age.

The mean number of trials increases very significantly with age: whereas Group 1 (36 years) needed 6 trials, Group 5 (79 years) needed 18 trials. This trend is shown in Fig. 1.

The progression of the number of trials is shown by the continuous line. The dotted line is the theoretical line, based upon the following facts: (1) two absolutely identical groups differing only in age (29 and 39 years) have a 1.5 trial difference; (2) the number of subjects for whom we have stopped the learning after 30 nonsuccessful trials (score 30) advances proportionally with age.

We shall now try to determine the importance of factors which may have an influence upon this learning.

Verbal intellectual background. With a high intellectual background the mean number of trials required is about 6 to 8 trials.

Figure 2 shows the progression in scores as related to verbal back-

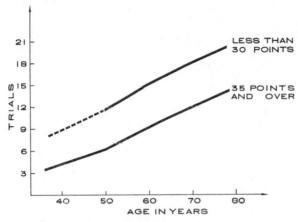

Fig. 2. Mean number of trials required to learn in relation to age for two groups of subjects: those with high (over 35 points) and those with low (less than 30 points) scores on the Wechsler Vocabulary Test

ground measured with the Wechsler Vocabulary Test. Our two extreme groups (35 and over and less than 30 points at this test) are also shown. We made an extrapolation for the younger group, having only three subjects at our lowest background. This extrapolation has been made in connection with the median group data.

The cultural background. As judged by university degrees this gives the same results as above.

The intensity of intellectual activity. This was judged by specified criteria. We ignored the subjects with low intellectual activities since there were too few in our sample (however, their learning possibilities seem to decrease markedly). Between the subjects with high intellectual activities and the medium ones, the difference is rather small (about 1.5 trials to the benefit of the first).

Reaction-time. With subjects of the same age, better scores are shown by the fastest ones, i.e., a difference of about three trials when compared to the slowest subjects.

Intellectual efficiency. We defined this as the realization of intellectual possibilities; it is highly influenced by age and we have been able to show that it could be measured by a simple code-writing test.

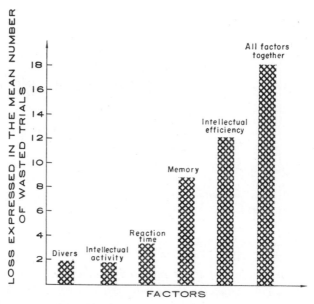

Fig. 3. Relative contribution of various factors to learning

With subjects of the same age, there is a mean increase of about 12 trials between subjects of high and low intellectual efficiency.

Memory as measured with the Wechsler test. With subjects of the same age, a mean difference of about 9 trials is associated with high and low memory scores.

Light sensitivity. This does not alter the data in any way.

Driving a car. Frequency of driving an automobile had no relation to learning scores. This was examined, however, since it could have been thought that the fact of being used to giving motor-responses adequately to various stimuli (as in driving) might have made psychomotor learning easier.

Physical activity. As judged by interviews, this had no relation

except when very low, when an increase of the number of trials may be found.

CONCLUSIONS

We have surveyed the effects of various factors on the data of our learning test. Figure 3 gives an idea of the relative importance of the factors we have controlled.

Among the factors, intellectual efficiency stands first. It is much more important than the other factors which, though playing a part, are effectively linked to intellectual efficiency, especially the Wechsler Memory Test. It can be seen that these factors are not altogther additive. Each of them increases but little the influence of intellectual background. Intellectual efficiency itself, of course, also decreases with age. Therefore, we think the greatest amount of loss in learning faculties is to be attributed to losses in intellectual efficiency.

We have ignored the influence which the "motivation" factor might have had, because our subjects did their task willingly and their remarks indicated that they took it seriously.

Age would seem to result in a greater difficulty in keeping the mnemonic traces left by a given stimulation and the proper response to it, while a greater and greater difficulty in inhibiting bad responses grows concomitantly. It has been shown that it was more difficult to establish a conditioned reflex in the aged than in the young subjects, and undesirable responses were more difficult to inhibit in early trials; the extinction of the conditioned reflex took, on the other hand, longer in the aged.

As Birren (1955) has shown, with age there is a decrease in central nervous system excitability, the processes of inhibition being more affected than facilitation. This decrease of excitability would show through the delay of voluntary responses. A number of investigators have shown that old organisms require additional time to integrate or perceive information and to program the appropriate responses. If additional time cannot be provided and if a more difficult selection of appropriate responses is added, tasks requiring the organization of mnemonic traces of successive excitations become more and more difficult.

The effect of cultural background on learning cannot be doubted, and it may be that the training of the intellectual functions influences their retention.

REFERENCE

Birren, J. E. 1955. Age changes in speed of simple responses and perception and their significance for complex behavior. *In* old age in the modern world, pp. 235–47. London: E. & S. Livingstone.

Effects of Dextro-Amphetamine, Meprobamate, and a Placebo on Problem Solving and Mood of Aged Subjects

ARNOLD D. KRUGMAN, SHERMAN ROSS, FRANK L. VICINO, AND DEAN J. CLYDE

AT the Veterans Administration Center in Martinsburg, West Virginia, there are housed approximately 1300 veterans of the United States Armed Forces. The Center is composed of a hospital unit and a domiciliary. The hospital section consists of a 250-bed TB service, a 350-bed medical and surgical service, and a 250-bed intermediate service. The domiciliary contains about 450 male and 50 female veterans who are not sick or disabled enough to warrant hospital care, but who are not able to get along adequately in the community because of social, economic, physical, or emotional deficits. These veterans, however, are capable of self-care, are ambulatory, and are participating members in the domiciliary community. The nature of their participation in domiciliary and center life is a function of several variables: their physical tolerance, their personal needs and therapeutic goals, their rehabilitative potential, and the needs of the domiciliary.

It is with this domiciliary population that we have invested a fair amount of our psychology research effort. There are several reasons for this: a large portion of the group is relatively stable in terms of their stay in the domiciliary. This permits us opportunities for long-range programming and studies.

With regard to age, the average age in our domiciliary is in the middle sixties with upper limits in the high eighties. This permits us opportunities to learn about problems of aging. Although the population as such does not represent a highly successful one in terms of socioeconomic, educational, or vocational achievements, it is possible to point to college graduates, medical and other professional school alumni, businessmen, civil service supervisory employees, stable family men, etc., in the group. In this regard, then, some similarity to a nondomiciled population can be noted.

However, if we intend to generalize from results of any of our investigations to a comparably aged community population, we must ask ourselves how close our group is to a community population. An earlier survey indicated that our group was not too far removed from a noninstitutionalized one with respect to educational achievement. We averaged somewhere between seventh and eighth grade schooling; intellectual functioning was within average limits (90/110); our vocational level was in the semiskilled area predominately, with a scattering of skilled, subprofessional and professional occupations in the group, as noted above (Fogel *et al.,* 1956).

One of the large differences between our older domiciled population and a comparable community group appears to lie in the personality area. Earlier studies have indicated personal inadequacies, less motivation and purpose, and a kind of noncompetitive spirit on the part of the domiciled veteran (Fogel *et al.,* 1956). Any generalizations we might make to aging as such must be tempered with these interacting variables.

It should be stressed, however, that at Martinsburg, our primary concern has been with the nature of our institutionalized or domiciled group. We have set up a series of progressive studies, each telling us a little bit more about some of the processes associated with an aging and aged domiciled population.

For example, we were interested in how goal setting or level of aspiration behavior might be expressed by this group. We selected one of the level-of-aspiration measures in use in the field and obtained protocols from 39 males who ranged in age from 70 to 86. These were nonpsychiatric members with apparently normal (for this age group) mental functioning. We compared their protocols to those obtained from 36 male nursing assistants ranging in age from 22–36. Educational level was approximately equal for both groups (eighth or ninth grade).

The findings revealed that, despite the wide difference in age, both groups exhibited low, but practically equal, aspiration levels. However, the older group appeared significantly less flexible in adjusting to success and failure at the task. They exhibited greater ego needs for self-protection, more vulnerability to stress and more maladaptive patterns of test behavior (Krugman, 1959).

The findings of less flexibility in approach and more vulnerability to stress have been noted by other investigators in the aging field. It led us to consider how our older population would handle a complex problem-solving task, and, further, to determine if we could establish a relationship between problem-solving ability and abstract-reasoning ability. The experimental task itself incorporated learning, need to shift goals, and need to change an unworkable pattern of performance. I will describe our problem-solving apparatus in greater detail later.

In this study we observed 29 domiciliary members with an age range from 65 to 77. We found several things of interest. As the level of difficulty of the problem-solving task increased, the number of errors increased. Most errors, at each level, were made by those subjects whose abstract-reasoning ability was poorest. The correlation between problem solving and abstract reasoning was .53 (significant beyond the .005 level). However, approximately half the group experienced little to no difficulty with either the problem-solving task or the abstract-reasoning material (Ross *et al.,* 1960).

In this group, as in the previous one studied by means of our level-of-aspiration technique, we felt that feelings of insecurity were fairly pronounced in our less successful subjects. These feelings, conceivably, were being expressed as anxiety and were serving to impede the learning and problem-solving process. We wondered next about the influence of an anxiety-reducing drug and its relation to learning and problem solving in our older, domiciled population.

We selected two centrally acting drugs: Meprobamate and dextro-amphetamine, decided to use a placebo in addition, and explored their effects on the problem-solving performance, and also on the mood of some aged domiciliary members. Meprobamate has depressant or sedative qualities with short-acting central-muscle relaxant properties. It has been used clinically for anxiety and tension states with varying degrees of success. Reports in the literature indicate that at single-dosage levels from 400 to 800 mg in young adults, the drug does not affect psychomotor efficiency, visual acuity, depth perception, visual balance, motor steadiness, or ability to make rapid judgments in simulated stress situations. Within this dosage level there has been found no impairment of complex problem-solving ability to adults; and at 1600-mg dosage only slight impairment of problem-solving ability has been found.

Dextro-amphetamine has been described in the literature as a stimulant drug tending to elevate ego strength and feelings of self-esteem. Small doses of the drug (5–10 mg) have been reported to increase the feeling of well-being and the energy level of a group of elderly females (average age 78) without causing deviant physical or physiological effects. In a study on children it was found that d-amphetamine altered positively the emotional attitudes toward unpleasant tasks and resulted in increased intellectual performances.

In our study we selected 31 subjects who ranged in age from 59 to 83. The subjects were randomly assigned to 1 of 3 groups; 12 subjects received a 400-mg dose of meprobamate, 10 subjects received a 5-mg dose of dextro-amphetamine and 9 subjects received a placebo (5 mg of sodium-bicarbonate). Aside from the drugs the experimental procedure was the same for each subject. On the first day of the experiment the subject was administered the vocabulary section of the Shipley Institute of Living Scale. This was followed by our problem-solving task, which was followed by the Clyde Mood Scale. On the second day, approximately 1 hour after the subject received his drug, he repeated the problem-solving task, and, when finished, he repeated the mood scale.

The vocabulary test was used to provide a gross measure of intellectual level. The test is a self-administered 40 word multiple-choice list which requires the subject to select the proper definition for each word on the list. Scores are converted into vocabulary age and consequently into mental-age levels.

At this point we can describe our problem-solving apparatus. This and the problem task are essentially the same as that originally used by Kay (1954). Our version consists of a 5 ft high, 2 ft wide display board with a row of 12 signal lights at the top, and a response board with 12 pushbuttons at the base. An index card containing a random arrangement of the numbers from 1 to 12 is placed in a different position for each of the 3 test stages. These test stages represent different levels of difficulty. In Stage I the index card is placed immediately above and behind the push buttons. In Stage II the card is midway between the lights and the button. In Stage III the card is immediately below the lights.

Instructions follow those of Kay and are fairly simple. The subject is told to: "Think of the lights as being numbered from 1 to 12. When a light comes on, decide which number it is. Then look for that number on the index card and press the button immediately below that number. The light will go off when you press the correct button. Then another light will go on and your job, again, will be to select the correct button to press for the light to go off." The experimenter demonstrated the technique, answered all questions asked by the subject, and set up a couple of practice trials for the subject to familiarize himself with the task. When the practice trials were completed, the task began. Ten trials were made at each stage. Each trial began as soon as the correct response to the previous trial was made. The number of errors or incorrect responses for each trial provided the measure of problem-solving ability.

The Clyde Mood Scale is a 133-item 6-factor scale which was designed to measure aspects of mood which could be influenced by drugs. The factors measured are: "friendly," "energetic," "clear-thinking," "aggressive" "jittery," and "depressed." Each of the 133 items is printed on a separate IBM card which is sorted by the subject into one of four categories: "not at all," "a little," "quite a bit," and "extremely." The subject is asked to "sort these cards into one of four piles to show how you feel today." Examples of the items employed are "agreeable," "lively," "able to concentrate," "bossy," "troubled," "excitable." Each item is scored 1 if sorted in the "not at all" category, 2 if sorted in the "a little" category, 3 if sorted in the "quite a bit" category, and 4 if sorted in the "extremely" category. Thus the larger the numerical value of each score, the more that adjective describes the subject's feelings at that time.

We found that the 3 groups did not differ appreciably from one another in their vocabulary age: the dextro-amphetamine group was approximately 15.7 years, the placebo group was approximately 14.5 years, and the meprobamate group was 14.3 years. We related vocabularly scores to post-drug problem solving error scores and again did not find significant differences among the groups. In another analysis in which we held the pre-drug error scores constant we could not find significant differences among the groups in their post-drug problem-solving performances.

At this point we were concerned about the limited range of the problem-solving scores and the relative skewness of the data. Because of these factors the possibility of unreliability of scores existed, and, if the scores were unreliable, they would not reveal drug effects even if effects were present. However, we obtained test-retest coefficients for the 3 groups, ranging from .75 to .83. We concluded that the scores were reliable enough for the purposes of this experiment and felt that if marked drug effects had occurred, the test was reliable enough to have shown them.

Despite the lack of differences among and between the drug groups in their pre- and post-problem-solving scores, another analysis indicated that one possibly significant effect of the drugs and placebo preparations occurred on the clear-thinking score of the Clyde Mood Scale. Here we found that the means on the clear-thinking scale for the 2 drug groups were virtually the same before and after taking the drugs, while the placebo group had an increase of about 7 points.

These results suggested that the subjects felt somewhat less clear-thinking (less able to concentrate, less efficient, less alert) after meprobamate, and much less so after dextro-amphetamine, than after the placebo.

Generally, then, the similarity in the vocabulary scores obtained from each of the groups suggested that intellectual level was similar in all groups. Comparison of problem-solving error scores indicated that although each of the groups made fewer errors in their post-drug problem-solving performances, differences between drug and placebo performances were not significant. The drugs, then, at the levels used did not appear to have an effect on problem-solving performance. The test-retest correlations we reported earlier are evidence that there was little if any differential effect from subject to subject since those who earned high scores on the pre-drug trial were generally high in the post-drug trials and conversely.

This consistency in functioning is particularly noteworthy since those subjects who received meprobamate saw themselves as less clear-thinking than the placebo group following the drug, while those subjects who received dextro-amphetamine scored even lower in this aspect of the mood scale. Conceivably those subjects who received the placebo improved in their clear-thinking as a result of something we might call the "placebo effect." On the other hand, the somatic sensations produced by the drugs may have counteracted the placebo effect in the meprobamate and dextro-amphetamine groups. Our attitude at this point is that further investigation is very much in order.

We have in progress now a study which we hope will be able to tell us something about the uniqueness and the additivity of pharmacological and placebo effects as related to an aged population. This is a crucial kind of question because we are beginning to recognize that an aged population has features both like and unlike other populations. With our program plans we are preparing to answer some related questions regarding response to drugs—effects of different dosage levels, timing, and recoverability—to name a few variables in this area.

In addition to our involvement with drugs, we are preparing also to look at other areas vital to oldster veterans living in institutional settings. For example, we have begun a pilot study in which we are recording, tabulating, and quantifying the extent of patient participation in ward and off-ward activities. Here we are concerned with the interacting relationships between aging, physical illness, social participation and relations, and adjustment. The activities of each patient will be plotted against his age, physical ability, and hospital adjustment. We are hypothesizing that the less extensive the individual's participation is in activities, the more disabled, more poorly adjusted, and psychologically older he will be. From this pilot study we hope to be able to generate additional hypotheses for testing on a wider population.

REFERENCES

Fogel, E. J., Swepston, E. R., Zintek, S. S., Vernier, C. M., Fitzgerald, J. F., Jr., Marnocha, R. S., and Weschler, C. H. 1956. Problems of the aging: conclusions derived from two years of interdisciplinary study of domiciliary members in a Veterans Administration center. Am. J. Psychiat., 112: 724–30.

Kay, H. 1954. The effects of position in a display upon problem solving. Quart. J. Exper. Psychol., 6: 155–69.

Krugman, A. D. 1959. A note on level-of-aspiration behavior and aging. J. Gerontol., 14: 222–25.

Ross, S., Vicino, F. L., and Krugman, A. D. 1960. Effects of position in a display on problem-solving ability in aged subjects. J. Gerontol., 15: 191–94.

Decay of Heuristic Processes in the Aged

EDWARD A. JEROME

JUST about a year ago, we began to plan a project designed to evaluate, in the aging individual, the operation of those processes commonly referred to as the higher cognitive functions of man. Naturally, it was necessary to shrink this global concept somewhat before anything sufficiently concrete to serve as a starting point emerged. The familiar fact that a person entering upon the threshold of old age is usually beset by a swarm of problems of adjustment suggested a further concentration of interest on an appraisal of the problem-solving activities of such people. Finally, the fact that the data that most strongly impugn the problem-solving capacities of older generations fail to indicate the particular heuristic processes responsible for the observed deficiency, suggested a further restriction of attention to procedures with demonstrable capacities for facilitating the identification of defective processes. We are, at present, engaged in the task of assembling a collection of problems that satisfy this requirement and, at the same time, appear appropriate to the special work capacities of our subjects. It is the purpose of this paper to communicate some of the data secured from an initial study with one of the problems being considered. Although this exploratory venture was not extensive, its results seem sufficiently clear to dictate a change in emphasis in our future research.

LOGICAL ANALYSIS PROBLEMS

The original design of, and work with, the device described in this paper was reported by Roy John (1957). About 3 years ago J. Miller and R. John gave the device to the Psychological Corporation in New York for further development and Charles Langmuir undertook the project of improving it instrumentally, of securing standardization data, and of effecting its application. The device is now in a very convenient form instrumentally, a series of problems have been administered to a large number of college freshmen who, when they are about to graduate, will be retested as seniors, and the Psychological Corporation has been using it as a selection device for candidates for computer programming courses. A considerable amount of data relevant to evaluating performance on these problems should, therefore, become available in the near future.

Appearance of the device

Except for its discrete event recorder, the whole device is shown in Fig. 1. The control unit with a problem key marked "Example 1–4"

Fig. 1. Logical analysis device

is shown in the upper left; the small metal box in the lower right contains the experimenter's control keys; the subject's display and response panel with a removable information plate is shown in the upper right. We shall not be concerned with the control unit or the experimenter's keys, but the subject's panel will be discussed at length in connection with a detailed description of the instructions to the subject. Because this figure is a two-tone reproduction, it is necessary to ask the reader to bear in mind that buttons 4, 5, and 6 at the bottom of the display panel are red, whereas all the others are black. This color distinction is essential to an understanding of the problem.

Description of the task and instructions to the subject

Attention is directed to the small light marked "time" in the upper left-hand corner of the display panel. It has a cycle of 3 sec on and 3 sec off that is repeated continuously throughout the experiment. Its sole function is to divide time into arbitrary units, the relevance of which will become clear.

Next it will be noticed that the display panel consists primarily of a centrally placed light surrounded by a ring of nine lights. Each of the lights in the outer circle has associated with it a numbered push-button that turns it on during one and only one of the two periods defined by the "time" light, i.e., some of the lights in this ring can be turned on only when the "time" light is on, others only when it is off. No light can be turned on during both periods, but it is not necessary to remember during which period a given light will act. If a button is pressed, and its associated light fails to go on, the subject need only wait for the next time period and press it again. This time the light in question will certainly go on. All buttons can be used singly or in any combination.

Attention is now directed to the center light, which has no button associated with it. It is really a success signal and can be turned on only by achieving a prescribed set of light conditions in the outer ring. How one goes about discovering what these conditions are will be described.

In all problems, there are three and only three relations that may exist between lights; they are the following.

The effector relation is demonstrated with the assistance of the first information panel shown to the subject. These panels are small removable plates that fit into the ring of lights and display several arrows each of which has an origin on one of the lights and a terminal head on another. The plate used in this demonstration has a single arrow pointing from the light numbered "6," say L6, to the light numbered "3," say L3. The subject is shown that L6 can be turned on during only one of the two time periods and that if it is on during any given period, L3 will be turned on automatically during the next time period. At this point the subject is also shown a notation for recording the effector relation, viz., "6 → 3," and it is explained that this symbol for the effector relation means that any time L6 is on during a given period L3 will go on automatically during the next period unless prevented from doing so by some other operation.

The combinor relation is explained with the aid of another information panel that has an arrow from L9 to L2 and an arrow from L4 to L2. It is shown that neither L9 nor L4 alone will give L2, and hence that neither is a simple effector. It is then shown that if L9 and L4 are turned on during some single time period, L2 will go on during the following period. The notation for this operation, "94 → 2" or "49 → 2," is given and is interpreted to mean that if L9 and L4 are on during any given period, during the next period L2 will be turned on automatically unless prevented by some other operation.

The preventor relation is demonstrated with an information plate having an arrow from L1 to L7 and another from L5 to L7. It is first shown that L5 is a simple effector for L7, and it is then shown that if L5 and L1 are on during any single time period, L7 will not be turned on automatically during the following period. The notation "1 → $\overline{7}$" is introduced to mean that L1 prevents L7. It is pointed out that the preventor relation takes precedence over the other two relations and that this is exemplified by the fact that although "5 → 7," "15 → $\overline{7}$" implying that the effector relation between L5 and L7 has been nullified by the preventor relation between L1 and L7. Attention is directed to the fact that two operations are necessary to prove explicitly that L1 is a preventor of L7: first that L5 is sufficient to produce L7, i.e., "5 → 7," and then that it will not do so if combined with L1, i.e., "15 → $\overline{7}$." It is further pointed out that the fact that L1 alone leads to nothing, i.e., "1 → 0" means only that L1 is not a simple effector for L7, but does not rule out the possibility of its being a combinor.

The subgoal condition is then demonstrated with an information plate with three arrows pointing toward the center light X—one from each of L2, L3, and L8. The experimenter tries each of these lights singly and points out that since none of them leads to X being turned on, none of them is a simple effector for X. If the subject does not volunteer the information, it is then pointed out that if there is any way of turning on the center light, it must be by a pair of combinors. The indicated lights are then tried in pairs until it is found that only the combination "38" will yield the center light, i.e., "38 → X."

It is then stressed that in an actual problem-solving effort it would not be sagacious to be satisfied with the knowledge that "38 → X" and to omit determining what relation exists between L2 and X. It is pointed out that, in this case, it can be inferred with confidence that L2 prevents X, since it has already been shown that it is not a simple effector nor a combinor with any other light. At this point the following inferential basis is stressed: if there is an arrow between two lights, there is a relation between them; if there is a relation between two lights, there will be an arrow between them indicating the direction of the relation; if there is a relation between two lights, it will be one of the three relations defined above, viz., effector, combinor, or preventor.

The subject is then asked to demonstrate the explicit test required to show that L2 is a preventor of X, i.e., he is expected to show that "38 → X" and that "238 → 0." He is then shown a notation for this subgoal condition, viz., "$\overline{2}$38 → X." It is then stressed that in all problems that he will encounter there will be a subgoal condition that will have to be realized in order to solve the problem and that all of the lights belonging to this subgoal condition can always be identified immediately from inspection of the information plate by the fact that each will always have an arrow leading from it to the center.

A proper solution is demonstrated with the aid of an information plate for a sample problem of about the same difficulty as the first experimental problem. By way of introduction, the experimenter explains at this point that the problem-solving effort in this situation can be regarded as comprised of two periods: first, an exploratory phase in which the nature of the various indicated relations are identified, and, second, a phase during which an effort is made to enter a proper solution. The proper solution is then defined as one that satisfies all of the three following conditions: (1) it begins at any null time, i.e., after any arbitrary time interval during which none of the lights in the display ring were on; (2) it consists of a set of button pressing operations confined entirely to *red* buttons, i.e., buttons 4, 5, and 6; and (3) it terminates by lighting the center light.

It is emphasized that during the exploratory, or information-gathering phase, it is not only permitted but is actually highly desirable to use both red and black buttons either singly or in any combination. At this time, it is also explained that since some of the problems that will be offered are rather complex, it will be to the subject's advantage to keep careful notes on the information elicited during this exploratory period and to make use of the vertical rulings on his note paper to keep track of time relations. It is further pointed out that the experimenter, in all of the demonstrations and solutions that he performs, will use a single-solution strategy called the "backward solution procedure" which he explains in detail with every demonstration. The subject is encouraged to learn this strategy and to ask questions about it whenever they arise. The experimenter then solves the demonstration problem, X-A, using a rather verbose "talking-out" method.

Procedure

On the first day of testing with a particular subject, he was given the general orientation described above and an opportunity to work on an additional demonstration problem, X-C, by himself. If he asked for help, or if the experimenter felt that he seemed confused, assistance was given by reviewing that part of the instructions that seemed relevant to the difficulty. When this problem was completed, the first day's work was terminated. The session lasted about 40–60 minutes.

The second session was begun by asking the subject to read a typewritten copy of the instructions as described above. He was encouraged to ask for elucidation of any point that was unclear and was reminded that he was free to refer to his copy of the instructions at any time. The backward solution procedure was then reviewed by the experimenter's demonstration of Problem X-C, the last problem solved on the previous day's testing. The subject was again encouraged to ask questions about anything that was unclear. When these matters were disposed of, Problem 1-A was administered. The subject was told that he would be allowed a full half-hour to solve it and that he would be questioned at the end of the session about specific relations obtaining in it. If the subject solved the problem within the allotted time, he was immediately given a quiz that enabled the experimenter to detect any details of the relations that might not be clearly understood. Any misconceptions thus identified were corrected immediately. If the subject did not solve the problem within the allotted time, he was interrupted and given the quiz. After supplying any information that seemed necessary from the quiz results, the experimenter demonstrated the backward solution of the problem, answered any questions that the subject asked, and then terminated the session.

On the next day of testing, which might or might not be the day after the first test, depending on the subject's convenience, after a review of the instructions, the experimenter again demonstrated the backward solution of Problem 1-A and offered to answer any questions. This having been done, Problem 1.5-A, representing the second level of difficulty, was administered if the subject had solved Problem 1-A himself in the preceding session. If he had not solved this problem, he was given Problem 1-C, an equivalent form of 1-A obtained from the latter by a number permutation. Again, after solving the problem, or after an unsuccessful half-hour's work, a quiz on the specific relations involved in the problem was given. If the subject failed the C-form of any problem, he was discontinued.

The general form of this procedure, i.e., review of instructions by the subject, review of the backward solution of the previous day's problem by the experimenter, work on a new problem by the subject followed by a quiz on the specific relations involved, and, if the subject failed, demonstration of the backward solution of the new problem by the experimenter, was repeated from day to day until the subject had passed all four levels of difficulty or had failed some one level twice.

SUBJECTS

A group of 12 females, mean age 23 years, most of whom were college students, were compared with 11 retired government employees or their wives, mean age 66 years, range 60 to 85, most of whom were high school graduates. Five of the older subjects, a chemist, three engineers, and a retired editor, had certainly had considerably more formal education than any of the younger group.

RESULTS

The performances of the older subjects were strikingly inferior to those of the younger not only with respect to maximum and minimum achievement but also with respect to the manifest quality of the heuristic processes brought to bear in the efforts to produce solutions. The number of subjects in each age group achieving and failing various levels of difficulty is shown in Table 1.

Table 1. Numbers of subjects passing at various levels of difficulty

Forms	Age group[a]	Difficulty levels			
		1	*2*	*3*	*4*
First	Young	10	10	10	
	Old	3	5	1	0
Second	Young	2	2	2	4
	Old	5	1	0	0
At least one	Young	12	12	12	11
	Old	8	6	1	0

[a] Young group, N = 12; old group, N = 11.

There is very little suggestion that the two groups were at all comparable with respect to their abilities to solve this type of problem.

Thus, for example, it will be noted that only 2 of the 12 younger subjects needed a second chance on the first level of difficulty and that they both succeeded on the second form, while 8 of the 11 older subjects failed the first form at this level and 3 of those attempting the second form failed it. Conversely it will be noted that 11 of the 12 younger subjects passed at least one of the problems at the highest level of difficulty, whereas only one of the older subjects succeeded at the third level of difficulty. Striking though these differences in levels of difficulty achieved may be, there are additional indications of the inferiority of the older subjects derivable from Table 1. For example, the younger subjects, in spite of the fact that they were, on the average, working at higher levels of difficulty than the older, solved more than 79 percent of the problems that they attempted as compared with a 35 percent success among the older subjects. Similarly, more than 78 percent of the younger subjects' successes, but only 60 percent of the older subjects', were achieved at the first attempt. Rather than elaborate further on the magnitude of the observed difference in achievement, or product, it is more to the purpose of this study to direct attention to certain details of performance which contribute to the identification of the process deficits that appear to be primarily responsible for the observed disparities in problem solving proficiency.

The figures in Table 2 refer to certain aspects of the problem-solving process that seem to explain the difficulties experienced by the older subjects. All values in this table are medians, which were chosen as indices in preference to averages because the latter would be too heavily weighted for the old subjects, by performances that were failures. The first two rows of this table simply show that there were no marked differences in the rates at which the two groups worked. The time per inquiry was obtained for each subject by dividing the time that he worked on a given problem by the number of inquiries made, an inquiry being defined as any button-pressing operation, or set of operations, that began and terminated with a null period. The entries in the first row of Table 2 are the medians of the individual values obtained in this manner. Waiting times were measured in terms of the number of periods between the second null period after the termination of a given inquiry to the beginning of the next one, i.e., a waiting time was 2 less than the number of periods between inquiries so that, if a given inquiry was started during the first two periods after the termination of the preceding inquiry, the intertrial interval was not counted as a waiting time. The percent waiting time was obtained by dividing the sum of the waiting times for a given problem by the total number of periods before the first operation of the first proper solution.

The entries in the table are the medians of the individual percentages for each of the age groups at the two levels of difficulty analyzed. It will be observed from these data that there were no marked differences between the two age groups with respect to the rates at which they worked.

Table 2. General analysis of inquiry (medians)

Factors	First level		Second level	
	Young	*Old*	*Young*	*Old*
Seconds per inquiry	37	36	27	21
Percentage waiting time	45	50	46	52
Number of inquiries	20	56	30	85
Redundant inquiries	7	40	15	65
Percentage redundancy	35	72	49	75
Goal-effector condition	7	41	6	33

The third row of Table 2 shows the median numbers of inquiries made before reaching a solution for the two age groups at the two levels of difficulty. The total number of questions put to the machine during the half-hour work period was taken as the score for a subject who failed a given problem; this, of course, is an underestimation of the number of inquiries necessary for the subject to solve the problem in question. These data indicate that the older subjects made about three times as many inquiries as the younger subjects did on the first level of difficulty and more than twice as many on the second level. This result is the more remarkable in view of the fact that about 80 percent of the attempts by the younger subjects were successful, whereas more than 50 percent of the attempts by the older subjects were failures. Thus, the younger subjects produced much more satisfactory results from fewer questions than the older subjects did from many more. The general increase in the number of questions from the first to the second level probably reflects the difference in difficulty between levels. The fact that the relative increase between levels was less for the older subjects than for the younger ones can be attributed to at least two factors: (1) three old subjects who failed at the lower level were not tested at the second one; (2) the fact that more old subjects failed at both levels tended to keep the number of inquiries close to a maximum at both levels.

The next row provides some explanation of why the older subjects showed so little return for their numerous questions. Their augmented number of inquiries elicited no more information than the fewer questions of the younger subjects, because their questions were highly repetitious. The entries in this row show the number of inquiries made relative to information that had already been elicited; they were obtained by subtracting the number of different inquiries from the total number of questions. It will be observed that the older subjects asked 4 or 5 times as many redundant questions as the younger, but this might be anticipated, to a certain extent, from the fact that they generally made more inquiries, so that they would have a greater number of redundant questions even if their relative redundancy were the same as that of the younger subjects. The index of relative redundancy, in the next row, was obtained by dividing, for each subject, the number of repetitious inquiries by the total number of questions. The results show that even in this relative sense the older subjects exhibited a remarkable degree of redundancy, almost three-quarters of their inquiries being repetitious. At both levels of difficulty, the younger subjects devoted a much smaller proportion of their time to redundant questions.

The entries in the row labeled "goal-effector condition" are the median numbers of trials preceding the elicitation of explicit identification of the immediate effector antecedents of the center light. It will be recalled from the instructions that this item of information is the first object of inquiry in the backward solution procedure. Without it, the problem-solver has no goal that is specific to the problem under consideration; the turning on of the center light as a signal of success is not a goal specific to any problem, but is common to all, and is useful primarily as a correctness criterion that should be deliberately employed to identify the specific goal of each particular problem. This identification can always be achieved with 6 inquiries by the backward solution procedure, and it will be noted that this is very close to the median number of questions employed by the younger subjects to elicit it at both levels of difficulty. The older subjects, on the other hand, employed about 6 times as many questions to elicit the same information, indicating that, in general, they did not have explicit knowledge of the goal of a particular problem until very late in the total exploratory effort.

DISCUSSION

Rate of inquiry. The failure to detect important age differences in the rate of inquiry under the conditions of this experiment should not appear remarkable in view of the fact that sensory-motor coordination and speed and accuracy of movement could have influenced only an exceedingly small portion of the total time involved in the problem-solving efforts analyzed. Relatively great proportions of this time were devoted to decision-making, to selection of promising orders of inquiry, and to the integration of information, though this seems to have been more true of the younger than of the older subjects. It is, of course, permissible to speculate to the effect that the older subjects operated under an extraexperimentally induced compulsion to maintain an arbitrarily chosen rate of inquiry which, though adequate for younger people, failed to provide sufficient opportunity for effective reflection under their own decelerated rate of mental operation. It seems less tortuous, however, to simply indicate the fact that it is not the speed but the quality of the older person's inquiry that is impugned by the results of this experiment.

Redundancy. The most prominent indication of the inferior quality of the oldster's performance was the remarkable redundancy of his search behavior. In order to cope successfully with the problems employed in this experiment, he had to elicit a considerable amount of information, piece by piece, that could not be used immediately, but was needed for an ultimate integration by parts. It is obvious, as Welford (1958) suggests in comment on the results of problem-solving tasks making this kind of demand, that if the older subject suffers an impairment of short-term memory, storage or retrieval of necessary information is defective, and redundancy of inquiry is a natural compensation. It should be noted, however, that the subject had access to a much less troublesome and a completely effective means of permanent storage.

Note-taking. It will be recalled from the section on instructions that the subject was provided with a convenient notational system and was encouraged to take notes. Moreover, the experimenter made a deliberate effort to inculcate this useful practice upon the subject not only by repeated urging but also by providing good example in all of his demonstration solutions. Meagerness of notes was a distinctive characteristic of the oldsters' performance. This finding is quite in agreement with Welford's (1958) report of a problem-solving experiment by Clay. When, in compliance to rather insistent exhortation, an older subject occasionally did produce an appreciable quantity of notes on a given problem, he usually complained that he could make no use of them and could see no reason for writing them.

The experimenter was inclined to agree. In most cases, the old subject's notes were indecipherable to the subject himself, during the quiz that immediately followed the problem the solution of which they were intended to facilitate. Though it would seem to be an unpromising enterprise to attempt to distinguish between young and old subjects on the basis of decipherability of notes, the young subjects appeared to feel that they were very useful and frequently chided themselves for their inability to decipher them. It is possible that illegibility was responsible for much of the younger subject's redundancy, but the older subject's inability to derive advantage from his notes appears to be more irremediable in that it is associated with the following more fundamental impediment to efficient solution.

Order of exploration. A review of the general plan of the problems and of the rationale of the backward solution procedure provides a clue to a possible explanation of the inadequacy and, hence, the paucity of the older subject's notes. After the identification of the specific goal, a typical problem reduces to finding three sequences of related lights each leading from a set of red-button operations to one of the three lights having an arrow on the center light. The subject was repeatedly advised to trace out each of these paths separately without concerning himself with the other two during the exploratory phase of his attempt to find a solution. If this is done systematically, the sequence of events from any required set of red-button operations to the subgoal light that it activates can usually be written as a single formula having less than 4 or 5 links (→). Usually there are only three such formulas that need to be integrated temporally in order to achieve appropriate time relations. The backward search procedure has the properties of a solution strategy (Bruner *et al.*, 1956) in that it determines an order of inquiry that controls the probability of securing relevant information from each question and reduces the cognitive strain of searching for the solution by determining an effective order of inquiry, by organizing questions into groups in such a manner that only the answer to the last question in a group needs to be stored, and by guarding the work on any single group against interference from materials relevant to other groups.

It was characteristic of the older subject's search behavior that it failed to suggest concentration on single paths until each was completely traced, but showed, rather, considerable fluctuation from one path to another with an apparent disregard of red-button terminations. As a result of this lack of order in the search plan, information concerning any given conceptually unified sequence was temporally distributed in an apparently haphazard fashion. This probably increases very greatly the difficulty of perceiving the relatedness of the several components of the sequence.

Goal identification. All of the problems employed in this experiment had certain aspects in common and among these were the following: (1) all information plates indicated three lights that had arrows pointing toward the center light; (2) the activating condition for the center light was a combinor relation involving one of the three pairs that could be formed from the three lights mentioned in (1); (3) one of the three lights mentioned in (1) was a preventor. Identification of the specific goal for a given problem always consisted in finding out which of the pairs mentioned in (2) was the activating combination. This having been done, it could usually be inferred that the remaining member of (1) was a preventor. There was only one way to find out which pair of lights combined to activate the center, and that was by direct test.

Until this test was performed the subject had available to guide his inquiry only the vague idea that the important lights were among the three lights having arrows on the center, and that paths to these lights from red-button lights would have to be found: the relevant sequences were not clearly identifiable or completely meaningful until the specific subgoal was identified. It was a prominent characteristic of the older subjects' performance that they explored many relations quite remote from the specific goal before they performed the test necessary for identifying it. During this period, frequently 15 or 20 minutes long and often involving more than half of the total exploration, the subject's search could have been no more than vaguely goal-oriented.

This lack of goal-orientation during most of his exploration explains the older subject's failure to produce solutions and also explains many of the details of his inadequate performance. Thus, without having identified the goal, he was unable to direct his early search along the relevant paths and, in consequence, distributed his inquiries more or less randomly among the important sequences. This, in turn, made it difficult to recognize which items of information were related and which were not. With a haphazard order of acquiring information, it was necessary to record every item elicited because it could not be immediately assimilated, but had to be preserved for possible future use. Hence, note-taking became exhaustive and tedious, and because there was little order even in the notes, they were extremely difficult to use, and it is little wonder that the older subjects abandoned note-taking quite early in the exploration. As a result of having rejected the only storage device available other than his memory, the older subject soon found himself overwhelmed with a multitude of unrelated facts, and his information began to decay rapidly. In this distressing situation, he kept repeating his inquiries in a rather hopeless effort to maintain his insecure stock of information. It is quite true that we cannot be sure that all the inadequacies of the older subject's problem-solving behavior, as observed in this experiment, were consequences of his failure to observe the fundamental rule of heuristics, "Always be sure you know exactly what is required by the problem before you try to solve it!" but neither can we be sure that this was not the case. What seems to be needed, at the present time, is an item by item experimental check on the older person's capacity to reacquire the ability to apply the fundamental heuristic principles interpreted in the backward solution procedure for the logical analysis problems.

DECAY OF HEURISTIC BEHAVIOR PATTERNS

It has been noted above that the backward solution procedure is a solution strategy and that the results of our experiment indicate that the older subjects, in very marked contrast to the younger ones, were unable to apply it effectively. Superficially this resembles a failure to learn the backward procedure, and this is quite true, as far as it goes. Such an interpretation disregards, however, the essential property of a strategy and what it is that a person should see in, and do, with a strategy. First of all a solution strategy is simple, because it is intended to simplify the finding of the solution. It is, in fact, merely a particular interpretation or application of a small set of heuristic principles especially relevant to a class of problems to which the strategy is intended to apply. For example, the backward search procedure is intended to tell the subject how to apply, to the set of logical analysis device problems, a few elementary rules of heuristics given, among others, by Polya (1948, 1954) in a form somewhat like the following: (a) What is the unknown? What is the condition? (b) Separate the various parts of the condition. Can you write them down? (c) Could you solve part of the problem? Keep only a part of the condition, drop the other part. (d) Can you coordinate the parts you have solved?

Clearly, we do not want the subject to memorize particular backward search procedures, and neither the young nor the old subjects gave the slightest sign of doing so. We want him to recognize the small set of familiar and, we hope, well-practiced heuristic principles in a new form. Demonstration of the strategy simply shows him how to apply these ancient precepts to the test situation. In fact, giving a demonstration really detracts deplorably from the sophistication of the experiment and deprives the really capable subjects of an opportunity to demonstrate their superiority. It is quite reasonable to expect a normal person to develop the backward search procedure for himself from his long-standing familiarity with the heuristic principles required.

An investigation of the ability to develop, on the basis of experience with a class of problems, strategies and applications of heuristic principles appropriate to their solution will have to be undertaken eventually; to transfer the heuristics that he knows from the abstract to the concrete is the only real test of ability to apply them. This type of behavior seems to be the essence of creativity.

The present study indicates that the patterns of heuristic behavior, so laboriously built up during youth through formal education and emulation of skillful acquaintances, decay with age. What seems to decay is some kind of facility for recognizing occasions for the application of heuristically controlled behavior. Unfortunately, heuristics, as here understood, is an allegedly dead branch of logic and philosophy which for some unknown reason has not been consciously and deliberately revivified by psychologists. Polya (1948, 1954), the modern proponent of this lost discipline, offers the following by way of definition: "Modern heuristics endeavors to understand the process of solving problems, especially the *mental operations typically useful* in this process."

Most psychologists will, of course, insist that, according to this definition, it is a gross exaggeration to say that the study of heuristics is moribund. Even a cursory review of the literature of problem-solving will reveal a very lively interest in most of the topics included in Polya's dictionary of heuristics (1948). What may have been dead is the word and an interest in the subject matter it denotes as a discipline with its own rubrics. It may, however, be to the advantage of the psychology of aging to encourage the revitalization of this ancient category of distinction because the behavior governed by its content appears to be especially sensitive to the depredations of age, and, therefore, worthy of intensive systematic study. The isolation of this type of age change also directs attention to the fact that the behavior in question is obviously initiated, elaborated, and sustained by education and practice, and, consequently, may well be responsive to both preventive and remedial measures. We interpret the results of the experiment reported here to suggest that a strong effort should be made to study the possibility of reeducating the aged in the heuristic principles that seem so clearly to have decayed.

REFERENCES

Bruner, J. S., Goodnow, Jacqueline, J., and Austin, G. A. 1956. A study of thinking. New York: John Wiley & Sons.

John, E. R. 1957. Contributions to the study of the problem-solving process. Psychol. Monogr., 71, No. 18: 1–39.

Polya, G. 1948. How to solve it; a new aspect of mathematical method. Princeton: Princeton University Press.

———— 1954. Mathematics and plausible reasoning. Princeton: Princeton University Press.

Welford, A. T. 1958. Ageing and human skill. London: Oxford University Press.

Some Examples of Nonparametric Statistics in the Study of Age Differences in Intellectual Decline

DENNIS B. BROMLEY

THIS report describes in nontechnical language some of the ways in which nonparametric statistics have been used in studies of the psychological concomitants of aging. The emphasis is on the *uses* to which nonparametric methods may be put rather than on the *theory* underlying them. The intention is to show how some common problems of experimental design and inference in the psychological study of aging may be conveniently handled by these methods.

Birren (1959) says that the validity of a cross-sectional study of aging is limited to the question of whether or not age differences exist; but it can be argued that a cross-sectional study can answer questions only about the differential effects of aging. There are restrictions imposed upon mental tests as measuring instruments such that we cannot answer questions like, "How much decline with age, if any, is there in this particular intellectual ability?" But we can answer questions like "Does this particular ability decline with age more or less than this other ability?" For example, we cannot, except in an arbitrary way, compute the percentage decrement with age in short-term memory, but we can demonstrate that short-term memory declines with age more rapidly than does the availability of general information; again, we can say that symptoms of thought pathology show an increase with age, even in normal and high-grade subjects, relative to vocabulary or IQ.

Before one can say anything about age-differences in dependent variables such as general information, short-term memory or concept-formation, one must establish some sort of baseline. In cross-sectional studies this is usually done by showing that several groups of subjects, differing in age, are nevertheless comparable in respect to certain control variables such as vocabulary or IQ. It is as if one were saying, "The younger subjects in my sample will grow up to be like the older men" or, "The older men in my sample used to be like the younger men," and one goes on to specify the ways in which the subjects have been selected. For example, the subjects taking part in the studies relating to this report were selected on the basis of their vocabulary, IQ, and educational-occupational status. The usual assumption is that age differences in intellectual abilities cannot be assessed unless such variables are held constant, but in fact there is nothing in the logic of the procedure to justify this assumption; one might just as well match the several age groups for, say, maze learning and then observe age differences in other variables relative to this base line. One would expect vocabulary, IQ, socioeconomic status, and education to increase with age relative to maze learning. The same argument seems to apply not only to cross-sectional studies but also to longitudinal studies because, for example, even if one were able to demonstrate increases of score on retest after an interval of years one could safely interpret these increases only relative to some other longitudinal changes in score.

Before any conclusions can be drawn about the effects of age on the dependent variables, one normally tests the hypothesis that the age groups are in fact comparable in respect to the "matching" or "independent" variables. If both men and women are being studied, it is desirable to show that sex differences on the independent variables have been eliminated. If traditional parametric methods are used to test hypotheses about age differences or sex differences, then statistical procedures such as analysis of variance, t-tests, product-moment correlations, or regression equations would be appropriate. Such statistical procedures, powerful when properly used, have to be supported by a number of assumptions which the investigator cannot always meet, e.g., assumptions about the size of the sample, the normality of the distributions, the equality of the variances, and the metrical properties of the test. Informed opinions seem to differ on the question of what the investigator should do when he cannot make the assumptions. Some say, "Go ahead, the tests are robust anyway and they are not unduly affected if the assumptions are not met." Others say, "Why expose yourself to such risks when you can use methods which do not require you to make such dubious assumptions?"

The arguments for and against the use of nonparametric statistics in the psychological and social sciences have been summarized by Siegel (1956). Many psychologists find nonparametric methods more satisfying to work with and more meaningful; and they constantly remind the experimenter that his findings depend not so much on the elegance of his statistical treatment as on the validity and reliability of his observations. The possibility that slight age differences may not be

detected by nonparametric methods seems to be of no great consequence, and the possibility of error exists for parametric methods if
their assumptions are not met. The important point is not that nonparametric methods are crude but that parametric methods are invalid
to the extent that their assumptions are not met. Additional reasons
for adopting nonparametric statistics in the research work relating to
this report were: (a) that the results might provide interesting comparisons with the results obtained by other workers using parametric
statistics; and (b) that Welford (1958) has recommended the use of
a wide variety of small-scale investigations to explore the psychological
aspects of aging and to replicate earlier studies, for which nonparametric statistics seem appropriate.

EXAMPLES

The first example is the use of the Wald-Wolfowitz Runs Test
to test the hypothesis that the 80 male and 80 female subjects in the
main sample ($N = 160$) do not differ in chronological age. An interesting feature of this example is that the age distribution is rectangular;
this was intended, and normalizing it would have been absurd. The
procedure is to rank all subjects in order of chronological age and then
to count the number of *runs* of males and females. The expected
(chance) number of runs is 81, whereas the observed number is 93.
This gives a z-value of 1.9, but z-values need to be tested for significance only when $r_o < r_e$. The decision is to accept the null hypothesis
that the age distributions of men and women in this sample do not
differ in respect to central tendency, variability, or skewness.

However, of these three characteristics, central tendency is perhaps
the most important, and it can be examined more efficiently by the
Mann-Whitney U *Test*. Siegel (1956) says that it is one of the most
powerful of the nonparametric tests and a useful alternative to the
parametric t-test. This is the second example; the procedure is to
rank the subjects in order of age and to count the number of men that
precede each woman. The expected value of this statistic U is 3200,
whereas the observed value is 3036; the z-value of this difference is
-0.56, which is not significant, and the decision is to accept the null
hypothesis that the age distributions for men and women do not differ
in central tendency.

The third example is the use of the Kolmogorov-Smirnov two-
sample test to examine the hypothesis that the men and women in
the main sample are comparable in respect to vocabulary, Wechsler-

Bellevue IQ, and social background rating. For each variable in turn, this test compares the cumulative frequency distributions for men and women; in each case the distributions are not significantly different at any point and the decision is to accept the null hypothesis that the two groups do not differ in respect to central tendency, variability, or skewness.

The fourth example is the use of Spearman's well-known Rank Correlation Coefficient (Rho) to examine hypotheses relating to age differences. Rho has been paralleled recently by Kendall's Rank Correlation Coefficient (Tau) (Kendall, 1955); both are measures of association and both have their advantages and disadvantages. The following values of Rho are a few among many observed between chronological age and test score, -0.10 for Wechsler-Bellevue IQ, $+0.11$ for Wechsler-Bellevue Vocabulary, -0.27 for Similarities. The absolute values are unimportant; what is important is the relative size and direction of the coefficients, particularly if corroboration is possible—this aspect of method will be discussed later. The Kruskal-Wallis One-Way Analysis of Variance can be used to test whether or not age relationships exist, but there is no point in using it if it is possible to use Rho or Tau which not only test for the existence of an age relationship but also show its size and direction.

The fifth example illustrates a method of cross-validation by means of Kendall's Coefficient of Concordance (W). This statistic measures the degree of association between k ranked variables. In the investigations to which this report refers, one sample of 160 subjects and two samples of 48 subjects are assessed on the Wechsler-Bellevue Form I (Wechsler, 1944) and Spearman Rank Order Correlations are computed between each of 11 subtests and chronological age for each of the three samples. Then, for each sample separately, these values of Rho are ranked in order from the largest positive to the largest negative value. Casual inspection of the three sets of rankings reveals considerable similarity of order, and the calculated value of W is 0.89 showing that there is a significant and substantial measure of agreement between the samples in the way the various Wechsler-Bellevue subtests are associated with age. Summing three ranks for each subtest and reranking these sums enables the experimenter to get a more reliable picture of the differential rates of decline with age of the various intellectual functions measured by the Wechsler-Bellevue Scale.

DISCUSSION

The results achieved by using nonparametric methods agree substantially with those achieved by Wechsler's methods. Unfortunately, Wechsler does not give age correlations or regression equations for his subtests, and his selection of "hold" and "don't hold" subtests is different in the WAIS (Wechsler, 1958) from what it is in WB I. In fact, one cannot distinguish clearly between "hold" and "don't hold" tests because the difference is one of degree not one of kind.

There are two disturbing features of Wechsler's method: (1) Although Wechsler admits that performance tests reveal age differences more clearly than do verbal tests, yet the results referred to in this report show that the least declining performance subtest is declining more that the most declining verbal subtest, and one could argue that verbal and performance functions which are not comparable in respect of age decline ought not to be grouped together as "hold" or "don't hold" tests for the purpose of computing a "deterioration quotient." (2) The margin of difference in age decline between a test which is included in, say, the "hold" group, and one which is not can be very small and leaves one with the impression that the final selection is both arbitrary and unreliable and certainly less efficient than it need be. Part of the interest of the present investigations is the search for a wider range of differential effects of aging. In the field of verbal functions one might expect word-learning and concept-formation not to hold up well with age, although Graham-White (1960) has presented evidence against the former. In the present investigations, proverb interpretation, analogies, and verbal measures of abstraction and generalization are all adversely affected by age. In the field of performance functions temporal-integration and concept-formation (Hearnshaw, 1956; Bromley, 1961) are adversely affected.

It is of interest to ask why verbal and performance tests should be so differently affected by aging—assuming that the speed factor in Wechsler's performance tests has not obscured the issue. It is well-known that some of the most useful diagnostic instruments are performance tests, e.g., those of Goldstein and Scheerer (1941), Halstead (1947), and Semeonoff and Trist (1958). It is curious that language functions should be so resistant to the deleterious efforts of normal aging; perhaps the explanation is that they are less likely than performance functions to suffer from decay through disuse. An example will illustrate how little we really know about language functions in relation to age. Vocabulary is usually measured by asking the subject to define words, and this ability holds up with age relatively well; suppose vocabulary were measured by asking the subject to find words to fit definitions, should we find that this ability too holds up with age? The answer is that we do not know.

One example of the use of nonparametric statistics in the psychological study of aging has been reserved for this section of the report. It describes briefly a method developed by the author (Bromley, 1959) which has not been widely published and requires further work in respect to its validity and usefulness. The method is called "rank order cluster analysis" and it is an attempt to apply the nonparametric approach to areas which are normally dealt with by factor-analysis. The method, taking a matrix of rank-order correlations as its starting point, separates out clusters of tests having similar correlation profiles, i.e., similar factorial compositions, and then defines an equal number of cluster-factors along which subjects can be ranked. The structure and pattern values for both cluster factors and normal factors (orthogonal to the cluster-factors), and the relations between the cluster factors can be calculated.

"Rank order cluster analysis" gives a solution analogous to the oblique simple structure solution in factor-analysis but this is not to say that the two methods are interchangeable. Like other nonparametric methods, "rank order cluster analysis" is crude compared with its parametric counterpart, and, like them, it has its own advantages and disadvantages. The aim of the procedure, of course, is to reduce the number of variables under consideration. The method, applied to the Wechsler-Bellevue results of the three samples of subjects already discussed, produced substantial but not perfect agreement between samples. Two cluster-factors were identified—a verbal cluster comprising vocabulary, information, comprehension similarities and possibly digit span, and a performance cluster comprising arithmetic, picture completion, picture arrangement, object assembly, block design, and digit symbol substitution. The pattern of loadings for the Wechsler-Bellevue subtests was so similar from one sample to the next as to give concordance (W) values of 0.77 and 0.96 for the two factors. The two cluster-factors were related to age in the same ways in each sample, in that the performance factor declined with age relative to the verbal factor; the rank-order correlations with age were −0.82 and −0.17, respectively, in the main sample. Work is in progress to apply the method of "rank order cluster analysis" to larger Rho matrices in order to explore the possibility of additional or subsidiary clusters, especially in the field of conceptual processes.

CONCLUSIONS

Some of the reasons why nonparametric statistics are desirable in psychological research on aging have been stated and some examples have been given of their use in research in progress. In general, the results are comparable with those obtained by parametric methods. This result is valuable in itself because it suggests that our beliefs about the effects of age on intellectual processes are reasonably sound. However, there is no guarantee that this comparability will hold for future findings, and the best research policy seems to be that of using a variety of methods on a variety of problems.

Nonparametric statistics are developing rapidly and it seems reasonable to look forward to the time when methods will become available for dealing, in a nonparametric way, with hypotheses which are not as yet amenable to this approach. In this connection, a method called "rank order cluster analysis" is being developed. Nonparametric statistics are not only of direct value in that they enable the experimenter to cope with certain sorts of data, but also of indirect value in that they help to reveal interesting problems, relationships, and anomalies which provide directions for further research.

REFERENCES

Birren, J. E. (ed.). 1959. Handbook of aging and the individual. Chicago: University of Chicago Press.

Bromley, D. B. 1959. Rank order cluster-analysis. (Unpublished manuscript, The University of Liverpool.)

───── Age differences in conceptual abilities. *In* Wilma Donahue, C. Tibbitts, R. H. Williams (eds.), Psychological and social processes of aging: an international research seminar. To be published.

Goldstein, K. and Scheerer, M. 1941. Abstract and concrete behaviour: experimental study with special tests. Psychol. Monogr., 53: 151.

Graham-White, J. 1960. The effects of age on learning and memory in people over 60. Bull. Brit. Psychol. Soc., No. 42, 98. (Abstract).

Halstead, W. C. 1947. Brain and intelligence: a quantitative study of the frontal lobes. Chicago: University of Chicago Press.

Hearnshaw, L. S. 1956. Temporal integration and behaviour. Bull. Brit. Psychol. Soc., 30: 1–20.

Kendall, M. G. 1955. Rank correlation methods. London: Charles Griffin & Co.

Semeonoff, B., and Trist, E. 1958. Diagnostic performance tests: a manual for use with adults. London: Tavistock Publishers.

Siegel, S. 1956. Nonparametric statistics. New York: McGraw-Hill Book Co.

Wechsler, D. 1944. The measurement of adult intelligence. Baltimore: Williams and Wilkins Co.

———— 1958. The measurement and appraisal of adult intelligence. London: Ballière, Tindall, and Cox.

Welford, A. T. 1958. Ageing and human skill. London: Oxford University Press.

Rigidity and Age

SHEILA M. CHOWN

STUDIES relating age to rigidity are rare, yet age differences in adaptability to new situations are often assumed to exist by those faced with practical decisions in industry and elsewhere. The area is therefore one of general importance.

Rigidity has been taken to mean lack of change of behavior where a change is necessary for success at the task, and where the subject knows that a change is likely to be demanded. The literature on such rigidity is immense, and has been surveyed elsewhere (Chown, 1959, 1960). Since rigidity-flexibility is almost certainly not a unitary trait, the relationship between its several aspects and age may be expected to vary.

The aims of the present research were first, to find out whether overlap occurred between types of rigidity named by other workers, and, second, to see what effects age had on performance in various rigidity tasks and on the relationships between these tasks.

In the present study eighteen tests were selected from many used by other workers. These included an inventory of liking for change, (Wesley, 1953), tests of psychomotor or disposition rigidity (Cattell, 1946*a, b*) and two types of intellectual rigidity (Guilford *et al.*, 1957). Tests of nonverbal intelligence and vocabulary were also used (Raven, 1938, 1943). It was hypothesized that spontaneous and adaptive flexibility would, on the basis of Guilford's work, remain distinct, and also that disposition rigidity, personality rigidity and speed would remain separate, since Schaie (1958) found them to be so. If overlaps occurred, it was expected that they would be between these groups and with intelligence.

The tests were all group-administered and were given to 200 subjects ranging in age from 20 to 82. Subjects were obtained from military hospitals, foreman courses, adult education classes, veterans clubs, and over-60s clubs.

The intercorrelations of 26 test scores in the form of stanines (including age) were factor-analyzed by Hotelling's principal components method. After obtaining 8 factors, which accounted for 63 percent of the variance, the analysis was stopped when the latent root of the ninth factor was less than 1.00. Hand rotations were carried out to remove two factors, those of nonverbal intelligence and age. The remaining six were subjected to Kaiser's normal varimax method of rotation and later tidied up by hand rotation.

Disregarding for the moment the intelligence and age factors, four of the five rigidities remained distinct, with separate factors and no overlap. These were spontaneous flexibility, personality rigidity, speed, and disposition rigidity (which in fact gave rise to two factors) (see Table 1).

Looking at the intelligence factor it can be seen that spontaneous flexibility, adaptive flexibility, and speed all load highly on it. Adaptive flexibility is almost totally accounted for by this type of intelligence measure. One aspect of personality rigidity—the second, previously found to be associated with lack of intelligence—loaded negatively on the factor.

On the age factor, verbal intelligence and one aspect of personality rigidity—liking for habit—were positively associated with aging. Nonverbal intelligence and two of the adaptive flexibility tests loaded negatively on the age factor. Scores on these three tests and on the double alternation disposition rigidity test were in fact ones which declined in an approximately linear fashion with age. Scores on the other tests showed a curvilinear or inverted-U shape in relationship with age.

The results suggest that much of what is regarded as "rigid" behavior in older people may be due to a decline in "g." It is almost impossible to separate out the two in real life, since if "g" is held constant and age varied, life experiences are likely to have been very different. However, over and above the rigidity accounted for by present low intelligence, there are various forms of rigidities which differ in extent from person to person: and these differences are only rarely linked to the age of the person concerned.

Table 1. Rigidity factors[a]

Hypothesized factors	Tests	Obtained factors							
		Age	"g"	SF	PR	DR₁	DR₂	Sp.	Alph.
Age	Age	.81							
"g"	Raven Nonverbal	−.54	.64						
	Mill Hill Vocabulary	.54	.56						
Adaptive flexibility	Matches	−.51	.41						
	Hidden figures	−.36	.70						
	Squares		.64						
Spontaneous flexibility	Brick uses		.46	.56					
	General uses		.58	.53					
	Object naming		.49	.42					
	Impossibilities		.40	.48					
	Blots		.32	.66					
	Pictures		.37	.57					
Personality rigidity	Wesley 1				.80				
	Wesley 2		−.30		.53				
	Wesley 3	.48			.32				
Disposition rigidity	Ready (ratio)	.50				.72			
	Double "						.54		
	Alternate "						.49		
	237 "					.69			
	Signs "							.76	
	Alphabet "								
Speed	Writing ready		.55				.30	.47	.86
	" sentence		.61					.53	
	" 237		.51					.58	
	Signs (normal)		.67					.44	
	Alphabet (forwards)		.57						.52

[a] Age range, 20–82; N = 200; only values ≥ .30 are included.

REFERENCES

Cattell, R. B. 1946*a*. The riddle of perseveration: I. Creative effort and disposition rigidity. J. Personality, 14: 229–38.

———— 1946*b*. The riddle of perseveration: II. Solution in terms of personality structure. J. Personality, 14: 239–67.

Chown, Sheila M. 1959. Rigidity—a flexible concept. Psychol. Bull., 56: 195–223.

———— 1960. A factor analysis of the Wesley Rigidity Inventory: its relationship to age and non-verbal intelligence. J. Abnorm. & Social Psychol., 61: 491–94.

Guilford, J. P., Frick, J. W., Christensen, P. R., and Merrifed, P. R. 1957. A factor analytic study of flexibility in thinking. University of Southern California, Reports from the Psychological Laboratory, No. 18.

Raven, J. C. 1938. Progressive matrices. London: H. K. Lewis and Co. Ltd.

———— 1943. The Mill Hill Vocabulary Scale. London: H. K. Lewis and Co. Ltd.

Schaie, K. W. 1958. Rigidity—flexibility and intelligence: a cross-sectional study of the adult life span from 20 to 70 years. Psychol. Monogr., 72, No. 9: 1–26.

Wesley, Elizabeth. 1953. Perseverative behaviour in a concept formation task as a function of manifest anxiety and rigidity. J. Abnorm. & Social Psychol., 48: 129–34.

The Structure of Psychological and Psychomotor Functions in Relation to Age, in the Light of Factor Analysis

SUZANNE PACAUD

A Thurstone Multiple Factor Analysis was carried out on results obtained from about 4000 subjects performing a battery of tests which included psychomotor, memory, attention, and various intellectual tasks and which yielded 15 distinct scores. The subjects ranged in age from 19.5 to 55 years and were divided into 5-year age groups. Within each age group there were two subgroups of different educational levels.

We used a methodological approach, never employed up to now as far as we know. The youngest group (from 19 years and 6 months to 24 years and 5 months old) with the lower educational level was used as a *pilot group,* and upon their results a set of rotations of axes was performed.

We started from the hypothesis that if the constellations of the functions studied remain constant with age, the rotations of the axes performed on the pilot group would, when applied to the results of other age groups, produce constellations similar to those observed for the pilot group.

If, on the contrary, modifications in the constellations take place in the course of aging and if these modifications are lawful, we ought to be able to discern a certain regularity in the variations, either in the saturation of the functions by the factors, or in the displacing of the functions from one factor to another.

Last, if the modifications of the constellations in the course of aging are not lawful but are disorderly fluctuations, we ought to find

This paper appears in full in Wilma Donahue, C. Tibbitts, and R. H. Williams (eds.), *Psychological and Social Processes of Aging: An International Research Seminar* (to be published).

once again in other age groups the constellations brought to light in the pilot group.

The results obtained showed that the constellations of psychological and psychomotor functions studied remained constant throughout the age groups when the rotations of axes performed on the pilot group were carried over to the eleven other groups. Such deviations from constancy as did appear were not large when it is recognized that rotations of axes made on one group were carried over rigidly to the others.

An exception must be made, however, for a cluster composed of speed tests. No constancy of constellation appeared for any factor in this function, except concerning Factor 1 (concerned with psychomotor coordination).

A reasonable explanation of this fact could be made along the following lines:

The maintaining of speed, whether perceptual or psychomotor, over the course of life, depends on manifold and very diverse biological and ecological factors, the influence of which can profoundly modify the normal organic factors.

These influences impinge especially upon the speed function so that the regularities or laws of decline observed in this which are due either to the organic or to the ecological factors which cause the senescence of the individual are very much influenced by the "biographical" factors specific of each individual's own history and by the personal style of his actual life.

For this reason, speed does not necessarily change with age at the same rate as other functions, and some of the linkages between the speed function and others may deteriorate and other links be established as age advances.

The speed functions of the sample of the less-educated subjects is much more saturated with Factor 1 (concerned with psychomotor coordination) than is that of the more educated. This difference of saturation between the two educational levels remains extremely constant in all age groups. We believe this difference can be explained by saying that performance under pressure for speed sets in action different forms of work-organization in the two groups: with the subjects of the less-educated level, the factor of exclusively psychomotor organization has primacy over all other forms of organization. For the other psychomotor, mental, and intellectual functions, the constancy of the constellations with age held for both educational levels in most cases. Also, the level of saturation was nearly the same. Certain cases where the constancy did not hold suggest that the differences result in considerable part from occupational and attitudinal causes based on experience and environmental demand and associated with education because it provides techniques of approach to certain of the tests, especially of memory function.

Longitudinal Study of Intellectual Changes in Senescent Twins

LISSY F. JARVIK, FRANZ J. KALLMANN,

IRVING LORGE, AND ARTHUR FALEK

"ALTHOUGH the primary interest in old age research tends to be focused upon age changes, our scientific evidence consists chiefly of data for different individuals in different age groups. Such records yield normative indications of age decline, but they tell us little about process or about dynamically associated factors." This statement was made by the late Harold E. Jones (1959, p. 717), and the present report is intended to supply some much-needed longitudinal data on intellectual changes.

Our psychometric study of senescent twins was organized in 1947 as part of a long-term investigation of the hereditary aspects of aging and longevity.

PROCEDURE

Details concerning the collection of the series of more than 2500 twins over age 60 in New York State and closely adjacent areas have been published elsewhere (Kallmann and Sander, 1948). The sample for the psychometric follow-up was selected from this twin population frame as follows: In order to be designated as potential test cases, both twin partners had to be alive, of the same sex, in good health, white, literate, English-speaking, and residing in the community (not institutionalized). Originally, 150 pairs were found to fulfill these requirements and incidental factors reduced the size of the initial test group to 120 pairs. Subsequently, it was possible to add 14 pairs from

This paper constitutes the tenth consecutive report on the progress of a study which has been supported by grants from the Rockefeller Foundation (1945–1951) and the Division of Research Grants of the National Institutes of Health (1952–1959).

the general frame, bringing the total up to 134 test pairs or 268 twin individuals. All pertinent details concerning the representativeness of the original sample with respect to sex, zygosity (one-egg or two-egg), age, residence, occupation, and education were reported previously (Feingold, 1950).

The major differences between the test cases and the general white population of New York State were traced to an underrepresentation of metropolitan residence (40 percent in the twin sample versus 80 percent in the New York State population) with a consequent excess of rural occupations, as well as to the exclusion of foreign-born persons with potential language difficulties. Hence, the range of intellectual abilities in the twin sample typifies an aged population of literate, white, native-born, healthy, noninstitutionalized persons as found especially among the residents of rural and small urban communities.

The distribution of test cases, according to sex and zygosity, has been given in Table 1. The largest group was that of one-egg female

Table 1. Distribution of twins tested in longitudinal study (1947–1957) according to sex and zygosity

	First	Second	Third	Fourth
Male one-egg twins	76	60	25	6
Male one-egg pairs	38	28	11	3
Male two-egg twins	40	28	7	1
Male two-egg pairs	20	13	3	
Female one-egg twins	100	78	36	6
Female one-egg pairs	50	38	17	2
Female two-egg twins	52	41	10	4
Female two-egg pairs	26	19	4	2
Both sexes twins	268	207	78	17
Both sexes pairs	134	98	35	7

twins (100) followed in order by one-egg males (76), two-egg females (52), and two-egg males (40) for the initial as well as for subsequent testings. The considerable excess of female twins and of one-egg pairs in the age group above 60 was in accordance with statistical expectation (Jarvik *et al.,* 1960; Kallmann, 1961).

As shown in the last two columns of Table 1, 207 twins (including 98 pairs) were retested with the same battery after a period of approximately 2 years (mean interval 2.02 years). The second test session took place 1 year after the first (mean interval 11.7 months) for 124 of the twins (62 pairs) in order to establish the reliability of the test battery. For the remaining 83 twins the corresponding interval was about 3½ years. It was possible to administer a third testing to 78 survivors about 6 years after the second test session (mean interval 6.4 years), and 17 of them were able to participate in the fourth test round another 2.6 years later. The various intertest intervals for the 17 pairs tested four times were somewhat shorter than the corresponding means, with the time span for the four testings covering about 9¼ years.

The particulars of the test battery and the reasons for its use in an aged population were specified previously (Feingold, 1950). Sufficient data were available for the present report on seven subtests of the battery. Five of the tests (Digits Forward, Digits Backward, Digit Symbol Substitution, Block Designs, and Similarities) were from the Wechsler-Bellevue[1] Intelligence Test Scale I (Wechsler, 1944, 1955), the sixth (Vocabulary) from List 1 of the 1916 Stanford-Binet (Terman, 1916), and the seventh, a simple paper and pencil tapping test, was added by us.

RESULTS

The results of the initial testing, reported some years ago (Feingold, 1950; Kallmann *et al.*, 1951; Kallmann, 1953), demonstrated that the scores of one-egg twin partners were more similar than those of two-egg twin partners on tests of various intellectual abilities. The intrapair correlations for the first 120 pairs tested are presented in Table 2.

Table 2. Intrapair correlations of scores at first testing according to sex and zygosity (based on initial test round comprising 120 pairs)[a]

	MALE PAIRS				FEMALE PAIRS			
	One-egg		Two-egg		One-egg		Two-egg	
Type of test	N[b]	r[c]	N	r	N	r	N	r
Vocabulary	34	0.78	19	0.57	41	0.85	26	0.37
Tapping	32	0.78	17	0.19	37	0.65	22	0.49
Digits Forward	34	0.27	19	0.22	41	0.48	26	0.17
Digits Backward	33	0.49	19	0.52	41	0.42	26	0.17
Digit Symbols	29	0.67	12	0.48	36	0.83	18	0.52
Similarities	32	0.58	19	0.45	40	0.72	24	0.30
Block Designs	32	0.73	17	0.42	36	0.70	18	0.48

[a] Adapted from Feingold (1950).   [b] Number of pairs.
[c] Intrapair correlation.

There is a higher correlation for one-egg than for two-egg twin partners on the 7 subtests in the female series, and for 6 of the 7 tests in the male series. On Digits Backward, the exception, the intrapair correlations are 0.49 and 0.52 for one-egg and two-egg pairs, respec-

[1] Digits Forward and Digits Backward together make up Wechsler's Digit Span.

tively. In 7 such comparisons, 6 would be expected to be in the same direction by chance less than 8 times in 1000, and for 13 out of 14 comparisons the chance is less than once in 1000 times. Thus, it was justifiable to conclude that gene-specific differences in intellectual functioning continued to express themselves during senescence.

After an interval of approximately 8 years, preliminary analyses of retest data demonstrated that mean intrapair differences were smaller in one-egg than two-egg pairs (Jarvik *et al.*, 1957; Falek *et al.*, 1960). Similar trends were observed in the latest analyses of intrapair correlations summarized in Table 3. To take advantage of modern data-

Table 3. Intrapair correlations of scores in those pairs where both partners completed all seven subtests on at least one occasion

Type of test	Group I[a]	Group II[b]		Group III[c]		
	First testing	First testing	Second testing	First testing	Second testing	Third testing
Vocabulary	0.75	0.77	0.78	0.76	0.72	0.60
Tapping	0.50	0.45	0.31	0.46	0.53	0.50
Digits Forward	0.34	0.39	0.33	0.20	0.37	0.58
Digits Backward	0.33	0.47	0.40	0.11	0.51	0.48
Digit Symbols	0.69	0.72	0.64	0.50	0.47	0.69
Similarities	0.54	0.51	0.53	0.56	0.49	0.49
Block designs	0.47	0.57	0.62	0.59	0.68	0.46

[a] Group I includes 76 pairs who were tested at least once.
[b] Group II includes 54 (of the 76) pairs who were tested at least twice.
[c] Group III includes 19 (of the 54) pairs who were tested at least three times.

processing equipment (IBM machines), the analyses were limited to those pairs where both partners completed all seven subtests, reducing the number from 134 to 76 pairs for the first test round (Group I). The corresponding figures were 54 instead of 98 pairs for the second testing (Group II), and 19 instead of 35 pairs for the third testing (Group III). The fourth testing has not been included because only 4 pairs had completed the four rounds.

In Table 3, intrapair correlations are given separately for each group on each testing. This arrangement permits the comparison of correlations obtained on the second and third testings with those for the same subjects on first testing as well as with the intrapair correlations for the larger group on first testing (Group I). Theoretically, intrapair correlations should decrease if twin partners age at different rates. Actually, the correlations obtained from second and third testings did not differ significantly (5 percent level of confidence) from those on first testings. For the current data, differences in intrapair correlations over time can be considered as chance variations.

Of course, the failure of intrapair correlations to show a significant change cannot be considered evidence of the stability of the scores over the 9-year follow-up period. Yet, the analyses (Table 4) disclose

Table 4. Mean scores achieved by senescent twins on longitudinal psychometric examinations (1947–1957)

	1st testing		2nd testing		3rd testing		4th testing	
Type of test	N[a]	Mean	N	Mean	N	Mean	N	Mean
Vocabulary	268	28.4	203	29.4	73	29.7	14	30.0
Tapping	230	66.6	194	66.7	76	59.6	17	60.0
Digits Forward	265	5.8	205	6.1	77	6.2	15	6.5
Digits Backward	261	4.1	204	4.2	75	4.2	15	4.3
Digit Symbols	197	28.4	173	27.2	77	26.2	16	26.0
Similarities	246	9.2	206	9.5	76	9.5	17	11.1
Block Designs	211	13.5	187	13.5	73	13.5	15	13.5
Age (in years)[b]	268	69.7	207	71.3	78	74.9	17	76.7

[a] N = number of twin individuals.   [b] Age = age at time of testing.

little change in four consecutive testings. The only evidence for decline comes from two tests of visual-motor coordination and speed, Tapping and Digit Symbol. The scores on the other five tests either remained stable or increased on successive testings despite an average age change from 69.7 to 76.7 years.

This first impression calls for investigation by a different type of analysis, if only because the number of twins examined was reduced successively from 268 on first testing to 17 on the fourth testing. If, for any reason, the retested subjects scored above the original first testing group means, then a decrement in their scores might have been obscured by the larger contribution to the means of those twins who were tested only once or twice.

With this possibility in mind, it was decided to limit the comparison to twins with repeated testings. One difficulty in this analysis arose from the fact that the data-processing program required that all subjects complete each subtest at each testing. Unfortunately, the numbers meeting this requirement varied considerably (Table 4). On the first testing, for example, all 268 twins were given the Vocabulary Test while only 197 took the Digit Symbol Test.[2] Since only nine persons had all scores on four testings, the longitudinal comparison was made on 48 twins with three complete testings. Similarly, although the third test series was administered to 78 subjects (Table 4), 30 lacked one or more subtests on at least one of the testings. Hence, only 48 twins furnished the required complete scores.

[2] The principal reason for omission of subtests was lack of time. The other causes ranged from arthritic complaints to interruptions by angry spouses.

Table 5. Longitudinal mean scores of 48 twin subjects who completed all seven subtests on three successive testings

Type of test	Mean scores and standard deviations			Change in score (second versus third testing, in percent)
	First testing (Mean age 67.5 ± 5.5)	Second testing (Mean age 68.4 ± 5.5)	Third testing (Mean age 75.7 ± 4.7)	
Vocabulary	29.1 ± 4.9	30.1 ± 5.2	29.5 ± 5.3	−1.99
Tapping	69.6 ± 15.0[a]	72.1 ± 12.5[a]	59.1 ± 14.7[a]	−18.03
Digits Forward	6.2 ± 1.1	6.2 ± 1.1	6.3 ± 1.2	+1.61
Digits Backward	4.2 ± 1.0	4.3 ± 1.1	4.2 ± 1.3	−2.32
Digit Symbols	29.8 ± 7.6[b]	28.9 ± 9.0	26.1 ± 8.1[b]	−9.69
Similarities	9.5 ± 4.1	9.8 ± 4.2	9.4 ± 4.4	−4.08
Block Designs	14.3 ± 5.0	14.7 ± 5.9	12.6 ± 5.7	−14.28

[a] Differences between first and third as well as between second and third testings were significant at 1 percent level of confidence.

[b] Difference between first and third testing was significant at 1 percent level of confidence.

The mean scores for this group of 48 twins are reported in Table 5, together with their standard deviations. Comparison of Tables 4 and 5 reveals that, indeed, the group with three complete testings exceeds the mean scores of the total test population on all seven subtests at both the first and the second testing. Nevertheless, if the results of the first test round are contrasted with those of the third, there are again losses on the Tapping (with mean scores of 69.6 versus 59.1) and on the Digit Symbol Tests (29.8 versus 26.1). These differences are statistically significant (at the 1 percent level of confidence). The observed decrement on the Block Designs from 14.3 to 12.6, however, is not statistically different (5 percent level of confidence). On the other four tests, the scores were essentially unchanged.

What should be noted especially is that the results of Table 5 suggest an almost uniform *increase* in score between the first and second testings. The only decrease was on the Digit Symbol Test (from 29.8 to 28.9), while the mean score on Digits Forward was unchanged at 6.2. Apparently, the functions measured changed little during the 1-year interval between the first two testings (mean ages of 67.5 to 68.4 years, respectively), possibly because this aged population acquired some "test wiseness" which may have counterbalanced a declining trend. Be that as it may, the oft-asserted downward tendency is unsupported by our data, regardless of whether or not experiential factors were responsible for the observed increase in scores. None of the differences between first and second testing were statistically significant (5 percent level of confidence), and the stability of the scores was emphasized in intertest correlations[3] of 0.71 and 0.93 for the Tapping and Vocabulary Tests, respectively. Lower correlations for Digits Forward (0.46) and Digits Backward (0.61) may be attributable to the restricted range of scores on these tests.

Despite the close agreement between the results of the first two testings over the lapse of about a year, the scores on the second session may be a better estimate of the level of intellectual functioning. Comparison of the mean scores of the *third* test round with those of the *second,* rather than the first, testing, reveals a decrease in all tests, except Digits Forward. The mean score for this test increases slightly (from 6.2 to 6.3) over the 7 years between the second and third testings. During that period, the age of the twin population went from 68.4 to 75.7 years. While the decrease in scores was generally limited, the difference on the Tapping Test was statistically significant (the 1 percent level of confidence). For whatever illumination they may provide, the changes by percent are given in the last column of Table 5.

To estimate the generality of the above findings for aged persons in the community with a satisfactory state of health, the means for the tests from the Wechsler-Bellevue Scale were converted into weighted scores in accordance with Wechsler's specifications (Wechsler, 1944). The results for the longitudinal twin samples are listed in Table 6,

Table 6. Comparative mean weighted scores of 48 twins with three complete testings and Wechsler's oldest standardization groups

	Digit Span	Digit Symbols	Similarities	Block Designs
Mean age (in years)				
Longitudinal twin data				
67.5 (N = 48)	7.8	7.2	8.2	7.6
68.4 (N = 48)	8.0	7.0	8.4	7.8
75.7 (N = 48)	8.0	6.4	8.2	6.8
Age group, Wechsler data				
50–54 (N = 55)	7.7	6.8	8.8	8.0
55–59 (N = 50)	7.5	5.9	7.9	6.7

together with the corresponding weighted scores reported by Wechsler for his oldest standardization groups, aged 50–54 and 55–59. On the first testing, the mean scores of the twins were consistently higher than those for Wechsler's oldest subjects, in spite of the fact that the latter were in the age group 55–59, while the ages of the twin sample ranged from 60–78 years with a mean of 67.5. It is of interest in this connection that the educational background of the twins closely resembled

[3] Table of correlations not included in this paper.

that of the New York State native white population of comparable age. In the twin sample, 29 percent of the subjects had a history of some form of secondary education, while the corresponding figure for the general population is 27 percent.

As a group, the twins maintained superiority throughout the second and third testings, although they had attained a mean age of 75.7 years at the time of the third testing. On the Digit Span[4] Test, the twins surpassed even Wechsler's 50–54-year-old group, while on Digit Symbols they fell below the 50–54-year norms only on the third testing. On Similarities and Block Designs, the initial weighted scores of the twin population failed to reach those of Wechsler's 50–54-year group.

Unfortunately, a similar comparison with the more relevant Kansas (Doppelt and Wallace, 1955) and North Carolina (Eisdorfer *et al.,* 1959) samples was precluded by the changes made in restandardizing and extending the Wechsler-Bellevue Test into the Wechsler Adult Intelligence Scale (WAIS). However desirable these changes may have been, they complicate longitudinal research, and make it more or less impossible to validate such observations by comparative data.

Another approach to the evaluation of our results as compared with those reported in the literature is provided by the intercorrelations of the various tests (Table 7). The intercorrelations for the first testing of the 76 pairs where both members completed all seven subtests are presented in the upper part of this table. The specific correlations are recorded for twins and their cotwins (76 in each group). In addition, correlations with age are given for each test. The division of each pair into "twin" and "cotwin" was arbitrary for pairs with complete testings. In the other instances, to be discussed later, the twin with the larger number of testings was designated as "twin" and his partner as "cotwin." In pairs with equal test sessions, the "cotwin" completed fewer subtests.

In the lower half of Table 7, Wechsler's data are given for the four subtests used in the present study (Block Designs, Similarities, Digit Symbols, and Digit Span, the last representing the combination of Digits Forward and Digits Backward) as well as for the WAIS Vocabulary. Notwithstanding the fact that the twin data are based on a different vocabulary test—the Stanford-Binet, 1916 edition—this comparison may have some value as long as the discrepancy is taken into consideration. After all, both tests purport to measure the same intellectual function with a high degree of reliability.

---

[4] Digits Forward and Digits Backward had to be combined since separate data for these tests were not available (Wechsler, personal communication).

Table 7. *Comparative intercorrelations of tests for twin and Wechsler samples (from first testing of 76 pairs who completed all tests)*

Tests	Tapping	Digits Forward	Digits Backward	Digit Symbols	Similarities	Block Designs	Age
Twin data							
Vocabulary	0.17[a]	0.22	0.27	0.25	0.63	0.26	0.18
	0.27	0.13	0.33	0.29	0.68	0.34	0.07
Tapping		0.11	0.27	0.52	0.20	0.31	−0.11
		0.29	0.22	0.58	0.35	0.38	−0.35
Digits Forward			0.32	0.15	0.24	−0.02	−0.02
			0.37	0.14	0.17	0.20	0.00
Digits Backward				0.38	0.46	0.30	−0.23
				0.22	0.32	0.19	0.06
Digit Symbols					0.48	0.53	−0.30
					0.42	0.58	−0.39
Similarities						0.38	−0.01
						0.32	−0.13
Block Designs							−0.03
							−0.16
Wechsler data							
Similarities						0.50[b]	
						0.54[c]	
Digit Symbols					0.57	0.50	
					0.51	0.61	
Digit Span				0.48	0.45	0.42	
				0.52	0.38[e]	0.42	
Vocabulary			0.53[d]	0.63	0.72	0.52	
			[e]				

[a] Twins on first line and cotwins on second line, respectively.
[b] WAIS age 45–54 on first line; Wechsler-Bellevue age 35–49 on second line.
[c] Wechsler-Bellevue age 15–49 since data lacking for age group 35–49.
[d] Intercorrelations for digit span since data not available for Digits Forward and Digits Backward separately.
[e] Data not available for Wechsler-Bellevue.

Two entries appear for each item under "Wechsler Data." The first-line entries are for the intercorrelations in the WAIS manual for the age group 45–54, the second line for the Wechsler-Bellevue data (Wechsler, 1944) for the age group 35–49 (or 15–49 where available data did not suffice for the older group).

Of the 42 intertest correlations derived from the twin data, 41 are positive. The single exception is the value of −0.02 for Digits Forward with Block Designs for twins, whose cotwins show a correlation of +0.20 for the corresponding variables. The correlations for Digit Span with Block Designs are 0.17 and 0.24 for twins and cotwins, respectively. The other correlations for Digit Span are as follows: with Vocabulary 0.30 and 0.28; with Similarities 0.44 and 0.30; with Digit Symbols 0.33 and 0.22; and with age −0.45 and +0.04 for twins and cotwins, respectively.

On the whole, the positive matrix is in agreement with previous reports, although the intercorrelations based on the twin data are generally lower than Wechsler's. The age span for the latter varied from 10 years (age group 45–54) to 35 years (age group 15–49), whereas it approximated 30 years (age group 60–90) in the twin sample.

In line with the findings of other investigators (Jones and Conrad, 1933; Miles and Miles, 1932), most correlations between chronological age and test score are negative, ranging from −0.01 with Similarities for twins (cotwins, −0.13) to −0.35 with Tapping for cotwins (twins, −0.11). The exceptions are the Vocabulary values which are positive (0.18 and 0.07 for twins and cotwins, respectively).

The highest intertest correlations are for Vocabulary by Similarities (0.63 and 0.68 for twins and cotwins, respectively), Tapping by Digit Symbols (0.52 and 0.58), and for Digit Symbols by Block Designs (0.53 and 0.58).

Table 8. Comparative longitudinal intercorrelations of tests (based on 54 and 19 pairs with complete second and third testings, respectively)

Tests	Tapping	Digits Forward	Digits Backward	Digit Symbols	Similarities	Block Designs	Age
Second testing							
Vocabulary	0.14a	−0.07	0.33	0.24	0.63	0.20	0.19
	0.13	−0.08	0.27	0.44	0.72	0.32	0.01
Tapping		0.30	0.29	0.41	0.10	0.21	−0.20
		0.08	−0.04	0.51	0.07	0.28	−0.36
Digits Forward			0.26	0.24	−0.01	0.38	−0.27
			0.33	0.08	−0.03	0.08	−0.20
Digits Backward				0.39	0.34	0.38	−0.11
				0.24	0.14	0.07	−0.02
Digit Symbols					0.38	0.46	−0.38
					0.46	0.54	−0.32
Similarities						0.22	0.09
						0.29	−0.05
Block Designs							−0.13
							−0.20
Third testing							
Block Designs							−0.26
							−0.07
Similarities						0.46	0.20
						−0.02	0.37
Digit Symbols					0.18	0.33	−0.47
					0.11	0.37	−0.60
Digits Backward				0.17	0.36	0.17	0.26
				0.00	0.29	0.22	−0.09
Digits Forward			0.31	−0.05	0.24	0.40	−0.02
			0.41	−0.02	−0.04	0.16	−0.04
Tapping		0.17	0.03	0.35	0.26	0.25	−0.25
		0.09	−0.16	0.48	−0.21	0.22	−0.52
Vocabulary	0.32	0.42	0.13	0.30	0.56	0.45	0.29
	0.04	−0.05	0.30	0.47	0.65	0.24	0.00

a Twins on first line and cotwins on second line.

It is evident from the data in Table 8 that the same relationships persist throughout the subsequent testings. Here, the intercorrelations recorded for the second and third testings are based on 54 and 19 pairs with all tests completed by both twin partners. The intertest correlations given for the WAIS age group 25–34 also correspond closely to those for the older age group (45–54). Consistently high correlations for twins and cotwins have been found for Vocabulary by Similarities, Tapping by Digit Symbols, and Digit Symbols by Block Designs. An unanticipated result is the high negative correlation between age and

Digit Symbol on the third testing (-0.47 and -0.60 for twins and cotwins, respectively).

In order to test for specialization by means of factor-analysis, the intercorrelations computed from two complete testings of 54 twin pairs were used. The data included seven subtests and age at first testing for twin and cotwin, and again for second testing, about a year later, for twin and cotwin. The dichotomy male-female and monozygotic (one-egg)-dizygotic (two-egg) were two additional variables making 34 in all. With factor rotation accomplished by the quatrimax method, eight factors were extracted, the first of which was chronological age (*first* factor). Surprisingly, only one test, Digit Symbol, showed consistently negative correlations with this factor for each twin at each testing. This finding confirmed the specialization indicated by the correlations between test score and age.

The *second* factor correlated highly with Vocabulary and Similarities. Hence, it represented a verbal component which was positively related to Digits Backward and Digit Symbol. It is significant that loading for the twins on this factor at first testing was 0.88 and at the second testing 0.90. For the cotwins the respective values were 0.89 and 0.91. Corresponding relations for Similarities were 0.62 and 0.61 for twins and 0.70 and 0.71 for cotwins. For Digits Backward, the values for first and second testing were, respectively, 0.36 and 0.36 for twins, and 0.32 and 0.35 for cotwins.

For the *third* factor, the highest loadings were associated with Block Designs as a specific. The loadings were 0.83, 0.81, 0.71, and 0.74 for the first and second testings, and for twin and cotwin.

The *fourth* factor had high loadings on Digits Forward and somewhat lesser ones on Digits Backward, both of which make up Wechsler's Digit Span. The values for Digits Forward were 0.64, 0.54, 0.64, and 0.57 for the twin pairs at the two testings, while those for Digits Backward were 0.35, 0.34, 0.39, and 0.63.

The foregoing factors emerged in both twins at the same time and at different times with approximately the same loading, suggesting stability of the functions by twins over time. The verbal component (factor two) accounted for 25 percent of the variance and the age factor for 20 percent, while factors three (Block Designs) and four (Digits Forward and Backward) were responsible for 14 and 11 percent, respectively.

A *fifth* factor was associated with Tapping and showed high loadings for the cotwins on first as well as second testings (0.78 and 0.72, respectively). The corresponding loadings for the twins were considerably lower (0.35 and 0.32, respectively). Also, there was some association between factor five and Digit Symbols for the cotwins, but not for the twins. The relevant values were 0.39 and 0.45 for the former on first and second testings, respectively, and 0.06 for the twins on both testings.

A somewhat similar situation obtained for the *sixth* factor which had high loadings on Digit Symbol for twins (0.76 on both testings) and lesser ones for cotwins (0.49 and 0.43 on first and second testings, respectively). This factor was also related to Similarities, with loadings of 0.45, 0.44, 0.21, and 0.40 for first and second testings of twins and cotwins, respectively. Factors five and six accounted for 8 and 12 percent of the variance, respectively.

The discrepancies between twins and cotwins for some of these factors may be attributed, at least in some measure, to the unreliability of the tests. This is particularly true for the Tapping Test where h^2 accounted for 50 percent of the total variance as against 88 percent for the Vocabulary Test.

The dichotomy monozygotic-dizygotic twins contributed the following information: One-egg twins had a higher loading on factor two (verbal) than did two-egg twins, while the reverse held true for factor three (Block Designs). The comparison of male versus female twins showed high loadings for females on factors two, four, five, and six, while factors one (age) and three (Block Designs) did not discriminate between the sexes.

A factor well known for its differential effect upon the two sexes is that of survival. Female life expectancies consistently exceed those of males in twins as well as in singletons (Kallmann and Feingold, 1949; Kallmann *et al.*, 1956; Falek *et al.*, 1960; Jarvik *et al.*, 1960; Kallmann, 1961). Since preliminary analyses of partial retest data suggested a positive relationship between test score and longevity (Jarvik *et al.*, 1957), a comparison of the mean scores according to subsequent survival was undertaken. The critical date selected for this purpose was 1955, because most of the third testings took place during that year. Of the 268 twins tested originally, 168 were still alive in 1955, while 100 had died. The two groups have been designated as "survivors" or "alive," and "deceased" or "dead," respectively. In Table 9, the mean scores and standard deviations obtained on the first test round are listed separately for the 168 survivors and the 100 deceased twins, according to sex and zygosity. In order to utilize the maximum number of subjects, the scores of all twins have been included and missing scores have been estimated at the mean for those for whom no data were available. This procedure has been followed with the full realization that any bias would be

Table 9. *Mean scores and age on first testing (1947–1949) of 268 twin subjects according to survival status in 1955*

Twin subjects	Vocabulary	Tapping	Digits Forward	Digits Backward	Similarities	Mean age on 1st testing
Male one-egg						
Alive (47)[a]	29.2 ± 5.4	69.8 ± 13.7	6.1 ± 1.1	4.4 ± 1.3	9.5 ± 4.3	68.2 ± 6.2
Dead (29)	28.6 ± 5.9	63.3 ± 13.8	5.7 ± 1.2	4.0 ± 0.8	8.5 ± 3.4	71.6 ± 8.0
Male two-egg						
Alive (19)	24.8 ± 4.5	63.5 ± 11.8	6.0 ± 0.8	4.4 ± 1.2	7.1 ± 3.0	67.2 ± 8.4
Dead (21)	29.2 ± 8.0	56.5 ± 16.5	5.6 ± 1.0	4.0 ± 1.1	9.7 ± 5.1	73.2 ± 6.7
Female one-egg						
Alive (73)	28.8 ± 5.9	69.4 ± 14.0	5.9 ± 1.1	4.0[b] ± 0.9	9.9 ± 4.6	67.8 ± 4.0
Dead (27)	28.6 ± 6.1	61.4 ± 11.1	5.7 ± 0.8	4.0[b] ± 1.2	9.1 ± 3.9	71.3 ± 8.0
Female two-egg						
Alive (29)	28.6 ± 5.4	76.0 ± 13.4	6.1 ± 1.3	4.5 ± 1.4	10.2 ± 4.7	68.2 ± 6.8
Dead (23)	27.0 ± 6.7	60.7 ± 17.2	5.3 ± 0.8	3.9 ± 0.9	6.7 ± 3.6	74.8 ± 5.8
All pairs						
Alive (168)	28.4 ± 7.1	70.0[c] ± 13.9	6.0[c] ± 1.1	4.2[d] ± 1.2	9.5 ± 4.5	67.9[c] ± 7.1
Dead (100)	28.4 ± 6.6	60.8[c] ± 14.5	5.6[c] ± 1.0	4.0[d] ± 1.0	8.5 ± 4.1	72.6[c] ± 7.2

[a] Number of twins tested, missing subtest scores estimated at mean for total sample.
[b] Actually 3.986 and 3.962 for living and dead, respectively.
[c] Difference between means alive-dead was significant at 1 percent level of confidence.
[d] Difference between means alive-dead was significant at 5 percent level of confidence.

opposed to the postulated difference favoring the survivors. If deceased twins tended toward lower scores, then the use of the group mean as the best guess for missing scores would raise the mean for the deceased group. Conversely, this estimate of missing scores would lower the mean of the survivors and minimize intergroup differences. For this reason, estimated scores have been limited to not more than 15 percent on any one test. Unfortunately, two tests were eliminated by this restriction (Digit Symbol and Block Designs), reducing to five the number of tests for this analysis. Using the first column of Table 4, it may be noted that the number of estimated scores varies from zero for the Vocabulary Test (all 268 twins had the test) to three for Digits Forward, seven for Digits Backward, and to 22 and 38 for Similarities and Tapping, respectively.

Distributing the subjects among the four groups, one-egg male and female and two-egg male and female twins, for each of the five tests, we have 20 subgroups for comparison. Table 9 shows that in 18 of the 20 comparisons the mean scores of the survivors (alive) exceed those of the dead twins. This result would be expected by chance alone less than once in a thousand times. The exceptions are for two-egg males, with the mean scores of 21 deceased twins exceeding those of 19 survivors on Vocabulary (29.2 and 24.8, respectively) and Similarities (9.7 and 8.5, respectively). However, the given differences are not statistically significant.

If the total group of 168 survivors is contrasted with the 100 deceased twins, the former have higher means on all five tests, although the Vocabulary difference is negligible (28.39 versus 28.38). The intergroup differences between living and dead twins are significant for Tapping and Digits Forward (1 percent level of confidence), as well as for Digits Backward (5 percent level of confidence).

An attractive explanation for the observed differences is offered by a discrepancy in the chronological ages of the two groups. The survivors, with a mean age of 67.9 years, were significantly younger at the time of the original testing than the deceased twins, whose mean age was 72.6 years. Though age was undoubtedly an important variable, the relatively low correlations between age and test score would seem to indicate that other factors have been primarily responsible for the relative inferiority of the deceased twins on Tapping, Digits Forward, and Digits Backward. The correlations with age for this group range from -0.09 for Digits Forward to -0.26 for Tapping, so that chronological age contributed less than 10 percent to the variance. The inference that high test scores are prognostic of long survival will be discussed later.

DISCUSSION

This study has been concerned with intellectual changes in senescent twins and, as a byproduct, has provided longitudinal information on a group of aged persons in the community. Intentional biases were introduced into the selection of the sample and institutionalized individuals were omitted entirely. The restriction to English-speaking, thus largely native-born, subjects was considered imperative for the adequate evaluation of psychometric data with a prominent verbal component. Limitation to "white" persons was necessitated by the underrepresentation of other groups. The stipulation of "good health," interpreted liberally, excluded bedridden, psychotic, and obviously senile cases.

While the selective effects of the above criteria are easily evaluated, a more difficult problem is posed by the fact that our research subjects were twins rather than single-born members of the community. Investigators from disciplines other than human genetics tend to be suspicious of twin data, mainly because of the old belief that twins are somehow inferior to singletons (Byrns and Healy, 1936; Howard, 1946; Mehrotra and Maxwell, 1949; Sandon, 1957; Tabah and Sutter, 1954; Zazzo, 1952). From the results of the present study (Table 6) it may be inferred with confidence that the intellectual abilities of twins, at least in the age group above 60, are well within the norms set for nontwins. Indeed, to be precise, the intellectual performance of the twins included in the present investigation (age 60–90) has been superior to that of Wechsler's 54–59-year-old group. This lack of evidence for the presumed "inferiority" of twin subjects is in agreement with the finding that twins have the same morbidity rates as single-born individuals for a variety of physical and mental disorders (Kallmann, 1938, 1953; Kallmann and Reisner, 1943) and do not significantly differ from the general population in their life expectancy (Falek *et al.,* 1960; Kallmann, 1961).

General population studies of intellectual changes in senescence have been based upon cross-sectional data. Since several extensive reviews are available (Lorge, 1956*a*; Jones, 1959; Birren, 1960), it may simply be stated here that it has been asserted that the course of intelligence during the life span shows a steep rise from childhood to adolescence, decelerates gradually, and begins to decline during the third and fourth decades, and declines more rapidly thereafter. The need for longitudinal studies "to verify whether age differences are identical with age changes" (Lorge, 1956*b*, p. 356) has been stressed repeatedly (Anastasi, 1956; Bayley, 1956; Birren, 1960; Jones, 1956; Lorge, 1957). The three longitudinal studies which dealt with young and middle-aged adults have been in sharp disagreement with the inferences based on cross-sectional evidence (Owens, 1953; Bayley and Oden, 1955; Jones, 1959). Even though a different intelligence test was used in each study and the interest periods ranged from 12 to 30 years, over an age span from early adolescence (age 12) to full adulthood (age 50), all three investigations demonstrated an increase, rather than the oft-asserted decrease, in score. A recent report of gains in intelligence test scores by mental defectives in Manitoba (age 15–64) over a five-year interval (Bell and Zubek, 1960) contrasted sharply with Kaplan's (1956) reported decline in older morons (average age 41 years over a 15-year period.

It would be of interest to know if the Canadian mental defectives had been given any tests prior to, or during the time of, that study. If not, then some of the observed increases in score may have been due to "test familiarity" as evidenced in the twin study between the first and second testing. According to expectation, there should have been a loss during the one-year intertest interval. It is because of such possible test-wiseness that longitudinal studies of a population without previous testing experience should strive for at least three time-separated sessions per individual.

Longitudinal as well as cross-sectional studies have shown a differential effect of age upon various functions. Changes are most easily detectable in performance tests, particularly when speed is involved. Also, tasks measuring learning ability, retention and recall of unfamiliar material, and immediate memory span tend to reveal a larger age deficit than tests of comprehension and reasoning. Of course, general information and vocabulary are most resistant to change.

The results of the present study show similar trends (Table 5). The only statistically significant declines have been for the two performance tests, weighted heavily by speed (Tapping and Digit Symbol). Digit Symbol has been the only test showing a heavy loading on the age factor.

The finding that memory for digits remained unchanged during the 8-year interval has been unexpected. In this connection, it is of interest that mental defectives in the age group 50–60 showed improvement on this test over the 5-year period in question (Bell and Zubek, 1960).

For the twin study the Digit Span test has been reported separately for Digits Forward and for Digits Backward, because it was believed that different intellectual functions are tapped by these subtests. Indeed, factor-analysis suggests that, in addition to the common factor, Digits Backward is associated highly with the verbal component whereas Digits Forward is not. Evidently, much useful information may be obtained in future studies were the data reported and analyzed separately for these two subtests.

In fact, we may have to revise our concepts so as to think not so much of "intelligence" in the aged but rather of several distinguishable intellectual functions. This change would eliminate the confusion caused by a term which has neither been properly defined nor adequately validated for older groups against independent criteria. In childhood and adolescence, reliable measures of global intelligence are very useful in the prediction of educational success, although assumed to measure primarily potential ability and not the ultimate actualization of this potential. In a group of senescent individuals, an estimate of potential educational achievement lacks applicability even were some valid measure available. Concentration upon separate mental abilities would do away with many fruitless arguments such as those concerning the importance of speed in assessing the "intelligence" of an aged population.

Basic support for this belief is furnished by the results of the present factor-analysis. In addition to the verbal component (25 percent of the variance), four specific factors were extracted which together accounted for 45 percent of the variance (from 8 to 14 percent each). In line with the distinct factors derived for Block Designs, Digits (particularly forward), Tapping, and Digit Symbols, it would seem essential to examine age changes separately for each of these variables as well as for verbal ability. Therefore, theories ascribing age decline in intellectual functioning to gradually increasing brain atrophy, as on the basis of generalized cerebral arteriosclerosis, should be revised.

It may be postulated either that certain neural pathways are subjected more easily to detrimental concomitants of the aging process, whatever they may be, or that intrinsic, as yet unmeasurable, differences exist in the cytochemical, metabolic, or neurophysiological substrates of these functions. Support for the latter inference stems from the observation that hereditary factors are likely to exert differential influences upon these functions. The strongest genetic components have been found for Vocabulary, Digit Symbols, Block Designs, and Tapping, and lesser effects for Similarities and Digits Backward; Digits Forward did not discriminate between the zygosity groups (Feingold, 1950). These observations were made in the original test group of the present study; hence, in an aged sample.

More recently, data reported on young twins corroborated our observations, although not strictly comparable (Cattell *et al.,* 1957; Vandenberg, in press). Significant effects of hereditary differences were demonstrated (Vandenberg, 1961) for the WISC (Wechsler, 1949) Vocabulary and for a number of dexterity and sorting tests (possibly related to the present Tapping). Less firmly established were effects (5 percent instead of 1 percent level of confidence) for WISC Digit Span. Contrary to aged twins, one-egg and two-egg pairs in the young group (age 12–20) could not be distinguished by the same Block Designs test.

A clear pattern of the relationship between genetic components and age changes has not emerged. Of the four tests with well-established genetic determinants, two showed significant declines with age (Tapping and Digit Symbols); one a definite trend toward decline (Block Designs); and one a negligible loss (Vocabulary). The two tests (Similarities and Digits Backward) with a less clearly established effect of genetic factors (5 percent level of confidence) showed a slight tendency to decline, while for the other test (Digits Forward) neither zygosity nor advancing age had a demonstrable effect. Elucidation of this problem requires further study which, ideally, should cover the entire life span of the subjects.

Such a program would also furnish evidence for or against the suggested association between mental fitness and survival. Actually, pertinent information might be gathered within our own generation, by utilizing scores attained several decades ago on some widely used intelligence test, such as the World War I Army Alpha subtest scores. Collection of survival data on suitably selected samples would present no major obstacles.

The rationale of more extensive research in this area is based on the hope that studies of this kind would help to clarify primary processes associated with aging. With a biological basis established not only for mental abilities but also for variations in survival, it may be hypothesized that the underlying genetic components are likely to share at least one common denominator. Hence, factors protecting against eventual age decrement may reveal themselves at a relatively early age in the profile of intellectual functioning.

SUMMARY AND CONCLUSIONS

In a longitudinal psychometric study of 268 senescent twins (1947–1957), the sample consisted of 134 noninstitutionalized, same-sex pairs who were over age 60 at the time of first testing, and were literate, white, English-speaking, and in satisfactory health. With the passage of time, the sample was reduced from 207 twins on the second testing to 78 on the third and to 17 on the fourth test round. The mean interval between the first and fourth testings was 9.25 years.

The analysis of the data extended to seven tests, five derived from the Wechsler-Bellevue (Digits Forward, Digits Backward, Digit Symbols, Block Designs, and Similarities), and one from the Stanford-Binet (Vocabulary). The seventh was a simple paper and pencil tapping test. For a variety of reasons, the numbers varied for different analyses from 268 to 48.

The original test data had shown a greater similarity in one-egg than two-egg twin pairs in the age group above 60. No significant change in intrapair correlations was demonstrated during the follow-up period.

The performance of the twins (age 60–90) equaled or exceeded the norms established for the general population at a younger age (50–54 and 55–59), despite similar educational histories. There is no reason for believing, therefore, that twins over age 60 are inferior to singletons with respect to the measured functions.

Retest results obtained after a 1-year interval showed a general *increase* in scores, indicating a marked stability of the functions tested as well as a possible influence of "test-wiseness." It seems advisable to plan a minimum of two retests in designing longitudinal psychometric studies of a naïve adult population.

Comparison of mean scores on first, second, and third testings revealed statistically significant losses only on the two speeded performance tests (Tapping and Digit Symbols). The decline trend on the other tests was less pronounced although there was an interval of 7 years between the second and third testings.

In the light of the heterogeneous age changes disclosed by performance on the various subtests and confirmed by factor analysis, a revision of our concepts of "intelligence" in the aged has been proposed. The suggested biologically orientated approach could serve to clarify many basic questions as to age-determined psychological changes.

It appears that there is a positive relationship between test score and survival. With evidence for the operation of significant genic elements in both phenomena a new avenue has been opened for research which, it is hoped, may provide a stimulus for further widespread investigation by gerontologists in various fields of specialization.

Acknowledgment. Grateful acknowledgment is hereby made of Mrs. Laine Ruut's tireless help in preparing the manuscript and constructing the tables.

REFERENCES

Anastasi, Anne. 1956. Age changes in adult test performance. Psychol. Rep., 2: 509.

Bayley, Nancy. 1956. The place of longitudinal studies in research on intellectual factors in aging. *In* J. E. Anderson (ed.), Psychological aspects of aging, pp. 151–54. Washington, D.C.: American Psychological Association.

———, and Oden, Melita H. 1955. The maintenance of intellectual ability in gifted adults. J. Gerontol., 10: 91–107.

Bell, Anne, and Zubek, J. P. 1960. The effect of age on the intellectual performance of mental defectives. J. Gerontol., 15: 285–95.

Birren, J. E. 1960. Psychological aspects of aging. Ann. Rev. Psychol., 11: 161–98.

Byrns, R., and Healy, J. 1936. The intelligence of twins. J. Genet. Psychol., 49: 474–78.

Cattell, R. B., Stice, G. F., and Kristy, N. F. 1957. A first approximation to nature-nurture ratios for eleven primary personality factors in objective tests. J. Abnorm. & Social Psychol., 54: 143–59.

Doppelt, J. E., and Wallace, W. L. 1955. Standardization of the Wechsler Adult Intelligence Scale for older persons. J. Abnorm. & Social Psychol., 51: 312–30.

Eisdorfer, C., Busse, E. W., and Cohen, L. D. 1959. The WAIS performance of an aged sample: the relationship between verbal and performance IQs. J. Gerontol., 14: 197–201.

Falek, A., Kallmann, F. J., Lorge, I., and Jarvik, Lissy F. 1960. Longevity and intellectual variation in a senescent twin population. J. Gerontol., 15: 305–9.

Feingold, Lissy. 1950. A psychometric study of senescent twins. (Unpublished doctoral dissertation, Columbia University.)

Howard, R. W. 1946. Intellectual and personality traits of a group of triplets. J. Psychol., 21: 25–36.

Jarvik, Lissy F., Falek, A., Kallmann, F. J., and Lorge, I. 1960. Survival trends in a senescent twin population. Am. J. Human Genet., 12: 170–79.

———, Kallmann, F. J., Falek, A., and Klaber, M. M. 1957. Changing intellectual functions in senescent twins. Acta Genet. Statis. Med., 7: 421–30.

Jones, H. E. 1956. Problems of aging in perceptual and intellective functions. *In* J. E. Anderson (ed.), Psychological aspects of aging, pp. 135–39. Washington, D.C.: American Psychological Association.

——— 1959. Intelligence and problem-solving. *In* J. E. Birren (ed.), Handbook of aging and the individual, pp. 700–38. Chicago: University of Chicago Press.

———, and Conrad, H. S. 1933. The growth and decline of intelligence. Genetic Psychol. Monogr., 13: 223–98.

Kallmann, F. J. 1938. The genetics of schizophrenia. New York: J. J. Augustin.

——— 1953. Heredity in health and mental disorder. New York: W. W. Norton.

——— Genetic factors in aging: comparative and longitudinal observations on a senescent twin population. (In press.)

———, Aschner, Bertha, and Falek, A. 1956. Comparative data on longevity, adjustment to aging, and causes of death in a senescent twin population. *In* L. Gedda (ed.), Novant' anni delle Leggi Mendeliane, pp. 330–39. Rome: Instituto Gregorio Mendel.

———, and Feingold, Lissy. 1949. Principles of human genetics in relation to insurance medicine and public health. J. Insur. Med., 4: 1–8.

———, Feingold, Lissy, and Bondy, Eva. 1951. Comparative adaptational, social, and psychometric data on the life histories of senescent twin pairs. Am. J. Human Genet., 3: 65–73.

———, and Reisner, D. 1943. Twin studies on the significance of genetic factors in tuberculosis. Am. Rev. Tubercul., 47: 549–74.

———, and Sander, G. 1948. Twin studies on aging and longevity. J. Heredity, 39: 349–57.

Kaplan, O. J. (ed.). 1956. Mental disorders in later life. Stanford: Stanford University Press.

Lorge, I. 1956a. Aging and intelligence. The neurological and psychiatric aspects of the disorders of aging. Proc. Assoc. Res. Nerv. Ment. Dis., 35: 46–59.

——— 1956b. Gerontology (later maturity). Ann. Rev. Psychol., 7: 349–64.

——— 1957. Methodology of the study of intelligence and emotion in ageing. *In* G. E. W. Wolstenholme and C. M. O'Connor (eds.), Ciba foundation colloquia on ageing (3), pp. 170–87. London: J. & A. Churchill.

Mehrotra, S. N., and Maxwell, J. 1949. The intelligence of twins: a comparative study of eleven-year-old twins. Population Studies, 3: 295–302.

Miles, Catherine C., and Miles, W. R. 1932. The correlation of intelligence scores and chronological age from early to late maturity. Am. J. Psychol., 44: 44–78.

Owens, W. A., Jr. 1953. Age and mental abilities. Genet. Psychol. Monogr., 48: 3–54.

Sandon, F. 1957. The relative numbers and abilities of some ten-year-old twins. J. Roy. Statis. Soc., 120: 440–50.

Tabah, L., and Sutter, J. 1954. Le niveau intellectuel des enfants d'une même famille. Ann. Human Genet., 19: 120–50.

Terman, L. M. 1916. The measurement of intelligence. Boston: Houghton Mifflin.

Vandenberg, S. G. A comparison of identical and fraternal twins on a battery of psychological tests. (In press.)

Wechsler, D. 1944. The measurement of adult intelligence. Baltimore: Williams and Wilkins.

———— 1949. Wechsler intelligence scale for children. New York: Psychological Corporation.

———— 1955. Manual for the Wechsler adult intelligence scale. New York: Psychological Corporation.

Zazzo, R. 1952. Situation gemellaire et development mental. J. Psychol. Norm. Pathologique, 45, 208–27.

Comparison of Attitudes toward Old Age, Mental Illness, and Other Concepts

JOHN ALTROCCHI AND CARL EISDORFER

INVESTIGATIONS of attitudes toward old age have been relatively sparse until recently. The early writings of Barron (1953) and Drake (1958) were primarily conceptual and emphasized the negative elements in most people's attitudes toward the aged. Barron's position was probably the most extreme, suggesting that attitudes toward older people resemble attitudes toward minority ethnic groups in American society. More recently there was a series of empirical studies by Tuckman and Lorge (1952a, b, 1953, 1954, 1958) concerned with extent of agreement with various stereotypic statements about old age. Golde and Kogan (1959) have pointed out that there are some methodological shortcomings in the Tuckman and Lorge studies, including failure to control for response set effects inherent in items of the yes-no type and the absence of control for the generality of the attitude, in that subjects may or may not attribute the same qualities to people in general that they attribute to old people. A current study by Axelrod and Eisdorfer (1961) has shown that Tuckman and Lorge's approach may have considerable general validity but that specific classes of items vary considerably. Their findings, however, lend some credence to Tuckman and Lorge's argument that mental deterioration is often seen as an increasing problem with advancing age.

Among the more important recent efforts in this area is a group of papers by Nathan Kogan (1960) and his associates, most of which are in the process of publication this year and of which Dr. Kogan kindly sent us prepublication copies. These studies have shown that attitudes toward old people are qualitatively different from—and not always more negative than—attitudes toward people in general, that older people themselves are ambivalent regarding their status, and that subjects are more likely to associate aging with a state of physical disability than with mental illness.

OLD MAN

Factor represented

Evaluative	foolish	_:_:_:_:_:_:_	wise
Evaluative	intelligent	_:_:_:_:_:_:_	ignorant
Evaluative	happy	_:_:_:_:_:_:_	sad
Activity	active	_:_:_:_:_:_:_	passive
Evaluative	trustworthy	_:_:_:_:_:_:_	untrustworthy
Evaluative	poor	_:_:_:_:_:_:_	rich
Understandability	predictable	_:_:_:_:_:_:_	unpredictable
Potency	weak	_:_:_:_:_:_:_	strong
Activity	slow	_:_:_:_:_:_:_	fast
Potency	rugged	_:_:_:_:_:_:_	delicate
Understandability	mysterious	_:_:_:_:_:_:_	understandable
Evaluative	warm	_:_:_:_:_:_:_	cold
Evaluative	clean	_:_:_:_:_:_:_	dirty
Evaluative	safe	_:_:_:_:_:_:_	dangerous
Evaluative	relaxed	_:_:_:_:_:_:_	tense
Evaluative	valuable	_:_:_:_:_:_:_	worthless
Evaluative	sick	_:_:_:_:_:_:_	healthy
Evaluative	good	_:_:_:_:_:_:_	bad
Evaluative	ineffective	_:_:_:_:_:_:_	effective
Understandability	familiar	_:_:_:_:_:_:_	strange

Fig. 1. Representative page from the semantic differential instrument used to measure attitudes

The present study seeks to compare attitudes toward old age specifically with attitudes toward average people and the mentally ill, using a quantitative measure of the quality of the attitudes (see also Altrocchi and Eisdorfer, in press). Subjects were 103 undergraduate summer school and nursing students at Duke University, the majority of them female, and 31 noninstitutionalized aged subjects from the surrounding area.

Attitudes were measured by a semantic differential instrument modeled after similar instruments used by Osgood *et al.* (1957) and Nunnally (1961). Figure 1 shows a sample page from this instrument. The concept to be rated—in this case "Old Man"—is at the top of the page. The subject checks each of 20 seven-point bipolar scales below it. The 20 scales were chosen to represent the four factors which Osgood and Nunnally have found in their factor analytic studies with semantic differential instruments. Thirteen of the scales—designated in the margin on this sample—represent the evaluative factor: for instance, "good . . . bad." Two scales represent the potency factor: for instance, "weak . . . strong." Two scales represent the activity factor: for instance, "slow . . . fast." And three scales, except for the older subjects where scales for this factor had been left out, represent the understandability factor: for instance, "predictable . . . unpredictable." Mean factor scores were used in all analyses.

All student subjects rated the concepts "Average Man," "Average Woman," "Old Man," "Old Woman," "Neurotic Man," "Neurotic

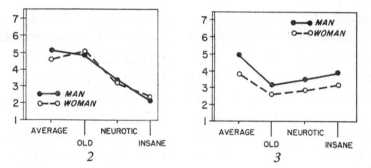

Fig. 2. Mean semantic differential evaluative factor scores for all subjects

Fig. 3. Mean semantic differential potency factor scores for all subjects

Woman," "Insane Man," "Insane Woman." The 31 aged subjects rated "Self" only.

Figures 2–5 summarize the results. For each factor, for Man and Woman separately, a repeated-measurements analysis of variance was carried out. Concept effects were significant at well beyond the .01 level for Man and Woman for all factors. All reference to statistical significance of the results will therefore refer to *t* tests, performed after the over-all analyses, using the .01 level of significance at all times. The results for the 31 aged subjects were not included in the statistical analyses but are included in the figures for purposes of comparison.

Figure 2 which gives results for the evaluative factor, shows that those for Man and Woman concepts were almost entirely parallel and identical. Average Man and Woman were rated significantly higher than Old Man and Woman, even though the difference was small. Old

Man and Woman, in turn, however, were rated significantly and very much higher than Neurotic and Insane Man and Woman. The older subjects rated Self noticeably higher than the younger subjects' ratings of Old Man and Old Woman.

Turning now to the potency factor in Fig. 3, it is immediately apparent that Man concepts were seen as more potent than Woman concepts. Considering that the two scales representing the factor were "weak . . . strong" and "rugged . . . delicate," this is quite understandable and reflects favorably on the validity of the instrument. Old Man was seen as much less potent than Average Man, significantly less potent than Insane Man, but not significantly different from Neurotic Man. The results for Woman concepts were entirely parallel.

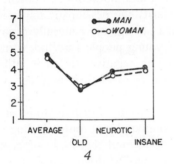 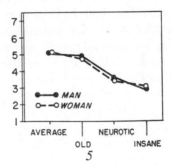

Fig. 4. Mean semantic differential activity factor scores for all subjects
Fig. 5. Mean semantic differential understandability factor scores for all subjects

The older subjects rated Self as much more potent than the younger subjects rated either Old Man or Old Woman.

Results for the activity factor in Fig. 4 show as one might expect, that Old Man was seen as significantly less active than Average, Neurotic and Insane Man, with the results for Old Woman being entirely parallel. Again the older subjects' rating of Self was much higher than the younger subjects' rating of Old Man and Old Woman.

For the understandability factor in Fig. 5, Old Man was seen as much more understandable—and highly significantly so—than Neurotic Man, and especially Insane Man—and as not significantly different from Average Man. For Old Woman, the results were the same. We shall not comment on the finding that Average Woman was seen as less understandable than Average Man!

Before turning to a discussion of these results, it might be useful to note that all the younger subjects were tested a second time after one or another kind of learning or training experience of several weeks' duration. The results of the second testing were almost identical with the results of the first testing, presented here, for Old Man and Old Woman. Thus the results for Old Man and Old Woman can be considered as somewhat stable over at least a few weeks' time.

It seems that whether attitudes of young people toward concepts of old age are positive or negative compared to their attitudes toward concepts of the average person depends on what specific aspects of attitudes are measured. These results are quite congruent with expectation and with Tuckman and Lorge's and Kogan's findings in this respect. For instance, Old Man and Old Woman were seen as being as understandable as Average Man and Average Woman, but slightly and reliably lower in value or goodness, and markedly less potent and active. Thus these findings help to clarify the pessimistic impressions of earlier writers that attitudes toward old age are generally negative. There are evidently some aspects of young people's attitudes toward old persons which are as positive—or as negative—as their attitudes toward the average person, and other aspects of their attitudes which are more negative toward older people, so that it might be reasonable to talk of older people as a minority group. Further study of this problem is needed. We would recommend not only dealing with specific aspects of attitudes but going beyond the study of abstract concepts like Old Man to study, as Kogan has done, sketches or pictures or movies of specific old and other people.

On all factors, and with only one exception, however, Old Man and Old Woman were seen as significantly different from concepts of mental illness as represented by Neurotic and Insane Man and Woman. Thus the present results suggest that younger people, at least, clearly discriminate between concepts of old age and concepts of mental illness—a finding which supports Kogan's position. An important next step would be to compare old age and mental illness with physical illness and disability.

Finally, it might be illuminating to compare the attitudes of older people toward old age, physical and mental disability, and people in general with the attitudes of younger people toward the same groups. Such an approach appears to have special relevance in view of the suggestion, by present results obtained by the brief testing of a few older people, that these older subjects' attitudes toward themselves were higher on all semantic differential factors than younger people's attitudes toward concepts of old age. The question arises, for instance, whether old people see old people in general or only themselves in a more positive light. We are now collecting more extensive semantic differential data from aged subjects in an attempt to answer such questions as this so as to clarify further the status of the aged in our society.

REFERENCES

Altrocchi, J., and Eisdorfer, C. A comparison of attitudes toward old age, mental illness, and other concepts. Ment. Hyg. (In press.)

Axelrod, S., and Eisdorfer, C. 1961. Attitudes toward old people: an empirical analysis of the stimulus-group validity of the Tuckman-Lorge questionnaire. J. Gerontol., 16: 75–80.

Barron, M. L. 1953. Minority group characteristics of the aged in American society. J. Gerontol., 8: 477–82.

Drake, J. T. 1958. The aged in American society. New York: Ronald Press Co.

Golde, Peggy, and Kogan, N. 1959. A sentence completion procedure for assessing attitudes toward old people. J. Gerontol., 14: 355–63.

Kogan, N. Attitudes toward old people: the development of a scale and an examination of correlates. J. Abnorm. & Soc. Psychol., 62: 44–54.

Nunnally, J. 1961. Popular conceptions of mental health: their development and change. New York: Holt, Rinehart, Winston.

Osgood, C. E., Suci, G. J., and Tannenbaum, P. H. 1957. The measurement of meaning. Urbana: University of Illinois Press.

Tuckman, J., and Lorge, I. 1952a. The effect of institutionalization on attitudes toward old people. J. Abnorm. Soc. Psychol., 47: 337–44.

———— 1952b. The influence of a course on the psychology of the adult on attitudes toward old people and older workers. J. Educ. Psychol., 43: 400–7.

———— 1953. Attitudes toward old people. J. Soc. Psychol., 37: 249 60.

———— 1954. The influence of change directions on stereotypes about aging, before and after instruction. Educ. Psychol. Measurement, 14: 128–32.

———— 1958. Attitude toward aging of individuals with experiences with the aged. J. Genet. Psychol., 92: 199–204.

Toward a Behavioral Scale for Biological Age

WARD C. HALSTEAD AND PHILLIP RENNICK

IN recent years, nonpatient populations consisting primarily of production workers and business executives have been under study by us at the University of Chicago Clinics and at several college testing centers in various parts of this country. Neuropsychological tests developed in the Laboratory of Medical Psychology for the measurement of higher brain functioning have been applied in conjunction with standard medical indicators bearing upon the general problem of mental and physical health. A collateral purpose of such studies is the elucidation of the incidence and nature of possible changes in higher brain functioning as have come to be commonly associated with the process called "aging." The studies are objective and quantitative in nature. The psychological indicators constitute the Halstead Battery of Neuropsychological Tests. These tests have been developed during the past 25 years and have proved to be relatively sensitive, reliable, and valid in defining the state of higher brain functioning independently of such considerations as calendar age, sex, amount of formal schooling, ethnic origin, occupational history, and psychometric intelligence or IQ.

So far as is known, this is the first "culture free" battery of psychological instruments for the measurement of adaptive brain power which have been validated directly on neurosurgical and neurological patients along with appropriate controls. The tests are essentially nonverbal in character and attempt to determine the ability of the brain to integrate information in time and space supplied to it through the modalities of vision, hearing, and sense of touch. Evidence bearing upon sensitivity, reliability, and validity as well as more detailed descriptions of the ten individual tests in the Battery have been published (Halstead, 1947; Reitan, 1955; Kløve, 1959; Chapman et al., 1958; Halstead et al., to be published).

This research has been supported in part by grants from the National Institute of Neurological Diseases and Blindness (Grant B–1507) and the Abbott Memorial Research Fund. Phillip Rennick was a National Science Foundation Cooperative Fellow, 1959–1960.

It should be noted that in applying these instruments to the problem of "aging," several considerations must be kept in mind. One of these is obviously the motivational factor. Are the tests interesting and enjoyable? Or are they dull and boring to take? Does repetition of the tests involve a substantial increment of learning? Are the tests too highbrow or intellectual in character for the general population? Is the meaning or purpose of each test so self-evident to the subject that willful distortion or malingering is likely? We believe that our combined experience, which now includes several laboratories, and the data for several thousands of individuals provide encouraging answers to each of the above questions. The test battery is novel and diversified in content and normally elicits a high level of motivation and cooperation. Many subjects describe taking the tests as "fun." The test-retest reliability is satisfactorily high. The nonverbal content of the tests requires special norms and objective scoring keys for evaluation of performance. Thus, the subject does not know at the end of testing whether he has performed well or badly. His attitude of cooperation and serious approach to the test is reinforced throughout by the attitudes and behavior of the testing personnel and by provision and maintenance of an appropriate test environment.

We have been impressed by the considerable range of individual differences exhibited by our older executive personnel in both the quantitative and qualitative aspects of their test performances. Men of the same calendar age often differ markedly in "quality of test decisions" and in their apparent efficiency in reaching them. This has led us to raise the question of whether this group of men was initially more homogeneous in ability and has become less so over time as a function of some X-factor such as "aging." On the assumption that this X-factor exists, we have taken preliminary steps toward construction of a behavioral scale which we hope will ultimately reflect *biological age* in meaningful terms. Theoretically, biological "age" could be assigned to an individual on the basis of measurements of the pattern of irreversible changes in the molecular make-up of several important physiological systems. Ideally, for each of these systems the probability for each chronological age that a certain type of molecular breakdown, or error, is present would be known. From measurements of a sufficiently large array of these variables arranged on age scales, the "aging" of some individuals could be determined, presumably with more predictive value in many applications than the age arrived at by counting years since birth. The differences in the rate of "aging" over time, in one species, could probably be attributed to three classes of variables: (1) Genetic differences in the perfection of the systems themselves, resulting in differing rates of production of "incorrect" molecules, in ordinary conditions; (2) Genetic differences in the self-corrective mechanisms involved in the prevention of breakdown during deviations from the ideal steady-state conditions, as in stress; (3) Environmental differences in the amount of interference with the operation of the systems from such factors as disease and injury.

An example of molecular breakdown might conceivably be found in the case of *memory*. It is a commonplace observation that "failing memory" and early senility are often associated in oldsters. Does this "memory loss" reflect the dropping out of neurones [at a rate possibly as high as 100,000 per day after age 30, according to Burns (1958)] or are para-neuronal structures and processes more directly involved? Halstead (1951) and Katz and Halstead (1950) have proposed this latter possibility as being in line with negative findings from ablation studies and compatible with modern conceptions of the gene as a memory device or trace. The ultra-structure of the nerve cell and its processes is considered to provide short-term memory storage capacity at the molecular level in nucleoproteins or chromatin materials (e.g., D.N.A. and R.N.A.). The possibility must be seriously considered that once neuronal R.N.A., for example, is encoded with experience, its capacity for self-replication extends beyond the neurone into the abundant, metabolically highly active R.N.A.-rich glial brain for long-term storage. "Memory" or recall would thus become a kind of molecular retrieving or matching appropriate to the needs specified contemporaneously by the neuronal brain. It is of interest that Hydén (1958) proposed a similar view of memory at the Fourth International Congress of Biochemistry in Vienna in 1958.

Assuming for the moment that such measurements are possible, it would still remain to be seen how valuable they might be. Perhaps scales of equal predictive value could be constructed from measurements of other variables which in general change over time, with individual differences. It would in fact be of great value in the unraveling of the mind problem if age scales of *behavioral* capabilities could be constructed so that the physiological age scales could be related to them. The problem of the causal analysis of the relationship between behavioral "aging" and physiological "aging" would be easier to open up if the behavioral scales used were validated on physiological criteria during their construction—even if these criteria are not the "molecular error" measurements used in constructing ideal age scales.

In the construction of such a behavioral age scale, an approach analogous to the search for "molecular errors" typical of certain steps in chronological age might well be used—provided that the variables measured showed about the same order of individual differences in healthy people of a given age as did the psychological variables, so that the confusion between age level and ability level was minimized, and so that the relationship between them was maximally clarified. Validation of the scales on physiological criteria during their construction is the most direct method of attaining such variables.

Since the Halstead Battery of Neuropsychological Tests was validated during construction on the criterion of known brain injury, it may serve as a lead in the formation of a biologically useful behavioral age scale. It is our purpose in this paper to discuss some of the possibilities inherent in this tool and to show some of the preliminary results in our use of it to measure biological age.

We now have over six-hundred battery scores on over four-hundred top-level executives. We test these men for indicators of brain impairment as part of their annual physical examinations at various college testing centers throughout this country and at the University of Chicago Clinics. It is our belief that we have here a group sufficiently homogeneous in individual abilities under conditions of good health to warrant a look at individual differences in terms of biological age. We intend to search out all three of the over-all scoring methods applicable to our test data for relevance: (1) we can look at the scores on subtests of the battery and perhaps construct profiles appropriate to age levels; (2) we can see what happens during aging to the established single score—the Halstead Index—which best predicted presence or absence of brain lesions in the validation studies (Halstead, 1947; Reitan, 1955); (3) we can check for the appropriateness in this context of Halstead's four-factor Biological Intelligence model, in the hope that individual differences in Betaweights on these factors are more directly related to differential aging than to original differential endowment in this population. This search is now being programmed for computer analysis, and we have already transferred all of our findings onto IBM cards for this purpose.

As an illustration of some of the assumptions on which one can base these computations we here present some of our preliminary work-ups on 76 of these executives—aged 46 or older (where differential aging begins to be especially significant in terms of external criteria). This particular group was of interest to us because we were able to secure from their company presidents merit judgments on each of them (to avoid contamination of predictor criteria, these companies never receive the results of our measurements). As noted by

Halstead, Merryman, and Klien (to be published) the agreement between the Halstead Impairment Index and a threefold rating from the company presidents was good enough to convince us that such biologically oriented measurements could be important determinants in predicting outcomes of some very important real-life situations.

Another important determinant in the companies' valuation of these men might be their chronological age. Let us divide the 76 men into three roughly equal groups according to chronological age and compare the distributions in these groups of the company ratings. Such a comparison is presented in Table 1. There is obviously some

Table 1. Relation between performance ratings of executives and chronological age[a]

Chronological age	Company rating					
	A		B		C	
46–50	9	(50.0%)	4	(22.2%)	5	(27.8%)
50–55	14	(45.2%)	14	(45.2%)	3	(9.6%)
Over 55	1	(3.8%)	15	(55.5%)	11	(40.7%)

[a] See Halstead, Merryman, and Klien (to be published) for scale employed in rating performance.

tendency for the older men to be downgraded in the evaluations of these companies. Only 1 of 27 men older than 55 is rated A by the companies, while 50 percent of the men aged 46–50 are so rated. Incidentally, over 85 percent of the executives at this high level aged 45 or below are rated grade A by their companies, which we take as evidence that these men are a relatively homogeneous, highly talented group before differential aging begins to sort them out after age 45.

To test the hypothesis that it is differential aging which sorts them out after age 45, we have chosen to experiment with means for correcting the chronological age of these men in terms of their performance on our measures of higher brain functioning. Thus a score would be obtained which (in view of the demonstrated biological validity of the Halstead Battery) one would feel somewhat justified in calling a "biological" age. In prediction applications, it seems justified to depart from the ideal of measuring "aging" independently of chronological age, to take advantage of the presumably valid predictive value of chronological age in estimating "aging." In setting up a biological age in this manner, one is governed by the ideal of maximal predictive value when assigning the corrections to be applied at a given chronological age for a given score. Using the Impairment Index as the basic score, and applying a correction factor for each Impairment Index which varies with chronological age, one can construct a table of biological ages to be assigned for each combination of Impairment Index and chronological age. As an example, a 60-year-old man might "earn" a biological age of 50 or 70 or any other age within reason depending on his Impairment Index and the size of the correction factor chosen in making up the table.

Taking the merit ratings on this group of 76 executives as the external criterion (assuming them to be approximately homogeneous in native endowment so that it is their differential aging which determines their current abilities), we have made up one table of biological age with the aim of obtaining a high predictive value. Some of the correction factors on this table are quite large—one 46-year-old man was assigned on the basis of his test scores the biological age of 34—but the correction factors were chosen systematically on the basis of empirical predictive value and common sense, rather than *a priori* considerations. Most of the correction factors are of the order of 4 or 5 years in this group. The 3 × 3 table of agreement between biological age and merit ratings is presented as Table 2.

Table 2. Relation between performance ratings of executives and biological age

	Company rating		
Biological age	*A* (*N* = 24)	*B* (*N* = 33)	*C* (*N* = 19)
Under 50	11 (60.8%)	7 (38.9%)	1 (5.3%)
50–55	9 (29.0%)	22 (71.0%)	0 (0.0%)
Over 55	4 (15.4%)	4 (15.4%)	18 (69.2%)

The agreement of the companies' ratings with the biological ages within Table 2 is very much greater than that with the chronological ages in Table 1. It is as if our tests were selecting those older executives who were "aging" less rapidly than their peers and assigning them biological ages more consonant with their retained abilities, and at the same time selecting those younger executives "aging" more rapidly than their peers and assigning them biological ages indicative of their failing abilities. The 59-year-old executive with no impairment might be more valuable to his company with his extra experience than the 49-year-old executive already exhibiting borderline impairment.

There are other criteria which could be used to suggest methods for correcting chronological age with neuropsychological data, one of which, based on a kind of profile analysis of the test data compared with ophthalmoscopic examination for evidence of vascular abnormalities, was presented by Halstead, Merryman, and Klien (to be published). This too was preliminary, and we are awaiting the results of computer analysis before we decide upon a workable system for constructing a behavioral scale for biological age. At this stage we do not yet know whether it will be possible from our data to assign an absolute biological age without using the measurement of chronological age as one of the indicators. It seems likely that biological intelligence declines on the average more regularly with "aging" post-maturity than psychometric intelligence does, but we shall have to test a wide range of subjects in various stages of health and disease to verify this assumption. It is interesting, however, that even in our executive population, with its annual physical checkups and top medical care, our measures show an *average* decline in abilities starting in the fourth decade.

REFERENCES

Burns, B. D. 1958. The mammalian cerebral cortex. London: Edward Arnold Ltd.

Chapman, L. F., Thetford, W. N., Berlin, L., Guthrie, T. C., and Wolff, H. G. 1958. Highest integrative functions in man during stress. *In* S. B. Wortis (ed.), The brain and human behavior. Baltimore: Williams & Wilkins Co.

Halstead, W. C. 1947. Brain and intelligence: a quantitative study of the frontal lobes. Chicago: University of Chicago Press.

—— 1951. Brain and intelligence. *In* L. A. Jeffress (ed.), Cerebral mechanisms in behavior, pp. 244–88. New York: John Wiley & Sons, Inc.

——, Merryman, P., and Klien, B. The Halstead Index and differential "aging." *In* Wilma Donahue, C. Tibbitts, and R. H. Williams (eds.), Psychological and social processes of aging: an international research seminar. To be published.

Hydén, H. 1958. Biochemical changes in glial cells and nerve cells and varying activity. *In* O. Hoffman-Ostenhof (ed.), Proceedings of the Fourth International Congress of Biochemistry, Vol. 3. New York: Pergamon Press.

Katz, J. J., and Halstead, W. C. 1950. Protein organization and mental function. *In* W. C. Halstead (ed.), Brain and behavior. (Comparative psychology monograph #103), 20: 1–94. Berkeley: University of California Press.

Kløve, H. 1959. Relationship of differential electroencephalographic patterns to distribution of Wechsler-Bellevue scores. Neurology, 9: 871–76.

Reitan, R. M. 1955. An investigation of the validity of Halstead's measures of biological intelligence. A. M. A. Arch. Neurol. Psychiat., 73: 28–35.

The Differential Relationships of Psychological Test Results to Electroencephalographic Criteria in Older and Younger Age Groups

HALLGRIM KLØVE

IN an earlier study (Kløve, 1959*a*) certain rather striking relationships between different electroencephalographic patterns and the distribution of Wechsler-Bellevue scores were demonstrated. These results can be summarized in the following manner: EEG disturbances maximized over the right cerebral hemisphere tended to lower the performance subtests, while with the electrical disturbance maximized over the left cerebral hemisphere, the verbal subtests tended to be depressed. Brain-damaged patients with generalized EEG disturbances and normal EEG failed to demonstrate significant differences between verbal and performance subtests. The general level of the results was better in the patients with normal EEG than in the other groups.

MATERIALS AND METHODS

In the present study, 45 control subjects and 216 patients with verified brain damage were examined. The patients represented general referrals for neuropsychologic examinations from the neurologic and neurosurgical services at Indiana University Medical Center. The patients were divided into two age groups, those who were 35 years and younger and those who were 45 years and older. These two groups were then each divided into the following subgroups according to electroencephalographic criteria: normal EEG with brain damage, generalized EEG abnormality over both hemispheres, EEG abnormality maximized over the right hemisphere, and EEG abnormality

This investigation was supported in part by Research Grant B–2416 from the National Institute of Neurological Diseases and Blindness, USPHS.

maximized over the left hemisphere. The descriptive variables for each group are presented in Table 1.

Table 1. *Descriptive variables for each of the groups*

			Age			Education (in years)		
	Male	Female	Mean	S.D.	Range	Mean	S.D.	Range
35 and younger								
Normal control (N = 33)	32	1	27.45	4.63	20–35	11.54	3.12	7–20
Brain-damaged								
Normal EEG (N = 40)	32	8	27.37	6.28	15–35	10.87	2.85	6–20
Generalized EEG								
abnormal. (N = 33)	24	9	27.18	5.84	15–35	9.58	2.65	2–14
Right EEG								
abnormal. (N = 34)	28	6	25.47	5.78	15–34	10.94	2.67	4–17
Left EEG								
abnormal. (N = 37)	28	9	26.57	6.36	15–34	10.00	3.08	2–16
45 and older								
Normal control (N = 12)	10	2	53.00	5.92	45–62	10.33	2.57	4–12
Brain-damaged								
Normal EEG (N = 22)	19	3	54.77	7.53	45–72	9.77	3.26	3–16
Generalized EEG								
abnormal. (N = 16)	13	3	52.12	5.29	45–62	9.81	2.86	5–16
Right EEG								
abnormal. (N = 17)	15	2	57.12	7.67	47–74	9.65	4.63	2–19
Left EEG								
abnormal. (N = 17)	12	5	53.94	6.66	46–71	9.35	2.75	3–14

No significant differences were found between any of the subgroups in respect to years of education except that among those aged 45 and older a comparison between the control group and the group with right EEG abnormalities revealed an age difference which just, although barely, reached the 5 percent level of confidence. These were the only two subgroups which differed significantly as regards age— the control group being significantly younger than the group with right EEG abnormalities. It should be emphasized that the groups labeled as normal EEG had unequivocal evidence of organic damage to the brain, as did of course, the patients with abnormal EEG. Criteria other than EEG were used to determine whether or not a patient was brain-damaged. Once brain damage was established, EEG served as a classification criterion as indicated in Table 1. The records were obtained from an eight-channel Grass electroencephalograph model III A. Bipolar recording technique with 14 electrodes was used. Each patient was hyperventilated for three minutes and photic stimulation was employed.

The Wechsler-Bellevue Scale of Adult Intelligence Form I (Wechsler, 1944) and the Halstead Impairment Index (Halstead, 1947) were obtained before composition of the groups. The raw scores were converted to T-scores in order to normalize the distributions and equate variances. Statistical comparisons between age groups were then performed.

RESULTS

In Fig. 1, the distributions of total verbal and total performance weighted scores are presented. The verbal weighted score was identical for the two control groups. However, in the younger group, the performance level was better than the verbal level while in the older group this relationship was reversed.

The same relationships between verbal and performance levels were present in the younger and older brain-damaged groups, except for the younger group with right EEG abnormalities and the older group with left EEG abnormalities. As one would expect from the study mentioned earlier, the performance scale was slightly lower than the verbal scale in the younger group with right EEG abnormalities, whereas the performance scale was slightly higher than the verbal scale in the older group with left EEG abnormalities. These relationships are in accordance with expectation concerning the differential effects of lateralized brain dysfunction on the verbal and performance scales of the Wechsler-Bellevue (Kløve, 1959*b;* Kløve and Reitan, 1958; Reitan, 1955) with the additional observation of an especial lowering of the performance scale in all of the brain-damaged groups. This latter effect augmented the difference between the verbal and performance scales in the older as compared with the younger groups with right EEG abnormalities and diminished the same difference in the older as compared with younger groups with left EEG abnormalities.

In Fig. 2, these data are rearranged in order to permit a more direct comparison between the two age groups for each EEG classification. The levels of significance of the differences are indicated in Table 2 for each comparison. On verbal subtests, there were no sig-

Table 2. Table of T-score means and level of confidence
(higher T-score corresponds with higher raw score)

Test group	WECHSLER-BELLEVUE VERBAL SCALE			WECHSLER-BELLEVUE PERFORMANCE SCALE			HALSTEAD IMPAIRMENT INDEX		
	Young	*Old*	*p <*	*Young*	*Old*	*p <*	*Young*	*Old*	*p <*
Normal Controls	58.33	58.08	N.S.	61.85	53.33	.001	63.36	57.83	.05
Normal EEG	52.92	52.68	N.S.	55.80	47.41	.005	53.57	45.09	.005
Generalized EEG abnormal.	50.36	46.50	N.S.	50.85	44.87	.05	52.15	46.62	N.S.
Right EEG abnormal.	50.97	52.88	N.S.	49.91	40.47	.005	53.35	45.12	.001
Left EEG abnormal	47.05	44.29	N.S.	52.70	45.88	.005	51.11	44.59	.05

nificant differences between the age groups while on performance subtests, the differences were highly significant. The Halstead Impair-

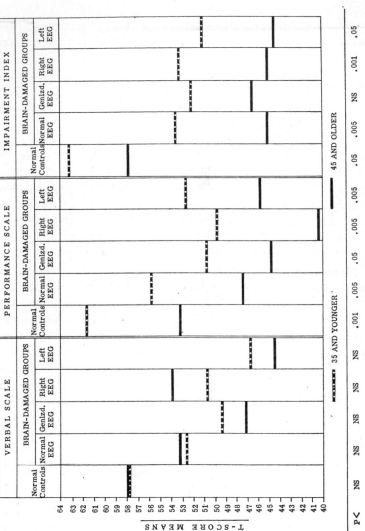

Fig. 1. Distribution of total verbal and total performance weighted scores for the younger and older age groups

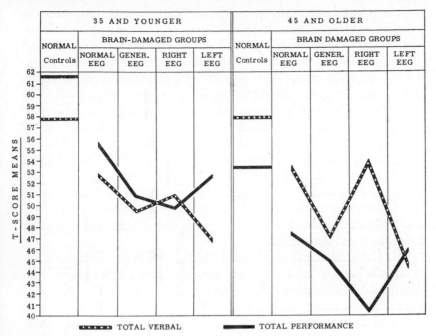

Fig. 2. *Comparison between the two age groups for each EEG classi-fication on the two Wechsler-Bellevue Scales and the Impairment Index*

ment Index also showed significant differences in all comparisons except for the groups with generalized EEG abnormalities.

COMMENTS

There may be several bases for expecting differential relationships to age among these variables in groups with lateralized cerebral dysfunction. Probably the most obvious one is that younger persons are not as frequently afflicted with massive lateralized lesions as are older persons. In our experience, gliomata, hemorrhages, and occlusions represent the types of lesions most often associated with selective impairment of either the verbal or performance subtests in the Wechsler-Bellevue Scale. The results of this study, however, suggest that roughly the same relationship between verbal and performance results was present in both the younger and older groups with lateralized dysfunction.

Another factor that may be represented by the aging process per se stands out much more prominently in the results. Between the younger and older control groups there was no difference on the verbal scale. However, comparison of the performance scale for these groups yielded a difference significant beyond the .001 level of confidence, the older group being poorer. This difference seems to represent an aging factor. Consequently, in our older patients with right hemisphere lesions, impairment on the performance scale was pronounced since both lateralization of the lesion and the effects of normal aging apparently contributed to the impairment. Verbal abilities, as indicated by several other studies (Wechsler, 1944; Reitan, 1957), are more stable and less susceptible to age changes than are performance-type abilities. Consequently, since the performance scale was depressed in all our older groups, the difference between the verbal and performance scales in the older group with dysfunction of the left hemisphere was diminished.

The Halstead Impairment Index yielded significant differences between the younger and the older groups except in the groups with generalized EEG abnormalities. The variations between the subgroups were smaller because the Impairment Index appears to be sensitive to lesions in either hemisphere. The differences between age groups were, however, more consistent than for the Wechsler-Bellevue Scale. Discriminations between the control group and the brain-damaged groups were, especially, more marked for the Impairment Index. The Impairment Index also clearly classified both the younger and older groups with brain damage but normal EEG at levels comparable to the other brain-damaged groups. This finding suggests that the Halstead Impairment Index is more sensitive in these subgroups to the organic condition of the brain than is the EEG.

SUMMARY

Younger (mean age, 26.80 years) and older (mean age, 54.19 years) groups were each subdivided according to the following EEG criteria: normal EEG with brain damage, generalized EEG abnormality, right EEG abnormality, and left EEG abnormality. Comparisons with Wechsler-Bellevue variables and with the Halstead Impairment Index were performed.

The younger and older groups with the same EEG classifications showed no significant differences in the verbal total scores, whereas significant differences were present in each comparison for the performance total scores. Consistent trends were noted in both the younger and older groups with lateralized EEG disturbances. The Halstead Impairment Index showed significant differences between older and younger groups in all comparisons except for the subgroups with generalized EEG disturbances.

REFERENCES

Halstead, W. C. 1947. Brain and intelligence. Chicago: University of Chicago Press.

Kløve, H. 1959a. Relationship of differential electroencephalographic patterns to distribution of Wechsler-Bellevue Scores. Neurology, 9: 871–76.

——— 1959b. The relationship of sensory suppression to distribution of Wechsler-Bellevue scores. (Paper read at Midwestern Psychological Association, Chicago.)

Kløve, H., and Reitan, R. M. 1958. Effect of dysphasia and spatial distortion on Wechsler-Bellevue results. Arch. Neurol. & Psychiat., 80: 708–13.

Reitan, R. M. 1955. Certain differential effects of left and right cerebral lesions in human adults. J. Comp. Physiol., 48: 474–77.

——— 1957. Differential reaction of various psychological tests to age. *In* Proceedings of the Fourth Congress, International Association of Gerontology, Merano, Italy, 4: 158–65. Fidenza: Tipografia Tito Mattioli.

Wechsler, D. 1944. The measurement of adult intelligence. Baltimore: Williams and Wilkins Co.

The Comparative Psychological Significance of Aging in Groups with and without Organic Brain Damage

RALPH M. REITAN

PREVIOUS studies by the writer have yielded results indicating differential results on psychological measures in accordance with chronological age for groups with and without brain damage. In one investigation (Reitan, 1955c), the Halstead Impairment Index was determined for 180 brain-damaged subjects and 101 neurologically "normal" subjects, each group ranging in age from 15 through 64 years. The Pearson product-moment coefficient of correlation and the correlation ratio between age and the Impairment Index for the group with brain damage were .23 and .27, respectively. For the group without brain damage, however, the corresponding values were .54 and .61. The regression line for the group with brain damage did not deviate from rectilinearity, but the hypothesis of rectilinearity for the group without brain damage was retained at a confidence level falling between .10 and .05. Inspection of the results for the two groups revealed that the brain-damaged group performed poorly at all age ranges, whereas the group without brain damage showed impairment only after the age of 45 years.

Another study (Reitan, 1956) investigated the comparative distribution according to age of the Halstead Impairment Index and the full-scale Wechsler-Bellevue Intelligence Scale weighted score. The results indicated that groups with and without brain damage showed larger differences among themselves on the Impairment Index than on the Wechsler measure. Correlations between age and the W-B measure for the brain-damaged and non-brain-damaged groups were .37 and .35, respectively. Correlation between age and Impairment Index for the brain-damaged group was .37, but the group without brain damage yielded a coefficient of .60.

These findings prompted a more detailed and directly controlled

Supported by Grant B–2416, National Institutes of Neurological Diseases and Blindness, National Institutes of Health.

study of possible differential relationships between age and ability measurements in groups with and without brain damage. The writer (Reitan, 1955*a*) had found previously that the most sensitive measures to brain damage in a large battery of tests studied at the Indiana University Medical Center were the Halstead Impairment Index, the Halstead Category Test, the Localization component of the Halstead Tactual Performance Test (Halstead, 1947), and Part B of the Trail Making Test (Reitan, 1955*b*; 1958). Consequently, these variables were selected for the present investigation.

PROCEDURE

Fifty subjects with established brain damage composed one group. The second group contained 50 subjects who had no history suggesting brain damage and who showed consistently negative findings upon neurological examination. No attempt was made to select brain-damaged subjects with respect to neurological criteria relating to factors such as type of lesion, severity of damage, duration of impairment, or recency of symptoms. The brain-damaged group, consequently, was rather heterogeneous with respect to neurological characteristics. Each group was divided into sub-groups according to chronological age as follows: 34 years and below, 20 subjects; 35–44 years, 10 subjects; 45–54 years, 10 subjects; and 55 years and above, 10 subjects. Within subgroups the subjects with and without brain damage were closely matched in pairs with respect to color, sex, age, and education. No significant differences in education were present either for the total groups or in comparison of any pair of the subgroups (Table 1).

Table 1. Descriptive statistics for subjects included in study

			Age		Education (in years)	
Age group	*Male*	*Female*	*Mean*	*S.D.*	*Mean*	*S.D.*
Brain-damaged						
34 and less	18	2	28.70	4.62	11.75	2.86
35–44	9	1	39.90	3.67	12.70	2.15
45–54	9	1	48.20	3.25	12.00	3.71
55 and more	9	1	58.00	2.86	11.30	4.20
Non-brain-damaged						
34 and less	18	2	27.95	3.78	11.70	3.12
35–44	9	1	40.30	2.83	13.00	1.79
45–54	9	1	48.50	2.87	12.50	3.78
55 and more	9	1	57.90	2.66	11.90	3.05

The psychological tests were administered and scored before any of the subjects had been identified for inclusion in the study. The Halstead Impairment Index is a composite value based upon the ten tests that Halstead found to be particularly sensitive to organic brain damage (Halstead, 1947). It is determined for each subject by counting the number of tests upon which the performance passes the criterion level into the range characteristic of brain-damaged subjects. The Category Test and Tactual Performance Test are also from Halstead's battery. The Category Test is an abstraction test, requiring the subject to discern a principle that runs through successive stimulus figures. Each response to the 208 figures composing the test is reinforced by a bell or buzzer, depending upon whether or not the answer is correct. The Tactual Performance Test requires the subject, while blindfolded, to place ten variously shaped blocks into a formboard. The subject does the task first with his preferred hand, next with his other hand, and finally with both hands. The board and blocks are then removed, and without having had an opportunity to see them, the subject is asked to reproduce the board and its various shapes in a pencil drawing. This drawing is scored for the number of shapes correctly reproduced (memory component) and for the number approximately in their correct positions (localization component).

The localization score was selected for use in this study because of its apparent sensitivity to brain damage (Reitan, 1955a). The final dependent variable was the score obtained from Part B of the Trail Making Test. Part A of this test requires the subject to connect numbers variously distributed upon a sheet of paper with a pencil line according to ascending numerical sequence. Part B of the test includes both numbers and letters. The subject is required to draw a line from 1 to A, from A to 2, from 2 to B, and so on, alternating between numbers and letters until completing the test. The score is recorded as the time needed to complete the test.

The raw scores for the two groups were combined into a single T-score distribution for each variable to effect approximate normalization of the distributions and to equate variance. The groups then were recomposed and T-scores were used in the analysis. Comparisons were made between the groups with and without brain damage in each chronological age interval. Additional comparisons were made between all combinations of subgroups in varying age intervals in both the brain-damaged and non-brain-damaged groups.

RESULTS

Figure 1 presents comparisons between groups with and without brain damage on each variable, subdivided into categories of subjects under and over 45 years of age.

Highly significant differences were present in each comparison except one (category test for patients of 45 years and older). Figure 1 shows no pattern of differential significance levels in accordance with age categories. The differences between groups appear to be approximately equivalent for either the younger or older groups. In every instance the younger brain-damaged group performed better than the older brain-damaged group and the same relationship was present for the older and younger groups without brain damage.

Figure 2 presents a more detailed analysis of the data. Mean levels are presented for each of the four age categories for both groups on each of the variables. The conversion to T-scores was done in such a way that the higher values represent the poorer performances. Each difference approaching or reaching a significant level ($p < .10$) either between or within groups is included in the figure.

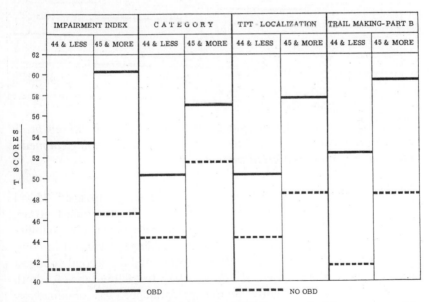

Fig. 1. Comparative performances of younger and older groups with and without brain damage on several psychological measures (higher T-scores represent poorer performances)

The graph presenting results obtained with the Impairment Index may be used to illustrate interpretation of Fig. 2. For each age category the brain-damaged groups performed more poorly than the groups without brain damage (probability levels ranging from < .01 to < .001). Comparisons of different age categories within the brain-damaged group or within the group without brain damage showed fewer significant differences. In the brain-damaged group, the youngest subgroup (aged 34 years and less) obtained a significantly better Impairment Index than did the two oldest subgroup (aged

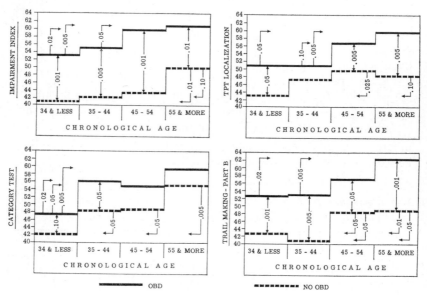

Fig. 2. *Comparative performances of groups with and without brain damage, subdivided into age categories, on several psychological measures (higher scores represent poorer performances)*

45–54 years and 55 years and older). The subgroup aged 35–44 years also performed significantly better than did the oldest group. The only differences between age subgroups with a chance probability of less than .10 in the group without brain damage occurred in comparisons of the youngest and oldest subgroups and the second youngest and oldest subgroups ($p < .01$ and $< .10$). In each instance for both groups, however, a slightly poorer performance was obtained by each successively older subgroup. Thus, while brain-damaged and non-brain-damaged subgroups of comparable age showed significant differences in each comparison on the Impairment Index, a minimum of a 10-year age gap was necessary for differences to begin to appear in comparisons of subgroups of varying age.

Results obtained with the other variables may be inspected in Fig. 2 as a basis for assessing further the effects of brain damage as compared with advancing age. However, some summary statements relating to all 4 test variables may be an aid in drawing conclusions. Comparisons of comparable age categories of the groups with and without brain damage yielded significant results $(p < .10)$[1] in 13 of 16 instances. A total of 6 comparisons between different age categories were computed for each variable within both the brain-damaged and non-brain-damaged groups. In the brain-damaged group, 11 of the 24 comparisons reached significant levels and the group without brain damage also had 11 significant differences in the 24 comparisons. Comparisons of the youngest and oldest subgroups contributed a majority of these significant differences in each group. Seven of the 11 significant differences in age categories occurred in comparing the youngest and oldest brain-damaged subgroups, and 6 of the 11 significant differences occurred in the comparable subgroups in the group without brain damage. Of the 11 significant age-category differences occurring in each group, only 2 in each group occurred in comparisons of adjacent age subgroups. In the other 9 instances for both the groups with and without brain damage, a gap of at least one age interval was present in the comparisons.

Differences between the oldest and youngest subgroups within both the brain-damaged and non-brain-damaged groups were consistently significant. The probability levels in these comparisons approached but generally were not quite as small as those obtained in comparisons of subgroups with and without brain damage but of comparable age. The youngest and oldest subgroups had mean ages approximately 30 years apart (see Table 1) and in no individual instance less than 20 years apart. Thus, an age interval of about 30 years was necessary within both the groups with and without brain damage to bring about differences that began to become comparable to those obtained as a result of brain damage with age held constant.

DISCUSSION AND CONCLUSIONS

The results indicated that fairly consistent and significant differences were present on selected psychological tests for comparably

---

[1] The significant differences had probability levels of less than .05 in a total of 31 of 35 comparisons. The 4 probability levels that were less than .10 but greater than .05 were included merely to indicate trends.

aged persons with and without brain damage. Each group, however, tended to show progressively poorer performances with advancing age. Within either group, a gap of at least 10 years was necessary for significant age-determined differences to begin to appear. Within the age ranges of the adults included in this study (21 to 64 years), the results suggested that the impairment shown by persons with clinically recognized brain damage as compared with non-brain-damaged controls of the same age began to be approached presumably as a function of normal aging in about 30 years.

While inferences of this type may be legitimate in terms of ability measurements they should not be construed as a basis for presuming that the effect of normal aging is necessarily one of a progressive approach to clinical brain damage. The marked similarity in effect on the psychological tests of advancing age in the groups with and without brain damage suggests that aging affects both groups comparably. Whatever the cumulative pathological changes that might accompany aging represent, one could hypothesize that they would affect these two groups differently if they were comparable to the broad range of disorders recognized clinically as effecting brain damage.

The psychological tests used in this study were selected because of prior evidence for their special sensitivity to organic brain damage. Possibly these tests are not the same as ones which might be especially sensitive to the normal effects of advancing age. Thus, the somewhat more consistent and significant differences obtained as a function of brain damage as compared with differences in various age categories may have been influenced by the selection of dependent variables. The results suggest that a meaningful additional step in this research approach would be to study more pointedly the question of whether those psychological measures specifically sensitive to brain damage are also the particular tests most sensitive to the effects of normal aging.

SUMMARY

Two groups of 50 subjects, one with and one without evidence of organic brain damage, were compared in an effort to determine the differential significance of brain damage and aging on psychological test results. The subjects in each group were closely matched in pairs with respect to color, sex, age, and education. The groups were divided into subgroups according to age (34 years and below, 35–44 years, 45–54 years, and 55 years and more) for purposes of the analysis.

The results yielded fairly consistent and significant differences for comparably aged subgroups of subjects with and without brain damage. Comparisons within the two groups of differently aged subgroups yielded less frequent significant differences than when the presence or absence of brain damage was used as the criterion for grouping. However, each significant difference in various age groups showed the older group performing more poorly than the younger group. The rate of advancing impairment with age was approximately comparable in both the groups with and without brain damage. The results suggest that within the age ranges used in this study, the impairing effects of normal aging require about 30 years to begin to become equivalent to the impairment brought about by clinically recognized brain damage.

REFERENCES

Halstead, W. C. 1947. Brain and intelligence: a quantitative study of the frontal lobes. Chicago: University of Chicago Press.

Reitan, R. M. 1955*a*. An investigation of the validity of Halstead's measures of biological intelligence. A. M. A. Arch. Neurol. & Psychiat., 73: 28–35.

——— 1955*b*. The relation of the Trail Making Test to organic brain damage. J. Consult. Psychol., 19: 393–94.

——— 1955*c*. The distribution according to age of a psychologic measure dependent upon organic brain functions. J. Gerontol., 10: 338–40.

——— 1956. The relationship of the Halstead Impairment Index and the Wechsler-Bellevue total weighted score to chronologic age. (Presented at the Ninth Annual Meeting of the Gerontological Society, Inc.).

——— 1958. Validity of the Trail Making Test as an indicator of organic brain damage. Percept. Motor Skills, 8: 271–76.

Changes in Cognitive Functioning in Relation to Intellectual Level in Senescence

CARL EISDORFER

ONE of the salient problems in the gerontologic literature involves intellectual and cognitive decline in senescence in relation to level of ability. Gilbert (1941) and Sorenson (1933, 1938) have demonstrated a differential decline based upon occupational levels but have attempted to explain their findings on the basis of the sustaining effects of more intellectual pursuits. Vernon (1947–1948) has investigated decline in performance on the Raven Progressive Matrices and has demonstrated that lower occupational levels are related to greater decline. This work is in general support of the findings of Raven (1948), which show a greater rate of decline among subjects scoring in the lower percentiles.

In longitudinal studies involving administration of the Army Alpha as a college entrance exam and subsequent reexamination of most of the initial group after 31 years, Owens (1953, 1957) reported that for his subjects, at least, there appears to be no evidence to indicate that age is any kinder to the initially more able. It must be remembered, however, that, at the outset, all of his subjects were entering college and so represented a restricted sample; in addition, the subjects were tested at approximately ages 19 and 49 thus further restricting the generality of this data.

In an investigation of change in specific information as defined by the Graduate Record Examination, Osborne and Sanders (1954) suggest that their investigation would support the hypothesis of a differential rather than a consistent rate of decline of acquired knowledge with age. A characteristic curve of mental decline occurred only for the "scientific" profiles. Unfortunately they do not include data on the initial level of their subjects nor is there any relationship established between pattern of decline and occupation. The work of Bayley and Oden (1955) suggests that for a limited age span, i.e., 30–42, there may even be some gains in conceptual ability with advancing age in a gifted group.

Among the problems which occur in interpreting many of these studies, we find that test procedures which serve as the dependent variables are heavily weighted with material favoring educated over noneducated groups, especially those individuals whose employment helps to maintain verbal skills, i.e., teachers, white collar workers, etc., as compared to those individuals who do not find it necessary to maintain such skills. It therefore seems valuable to investigate this problem with techniques that are relatively culture free, require no writing ability, and utilize perceptual as well as verbal skills.

Insofar as it is a complex perceptual task, the Rorschach Test seems appropriate for such an investigation. The use of this procedure in assessing developmental level of cognition and perceptual organization (as opposed to any specific clinical utility) has been well established at Clark University, Worcester State Hospital, Duke, and other centers.

PROCEDURE

The Rorschach Test was administered to 243 aged subjects who were volunteers from the community to the Duke Geriatrics Research Project. As one aspect of their examination, each of these subjects was administered the full-scale Wechsler Adult Intelligence Scale as well as the Rorschach. The Rorschach was then analyzed according to various factors, but the four variables to be reported upon in this study include: the number of responses (ΣR); the number of human movement responses (ΣM); and two developmental scores: the sum of functional integration (ΣFi), and content score (CS). The functional integration score was developed by Philips and his associates and is based upon Heinz Werner's (1948) approach to perception, i.e., that there is a developmental hierarchy in perception proceeding from the diffuse to the specific, to the integration of percepts. Functional integration is scored when the subject has successfully integrated two or more elements of the stimulus into a functional relationship. The content score developed by Grace (1956) involves the vocabulary of the perceptual responses and compares it with the developmental pattern of word usage for children and adults in the general population: it may thus be viewed as a developmental comparison of the language used in the various Rorschach percepts.

Subjects were divided into three groups on the basis of full-scale IQ scores on the WAIS; the average group included scores from 85–115, the high intelligence group, IQs of 116 and above, and the low IQ group for subjects with IQs below 85. Subjects were further subdivided according to age beginning with age 60 and including 5-year intervals, 60–64, 65–69, 70–74, and 75 plus. The result of this breakdown was twelve groups of subjects divided according to age and three levels of full-scale IQ. The Ns for each cell of the design ranged from 11 to 38.

RESULTS

Table 1 shows the number, age, and IQ composition of the subjects in these groups.

Table 1. WAIS IQs of subjects according to age and full-scale categories

IQ category and test	Age groups			
	60–64	*65–69*	*70–74*	*75+*
III (below 85)				
Number of cases	14	19	12	11
Verbal IQ	79.6	78.5	80.0	80.1
Performance IQ	75.1	72.1	74.9	76.0
Full-scale IQ	76.4	74.3	75.9	77.2
II (85–115)				
Number of cases	19	38	34	35
Verbal IQ	106.7	102.1	103.2	101.4
Performance IQ	94.7	93.2	92.9	94.7
Full-scale IQ	101.7	98.2	98.8	98 1
I (above 115)				
Number of cases	12	12	19	18
Verbal IQ	132.7	125.0	133.4	134.3
Performance IQ	112.1	113.2	117.9	118.0
Full-scale IQ	125.2	121.0	128.3	129.1

In view of the limited number of subjects in certain of the cells, and in order to retain as representative a sample as possible, cell numbers were left intact and the statistical analysis was based upon multiple *t*-tests between pairs of cells. Table 2 shows the means and S.D.s for each of the scores according to age and IQ subgroups for each of the four dependent variables.

For variable 1, number of responses on the Rorschach, Fig. 1 demonstrates the number of responses of the various groups on the Rorschach.

The results of the statistical analysis indicate that there is no definable decline in the high IQ category. Within IQ level I the only

Table 2. Means and standard deviations of Rorschach Test variables according to age and IQ groups

Age group	IQ group	N	Number of Rorschach responses		Number of human movement responses		Sum of functional integration		Content score	
			Mean	S.D.	Mean	S.D.	Mean	S.D.	Mean	S.D.
60–64	Iᵃ	12	22.0	10.3	2.0	1.8	6.2	4.3	14.2	1.6
	IIᵇ	19	18.3	11.2	1.2	1.7	4.8	6.3	12.8	3.4
	IIIᶜ	14	14.5	6.3	1.2	1.3	1.6	1.9	12.3	2.1
65–69	I	12	18.8	8.9	1.7	1.7	5.1	5.1	14.5	1.6
	II	38	18.9	9.8	1.2	1.4	4.1	4.8	13.6	2.0
	III	19	14.6	6.4	0.7	0.9	1.1	2.1	11.4	2.7
70–74	I	19	29.2	16.6	2.6	2.1	6.0	4.4	14.2	1.9
	II	34	16.1	8.2	1.0	1.4	3.0	3.4	12.6	2.5
	III	12	12.5	5.3	0.4	0.6	1.0	1.5	12.1	2.6
75+	I	18	21.1	6.9	2.5	1.8	7.0	5.4	14.8	1.8
	II	35	14.5	6.3	0.7	0.8	2.0	2.2	12.5	2.4
	III	11	9.8	3.2	0.4	1.3	2.0	3.6	10.0	2.1

ᵃ IQ group I = 116+.   ᵇ IQ group II = 85–115.   ᶜ IQ group III = below 85.

significant difference found was that between the 65–69 and the 70–74 year groups, the older subjects showed a larger number of Rs; t-test between these groups is significant at $p < .05$. This finding would appear to be the result of a sampling artifact and neither one of these subgroups is significantly different from the youngest or oldest age group in the same IQ category. For IQ level II, while the first two age groups do not differ from one another, the data suggest that there

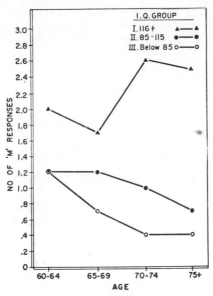

Fig. 1. Number of "M" responses arranged according to age and IQ groups

is a decline after age 69. The 70–74 year group does have significantly lower scores than the 65–69 year group; *t*-test is significant at $p < .05$. For IQ group III, the decline after 69 is similarly significant. Again there is no difference between age groups 60–64 and 65–69 and both of these groups show a significantly greater number of responses than the oldest age group (75 plus). In comparing the high to the low IQ levels (i.e., I and III), there are significant differences at every age period except for 65–69. Comparing the high to the middle IQ levels (i.e., I to II), there are no differences for the first two age categories but significant differences between IQ levels for the last two age

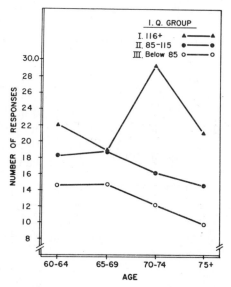

Fig. 2. Number of responses arranged according to age and IQ groups

categories (in both cases $p < .01$). Between middle and low IQ levels (II and III) the only difference exists between the 75 plus groups.

For variable 2, number of *M responses*: There are no significant differences between age groups within any of the IQ levels (see Fig. 2). Inspection of the differences between IQ levels does appear to be of importance, however. Thus, while there is no significant difference between IQ levels for the first two age groups, the high IQ category does differ from both the middle and the low IQ levels for the last two age groups. In both cases *p* is beyond the .01 level. The middle and low IQ categories differ only for the 70–74 year span. These results

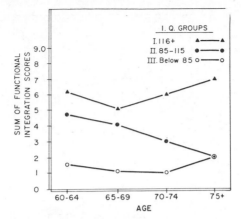

Fig. 3. Sum of functional integration scores arranged according to age and IQ groups

would again seem to suggest differential rates of decline with increasing age as a function of IQ level.

For variable 3, sum of functional integration: Again, no significant difference appears between age groups in the high IQ category. For IQ level II, there is no difference between the first and the second age categories but, as was the case for the number of responses, the second does differ significantly from the last age category. For this variable we find no difference between any of the age groups in the low IQ level; it seems clear from Fig. 3 that this is very probably the result of a base-line effect. The low and middle IQ levels differ for the first three age categories, eventually meeting at 75 plus.

For variable 4, Content Score: For this variable involving vocabulary level, we find no significant differences between the age groups within IQ category I; and, once again, we find that for IQ category II, while there is no difference between age groups 60–64 and 65–69, the latter group does differ significantly from the oldest age group. For IQ level III, we find that the difference between the youngest and oldest age groups is statistically significant. As we have seen before, IQ groups I and III differ at every age level. In addition, as also seen in two of the other variables (*M* and *R*), the high and middle IQ groups differ only for the last two age groups; IQ groups II and III differ at the second and fourth age groups. (See Fig. 4.)

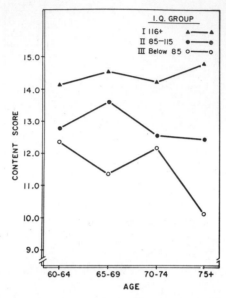

Fig. 4. Content score arranged according to age and IQ groups

DISCUSSION

There are clear difficulties in interpreting the results of this study. The data are cross-sectional, rather than longitudinal, the Ns for several of the groups are quite small, and, at this time, there is no convenient way to assess the relationship between the significant findings and chance probability associated with multiple *t*-test analysis. Certain consistencies do, however, emerge. The lack of decline in the performance of the high IQ groups seems especially notable. This is in contrast to the declines found in the middle IQ group between 65–69 and 75 plus (in three of the four variables) and in the low IQ group between 60–64 and the oldest or next oldest groups in three of four variables. In addition, while the high and low IQ levels differ quite consistently across age, this difference occurs between high and middle IQ levels only for the oldest two age categories.

The results clearly seem to suggest increasing differences between high and middle IQ levels with advancing age as well as an accelerating decline in the middle IQ range which follows a similar decline (appearing earlier) in the lowest IQ category. There are several possible interpretations of the results:

Insofar as any cross-sectional study includes a built-in bias involving differential environmental effects at different stages of life, the present results may represent data based upon a sampling artifact.

The findings suggest that there may be differential rates of decline in cognitive ability, with increasing age, as a function of intellectual level.

A third interpretation would reflect the role of differential levels of learning in relation to level of intelligence. This position is based upon the assumption that cognitive skills are learned according to the usual rules of learning. Thus, what we may be observing in results such as have been obtained in this study is the retention of skills which have been differentially reinforced. By this is meant that more intellectually gifted individuals are more inclined to utilize (and thus reinforce) higher-order cognitive skills. With this in mind it is especially interesting to observe that the content score, based upon vocabulary usage, is most consistent in demonstrating the differential decline in relation to intelligence.

SUMMARY

Two hundred and forty-three subjects who served as volunteers to the Duke Geriatrics Project were administered a full-scale intellectual evaluation (WAIS) and the Rorschach. These subjects were divided into three groups based upon full-scale IQ level. Each group was subdivided into four age categories. This (3 x 4) design made it possible to perform a cross-sectional examination of cognitive changes in Rorschach performance, as a function of age and intellectual level.

Total Σ of responses, Σ of human movement responses (M), vocabulary level score, and functional integration score were analyzed (*t*-tests were used throughout). While there is no significant decline with advancing age in the middle IQ groups, there appears to be an age-related decline of performance in the middle IQ group and an even more striking decline in the low IQ group. The findings may be interpreted to support the concept of differential rates of decline in cognitive functioning, with age, as a function of intellectual level, or differential experience.

REFERENCES

Bayley, Nancy, and Oden, Melita H. 1955. The maintenance of intellectual ability in gifted adults. J. Gerontol., 10: 91–107.

Gilbert, Jeanne G. 1941. Memory loss in senescence. J. Abnorm. & Social Psychol., 36: 3–54.

Grace, N. B. 1956. A development comparison of word usage with structural aspects of perception and social adjustment. (Unpublished doctoral dissertation, Duke University.)

Osborne, R. T., and Sanders, W. B. 1954. Variations in graduate record examination performance by age and sex. J. Gerontol., 9: 179–85.

Owens, W. A., Jr. 1953. Age and mental abilities: a longitudinal study. Genet. Psychol. Monogr., 48: 3–54.

———— 1957. Is age kinder to the initially more able? *In* Proceedings of the Fourth Congress of the International Association of Gerontology, 4: 151–57. Fidenza, Italy: Tipografia Tito Mattioli.

Raven, J. C. 1948. The comparative assessment of intellectual ability. Brit. J. Psychol., 39: 12–19.

Sorenson, H. 1933. Mental ability over a wide range of adult ages. J. Appl. Psychol., 17: 729–41.

———— 1938. Adult abilities. Minneapolis: University of Minnesota Press.

Vernon, P. E. 1947–48. The variation of intelligence with occupation, age, and locality. Brit. J. Psychol., Stat. Sec. 1–2, 1–2, 52–63.

Werner, H. 1948. Comparative psychology of mental development. (Rev. ed.) Chicago: Follett Publishing Co.

SYMPOSIUM

ON MEANINGFUL USE

OF FREE TIME

Organized by
ROBERT W. KLEEMEIER
Washington University, St. Louis, Missouri

The Nature and Values of Meaningful

Free-Time Activity

ROBERT J. HAVIGHURST

OF all the interesting problems which the twentieth century has presented to the human race, perhaps the most important, for the happiness of mankind, is that of meaningful use of free time.

Before this century, in all civilized societies, men lived under the rule of work as a necessity which lay upon them like a yoke of iron. One must work, and work hard, in order to live. Only in a few happy faraway South Sea Islands was it possible to live by picking one's food off the trees or out of the sea with little labor. There was also the Marxian dream of a productive, classless society in which each person would receive what he needed; but in which all must work to make this possible. Thus modern man came to devote himself to work and to productivity as a way and a goal of life.

Then, with twentieth-century technology came the "affluent society," which brought a much shorter work week for the common man, and made more free time during the working years.

At the same time there came a longer life, with more free time in the later years. The average man in the United States today has something like 8 years of retirement from work at the close of his life. In 1900 he had only 2.5 years of retirement. Thus a society whose goal has been productivity through work has succeeded so well that it has had to reduce the amount of time its members spend in work.

Men now have a great deal of leisure. But leisure, which was valuable in a workridden society, has lost some of its glamor. Men still feel a compulsion to work. We retain the image of man under a psychology of scarcity. Creative, productive work is seen as the most valuable use of time at any age. The child is expected to learn this attitude as early as possible. The adult is expected to maintain it as long as possible. Inactivity is valueless, except as rest in preparation for a new period of activity. Contemplation is viewed with suspicion as being not far removed from mere vegetation.

NEW CONCEPTS OF LEISURE

We need a new life pattern in which leisure has a well-understood and well-used function. In place of the old principle of *necessity to work,* which kept men constructively occupied all their lives, we need a new pattern of use of time—a new *necessity* which people feel and respect—to use time in a meaningful way in leisure as well as in work.

The new pattern, or the new image of man in a society of abundance, will recognize that the productive impulse of man may be expressed as well in play and in study as in work. We need to advance from the view of the ideal man as a one-dimensional *producer* to that of a three-dimensional person who combines work, study, and play into a coherent pattern throughout his life.

We also need a new view of the life cycle which does not divide life horizontally into discrete stages: childhood (play), adolescence (study), adulthood (work), and old age (retirement), each with its special concern. Rather, we need a view of the life cycle as a three-dimensional combination of play, study, and work in appropriate proportions at each age. The child will give more time to play than to study and work, but he should use some of his time for study and for work; the adult should continue to play and to study, although most of his time is given to work. The life cycle will not be divided into stages but into phases which are present at every age.

Is this possible? Is man plastic and adaptable enough to work out a new pattern of life and a new image of himself to fit the affluent society?

The great psychologist, Thorndike (1940) tried to answer this question toward the close of his own busy and fruitful life. He wrote:

The amount of time spent in physical entertainment by means of games and sports has probably increased also within the past generation. But the enormous increase has been in reading magazines, riding in automobiles, going to the pictures and listening to the radio. The time saved from wage-work and family work by reductions in hours and by gas, electricity, and household appliances has gone for increased entertainment, supplied mostly by these four means.

Some students of history and sociology will credit the present flood of entertainment to the great increase in the supply coupled with commercial methods of stimulating the demand. They will argue that men will, under fit environmental conditions, spend their free time in serving the state by fighting or otherwise or in serving the church by religious rites or in serving the family by labor and ceremonial. They will assert that men will follow true gods of truth or beauty or virtue or utility or the common good as readily as the false god of entertainment if they are shown the right path by example and have their feet set upon it by habit.

I hope that this is so. But I fear that the craving for entertainment is deeply rooted in man's nature and that very strong counter-attractions will be required to stem the present flood. I prophesy that historical and anthropological research will increasingly reveal that the great majority of people have spent their free time for entertainment up to or beyond thirty hours a week, if supply was available. The desire for approval may counteract it widely, as in waves of Puritanism or patriotism. Also, the desire to see others happy, which apparently has been held down by brutal and bigoted customs in most civilizations, may become a more and more potent alternative, at least in superior souls. The human nervous system is very adaptable and can learn to operate with satisfaction in a humdrum world. But its lines of least resistance go toward cheerful sociability, free play, sensory stimulation and emotional excitement. [p. 127]

One answer to Thorndike's question is given by a study of the values obtained by adults in their free-time activities, made by my colleagues and myself in the Kansas City Study of Adult Life. We studied the reports given by people aged 40 to 70 concerning their two favorite leisure activities. They described and discussed these activities at length to our interviewers and we were able to make a reliable rating on the *values* and *characteristics* of these favorite leisure activities, using the following characteristics for the ratings: autonomy versus other-directed; creativity and talent development; instrumental versus expressive; leisure complementary to work versus leisure contrasting with work; gregarious versus solitary; service versus pleasure; vitality and expansion of interests versus apathy and constriction of interests.

With a form of factor analysis we discovered groups of people with characteristic patterns of values they secured from their favorite leisure activities. There were three groups of people regarded by us as successful users of leisure time.

The challenging new experience group

These are the most successful users of leisure. They were rated high by our judges on the following characteristics of their favorite leisure activities: creativity, vitality, expansion of interest, talent, instrumental use of leisure, autonomy, enjoyment, and service. They were rated high on an independent scale of personal adjustment. They were generally middle-class people.

The instrumental service and expressive pleasure groups

In addition to the challenging new experience group there are two other groups who may be called successful users of leisure, though they have contrasting leisure styles. One is the instrumental service group, and the other is the expressive pleasure group. Both groups contain people who are autonomous and creative in their uses of leisure. The difference between them lies in the goals they seek.

The instrumental service people seek to *accomplish* something by means of their leisure activity. Their favorite activities are home decorating, home repairing, sewing, gardening, music, club work, church work, and League of Women Voters. They do not seek relaxation in these activities.

The expressive pleasure people are those for whom *leisure is fun.* They have no motive ulterior to the activity. Their favorite leisure activities are flying, golf, bowling, target practice, fishing, hunting, dog breeding, oil painting, ceramics, photography, traveling, reading, friendships, sewing, and gardening. They seek relaxation in these activities, or escape from the tensions of work.

It is to be noted that sewing and gardening appear in both lists, indicating that some people do these things for sheer pleasure, while others do them with an instrumental purpose.

Unsuccessful users of leisure

There were two groups whose uses of leisure were clearly unsuccessful. One consists of people who are apathetic about their leisure, have narrow interests, and lack autonomy and creativity in the things they do. The other, the *active escape* group, also fails to find the meaning they seek in their leisure. Mostly men, they are likely to be maladjusted socially or occupationally and they attempt to get through leisure what they cannot get in other roles. They use their leisure in a generally fruitless attempt to make up for deficiencies and to give their life some meaning. The men in this group, often alienated from work, or from spouse, or from the "community," attempt to adjust to this alienation by engaging in leisure activities where they invest a lot of energy and through which they can enjoy themselves and see themselves as acceptable. One of the subjects is a factory manager. He finds no satisfaction in this position but rather pictures himself as an intellectual and therefore spends a great deal of time reading. A second subject, an amateur pilot, directs his leisure away from a home where some emotional difficulties exist. Another man was trained as an engineer and has shifted over the years from one job to another finally going into a business with his wife which he does not enjoy. Like the factory manager he pictures himself as a scholar, and spends his leisure time reading oriental history.

The women in this group have difficulty in relating to their husbands and are emotionally insecure; they have degrees of feelings of un-wantedness and of not being loved. As an outlet they concentrate their energies into a single activity where they can achieve proficiency, such as sewing, embroidery, or petit-point; or in social activities where they can spend time with "the women" and gain status in the women's world.

RETIREMENT AND THE USE OF TIME

For the twentieth century man who has found the way to combine work, study, and play, retirement is simply a reduction of the work dimension in his life, and a corresponding and compensatory increase in the play and study dimensions. However, most people have not yet learned this art, and they will have difficulty in finding interesting and rewarding ways of using their time after they have dropped or substantially reduced the work role. Roughly a quarter of the Kansas City Study Group appear to have done a reasonably good job in this connection.

Retirement forces a revision of the time budget. There is much more time available, and not so much pressure to use it for socially prescribed purposes. Older people react in various ways to this situation. Some develop substitute uses of time to take the place of time earlier spent in work, and continue without much reduction of action. Others reduce activity and also withdraw emotionally from engagement in the world, spending more time in meditation and also more time in sheer inaction.

It is not clear to what extent these changes in the use of time during later maturity are brought on by the social environment or by physical aging of the muscles and the nervous system. It has been suggested, also, that an intrinsic psychic process of disengagement is causing the person to pay less attention to social expectations about the meaningful use of time and to do more nearly "as he pleases."

Thus, as a general summary statement, it appears that the use of time, whether meaningful or meaningless, remains on a plateau with respect to age from 40 to 65 or 75. It is a part of one's personality. Then comes a personality change which is reflected in a change of use of time. The personality change which comes in the 60s or early 70s depends upon the previous life of a person, as well as upon the physical and social conditions in which he finds himself at this point in his life. His use of time will in any case constitute the meaning of this last phase of his life, worthy or unworthy, pleasant or unpleasant. If he is fortunate, it will also lead to his fulfillment.

REFERENCE

Thorndike, E. L. 1940. Human nature and the social order. New York: Macmillan Co.

Meaningful Activity in a Family Context

WAYNE E. THOMPSON AND GORDON F. STREIB

IT is proposed to speak less in this paper of meaningful activity and somewhat more of the family context. In so doing there is a double risk: first, the risk of being accused of elaborating the obvious for little of what is said will come as any great surprise to most; second, the risk of appearing to regard problems of meaningful activity as unimportant, for in a broader context problems often become statistical rarities, deviations from the normal pattern, exceptions to the rule.

The venture seems worth these risks, however, for it is important to keep our subject matter in proper perspective. Committed as we are to the study of an important social problem, we tend too often to approach our subject from a clinical perspective. But life on the whole is not accurately portrayed by dramatic problem cases, not even for old people, and to assume that it is leads to wrong questions, wrong answers, wrong ameliorative efforts, and general misunderstanding.

It is so in the case of the meaningful use of time. The problem often is stated in a way which suggests an individual standing apart from a normal life setting who must then, as an individual, find or create interests, activities, and relationships for himself. In point of fact, this image of the isolated and solitary individual at once overstates the problem and overstates the individual's freedom of choice in effecting a solution. The overwhelming majority of people, young and old, live their lives in and through social relationships which pattern their use of time and determine, facilitate, or limit those courses of action which may be regarded as meaningful.

Family relationships are among the most important of these social relationships. They are important, first of all, because of their widespread incidence in the population. Effects of industrialization and urbanization to the contrary notwithstanding, family ties in America remain strong; in every class, almost no one is without some kind of contact with other members of his family.

Family relationships are important also because for each person they tend to be one of the most frequent forms of interaction. Among other things, at every age the household unit typically is composed of more than one member of a single family, a fact which ensures a high frequency of interaction.

A third reason for the importance of family relationships to the researcher is that they are important to the person himself. When we want to emphasize the closeness of friendship ties we say "He's like a brother," "She's like a mother," and so forth. To be sure, not all people like their relatives, and we also speak of "being saddled" with renegade relations. But even this implies a firm bond, and one must usually acknowledge relatives as among the most significant of significant others.

RELEVANCE OF FAMILY RELATIONSHIPS

Family relationships are relevant to the meaningful use of leisure time in many ways. In the first place, in its socializing function the family transmits to its constituent individuals the definitions, values, and patterns of the culture. Thus, interests and patterns of activity may be inculcated in childhood which will form the basis of preference for activity in the later years. Socialization is not restricted to the young, however, or is it solely a matter of transmission of culture from parent to child. In fact, as far as socialization within the family is concerned, it may be that for older people the direction is just as often the reverse. For example, the grandparent's role is increasingly defined by the young parents, thereby delimiting one important meaningful activity for older people. Moreover, it is often the child who defines the age role and identity of the parent, implicitly by the sheer fact of growing up or more explicitly by word or deed, thereby admonishing the parent to "act his age." Thus, among many other factors, family relationships set patterns which are expressed as individual habits. These, as important aspects of personality, must be taken into account in any consideration of choice of leisure-time activities.

Family relationships are also relevant to the meaningful use of time through the established patterning that exists within the relationships, either as an expression of general cultural patterns or as an expression of the unique patterns of the family's own traditions. In America, thousands still go "to grandmother's house" on the Thanksgiving holiday, for example; and grandmother very often wears herself out in the course of preparing the customary holiday spread. Yet the days and weeks of preparation and anticipation, the big event itself, and the weeks afterward are structured activities filled with meaning for the grandmother and, in fact, for all the relatives involved. Similarly, consider the possible range and meaning of activities implicit in the following statements, taken from interviews with 70-year-old retirees: "My daughter and I do our marketing together," "My son-in-law is all thumbs when it comes to fixing things around the house, so I help him out whenever I can," "My grandchildren like to raid the cookie jar, and it really keeps me hopping to keep ahead of them with my baking."

Most of the patterns of family relationships are realized in a group setting, of course; and the fact that the family is a social group is another point of relevance to meaningful activity in the mature years. Minimal obligations of group membership immediately place limits on free choice of activities; and as the properties of the group vary, so do the activities which are chosen. Often, the pursuit of activities considered meaningful is joint effort based on joint decision. In other instances, activities to be pursued are a basis of contention and a source of friction within the family group. In still other instances, the family setting may provide the older person with opportunities for participation and self-expression sometimes denied him in other contexts. Consider, for example, the 70-year-old who bowls with his grandchildren "because they expect me to."

Beyond all this, the significance of the family to meaningful activities may rest with the fact that family relationships may in themselves constitute meaningful activity for the older person. That is to say, the activity per se may be or may become irrelevant and the meaning may derive primarily from the family contact. As one older person puts it:

Yes, since I retired I have a lot of free time. What do I do with myself? Well, you know . . . just putter around, watch TV and sometimes go for a walk. And I like to spend as much time with the kids and grandsons as I can. That's what means the most to me.

What, then, are the normal family settings within which meaningful activity does—as it inevitably must—take place? In a pluralistic society such as ours there are, of course, widespread variations. There are ethnic differences; there are generational differences; there are regional differences; and there are important social-class and socio-economic-status differences.

Nevertheless, in broad structural terms, families move through a series of stages—what has been called the life cycle of the family—and these stages provide the immediate context for action as well as the basis for patterns appropriate to successive periods. Examining the latter half of the family cycle thus helps to delineate the facilitating and limiting factors for meaningful activity in the mature years.

THE LIFE CYCLE OF THE FAMILY

As a starting point, we note that within the age category 45 to 54 almost 90 percent of both males and females live in households which include one or more relatives. The overwhelming majority of these people are married and living with their spouse; and most still have dependent children living at home. At this stage of the family cycle, many of the patterns of activities within the family context represent an extension of whatever patterns were prevalent earlier. At this point, however, the relationship between parents and children is undergoing a significant transition as the child reaches the end of his period of dependency; and the patterns of activities associated with this relationship are undergoing transition as well. A wide variety of leisure-time pursuits, both formal and informal, which were associated with the parent-dependent-child relationship, lose their meaning at this point, and for the parents the stage is set for working out a *modus vivendi* for two.

In an important sense, the patterns of family relationships which are established in this period are crucial for all subsequent stages of the family cycle. Here parents and children establish the beginnings of their relationships as adults; and, closely related to this, here the two-generation family group is dismembered and the parent-child relationships are reformulated as an aspect of what has been called a network of social relationships. Success in establishing satisfactory relationships in this sense is clearly of first importance in all the later years.

In this transitional period, leisure-time activities which are not aspects of family duties become increasingly significant, for release from the obligations of parental responsibility provides an impressive amount of free time. This is especially true in the case of the wife, for whom "retirement" from the role of mother provides the opportunity for increased leisure-time activities. Clearly, "retirement" from the role of father also requires considerable readjustment. In the case of the husband, however, excessive free time is not so much an issue, and for this reason it may be that the wife plays the dominant role in choosing the patterns of meaningful activity to be pursued through the later years.

The next stage of the family cycle we call the family of preretire-ment. In this period, which includes people 55 to 64 years old, the differences in family composition between older males and females are beginning to be greater. The most striking of these, of course, is the greater incidence of widows: in this age range there are more than four times as many widows as widowers. Over-all, however, just as in the previous stage, the vast majority of both males and females are still living with their spouses in their own households.

But these families differ in an important way from the modal family of late maturity. Namely, by this time the percentage of families with dependent children has dropped sharply. In other words, at this stage of the family cycle, the fledglings typically have left the nest. Relationships with children persist, however, although in an altered form, for the emphasis has generally changed from responsibility to assistance.

The parent-child relationship at this point includes all the vicarious joys and woes involved in watching the children get established on their own. Further, more often than not, it involves the pleasures of grandparenthood. As we have suggested, however, an important difference between the parental role of this period and of earlier periods is the degree to which parental responsibility is involved. Despite ties of affection, despite vicarious attachment, despite contact and usefulness in helping the children get settled, both parents and children by this time come to subscribe to the norm of independence for children. Although parents who in fact maintain relationships with their children express little need to substitute new activities for extended family activities, they claim to be pleased to have more freedom to do what they desire. And, objectively, they are more free to pursue activities of their own choice.

At this stage, retirement from the occupational role also begins to come into focus. In fact, it may be that freedom from family responsibilities serves logically and practically as the point at which systematic preparation for retirement should begin. Putting it another way, in this period the family relationships of the couple are the prototype of the pattern of relationships in retirement; and the patterns of meaningful activity evolved here can be expected to serve in the later years, at least as long as both husband and wife survive in reasonably good health.

At the stage of the family cycle ranging from age 65 to 74, what we call the family of early retirement, there is a pronounced variation in the family living arrangements of men as compared with women, a further development of the trends we have mentioned previously. As before, the single most frequent living arrangement for both sexes is living with the spouse in their own household. However, this category constitutes less than half among the women. Moreover, nearly half of the women are widowed as compared with fewer than one-fifth of the men. In considering the family structure of people in early retirement, therefore, it might be useful to consider separately the family context of men and women.

About 65 percent of the men in early retirement are living with their spouse in their own household, more often than not with no other relatives present. Inasmuch as this is the period in which retirement becomes frequent, one might contend that the problems of meaningful activity here devolve upon the relationship between the husband and wife in their own home. The circumstances of retirement may markedly alter the range of possible activities for such older couples; but, to the extent that situational resources allow, the activities of the couples of this age probably represent an expression of interests which were developed earlier.

For some people, of course, retirement to hearth and home is not an unmixed blessing. Instead of being able to enjoy free time with the spouse, the older person may find the retirement years to be a long drawn-out hassle. On the face of it, this would not seem to be a particularly attractive way of life, although it might be well for those of us who would study meaningful activity not to prejudge what can and cannot be meaningful.

Among women between 65 and 74, exceptional family living arrangements become the rule. Although the most frequent single living arrangement is living with spouse in their own home, the most frequent marital status is widowhood. For those women in this age bracket who are widowed, the most frequent living arrangement is that of the primary individual, which usually means living alone. As in the case of the widower, this may involve a lonely existence. But for the widow, unlike the widower, the housewifely tasks usually do not represent a marked change of pattern and problem of adjustment. In fact, for a great many widows living alone the day-to-day tasks involved in keeping their house constitute a very important variety of meaningful activity; ability to maintain certain standards of good housekeeping often represents a challenge and a test of the degree to which the older woman is avoiding "getting old."

The widow who lives alone may have frequent contacts with her children and grandchildren, of course, and in many instances may be able to live a full meaningful life within a pattern that includes very little more than her house and these contacts. Among other things, the role of grandmother in our culture probably includes a wider range of meaningful activities than the role of grandfather and on this account may be a more important factor in the adjustment of the elderly widow. Moreover, insofar as women set the pattern of relationships with children, these patterns may differ very little from those which would obtain were the spouse still alive.

The period of late retirement, age 75 and above, marks the culmination of trends in changing family patterns which can be noticed earlier. Notwithstanding stereotypes of the aged to the contrary, there probably is less social structural and cultural standardization of individual and family behavior patterns in this last stage of the family cycle than in any other period. The keynote is diversity: diverse patterns of contact with children and grandchildren, diverse conditions of health and ability to care for one's self, and even diverse orientation toward life itself.

For many, of course, the patterns of meaningful activity are simply those which have been followed for the previous decade or two. But for others this late retirement period marks a decline in other meaningful activity, and contact with children and grandchildren becomes crucial. These relationships with the younger generations may take many forms. For some, the contact represents the harvest of a lifetime of good family relationships. Here the children and grandchildren interact with their aging relative largely because they want to, and for the elderly person this is a pleasant social relationship happily awaited and remembered. In such a relationship, benefits are reciprocal: the older person gives to the relationship as well as receives from it. In other instances, the benefits accrue largely to the old person and not to the "youngster." That is to say, the old person's dependence upon the child for interpersonal relationships may follow a pattern in which emotional sustenance is provided almost exclusively by the visits of the children or grandchildren.

All of this tends to assume, however, that the old person does enjoy and want contact with his children. In some instances this simply is not the case. Following the findings of the Kansas City studies, one might hypothesize that the process of disengagement from the norms of society would affect family relationships as well as other institutional commitments. That is to say, with increasing age the individual tends to return to a more or less egocentric outlook. At this advanced age the old person tends to stress individual satisfaction as the most important value rather than more normatively structured activities such as family relationships. At this age, interest in the feelings of others declines to a considerable degree and the old person becomes increasingly direct—even blunt and impolite—in his interpersonal relationships.

To the extent that disengagement occurs in this extreme sense, it might be suggested that, if such old people are physically and economically capable, they should be left alone and free to pursue whatever they choose to regard as meaningful activity in their idiosyncratic way. As it happens, however, disengagement as a correlate of aging is found much more frequently in the very advanced age levels—a time at which physical and mental decline also is more probable. Thus such egocentric old people very often may be found living with their children. This creates a dilemma not only for the children torn between generational loyalties but also for the old person himself.

For the egocentric old person, complete dependence of this sort may provide the opportunity to behave as a martinet; and such a person may derive considerable "meaning" from pushing the role to its hilt. For many old people, however, dependence in this sense is a personal disaster which precludes meaningfulness in old age. In fact, for those of clear mind this most probably constitutes the modal reaction to complete dependency. Given no other context than dependency for meaningful activity, life itself may lose meaning; in instances in which there are no alternatives, the old person quite literally would rather die.

SIGNIFICANT ACTIVITIES IN A FAMILY CONTEXT

In describing the varying family contexts at various stages of the family cycle, we have said very little of specific activities. Yet, ultimately, it is the specific activity which counts; and, one might ask, what are the activities which may be regarded as meaningful in the later years? In particular, what are the activities which are especially significant in a family context?

If we focus on the "cultivated act," creative endeavor, the unusual and the unique, the answer would seem to be that any single such activity might be selected as meaningful and might find a significant place in a family context. Putting it another way, any such activities may fill the bill as meaningful activities in a family context; but they are not predictable from a general analysis of the family for they are neither necessary to the family nor it to them.

If, however, we recognize that painting a picture may be no more meaningful than painting a wall, that collecting Picassos may be no more meaningful than collecting snapshots of grandchildren, that growing an orchid may be no more meaningful than growing some corn, then we bring into focus the true significance of the family. For humdrum and homely decisions and acts, the day-to-day tasks of living one's life garner meaning and purpose from the family context in which they are found.

The Use and Meaning of Time in Special Settings

ROBERT W. KLEEMEIER

IN this paper it is intended to discuss the influence of certain kinds of environments upon human activities and use of time. For want of a more precise term these environments have been referred to as "special settings for the aged." While this is a somewhat unsatisfactory term, it does have a degree of generality which allows us to subsume under it such diverse living arrangements as specialized housing for the aged; retirement communities; residential homes; settings for the ill-aged, such as chronic hospitals, nursing homes, even mental hospitals; and finally part-time or limited settings, which may include day hospitals, recreational centers, clubs for the aged and other diverse settings in which the person may spend a part of his day or week.

Specifically, the question in which we are interested is, "How do these various kinds of special settings influence the behavior, activities, and use of time of the older persons who live therein?"

It is obvious that this is not a simple question. In the first place the types of settings listed above range from those which are almost indistinguishable from the living accommodations of the ordinary community to those specialized settings designed to care for the sick and disabled or the senile and mentally frail.

Since this great divergence exists both in type of living arrangement or setting and in the type of older person served, special problems of analysis are involved if we are to propose ways of answering the question we have set for ourselves.

One obvious solution, of course, is to accept the differences implied by the names given to the various kinds of specialized settings and to study the activity patterns found in each. One soon encounters difficulty with this approach. Names and classifications are often unrelated to the function served by the particular setting. For example, a home for the aged upon investigation may actually be more like a chronic hospital than a residential home. A senile ward in a mental hospital, on the other hand, may be caring for many individuals who could adapt well, with some support, to semi-independent living in the community or in a residential home.

Such problems of nomenclature and classification force one to look elsewhere for a solution to the problem. One possible approach which suggests itself is to determine, if possible, the descriptive dimensions which would allow us to characterize the setting, not by misleading names, but by means of scales or indexes.

Should this prove possible, then the activities and time usage of residents in the various settings could be related to the dimensional aspects of the setting with the expectation that the findings would have greater generality.

Similarly, if the characteristics of the individual which are basic to his activities and behavior could also be so structured, then it might be possible to make predictions about the influences of certain general aspects of the environment on the behavior of specific individuals.

Needless to say, this is an ambitious program. It requires first an adequate conceptualization; second, tentative verification from existing factual information; and, finally, verification by field observation and, where possible, by experimentation. As a first step in this three-field approach, the following conceptualization may prove useful to future observation of fact.

First, three dimensions are proposed, by means of which various special settings can be characterized, differentiated one from the other, and ordered along measurable continua. These are the *segregate-nonsegregate* continuum, the *institutional-noninstitutional or control* continuum, and the *congregate-noncongregate* continuum.

The first of these dimensions, i.e., the segregate continuum, at one end refers to the condition under which older persons may live exclusively among their age peers, having little contact with other age groups. At the other end are placed those living arrangements which daily bring older persons together with people of all ages. The segregate continuum, therefore, refers to the degree to which the living arrangement permits the resident to associate with other age groups.

The institutional or control dimension, on the other hand, applies to the varying degrees to which the individual must adjust his life to imposed rules, discipline, and the various means of social control utilized by administrators, medical and other staff personnel, and by residents and patients themselves in order to bring about desired behavior patterns. While this dimension is more commonly thought of as applying to large group settings, it is, nevertheless, largely independent of the size and constitution of the group.

Finally, the congregate-noncongregate dimension refers to the group aspects of the setting; not only to the size of the group, but also to the closeness of individuals to each other and to the degree of privacy it is possible to obtain in the setting.

If we would know more about the influence of behavior setting upon activity, it is suggested that we approach the problem by determining the effects of these three environmental dimensions on behavior of the individual residing in the setting.

The activities in which a person engages, however, are not solely the products of environmental influences. Therefore, in addition to these, two personal factors or characteristics could be employed to assist in this analysis. These are: (1) the rate of energy expenditure of the individual, and (2) his behavior repertory.

Rate of energy expenditure is significant because it determines the total, daily amounts of activity exhibited by the person. While it will be agreed that sheer amount of behavior is at best only a remote indicator of the meaning or significance of activity, nevertheless, it does provide the basis for a quantitative index.

Although some studies of the behavior and activities of older persons have been carried out, we have nothing in this area to compare in completeness to the observations of Barker and Wright (1954) on the daily activities of children. These investigators, it will be recalled, have shown that it is possible to observe and quantify the amazing amounts of activity exhibited by children in their natural ecological settings. Their success with children suggests that comparable observations could be made on aged adults with appropriate modifications of methodology.

While crude amounts of activity, such as would be used in determining activity or energy levels, are important, personal adjustment and social effectiveness depend on the qualitative significance of the activity itself. This, in turn, depends upon the behavior repertory of the individual and upon his selection from among these available behavioral alternatives those best suited to deal with the situation. Simply stated, the behavior repertory is the number of things an individual can do—his skills, his habits, his vocabulary, his physical strength, and agility. While the behavior repertory changes throughout life, in the early years it is marked by expansion and during the later years of life it is undoubtedly diminished in its richness and variety.

What has been said here is simply that the activities of the individual depend upon his environment or source of stimulation; his rate of energy expenditure which would involve his motivation, his physiologic condition, and other related factors; and finally his behavior repertory as described above. The problem for research then is to relate, within the framework described in this discussion, the setting characteristics to the characteristics of the individual. Unfortunately, there is not time to go into these possible relationships in any detail here, but perhaps one illustration will suffice to indicate the direction suggested.

For this purpose let us consider the condition of the aged resident in a highly congregate, segregate, and institutional setting who exhibits a low level of energy expenditure but who has a relatively undeteriorated behavior repertory. This is the person who satisfies fairly well the generally accepted stereotype commonly aroused by the designation "old age." He is the capable person who likes to take things at a slower pace, who is conserving his energy, who has given up trying.

The following hypotheses are offered concerning this person's reaction to a highly congregate, segregate, and institutional setting. (1) The likely consequence of low energy expenditure is the creation of an isolated person, apparently content to sit in his room or in some favorite spot, following routines imposed upon him. (2) Since the expression of the behavior repertory is prevented by lessened energy reserves, reduction in the energy requirements for activity will result in increased activity. (3) Age segregation is likely to be accepted along with congregate aspects of the setting, because energy requirements of such situations are likely to be small. (4) Institutional or control aspects of the situation also tend to be accepted provided the requirements are viewed by the person as appropriate and in keeping with his self-concept.

Programs in the more traditional old age settings are designed with the low energy levels of residents in mind. Since this characteristic is shared by the majority, almost any sort of program appears acceptable provided the resident's bodily needs are properly cared for. Little complaint about lack of activity programs is heard even though potential interest and activity levels could be raised considerably. Low morale and actual dissatisfaction may be abundantly present, but unwillingness of residents to exert the effort necessary to express it, plus their failure to recognize the source of the problem, create the impression of acceptance. Alteration of this situation is dependent upon the skill with which the behavior repertory is tapped within the energy limits of the residents.

In this discussion of the possible behavioral influences of personal characteristics we have tended to hold the setting characteristics constant because at this stage it would not be profitable to attempt to explore the full range of interaction possibilities. Let us consider for a moment, however, the possible consequences of the setting characteristics in terms of resident activity.

Consider first activity and the congregate dimension. At the high end of this dimension many people live together closely with little privacy; contact with others is enforced by the very physical demands of the situation. This high level of social interaction fosters high levels of activity. In this situation the activity demands upon the individual may be so great that he is forced to take counter measures to safeguard his privacy and to conserve his energy; but, nevertheless, multiple sources of stimulation to activity are in the situation. At the opposite end of this continuum is isolation, the person by himself. In this situation the reduction in incoming stimulation is great, activity levels decrease, and serious personality disruptions can occur.

Following this reasoning we may state the relationship between activity and the congregate dimension in the following form: environmentally induced activity levels are positively correlated with the congregate dimension of the setting. It would follow from this postulate that the congregate aspect of living in residential homes for the aged and retirement communities fosters higher activity levels in older persons.

Consider now the segregate dimension and activity. This dimension refers to the degree of age segregation in the setting; at the high end would be groups composed of individuals drawn from a very narrow age range, while at the low end would be heterogeneous groups composed of persons of all ages. Using a concept developed by Barker and Wright, we may state the following hypothesis concerning the activity-influencing effects of segregation: the degree of *penetration into organized patterns of behavior or into group activities by members of an age group is positively associated with the degree of age segregation in the group.*

Penetration here refers to the role or to the degree of involvement or responsibility that a person assumes in the setting. At the low end is the person who is merely an onlooker, and at the high end is the person who is leader of the group or activity. Evidence from the Barker and Wright (1954) studies shows that those in the adult age group from 18 to 64 tend to monopolize leadership roles, or to penetrate more deeply into social settings than do other age groups.

What is being said here with reference to the hypothesis stated above is that in the absence of other age groups the more central functionary and leadership roles must be assumed by members of the segregated age group involved. Thus, *age segregation may be a condition conducive to higher activity levels than age heterogeneity.*

Concerning activity and the institutional or control dimension we are again drawn to this point. In a highly institutional setting, in which the proportion of staff members drawn from "adult ages" is likely to be high, the penetration of the aged residents into the institutional community activities will not be as great as in less institutional, more segregated residential settings for the aged. A community composed of both staff and residents cannot be considered as exclusively a community of the latter, even though it exists solely to serve the needs of this group. Thus we are suggesting that in highly institutionalized settings the presence of the staff tends to dilute or lessen the degree of age segregation which might otherwise be present. This lack of segregation can be reflected in lessened penetration of the aged into the behavior settings of the institution.

These hypotheses are frankly tentative and suggestive. All require greater refinement and a supporting body of factual evidence. Thus this is not a report of a research program, but a suggested basis upon which a need research program could be built. Basically such research would require the construction and testing of scales following the three dimensions of the special settings described in this paper. It would require the testing of the scales on a large variety of environmental settings for the aged. In addition it would be necessary to develop and sharpen means to observe the activities of residents in these settings— some method of establishing their energy levels, or activity levels. And finally these would be viewed in conjunction with various measures of present and past abilities and performance levels. This, it will be recognized, is an ambitious research program. The effort should, however, prove most rewarding in terms of both scientific return and practical application.

REFERENCE

Barker, R. G., and Wright, H. F. 1954. Midwest and its children. Evanston, Ill.: Row Peterson.

Life Cycle, Work Situation, and Participation in Formal Associations

HAROLD L. WILENSKY

MY assignment is to deal with the sources and effects of variations in secondary attachments among the aged. By "secondary attachments" I mean the entire range of formal organizational ties—membership and participation in workplace, church, and union, as well as voluntary associations such as fraternal order, political party, hobby club, ethnic club, and the like. In contrast are "primary ties"—those to family, relatives, and close friends. "Aged" will refer to persons in the later stages of the life cycle—solitary survivors and couples whose children are adult as well as those old in years. I will concentrate on one fact about participation, namely, that it shows a typical curve over the life cycle, something like that shown on the chart. I will then mention some limitations of the data from which I infer that curve. Finally, I will offer some ideas about the meaning of the participation cycle and deviations from it in the lives of certain groups.

How does participation change over the life cycle of the individual? With aging, is there a decline in memberships and activity? There are about thirteen American studies which are good enough in sampling procedures and data collection and detailed enough in age breakdowns to serve our purposes.

Where studies lump all formal organizations together, church, church-related, and labor union as well as other more voluntary associations, proportions reporting two or more memberships appear to be lowest among young people under 30. The membership peak is among those 30 to 44. There is a slight decline in subsequent years which becomes definite after 60 or so. Meeting attendance shows a similar curve.

Based on Chapter 8 of *Aging and Leisure: Research Perspectives on the Meaningful Use of Time,* edited by Robert W. Kleemeier, Oxford University Press, New York, 1961. For elaboration of the theoretical perspective and related data, see H. L. Wilensky, *Work and Leisure,* The Free Press, Glencoe, Illinois, to be published.

I think this finding of a cycle of participation reflects the truth, but we must be cautious, for several major difficulties beset all attempts to deal with participation and age—controls for type of organization, type of community, and social-economic level are lacking; participation is probably overestimated in cross-sectional surveys, especially for older people; and we have little knowledge of the quality of participation, its meaning to the member or attender. A word about these limitations.

Some leads in these data suggest that type of organization counts. For instance, it seems likely that church organizations and fraternal organizations have more holding power than other types—the former because of the imminence of death and other crises, the latter because of insurance benefits contingent upon continued membership. It appears that participation in churches does not drop off much until after 70 or 75. Yet few studies give attention to these organizational variations.

There are also hints that type of community affects the relationship between age and participation. I have only to mention mass-produced middle-class suburbs like Park Forest, Illinois, or the Levittowns where frantic participation and the "outgoing life" are the norm; the retirement communities of Florida and California; the slummy rooming houses in the heart of Chicago or Detroit; factory-dotted proletarian suburbs like those around Flint, Michigan, where life is not so "outgoing"; simply to list these is to realize that sheer opportunity for participation (whatever one's age or inclination) varies greatly according to the community environment in which one finds oneself. Professor Havighurst's (1960) studies indicate some European countries (notably Holland) in which the portion of the population over 65 participating in old people's clubs is as much as one in ten—a rate five times that in America.

Clearly we need more systematic comparisons of aging and participation in various nations and in various types of communities.

Finally, and most important, there is near-unanimity that the number of secondary attachments is closely related to education, social-economic status, and residence (urban and rural nonfarm versus rural farm). Those with high-school education or more, in higher economic brackets and higher occupational strata, and living in urban areas participate most. Yet only one of the thirteen studies considered relates participation to age and at the same time controls for even one of these crucial variables so that we may see which older and younger persons are participating.

In short, the unique effect of aging cannot be sifted out until we give closer attention to type of organization, type of community, and social-economic level, all of which condition the relationship of age to secondary attachments.

A second caution is this: participation is probably overestimated in cross-sectional surveys, especially for older people. Even in the most carefully designed survey there tends to be an undersampling of social isolates. For practical reasons, large rooming houses are often eliminated. For reasons of physical and mental incapacity and other resistances, nonresponse rates among older respondents are high. In recent Detroit surveys, only 78 percent of the designated older respondents (60 or more years of age) could be interviewed, compared to 91 percent of those 21 to 34. Contacting and interviewing widows, widowers, and single adults has proved to be especially difficult. The sociology of isolation may thus remain underdeveloped, a casualty of the cost not only to society but to the researcher of reaching the isolate.

This underrepresentation of the aged means that the actual dropoff in participation among the aged may be more marked than available data show.

A final caution: there is little knowledge of the quality of social participation—its meaning to the member or attender. Think of the quiet pleasure of a retired worker playing checkers at a union drop-in center, then look at the anxious attachment of a California pensioner to the noisy radio voice of George McLain, whose mass movement is so well described by Pinner, Jacobs, and Selznick (1959) in *Old Age and Political Behavior*. These suggest a vast range in the quality of secondary attachments. As we list the number of memberships and look for changes with aging, we must recognize the varied meanings a "membership" may have.

Despite these warnings, some things can be said with reasonable confidence. Only a small portion of the total adult population—one in five, at most two in five—have secondary ties beyond church and union. This means that most nonparticipants among the aged are continuing well-established patterns; they are lifetime nonparticipants. And, among the minority who do get into the organizational act, there are participation "careers," typical sequences of membership and activity. The most general pattern is the one pictured in Fig. 1, a slump among young married couples, a peak among married 30 to 45-year-olds, and low rates among those over 65.

Accepting these statements as fact, I now come to the core of my argument—some speculation about the causes and effects of variations in secondary attachments. The first point I will make is that

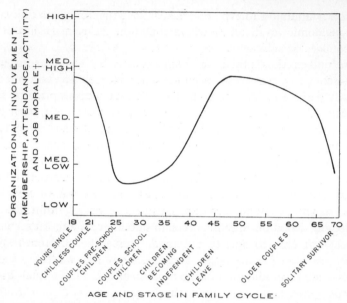

Fig. 1. Hypothetical picture of the participation and morale curve for the general population of an urban-industrial society

Inferred from existing data for the United States on variations by family life cycle and/or age in economic rewards and aspirations, consumer behavior and aspirations, and participation in formal organizations. Sources cited in Harold L. Wilensky, "Life Cycle, Work Situation, and Participation in Formal Associations," in *Aging and Leisure,* edited by R. W. Kleemeier, Oxford University Press, New York, 1961, Chap. 8. Think of "high" as a man who loves his work, belongs to a union or professional association, a church, and three or four other organizations, is active in them and enjoys them. Think of "low" as a man who is unemployed, involuntarily retired, or work-alienated, and who belongs to nothing.

cycles of participation are linked to interdependent cycles of family life, consumption, and work. Second, where we find major deviations from the general pattern, they are due largely to specific variations in work situation and mobility experience and aspirations. Finally, I will discuss the implications of an impoverished secondary group life for democracy.

Let us look at this idea of interlocking cycles. Students of aging, of family life, and of consumption and leisure have each in their own areas been alive to the flow of time. But I know of no systematic studies which focus either on "participation careers" (typical sequences of membership and attendance over the life cycle), or on interlocking cycles of family life, work, consumption, and participation. Yet it is obvious that labor-market experience leaves its mark on the participation pattern: for reasons of both motive and opportunity (including job-linked health factors), the man on the assembly line, if he lives on, will sever his work ties earlier and more completely than the professor or physician. Other secondary attachments, too, will be affected by both work experience and the family cycle: when children arrive, the church and the PTA will seem appropriate; when the nest is empty, the PTA no longer attracts; when retirement approaches and no strong commitments to work have been developed, occupational associations (unions and other work-based contacts) quickly fade into the background.

A better grasp of variations in secondary attachments can come from analysis of these interlocking cycles. For example, there are literally scores of studies of job satisfaction whose contradictory results could well be reexamined from this point of view, for they yield a picture of lifetime variation very similar to that derived from studies of aging and social participation—a low period in the twenties, a climb to a peak in the middle years, a slight dropoff and then a final sag in the sixties.

I would suggest this interpretation: job satisfaction is a function of disparity between rewards (what we get in income and job status) and aspirations (what we want in goods and services and job status); both payoff and demand are likely to show a chronology linked to family life cycle and work history. Leaving aside the college crowd and the unusually ambitious, the young man fresh from high school, for a few years at least, finds himself with a happy combination of modest aspirations, limited responsibilities, and an income that seems large—even for the purchase of tailor-made suits and expensive dates with the girl friend or outings with the wife.

A sharp change occurs, however, when home and children come into focus (i.e., about age 22–35). As family pressures mount, the demands for credit in the product market and income in the labor market begin their swift ascent. The appetite for consumer durables and the demand for money and job security reach a peak in the thirties among married men with children. But the peak in actual income and security is seldom reached in this critical period (25–35). For the manual worker most subject to instability of employment, seniority protection is as yet weak, and for all categories, the period of maximum economic rewards comes later. A working wife is one solution, but the double-earner pattern is least frequent among the very families which feel squeezed, i.e., young couples with children at home. The result: a morale trough which lasts until job aspirations and family pressures decline, rewards increase, or both. When children leave home and debts are paid off, job morale, indeed all satisfactions unconnected with child-rearing, should climb. Later, with retirement impending, the morale curve will vary depending upon the type of career and strength of work commitment, but a final sag in morale seems most frequent.

It would appear that while all societies define human potentialities and obligations by age grades, the timing and balance of obligations in the economic, kinship, and other spheres is vastly varied. Thus, in some preindustrial societies, that period of a man's life when he is most busy building up a family is the time when he is relatively free of such other obligations as his earlier commitment as a warrior or his later activity as an "elder" in the age-group system. Our own society has so structured this balance that peak demands in economic life (launching a career, getting established in a job) coincide with peak demands in procreation and hence consumption, doubtless a source of strain for both person and social structure.

Another structured imbalance appears at the other end of the life cycle, where the accent on youth clashes with the facts of aging.

Many scholars have noted the activist and equalitarian bent of American culture. Whether it is a reflection of the "Protestant ethic" or something else, American elites seem to approve both an active, rational mastery over worldly things and ideas (versus a passive, contemplative stance) and equality of economic opportunity—the treatment of all men by the same impersonal standards. These values are shared by all major segments of American society; they have deep roots in social structure and culture.

Some of the activism and one version of equalitarianism may be due to populist traditions unique to only a few industrial societies, notably America and France, i.e., hostility to established hierarchy (including aged elites), a belief in the supremacy of popular will and its direct and unconstrained expression ("We, the people, are not just equal to our rulers and the classes they represent, we're better and we can darn well do something about it").

The hold of these values is also due to universal features of industrial societies. While seniority still counts in some segments of the economy and "elder statesmen" flourish, while nepotism, "pull," and discrimination operate alongside testing and merit-rating, industrial societies nevertheless tend to be more ruthless in their application of ability criteria in the allocation of people to jobs. What you can do or learn to do quickly, how you can perform, visibly and actively, is emphasized. At minimum, few organizations allocate positions exclusively on the basis of age.

These values are expressed in a cult of youthful pep which affects old and young alike, even those who cannot possibly act it out. A study done in 1934 notes what people would like to do with their leisure time as opposed to what they did. Nine of the ten most-preferred leisure pursuits were in the get-up-and-go category—tennis, swimming, boating, golf, camping, auto-riding, theater-going, etc. Our euphemisms for old-age—"later maturity," "middle years," "golden age," "senior citizen"—may reflect this desperate ideological commitment to youthful appearances.

In practice, however, older Americans apparently steer clear of activism. As we have seen, secondary attachments other than church fall off in the sixties. Other data on variations by age in leisure activities and expenditures also suggest a gradual withdrawal from the strenuous life.

Thus, as the person moves through the life cycle in an industrial age-grading system (reinforced by American values), he is subjected to two built-in episodes of strain: first, the incongruous demands of economic and kinship spheres on young family men; and then, toward the end, when energy declines and abilities are blunted, the incongruity of activism as an ideological norm and apathy as the fact.

The participation curve, it should be noted, parallels the job-satisfaction curve, and both are products of interdependent cycles of family life, consumption, and work.

At this point many exceptions to the picture of the typical participation career on the chart have undoubtedly arisen. And it is true that changes common to major stages of the life cycle cannot explain variations in rates and kinds of participation at every age grade and at every social-economic level. To understand these variations we must look to more specific characteristics of the work situation and career pattern.

That much participation is career-connected, especially among more mobile segments of the middle class, seems plain. David Sills (1957), in a systematic survey of the phenomenally successful Polio Foundation, shows that the Polio Chapter and March-of-Dimes volunteers tend to be "main streeters" (or their wives); most of the three million are middle-class Protestant businessmen and professionals; about half also work on Red Cross and Community Chest. In orientation, most recruits are "self-oriented" joiners, vague on organizational goals; their motives are phrased in terms of job-obligation or status striving. We have the young lawyer seeking a clientele, the retail merchant or insurance salesman solidifying his customer base, the local executive on the make, a "philanthropic career" unfolding with his business career (incidentally, many talk more like "draftees" than "volunteers"). Two in three of these multiple participants are 31–50 years of age, highlighting again a major source of the general participation peak: the career contingencies of mobile business and professional people.

In other words, participation in community life is a natural extension of participation in the labor market; orderly and pleasant experiences in the latter provide motive and opportunity for the former. For work-committed executives, merchants, professionals, and craftsmen whose careers demand broad-ranging contact, participation in the later years is a continuation of an established pattern of life and, in fact, goes on well into the fifties and sixties.

We must recognize, however, that most work situations, middle-class or working-class, provide little motive and opportunity to elaborate the work role beyond the workplace and into a life plan. Indeed, the mass of men withdraw both from work and the larger communal life well before they grow old. "Aging" for them in a sense begins at 35 or 40. Their work becomes little more than a source of income, a source which is often uncertain. High aspirations—for income, occupational prestige, power—are unrealistic; they are typically scaled down. If these men belong to any formal organizations beyond church and union, the participation peak is 30–45, the time devoted to them is slight, the membership casual. What happens as they move through the middle years and approach the sixties?

To the extent that people are exposed to disciplined work routines yielding little gratification, or have careers which neither afford continuity of personal experience nor necessitate wide community participation, their retreat from work is accompanied by a gradual decline in the number and strength of secondary attachments (Wilensky, in press).

Does the task offer little variety? Is there little discretion in methods, pace, or schedule? Then, like some dentists and assembly-line workers we have studied, our nonmobile man-in-the-middle will do his job in a reliable way, go home, segregate his work from life, and retire into the heartwarming circle of kin and friends.

Does the job yield no readily visible status claim? Then it is as neighbor and family man that he will find his chief identity. Ask a "hindleg toenail remover" what he does and he will tell you that he works at Swifts; but the white-collar "console operator," too, will name the company, not the job, because nobody has heard of this latest example of automation. The work role, if it is status-invisible, will be checked at the workplace door.

Is the work history punctuated by unexpected periods of unemployment, disorderly shifts among jobs, occupations, and industries? Then the kind of life plan afforded by the established professions and crafts, the civil service, and military establishment is impossible, and preparation for retirement, including the search for satisfying voluntary associations, is unlikely.

Finally, is it a career which does not necessitate sustained cultivation of customer or client? Then one of the principal motives for getting into civic affairs is removed and participation in fund-raising drives and good works will be left to the ad man, the solo lawyer, or the executive on the make.

In this context, the structural base for anything more than a modest growth in secondary attachments among the aged is lacking. By the time the children leave, a leisure routine which is profoundly local, centered in family and neighborhood, is too firmly established. It is not surprising, then, that no more than two in a hundred of our older citizens are able to find their way to old people's clubs and that only tiny fractions participate in anything beyond the church.

Let us turn now to the question of the effect of the quality and quantity of participation on the viability of a democratic political order.

I suggest one major hypothesis: The dearth of strong, stable secondary ties among the very young and the old, coupled with the structured strains to which they are subject, makes them peculiarly vulnerable to irresponsible political leaders.

In urban-industrial societies self-governing formal associations are becoming more important in binding persons to larger communal ends. Local primary groups are decreasingly effective in determining these ends (e.g., welfare state and garrison state policies) and in linking persons to them.

We do not have to argue that, in the modern world, political and economic crises are more frequent than before. (There have always been wars and rumors of wars.) Nor do we have to argue that the mass media are more efficient means of mobilization in such crises than the means available to preindustrial elites. We hold merely that the number of issues and areas of life for which local groups provide no stable guide to good and bad, real and unreal, have increased.

Thus, to be an effective source of social integration, a vital primary group life (lively ties to family and friends) must be accompanied by a vital secondary group life. Something must mediate the relations between the individual, immersed in his parochial concerns, on the one hand, and a powerful state and the great mass organizations of the city (corporation, labor union, political party, and the agencies of mass communication), on the other. Where the workplace, the local union, and the precinct organization foster stable, close friendships which function as transmission belts from leader to member, then an organization massive in size is not a "mass" in a sociological sense. When the senator's speech, the TV program, and the news story are discussed in such lively organizational contexts, once again the power of the "mass" media is blunted and its content reinterpreted to fit the interests and values of groups closer to home. But not every membership results in deep attachment, not every distant symbol or event is interpreted by local groups. In the absence of effective mediating ties, of meaningful participation in voluntary associations, the population becomes vulnerable to political extremism, more susceptible to personality appeals in politics, more ready for the demagogues who exploit fanatical faiths of nation and race.

American studies of the correlates of participation are consistent with this idea, but do not allow a crucial test of it. It has been shown that those with secondary ties are more likely to vote, contribute to charity, and be interested in public affairs. Conversely, lack of secondary attachments fosters antidemocratic tendencies. It permits the mobilization of the depressed, deprived, and marginal portions of the population against any target. For instance, deepest and most sustained conflict over desegregation, alleged Communist subversion, and even fluoridation of drinking water, seems to occur in those communities and among those populations having the least lively associational life.

Unfortunately, this remains speculative. Aside from the problems of interpretation discussed above—lack of controls for class, type of organization, and, soon, weakness of data on the isolated, and on the quality of participation—none of these studies of the impact of participation tells us whether people in voluntary associations are also those with a more stable family life and a wide range of informal contact with relatives, friends, and fellow workers (which could also account for their constrained community behavior). None of them reports data on the effect of social ties to local versus ideological attachments to national units of these big organizations.

How does this hypothesis about the increasing importance of secondary ties relate to the facts on rates of participation among the aged and our picture of "participation careers"?

American society may still have a sufficiently vital associational life to avoid the proliferation of antidemocratic mass movements; but in the next decade or so, rapid growth in numbers of people at the most strainful stages of the life cycle (hard-pressed young family men, older couples, and solitary survivors) may increase the potential for political disruption and the deterioration of the common life.

First, these stages mark the low points in participation beyond the immediate family. Second, for the aging, the ties that weaken most and earliest are the very ties that are most effective as integrators, i.e., work-based associations. Finally, the aged are likely to be segregated residentially (an aspect of the decline of the extended family system); since older people are disproportionately represented among low-income families, many are also segregated socially. Physical and social segregation of age grades everywhere brings a gap in values, beliefs, and interests between them and the rest of the population. It is a general problem of modern society to integrate such specialized groups and strata. Thus, organizations which mix age grades, especially churches, workplaces, unions, and professional associations, have strategic significance as softeners of the natural conflict between generations. When ties to such organizations are severed, the person is more likely to become estranged from community and society.

The common picture of the aged as apathetic and conservative may be accurate. But, as with the apathetic everywhere, they stay on the sidelines of community controversy only until something triggers them off. In Northhampton, Massachusetts, normally apathetic older people (who were also less educated, and more science-resistant) were easily mobilized to defeat a fluoridation plan. Although data are clearly lacking, it seems plausible that other situations of extreme conflict, too, bring out the socially isolated and politically apathetic, and the aged may contribute a disproportionate share. Their free-floating aggressions can be turned against everything from new residents to suspect library books, from school-bond issues to political liberals. Some of this is simple self-interest (those low-income homeowners whose children are through school want low school taxes); but much of it reflects an easy availability for manipulation by demagogues, whatever the issue. The aged must be seen as a peculiarly potent pool of extremism; apathy and activism may, in the end, be blood brothers.

When every morning sees one thousand more men and women 65 and over, when the typical case feels more deprived emotionally and financially than the rest of the population and has fewer and weaker secondary ties to constrain the response to deprivation, the threat to democratic political order and responsible community action is real.

Is there any message here for the gerontologist, for the welfare administrator? I think so. Your efforts to make the aged more secure economically, to make retirement more voluntary and at the same time cushion its shocks, your programs to encourage those great age-grade mixers, unions and industry, to face the problems of the aged, your attacks on the means tests, on eligibility rules which keep the aged poor from productive labor and otherwise reinforce their isolation—in general, your search for ways to avoid too radical a segregation of their activity and residence—all these not only pay off in more happiness and self-respect for the older person, but also constrain the kind of political extremism that makes democracy precarious in the modern world.

REFERENCES

Havighurst, R. J. 1960. Life beyond family and work. *In* E. W. Burgess (ed.), Aging in western societies, pp. 299–353. Chicago: The University of Chicago Press.

Pinner, F. A., Jacobs, P., and Selznick, P. 1959. Old age and political behavior: a case study. Berkeley: University of California Press.

Sills, D. L. 1957. The volunteers. Glencoe, Ill.: The Free Press.

Wilensky, H. L. 1961. Life cycle, work situation, and participation in formal associations. *In* R. W. Kleemeier (ed.), Aging and leisure, pp. 213–42. New York: Oxford University Press.

—————— Orderly careers and social participation. Am. Sociological Rev. (In press.)

—————— Work and leisure. Glencoe, Ill.: The Free Press. (In press.)

Contributors

Abel-Smith, Brian, Lecturer, London School of Economics, London W.C. 2, England

Albrecht, Ruth, Head, Department of Family Life, University of Florida, Gainesville, Florida

Altrocchi, John, Assistant Professor, Department of Psychiatry, Duke University Medical School, Durham, North Carolina

Arth, Malcolm J., Anthropologist, Geriatric Hospitalization Project, Boston State Hospital, Boston, Massachusetts

Ashley, E. Everett, III, Director, Statistical Reports and Development Branch, Office of the Administrator, Housing and Home Finance Agency, Washington, D.C.

Axelrod, Seymour, Assistant Professor of Medical Psychology, Department of Psychiatry, Duke University Medical School, Durham, North Carolina

Baumert, Gerhard, Director, DIVO Institute, Am Hauptbanhof 12, Frankfurt am Main, Germany

Beard, Belle Boone, Associate Professor of Sociology, Sweet Briar College, Sweet Briar, Virginia

Beyer, Glenn H., Professor of Housing and Design, Director, Housing Research Center, Cornell University, Ithaca, New York

Birren, James E., Chief, Section on Aging, National Institute of Mental Health, Bethesda 14, Maryland

Blau, David, Director, Geriatric Hospitalization Project, Beth Israel Hospital, Boston 24, Massachusetts

Botwinick, Jack, Research Psychologist, Section on Aging, National Institute of Mental Health, Bethesda 14, Maryland

Braun, John C., Texas Christian University, Fort Worth, Texas

Brinley, Joseph F., Research Psychologist, Section on Aging, National Institute of Mental Health, Bethesda 14, Maryland

Bromley, Dennis B., Lecturer, Department of Psychology, University of Liverpool, Liverpool, England

Burgess, Ernest W., Consultant, Industrial Relations Center, The University of Chicago, 1225 East 60th Street, Chicago 37, Illinois

Busse, Ewald W., Professor and Chairman, Department of Psychiatry, Director, Regional Center for the Study of Aging, Duke University Medical Center, Durham, North Carolina

Cesa-Bianchi, Marcello, Professor, Faculty of Medicine and Surgery, University of Milan, Via Lanzone N.2, Milan, Italy

Chevry, G. R., Director of Demography and Research, National Institute of Statistics and Economic Studies, Paris, France

Chown, Sheila M., Medical Research Council, Psychologist, Unit for Research on Occupational Aspects of Aging, University Department of Psychology, University of Liverpool, 7 Abercrombie Square, Liverpool 7, England

Christ, Adolph E., The Langley Porter Neuropsychiatric Institute, Parnassus and First Avenues, San Francisco 22, California

Clague, Ewan, Commissioner of Labor Statistics, Bureau of Labor Statistics, U.S. Department of Labor, Washington 25, D.C.

Clément, F., Director of Studies, Centre de Gerontologie Claude Bernard, Institution Sainte-Perine, 11 Rue Chardon-Lagache, Paris 16, France

Clyde, Dean J., Research Psychologist, National Institute of Mental Health, Bethesda 14, Maryland

Cohen, Louis D., Professor of Medical Psychology, Department of Psychiatry, Duke University Medical School, Durham, North Carolina

Cohen, Wilbur J., Assistant Secretary, U.S. Department of Health, Education, and Welfare, Washington 25, D.C.

Colombo, Ugo M., Director, Department of Public Assistance of Milan, 39 Viale Romagna, Milan, Italy

Crook, Guy Hamilton, Research Psychologist, Geriatric Research Project, Langley Porter Neuropsychiatric Institute, Parnassus and First Avenues, San Francisco 22, California

Cuzzaniti, Roberto, President, National Institute for Pensioners, Milan, Italy

Davidoff, Melvin D., U.S. Civil Service Commission, Washington, D.C.

Davies, George Vernon, Medical Officer, Department of Mental Hygiene, Mont Park, Melbourne, Victoria, Australia

Dibner, Andrew S., Clinical Psychologist, V. A. Outpatient Clinic, Boston, Massachusetts

Donahue, Wilma, Chairman, Division of Gerontology, Institute for Human Adjustment, The University of Michigan, Ann Arbor, Michigan

Eisdorfer, Carl, Assistant Professor of Medical Psychology, Department of Psychiatry, Duke University Medical School, Durham, North Carolina

Epstein, Lenore A., Assistant Director, Division of Program Research, Social Security Administration, U.S. Department of Health, Education, and Welfare, Washington 25, D.C.

Falek, Arthur, Department of Medical Genetics, New York State Psychiatric Institute, Columbia University, New York 32, New York

Fields, Gene L., University of Missouri, Columbia, Missouri

Fiske, Marjorie, Co-Principal Investigator, Studies in Geriatric Mental Illness, The Langley Porter Neuropsychiatric Institute, San Francisco 22, California

Fleming, Christopher E., Lecturer in Social and Industrial Medicine, The University of Sheffield, Sheffield, England

Forssman, Sven, President, Swedish Employers' Confederation, Division of Occupational Health, Stockholm, Sweden

Friedsam, H. J., Director, Department of Economics and Sociology, North Texas State College, Denton, Texas

Friis, Henning, Director, Danish National Institute of Social Research, Nyhavn, 38, Copenhagen, Denmark

Gaitz, Charles M., Department of Psychiatry, University of Houston, Houston, Texas

Goldfarb, Alvin I., Chief, Neuropsychiatry Department, New York Home for Aged and Infirm Hebrews, 121 West 105th Street, New York 25, New York

Gordon, Margaret S., Associate Director, Institute of Industrial Relations, University of California, Berkeley 4, California

Grad, Jacqueline, Medical Research Council, Graylingwell Hospital, Chichester, England

Griew, Stephen, Research Associate in Psychology, University of Bristol, 27 Belgrave Road, Bristol, England

Halstead, Ward C., Professor of Medical Psychology, The University of Chicago, 5537 University Avenue, Chicago 37, Illinois

Havighurst, Robert J., Professor of Education, Committee on Human Development, University of Chicago, Chicago, Illinois

Heron, Alastair, Medical Research Council, Unit for Research on Occupational Aspects of Aging, University of Liverpool, Liverpool, England

Hudson, Atwood, Director, The Speech and Hearing Clinic, Rockford College, Rockford, Illinois

Hydén, Sven, Svenska Arbetsgivareföreningen, Box 16120, Stockholm 16, Sweden

Inglis, James, Assistant Professor of Clinical Psychology, Department of Psychiatry, Queen's University, Kingston, Ontario, Canada

Jaffe, A. J., Director, Manpower and Population Program, Columbia University, New York, New York

Jambor, Helen M., Research Social Worker, Geriatric Research Project, The Langley Porter Neuropsychiatric Institute, Parnassus and First Avenues, San Francisco 22, California

Jarvik, Lissy F., Department of Medical Genetics, New York State Psychiatric Institute, Columbia University, New York 32, New York

Jeffers, Frances C., Regional Center for the Study of Aging, Duke University Medical Center, Durham, North Carolina

Jerome, Edward A., Research Psychologist, Section on Aging, National Institute of Mental Health, Bethesda 14, Maryland

Jones, Marcia J., Assistant, School of Social Work, University of Missouri, Columbia, Missouri

Kahn, Robert L., Senior Research Psychologist, State of New York Department of Mental Hygiene, 80-45 Winchester Boulevard, Queens Village 27, New York

Kallmann, Franz J., Associate in Psychiatry, Department of Medical Genetics, New York State Psychiatric Institute, Columbia University, New York 32, New York

Katz, Lawrence, Clinical Psychologist, Letterman Hospital, San Francisco 22, California

Kettell, Marjorie E., Psychologist, Geriatric Hospitalization Project, Beth Israel Hospital, Boston 24, Massachusetts

Kiser, Clyde V., Head of Population Branch, Milbank Memorial Fund, 40 Wall Street, New York 5, New York

Kleemeier, Robert W., Professor, Department of Psychology, Washington University, St. Louis 30, Missouri

Kløve, Hallgrim, Department of Neurology, Indiana University Medical Center, Indianapolis 7, Indiana

Köckeis, Eva, Research Assistant, Vienna University, Vienna, Austria

Kooy, Gerrit A., Professor, Department of Sociology, Agricultural University, Wageningen, The Netherlands

Krugman, Arnold D., Chief, Clinical Psychology Service, Veterans Administration Center, Martinsburg, West Virginia

Lake, Wilfred S., Dean, College of Liberal Arts, Northeastern University, Boston, Massachusetts

Lakin, Martin, Assistant Professor of Psychology and Psychiatry, Duke University Medical Center, Durham, North Carolina

Lamale, Helen H., Chief, Branch of Consumption Studies, Bureau of Labor Statistics, U.S. Department of Labor, Washington 25, D.C.

Lipman, Aaron, Assistant Professor, Sociology Department, University of Miami, Coral Gables, Florida

Lorge, Irving, Professor of Education, Executive Officer, Institute of Psychological Research, Teachers College, Columbia University, New York 27, New York

Lovald, Keith A., Assistant Professor of Sociology, University of Massachusetts, Amherst, Massachusetts

MacFarland, M. Carter, Director, Division of Economics and Program Studies, Housing and Home Finance Agency, Washington, D.C.

McConnell, John W., Dean, New York State School of Industrial and Labor Relations, Cornell University, Ithaca, New York

Milavsky, J. R., Research Assistant, Bureau of Applied Social Research, Columbia University, New York, New York

Milhøj, Poul, Danish National Institute of Social Welfare, Nyhavn, 38, Copenhagen, Denmark

Naville, Pierre, Directeur de recherches au Centre national de la recherche scientifique, Paris, France

Neugarten, Bernice L., Associate Professor, Committee on Human Development, The University of Chicago, Chicago 37, Illinois

Nichols, Claude R., Regional Center for the Study of Aging, Duke University Medical Center, Durham, North Carolina

Nierstrasz, F. H. J., Economist, Bouwcentrum, Rotterdam, Holland

Nimkoff, M. F., Chairman, Department of Sociology, Florida State University, Tallahassee, Florida

Okada, Yuzuru, Professor of Sociology and Anthropology, Tokyo Kyoiku University, Tokyo, Japan

Oppenheim, D. J., Interne in Medicine, Geriatric Hospitalization Project, Beth Israel Hospital, 591 Morton Street, Boston 24, Massachusetts

Orbach, Harold L., Assistant Director of Social Gerontology Project, Division of Gerontology, The University of Michigan, Ann Arbor, Michigan

Pacaud, Suzanne, Chief of Research at the National Center of Scientific Research, Assistant Director at the Technical School of Advanced Studies, 17 Rue Mechain, Paris 14, France

Pagani, Angelo, Operations Research Center, Sociological Section, Bocconi University, Milan, Italy

Paillat, Paul, Institut National d'Etudes Démographiques, 23 Avenue Franklin Roosevelt, Paris 80, France

Peck, Arthur, State of New York, Department of Mental Hygiene, 80-45 Winchester Boulevard, Queens Village 27, New York

Pollack, Max, Senior Research Psychologist, State of New York Department of Mental Hygiene, 80-45 Winchester Boulevard, Queens Village 27, New York

Reichard, Suzanne, Associate Research Psychologist, Institute of Industrial Relations, University of California, Berkeley 4, California

Reitan, Ralph M., Associate Professor, Indiana University Medical Center, 1100 West Michigan Street, Indianapolis 7, Indiana

Rennick, Phillip, The University of Chicago, Chicago, Illinois

Rhudick, Paul J., The Age Center of New England, Inc., 160 Commonwealth Avenue, Boston 16, Massachusetts

Richardson, I. M., Senior Lecturer, Department of Public Health and Social Medicine, University of Aberdeen, Aberdeen, Scotland

Riegel, Klaus F., Assistant Professor, Department of Psychology, The University of Michigan, Ann Arbor, Michigan

Robins, Arthur J., Professor, School of Social Work, University of Missouri, Columbia, Missouri

Rosenmayr, Leopold, Professor of Sociology, Vienna University, Vienna, Austria

Rosow, Irving, Associate Professor of Sociology, Western Reserve University, Cleveland, Ohio

Ross, Sherman, Special Consultant, National Institute of Mental Health, Bethesda 14, Maryland

Sainsbury, Peter, Medical Research Council, Clinical Psychiatry Research Unit, Graylingwell Hospital, Chichester, England

Sanderson, R. E., Queens University, Kingston, Ontario, Canada

Schaie, K. Warner, Assistant Professor, University of Nebraska, Lincoln, Nebraska

Shanas, Ethel, Senior Study Director, National Opinion Research Center, The University of Chicago, 5736 South Woodlawn Avenue, Chicago 37, Illinois

Shultz, Edwin B., Professor, New York State School of Industrial and Labor Relations, Cornell University, Ithaca, New York

Simmons, Walt R., Statistical Advisor, U.S. National Health Survey, National Center for Health Statistics, U.S. Department of Health, Education, and Welfare, Washington 25, D.C.

Singer, Margaret Thaler, 17 El Camino Real, Berkeley 5, California

Slavick, Fred, Associate Professor, New York State School of Industrial and Labor Relations, Cornell University, Ithaca, New York

Smith, Patricia Cain, Assistant Professor, New York State School of Industrial and Labor Relations, Cornell University, Ithaca, New York

Streib, Gordon F., Professor of Sociology, Cornell University, Ithaca, New York

Suci, George J., Research Associate, Department of Child Development and Family Relations, Cornell University, Ithaca, New York

Swenson, Wendell M., Clinical Psychologist, Mayo Clinic and Mayo Foundation, University of Minnesota, Rochester, Minnesota

Szafran, Jacek, Professor of Psychology, Psychological Laboratory, Gandy Street, University of Exeter, Exeter, England

Tachibana, Kakusho, Professor of Psychology, Osaka University, Osaka, Japan

Talmon-Garber, Yonina, Professor, Department of Sociology, The Hebrew University of Jerusalem, Jerusalem, Israel

Tartler, Rudolf, Institut fur Wertschafts-und Socialwissenschaften, Universitatstrasse 14–16, Münster, Germany

Thomae, Hans, Department of Psychology, University of Bonn, Bonn, Germany

Thompson, Wayne E., Assistant Professor of Sociology, Cornell University, Ithaca, New York

Tibbitts, Clark, Deputy Director, Special Staff on Aging, U.S. Department of Health, Education, and Welfare, Washington 25, D.C.

Townsend, Peter, Lecturer in Social Administration, London School of Economics and Political Science, University of London, London, England

Tréanton, Jean-René, Professor of Sociology, University of Lille, Lille, France

Trentini, Giancario, Institute of Psychology, Catholic University of Milan, Milan, Italy

Troclet, Léon-Eli, Sénateur, Ancien Ministre du Travail et de la Prévoyance Sociale, Liége, Belgium

Vicino, Frank L., Veterans Administration Center, Martinsburg, West Virginia

Vinson, David B., Lecturer, Department of Psychiatry, University of Houston, Houston, Texas

Warren, Richard M., Research Psychologist, Section on Aging, National Institute of Mental Health, Bethesda 14, Maryland

Weir, R. D., Department of Social Medicine, University of Aberdeen, Scotland

Weiss, James M. A., Associate Professor of Psychiatry, Acting Chief, Department of Psychiatry, University of Missouri School of Medicine, Columbia, Missouri

Welford, A. T., Lecturer and Fellow in Experimental Psychology, St. John's College, Cambridge University, Cambridge, England

West, J., Geriatric Hospitalization Project, Beth Israel Hospital, 591 Morton Street, Boston 24, Massachusetts

Wilensky, Harold L., Assistant Professor, Department of Sociology, The University of Michigan, Ann Arbor, Michigan

Willis, Barbara Barney, Assistant, School of Social Work, University of Missouri, Columbia, Missouri

Wolfbein, Seymour L., Deputy Assistant Secretary, U.S. Department of Labor, Washington 25, D.C.

Yap, P. M., The Mental Hospital, University of Hong Kong, High Street, Hong Kong, B.C.C.

International Association of Gerontology

SOCIAL SCIENCE RESEARCH COMMITTEE 1957–1960

AMERICAN BRANCH

Burgess, Ernest W., *Chairman*
  Consultant, Industrial Relations Center, The University of Chicago, Chicago 37, Illinois
Tibbitts, Clark, *Secretary*
  Deputy Director, Special Staff on Aging, U.S. Department of Health, Education, and Welfare, Washington 25, D.C.
Ashley, E. Everett, III, Director, Statistical Reports and Development Branch, Housing and Home Finance Agency, Washington 25, D.C.
Barkin, Solomon, Director of Research, Textile Workers of America, 99 University Place, New York 3, New York
Birren, James E., Chief, Section on Aging, National Institute of Mental Health, Bethesda 14, Maryland
Cohen, Wilbur J., Assistant Secretary, U.S. Department of Health, Education, and Welfare, Washington 25, D.C.
Donahue, Wilma, Chairman, Division of Gerontology, Institute for Human Adjustment, The University of Michigan, Ann Arbor, Michigan
Gordon, Margaret S., Associate Director, Institute of Industrial Relations, University of California, Berkeley 4, California
Havighurst, Robert J., Professor, Department of Education, Committee on Human Development, The University of Chicago, Chicago 37, Illinois
Kleemeier, Robert W., Professor, Department of Psychology, Washington University, St. Louis, Missouri
Simmons, Leo W., Executive Officer, Institute for Research and Service in Nursing Education, Teachers College, Columbia University, New York 27, New York
Spector, Sidney, Staff Director, Committee on Problems of the Aged and Aging, United States Senate, Old Senate Office Building, Washington 25, D.C.
Willard, Joseph E., Research and Statistics Division, Department of National Health and Welfare, Ottawa, Canada
Williams, Richard H., Acting Chief, Professional Services Branch, National Institute of Mental Health, Bethesda 14, Maryland
Wolfbein, Seymour L., Deputy Assistant Secretary, U.S. Department of Labor, Washington 25, D.C.

EUROPEAN BRANCH

Friis, Henning, *Chairman*
  Director, Danish National Institute of Social Research, Nyhavn, 38, Copenhagen, Denmark
Sanderson, W.A., *Secretary*
  Executive Director, The Gulbenkian Foundation, 3 Prince Albert Road, London, N.W. 1, England

Behrends, Hanna, German National Old People's Welfare Committee, Beethovenstrasse, 81, Frankfurt am-Main 16, Germany

Berggren, Ali, Chief, Division of Social Care, The Royal Social Board, Birger Jarlstrog 14, Stockholm, Sweden

Bravo, A. L., Chief of Social and Occupational Health Section, World Health Organization, Palais des Nations, Geneva, Switzerland

Cavalieri, Ugo, Chief, Medical Services, Institutions for the Ageing, l'Ente Communale Assistenza di Milano, Via Marcona 45, Milan, Italy

Colombo, Ugo, Director, Department of Public Assistance of Milan, Viale Romagna 39, Milan, Italy

Fleetwood, J. F., Professor, Department of Physiology, R. C. S. I., Glenvera, Proby Square, Dublin, Ireland

Huet, J. A., Centre d'Etudes et de Recherches Gerontologiques, 1 Place d'llena, Paris 16, France

Karsten, Anitra, Professor, Swedish School of Economics, Kaserngatan 14 A, Helsingfors, Finland

Le Gros, Clark F., 34 Hyddelton Square, London, E. C. 1, England

Pagani, Angelo, Operations Research Center, Sociological Section, Bocconi University, Milan, Italy

Paulus, J. J., Professor, Department of Psychology, University of Liége, Liége, Belgium

Reigel, Klaus F., Assistant Professor, Department of Psychology, the University of Michigan, Ann Arbor, Michigan

Roth, J., Swiss National Foundation for Old Age, Seestrasse 2, Zurich 8, Switzerland

Ström, Axel, Professor, Department of Social Medicine, University Hospital, Oslo, Norway

Titmuss, R. M., Professor, Department of Social Science and Administration, The London School of Economics and Political Science, University of London, London, England

Tréanton, Jean-René, Professor of Sociology, University of Lille, Lille, France

van den Bunk, T., Head of Division for Censuses, Centraal Bureau voor de Statistick, 's-Gravenhage, The Netherlands

van Zonneveld, Robert J., National Health Research Council, TNO, Zilverschoonstraat 14, 's-Gravenhage, The Netherlands

Periodical Abbreviations

Acta Genet. et. Statis. Med.	Acta Genetica et Statistica Medica
Acta Med. Scand.	Acta Medica Scandinavia
Am. Economics Rev.	American Economics Review
Am. Imago	American Imago
Am. Law Rep.	American Law Reports
Am. J. Hum. Genet.	American Journal of Human Genetics
Am. J. Ment. Defic.	American Journal of Mental Deficiency
Am. J. Occup. Ther.	American Journal of Occupational Therapy
Am. J. Orthopsychiat.	American Journal of Orthopsychiatry
Am. J. Psychiat.	American Journal of Psychiatry
Am. J. Psychol.	American Journal of Psychology
Am. J. Sociology	American Journal of Sociology
A.M.A. Arch. Gen. Psychiat.	American Medical Association Archives of General Psychiatry
A.M.A. Arch. Neurol. & Psychiat.	American Medical Association Archives of Neurology and Psychiatry
A.M.A. Bull.	American Medical Association Bulletin
Am. Practit. & Digest. Treatment	American Practitioner and Digestive Treatment
Am. Psychologist	American Psychologist
Am. Rev. Tubercul.	American Review of Tuberculosis
Am. Sociological Rev.	American Sociological Review
Ann. Am. Acad. Political & Social Sc.	Annals of the American Academy of Political and Social Science
Ann. Hum. Genet.	Annals of Human Genetics
Ann. Otolaryng.	Annals of Otolaryngology
Ann. Rev. Psychol.	Annual Review of Psychology
Architect's J.	Architect's Journal
Architectural Rec.	Architectural Record
Arch. Neurol. & Psychiat.	Archives of Neurology and Psychiatry
Arch. Otolaryng.	Archives of Otolaryngology
Arch. Psicol. Neurol. & Psychiat.	Archivio di Psicologia, Neurologia e Psichiatria
Brit. J. Med. Psychol.	British Journal of Medical Psychology
Brit. J. Preventive Med.	British Journal of Preventive Medicine
Brit. J. Psychol.	British Journal of Psychology
Brit. J. Sociology	British Journal of Sociology
Brit. Med. J.	British Medical Journal
Brit. Sociological Rev.	British Sociological Review
Builder	Builder
Bull. Brit. Psychol. Soc.	Bulletin of the British Psychological Society
Bull. Menninger Clin.	Bulletin of the Menninger Clinic
Bull. Nat. Old People's Welfare Council	Bulletin of the National Old People's Welfare Council
Bull. World Health Organ.	Bulletin of the World Health Organization
Child Development	Child Development
Economie et Humanisme	Economie et Humanisme

Educ. Psychol. Measurement	Educational and Psychological Measurement
E. E. G. Clin. Neurophysiol.	Electroencephalography and Clinical Neurophysiology
Ergonomics	Ergonomics
Etudes et Conjuncture	Etudes et Conjuncture
Federal Reserve Bull.	Federal Reserve Bulletin
Genet. Psychol. Monogr.	Genetic Psychology Monographs
Geriatrics	Geriatrics
Gerontologia	Gerontologia
Giorn. Geront.	Giornale di Gerontologia
Harvard Business Rev.	Harvard Business Review
Hum. Relat.	Human Relations
J. Abnorm. & Social Psychol.	Journal of Abnormal and Social Psychology
J. Am. Geriatrics Soc.	Journal of the American Geriatrics Society
J. Am. Inst. Planners	Journal of the American Institute of Planners
J. A. M. A.	Journal of the American Medical Association
J. Am. Psychoanal. Assoc.	Journal of the American Psychoanalytic Association
J. Appl. Psychol.	Journal of Applied Psychology
J. Chronic Dis.	Journal of Chronic Diseases
J. Clin. & Exper. Psychopathal.	Journal of Clinical and Experimental Psychopathology
J. Clin. Psychol.	Journal of Clinical Psychology
J. Comp. Physiol. Psychol.	Journal of Comparative and Physiological Psychology
J. Consult. Psychol.	Journal of Consulting Psychology
J. Exper. Psychol.	Journal of Experimental Psychology
J. Genet. Psychol.	Journal of Genetic Psychology
J. Gerontol.	Journal of Gerontology
J. Hered.	Journal of Heredity
J. Hillside Hosp.	Journal of Hillside Hospital
J. Housing	Journal of Housing
J. Insur. Med.	Journal of Insurance Medicine
J. Invest. Dermatol.	Journal of Investigative Dermatology
J. Ment. Sci.	Journal of Mental Science
J. Nerv. & Ment. Dis.	Journal of Nervous and Mental Diseases
J. Neurol. Neurosurg. & Psychiat.	Journal of Neurology, Neurosurgery and Psychiatry
J. Neurophysiol.	Journal of Neurophysiology
J. Pediatrics	Journal of Pediatrics
J. Personality	Journal of Personality
J. Proj. Tech.	Journal of Projective Techniques
J. Prophylactic Med. & Social Hygiene	Journal of Prophylactic Medicine and Social Hygiene
J. Psychol.	Journal of Psychology
J. Roy. Stat. Soc.	Journal of the Royal Statistical Society
J. Social Casework	Journal of Social Casework
J. Social Issues	Journal of Social Issues
J. Social Psychol.	Journal of Social Psychology
J. Speech & Hearing Disorders	Journal of Speech and Hearing Disorders
Kol. Z. Soziol. Soz-Psychol.	Kolner Zeitschrift für Soziologie und Sozial-Psychologie
Lancet	Lancet
Laryngoscope	Laryngoscope
Los Angeles Bar Bull.	Los Angeles Bar Bulletin
Med. Officer	Medical Officer

Ment. Hygiene	Mental Hygiene
Merrill-Palmer Quart.	Merrill-Palmer Quarterly
Milbank Mem. Fund Quart.	Milbank Memorial Fund Quarterly
Min. of Labour Gazette	Ministry of Labour Gazette
Month. Labor Rev.	Monthly Labor Review
Neurology	Neurology
Newsletter (Gerontol. Soc.)	Newsletter of the Gerontological Society
Note Terap. Pract.	Note di Terapia Practica
Notiz. dell' Ammenstrazione Sanitaria	Notiziario dell' Ammenstrazione Sanitaria
Pediatrics	Pediatrics
Percept. Motor Skills	Perceptual and Motor Skills
Population	Population
Previdinza Sociale	Previdinza Sociale
Probl. Fiziol. Optiki	Problemy Fiziologicheskai Optiki
Progress in Health Serv.	Progress in Health Services
Psychiat. Quart.	Psychiatric Quarterly
Psychiatry	Psychiatry
Psychoanal. Rev.	Psychoanalytic Review
Psychol. Bull.	Psychological Bulletin
Psychol. Issues	Psychological Issues
Psychol. Monogr.	Psychological Monographs
Psychol. Rep.	Psychological Reports
Psychol. Rev.	Psychological Review
Psychol. Serv. Cent. Bull.	Psychological Service Center Bulletin
Psychol. Forsch.	Psychologische Forschung
Pub. Health News	Public Health News
Pub. Health Rep.	Public Health Reports
Pub. Opinion Quart.	Public Opinion Quarterly
Quart. J. Exper. Psychol.	Quarterly Journal of Experimental Psychology
Rev. Psychol. Appl.	Review de Psychologie Appliquée
Riv. Gerontol. Geriat.	Rivesta di Gerontologia e Geriatria
Social Forces	Social Forces
Social Issues	Social Issues
Social Security Bull.	Social Security Bulletin
Sociometry	Sociometry
Stanford Med. Bull.	Stanford Medical Bulletin
Trans. Actuarial Soc. America	Transactions of the Actuarial Society of America
Trans. Assoc. Industrial Med. Off.	Transactions of the Association of Industrial Medical Officers
Univ. Minn. Med. Bull.	University of Minnesota Medical Bulletin
Virginia Med. Month.	Virginia Medical Monthly
Vita Hum.	Vita Humana

Index